D1370444

THE NEW WORLD OF TRAVEL

1991

THE NEW WORLD OF TRAVEL 1991

BY

ARTHUR FROMMER

PRENTICE
HALL
PRESS

NEW YORK □ LONDON □ TORONTO □ SYDNEY □ TOKYO □ SINGAPORE

FROMMER BOOKS
Published by Prentice Hall Press
A Division of Simon & Schuster Inc.
15 Columbus Circle
New York, NY 10023

Copyright © 1988, 1989, 1990, 1991
by
Arthur B. Frommer

All rights reserved
including the right of reproduction
in whole or in part in any form

PRENTICE HALL PRESS and colophons are registered trademarks
of Simon & Schuster Inc.

ISBN 0-13-333196-2
ISSN 0893-1895

Book Design by Robert Bull

Research Assistance
by Andi Vaida and Pauline Frommer

Photo Research
by Andi Vaida

Manufactured in the United States of America

*To Pauline
from her proud father*

Contents

CONTENTS

Preface

"NEL MEZZO DEL CAMMIN DI NOSTRA vita"—at a midpoint in the path of my life, to crib from Dante, I felt a sharp malaise about the state of American travel, and with my own role in it.

After 30 years of writing standard guidebooks, I began to see that most of the vacation journeys undertaken by Americans were trivial and bland, devoid of important content, cheaply commercial, and unworthy of our better instincts and ideals.

And overpriced, even in the budget realm.

Those travels, for most Americans, consist almost entirely of "sight-seeing"—an activity as vapid as the words imply. We rove the world, in most cases, to look at lifeless physical structures of the sort already familiar from a thousand picture books and films. We gaze at the Eiffel Tower or the Golden Gate Bridge, enjoy a brief thrill of recognition, return home, and think we have traveled.

Only later do we ask: To what end did I travel? With what lasting rewards?

And these disappointments are not always reduced or affected by the decision to travel cheaply—as I once largely believed. Though the use of budget-priced facilities will *usually* result in a more meaningful trip—because they bring us closer to the realities of the countries through which we pass—they do not guarantee that condition. Even people staying in guesthouses and pensions can pass their days in senseless "sight-seeing," trudging like robots to Trafalgar Square and various Changings of the Guard.

No. To me today, travel in all price ranges is scarcely worth the effort unless it is associated with people, with learning and ideas. To have meaning at all, travel must involve an encounter with new and different outlooks and beliefs. It must broaden our horizons, provide comparative lessons, show us how those in other communities are responding to their social and industrial problems. At its best, travel should challenge our preconceptions and most cherished views, cause us to rethink our assumptions, shake us a bit, make us broader-minded and more understanding.

It is toward achieving that kind of travel—that infinitely more memorable form of travel—that this yearly book hopes to contribute. Its method is to turn a spotlight on a host of little-known travel programs and organizations that surface each year, usually to benefit only the smallest portion of our population.

All over the world, and at home as well, a tiny segment of the travel industry is laboring to add valuable content to the travel experience:

• These are the people who operate ambitious study trips and scientific tours; they offer challenging, politically oriented journeys and excursions into the Third World.

• Their aim is to change your life. They experiment with new lifestyles and spiritual quests at yoga retreats and utopian communities, at tented Caribbean resorts and macrobiotic farms, at personal growth centers and adult summer camps.

• They sail the smallest of cruise ships into tiny ports and fishing villages unsullied by mass tourism.

• They practice "integrated tourism," using local facilities, and broadcast appeals for ethical tourism and tourism for the poor.

• They go on treks into the Himalayas or bicycle tours into the Dordogne.

• They enable Americans to study foreign languages at overseas schools, stay as guests in the homes of private families abroad, share the life and rhythm of Australian sheep farms, study 16th-century art with a connoisseur in the Belgian Ardennes.

• They promote homestays among people of accomplishment in Britain, or volunteer workcamps on the coasts of four continents.

But they are fledgling travel companies without funds to properly advertise their new approach; their trips, in consequence, are confined to the barest few.

In this book, hopefully, they will find their voice. Each new edition will attempt to introduce the best of them, and especially those with novel travel ideas: new themes of travel, new travel methods, new programs, new vacation possibilities, new and better ways of visiting old destinations, new destinations. Out of the welter of obscure new travel organizations emerging each year, surely one will lead to at least one new vacation activity for each of our readers.

One, did I say? Why not two or three? Travel should be no occasional fling, but a normal and frequent, integral part of one's life. Because alternative vacations are nearly always cheaper than the standard ones, they are the very best means for stretching your travel dollar; they are more effective in that regard than a whole host of heavily promoted rules for reducing travel costs. Though the traditional tourist will do well to continue obeying those rules, the unconventional traveler will reap the pleasures and rewards of far more frequent, far-ranging foreign travels.

Our ability to engage in that sort of travel is nothing short of a miracle. We are the first generation in human history to fly to other continents as easily as people once boarded a train to the next town. We are the first generation in human history for whom travel is not restricted to an affluent few, but is available to many.

We should not squander our opportunity. Travel, for too long, has been trivialized in the popular press and by the promoters of popular tours; it deserves better. It is an enduring subject of human concern, the essential requisite for a ·civilized life, perhaps the most effective tool for reducing foolish national pride and promoting a worldview.

It is too important a subject to be left to the commercial megaliths of the travel industry.

Hence, this book.

See you next year.

ARTHUR FROMMER
January 1991

A REQUEST FOR COMMENTS:
The best of books is a collaboration between author and reader. In subsequent editions of this book, we hope to supplement our own recommendations with yours. If you know of additional travel organizations or programs of the sort we've cited, or if you have comments of any sort relating to our text, won't you let us know of them?
Send your comments and/or selections to:
Arthur Frommer
c/o Prentice Hall Press, Travel Division
15 Columbus Circle
New York, NY 10023.

Introduction to a New Form of Vacation

THIS IS THE FOURTH ANNUAL EDITION OF *The New World of Travel*, expanded in size, broadened in subject matter, and made up-to-date for 1991. But its central theme remains the same. It deals with the growing gap between the vacations mass-produced by standard travel companies and those desired by an increasing number of spirited, intellectually curious Americans.

That gap becomes more glaring with every passing year. At a recent trade show of the travel industry in Berlin, I spent several days wandering past the booths of the world's largest tour operators, cataloguing the vacations they sell. And there they were: beach vacations and ski vacations, ballooning vacations and camping vacations, motorcoach sightseeing and mountain vacations, tennis vacations and golf vacations, vacations that toned the muscles, vacations that supplied rest for weary bones.

Not a single booth dealt with the mind. It was as if, by common agreement, thinking ceased on vacation, as though the whole, vast panoply of culture, literature, and learning was an unfit subject for one's leisure time.

THE CURRENT CONDITION

What sort of travel world has been created by those limited attitudes? A distressing one, I fear. To Americans of taste and intelligence, the standard holiday trip has frequently become, at best, a crushing bore, at worst a horror, a nightmare. All over the world, small-minded entrepreneurs, urged by profit, have nullified the charm, complexity, and distinctive qualities of numerous leading destinations.

And if this seems an exaggerated complaint, then let me cite several typical experiences familiar to every person who has recently traveled.

• You succumb to the ads for a winter charter program going to a once-quaint fishing village on Mexico's Pacific Coast. You arrive at a mini-metropolis thronged with crowds and lined with gaudy shops displaying mountains of earrings and mass-produced rugs. At the doors to restaurants, the wait for tables is three-quarters of an hour. In the lobbies of hotels, massed ranks of viewers watch U.S. football on satellite TV. Escaping to the beach, you are besieged by hawkers, assaulted by teenagers dropping from the skies in parasails, deafened by the motors of waterski boats.

• You join the strolling crowds in Spain's Toledo, heading for the church that displays El Greco's *Death and Burial of Count Orgaz*. Arriving at the site, you jostle with 200 other clamoring visitors for a fleeting glimpse of the glass-protected painting, distanced by a crush of human bodies. You experience the same mob scenes at the Sistine Chapel, the Louvre, the Church of St. Bavo, the Nikko Shrine.

• You visit a medieval cathedral on the castle hill of Prague, and find yourself surrounded by a dozen clusters of tourists straining intently to hear the burst of commentary emerging from their suffering guides. As you seek to concentrate on the art and mood of the High Gothic era, you hear instead the distracting mini-lectures of a dozen touring companies, delivered in French and Russian, German and Japanese.

• You arrive, 10 minutes before curtain time, in the red-velvet-and-gilt setting of a Parisian music hall, where not a single other person is yet in sight. Suddenly the tour buses appear and the hall is instantly awash with foreigners carrying cameras and guidebooks. Tired dance numbers slouch onto the stage, their music canned, their theme without the slightest reference to even the popular culture of France. Broadly exaggerated imitations of French music hall variety ensue, done without finesse or talent—and hardly rehearsed. Totally contrived for the tourist, simple-minded, and infuriating.

Why are these scenes so frequently encountered?

• Because certain areas of the world are simply being visited by too many.

• Because tour buses, charter flights, and crowds of frantic, camera-toting visitors are spilling over from celebrated plazas, squares, beaches, and airports in the more popular, standard cities or islands.

• Because key attractions are besieged by throngs.

• Because, in response to the numbers, multinational chains have thrown up massive, towering hotels that soon preempt the field, but only serve to separate their guests from the life and atmosphere surrounding them.

• Because large tour companies, intent on the bottom line, follow the course of least resistance, take you only to the famous and familiar, seek to simplify the travel experience, and make it as dumbly comforting, both mentally and physically, as possible.

THE "NEW WORLD" OF TRAVEL

How, under these circumstances, can a self-respecting, intellectually curious, spirited individual continue to travel?

The answer lies in a new approach, to new destinations, using new modes of travel and lodging, in search of learning. That "New World" of travel is broadly available to any reasonably energetic person, at lower costs than the standard form of vacation travel, and it is invigorating beyond compare, producing all the rewards (and more) that travel brought before the world became homogenized and mobbed. No matter what your age or resources, once you have taken a nonstandard trip, you will never again return willingly to the hackneyed variety.

The key objective is to experience events, lifestyles, attitudes, cultures, political outlooks, and theological views utterly different from what you ordinarily encounter at home. Unless that happens, why travel? Why endure the fatigue of transportation, and its associated burdens, just to reach a replica of your familiar surroundings? Unless vacation travel is a learning experience, unless it leaves you a bit different from what you were when you began, it is, in my view, a pointless physical exercise.

In seeking these rewards of nonstandard travel, you are now assisted by a growing multitude of small, alternative-travel companies or resorts—more than 1,200 described in this book—of which only a handful existed as recently as 10 years ago. The all-but-unnoticed emergence of this new segment of the travel industry—new tour operators, new facilities, new programs, new forms of lodging—is a major phenomenon. It reflects a massive dissatisfaction by large numbers of Americans with the simplistic travels offered by established travel firms and facilities. In effect, tens of thousands of our fellow citizens have opted for adventures of the mind when they travel, a New World of Travel.

Some, for want of assistance, have relied on do-it-yourself methods to enter the "New World," and those, too, are described in this book. Essentially, the effort is to stay ahead of the crowds, attempting always to select new destinations and unvisited areas for vacation travel. In each yearly edition of this book, I shall be searching for the as-yet-undiscovered: the places that deserve to be visited, but which for one reason or another—lack of government publicity, difficulty of access—have not to date become the subject of mass-volume commercial travel. And these, I suggest, are always the sites of memorable vacations.

But usually the process of alternative travel requires an organization; it often involves booking a program or facility that pursues themes or beliefs outside one's normal ken: New Age therapies or Eastern theologies, holistic healing or macrobiotics, utopian living or rebellious politics, Nicaragua or abstract art.

One engages in these novel travel pursuits not necessarily out of a sympathy for such credos, but to be fully alive, open to all thought, constantly questing. I happen to be, in my own beliefs, very much a rationalist, agnostic, suspicious of spiritual claims or sudden panaceas. And yet the most rewarding travels of my life have been those when I exposed myself to diametrically opposing beliefs, in a residential setting, among adherents to those other beliefs, and with an open mind.

Such is the classic travel experience, exhilarating and enlarging; the rest is mere tourism, and painfully dull. Not to have heard alternative viewpoints in the places where they prevail, not to have visited countries of the Third World or nations of Eastern Europe, not to have met the people of other cultures in a nontouristic setting, is not to have lived in this century.

Which brings me to the final, key ingredient of productive, rewarding travel: *people*. We all know that the encounter with foreign people, on a human scale, away from hotels and tour buses, is the single most memorable event of any trip. Yet most of us pursue that goal of meeting people in an unplanned, helter-skelter fashion, simply hoping that lightning will strike.

The new approach to travel brings careful deliberation, even organization, to such meetings:

• First, by utilizing lodgings that are not standard hotels, but accommodations indigenous to their surroundings, operated by people representative of their respective cultures, and patronized by the world's most interesting tourists—dynamic, spirited, free-thinking people from around the world who disdain the normal channels of commercial tourism and gravitate to such alternative lodgings.

• Second, by choosing tour operators who expose you to the realities of life at each destination, and not simply to sights gussied up or contrived for the visitor. That, too, is a major theme of this book, and the subject of considerable discussion.

• And finally, by utilizing those many nonprofit programs that actually place you in the home of a foreign family, or at least arrange for a social encounter, over tea or at meals.

AN UNSERVED AUDIENCE

How many people crave to enjoy this "New World" of vacation experience? Far more than the commercial travel industry realizes. With due apologies to American Express and British Airways, to Russia's Intourist and the Caribbean Travel Association, to Carnival Cruises and all the other travel behemoths, let me suggest that they overlook the fastest-growing segment in travel today—one that could account for as many as 40% of all the people who travel. That figure is suggested not only by the success of the first three editions of *The New World of Travel*, but by an important statistical survey conducted by the well-respected Lou Harris organization. In a little-noticed report on vacation motivations, recently issued on behalf of *Travel & Leisure* magazine, Harris concluded from hundreds of interviews that routine travel activities—sunbathing, swimming, visiting relatives—still account for the majority of all vacations. But to his astonishment, he also discovered that a large minority—fully two-fifths of his respondents—cited personal growth as their chief vacation aim: the desire to encounter new ideas, expand horizons, meet new people.

Indeed, among all the several categories of vacation desires, "life enhancement" (with its 40% of the vote) was the single largest.

Alternative travel is thus clearly here to stay, and will henceforth receive a growing amount of attention from travel journalists and travel publications. But when will the standard travel companies awake to these undeniable new trends? How long will the "majors," with their immense resources, continue to cater solely to those 60% of travelers who turn off their minds when they travel, and pay no attention at all to those 40% who do the opposite?

How long, for that matter, will real-estate developers keep opening endlessly duplicated, mindless, cookie-cutter resorts that scarcely differ from one another: rooms, swimming pool, tennis courts? When, in short, will they stop producing hotels in which one expires from boredom?

Imagine the improvement in the vacations of all of us if further resources were applied to learning vacations. Imagine, for example, a resort hotel with all the standard recreational activities, but with two covered walkways leading to two separate buildings. One would be a spa facility, for physical self-improvement. The other would be a complex of classrooms, workshops, and small theaters, for life enhancement.

I'd patronize a resort like that. And I have a feeling that multitudes of other Americans would do so, too.

Pending the awakening of the travel giants, we rely instead on the 1,200-odd smaller entrepreneurs who have created the vacations described in this book. Long may they flourish.

A wise man once said that Hell consists of being condemned to stay at a different Holiday Inn every night unto eternity. No such fate awaits our readers. With joy and enthusiasm, let's embark now for "The New World of Travel."

I

VACATION "RESORTS" THAT STRETCH YOUR MIND AND CHANGE YOUR LIFE

Vacationing at a "Personal Growth Center": Esalen and Others

Their Aim Is to Fulfill the Human Potential, to Expand Consciousness and Improve Personal Relationships

ON A BROAD LAWN LEADING TO A STEEP cliff, above the rocky surf and sea lions of the Pacific Ocean, couples hugged or stroked each other's arms. Occasionally they reached out to pat the cheek of a passing stranger.

Others raged in response to a trivial slight. Some of them arm-wrestled, grimly, to settle a dispute.

In scenes such as this, flung across the covers of *Life* and *Look,* the Esalen Institute of Big Sur, California, introduced America in the 1960s to "encounter therapy" and related offshoots of the "human potential movement." Drunk with the vision that they could lead humankind into a new era of heightened insight, sensitivity, and understanding, the personalities associated with Esalen—Michael Murphy, Fritz Perls, Ida Rolf, Abraham Maslow, Will Shutz, Virginia Satir, Rollo May, Gregory Bateson—converted that isolated stretch of seafront heights into a place of unfettered experimentation in psychology, and fired the thought of millions, while offending or frightening legions of others.

ESALEN NOW

What has happened to Esalen in the ensuing years? Though no longer in the news, it perseveres, even thrives, but at a more measured pace, thoughtful and cautious. And it has spawned over a dozen imitators: residential retreats where hundreds of Americans devote their vacations to exploring a range of psychological subjects so broad as to require college-like catalogs to list them all. Encounter therapy—that almost-instant process of shedding inhibitions and re-sponding to every repressed emotion—is now only one of numerous treatments under study at America's personal growth centers.

For one thing, the early leader of the encounter movement—Michael Murphy, co-founder of Esalen—is no longer certain of the long-term benefits of the art. It is, he believes, only a start—this stripping away of defenses through encounter techniques—which must be succeeded by longer-lasting and less dramatic work. Others have concluded that encounter therapy can be positively dangerous, exposing serious underlying pathologies without providing a trained therapist to deal with what's exposed.

And so the core curriculum of the centers is currently devoted to such multiple emerging sciences as gestalt therapy, psychosynthesis, Ericksonian hypnosis, shamanic healing, neurolinguistics, Feldenkrais, and Rolfing. From these basic inquiries emerge, at some centers, more popular discussions: "Intimate Relationships: Keeping the Spark Alive," "Burn-out: Causes and Cures," "Letting Go—Moving On," "Building Community: A Learning Circle," "Agenda for the 21st Century." All are aimed at expanding human potential, tapping into energies and abilities as yet unknown.

At Esalen, instruction is through seminars or workshops extending over a weekend ($325, including room and board) or five days midweek ($630); a handful of bunk beds, and space for sleeping bags, offer lower-rate possibilities. Many first-timers select the orientation workshop simply known as "Experiencing Esalen" (sensory awareness, group process, guided fantasy, meditation, massage), or the somewhat simi-

At Big Sur on the California coast: the model for a dozen other, quite remarkable "resorts."

lar "Gestalt Practice"; others choose from more than 100 other widely varied subjects taught throughout the year.

Studies are combined with exquisite relaxation, in a lush oasis of gardens, birds, and natural hot springs; the springs bring 110° sulfurous water into bathhouses where residents can soak for hours while watching the sun or moon set into the ocean below. Rooms are comfortable and pleasantly decorated, but must be shared with others (usually), and lack telephones, TV sets, or radios; a retreat atmosphere is maintained. Meals are served in a dining hall where dress and decor are casual but the cuisine is gourmet. The Esalen gardens and nearby farm supply the majority of the many options in the daily salad and vegetables bar.

When the 100 guest beds are not fully booked (which is common during the winter season and sometimes happens during midweek in summer), it is possible simply to stay at Esalen without enrolling in a seminar. The cost of this varies, but falls into the $75 to $95 range for a night and a day, including dinner, breakfast, and lunch, or for even less than that if you bring a sleeping bag or occupy one of the few bunk beds. Often people come to Esalen simply for a bout of quiet writing, or during a time of life transition. As workshops and bed spaces fill up early (especially in summer), it is important

They will cause you to discover, at the very least, important new aspects of your inner life and relations with others.

to plan a trip to Esalen well in advance. You may phone for a catalog or to reserve a workshop on your credit card (call 408/667-3000), but the preferred method is to write c/o **Reservations, Esalen Institute, Hwy. 1, Big Sur, CA 93920.** The location is 300 miles north of Los Angeles, 175 miles south of San Francisco, between the spectacular coastal highway and the 100-foot cliffs overlooking crashing waves below.

Class at Omega Institute

Omega Institute

And how do people respond to that setting? I can best report the reaction of a middle-aged couple from Santa Barbara who come here for a semi-annual "fix," to "feel alive and revitalized." Apart from their interest in Aikido movement/meditation (subject of their workshop), they feel that Esalen "has the nicest piece of real estate in the world—beach, rocks, surf, sea, air, mountains, hot tubs, good food, and loving people—who could ask for anything more?"

AND FARTHER AFIELD

Though Esalen was the first, it is now but one of a dozen such "personal growth" retreats on both coasts of the United States and in between.

Their goal? It is again to fulfill the "human potential," to expand consciousness and improve personal relationships, to tap into the same mysterious sources of energy and spirit that enable mystics in other lands and on other levels to enjoy trances and visions, to walk on nails or fast for days.

Their method? Workshops of a week's or a weekend's duration, attended by vacationing members of the public, who offer up their own psyches to these new therapies or to classroom training.

Unlisted in any directory of which I am aware, and marketed through severely limited mailings or classified ads in magazines of small circulation, they are nonetheless open to all and worthy of far broader dissemination.

EAST COAST

Omega Institute, Lake Drive (R.D. 2, Box 377), Rhinebeck, NY 12572 (phone 914/338-6030 from September 15 to May 15 and 914/266-4301 from May 15 to September 15), is—apart from Esalen—the lodestone; it attracts up to 500 people a week during its summer operating period from mid-June to mid-September. On a broad lake flanked by extensive, hilly grounds of forest and clearings, in a joyful atmosphere of kindness and smiles, it presents weekend and weeklong workshops ranging from the clearly lighthearted ("Vocal Joy," "Delicious Movement") to the softly therapeutic ("Working with Dreams," "The Fear of Losing Control," "Choosing to Connect") to the arcane and abstruse ("Oriental Diagnosis," "Interfacing Psychology and Spirituality," "The Tibetan Path of Love and Compassion"); many of the most famous figures in the human potential movement— Ram Dass and Ashley Montagu, Ilana Rubenfeld and Per

Vilayat Inayat Khan—make an appearance. Tuition averages $60 a day; housing and meals (vegetarian) add $35 or $45 in campsites or dorms, up to $55 and $65 in private cabins. You can contact Omega directly for a copy of their 80-page catalog, which will also alert you to a January program on the island of St. John in the U.S. Virgin Islands.

Camp Lenox, Rte. 8, Lee, MA 01238 (phone 413/ 243-2223): In the southern Berkshires, on 250 hillside acres overlooking a lake, it accepts adults in June and September only, in facilities otherwise operated as a children's summer camp in July and August. Seminars are on weekends only, cost $140 to $215 per person including full board (gourmet vegetarian), and pursue such themes as "Living in the Spirit," "An Invitation to Radical Aliveness," and "The New Sacred Psychology." From October through May, when the facility is closed, write for information or reservations to: Richard Moss, 345 Riverside Dr., Apt. 4C, New York, NY 10025, or phone 212/662-3182.

Aegis, The Abode, R.D. 1, Box 1030D, New Lebanon, NY 12125 (phone 518/794-8095): On three-day weekends from May through October, supplemented by five-day midweek sessions in June and July, and occasional workshops in other seasons, outsiders come to study on this mountain in the Berkshires with a permanent community of "Sufis"—the gentlest of people who have made an eclectic choice from the prophetic messages of all religions, both Western and Eastern. Faculty includes a Benedictine monk, a rabbi, and a Native American. Sample workshops: "Optimal Functioning in Daily Life," "Healing and Wholeness in Psychotherapy," "The Shared Heart," "Dances of Universal Peace," "Sufism"; there is much meditation. To weekend tuition costs averaging $125, add room and board charges of about $30 a day in a dorm or cabin, $20 a day in a campsite.

Wainwright House, 260 Stuyvesant Ave., Rye, NY 10580 (phone 914/967-6080): A stately mansion on elegant grounds, just north of New York City, it offers year-round daily workshops—some for only a day in duration—in Jungian studies, spiritual disciplines, "health and wholeness," and other topics of psychology. Themes are far-ranging— "Depth Psychology," "Spiritual Development," "Global Issues," "Sonic Meditation," "The Psychology of Illness"— and speakers more eclectic still: They include Ram Dass, Dr. Bernie Siegel, James Hillman, Barbara Marx Hubbard, and Robert Johnson. One-day tuition ranges from free to $50, and overnight accommodations, including breakfast, run

Celebration Week, Omega Institute

$26 (dorm) to $36 (per person, double room). Other meals are offered in the dining room at additional cost. And a catalog of courses is free for the asking.

WEST COAST

Naropa Institute, 2130 Arapahoe Ave., Boulder, CO 80302 (phone 303/444-0202): Summer primarily, but in other months as well; it's best to inquire. In a partly urban setting, yet on the slopes of the Rockies, it is serious and intellectual, but with a heavy emphasis on innovative, psychological approaches to music, theater, dance, and creative writing. Nevertheless, workshops also include "The Intimate Relationship as a Practice and Path," "Nurturing," "Contemplative Psychotherapy," "Christian and Buddhist Meditation." Most short-term guests (less than a month) use nearby University of Colorado housing for room and board costs of about $150 a week, to which average tuition fees of about $250 should be added.

Feathered Pipe Ranch, P.O. Box 1682, Helena, MT 59624 (phone 406/442-8196): Open in spring, summer, and fall only, using log-and-stone ranchhouse accommodations in a stunning Rocky Mountain location bordered by a national forest. The program consists of "holistic life seminars," heavily spiritual, but also including standard yoga workshops (sometimes presented by Angela Farmer, the

Their goal? To fulfill the "human potential," to expand consciousness, releasing energy and spirit.

Hollyhock

most sought-after yoga instructor in the country), studies in holistic health, male/female relationships. Ilana Rubenfeld presented her widely acclaimed five-day "synergy" workshop (gestalt therapy combined with Feldenkrais and other forms of "body work") at Feathered Pipe recently; such other prominent figures in the personal-growth movement as Alan

Cohen and Jane Bolen (the latter the author of the bestselling *Goddesses in Every Woman*) are also frequent lecturers here. Charges average $700 a week for instruction, meals, and dorm-style lodging, but rates are reduced considerably for individuals participating in a "work retreat" program; inquire.

Ojai Foundation, P.O. Box 1620, Ojai, CA 93024 (phone 805/646-8343): Workshops with intensely spiritual themes are conducted throughout much of the year on these 40 acres of semi-wilderness land two hours north of Los Angeles. "Ritual Geomancy and Celebration," "Engaged Buddhism," "The I-Ching," and "Taoist Yoga" are among the studies pursued. Tuition (including lunch) is $125 to $195 (depending on the course) for a weekend, $325 for five days; campsite use, brunch, and dinner are $25 a day more. An interesting alternative, and a superb value, is a simple retreat program at Ojai, without courses: $25 a night for a campsite and all three meals; $40 a night to rent a "dome" or other structure, again including all three meals.

Hollyhock, P.O. Box 127, Manson's Landing, Cortes Island, BC, V0P 1K0, Canada (phone 604/935-6465): One hundred miles north of Vancouver, in the Strait of Georgia, this is a warm-weather-only (May through October) facility on an expanse of beach and 48 acres of gardens, orchards, and forest. Workshops are generally five days in duration, average U.S. $525 (and less) for tuition, room, and board, and explore such subjects as "Tibetan Buddhism," "Exploring the World of Alternative Medicine," "Vipassana Meditation," "Jungian Dreamwork," and "Tai-Chi Chu'an." Simple retreats without the workshops, but including morning yoga and meditation, in addition to lodgings and three meals a day, are $78 (Canadian) a day, or $495 (Canadian) for a week.

Each center issues catalogs or other descriptive literature, to be carefully perused before enrolling. From personal experience, I can assure you that a stay will cause you to discover, at the very least, important new aspects of your inner life and relations with others.

A Summer in the New Age

On a Rising Tide of Public Interest Spurred by the Works of Shirley MacLaine, Consciousness-Exploring Resorts and Retreats Have Emerged All Over the Nation

WHEN SHIRLEY MACLAINE FIRST REVEALED in a spate of bestselling paperbacks that she had lived past lives, gained strength from crystals, and experienced other cosmic phenomena, she did more than simply popularize a set of beliefs—she all but created a new segment of the travel industry. Because her writings had swayed a mass audience, other enthusiasts of the "New Age" were able to open holiday resorts and vacation villages to explore the subject in weekend and week-long seminars, workshops, and "retreats." Today, on a rising tide of success, and in more locations than many suppose, the countryside centers they founded are busily erecting new log cabins, more communal dining halls, additional meditation tents, and extra dormitory *yurts* (quaint, dome-topped lodges) to house a growing clientele.

But unlike their star performer, most New Age resorts want nothing to do with magic crystals, channeling, and past-life regression. Rather, they are peopled for the most part with fairly sober types—including eminent academic figures—whose most extreme belief is to suspect that humankind is poised on the brink of a major, evolutionary expansion of consciousness, whose frontiers they wish to explore. Or else they search for a single, universal force that may animate all living things on earth, holding out hope for eventual communication between species (animals, plants) and a growing closeness with nature. Or else they simply attempt to create a more caring, nurturing society through attention to spiritual concerns of a nondivisive sort.

A vacation at a New Age resort is therefore infinitely less exotic than most assume. It is, according to numerous reports, and based on my own one experience, relaxed and unpressured, nonjudgmental, but intellectually invigorating, and spent among a great many open-minded people. Certainly it can do you no harm, and the advantages are considerable: an open-air vacation in which all the standard recreations are available to supplement or substitute for the seminars, and all at costs that are among the lowest in the vacation field.

FIVE MAJOR RESORTS

Shenoa Retreat Center, P.O. Box 43, Philo, CA 95466 (phone 707/895-3156): Like most of the New Age resorts, it occupies a glorious physical setting, adjoining a virgin redwood forest and state park, above a 60-acre meadow bordered by three bubbling streams. You are in Mendocino

Shenoa Retreat Center

Directions to Shenoa:
Take Hwy. 101 north through Cloverdale. Past Cloverdale turn west on Hwy. 128. Stay on 128 through Boonville to Philo (about 55 minutes from Hwy. 101). In Philo turn left onto Ray's Road which is next to the BP Gas Station and proceed .3 of a mile to a fork in the road. Take the left fork (a gravel road) and avoid turning down any residential driveways. **You still have 1 mile to go to reach Shenoa.** Follow this road as it curves down to and across the Navarro River, and meanders up our hill until you see a sign directing you through the gate. You've made it!

County north of San Francisco (but warmer than that sometimes-chilly city), a half hour from the Pacific, in a facility of several rustic buildings (dining lodge, cabins), pleasant swimming pool, and tennis courts. The remarkable cost? $45 a day per adult in cabins, $25 camping, including all three meals (another $5 on weekends); plus a quite reasonable but varying sum (as little as $40 for three full days) for attendance and instruction at purely optional workshops and seminars in core subjects of the New Age: "Intuitional

---

Most New Agers believe that humankind is poised on the brink of a major, evolutionary expansion of consciousness.

Work and Dream Process," "Consciousness Healing," "Community Building," "Using Mental Images to Resolve Issues," a "Course in Miracles," or "The Manifestation of Spirit in the Life of the Planet at This Time." Some guests skip the seminars, savor the setting, and pay only $40 daily for everything else. Founded by alumnae of the famous Findhorn community in northern Scotland—first of the classic New Age retreats (1962)—Shenoa attempts to emulate Findhorn in its broad and tolerant approach, and permits proponents of every sort of spiritual belief to appear at its rostrum. Studies occupy half the day, after which guests can, in the center's words, "read, play, dream, swim, go for long walks in the forests or along the river, become renewed, refreshed, and inspired in this special place with like-minded, like-hearted people."

Chinook Learning Center, P.O. Box 57, Clinton, WA 98236 (phone 206/321-1884): On a stunning 72 acres of evergreen forest and meadowland, with a view of the Olympic Mountains, and close access (three miles) to the beaches of Puget Sound, the 19-year-old Chinook has a main house and scattered cabins housing 20 or so guests, but accommodates the bulk of its visitors (130 more) on campsites serviced by a nearby kitchen. Because of the camping emphasis, fees can run as low as $95, but generally average $175, for a long-weekend, three-night "program" of accommodations, all meals, and instruction on such typical themes as "An Inquiry into 'Gaia'" (the theory that all the earth is a single, living organism), "Spirit and Soul," "Guiding Myths for Men and

Women," "Holding Your Dreams in Community," and "Bonding with the Earth Through Meditation and Ritual." Other summer sessions run from four days to a full week or more, and some include workshops in various arts and crafts.

High Wind Farm, W7136 County Road D, Plymouth, WI 53073 (phone 414/528-7212): Primarily a permanent ecological community pursuing a wide variety of researches into energy conservation, organic gardening, and cooperative living. But a strong spiritual tone underlies the rational practices, and every summer—late June to early August—High Wind invites a number of New Age groups and speakers to present workshops for transient guests in such topics as "Our Role in a Holistic Universe," "Wonders of the Inner Mind," "Accelerating Human Consciousness," "Social/ Global Transformation," and "The Well-Being of Body, Mind, and Spirit." One such summer program, a full eight days and eight nights in length, costs a total of $385 per person, including room, all three meals, and all instruction. At most other times of the year, guests are invited simply to observe and share the experience of High Wind Farm for $30 per person per day, including accommodations and all meals. On such latter stays, as the group explains, you can "walk in the woods and fields, retreat, study, chat with available staff, lend a hand with cooking if you like." The farm complex, with its numerous, separate structures and homes, Community Center, "bioshelter," greenhouses, and big, red barn, occupies 128 verdant acres of rolling hills. Request, in particular, the 28-page tabloid newspaper of High Wind, called *Windwatch*, sent to persons remitting $25 for associate membership.

Joy Lake Mountain Seminar Center, P.O. Box 1328, Reno, NV 89504 (phone 702/323-0378): A large, 40-page catalog is required to list and describe the dizzying array of New Age topics and therapies taught in more than 80 three- to seven-day workshops, from May through September, at this forested, mountainside setting overlooking Joy Lake in the eastern Sierra Nevadas, a half hour's drive from Reno. Courses range from such highly arguable themes (to put it mildly) as "The Therapeutic Use of Crystals," "Past Life Recall Through Memo Therapy," and "Herbal Wisdom," to a host of utterly respectable, well-supported disciplines. The latter category includes lectures by such eminent authorities as Dr. Fritjof Capra, author of the widely acclaimed *The Tao of Physics*. Some of the workshops are taught outdoors—on the meadow, under Ponderosa pines, amid wildflowers and the chirping of pheasants in the Joy Lake aviaries. Afternoons, participants can simply relax "in a hammock listening to the creek bubble," says one brochure. For all this, room and board total only $45 (approximately) per person per day, with accommodations provided in either cabins or four-person *yurts* (with nomadic-style domes). You then add tuition costs, which average $150 for a three-day workshop, but vary widely.

High Wind Farm

The Center of the Light, P.O. Box 540, Great Barrington, MA 01230 (phone 413/229-2396): A strange amalgam of New Age beliefs and broad Christian doctrines, the center is administratively staffed, in large part, by ministers of the "Church of Christ Consciousness" (which claims to be wholly nondenominational), but teachers include students of the Kabbalah, holistic health practitioners, body awareness specialists, faith healers, researchers in paranormal experiences, and neurolinguistic educators. The curriculum is eclectic, to say the least. The summer program consists of two- to five-day workshops costing $90 to $150, to which you add $40 a day for room and board, using rustic dormitory cabins (bring your own sheets and blankets) segregated by sex; a limited number of "doubles" cabins, for couples, are available at the same $40-per-person charge. If guests wish, they can stay at the center in summer without taking a workshop, simply for the daily $40 charge. The prospect is tempting: you are in the western Berkshires, near Tanglewood and Jacob's Pillow, surrounded by orchards, lawns, gardens, fields, woods, and lakes. Facilities include a pool, tennis court, ball fields, and hiking trails. And the natural-foods cuisine, primarily vegetarian, is tasty and abundant.

Some critics charge that New Age beliefs are a substitute for political or social commitment, or a flight from serious, practical concerns, and a part of me shares those doubts. Nevertheless, while acknowledging my own preference for the rational over the mystical, and therefore a prejudice against the New Age, I have to admit the importance of these speculations and the reasonable possibility that they may be on the right track (although centuries away from corroborating their instincts). As a vacation activity, these pleasant mental exercises are among the more agreeable of all available options—certainly they're superior to the stressful programs of most resorts—and enjoyed in the company of kind and gentle people. Why not give them a try?

But unlike their star performer, most New Age resorts want nothing to do with magic crystals, channeling, and past-life regression.

A Visit to Famous Findhorn

Thousands Enjoy an "Experience Week" at the World's Most Celebrated "New Age" Community

FIRED FROM HIS JOB AS A HOTEL MANAGER, A restless Peter Caddy moved with his wife, three children, and a family friend to a car-trailer parked on a bleak stretch of sandy seacoast in northeastern Scotland, near a village named Findhorn.

And there, in 1962, he grew cabbages weighing 42 pounds. Claiming to tap into a life force that animates the universe, using meditation and "attunement" to feel at one with nature, this rather conventional Englishman created a garden so fertile as to cause dozens of others to join him in building a New Age community on the surrounding site. Its aim: to expand the human consciousness and thus change the world.

Today the cabbages are no more. Residents of the Findhorn Foundation joke about the phenomenon that brought them worldwide attention. "And anyway," said one to a recent guest, "why should anyone want to eat cabbage for a month?"

But what survives is an impressive, sprawling, residential-and-classroom complex of 180 permanent members, another hundred or so visitors pursuing successive, one-week courses of instruction—and a potent tourist attraction. By the thousands each year, adherents of a dozen, radically differing theories of the human potential, joined by others who are simply curious, flock to what has by now become the single most famous utopian community on earth.

THE EVOLUTION IN ITS FUNCTION

But Findhorn today is more a learning center than a community. Though the cultivation of its famous garden (books have been written about it) continues to be a major activity, Findhorn is far from self-sufficient in food or other products, and only a handful of its members work at life-sustaining tasks. Rather, the bulk of its population are administrators, publicists, teachers, or loyal volunteers at housekeeping (kitchen, transport, maintenance, accounts). Through those labors they keep the area alive with periodic workshops, seminars, and conferences exploring the spiritual bases of life. And these are attended by guests from around the world.

The goal is a breathtaking one, massively ambitious. "We believe humanity is on the verge of a major evolutionary leap," says one explanatory leaflet, "an expansion of consciousness" creating "new patterns of civilization and a . . . culture infused with spiritual values. . . . We seek [to discover that] new awareness in our own daily lives."

The steps toward the goal are more modest, and pursued in a highly reasonable manner. Findhorn teaches no single creed, explores the principles of all spiritual outlooks, grants total freedom of expression, and tends to ignore exotic dogmas. In its directory of workshop topics, not a single one

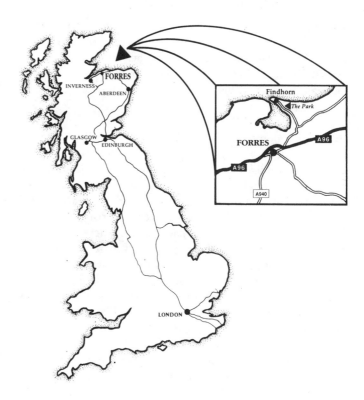

deals with Shirley MacLaine–type speculations into reincarnation, channeling, or magic crystals. Rather, it is the subconscious and the intuitive, the impact of mind upon body, the potential of human imagination, that form the core of discussions listed under such headings as "Meditation as a

Its aim: to expand the human consciousness and thus change the world.

Way of Life," "Reawakening the Metaphoric Mind," "Dreams and the Spiritual Path," "Learning to Love," "Coming Alive," "A Working Retreat for Managers," "Holistic Healing"—in short, the entire range of the more defensible forms of New Age thinking.

Workshops average £200 to £220 ($360 to $396) a week, including room and full board, and most are one week in duration.

THE EXPERIENCE WEEK

The strict prerequisite for attending a workshop, however, is prior participation in an "Experience Week" offered Saturday to Saturday throughout the year, and costing £200 ($360) for all-inclusive arrangements; that weekly sojourn is the major means for visiting Findhorn on a touristic or temporary basis.

"Experience Week" guests stay for seven nights in two- to six-bedded rooms of Findhorn's Cluny Hill College, a large, old (but well-maintained) former hotel overlooking a golf course; there they also take their meals (vegetarian, fresh, delicious). Throughout the week they tour every part of the Findhorn Foundation, including its work "departments," hear lectures by staff and celebrated theorists, engage in "sharings" (communal social gatherings), "sacred dancing," and innovative games designed to strip away repressions and wasteful defenses. They talk endlessly and lovingly with fellow guests about personal problems and goals. For each of five weekdays they also work for four hours in Findhorn's garden or kitchens, because work is regarded as a "cement" that brings community members together spiritually, a caring gesture more than a task.

Before each work period, members and guests hold hands in a brief meditation to "attune" to each other and the

Findhorn Foundation

project ahead. They talk with one another as the work proceeds, express mutual affection, become a close-knit group. Numerous observers (including my college-age daughter, Pauline, who visited Findhorn on my behalf) have commented on the energy and enthusiasm that go into such projects, and their impact on Findhorn, where grounds and structures are remarkably well kept and clean. In the kitchen, she reports, "work was done quickly and efficiently, and was more enjoyable than burdensome."

Although Findhorn's "Experience Weeks" have a large capacity, they are always heavily booked, especially in summer, when applications six to nine months ahead are advisable. Write for application forms, and further information, to **Accommodations Secretary, Findhorn Foundation, Cluny**

Cluny Hill College

Hill College, Forres, Scotland IV 36 ORD (phone 309-73655). Another Findhorn number for more general information is 309-72288.

Visiting children are not accepted, and have little role at Findhorn, except during occasional "Family Weeks."

ALTERNATIVE POSSIBILITIES

For would-be visitors unable to spend a full week at Findhorn, three lesser and last-minute alternatives are available.

First, you can simply wander through Cullerne, the main gardening area of the foundation, open to the public from sun-up to sundown. Some casual visitors have been known to work in that garden; in a large barn on the site, a downstairs coatroom provides raincoats and galoshes to poorly equipped, impromptu volunteers.

Or you can take a guided, but free, two-hour tour of the foundation's grounds, starting daily at 2 P.M. in spring, summer, and fall, but on Tuesday and Saturday only in winter. Tours set out from the Phoenix Shop (a combination bookstore and health-food purveyor) in The Park, which is the large area of trailers where Peter and Eileen Caddy first placed their home. The epochal, small green trailer is still there, but used as an office, and found directly across from the guest reception center. Nearby is the Universal Hall, Findhorn's showplace for conferences and performances; the Sanctuary (for meditation); the Apothecary Shop (herbal medicines prescribed by holistic physicians who have seen the light); a Community Center with food service; craft studios; pottery and weaving barns; a graphic design shop; a printing plant; and more.

Perhaps the best alternative visit is an unplanned, three-

Findhorn teaches no single creed, grants total freedom of expression, and tends to ignore exotic dogmas.

"Attuning" in the herb garden

day stay as a "short-term guest." Here, you generally arrange your own accommodations—either pitching a tent or using one of the many £10-a-night ($16) B&Bs or guest-accepting farmhouses in the vicinity—but present yourself daily to Findhorn for three hours of work (in your choice of departments, morning or afternoon), supplemented by participation in various gatherings and evening fests to which you'll then be invited. You simply show up unannounced at the Visitors Centre in The Park, or better, write or phone ahead to the **Findhorn Foundation (Short Term Guests), The Park, Forres, Scotland IV 36 OTZ (phone 309-30311)**, in which latter case you'll sometimes—but rarely—receive a bed in Cluny Hill College.

Despite your daily three-hour stint of work, you'll pay a "short-term charge" of £10 ($16) a day, or whatever you are able to afford (my backpacking daughter offered, and paid, £6), plus £2 ($3.60) for every meal taken. Unlike Experience Week guests, who are often bused from place to place on the extensive grounds of Findhorn, short-term guests make their own way to and from, and are probably best advised to have a car.

Bear in mind that the Findhorn Foundation is wholly distinct from the adjoining, tiny village of Findhorn—the latter a former fishing town, today a resort whose docks berth pleasure craft. In walking distance from the village's center is a long and lovely beach known as the "Riviera of Scotland" (but normally too cold for swimming).

The nearest larger village is Forres, about five miles away, and nationally acclaimed for its own gardens. In the vicinity is the well-preserved Cawdor Castle, full of armor, traditional furniture, and portraits of the Cawdors.

A larger nearby city is Inverness, 30 minutes by car from Findhorn, and proud possessor of a major airport. But trains stopping at Forres can also bring you to Findhorn.

Elsewhere in this book, I've written about an easily visited rationalist community in Britain, the Centre for Alternative Technology near Machynlleth, Wales, where residents apply logic, science, and egalitarian principles to the conduct of community life. In Findhorn, you have the contrasting spiritual approach to many of the same concerns, and both communities provide the basis for a profoundly important, endlessly fascinating, vacation trip to the U.K.

On the Road to Utopia

At "Intentional Communities" Across the U.S.A., Short Stays and Visits Are a Mind-Expanding Experience

SHOW ME A UTOPIAN COMMUNITY AND I'M soon walking on air. The very thought of people uprooting themselves and reassembling to lead a rational life brings goosepimples to my flesh, awakens youthful dreams of a better world.

Well, wonder of wonders, our nation harbors a hundred and more utopian communities, and some of them accept short-term visitors. Can you think of a more rewarding weekend or week-long stay than at a modern Walden, an Erewhon, a Shangri-La?

None of them, of course, would be so bold as to style themselves by those long-hallowed names. Rather, they are simply "intentional communities"—the modern term for those who have gathered onto a rural or small-town site to pursue a carefully planned life of cooperation and sharing.

Some are simply working farms occupied by three or four families, and obviously unsuitable for visiting tourists. Others, a growing number, are elaborate villages, with 60 to 100 residents, that encourage visitors and maintain overnight lodgings for them. From there they take you to classrooms, tour you through the site, lecture and prod you to reexamine your own harshly competitive life.

If all this seems threatening, or against your political grain, you might pause to consider that throughout history, similar intentional communities—both here and abroad— have introduced approaches to life, and forms of social organization, that later became commonplace.

The communal homes of a Denver or Washington, D.C., in which young single people share costs, are outgrowths of the experience of intentional communities. So are the ever-more-frequent platonic households of two singles of the opposite sex sharing an apartment.

The very same intentional communities first launched to a broader audience the current, widespread consumption of health foods, the growing practice of holistic medicine, protection of the environment, energy conservation and the use of nonfossil fuels, the soaring interest in Eastern philosophies and religions (zen, tao, yoga), humane attitudes toward animals.

"We are like laboratories for research into the future," said a member of one community in the course of my own visit. "We are testing the methods that people a hundred years from now will use to improve their lives."

THEIR VISITOR PROGRAMS

Care to observe? The most rewarding vacations I know are spent as a guest (or working guest) on the grounds of a hundred such villages that avidly encourage visitors as a means of spreading their utopian views. They house and feed you for the most nominal charge, because their goal (to put it bluntly) is to change your life—and the life of this planet.

Yet though they proselytize, they do not brainwash. The mildest of people, they fully expect you to recoil initially from such community concepts as "transspecies interaction" (communication with animals, insects, and plants)—and they take no offense at your own disbelief. They are just as accustomed to resistance when first they introduce you to "communal childcare," "planetary citizenship," or "extended families." Instead of arguing, they return calmly to

Can you think of a more rewarding weekend or week-long stay than at a modern Walden, an Erewhon, a Shangri-La?

work while you, in dazed confusion, ponder upon an unsettling eruption of new ideas.

And ponder them you will. Just wait until you encounter "variable labor credits" or "flexible work weeks"! Your mind will almost audibly stretch as you learn that, at some communities, members performing desirable work (like childcare) receive fewer hours of credit than members performing undesirable work (like cleaning latrines). By opting for the latter, aspiring artists and writers can reduce their communal labors to two or three days a week—and isn't that sensible?

Among the communities that take visitors are these prominent examples (rich opportunities for your next holiday trip):

TWIN OAKS, VIRGINIA

Twin Oaks, near Louisa, Virginia: Nearly 100 people live in this 23-year-old collection of farm buildings on 400 acres of woods, creeks, hilly pastures, and meadows—their goal an eventual community of 200 to 300. To promote both membership and viewpoints, visits are permitted, but only on most (not all) Saturday afternoons from 2 to 5 P.M. (no food is served), for $3 per adult, and only through prior arrangement by phone. Those more seriously interested in joining are then allowed to make a three-week visit, for a total of $40, using self-supplied sleeping bags on the floor of several houses, or a dozen actual beds in the eight rooms of a visitors' building.

Heavily influenced by the utopian novel of the Harvard psychologist B. F. Skinner, *Walden Two*, the community attempts to be a "model social system" through rational approaches to life that avoid the spiritual emphasis of several other communities. Political solutions are stressed, logic is the tool, and all forms of modern media—books, records, tapes, and magazines, everything except television (because it promotes "those values and products that we are trying to avoid")—are amply available on site.

At Twin Oaks, all labor, property, and resources are held in common, but personal privacy is fiercely protected. Children are raised as in an Israeli kibbutz, occupying their own residence and raised by all adult members. Supervision of economic life is by numerous planner-managers elected to short terms, and the community is self-sufficient through the manufacture of handcrafted hammocks and chairs, other small industries, and the cultivation of extensive organic gardens serving a mostly vegetarian table.

Twin Oaks is easily reached by bus or car from Washington, D.C., but is even closer to Richmond, Charlottesville, or Culpeper. For literature, or to schedule a visit (even the afternoon visit must be booked in advance), contact **Visitor Program, Twin Oaks Community, Louisa, VA 23093** (**phone 703/894-5126**).

EAST WIND, MISSOURI

East Wind, near Tecumseh, Missouri, in the Ozark hills, is another kibbutz-like, B. F. Skinner–influenced community of 50 or so members pursuing a "peaceful, cooperative, and egalitarian" life free of "racist, sexist, and competitive behavior." Constantly experimental, open-minded, and diverse, it places a music practice space next to a dairy barn, a trailer-library alongside the inevitable shops for producing hammocks, sandals, and—a proud specialty—"nut butter." Members, each with a full vote, have substantial labor or production quotas, but enjoy weekend rest, plus three weeks of vacation a year, and can earn additional vacation by producing "overquota." Children are raised by "metas"—members who have chosen childcare as their work—but have at least three other "primary people" in their lives: their parents, and one or two others chosen by the parents.

Because East Wind is anxious to expand, it encourages visits (costing only $2 a day) for up to three weeks by people who then work the same number of hours as members and spend only the amount of money on site as would equal a member's allowance. Any fears of a spartan life that these rules may evoke are soon overcome by the idyllic natural setting of the site, an area renowned for its swimming, canoeing, hiking, and other outdoor recreation.

Write ahead for reservations (and don't simply drop in) to **East Wind Community, P.O. Box FB5, Tecumseh, MO 65760** (**phone 417/679-4682**).

SIRIUS, MASSACHUSETTS

Sirius, near Amherst, Massachusetts, emphasizes spirituality to the same or even greater extent than its political notions of cooperation and sharing; indeed, it differs from numerous other communities by encouraging members to earn their own incomes, sometimes at jobs in neighboring towns. But most of the members purchase food jointly, take most meals communally, own the 86 acres of their site jointly, reach community decisions by consensus—and meditate until all members acquiesce in the "rightness" of the decisions taken.

Like Thoreau, the Sirius participants have built their homes "in the woods," and there they engage in organic gardening, holistic health practices, and solar design. But it is personal growth to which most attention is paid. Though members are free to pursue varying spiritual disciplines, they believe in the God within each human being and the "interconnectedness" of all nature (animals, plants, humans). Several prominent members are alumni of the famous Findhorn Community in Scotland (we've already visited that magical place in a previous essay) and apply the same loving care to gardens and forests that Findhorn regards as a moral imperative.

Personal growth, so claims the Sirius group, results from

the demands of harmonious group living. Members rid themselves of old patterns, become "agents of change," build for themselves and others "a more peaceful, loving world."

Visits by outsiders can be made for several days or up to several weeks. Less intensive, free open houses are held on the first and third Sundays of every month, starting with a "New Age Sunday Service" at 11 A.M., meditation at 12:30 P.M., a "potluck lunch" (you either bring your own or make a small donation) at 1 P.M., and then a tour of the community at 2 P.M. On overnight stays of any duration, guests either join in community work or spend the time in quiet contemplation; accommodation fees are on a sliding scale according to the guest's income, include all three meals daily, and range from $20 to $60 a day. Guests are always asked (even for attendance at a free Sunday open house) to phone first for instructions and to let Sirius members know that they are coming.

Contact **Sirius Community, Baker Road, Shutesbury, MA 01072 (phone 413/259-1251).**

SUNRISE RANCH, COLORADO

Sunrise Ranch, near Loveland, Colorado, one of the oldest (1940s) and most successful (150 residents) of the alternative communities, places its emphasis almost entirely on personal, spiritual growth, and not on communal, social, or economic practices. Still, a major activity is organic gardening (supplying most of the ranch's foodstuffs), followed closely in the use of personnel by clerical functions supporting the worldwide activities of the Society of Emissaries, the sponsoring organization. The latter's doctrines are a mild, broad, and initially hard-to-comprehend philosophy of "quality living" through "alignment with the rhythms and cycles of life." "Manipulation," says Sunrise teacher Nick Giglio, "as well as hidden agendas and tools of persuasion are unnecessary excess baggage."

Visiting facilities are extensive, cost only $25 to $30 a day (the suggested "donation"), including all three meals (plus the cost of any particular seminar or presentation at the time of your visit), and should be reserved in advance by writing to **Sunrise Ranch, 5569 N. County Rd. 29, Loveland, CO 80538 (phone 303/679-4200).** Loveland is 50 miles north of Denver, and the ranch is seven miles from Loveland.

STELLE, ILLINOIS

Stelle, 90 miles south of Chicago and 30 miles southwest of Kankakee, at the opposite end of the political spectrum from the communal societies described above, is a small (125 residents), planned village (like a miniature Columbia, Md., or Reston, Va.) in which homes are privately owned and incomes privately earned. But various cooperative (not communal) institutions bind the residents together, including bulk purchases of food, joint operation of a local telephone exchange, periodic "celebrations," and a town-hall form of pure democratic government. Residents consider themselves an extended family.

The village is most productively visited for exposure to the library, publications, and audio-visual presentations of its quarterly, *Communities Magazine*, dealing with subjects that affect the operation of intentional communities. You do this either on a day trip or overnight for $25 single, $40 double, including breakfast, at any of about 20 bed-and-breakfast houses. Write or phone in advance to **Communities, 105-127 Sun St., Stelle, IL 60919 (phone 815/256-2200).** Or you can arrange a day visit, or one to have lunch with residents on Tuesday or Friday (at a cost of $3 to $5), by phoning the **Stelle Group Office (phone 815/256-2212 between 8 A.M. and 5 P.M.).** Generally, they will have someone available to talk with you and take you on a short tour, occasionally stopping to converse with residents.

FIVE MORE COMMUNITIES

Appletree, near Eugene, Oregon: A tiny, rural commune of rational, egalitarian practices. Overnight or week-long visitors pay $4 and contribute three hours of work a day, and are asked to apply at least two weeks in advance. Persons staying in nearby towns can visit for part of a day by simply phoning at least a day ahead. Write **Appletree, P.O. Box 5, Cottage Grove, OR 97424 (phone 503/942-4372).**

Mettanokit, in southern New Hampshire: An income-sharing, decision-sharing group of 20 individuals seeking to create a society (in their words) of "loving, cooperative, zestful, intelligent, creative human beings." They work by consensus, apportion all household and cleaning tasks

Some are elaborate villages, with 60 to 100 residents, that encourage visitors and maintain overnight lodgings for them.

equally, and enjoy receiving a constant flow of prenotified visitors who pay $10 a day for room and board on visits of several days (visitors share in the work and social activities of the community). Contact **Mettanokit, Another Place, Rte. 123, Greenville, NH 03048 (phone 603/878-9883 or 603/878-3117).**

The Foundation for Feedback Learning, on Staten Island, New York: Minutes from the towers of downtown Manhattan, a 45-member group inhabits five large houses in which they pursue researches so eclectic as to defy generalization: language training, psychodrama, biofeedback, and furniture repair, in addition to multiple new approaches to communal living and personal relationships, the constant exchange of thoughts and feelings. Visitors to New York may stay with them for a day or two for free, or for one-month periods for $400 to $550 per person (less per person for couples), including all meals. Contact the **Foundation for Feedback Learning, 135 Corson Ave., Staten Island, NY 10301 (phone 718/720-5378).**

Breitenbush Retreat Center, 60 miles from Salem, Oregon: Here are 40 adults (with 9 children) of widely divergent political and spiritual views, but all with a fierce urge to enjoy a life in nature, and warm, caring relationships. At a 2,500-foot elevation in the western Cascade Mountains, they found and restored this isolated hot-springs resort, where they provide guests with vegetarian meals, holistic health care, meditation, and other such "therapies" for as little as $40 per person per day, cabin and full board. Those more seriously interested in the communal practices of Breitenbush may occasionally stay for a week entirely free on a Volunteer Work Program involving 40 hours of moderate duties and full opportunity to attend all meetings and discussions. Contact **Breitenbush Community, P.O. Box 578, Detroit, OR 97342 (phone 503/854-3314 or 503/371-3754).**

Green Pastures Estates, in Epping, New Hampshire: A spiritual community in a small New England village. The 80 or so members aged 11 to 85 occupy a compound of period structures clustered around a central dining room where meals (both vegetarian and non-) are taken communally. Some members "live in" but "work out" at jobs in neighbor-

Foundation for Feedback Learning

Thrift Store, Foundation for Feedback Learning

ing towns, and then pay Green Pastures for their room and board. Others work the adjoining 160-acre farm. All pursue a goal of spiritual growth or maturity that stresses the responsibility of each individual for his/her own emotional state. By attaining that growth (taught, among other topics, at four evening "services" each week), members aid the community to become a joyful, creative, smoothly interacting

Throughout history, similar "intentional communities" have introduced approaches to life, and forms of social organization, that later became commonplace.

Breitenbush

group. Visitors wishing to participate for a short stay will receive room and board for only $25 a day (a suggested donation) by writing in advance to **Green Pastures Estates, 38 Ladd's Lane, Epping, NH 03042 (phone 603/679-8149).** Epping is about seven miles from Exeter.

AND STILL OTHERS

Since most intentional communities receive frequent visits by like-minded members of other such communities, members are usually aware of the distinctive features, pros and cons, of several. They share this knowledge with visitors, network-

ing in open, unabashed fashion. Soon you become aware of both the nationwide and international ramifications of the "intentional communities" movement, enriching your knowledge of the contemporary world, and perhaps learning how people will live in future years.

The current-day community members total as many as 200,000 people. In hundreds of small farm settlements or tiny villages, or more frequently in thousands of urban communal households, they have rejected the current forms of society and sought Utopia: a life of cooperation, not competition; of sharing, not owning; of full equality and democracy, without direction or domination from above.

America on $35 a Day, Via the Yoga Route

Remarkable Vacations, Rewarding and Cheap, at Ashrams Clustered Near Both Coasts

I AM NOT A YOGI. AND CONSIDERING MY FE-verish lifestyle, horrendous eating habits, and stubborn rationalism, that's the understatement of the year.

But yogi or not, some of my happiest holidays have been spent at yoga retreats. When it comes to inducing sheer serenity, restoring vigor, flushing toxins from both mind and body, nothing beats these mystical *ashrams* (schools, places of learning) with their vegetarian meals and quiet hillside settings, their twice-daily *asanas* (languid stretching exercises) and moments of meditation, their gentle people.

And when it comes to cost, nothing else in the vacation field even remotely compares. At a score of residential, countryside ashrams clustered near both coasts, the charge for room and all three meals amounts—if you can believe it—to $35 and $45 a day.

Why so cheap? Because the meals are vegetarian, the sites are often donated, and the staff works for free, performing karma yoga (selfless service).

Why, then, aren't they inundated with guests? Because the public, in general, recoils from Eastern thought, equating all such teachings with those of Sun Myung Moon, assuming dreadful acts of brainwashing or abandoned conduct, as at the turbulent Rajneeshpuram in Oregon or the doomed Guyanese community of mad Jim Jones.

As applied to the yoga movement, nothing could be further from the truth. A philosophy of life, not a religion; a questing science, not a dogma—yoga is the most tolerant of creeds, its practitioners good-humored, broad-minded, and modest, non-authoritarian. At the U.S. ashrams, nothing is mandatory other than attendance at the asanas (physical exercises or postures) and silent meditations—and that, only to screen out persons who are simply seeking a cheap crashpad for their vacations.

Apart from those two limited daily sessions, no one cares what you do or where you go, or whether you even attend lectures of the guru. He or she is regarded with affection, called *guruji* or *swamiji* (dear little guru, dear little swami), but treated as fallible, and certainly not as a Godhead. Some instructors at the ashrams—even a director or two—will stress their distance from Hindu theology and their pursuit of yoga primarily for its physical and calming benefits.

Though the residential ashrams in North America number far more than a score, not all have guaranteed staying-power. Those that do include:

THE SIVANANDA RETREAT

On Paradise Island, the Bahamas: You've heard of Club Med; now meet Club Meditation (at a fifth the price). The ashram that's a 150-bed tropical resort, it sits next to sugary-white sands, across the bay from Nassau on four beachfront acres donated to the Sivananda Vedanta movement by an admirer; the popular, otherworldly complex is now in its 24th year. You arise at dawn to meditate on the beach, proceed immediately (and before breakfast) to a two-hour exercise class (asana), partake at last of a mammoth vegetarian brunch, and are then allowed to do nothing at all (except swim, snorkel, and sun) until 4 P.M., when a second round of asanas is followed by supper at 6 P.M., meditation at sunset, and bed. Accommodations range from airy dorms in a colonial building ($45 per person per night, including meals and exercise classes) to double rooms in modern cabins ($50) to "meditation huts" ($55) overlooking the sea, to single rooms affording privacy and great calm ($75). Contact **Sivananda Ashram Yoga Retreat, P.O. Box N7550, Paradise Island, Nassau, Bahamas (phone 809/363-2902)**, for reservations or literature; or you can speak with the New York office: **Sivananda Yoga Center, 243 W. 24th St., New York, NY 10011 (phone 212/255-4560)**.

Sivananda Yoga Vedanta Center, Nassau

KRIPALU CENTER

Near Lenox, Massachusetts: In the many wings and 400 rooms of a former Jesuit monastery, on a hillside overlooking Lake Mahkeenac in the Berkshire Mountains of western Massachusetts, Kripalu is one of the largest of all ashrams, with one of the most varied programs—its brochure resembles a college catalog crammed with courses and options. Soothed by the ministrations of a largely unpaid staff of volunteers, you exercise, meditate, wander, and soak, attend lively seminars and yet dine in complete silence at thrice-daily vegetarian buffets, hear lectures by the impressive Yogi Amrit Desai (*gurudev*—beloved teacher). Accommodations are comfortable, in spacious dorms (10 to 22 people) of wide-frame, wooden double-deckers, or in pleasant private rooms, and yet the all-inclusive charge—for housing and all three meals, exercise classes, and most other activities—is only $60 per person in the dormitories, $70 per person in a standard double room. Write or phone **Kripalu Center, P.O. Box 793, Lenox, MA 01240 (phone 413/637-3280 Monday through Saturday).**

TWO IN NEW YORK STATE

The Yoga Ranch, at Woodbourne, New York: About two hours by bus from New York City, it occupies a stunning setting atop a wooded hill, looking down into a valley and up onto another hill, the mountains of the Catskills receding into the distance. Dotted about are open areas devoted to organic farming or used by grazing deer. On the extensive grounds, a one-acre pond is deep enough for swimming, while nearby stands a stone-faced sauna, wood-fired, rock-heated, and steamed by pure, mountain spring water—one-of-a-kind. "You'll be doing good for a lot of people if you recommend us," said the co-director at the end of our talk. "They come here with jangled nerves, and then leave completely restored." The charge for that revival is an astonishing $30 per person per day (half price for children under 15, free for children under 5), including yoga asanas (exercises), meditation, accommodation in twin or triple rooms, and two vegetarian meals. Write or phone **Sivananda Ashram Yoga Ranch, P.O. Box 195, Woodbourne, NY 12788 (phone 914/434-9242).**

Ananda Ashram, near Monroe, New York: Despite its resident guru (a soft-spoken, self-effacing, former physician, now Shri Brahmananda Sarasvati) and classic activities (which include lessons in the much-stressed science of

When it comes to inducing sheer serenity, nothing beats these mystical retreats with their vegetarian meals and quiet hillside settings, their twice-daily asanas (languid stretching exercises) and moments of meditation.

Ananda Ashram

pranayama—breath control), the 27-year-old Ananda Ashram has a far-less-pronounced Eastern orientation than some others: it schedules meditation for as late as 9 A.M. on weekends, invites guest teachers from all religious disciplines, and presents classes in creative music, drama, dance, video production, and visual arts. Less than 90 minutes by bus from New York City, at the base of the Catskill Mountains, it occupies 100 wooded acres, including a large private lake, and houses 40 visitors in two main guesthouses, for an all-inclusive room-and-meals charge (on seven-night stays) of $200 per week. Lesser stays are $35 per person per day in midweek for room and meals, $45 per day on weekends. Contact the **Ananda Ashram, R.D. 3, Box 141, Monroe, NY 10950 (phone 914/782-5575).**

THREE IN CALIFORNIA

The Yoga Farm, at Grass Valley, California: Cheapest of the residential ashrams ($30 a night, mainly in triple rooms, including vegetarian meals), but the smallest also, with space for just 30 guests, the farm is the personal favorite of the eminent Swami Vishnu Devananda, head of the Sivananda movement. Like thousands of others over the years who have driven up the 50 or so miles from Sacramento and then followed dirt roads to the isolated setting, he values the special simplicity and quiet of this rustic, two-building resort, with its changeless routine of meditation/exercises/free time. In the free-time period, as you hike to the top of an adjoining hill and lie daydreaming on its crest, you see the

Sivananda Ashram Vrindavan Yoga Farm

foot central building provides some of the accommodations, but most guests stay in three- to four-person yurts scattered about the 40 acres of grounds. Personal retreats and classes in yoga can be pursued at any time of the year, at a $35-per-day charge, which does not include meals (participants buy and cook their own food in a central kitchen), but more elaborate one-week and 16-day "intensives" are scheduled at frequent intervals throughout the spring, summer, and fall, and these include meals prepared by two noted vegetarian chefs, as well as morning-till-night classes (in-depth yoga training) at a cost of $675 to $750 for the one-week sessions, $1,500 for the 16-day "intensives." Since the weather of Santa Barbara is mild even in the winter (daytime temperatures in the upper 60s or low 70s), yoga-inclined travelers might schedule a personal visit at that time of year, at the $35-a-day tariff. To reach this very contemporary, eclectic yoga center, contact: **The White Lotus Foundation, 2500 San Marcos Pass, Santa Barbara, CA 93105 (phone 805/964-1944).**

Ananda, The Expanding Light, near Nevada City, California: A strange amalgam of faiths, this is the yoga ashram located on the grounds of a larger utopian community known as the Ananda World Brotherhood Village. The "town," 1,000 acres in size, was formed in 1967 by devout Christians who are also practitioners of yoga, and regard it as complementary to the other faith. Today, at the Brotherhood Inn and other scattered structures and (in summer) tents, 200 visitors of all faiths and backgrounds can engage in a retreat of classic yoga practices—early-morning and late-afternoon asanas and meditations—supplemented by classes and workshops on yogic themes. For week-long stays, the daily charge is $27 for campers bringing their own tents, $35 in shared tents, $40 per person in a double room, $55 for a private single room, including all three vegetarian meals and classes. Guests volunteering for a "work exchange" program, doing some cooking or cleaning, pay only $18 a day. Ananda is 15 miles from Nevada City, the latter is 70 miles north of Sacramento. Contact **The Expanding Light, c/o Ananda World Brotherhood Village, 14618 Tyler Foote, Nevada City, CA 95959 (phone 916/292-3494, or toll free 800/346-5350).**

majestic Sierras spread out before you. A very special place. Write or phone **Sivananda Ashram Vrindavan Yoga Farm, 14651 Ballantree Lane, Grass Valley, CA 95949 (phone 916/272-9322).**

The White Lotus Foundation, in elegant Santa Barbara, California: Some 1,800 feet up the mountains just behind the city, overlooking the Pacific Ocean and the Channel Islands, and founded in 1967 and currently directed by Ganga White, author of the book *Double Yoga*, its principal emphasis is on yoga and related disciplines (bodywork, shiatsu, acupuncture, acupressure), conveyed to guests through workshops, seminars, and classes throughout the year. A 5,000-square-

A philosophy of life, not a religion; a questing science, not a dogma—yoga is the most tolerant of creeds, its practitioners good-humored, broad-minded, and modest, non-authoritarian.

STILL OTHER POSSIBILITIES

The Himalayan Institute of Pennsylvania is yet another major center of yoga practice and studies, yet so diverse in its programs that it is practically impossible to describe. A 48-page catalog lists all its weekend, week-long, 10-day, and month-long investigations throughout the year into every aspect and theory—sometimes conflicting—of the yoga literature; it is for serious students of the art, and beginners may feel "in over their heads"! Figure $45 a day, all inclusive, for most week-long and longer programs, which do include beginners' classes in hatha yoga (physical exercises). If you do attend, you'll be housed on a 422-acre campus in the hills of the Pocono Mountains region of northeastern Pennsylvania, six miles north of the town of Honesdale, overlooking spectacular wooded hills and valleys. Contact **The Himalayan Institute, R.R. 1, Box 400, Honesdale, PA 18431 (phone toll free 800/444-5772).**

I have not described the important 2,000-bed Muktananda Center (the "Syda Foundation") in South Fallsburg, New York (phone 914/434-2000), because of its heavy (and somewhat atypical) theological emphasis, which stresses chanting and meditation to a far greater extent than hatha (physical) yoga and exercises. The Syda Foundation discourages casual visitors but is happy to accept potential acolytes.

Nor have I mentioned large retreats in Canada and Baja California.

To find other residential ashrams, phone the in-city centers listed under "Yoga Instruction" in the *Yellow Pages,* and ask the personnel to name the countryside location, if any, to which they go for an occasional retreat. I'd be grateful if

The Himalayan Institute

you'd also pass on the information to me, at the address listed in the Preface; and in gratitude, I press my hands together beneath my lips, and intone: "Jai Bhagwan" ("I honor the spirit within you").

THE NEW WORLD OF TRAVEL 1992

The lifeblood of the Arthur Frommer travel guides is the correspondence received from readers, commenting on the establishments recommended in the texts and recommending new establishments. Each such letter is carefully studied, and when a particular lead seems promising, it is followed up and personally checked.

It is hoped that *The New World of Travel* will receive similar assistance from its readers. A yearly publication, issued near the start of each year, *The New World* will constantly grow. And since much of its content relates to

organizations that lack the means to market themselves properly, or come to the attention of a travel journalist, your help is invaluable in alerting me to the organizations—hospitality exchanges, alternative resorts, new travel clubs, and the like—that you have discovered.

If you become aware of a new travel organization, program, or development that deserves to be described in our next edition, *The New World of Travel 1992*, won't you please let me know about it? Send your letters to Arthur Frommer, *The New World of Travel*, c/o Prentice Hall Press, Travel Division, 15 Columbus Circle, New York, NY 10023. All letters will be acknowledged, and all are warmly appreciated, in advance, by the author.

II

POLITICAL TRAVEL, TO SEE FOR YOURSELF, TO WIDEN YOUR VIEW

Meet the Political Travel Agent, a New Breed

Their Trips and Tours Are Sharply Different from the Usual Variety—Profound and Stimulating

THEY ARE FED UP AND FURIOUS WITH THE Changing of the Guard, the beach at Copacabana, the Golden Gate Bridge.

Though they are travel professionals, they are grieved by the often trivial content of their profession. Unlike the usual travel agent—who tends to be a rather conservative retail merchant, glued to the bottom line—they are passionate idealists out to change the world.

Travel, they believe—properly conducted and serious in content—can change the consciousness of the traveler, and thereby alter the United States. Whether to the right, left, or center, and in however small a way, they feel they can make a difference.

Meet four examples of the "political travel agent" or "public affairs travel agent":

GATE (GLOBAL AWARENESS THROUGH EXPERIENCE)

Here is the reflection in travel of the surging "Liberation Theology" movement in the Catholic church. Determined to expose a wider public to the realities and sufferings of Third World nations, nuns of the Sisters of Charity founded the odd travel agency called GATE in Mount St. Joseph, Ohio, nine years ago, then moved its offices in late 1990 to a college in La Crosse, Wisconsin, for greater effectiveness. From there each month, photocopies of typewritten travel brochures— like none you've ever seen—go cascading forth to every part

Travel, they believe, can change the consciousness of the traveler, and thereby alter the United States.

Managua, Nicaragua

of the country, advertising GATE-led tours to Nicaragua and the barrios of Peru, or to "base communities" in Mexico. In place of "today we journey to the famous waterfall," GATE's literature talks of "dialogues with ministers, professors, and the poor," attendance at "meetings of popular movements . . . supporting their search and struggle for freedom in their country." Tour rates (and amenities) are moderate in level; participation is ecumenical and increasingly promoted also by Protestant groups; tour leaders and destination representatives (some of them on-the-spot missionaries) are opinionated but noncontrolling. Some tours go to countries of Eastern Europe.

But the emphasis is nonetheless on themes of Liberation Theology. As defined by Sister Patricia McNally, a former U.S. GATE coordinator, it is "a theology in which we are all brothers and sisters, achieving equality, freeing and then empowering the oppressed to achieve their full dignity, enabling them not always to be dominated by some white-faced person. . . ." For literature, send a stamped, self-addressed envelope to **Sister LaVonne Abst, GATE, Viterbo College, La Crosse, WI 54601 (or phone 608/791-0462).**

PEOPLE TO PEOPLE INTERNATIONAL

This is the "centrist" of the political travel agencies, more heavily involved in broad public affairs than in special-interest advocacy or politics, and so prestigious as to be frequently mistaken for a U.S. government agency.

It once was. President Dwight D. Eisenhower founded it in 1956 out of a belief that people-to-people contacts across national boundaries were as vital as government efforts to

Guatemala

maintain world peace. He initially made the organization a part of the U.S. Information Agency, then in 1961 persuaded his friend, Joyce Hall, of Hallmark Cards in Kansas City, to fund the transition to a private, nonprofit corporation for which the then former President Eisenhower was the first chairman of the board. Today, in addition to its several Student Ambassador Programs sending teenagers abroad, and American-homestay plans for foreign visitors to the U.S., PTP organizes trips by several thousands of adult Americans each year to visit with their counterparts abroad: lawyers with lawyers, teachers with teachers, scientists with other scientists in their field. The goal: to "unleash the common interests among citizens of all countries and avoid the difference of national self-interest." More than 180 overseas

The goal of People to People International: to "unleash the common interests among citizens of all countries and avoid the difference of national self-interest."

chapters in 34 countries make the arrangements for personal contacts; several prestigious U.S. tour operators handle the technical arrangements. Because itineraries involve an intricate schedule of meetings, briefings, speeches, and seminars, the trips aren't cheap. Contact **People to People International, 501 E. Armour Blvd., Kansas City, MO 64109 (phone 816/531-4701).**

OTHERS, CENTER AND LEFT

Friendship Tours, of Modesto, California: Another "centrist" approach to political touring, non-ideological but people-to-people in its orientation. To a broad variety of standard trips (Guatemala, Honduras, American Appalachia, the Soviet Union, Africa), Friendship Tours attaches university lecturers or noted journalists, then works to schedule meetings and interviews with relevant individuals at the destination. For information, contact **Jo Taylor, Friendship Tours, 1905 E. Orangeburg Ave., Modesto, CA 95355 (phone 209/576-7775).**

Forum Travel, of Pittsburgh, Pennsylvania: A traditional, full-service travel agency, Forum nevertheless specializes in study tours of the Middle East, devoting special attention to issues in the Israeli-Palestinian conflict. Tours go to Israel, Jordan, Egypt, and Syria; to kibbutzim, West Bank settlements, and Arab villages; and to the homes of both Israeli and Arab families. Though most groups desiring such tours are already organized before they come to Forum for assistance and arrangements, Forum can occasionally place individual applicants with groups already created and scheduled to depart. Contact **Forum Travel, 4608 Winthrop St., Pittsburgh, PA 15213 (phone 412/681-4099, or toll free 800/888-4099).**

Anniversary Tours, of New York City: Specialists in travel to the USSR and the nations of Eastern Europe, Anniversary Tours takes an intensely political approach, even earthily so: some tours proudly include "visits to four different factories" or "a round-table discussion with workers and scholars on the current nature of restructuring (*perestroika*)." Generally speaking, they are not for aesthetes or people of standard views, although some tours feature "theater and the arts," Soviet style. Anniversary is also the only tour operator I know that occasionally uses the lower-cost hotels administered by the Soviet Union's Central Trade Union Council (as opposed to the tourist hotels controlled by the official Soviet travel organization, Intourist). When it does so—and passengers are always specifically advised of such use in advance—resulting tour prices are generally $200 to $300 less than for similar programs using Intourist hotels. But more important, staying in hotels not ordinarily assigned to tourists, but used by Soviet citizens, has the added

Cajamarca, Peru

Friendship Tours to China

benefit of putting tourists in contact with ordinary Soviet travelers, and not simply other international tourists. For brochures and other information, contact **Anniversary Tours, 330 Seventh Ave., New York, NY 10001 (phone 212/465-1200, or toll free 800/223-1336 outside New York State).**

Although the bulk of the new "political travel agents" send their clients to all parts of the world, a number focus solely on problems of the Third World. Because the latter approach is somewhat different, I've split off the Third World specialists from the preceding discussion and dealt with them mainly in the very next essay. Please read on.

Reality Tours to the Third World

On "Travel Seminars," in Nations with Three-Quarters
of the World's Population, Americans Are Exploring
the Most Important Issues of Our Time

HOW MANY "WORLDS" DO YOU KNOW? TO how many "worlds" have you traveled? Apart from a periodic jaunt to Mexico or the Caribbean, have you traveled to the "Third World"? And can those beach vacations at a Club Med in Cancún, or a casino-resort in Curaçao, really be regarded as trips to the Third World?

Five organizations outside the bounds of the normal travel industry have set about operating "reality tours" to the true Third World. Their aim is enlightenment rather than recreation or rest. Their area of activity is the poorest part of what is also called the "developing world": most of Central and South America, most of Africa, much of Asia. Their method is to stress contact with ordinary people of the Third World, to expose tour passengers to conditions experienced by residents of that "world" (who make up three-quarters of the population of the earth). And their search is for solutions: to poverty and debt, domestic instability and disease, the unequal allocation of income and resources.

So is the trip a chore, an exercise in self-flagellation? Far from it, say the backers of these odd travel ventures. For this, it is claimed, is "transformational travel" that irrevocably broadens the mind and liberates the spirit of those who engage in it, makes them clear-headed and emphatic in their public judgments, enhances their love for humankind, gives them goals and purpose. And some concessions are made to personal comfort: the use of modest hotels in place of mud huts, an occasional stay in modern dormitories or pleasant private homes.

LARGEST OF ALL

The Center for Global Education, Augsburg College, 731 21st Ave. South, Minneapolis, MN 55454 (phone 612/ 330-1159), is the largest of the Third World tour operators. Though its base is that of a small Lutheran school with limited funds, it successfully sends out more than 40 groups a year—often a departure a week—to countries of the Middle

East and Central America for the most part, but occasionally to the Philippines and islands of the Caribbean, and rarer still, to South America (Chile is a prominent choice). Most tours are planned to visit combinations of two and three countries—say, Guatemala and El Salvador, or Mexico, Honduras, and Nicaragua—for 10 to 14 days, at total tour costs of $900 to $2,200 per person, including air fare, accommodations, and all meals.

Trips here are called travel seminars, and seminars they most emphatically are: discussions from morning till night with a multitude of individuals and groups. In recent brochures, participants are scheduled to meet, on the one hand, with officials of the U.S. embassy in each capital, and with members of the U.S. business community there, for one viewpoint, but also with contrary-thinking clergy from "base Christian communities" in each nation. And then, to inject still more "voices" into the talk:

In Honduras: "Dialogue with officials of the Honduran government . . . with peasants and labor union leaders. . . . Visit to U.N. refugee camps . . . to a Honduran military base and discussion with U.S. military personnel. . . . Dialogue with religious and human rights organizations. . . . Visits to development projects in rural Honduras."

In El Salvador: "Discussion of foreign policy issues with Salvadoran government officials. . . . Dialogue with mothers of disappeared persons. . . . Visit to church-sponsored refugee camps. . . . Dialogue with representatives of the church."

In Mexico: "Visit to a squatter settlement in Cuernavaca and discussion with residents about their situation. . . . Visit to a rural village and discussion with peasants."

Heavily influenced by the Brazilian educator Paulo Freire, the center's officials take pains to emphasize their use of his theories: that "experiential education" (here, a short-term immersion in travel) is the most potent form of self-education; that dialogue, in which people critically assess their own situation, can liberate them from prejudice and lead to beneficial social action; that even the illiterate can gain from such dialogue; and that communication can be achieved between the poor and nonpoor, greatly benefiting both.

Accordingly, the center stresses advance preparation for travel, which "helps people recognize their biases and provides them with tools to discern the truth in the voices they will hear." En route, it exposes passengers to "a variety of political points of view so that they can reflect more critically on all the voices they hear." And though it seeks to meet with leaders and decision-makers in the countries it visits, it "places emphasis on learning from the victims of poverty and oppression—those who do not often have an opportunity to speak."

Accommodations in most nations are in modest hotels, or in the organization's own dormitory-style residences in Mexico and Nicaragua. For literature, contact the center at the address above.

TOWARD "TRANSFORMATIVE EDUCATION"

Plowshares Institute, P.O. Box 243, Simsbury, CT 06070 (phone 203/651-4304), operates a similar if smaller program, but to a broader array of geographical areas—Africa, Asia, India, South America—and with a particular emphasis on critical issues of U.S. foreign policy toward the Third World, debt and apartheid among them. The organization was founded in 1982 by a Protestant minister, the Rev. Robert Evans, whose life and outlook were profoundly changed by a stint as visiting professor in the African nation of Uganda; he resolved soon after to use travel as a means of "transformative education," and has since co-authored an important book often cited by others in the field, *Pedagogies for the Non-Poor* (Maryknoll, N.Y.: Orbis Books, 1987; $13.95).

The strategy of Plowshares is to visit areas and organizations of the Third World where active solutions are afoot to the area's classic problems; the group feels it is nonproductive simply to dwell upon festering conditions or to feel rage without hope. Once at the destination, according to program director Hugh McLean, "we find articulate voices on all sides of each issue; the goal is to listen to as many voices as possible." On a recent visit to Mexico, Plowshares travelers met with officials of IBM, but then with landless peasants; with members of the "PRI" (Mexico's ruling political party), but then with social workers and "base Christian communities in the barrios"; they lived in a dormitory of the Lutheran Theological Seminary in Mexico City, but then traveled to the poor and rural province of Hildalgo in the north to visit creative development projects.

Tours are frequently co-sponsored by a variety of other religious organizations, including New York's Union Theological Seminary, but also by a host organization at the destination; in 1991, for instance, Plowshares will go to the Union of South Africa to "dialogue" with the South African Council of Churches as well as senior members of the government (an 18-day trip for $2,950, including air fare, meals, and all else).

Some concessions are made to personal comfort: the use of modest hotels in place of mud huts, an occasional stay in modern dormitories or pleasant private homes.

As they did in past years, they will visit the black ghetto of Soweto, and some participants will stay overnight in Soweto homes, in addition to visiting Afrikaaner families in Pretoria.

Plowshares passengers sign a "covenant": that they will engage in considerable preparation for the trip, live "at the level" of their hosts (dormitories, government rest houses, private homes), and tell of their experiences to others, in both formal and informal talks, for at least a year following the trip. For brochures, write to the address above (enclosing a stamped, self-addressed envelope).

THE NEWEST ENTRANT

Global Exchange, 2940 16th St., #307, San Francisco, CA 94103 (phone 415/255-7296) is a dynamic, new company operating politically sensitive tours. Dissatisfied with the limited tour departures of their former travel affiliation, officers of Global Exchange began scheduling and successfully operating multiple tours to Third World nations in 1988–1990, and have mounted an even more ambitious effort for 1991, including such two-week immersions in present-day realities

as "Environmentalism in India," "Southern Africa—Mozambique and Zimbabwe," and "An Inside Look at Development in the Dominican Republic and Haiti," in addition to the probable repeat of earlier popular tours to Brazil; Honduras and Nicaragua; the Philippines; Israel and the Occupied Territories; Appalachia and the U.S./Mexican border. Prices are kept low ($960 to $2,300), but include air fare, all three meals daily (mostly local fare), and clean, proper accommodations (but don't expect five-star hotels). And daily schedules consist almost entirely of constant dialogue—seminars—with religious leaders, peasant farmers, government officials, labor organizers, peace activists, environmentalists, and scholars.

OTHER IMPORTANT GROUPS

Food First, 145 9th St., San Francisco, CA 94103 (phone 415/864-8555), is primarily an educator and publisher on the root causes of world hunger: why it occurs, what can be done. In 1986, with sponsorship of a first tour to Haiti and the Dominican Republic, it decided to use travel experiences

Nicaragua

Sharing lunch, Papua New Guinea

in agricultural communities as a "window" (their term) onto broader structural issues: how a society deals with its social and political problems. Soon it was offering several tours a year, primarily to rural villages abroad, meeting with both government officials and private persons, in places as diverse as Honduras, the Philippines, and Nicaragua. Participants stay in private homes or very modest hotels, which brings costs down to a low $1,850, for instance, for a two-week trip to the Philippines from the West Coast, air fare and all else included. There, after meetings and briefings in Manila, the Bataan export processing zone, and the Subic Bay naval base, tours split into groups of as few as three people to visit the sugar-producing province of Negros (where malnutrition is rampant), or to meet with land-seeking peasants in the prov-

ince of Cagayan de Oro. Write for literature to the organization's "reality tours" department, but this time enclose $2 for postage and handling.

Our Developing World, 13004 Paseo Presada, Saratoga, CA 95070 (phone 408/379-4431), is another secular West Coast heavyweight in the Third World field. A nonprofit group whose directors are mainly educators from cities in northern California, it schedules its departures primarily from Los Angeles and San Francisco, but also permits participants to join up in Miami on those of its tours that go to Central America, and uses New York as its gateway to Africa. A major focus is on problems of development in southern Africa (Zimbabwe and Mozambique); a frequent practice is to "theme" each tour to concentrate on one partic-

Their search is for solutions: to poverty and debt, domestic instability and disease, the unequal allocation of income and resources.

Drying rice, Indonesia

ular subject matter per destination: "Women's Role in Development," "Appropriate Technology," "Education and Health Care," and so on. Except for the occasional one-month trip to Africa from New York (costing a high $4,000, all inclusive), trips are two to three weeks in duration, usually range from $1,700 (for two weeks) to $2,399 (for three weeks), using West Coast departure points, are also all inclusive, and (in the words of co-director Vic Ulmer) "bring the realities of the Third World into the consciousness of North Americans through direct contact with the people of those areas." Thus a three-week summer tour to study "Human Services in Honduras and Nicaragua" will meet with peasants, social workers, church leaders, "members of Christian base communities," trade unionists, and government officials, and will visit facilities ranging from medical clinics to day-care centers. U.S. participants are particularly sought from among teachers, social workers, and health-care professionals; but any concerned member of the public can come.

The Church Coalition for Human Rights, 110 Maryland Ave. NE (P.O. Box 70), Washington, DC 20002 (phone 202/543-1094), supplies information on numerous locally sponsored, church-endorsed "travel seminars" to Third World nations. Costs are in the low to mid-$2,000s, all inclusive, and while preference is given to members of the sponsoring denomination, places are open to all.

Finally, **GATE (Global Awareness Through Experience), c/o Viterbo College, La Crosse, WI 54601 (phone 608/791-0462)**, is a small group of Catholic nuns who operate tours to Third World areas where other Catholic clergy are engaged in "liberation theology," a struggle to empower the poor. Assisted by resident priests and other church workers at the destination, tour participants look and listen, debate and discuss, while occupying lodgings so modest that GATE's tours are among the cheapest in the field: $400 plus air fare for 10 all-inclusive days in Mexico, $1,100 plus air fare for two such weeks in Peru, $1,000 plus air fare for 11 days in Nicaragua. Enclose postage in requesting their largely typewritten literature.

The Third World. Our understanding of the human condition is stunted so long as we delete it from our travel plans. Thanks to the efforts of seven unusual "tour operators," that needn't be the case.

The Bold, New World of the Feminist Tour Operator

Organized Travel for Women Only

SHOULD WOMEN TRAVEL ONLY WITH OTHER women? Should they do so on occasion?

If the trip is one of outdoor adventure, involving physical challenge, should they travel only with other women? Should they agree to include men on a group tour only if the group is led by a woman?

Because so many women are responding to one or more of the above questions with a resounding "Yes," a sizable new segment of the travel industry has emerged to serve their wants. As surprising as it may seem, more than 50 tour companies in a dozen major states are now openly feminist in their orientation, and limit their clients or leadership to women only.

The reason is unrelated to sexual proclivities or the lack of them. From a review of their literature, not one of the 50 new firms seems operated for homosexuals, and most stand carefully apart from a wholly separate group of tour companies openly appealing to gay men or gay women.

THE PREMISE OF FEMINIST TRAVEL

Rather, the move to feminist travel seems motivated by a combined goal of consciousness-raising and female solidarity, and by the belief that women enjoy a holiday change of pace, stress-free, relaxing, when they travel only with other women. Though the philosophy is rarely articulated in the feminists' tour brochures, and is obtained with difficulty even in conversations with feminist tour operators (I've now spoken with several), the gist of it seems as follows:

When women travel with men, and especially on outdoor trips, both they and the men, say the feminists, tend to fall into predetermined gender roles: the men do the heavy work, the women putter about and cook. Traveling only with other women, women accept greater challenges, court greater responsibility, acquire new skills, gain confidence and a heightened sense of worth.

Male travelers are conditioned by society to be excessively goal-oriented: they must conquer this or that mountain, show prowess and strength, domineer. Most women, by contrast, enjoy the mere experience of travel, the joy of encountering nature, all without stressful competition or expectations. They have less need to boast and strut; they lack the male's inner urge (from early upbringing) to seem always skillful, strong, serene, and protecting. "I don't want to be protected on vacation," say many women; "I want to be myself."

Womantrek

In Mongolia with Womantrek

In the presence of the other sex, so goes the argument, both sexes find it difficult to "let down their hair." On a tour limited to women, say the feminists, these tensions subside. Women spend less time on personal appearance and grooming, dispense with sexual role-playing, care only for themselves.

"And why should men feel threatened by that need?" asks one prominent female tour operator. "Why should an all-female tour be the subject of sneers? Men have been going off to hike or fish 'with the boys' for centuries."

Practical considerations: Since everyone on a woman-only trip is "single," participants pay no single supplement, but instead share rooms and costs. Since some male spouses don't care for outdoor trips, feminist tours often provide the only vacation outlet for women who genuinely enjoy the attractions of nature. Then, too, women who are recently widowed or divorced are enabled by such tours to meet others in the same situation; the experience is healing, restorative. But mainly, the women "take charge" of their holiday, free from the customary domination of men.

HUB OF THE MOVEMENT

The largest (70 departures a year) and oldest (14 years) of the feminist tour operators, and a clearinghouse for all the rest, is Woodswomen, of Minneapolis. Nonprofit, and eager to promote the offerings even of its competitors, its quarterly publication, *Woodswomen News,* is replete with the ads of dozens of widely scattered feminist travel firms. Most of the latter are engaged in purely local operations.

While Woodswomen is also heavily oriented toward its own state of Minnesota (and the nearby Northwest), it supplements that emphasis with expeditions to California, Alaska, Massachusetts, and France (for biking), the Swiss Alps (for hiking), and Nepal (for trekking, an organized walk along the lower slopes of the Himalayas). Send either $2 (for postage and handling) for a copy of the organization's 12-page *Woodswomen News,* or else $20 for a year's membership (including all publications and related services), to **Woodswomen, 25 W. Diamond Lake Rd., Minneapolis, MN 55419 (phone 612/822-3809).**

ACTIVE AND THRIVING

Runners-up to the leader? Marion Stoddart's Outdoor Vacations for Women Over 40, of Groton, Massachusetts, and Bonnie Bordas's Womantrek, of Seattle, Washington, vie for the No. 2 spot. The first is active mainly in the northeastern states; the second (Womantrek) ranges far afield to China, the USSR, Nova Scotia (on bicycle tours), Peru, Nepal, Crete, and northern India (for trekking), Thailand, Tibet, the Galápagos, Africa, and Baja California (the last for sea kayaking, open to "absolute beginners"). Contact **Outdoor Vacations, P.O. Box 200, Groton, MA 01450 (phone 508/448-3331),** or **Womantrek, 1411 E. Olive Way (P.O. Box 20643), Seattle, WA 98102 (phone 206/325-4772 or 800/477-TREK),** requesting literature on the areas that interest you. Womantrek offers particularly exciting trips to the Himalayas, Peru, the Baja Coast (for sea-Kayaking) and Africa (wildlife safaris), among others.

Still another relatively large firm is Womanship, of Annapolis, Maryland, offering a learn-to-sail program in a field of sport heavily dominated by men. Because (according to

A sizable, new segment of the travel industry has emerged to serve the feminist cause.

founder Suzanne Pogell) men tend to handle the main tasks on sailing expeditions, women are rarely able to do more than prepare the sandwiches; certainly they never "take charge" of the vessel. With Womanship, they do, gaining confidence, achieving independence. Weekend, weekday, and week-long cruises are offered for both beginners and advanced sailors aged 20 to 70, in locations ranging from Chesapeake Bay, New England and Long Island Sound, the

Womantrekkers

Womanship

New Routes, Inc.

west coast of Florida, and the Pacific Northwest (San Juan and the Gulf Islands) to the U.S. and British Virgin Islands. Contact **Womanship, Inc., 137 Conduit St., Annapolis, MD 21401 (phone 301/269-0784 or 301/267-6661).**

Other major feminist tour operators include **New Dawn Adventures, P.O. Box 1512, Vieques, PR 00765 (phone 809/741-0495),** heavily emphasizing camping retreats at their bunkhouse on the island of Vieques, Puerto Rico (the mainland office is located at 518 Washington St., Gloucester, MA 01930; phone 508/283-8717); **Mariah Wilderness Expeditions, P.O. Box 248, Point Richmond, CA 94807 (phone 415/233-2303 or toll free 800/4-MARIAH),** with an impressive four-color catalog featuring white-water rafting, kayaking, and ballooning; **Adventures for Women, P.O. Box 515, Montvale, NJ 07645 (phone 201/930-0557),** centering on New Jersey and New York; **Alaska Women of the Wilderness, P.O. Box 775226, Eagle River, AK 99577 (phone 907/688-2226),** which has thus far provided confidence-building programs to more than 1,000 women (highly recommended); **Earthwise, 23 Mt. Nebo Rd., Newtown, CT 06470 (phone 203/426-6092); and New Routes, Inc., R.R. 2, Box 2030, Brunswick, ME 04011 (phone 207/729-7900).**

Male travelers, they believe, are excessively goal-oriented; most women, by contrast, enjoy the mere experience of travel, the joy of encountering nature, all without stressful competition or expectations.

A Visit to the World of "Small Is Beautiful"

At the Centre for Alternative Technology in Wales, the Most Basic Assumptions of the Industrial West Are Attacked and Derided

WHAT DO WE REALLY SEEK ON A HOLIDAY abroad? Should we travel simply to feel pleasure? Or should we travel sometimes to get mad? I opt for the brand of travel that disturbs mental calm, compels you to think, challenges your most cherished beliefs, supplies new ideas and comparative lessons, leaves you a bit different from when you began.

In the alpine-like center of Wales, near the dreamy little town of Machynlleth (pronounced "mah-hun-lith"), Britain's Centre for Alternative Technology does just that. It disputes the very need for industrial development, rejects all arguments for large-scale commercial growth, condemns the activities to which the greater number of Americans have devoted their lives. In so doing, it acts as the cutting edge for an ideological movement that has won the loyalty of millions of Europeans, and even achieved a semblance of political power in Germany. To the "Greens" of Europe, the extreme ecologists, the fierce, anti-nuclear-power activists, the advocates of "Small Is Beautiful," and to similar groups in 21 European nations, the Centre has become a secular Mecca to which more than 50,000 people make visits each year. No one understands contemporary Europe who does not understand the movement it represents.

You reach Machynlleth by British Rail in four comfortable hours from London's Euston Station, changing at Shrewsbury (pronounced "shroze-berry") and proceeding from there through the "harp-shaped hills" of Wales (Dylan Thomas's phrase) into one of the least populated areas of the British Isles—a scene of rocky heights dotted with patches of dark-green outcroppings. At Machynlleth, a three-mile ride by taxi or bus takes you to the bottom of a soaring but thoroughly exhausted slate quarry where signs advise you, in Dante-esque fashion, to abandon your car and ascend the steep hill on foot.

You are leaving behind civilization as we know it. The Centre—a tiny, working village—is unconnected to the electric grid of Britain, or to water mains. It provides its own power from wind, solar, or hydro sources; produces much of its own food from organic gardens, fish ponds, and poultry yards on the site; replaces worn-out machinery with parts forged by its own blacksmith. Within its bounds, nothing is wasted: organic refuse is recycled into compost-created fertilizers; metal is fired down and reused; sludge is collected from septic tanks and placed into methane digesters for the production of combustible gas and fertilizer by-products; homes are insulated to an extraordinary degree; even human urine is preserved for soil fertilization via amusing, odorless "pee collectors" discreetly placed at convenience stops. On the grounds, past a forest of solar panels, near a grove of

The Centre is a working city meant to be visited and observed by a steady stream of tourists—a teaching device as much as a laboratory.

ALTERNATIVE LIVING

Some may consider the trend as the modern alternative to Welsh mysticism. Others may see it as a kind of back-to-the land revivalist movement. But organic farming and alternative technology have gained a strong foothold in the rough hill country of West Wales.

Led by a band of quintessential English refugees from the rat race of London and the southeast shires, these born-again farmers have formed a growers' cooperative and set up shop on an industrial estate in Lampeter. A market town since 1284, Lampeter has become the UK's largest centre for the preparation, packaging and distribution of organic fruits, vegetables and dairy products.

Some of the exotic fruits and vegetables, raised without the boost of chemical fertilisers or the protection of potentially harmful pesticides, are imported. But an increasing amount of the seasonal produce is home-grown on abandoned farms and small holdings (about two dozen at last count) within a 100-mile (160-km) radius of Lampeter.

Many of the growers are new farmers, like Oxfordshire-born Giles Bowerman, who manages the Organic Growers West Wales cooperative. Tired of city living and with a desire to become self-sufficient, he and a girlfriend emigrated to Wales six years ago and found a small holding to rent just south of Carmarthen. While he now looks after the cooperative growers, his partner tends to the crops: 10,000 heads of little gem lettuces, five acres (two hectares) of carrots, an acre of courgettes, hoop houses filled with cucumbers and tomatoes and an experiment in raising Chinese leaf.

Nick Rebbeck, a film director-turned farmer who was born in West Sussex and became captivated by Wales while on holiday there in the mid-1970s, is now a partner in Bwlchwernen Fawr, an organic dairy farm near Lampeter. In between film engagements, he oversees the herd and, as a first-time organic vegetable farmer, suffered his first unarmed bout against a swarm of predatory caterpillars which had infested the 90,000 red cabbage plants he had contracted to raise for the cooperative.

Bwlchwernen Fawr's milk is processed into cheese at Welsh Organic Foods, a new dairy cooperative run by Australian-born, London-bred Dougal Campbell. A veteran Swiss-trained cheesemaker, Campbell and his Cambridgeshire-born wife, in wellies and shorts, churn out 10 tonnes a year of their own label "Tyngrug", a rough unpasteurised farmhouse Cheddar/Caerphilly cross they sell from their 120-acre (48-hectare) hill farm near Lampeter.

Their surplus milk, along with milk from other organic member dairy farms, is bought by the cooperative at twice the price the government-regulated Milk Marketing Board pays farmers. At the modern Lampeter dairy cooperative plant, the milk is processed into "Pencarreg", a soft pasturised brie-type, and two other Welsh brands of organic cheese, which are sold to UK supermarkets.

West Wales has a long tradition of cooperative and organic farming. In the old university town of Aberystwyth, 23 miles (37 km) northwest of Lampeter, the University of Wales has just begun offering a full-year course in organic farming. It is the first university in the UK to do so.

Further north, just off the A487 three miles (five km) past Machynlleth, lies an unusual microcosm of what some see as tomorrow's world: the Centre for Alternative Technology. Built on the foundations of an abandoned slate quarry, the Centre is both a museum and a real-life application of techniques which save resources and eliminate waste and pollution.

It runs not on mains electricity but on renewable energy sources: windmills, water turbines, solar energy and biofuels. Cottages are built of recycled materials and heated by solar power and wood stoves. Even human sewage, provided by visitors using the Centre's public lavatories, is recycled into organic fertiliser for the organic vegetable garden. Transport of people and materials is confined to non-pollutant bicycles, water turbine-charged electric vehicles and a hand-operated steel track railway.

The Centre, open daily from 10 a.m. to 5 p.m., also offers short residential courses on alternative energy, low-cost building and organic gardening.

182

modern metal windmills of every shape and size, runs an electric truck recharged by on-site water turbines powered by rushing streams. Using and displaying such "alternative technology," a utopian community enters its 17th year in mid-1991, locked in combat with the enemies that its chief theorist, the late E. F. Schumacher, succinctly ticked off as "urbanization, industrialization, centralization, efficiency, quantity, speed."

The combatants in this awesome battle, permanent residents of the Centre, are a slowly changing group of 32 young Britons whose average tenure here is about four years. A highly attractive lot, neatly if simply dressed in work clothes, well educated and articulate, they defy the stereotyped image of the "eco-freak," and emerge from a broad mix of schools and skills. Two are Ph.D.s in electrical and mechanical engineering; three are registered architects. All receive the same subsistence-level salary, except those with dependent children, to whom a "need-related" supplement is given. They eat communally (of a largely vegetarian diet), govern themselves by consensus reached at fortnightly meetings, confront daily decisions in 15-or-so, four-member "topic groups," each dealing with specialized work areas. They receive no major government support, and are a nonprofit organization subsisting almost entirely on the admission and study-course fees paid by members of the public.

GOING BEYOND CONSERVATION

Why have they come together at the Centre to lead lives that, to the outsider, seem so harsh and confined? It is because they share a common vision that goes far beyond the well-publicized conservationist goals of preserving natural beauty and reducing harmful pollution. To the European ecological movement, simple technology and decentralized economic organization are part of a happier, healthier approach to life, as well as a moral imperative. By using renewable sources of energy present in nature, by keeping technology simple and small, one preserves meaningful work opportunities for more and more people, they argue; one spreads the activity of production over broad rural areas, slows the movement to cities and the creation of inhumanly large industrial complexes, keeps nations democratic and people healthy, promotes nonviolence in all spheres of life, teaches personal responsibility, and—most important—shares the dwindling supply of finite fossil resources more equitably among all the people of the earth.

To these ends, all 32 of "The People," as the Centre styles its staff, are researchers relying for their daily existence almost entirely on small machines and devices that make use of wind, sun, water, and biomass for their energizing forces. Though the technology itself emerges from universities and laboratories around the world, it is the Centre's task, they believe, to "live with" the machines, discovering the necessary modifications and improvements that only actual experience can provide.

SCHOOL AND LABORATORY

Are they, then, simply a test-tube community? They are more. Though officials of the Walt Disney organization would blanch at the comparison, they are perhaps a tiny version of what the late Walt Disney once envisioned as his EPCOT Center in Orlando, Florida: an actual working city that would, at the same time, be visited and observed by a steady stream of tourists—a teaching device as much as a laboratory. While Disney obviously failed to pull off the feat of combining two such antagonistic functions, the Centre quite demonstrably does.

It teaches. Its staff supplies a running commentary as they go about their tasks. You compliment a chef on the bean-sprout salad served in the Centre's superb vegetarian restaurant and he runs into the kitchen to extract a large bell jar in which the sprouts are grown, explaining how you, too, can enjoy such daily treats from the moistened seeds of simple alfalfa. You gaze over the shoulder of an engineer adjusting a "biomass gasifier" and she hastily explains how a renewable supply of wood, burned in a near-vacuum, will result in a combustible gas capable of powering an electric generator. Everywhere are colorful, cartoon-illustrated explanations and exhortations, such as: "Use Less/Build to Last/Reuse/Repair/Recycle." "What good is efficiency if it puts people out of work and uses up resources?" "Gross product per head measures only the quantity of our wealth, not the quality of our lives. Are we happier?"

The Centre's staff heatedly deny that their work is of exclusive relevance to the Third World, responding to a frequent comment. It is morally and politically indefensible, they affirm, that the advanced West should make such a lavish disproportionate use of the world's resources, especially fossil fuels (America, with 6% of the earth's population, uses 40% of the world's primary resources). And there are insufficient such resources for the entire world to follow

Snowdonia National Park

the wasteful, indulgent course of the West; consequently, that course must change—in all areas.

They also deny that the glut in oil before the Persian Gulf Crisis was at all significant; it was a brief lull in the crisis, a fool's paradise. Even were those supplies sufficient, their use exacts too high a human toll in acid rain, pollution, industrial blight, ruined lives; and fossil sources can, in any event, be put to better use than as energy. So goes the argument of Wales's Centre for Alternative Technology, in seminar presentations, group discussions, gardenside chats, quiet admonitions from engineers tinkering with a solar roof, a waterless toilet, a compost heap, or an "aerogenerator" manufactured at the Centre and sent around the world.

PLANNING A VISIT

Two days set aside from the normal routines of a British vacation, or added to it, suffice for a thorough visit to the Centre. After traveling there by train from London (£30, approximately $60, round-trip), most visitors base themselves in Machynlleth (where the Wynnstay Hotel, phone 2289, is your best bet, followed in distant second place by the Glyndwr, phone 2082) or in Corris, two miles from the Centre (Hotel Braich Goch, phone 73/229), or in several guesthouses in the area.

The Centre is open to visitors every day of the year except Christmas, for an admission charge of £3 ($6) for adults, less for seniors, students, and children. Two weekends a month from October to June it offers two-day courses in which you pursue one topic per weekend: blacksmithing, low-energy buildings, solar collectors and systems, organic gardening, wind power, etc. Free time involves explorations of Machynlleth, mid-Wales, and the Cambrian Coast. For specific dates, subjects, and application forms, contact the **Courses Coordinator, Centre for Alternative Technology, Machynlleth, Powys, Wales, U.K. SY20 9AZ (phone 06/54-2400).**

Visits of lesser duration are best followed by self-drive tours through awesome Wales, perhaps starting at the nearby small (but active) seaside town of Aberystwyth, heading north from there to Snowdon, highest mountain in Wales, visiting abandoned lead mines en route. Richard Llewellyn's Welsh classic, *How Green Was My Valley,* is your best preparatory reading.

But now it is dusk, at the end of a day of "alternative technology," and you are coming down from the mountain, perhaps jarred and disquieted, perhaps exhilarated, always alive with new ideas. This new approach—this confrontational approach—to travel has converted a routine British vacation into a memorable one, of lasting value.

The Centre disputes the very need for industrial development, rejects all arguments for large-scale commercial growth, condemns the activities to which the greater number of Americans have devoted their lives.

III

CEREBRAL VACATIONS, IN THE SUMMERTIME

Summer Camps for Adults

Audubon Camps, Sierra Camps, Unitarian Camps, and Political Camps Use "Sleepaway Camps" for Grownup Needs

YOU APPROACHED IT THROUGH A FOREST, ON a dirt road, beneath a canopy of leafy boughs. You slept there in a rustic cabin or a lean-to made of logs. You ate in a wooden mess hall, at long, communal tables; swam in a lake; sat around an open fire at night.

And paid very little.

Sleepaway camp. Was there ever a better vacation? A more treasured time of childhood? And can those joyful, vibrant, inexpensive holidays be reexperienced at a later time, as an adult?

The answer is a limited yes. Provided you apply soon enough—say, by early spring, before the rolls are filled and closed—you can stay at one of nearly 50 widely scattered camps that operate for people of all ages, 18 to 80, in a setting almost identical to those cherished memories of youth.

AUDUBON ECOLOGY CAMPS

These have existed for 55 years. On a thickly wooded 300-acre island off the mid-coast of Maine, at a lofty ranch in the Wind River Mountains of northwestern Wyoming, and in a large nature sanctuary near Greenwich, Connecticut, the National Audubon Society has enabled adults from all over the nation to enjoy an intense, camp-style experience, for one or two summer weeks, with all forms of plant and animal life: birds and marine mammals, insects, herbs and wild-flowers, mink, beaver, otter, and eagles. You go birding or canoeing at 7 A.M., take leisurely hikes through open meadows or on mountain trails, make field trips to a hem-lock gorge, and alternate all the outdoor activity with atten-dance at classroom lectures by expert naturalists. The simple aim is to reintroduce you to nature and its delicate balancing act; to show how all life is interdependent, and what you can do to protect it.

In the undeveloped, wilderness settings of all three camps, you quickly forget all urban concerns, but enjoy a reasonable standard of comfort at the same time: original

homestead cabins in Wyoming (mostly dormitory in style, but with some facilities for couples), wood-frame dormito-ries and a restored 19th-century farmhouse on Hog Island in Maine, slightly more modern facilities and private rooms in Connecticut. Hearty meals are served buffet style, three times a day.

Connecticut camp sessions, from late June to mid-August 1991, are run for one week and cost a flat $450 per person,

Trumpeter swans, National Audubon Society

44

Field ecology camp, National Audubon Society

including all instruction, room and board, all field trips and recreation.

Wyoming's camp is also operated from late June through the middle of August 1991, and consists of both one-week and two-week sessions in "field ecology," costing $525 for one week, a remarkable $725 for two weeks, again all inclusive.

The camp in Maine runs from early July to early September 1991, and consists of one- and two-week sessions in "field ecology" ($525 for one week, $725 for two weeks, all inclusive) and one-week sessions in "field ornithology" (for $595, all inclusive).

There's not another cent to pay (except your transportation to the camp), nowhere at all to spend additional money, and no supplement for single persons traveling alone.

Who attends the Audubon camps? Adults of all ages and backgrounds: an accountant from Atlanta alongside a professional educator from San Francisco, college students, firemen, and retired senior citizens—their common tie, the urge for a vacation "with more substance to it than sitting on a

beach," in the words of Philip Schaefer, Audubon's director of camps and summer programs. Returning to nature, he adds, is an "emotional as well as a learning experience," and at the final campfire, "there isn't a dry eye."

For extensive, colorful literature and application forms relating to all three camps, contact the **National Audubon Society, Audubon Camps and Workshops, 613 Riversville Rd., Greenwich, CT 06831 (phone 203/869-2017).**

SIERRA CLUB "BASE CAMPS"

Here's an even older program of adult summer camps, a small part of the much broader year-round schedule of "outings" operated since 1901 by the fierce and powerful (500,000 members) environmental organization called the Sierra Club. In "wild places" of the United States, at least a dozen times each summer, experienced Sierra volunteers establish "base camps" at small cabins or lodges, or at tented camp areas, to which other participants then usually hike in from a road several miles away. Once established at the base

You are in a setting almost identical to those cherished memories of youth.

SIERRA CLUB

SIERRA CLUB CENTENNIAL 1892 - 1992

BURRO

The friendliest and gentlest of pack animals, burros are your companions on these wilderness outings. ♦ Suitable for novice camper or seasoned outdoorsperson of any age, a burro trip is truly a different type of outing. The burros are led by participants and carry most of the trip load. Everyone takes part in the trip activities, including burro care and wrangling, as well as cooking and dishwashing. Most routes are at high elevations (8,000 to 12,000 feet), and a typical day covers 5 to 10 miles. ♦ Participants must be in good physical condition. Leader approval is required for all burro trips.

Heart of the Cathedral Range, Yosemite Park, Sierra—July 28–August 4. This loop trek through the Cathedral Range provides for refreshing adventure. Following Rafferty, Fletcher, and Lewis creeks, we stop at several subalpine and alpine lakes to camp, fish, and enjoy the scenery of one of Yosemite's most scenic regions. Elevation change on our route is moderate. *Leader: John McClure. Price: $425 Dep: $50.* [90204]

The Hee Haw Vogelsang Family Trip, Yosemite Park, Sierra—August 4–11. Moderate trails, spectacular scenery, and ready access beckon to the family traveler. Vogelsang's glacial landscapes provide a sharp contrast to our humble burros. Abundant lakes offer fishing and easy peaks to scramble up nearby. We will spend nearly all our trip in the subalpine zone, where we can take pleasant dayhikes up into the tundra or down into the dense forests. *Leaders: Linda and Ted Bradfield. Price: adult $435, child $360; Dep: $100 per family.* [90205]

Tuolumne Meadows to Green Creek, Yosemite Park and Inyo Forest, Sierra—August 11–18. On this moderate trip, we head north from Tuolumne Meadows through Glen Aulin into the beautifully glaciated Virginia and Spiller canyons. From a zone of lodgepole pines, we ultimately reach the alpine region of Summit Lake before descending to the lush Green Creek drainage on the east side of the Sierra. Along the way we'll take time for dayhikes, swimming, and burro wrangling. *Leader: Dan Holmes. Price: $425; Dep: $50.* [90206]

Fish Valley Family Trip, Sierra Forest, Sierra—August 19–26. This trip gives families

On the way to Bear Creek in the John Muir Wilderness, Sierra.

with young children (ours are four and seven) a chance to enjoy the upper Sonoran forest environment of the High Sierra (6,400 feet). Lovable and gentle burros will carry the gear for a total of four moving days to and from a base camp, where we'll organize dayhikes, nature walks, and fishing trips as we like. *Leaders: Cathy Neuhauser and Jack Holmes. Price: adult $435, child $360; Dep: $100 per family.* [90207]

camp, to which supplies have been brought by mule or vehicle, campers make day hikes into the surrounding countryside, or simply enjoy the outdoor pleasures of their wilderness base. Most of the base camps are in California, Washington, or the Sierra Mountains of California/Nevada; a few are in Arizona, Oregon, New Mexico, Virginia, and the Great Smoky Mountain Park of Tennessee/North Carolina.

With a minor exception or two, charges are remarkably low, even though all inclusive: as little as $400 for some one-week stays, an average of $500, a top of $725. That's because all campers pitch in to perform camp tasks, including cooking, supervised by the camp staff.

Sample base camp stays planned for 1991: in the Tahoe Forest of California/Nevada, near early Native American habitats, abandoned mines, and ghost towns; near the Donner Pass amid majestic rock cathedrals and trout-stocked lakes; on a Navajo reservation near Canyon de Chelly National Monument of Arizona; in a nationally protected area of fossil beds in Oregon; in the densely wooded Monongahela Forest of West Virginia. Though the accent throughout is on fun—the sheer pleasure of removing oneself for a week or two to an untouched, untrammeled wilderness—participants (of all ages, and including families) have the added opportunity to "network" with other kindred sorts, the dedicated environmentalists of our nation.

The full list of base camps appears in a larger directory of club outings bound each year into the January/February edition of *Sierra*, the club's magazine. For a copy, send $2.50 to **Sierra Club, 730 Polk St., San Francisco, CA 94109**; and for other specific information or longer leaflets on individual base camps, contact the **Sierra Club Outing Department, 730 Polk St., San Francisco, CA 94109 (phone 415/776-2211)**. Since base camps are open only to Sierra members or "applicants for membership," you'll later need to include your membership application and fee ($15 for seniors, students, and people of limited income, $33 for all others) with your reservation request.

UNITARIAN CAMPS

And then you have the often more comfortable and more numerous adult summer camps of the merged Unitarian/Universalist church, each one of which is open—as a matter of firm church policy—to Americans of all religious persuasions and of none. Acting from the same tolerant impulses that led them to found the American Red Cross, the ASPCA, and much of the public school movement, Unitarian/Universalists have here created a major travel/vacation resource, yet one that is unknown to much of the traveling public.

Why do they invite people of all religious persuasions to make use of their summer camps? Certainly not to proselytize or seek converts—they don't believe in that. Rather, as it's been explained to me, because they seek to discover common bonds among all humankind, and common spiritual truths; because their creed is without dogma and broadly compatible with all other faiths. What better place to experience such unity, they theorize, than at a summer gathering, in a pleasant, unstressed, cooperative camp?

Because some of the Unitarian/Universalist camps fill up by summer, you'd be well advised to apply quickly to one of the following:

Star Island Camp, New Hampshire: A rustic, rocky, sea-enclosed marsh connected to the mainland by a single telephone line, Star Island is one of the historic "Isles of Shoals" off the New England coast (reached by ferry from Portsmouth, N.H.). A naturalist's dream, a photographer's vision, it has been owned by the Unitarians since 1915, and used as an adult summer camp (swimming, boating, fishing, hiking, tennis, softball) open to all, but mainly patronized by Unitarian/Universalists. From mid-June to early September, singles, couples, and families can opt for "theme weeks" focused on the arts, natural history, international affairs, psychology, and the like. They stay either in a wooden main building or a number of cottages (comfortable but not modern) at charges averaging $290 per adult per week for room, full board, and all activities. Prior to summer, contact **Star Island Corporation, 110 Arlington St., Boston, MA 02116 (phone 617/426-7988)**; thereafter, **P.O. Box 178, Portsmouth, NH 03801 (phone 603/964-7252)**.

De Benneville Pines Camp, near Angelus Oaks, California: Half an hour from the better-known town of Redland on the mid-Pacific coast, in a heavily wooded area laced with hiking trails, is De Benneville Pines Camp. Its Unitarian programs—usually open to all—consist primarily of a "family week" in August, a "singles week" in late July, and a "theme week" (which was chamber music in 1990) in late August. Family week is devoted to classic summer recreations, with the Unitarian theme largely limited to evening campfire discussions of broad ethical themes. Accommodation is in cabins; meals, according to staff, are "honest-to-goodness homemade—i.e., bread done from scratch"; all-inclusive weekly charges average $200 per adult for family weeks, much less for children; under $300 per adult for the theme-week session (which is occasionally, but not always, closed to the general public). Contact **De Benneville Pines, HC–01, Box 13, Angelus Oaks, CA 92305 (phone 714/794-2928)**.

Mountain Highlands Camp of North Carolina: This consists of cabins and lodges atop Mount Little Scaly (4,200 feet), overlooking the Blue Valley of the Blue Ridge Mountains. "Our camp," says guest relations coordinator Louis Bregger, "is completely surrounded by national forest and thus affords us beautiful, unthreatened vistas." Except for a single week reserved for training Unitarian leaders (mid-July), all other summer weeks (early June through August) are open to those of all religious backgrounds and of any age. Themes, which supplement a daily routine of swimming (in a small, spring-fed lake), hiking, arts and crafts, include "Singles Week," "River-Rafting," "Folklore and the Truth,"

Though sponsored by a church, they seek to discover common bonds among all humankind, and common spiritual truths.

"Life's Purposes," "Adventures for All Ages," and "Dare to Explore." Cabin accommodations, high-quality meals—figure about $350 per adult per week for everything. Contact **Mountain Highlands Camp, 841 Hwy. 106, Highlands, NC 28741 (phone 704/526-5838).**

Camp Unirondack, of upstate New York: On a peninsula jutting into Beaver Lake, near the western edge of Adirondack Park, this one is surrounded by thousands of acres of "forever wild" forest preserve, rugged hills, and abundant wildlife. Though most of its summer program is devoted to young people, two one-week sessions are reserved for "intergenerational families" and also accept adults without children in tow. In early July it's music-related activities for all ages; in early August, a "creative" week of singing, folk dancing, arts and crafts—all in addition to the usual hiking, canoeing, sailing, and swimming. Totally absent: religious pressures. "We respect different traditions," says one of its Unitarian administrators. "Our themes are simply participatory democracy, a reverence for the natural world, a search for excellence and personal growth." Accommodations are cabins or a log-style dorm with hot and cold running water, all near a large shower house. Adult prices average $190 a week for room, board, and activities; children pay $80 to $150, according to age. Contact **Dan Gottfried, 90 Park Terrace East, #2F, New York, NY 10034 (phone 212/569-5113).**

Aurora Institute, Alberta, Canada: In the awesome foothills of the Canadian Rockies, this one-week Unitarian camp (usually scheduled for late August) makes use of cedar-log buildings on the grounds of the Goldeye Center, a private camp operated by Canadian co-op associations. It is definitely open to U.S. citizens and to people of all faiths, "who will not feel uncomfortable," says Katie Sather, director of the institute. "We are very much *not* evangelical." Normal camp activities (lake canoeing, nature walks, choir, and crafts) alternate with a broad range of multiple workshops (purely optional): "Beyond War (Peace Consciousness)," "Essentials of Worship," "Clarifying Your Relationships with Money," "Gay-Straight Dialogues," "Tarot," "Family Puzzles," "Readers' Theater," among others. Fees are re-markably low: as little as $200 per adult for the entire week, meals included, if you stay in the dorm; about $100 more in smaller log guesthouses. Write **Aurora Institute, P.O. Box 1794, Lacombe, AB, T0C 1S0, Canada.**

The Hersey Retreat, on Penobscot Bay, Maine: A small "resort" off the mid-coast of Maine, this shingle-style lodge (built in 1909) and adjoining farmhouse are owned by the Universalist church, but open to all—including families—in the month of August. "In keeping with our liberal tradition," says the group's brochure, "we invite others to share our facility in summer." Afternoons make use of broad recreational opportunities in a superb, beach-lined setting; mornings are given over to discussion of the following 1991 themes: "Religious Education: Spirit Quest" (early August), "Family Dynamics" (mid-August), and "Music Week" (late August). August sessions are known as "family camps" and average $180 per adult, $90 for children 3 to 18, free for children 2 and under. Prior to summer, write **Hersey Retreat, P.O. Box 1125, Bangor, ME 04401;** thereafter, **P.O. Box 1183, Stockton Springs, ME 04981.** Or phone the director of Hersey, David Greeley (207/722-3405 or 207/567-3420).

Ferry Beach Center, on the coast of Maine: For its summer-long, ten-week program of adult activities, open to all without question, Ferry Beach makes use of 30 woodland acres on Saco Bay, and adjoining sand dunes and pine groves, with access to bike paths and walking trails in a state park. Though participants are free to romp and relax, they can also attend week-long conferences from the end of June through the Labor Day weekend. Conference themes will be in the spirit of these from the 1990 season: "Exploring the Maine Coast," "Creative Leisure," "Single Parents," "Gay Week," "Tai-Chi and Fine Arts." Expect to pay about $325 per adult for a week's room, board, registration, and activities, slightly less for children, much less for those occupying tented campsites. Contact **Ferry Beach Park Association, 5 Morris Ave., Saco, ME 04072 (phone 207/282-4489).**

Camp UniStar, in northern Minnesota: A Unitarian camp maintained, this time, exclusively for adults and families through all of June, July, and August. On the northeast tip of isolated Star Island in Cass Lake, accessible only by pontoon boat, Unitarians and "like-minded individuals" occupy cabins and lodges of a simple nature, but all with private facilities. They take meals communally in a nearby dining hall from which smoking has been banished. While the key aim is relaxation, pursued in unstructured fashion, lecture/discussions are had from 10 A.M. to noon daily on such weekly themes as "Writing and Reading Fiction," "Sailing and Shiatsu," "Israeli/Palestinian Tensions," "Philosophy and Fishing," "An Examination of American Identity." Charges run to approximately $175 per adult for the week (including the boat over and back), as little as $90 per child. Prior to June 1, contact **Judy Burtis, 7325 Fremont Ave. South, Richfield, MN 55423 (phone 612/866-8248);** there-

In undeveloped wilderness, campers quickly forget all urban concerns.

World Fellowship Center

after, **Camp UniStar, Star Island Water Rte. 51, Cass Lake, MN 56633 (phone 218/335-2692).**

Rowe Camp, in the Berkshires of northwestern Massachusetts: A Unitarian children's camp for much of the summer, Rowe largely replaces the youngsters with adults during three warm-weather periods: for a week in July ("Recovery Camp," for adult children of alcoholic parents), a week in early August ("Women's Week"), and a week in late August ("Liberation Camp"); the second is a consciousness-raising program for females only, while the third attempts to free all participants—singles, couples, families—"from whatever confines their spirits." In all three, daily workshops deal with growth in the physical, emotional, spiritual, and political realms; and all is combined with swimming, dancing, canoeing, silk-screening, and picnics—a joyful, dynamic, but intensely spiritual atmosphere. Scattered wooden cabins and main lodges resemble the camps of your own youth. The all-inclusive cost for a week averages $350 per adult, $240 to $260 per accompanying child, depending on age. Contact **Rowe Camp, Kings Highway Road, Rowe, MA 01367 (phone 413/339-4216).**

A POLITICAL SUMMER CAMP

Finally, a group of proud and unrepentant, happy and defiant liberals from all over the nation (of all ages, families and singles) converges each summer on the World Fellowship Center in the White Mountains of New Hampshire for a special vacation.

With its 300 acres of forest, mile-long Whitton Pond for swimming and boating, cookouts, campsites and rustic lodge buildings, WFC would seem at first to be a standard resort for standard, warm-weather relaxation.

But from mid-June to early September, every week of the

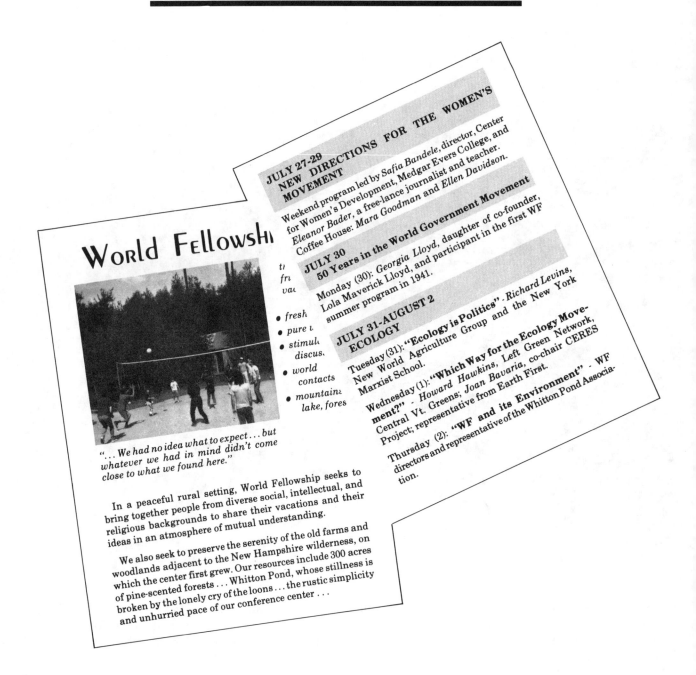

World Fellowsh

t
fri
va

- fresh
- pure w
- stimul
  discus.
- world
  contacts
- mountain:
  lake, fores

JULY 27-29
NEW DIRECTIONS FOR THE WOMEN'S
MOVEMENT

Weekend program led by *Safia Bandele*, director, Center
for Women's Development, Medgar Evers College, and
Eleanor Bader, a free-lance journalist and teacher.
Coffee House: *Mara Goodman* and *Ellen Davidson*.

JULY 30
50 Years in the World Government Movement

Monday (30): *Georgia Lloyd*, daughter of co-founder,
Lola Maverick Lloyd, and participant in the first WF
summer program in 1941.

JULY 31-AUGUST 2
ECOLOGY

Tuesday (31): **"Ecology is Politics"** - *Richard Levins*,
New World Agriculture Group and the New York
Marxist School.

Wednesday (1): **"Which Way for the Ecology Move-**
ment?" - *Howard Hawkins*, Left Green Network,
Central Vt. Greens; *Joan Bavaria*, co-chair CERES
Project; representative from Earth First.

Thursday (2): **"WF and its Environment"** - WF
directors and representative of the Whitton Pond Association.

*"... We had no idea what to expect ... but
whatever we had in mind didn't come
close to what we found here."*

In a peaceful rural setting, World Fellowship seeks to
bring together people from diverse social, intellectual, and
religious backgrounds to share their vacations and their
ideas in an atmosphere of mutual understanding.

We also seek to preserve the serenity of the old farms and
woodlands adjacent to the New Hampshire wilderness, on
which the center first grew. Our resources include 300 acres
of pine-scented forests ... Whitton Pond, whose stillness is
broken by the lonely cry of the loons ... the rustic simplicity
and unhurried pace of our conference center ...

summer there is devoted to such atypical, even unsettling, "resort" themes as "Care for the Poor," "Central America—Witness to War," "Revolution in Eastern Europe," "Confrontation in the Third World," "A Women's Movement for the '90s," "Bretton Woods Revisited," "Peace Priorities." Noted lecturers take to the stump on each week's topics; and twice-daily discussions, at 10:30 A.M. and after dinner at 8 P.M., alternate with lighthearted blueberry-picking, exercise sessions, and swimming.

All three meals are included in the room rates, and yet those charges amounted last season to only $210 to $260 per person per week (depending on room category) or to only $160 per week for people bringing a tent. At those price levels, space fills up fast.

For information and applications, contact **World Fellowship Center, c/o Christoph and Kathryn Schmauch, Birch Street (R.R. 2, Box 53), North Conway, NH 03860 until June 1, and thereafter R.D. Box 136, Conway, NH 03818 (phone 603/447-2280 in summer, 603/356-5208 the rest of the year).**

Campus Vacations

Like the TV Hosts of "Fantasy Island," They Enable You to Briefly Re-experience the "Shortest, Gladdest Years of Life"

REMEMBER THEM? THOSE WONDROUS years? You lived in a dorm, next door to a dining hall. Your days stretched on without limit, it seemed, and there was time for everything: discussions lasting hour after hour, a movie at night, the stillness of library and lab, your mind pulsing with new ideas and challenging thoughts.

"Bright college years"—through a wise use of vacation time, you can touch them again, feel the glow, recharge the spirit. At scattered colleges and universities, a number of short-term summer programs enable adults of all ages to briefly re-experience "the shortest, gladdest years of life."

There are, by my reckoning, 14 such schools. For a week in summer, when the campus blooms, they open their residences, dining halls, and classrooms to every sort of student from around the nation, without conducting tests or issuing grades, and at wonderfully low costs. Few other short vacations offer so much pleasure, and yet such mental growth.

And how do these programs differ from the "learning vacations"—an exotic cruise, an archeological dig—that we, as alumni, are so often offered in the mails? First, because they are offered to alumni and non-alumni alike. Second, because they are operated by the university itself, on a nonprofit basis, and not by a commercial tour operator or professor-turned-entrepreneur. Third, because they take place on campus. Fourth, because, unlike other classier, costlier seminars conducted on campus, these place you not in nearby hotels but in simple college dorms, from which you take your meals in adjacent student cafeterias, exactly as you did at the ages of 19, 20, and 21. And last, because, unlike the somewhat similar Elderhostel programs, they are available to youngsters in their 30s, 40s, and 50s as well.

14 CAMPUS CHOICES

Cornell's Adult University is the most ambitious of the lot, four one-week sessions in July 1991. At least 300 people attend each week, enjoying comfortable student lodgings and highly regarded food, eminent professors, bright fellow "students," the verdant surroundings of Cornell's famous hillside campus ("high above Cayuga's waters"), and sensible prices: $585 to $680 per week per adult, including tuition and full room and board; $200 to $310 per child, depending on age. Most adults opt for a single one-week topic, taught in daily sessions (they let out in midafternoon) throughout the week: "Decadence and Creativity in Nero's Rome," "Frontiers of Technology," "Louis XIV and Versailles," "The Physics of Everyday Things," "Poets and Prophets: The Heritage of the Greeks and Hebrews," and "Figaro and Don Juan," are highly illustrative samples from previous years' curricula. The quality of instruction, and convivial afternoon and evening recreation, create a setting so compelling that some guests need almost to be evicted after their week in "Brigadoon"; though the literature doesn't say so, guests are encouraged to stay for only a single week (but may add another), and early applications are advisable. Contact **Cornell's Adult University, 626 Thurston Ave., Ithaca, NY 14850 (phone 607/255-6260).**

Brown's "Summer College" invites both alumni and "friends" of the university to enjoy a remarkable week (mid- to late June) of high-quality lectures and discussions by eminent Ivy League professors. Each year's program pursues one common topic in morning sessions throughout the week, which are then followed by one's choice of varying afternoon

Unlike other classier, costlier seminars, these place you not in nearby hotels but in simple dorms.

51

subjects: 1988's theme was the pre-Columbian civilization of the Aztecs, Maya, and Incas; 1989's program explored the difficult task of American secondary education in building both competence and character, both "cleverness" and "goodness"; 1990's participants explored the "European Shuffle from the Atlantic to the Urals," as led by former national security adviser to John F. Kennedy, McGeorge Bundy; 1991's theme hasn't been chosen as we go to press, but will probably deal with structural problems of the U.S. Congress. Brown University, along with Dartmouth (discussed below), was the grandparent of continuing education in America and one of the earliest operators of short-term, residential, summer courses for adults. With room, board, and tuition included, expect to pay about $650 per person. Contact **Brown's Continuing College, c/o William J. Slack, P.O. Box 1920, Brown University, Providence, RI 02912 (phone 401/863-2474).**

"Summer of '91" at the College of Wooster, Ohio, consists of lectures from 8:30 A.M. to noon, followed by buffet luncheons and afternoon excursions to attractions in the area, followed by films or light opera (*H.M.S. Pinafore, Wiener Blut*) at night, and gala dinners consisting occasionally of barbecues in a giant tent. All this occurs from June 9 to June 15, 1991, with academic matters pursued for six straight days, through noon of Saturday. One typical theme topic of an earlier year was "Paris and Vienna 1889," as presented by eminent faculty members; 1991's discussion will explore "Earth—Our Home, Our Resource, and Our Future." Although organized by the Office of Alumni Relations, its staff members assure me that mere "friends" of the college are admitted to the program and to use the near-pastoral setting of a 300-acre campus and its many recreational facilities. Room, full board, and tuition total $386 per person for the entire week, using university dorms and the Lowry Center Dining Hall. Contact **Summer of '91, Office of Alumni Relations, The College of Wooster, Wooster, OH 44691 (phone 216/263-2263).**

The Vacation College of Slippery Rock University, Pennsylvania, occupies a 600-acre campus 50 miles north of Pittsburgh, in the rolling, tree-lined hills of western Pennsylvania. This is a far less academically intense program of such courses as "Word Processing," "Stained Glass," "Tombstone Geography," and "The Power of Laughter," all interspersed with golf, tennis, swimming, excursions, and organized evening events. You can schedule attendance at as many as three topics in your one-week stay, which starts in late June of 1991. As at all the other schools, you face no examinations, receive no grades, stay in university residence halls (here, with separate bathroom facilities for men and women on each floor). "Early-bird" registrants (applying before May 15) pay only $275 per person for a full week's room, board, and tuition; otherwise, $325. Participants are adults only, without their children, most in their early 40s, some in their 70s. Contact **Vacation College, Office of Continuing Education, Lowry Center, Slippery Rock, PA 16057 (phone 412/738-2633).**

"The Mini University" of Indiana University is from June 16 to June 21, 1991, and consists of 112 lectures on 112 separate subjects delivered by 114 faculty members of the great Hoosier center of learning; you are encouraged to attend as many as you can manage in the course of a six-day, five-night stay in Halls of Residence costing an average of $250 per adult for a week's room, board, tuition, and registration. Children coming along are sent to a separate campus "gym camp," but stay with their parents at an average cost of $180 per week, including registration and all meals. Costs are kept low by the fact that all profs donate their services free, as they speak on topics clustered under such headings as "Humanities," "Sciences," "International Affairs," "Arts," "Business," "Domestic Issues," "Health, Fitness, and Leisure." Contact **Mini University '91, Indiana Memorial Union M-17, Bloomington, IN 47405 (phone 812/855-6120).**

Grace Graham Vacation College, at the University of Oregon in Eugene, takes place in mid-August, and one year featured a thorough, full-week discussion (morning, afternoon, and evening) of "Creativity and Criticism: Tasting and Judging the Lively and Literary Arts" (1991's subject matter hasn't been announced as we go to press in late 1990). Lectures and seminars are delivered or led by a multidisciplinary faculty from the Law School, School of Journalism, and Department of Philosophy, and are impressive, indeed, in their depth and serious approach; but no tests follow the brainy debates! Students of all ages—but mostly middle-aged—stay in a high-rise residence located between the campus and downtown Eugene, take their meals in university dining rooms, and pay $440 per person in double rooms, $490 single. Contact **Grace Graham Vacation College, University Housing, University of Oregon, Eugene OR 97403 (phone 503/346-4265).**

The Vacation College of the University of North Caro-

They are operated by the university itself, on a nonprofit basis.

Brain." In true Johns Hopkins tradition, the talk is on a lofty plane, and has ranged over the years from Greek philosophies to present-day notions of genetic engineering and artificial intelligence. Evenings involve slide shows of pagan and early Christian art as a "change of pace." "This is always the best week of my whole summer," wrote one enthusiastic participant after a recent session. Contact the **Johns Hopkins Alumni College East, 3211 N. Charles St., Baltimore, MD 21218 (phone 301/338-7963).**

A recently instituted variant on Johns Hopkins Alumni College East is a western program conducted on two week-long occasions in July in Santa Fe, New Mexico. One such program gathered an eminent faculty from the departments of Near Eastern Studies, Classics, English Literature, and Film Criticism, to present joint classes in "Ancient Magic" one week, "Postmodern Culture: 'Reading and Writing'" the other. You can expect something equally arcane, abstruse, and weighty in 1991—an exciting prospect for well-educated travelers. Lodgings are at the elegant La Posada Hotel, and the program price, exclusive of air fare but including room, most meals, three field trips, and six days of instruction, is $995 per person double occupancy. This time, contact **Johns Hopkins Alumni College West, 3211 N. Charles St., Baltimore, MD 21218 (phone 301/338-7963).**

Smith College Adult Sports and Fitness Camp, for both men and women, is a highly active week of classroom instruction in fitness, nutrition, and stress management, alternating with active participation in yoga, cycling, hiking, swimming, windsurfing, tai-chi, canoeing, badminton, squash, tennis, and other forms of aerobics. The college's facilities for all this are among the best in the nation, and applications (from adults of all ages) are so heavy that two separate sessions have been scheduled for 1991: the second and third weeks of June. A single fee of $600 per person covers sports, instruction, and room and board (single or double rooms) from dinner Sunday through breakfast the following Saturday. Contact **Jim Johnson, Adult Sports and Fitness Camp, Scott Gymnasium, Smith College, Northampton, MA 01063 (phone 413/584-2700, ext. 3975).**

The Dartmouth Alumni College, in Hanover, New Hampshire, operating for 12 consecutive days in mid-August of 1991, is among the oldest and most serious of summer campus sessions for adults, and assures me it is open to non-alumni. Each morning of the nearly two-week period, two lectures are followed by small-group discussions with faculty, but afternoons are left mostly free for tennis or golf on campus, boating, or hiking in the White Mountains. Evenings are devoted to films, special lectures, concerts, or plays related to that summer's theme, which in 1990 was "Perestroika, Glasnost, and the Lessons of History." Professor Robert Henricks presided over a program of "major national names" as guest speakers, in addition to eminent faculty members from all departments of the college, including even

Adult Sports and Fitness Camp, Smith College

lina at Chapel Hill draws its faculty from the several noted universities in the area (including Duke), a resource so rich that two separate weeks are offered and two alternative subjects per week are taught throughout the day. Dates in 1991 will be June 23 to June 28 and July 21 to July 26, and topics will be akin to last year's "France from Napoleon to Napoleon (1800 to 1870)," "The USSR from Lenin to Gorby," and "Contemporary Japan." Musical programs or appropriate films are the relaxing evening activity. Tuition for the week is $240 per person, but meals and lodging in campus dormitories are billed separately, at a yet-to-be-determined (but moderate) charge. Contact **Humanities Program, CB #3420, 209 Abernethy Hall, University of North Carolina, Chapel Hill, NC 27599 (phone 919/962-1106).**

The Johns Hopkins Alumni College, which readily admits non-alumni to its sessions, will probably remain in 1991 at the Wintergreen Resort near Charlottesville, Virginia, because of ongoing dorm renovations at its normal location. The use of deluxe condominiums at that elegant mountain center causes prices per person to be a high $845 for the week, including tuition and full board. Four noted psychologists chaired the one-week session recently, discussing "Cognitive Neuroscience: The Relationship Between Mind and

Skidmore College, Summer Special Programs

the physical sciences. Participants pay $910 for the two weeks (that's per person, double occupancy, for those out of college for more than 10 years; younger grads get a discount of about $250 per person), including accommodation in Dartmouth dorms, books, instruction, and all meals (of which two are festive banquets). Contact **Dartmouth Alumni College, Dartmouth Continuing Education, 308 Blunt Alumni Center, Hanover, NH 03755 (phone 603/646-2454).**

The Alumni College of Penn State is yet another of those mistitled programs meant mainly for alumni, but firmly open to all. It is also somewhat less of an academically rigorous program than a partly recreational week for the entire family. Thus, recent classroom discussion pursued the theme "The World Around Us: An American Perspective," and included lectures on the "Greenhouse Effect," AIDS, nutrition, hydro-

farming, and other current topics. Oxford it's not, but rather a type of "cruise with faculty," according to one staff member. A fee of approximately $70 a day covers your accommodation in university residence halls (bath down the corridor), all meals, and all tuition. Dates are July 13 to July 20, 1991, and you can contact **Mary Jane Stout, Alumni Vacation College, 102 Old Main, Penn State University, University Park, PA 16802 (phone 814/865-6517).**

Skidmore College's Summer Special Programs, near Saratoga Springs, New York, invites several different groups to use its campus in summer for residential adult study programs, and some of the latter are open to the public at large. I'm particularly impressed by the two- to four-week creative-writing course of the New York State Writers Institute (mid-July of 1991: $900 for two weeks, $1,700 for four weeks, all inclusive), and by the nine-day conference and workshops of the International Women's Writing Guild (late July of 1991: approximately $650 for tuition, room, and board). Contact **Prof. R. Boyers, N.Y. State Summer Writers Institute, Skidmore College, Saratoga Springs, NY 12866; International Women's Writing Guild, P.O. Box 810, Gracie Station, New York, NY 10028; or Office of the Dean of Special Programs, Skidmore College, Saratoga Springs, NY 12866 (phone 518/584-5000, ext. 2264).**

Finally, Colby College of Waterville, Maine, plays host each August to the Great Books Summer Institute, an intensive discussion and analysis of four outstanding books that participants (up to 250 of them) have already read and pondered prior to arriving for their one-week stay. This year's session is in mid-August, 1991; this year's fee is $340, either single or double occupancy, including all lodging in college residence halls, all meals, and all tuition, as well as the four books sent to you via U.P.S. about a month in advance. During the session attended several years back by a friend of mine, books for discussion included Thomas Mann's *The Magic Mountain*, Frijthof Capra's *The Tao of Physics*, and William Barrett's *Irrational Man;* participants discussed the interrelationship of the books and their themes, in a week that was described to me as quite remarkably stimulating and satisfying. More recently, selections were: *The Aquarian Conspiracy, Wholeness and the Implicate Order, The Universe Is a Green Dragon*, and Thornton Wilder's *The Skin of Our Teeth*. One note: Discussions are led by a lay "moderator," not a professor, whose role is to elicit student comments and not to hand down scholarly judgments from above. For information, contact **Great Books Summer Institute, 680 Elton Ave., Riverhead, NY 11901, Attn: Bill Thurston (phone 516/727-8600).**

At all such schools: When the week is over and "students" depart, what usually is their appraisal of the experience? "It was a stimulating relief from my day-to-day office routine that I do not find lying on a beach," said one. "It was good to talk ideas with my spouse," said another, "and know both of our heads were still very much alive."

THE NEW WORLD OF TRAVEL 1992

The lifeblood of the Arthur Frommer travel guides is the correspondence received from readers, commenting on the establishments recommended in the texts and recommending new establishments. Each such letter is carefully studied, and when a particular lead seems promising, it is followed up and personally checked.

It is hoped that *The New World of Travel* will receive similar assistance from its readers. A yearly publication, issued near the start of each year, *The New World* will constantly grow. And since much of its content relates to organizations that lack the means to market themselves properly, or come to the attention of a travel journalist, your help is invaluable in alerting me to the organizations—hospitality exchanges, alternative resorts, new travel clubs, and the like—that you have discovered.

If you become aware of a new travel organization, program, or development that deserves to be described in our next edition, *The New World of Travel 1992*, won't you please let me know about it? Send your letters to Arthur Frommer, *The New World of Travel*, c/o Prentice Hall Press, Travel Division, 15 Columbus Circle, New York, NY 10023. All letters will be acknowledged, and all are warmly appreciated, in advance, by the author.

Vacationing at a Cultural Folkdance Camp

With an Intensity That Must Be Seen to Be Believed, Some Americans Devote Their Holidays to Exploring the Folkways of Ethnic Cultures

On WINTER EVENINGS IN DESERTED GYMS, they dance to the music of a dozen cultures, learning the steps as they go along, helping their partners, uncritical of the efforts of a sheer beginner.

Summers, from late June to early September, they repair to wooded settings near lakes or mountains to dance the entire day and evening. For a full week, or at least a long weekend, residential, rural folkdance camps provide an increasingly popular holiday/vacation alternative to tens of thousands of Americans.

Their atmosphere is among the most democratic of all our holiday institutions. Participants are wholly intergenerational and range from college sophomores to dynamic seniors in their 70s—some bearded, some in bold gypsy skirts or country dirndls. Without introduction, they take your hand to start a dance, then hand you off without skipping a beat to the next in a circle or line of whirling, or foot-stomping, or waltzing, dancers. There are no awkward social barriers, no inquiries into background or tastes, no attention paid to beauty or dress.

The music to which you dance, and the steps, are those that descend not from a paid composer or choreographer, but from the people, mainly poor people, and are then handed down from decade to decade by oral tradition or direct demonstration. It is intensely ethnic music and dance, and usually jumps from country American to Balkan to Greek and Israeli in the course of a single set.

It is also soul-stirring, insistent, pulsating music and dance that makes you joyous to be alive, and exercises every faculty of mind and limb. If you've never been to a folkdance camp or even folkdancing, you might think of taking the plunge, because the steps are easily learned and sheer beginners are accepted at virtually every camp.

The major camps—as best I've been able to determine—are the following:

ON BOTH COASTS

Pinewoods Camp, near historic Plymouth, Massachusetts: Here is perhaps the most extensive of the residential folkdance programs, a series of seven one-week sessions running from late June to early September. But all are focused on English, Scottish, and American forms of the art, without the enlivening digressions (in my opinion) into the Balkan or Mexican varieties that mark so many other camps. Still, for lovers of those familiar steps, here are several hours daily of dancing paradise, in spacious and airy wood pavilions scattered over 24 acres of pine groves. Housing, almost always double occupancy, is in rustic, screened cabins located among the trees, but none far from two clear-water lakes for swimming and boating. Seven of the weeks are sponsored by the Country Dance and Song Society, cost $389 a week (in all but one instance) for room, full board, and dancing, and inquiries should be sent, prior to around June 30, to **CDSS, 17 New South St., Northampton, MA 01060 (phone 413/584-9913)**, and thereafter to **CDSS, Pinewoods Camp, Off West Long Pond Road, Plymouth, MA 02360 (phone 508/224-4858)**. One session (early July, and usually $375, all inclusive) is sponsored by the Royal Scottish Country Dance Society, and features the three or so basic steps of Scottish folkdancing in endless combinations. A bagpiper wakes you in the morning! Contact **RSCDS, c/o Ken Launie, 15 Salem St., Cambridge, MA 02139 (phone 617/491-6855)**.

Centrum Foundation, Port Townsend, Washington: A nonprofit arts-and-education group sponsoring summer music, theater, and writing conferences at a 100-year-old former army base called Fort Worden; participants stay in single or double rooms carved out of barracks now owned by the State Parks Department. The site overlooks the awesome Cascade and Olympic Mountains on one side, the Strait of Juan de

Lady of the Lake, northern Idaho

Fuca, with its long, sandy beach, on the other. The last week of August is the usual period for "International Folk Dance and Music Week," teaching and practicing four different types of international dances. Tuition, room, and board run $300 per person. Contact **Centrum Foundation, P.O. Box 1158, Port Townsend, WA 98368 (phone 206/385-3102).**

Stockton Folk Dance Camp, in Stockton, California: One of the nation's oldest, in its 44th year, it always takes place the last week of July and the first week of August, Sunday through Saturday. With several two-hour classes running simultaneously, it isn't possible to sample everything, and many people therefore go for both weeks. According to one teacher, Stockton is not well suited for beginners, but is rather a skilled "work camp" for learning new dances. Accommodation is in University of the Pacific dorms, and fees for tuition, room, and board run about $435 per week. Contact **Stockton Folk Dance Camp, c/o Bruce Mitchell, Director, University of the Pacific, Stockton, CA 95211 (phone 916/488-7637).**

Maine Folk Dance Camp, near Bridgton, Maine: Another highly important one, it consists of nine week-long sessions held from July 1 through the Labor Day weekend, at a 37-acre, lakeside camp setting about an hour to the northwest of Portland, Maine. Housing is in individual cabins sleeping two people. Each day features the dance repertoire of a different nation: you wake one morning, let's say, to Mexican music, eat Mexican food, learn Mexican dances, and have a fiesta at night. Some participants claim the regimen to be better than actual international travel, since they experience "real" aspects of a culture, not tourist ones. Room, board, classes, and festivals cost under $400 a week, depending on the accommodation. Prior to early June (by which time much space is booked), contact **Maine Folk Dance Camp, P.O. Box 2305, North Babylon, NY 11703 (phone 516/661-3866);** thereafter, **Maine Folk Dance Camp, P.O. Box 100, Bridgton, ME 04009 (phone 207/647-3424).**

AND ELSEWHERE

Lady of the Lake, of northern Idaho: In the popular resort area of Lake Coeur d'Alene, an hour from Spokane, Washington, this is an almost frantically intense week (the last full week of June) of folkdancing that starts at 9 A.M. each day and roars on till 11 P.M. You do "contras," squares, clogging,

The world of folk life and art is a vast one, yet largely "underground" and little known.

Augusta Heritage Arts Workshops, at Davis & Elkins College, West Virginia

"swing," and "vintage" (turn-of-the-century) dancing, aided by accomplished instructors and musicians, all for the remarkably low weekly charge of $295, including meals and accommodations in rustic cabins housing 6 to 10 people. Children aren't encouraged to come. Contact **Lady of the Lake, c/o Penn Fix, 703 W. Shoshone, Spokane, WA 99203 (phone 509/838-2160).**

Buffalo Gap Camp, near Capon Bridge, West Virginia: A 2½-hour drive from Washington, D.C., Buffalo Gap Camp (on a spring-fed, clear-water lake) becomes an international dance camp on the three-day Memorial Day and Labor Day weekends, charging $200 per weekend for dancing, ethnic meals, and lodging in dorm-style cabins. Teachers are brought in from around the world to supervise exotic, foreign folkdances from 9 A.M. to 5 P.M. (repeated at evening

dance parties), and yet total beginners are invited to the camp. In between the opening and closing dates for summer the camp is rented to outside groups for week-long sessions of specialized dancing ("Scandinavian Week," "Balkan Week"). For information on the full summer program, contact **Buffalo Gap Camp, c/o Mel Diamond, 2414 E. Gate Dr., Silver Spring, MD 20906 (phone 301/589-9212 during office hours, 301/871-8788 evenings and weekends).**

Mendocino Country Dance Camp, in northern California: Living in small cabins sleeping five to six people, in a natural redwood grove of magnificent mammoth trees, or in tents along the Gualala River, you dance English and American squares and "contras" from 9 A.M. to 5 P.M., enjoy a short break, and then continue at an evening dance party that starts at 8 P.M. and officially ends at 11 P.M.—but frequently continues for most of the night! Beginners are very much encouraged and supported. Dates are July 13–20 and July 20–26, 1991, and the approximate cost is $350 for housing, meals, and instruction. Contact **Mendocino Country Dance Camp, c/o Jerry Allen, 3372 Victor, Oakland, CA 94602 (phone 415/531-7476).**

Kentucky Summer Dance School, at Berea College in Berea, Kentucky: Always the last week in June, it's in a sylvan place—a historic small town set in the foothills of the western Appalachians, and at a college noted for its support of the folk arts. Instruction ranges from traditional American dances to the most esoteric of the British and Scottish steps, and much of the classroom music is live. Charges average $300 for adults, $220 for teenagers, $175 for children 6 to 12 (who pursue a separate program), for meals, tuition, and lodging in college dorms. Note: The location in 1991 may change to another site in Kentucky, not yet chosen as we go to press. Contact **Kentucky Summer Dance School, P.O. Box 4128, Frankfort, KY 40603 (phone 502/227-4466).**

Augusta Heritage Arts Workshops, at Davis & Elkins College, West Virginia: In the context of a much broader, summer-long program delving into every conceivable folk art and craft, specialized dance weeks take place in mid-July (for Irish, English, and French-Canadian "step dances" only) and in early August (for southern squares, contras, swing dances, Cajun dances, clogging, and callers' workshops). Work is intense but open to all levels of expertise; lodging is in college residence halls, on the hilly, 170-acre campus of Davis & Elkins in the highlands (2,000 feet) of central West Virginia. Cost for a week: just over $350 for tuition, meals, and semiprivate room. Contact **Augusta Heritage Center, Davis & Elkins College, 100 Sycamore St., Elkins, WV 26241 (phone 304/636-1903).**

John C. Campbell Folk School of Brasstown, North Carolina: "Dance Weeks" at this noted, 63-year-old school for folk arts and crafts take place on scattered dates throughout the year, and are almost wholly devoted to steps and formations of the home-grown variety, thoroughly American. Grounds are a 365-acre campus nestled between the Smokies and the Blue Ridge Mountains, a 2- to 2½-hour drive from such cities as Atlanta, Chattanooga, Knoxville, Asheville, and Greenville. Meals, as you'd expect, are southern, home style, and accompanied by home-baked bread. And weekly charges average only $300 in dorms, slightly more per person in double rooms, for tuition, meals, and lodging. Contact **The Registrar, John C. Campbell Folk School, Brasstown, NC 28902 (phone 704/837-2775 or 704/837-7329).**

Fiddle and Dance Workshops, in the Catskill Mountains of New York State: The camp is Ashokan, along a lake at the base of heavily forested hills, 2½ hours north of New York City by car. And there, for five consecutive weeks starting in late July 1991, dedicated folkdancers (including beginners) attend either the "Northern Week" (squares, contras, and couple dances of New England, Britain, France, Sweden, and Canada), the "Southern Week" (Appalachian, Cajun, and "old-time," plus buckdancing, clogging, and "flat-footing"), the "Celtic Week" (Irish, Scottish, and Cape Breton), or the "Western and Swing Week" (country, western, cowboy, Texas two-step, jitterbug, and lindy). Just $375 a week covers tuition, meals, and lodging in bunkhouse dorms, 15 to 20 people per room; less than that if you camp out in your own tent or trailer. Contact **Fiddle and Dance, R.D. 1, Box 489, West Hurley, NY 12491 (phone 914/338-2996).**

Flying Cloud Academy of Cincinnati, Ohio: Every year in the third week of June, it sponsors a "Vintage Dance Week" for instruction in 19th-century and ragtime-era social and couple dances. "This is what our great-great-grandparents did," says director Richard Powers, "with original orchestrations, taught by the best teachers. Beginners need not fear; we'll instruct them." Tuition charge is only $160, and housing expenses vary from either nothing at all (in the homes of "friends of the Academy") to the standard rates of motels, B&B houses, and college dorms in the area; a committee assists with lodging, and can often secure university dorms for as little as $10 a night. Contact **Richard Powers, 3623 Herschel Ave., Cincinnati, OH 45208 (phone 513/321-4878).**

Oglebay Dance Camp of Wheeling, West Virginia: This dance camp, the oldest in the country, schedules three-day/two-night camps each year for the Memorial Day and Labor Day weekends in a 1,400-acre park outside the city limits, on the landscaped grounds of a former farm set in rolling hills. Participants sleep in bunk beds like those of a

Participants are wholly intergenerational and unconcerned with your own background, appearance, or dress.

Folk dancing, Oglebay Dance Camp, West Virginia

children's summer camp, and spend their days and evenings in ethnic-dance classes supervised by three specialist instructors. Total cost: $135, including meals, lodging, and instruction. Contact **Oglebay Dance Camp, 1330 National Rd., Wheeling, WV 26003 (phone 304/242-7700)**.

BUT ARE YOU UP TO IT?

A word of warning before you enroll in any program: Be sure you can take the pace. Sessions involve as many as nine hours of movement per day—the most protracted "aerobic exercise" in America—beginning with up to six hours daily of workshops, followed frequently by three hours of "partying" (continual dancing) at night. And be sure you can move in rhythm to music. Some retirees looking for a new vacation experience, but physically awkward or unable to last on the floor for more than an hour, have had a miserable time at dance camps. Try looking up a local teacher before you leave.

Despite this caution, most dance camps are open to sheer beginners, although some are more attuned to them than others. Mendocino has been mentioned to me by several people as particularly suitable for duffers, but Stockton isn't.

Finally, bear in mind that the world of folk life and art, represented in part by the folkdance movement, is a vast one, yet largely "underground" and little known. Though I've mentioned the major camps, dozens of smaller ones have been necessarily overlooked. Once you tap into the rich folklife culture, you'll quickly discover many other such opportunities, and add new dimensions to your life.

Brainy Tours for High IQs

Vacations That Turn Your Mind On, Not Off

How CAN YOU SAFELY BOOK ONTO AN organized tour if you can't stand the company of people less intelligent than yourself? How can you ensure that other tour members will be congenial companions, alive to new discoveries, thoughtful and bright?

For years, brainy tourists have sought to solve that conundrum by confining their choices to tours that were advertised as having a serious theme, or a scholarly content, or a famous professor to provide the lecture commentary. The theory was that tours described in lugubrious tones would scare off the sluggards and the philistines, and attract instead the readers of books, the lovers of art, the collectors of degrees—all like a form of Darwinian selection.

The trouble was, and is: such tours are few and scattered. They come to your attention only by chance, in random mailings from alumni groups or museums to which you may or may not belong. Rather than appearing in a year-long catalog of departures, to be consulted when the travel urge hits, they materialize at odd and inopportune times when you're simply unable to go.

With seven major exceptions:

Swan Hellenic Cruises, represented by Esplanade Tours of Boston, is the oldest of the brainy tour companies operating year round. Owned for half a century by the prestigious P&O Lines of Britain, and largely booked by British vacationers, it places not one but several guest lecturers—each a noted historian or archeologist—on each of its cruises to the eastern Mediterranean and its more recently instituted motorcoach tours to other important destinations around the world. Thus you travel with the likes of Oxford "dons" (teaching masters), Egyptologists and Greek classicists of renowned museums, authors of encyclopedic works—all in an atmosphere of high erudition, sharing the experience with other well-read travelers. Possibly because the clientele is mainly British, rates are moderate: an average of $200 to $250 a day for air/sea/land arrangements so comprehensive that they include all shore excursions and even tipping on the particularly popular journeys to classic sights in the Aegean (on a ship limited to fewer than 300 passengers). They thus attract a cross-section of thoughtful, intelligent people from all walks of life. For literature and reservations, contact **Swan Hellenic Cruises, c/o Esplanade Tours, 581 Boylston St., Boston, MA 02116 (phone 617/266-7465).**

Prospect Ltd., of England, is a more recent entrant, another British company that markets its tours in the U.S., and with such early success that its large catalogs are already three in number—"Art Tours of Europe, North America, and the Middle East," "Music Tours," and "Music and Art Tours in Great Britain and Ireland"—and nearly 200 year-round departures in scope. For each tour a specific tour leader is listed, and biographies at the back identify each as a noted academic with impressive credentials. These are no

---

Often, tours described in lugubrious terms scare off the sluggards and the philistines, and attract the readers of books, the lovers of art.

glib "personality kids" of the sort encountered on a standard tour, but—in one example—a scholar who "obtained his doctorate on Gothic architecture in Spain before becoming curator for Spanish and late Italian art at the National Gallery." Their commentary is not for the viewers of TV sitcoms. Tours explore history, art, music, and architecture for the most part; are one to three weeks in length and usually limited to 20 or 25 people apiece; and cost an average of only $100 to $140 per day in Britain, $150 per day in Europe, including (in the latter case) round-trip air fare from London to the jumping-off point for each tour. For literature and reservations, go directly to **Prospect Music & Art Tours Ltd., 454 Chiswick High Rd., London W4 STT, England (phone 081/995-2151, or toll free 800/752-4628 direct from North America; for brochures only , toll free 800/727-2771 in the U.S.).**

The Humanities Institute of Belmont, Massachusetts, offers the most intensive of the cerebral vacations, devoting each Monday through Thursday morning to actual classroom instruction in a foreign land, and then reserving the weekday afternoons and the weekends (Friday through Sunday) for actual touring of the areas outside the academic base. Instructors are distinguished academic figures of the country in question (England, Scotland, Ireland, Greece, Italy, Israel, Australia, Canada, China); "students" are mainly adults aged 30 to 60, who simply audit the courses without receiving credit but are required to complete specified readings; and tours/classes are generally three weeks in duration, on themes such as "Tensions in Irish History from Henry VIII to Cromwell" (at Trinity College, Dublin), "British Poetry After Eliot" (at Cambridge), "Renaissance Art and Architecture" (in Florence, Italy), and "The Oral and Literary Tradition of Greece" (in Athens, the Peloponnese, the Greek islands, and Crete). Figure $2,600 for three weeks, $2,000 for two weeks, including transatlantic air fare, tuition, accommodations, excursions, and many meals, for most of these "travel-and-learn" experiences, offered summer only. Contact **The Humanities Institute, P.O. Box 18, Belmont, MA 02178 (phone 617/484-3191, or toll free 800/327-1657 outside Massachusetts).**

The Smithsonian Study Tours, of Washington, D.C.'s famed Smithsonian Institution, offers 150 different "study trips" throughout the year, as an educational benefit of membership in the parent organization (which costs $20 a year). Each tour is led by either an art historian, ethnologist, marine biologist, ornithologist, or astronomer; and those specialties reflect the broad categories of the program. Small Smithsonian tour groups rove the world over, from Soviet Central Asia to Zapotec and Mayan Mexico; for periods of widely differing durations; pay from $1,200 to $3,500 for varying trips, or an average of $150 per day for domestic tours, $250 per day for foreign ones. Surprisingly, according to deputy

MEDITERRANEAN CRUISES

Civilised travel to where civilisation began. There are 19 different cruises to choose from, visiting the Aegean, the Mediterranean, the Black Sea and the Red Sea; each an exploration of the cultural, religious and social history of the ancient world.

Travelling with you are a number of guest lecturers, experts in art, architecture and history, whose informal talks will bring to life the places we visit.

On board the 250 passenger 'Orpheus', you can enjoy an informal lifestyle and the congenial companionship of your fellow travellers who will doubtless share your interest in and appreciation of the lands and cultures to be explored.

RHINE CRUISES

A leisurely cruise along a river noted for its history and the beauty of its scenery, on board our river boat commissioned exclusively for Swan Hellenic passengers.

Our itineraries have been carefully planned to give ample time to explore the highlights of the Rhine and Mosel. Once again, the sharing of knowledge and interests between your fellow travellers, guest lecturers and guides will create a stimulating and particularly satisfying holiday.

SPICE ISLAND CRUISES

Explore the islands of the Indonesian archipelago on board our 40-passenger luxury cruisers. In addition to a glimpse of the local culture, the itineraries offer a range of interests, including rare tropical sea life and exotic flora and fauna, such as the fabled Komodo dragon. You can also indulge in your favourite water recreations, with facilities available on board including windsurfers, water skis and snorkelling, diving and fishing equipment.

ART TREASURES TOURS AND NATURAL HISTORY TOURS

A deeper appreciation of the world's art treasures; tours in quest of the world's natural treasures. Those who enjoy an active holiday and have an enquiring mind will enjoy a Swan Hellenic tour.

With us, you can discover the world's treasures during a carefree journey with people whose outlook and objectives will almost certainly match your own.

Following carefully planned itineraries, our groups of between 20 and 30 people are always accompanied by a specialist guest lecturer who will add immeasurably to your appreciation of all there is to be seen.

17

Swan Hellenic tour, Temple of Apollo at Didyma

manager Prudence Clendenning, two-thirds of all tour passengers are single, despite the fact that the median age of participants is a fairly low 50. "Our participants are bright, thoughtful people who don't fit the stereotype of the 'casual tourist,'" she adds. Contact **Smithsonian Institution Study Tours, 1100 Jefferson Dr. SW, Washington, DC 20560 (phone 202/357-4700)**.

Citisights of London is for serious, short tours of Britain—one to three days in length—guided by professional archeologists and historians, and meant to be mixed and matched with standard touring or stays in the British Isles; they are also heavily booked by intellectually curious residents of Britain. Though touring is done by motorcoach, there all resemblance ends to the ordinary "once-over-lightly" approach of the usual programs. Three-day tours, leaving on Friday or Saturday, explore such weighty themes as "Wessex—Its History, Legends, and Thomas Hardy," or "Saxon Churches: The Arrival of Christianity in the North."

Swan Hellenic places not one but several guest lecturers—each a noted historian or archeologist— on each of its cruises.

Smithsonian Study Tours at Petra, Jordan (top), *and Abu Simbel, Egypt* (bottom)

Whale-watching with Biological Journeys of California

One-day tours, from February through October, delve into "The Peasants Revolt," "A Bronze Age Lake Village," "Chaucer's Canterbury Trail," and "Inside Roman and Medieval Colchester." Originally an operator of London walking tours, and still heavily into that worthy activity, Citisights is fast expanding into intellectual vehicular sightseeing, and is gaining acclaim not only for its refusal to pander to superficial touring attitudes but also for the moderate price level of its program: $40 for the average one-day tour, $265 for the average three-day variety. Contact **Citisights of London, 213 Brooke Rd., London E5 8AB (phone 71/739-2372).**

Biological Journeys of McKinleyville, California, operates whale-watching and other natural-history expeditions of serious scientific content but open to the public at large. Departures, nearly 50 of them, are for one and two weeks in every month other than December; go mainly to the waters of Baja California, Alaska, and South America; average $200 to $250 a day, all inclusive; and are each led by a prominent naturalist. You can be fairly certain that your fellow passengers—usually limited to 10 per trip—will have outlooks and imaginations similar to yours. Contact **Biological Journeys, 1696 Ocean Dr., McKinleyville, CA 95521 (phone 707/839-0178, or toll free 800/548-7555 outside Calif.).**

And finally, Dailey-Thorp Travel, of New York City, is the nation's leading operator of year-round opera and music tours to music festivals in the United States, Britain, and at sea; to massive doses of opera-going in Europe; and to opera and concerts in New York. These attract the dedicated music-lover, but the fairly affluent one, as tours—with their expensive admission tickets included—sometimes range as high as $300 to $400 per day. Contact **Dailey-Thorp Travel, 315 W. 57th St., New York, NY 10019 (phone 212/307-1555).**

To repeat a point: I am of course aware of the scores and scores of serious university, alumni, and museum tours that are sponsored by different institutions, and largely marketed to their members or mailing lists on a local basis, but here I've tried to identify the nationwide operators of intellectual tours that offer these on a consistent basis throughout the year, and reliably year after year. If I've omitted any major players, please advise me, c/o my publisher, Prentice Hall Press, Travel Division (15 Columbus Circle, New York, NY 10023, *The New World of Travel* Dept.), and we'll remedy the omission.

THE NEW WORLD OF TRAVEL 1992

The lifeblood of the Arthur Frommer travel guides is the correspondence received from readers, commenting on the establishments recommended in the texts and recommending new establishments. Each such letter is carefully studied, and when a particular lead seems promising, it is followed up and personally checked.

It is hoped that *The New World of Travel* will receive similar assistance from its readers. A yearly publication, issued near the start of each year, *The New World* will constantly grow. And since much of its content relates to organizations that lack the means to market themselves properly, or come to the attention of a travel journalist, your help is invaluable in alerting me to the organizations—hospitality exchanges, alternative resorts, new travel clubs, and the like—that you have discovered.

If you become aware of a new travel organization, program, or development that deserves to be described in our next edition, *The New World of Travel 1992*, won't you please let me know about it? Send your letters to Arthur Frommer, *The New World of Travel*, c/o Prentice Hall Press, Travel Division, 15 Columbus Circle, New York, NY 10023. All letters will be acknowledged, and all are warmly appreciated, in advance, by the author.

The Religious Retreat as a Form of Vacation

More Than a Million Americans Each Year Devote Large Portions of Their Leisure Time to Sojourns in Retreat Houses

THE RELIGIOUS RETREAT IS A FORM OF vacation activity that most professional travel observers seem to have overlooked. Yet more than a million Americans each year—the figure could amount to 1,500,000—devote large portions of their leisure time to sojourns in retreat houses. And while the greater part of them limit the stays to weekends, and to locations close at hand, a large number go for a week or two and many hundreds of miles away, and to centers whose broad range of subject matter and activities go well beyond the normal conception of a personal retreat.

As best as I can determine, there exist slightly more than 500 Catholic retreat centers and houses throughout the U.S. and Canada, about 150 Protestant centers, a dozen or so Jewish ones, and an emerging handful of Buddhist retreats. For a near-comprehensive listing of the Christian retreats, send $10 to **Retreats International, P.O. Box 1067, Notre Dame, IN 46556 (phone 219/239-5320)**, for the 1991 edition of their 60-page "Directory of Retreat Centers," which lists 594 such houses (520 or so Catholic retreats, about 75 Protestant ones), state by state, in pared-down fashion: addresses and phone numbers, name of director, months of operation, number of rooms, heavily abbreviated references to basic approaches and programs. You'll really need to phone the centers listed for your area to determine which best meet your needs.

For a more complete list of Protestant retreat houses (totaling about 150 in all), contact the **North American Retreat Directors Association, Olmsted Manor, Ludlow, PA 16333 (phone 814/945-6512)**. While theirs is simply a mailing list, not a directory with descriptions, they'll be pleased to furnish a copy free (after which you can phone the houses in your state for more details). Despite that kind offer, it would be a nice gesture to enclose $2 for postage and handling.

Upward of a hundred retreat houses have from 50 to 100 or more rooms apiece, while the remainder average 20 to 40 rooms. At the smaller houses, you obviously can't expect a complete activities program. Rather, in the monastic tradition of some (especially Catholic) retreats, the experience is largely a personal one, and guests take advantage of the stressless atmosphere and freedom from business and family

The experience is largely a personal one, and guests take advantage of the stressless atmosphere and freedom from business/family pressures to ponder the eternal verities.

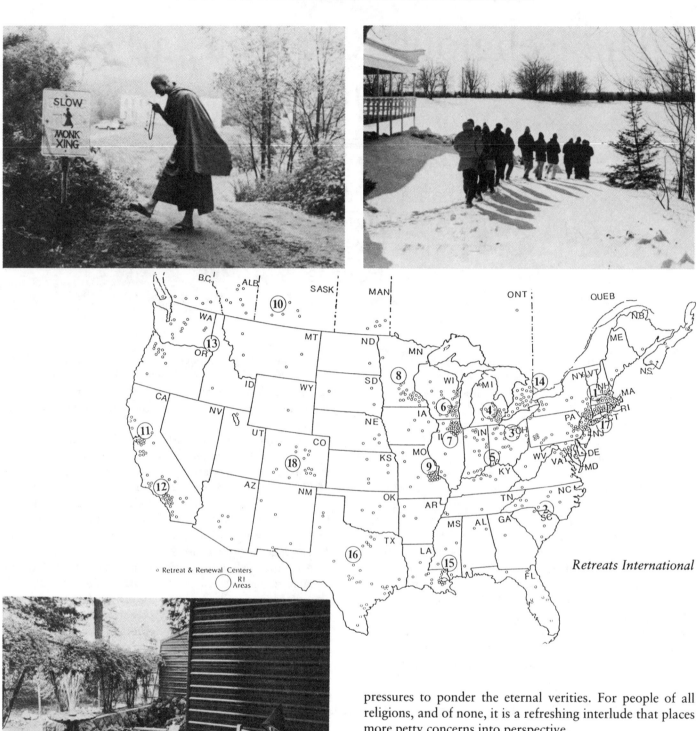

Retreats International

pressures to ponder the eternal verities. For people of all religions, and of none, it is a refreshing interlude that places more petty concerns into perspective.

The larger retreats have elaborate programs, often themed to major religious, social, or political issues. Probably the most extensive program (35 separate instructors, including widely known theologians, therapists, and authors) is the month-long summer institute conducted every July on the campus of Notre Dame University by the before-mentioned Retreats International. Here, in the casual setting of summertime, nearly 400 people (teachers, counselors, clergy, nurses, social workers, and other concerned adults) are in attendance each week (and one week is all you need stay), auditing courses and seminars in spiritual and other church-related issues, but also dealing with family and youth problems, intimate relationships, morality and self-healing, community needs. Housing for the entire week amounts to only $55 to $75 per person (depending on the room), meals add about $10 to $15 a day, and week-long courses (five two-hour sessions) are $100 for tuition, in addition to an overall $30 registration fee. Write for literature to the address earlier given.

Genesis Spiritual Life Center, in the Berkshire Mountains of western Massachusetts, is a far less typical example of the large retreat center, in that it is purposefully ecumenical in nature, appealing to people of all religious beliefs, even though it is administered by the Sisters of Providence, a Catholic order. "We believe," says their credo, "that when persons of differing lifestyles and spiritualities connect, God's creative and healing energies are released. . . . We give preference to those who often feel alienated from their church or society." Heavily influenced by theories of the "New Age," the center's themed retreats include courses ranging from "Meditation Techniques" to "Guided Imagery and Music" to "A Jungian Look at the Christian Message," as taught by an equally ecumenical faculty that at times has included Lutherans, followers of Joseph Campbell, massage therapists, and psychoanalysts. Programs are offered throughout the year, as are "private retreats" ($25 a day for room, board, and the spiritual assistance of a Genesis staff member). All this in a peaceful wooded setting dotted with flower and vegetable gardens, an old restored carriage house, a chapel, a library, and two dining rooms. For their fascinating literature, contact **Genesis Spiritual Life Center, 53 Mill St., Westerfield, MA 01085 (phone 413/562-3527).**

The Maryknoll Sisters Center in upstate New York, welcoming people of all churches and cultures, is the site for year-round group retreats that often deal with social change and other partly political issues, in the context of the intense religious missions for which the Maryknoll order is so well known. Six-day retreats range in subject matter from "Biblical Reflections," "Creation-Centered Spirituality," and "The Gospel in Context," on the one hand, to "Dismantling Racism," "U.S. Foreign Policy," and "Cultures Shaping People," on the other. Die-hard conservatives will not feel at ease

here, although they will like the rates: $24 a day for room and full board, $50 for registration and week-long tuition. Contact the **Maryknoll Mission Institute, Maryknoll Sisters Center, P.O. Box 529, Maryknoll, NY 10545 (phone 914/941-7575).** Maryknoll is at Ossining, New York, about 35 miles north of New York City.

In other areas of the country, the key, larger retreats include Covecrest Christian Renewal Center, in northern Georgia, a year-round Methodist complex with extensive program and facilities, and low rates of $17.50 to $23 per person per day for lodgings (much less for recreational vehicles and tent campers parked alongside the sweeping lawns). Write or phone **Covecrest Christian Renewal Center, Rte. 1, Box 1808, Tiger, GA 30576 (phone 404/782-5961).**

On the West Coast, but much smaller and radically different in atmosphere, is the highly regarded, Anglican-run Mount Cavalry Retreat House near Santa Barbara, California, overlooking the Pacific from a high vantage point. In the quiet atmosphere of this Protestant monastic community, in a large Spanish home with well-stocked library, individuals enjoy the essence of the retreat experience, for a suggested daily donation of $45 for room and board. Write or phone **Mount Calvary Retreat House, P.O. Box 1296, Santa Barbara, CA 93102 (phone 805/962-9855).**

The available Jewish retreats are almost all long weekends in nature, and include, most prominently:

The Brandeis-Bardin Institute, 1101 Peppertree Lane, Brandeis, CA 93064 (phone 818/348-7201), has cottages amid rolling hills 45 minutes from Los Angeles, and offers a wide variety of themed programs on religious practices in the tradition of Reform Judaism. Cost is $140 per weekend, including full board.

Hadassah "Kallahs" are summer study weekends led by distinguished biblical scholars, at locations in several states and on themes ranging from "Family Relations in the Old Testament" to "Jews and Islam." For dates, locations and prices, write: **Hadassah Jewish Education Department, 50 W. 58th St., New York, NY 10019.**

Discovery Seminars, 2½-day presentations, Friday evening to Sunday afternoon, of basic elements in the Jewish heritage, are offered mainly to those with little background, in several locations throughout the country, from September through early summer. Cost is $150 per person for tuition, room, and board. For information, write or phone **Discovery**

The larger retreats have elaborate programs that go far beyond the normal perception of their functions.

Seminars, 1220 Broadway, Suite 610, New York, NY 10001 (phone 212/643-8800).

Jacobs Camp, in Mississippi, has three large weekend retreats each year, September through May, discussing Jewish issues in a countryside setting that now also contains an 8,000-square-foot Museum of the Southern Jewish Experience, operated by the Union of American Hebrew Congregations. The all-inclusive charge is only $65 per person from Friday evening to Sunday evening. Contact **Jacobs Camp, P.O. Box C, Utica, MS 39175 (phone 601/885-6042).**

Camp Olin-Sang-Ruby, in Oconomowoc, Wisconsin, hosts a variety of midweek and weekend retreats—some for adults only, others for families or mature adults only—on themes such as "Spirituality and the High Holidays" and "Jewish Literature and the Arts." The all-inclusive charge is $125 to $150 for three days, for lodgings and meals in an extensive complex on 180 acres along the shores of Lake LaBelle. For information, write or phone **Camp Olin-Sang-Ruby, 100 W. Monroe St., Chicago, IL 60603 (phone 312/782-1477).**

For a complete directory of Buddhist retreats in North America, send $15.70 (which includes postage and handling) to **John Muir Publications, P.O. Box 613, Santa Fe, NM 87504,** for a copy of their recently published, 312-page *Buddhist America: Centers, Practices, Retreats*, by Don Morreale.

Museum of the Southern Jewish Experience, Jacobs Camp, Mississippi

IV

VOLUNTEER VACATIONS, FOR FREE OR ALMOST FOR FREE

Volunteer Vacations
for Vital Adults

At Locations Ranging from Wilderness Lands in the
U.S. to Collective Farms in Israel, the Donation of Your Labors Can
Result in a Free or Almost-Free Stay

SOME OF US DEVOTE OUR VACATIONS TO frantic aerobics—jogging, jumping, straining, pulling, and clamping on Sony Walkmen to ease the crushing boredom of the aimless sport.

Other, more enlightened sorts gain the very same aerobic benefits—and personal fulfillment of the highest order—by engaging in voluntary physical labor at a socially useful project, in mountains and deserts, forests and farms. Though most such "workcamp" activity is designed for the vacations of young people, a number of other major programs are intended for adults of all ages, or—in some instances—for adults up to the age of 40.

A HUNDRED HOLIDAY "DIGS"

All over the world, but at home as well, archeological excavations utilize volunteer labor by adults with no previous experience in the art. In many cases the projects pick up all expenses of your stay (other than transportation to the site); in some instances they also pay you a small salary; in most, they charge a fairly nominal fee for your spartan room and board.

And though the work is often limited to the painfully slow removal of earth from fragile fossils—with a tooth-brush, no less, delicately, as you crouch over a slit trench in the baking summer sun—it leaves you full of fatigue, drenched with sweat, and pounds lighter, at the end of each day's stint. Who needs the Golden Door?

Minimum stays range from three days to the entire summer. Examples? In Arizona, California, and Oregon, in the warm-weather months, a government-sponsored archeological survey will use summer-long volunteers to "identify and record prehistoric and historic sites . . . in rough terrain. . . . Volunteers will receive partial insurance coverage, on-the-job transportation, training, room, and board." At the east Karnak site of Luxor, Egypt, volunteers for six weeks are needed in May and June of each year to unearth building blocks used for the sun temples of the Pharaoh Akhenaten; "lodging and meals on site are provided without charge, except on Fridays (the day off)." In York, England, volunteers throughout the year pay $120 a week for the expense of participating for as little or long as they like in excavating stratified Roman, Anglo-Saxon, Viking, and medieval ruins of that historic city. Near Pisa, Italy, two-week volunteers are currently being sought this summer for excavations of 12th- to 15th-century structures in the Ripafratta area; volunteers pay $130 a week for room and board.

The chief source of information is the 80-page *Arche-*

*La Sabranenque's goal is to restore a host of decaying,
crumbled medieval villages at hillside locations
throughout southern France and northern Italy.*

72

ological Fieldwork Opportunities Bulletin, listing a hundred domestic and foreign "digs," issued each January by the Archeological Institute of America. (Some listings, you should be warned, are of "field schools" rather than "fieldwork," and involve substantial tuition charges.) Send $10 for a copy to the **Archeological Institute of America, 675 Commonwealth Ave., Boston, MA 02215 (phone 617/353-9361)**, and add $2.50 more if you wish it sent by first-class mail.

A STINT AS A STONE MASON

La Sabranenque is the strange but melodious source of this next volunteer vacation; it sends you to labor in the summer months in what many consider to be the most attractive areas in all of Europe: southern France and northern Italy. Non-

profit, and international, its goal is to restore a host of decaying, crumbled medieval villages at hillside locations throughout the historic area. It did so first in the early 1970s, with spectacular success, in the village of St-Victor-la-Coste, France, returning to their original form the 14th- and 15th-century stone farm buildings, chapels, and other community structures that had become heaps of rubble in the ensuing centuries. So favorable was the reaction of historians (and the French government), and so improved was the life of the village, that several other French and Italian villages immediately invited the group to attempt similar reconstructions of their own medieval ruins. Today, a half dozen such projects are pursued each summer, all utilizing international volunteers to set the stones and trowel the mortar for fences and walls.

Because the ancient structures of a European rural village

Restoration work in southern France, La Sabranenque

are rarely more than two stories high, the work requires no special construction or engineering skills; stone-laying is quickly taught at the start of each two-week or three-week session. Charges to the volunteers for housing, full board, and all activities are $450 for two weeks (spent in France only, at St-Victor-la-Coste), and $780 to $830 for three weeks (spent in both France and Italy; round-trip transportation between France and Italy is included). For more detailed information, contact **La Sabranenque Restoration Projects, c/o Jacqueline C. Simon, 217 High Park Blvd., Buffalo, NY 14226 (phone 716/836-8698).**

MAINTAINING THE "WILD LANDS"

You achieve this next worthy end by participating in a Sierra Club Service Trip operated in nearly 20 U.S. states by the mighty conservationist organization called the Sierra Club, now 500,000 members strong. Because many of the trips are subsidized by corporate donations, fees are low: as little as $175 for all the expenses of a 10-day tour of duty, except for transportation to the site—and that's a fairly average charge for the 50-odd service trips offered from April through late September; one-week trips cost even less, $125 in many cases.

You perform your "service" in some of the most enchanting places in all of America, not the standard, popular national and state parks, but the remote and less accessible ones, like the Gila Wilderness of New Mexico, the Washakie Wilderness of Wyoming, the Adirondack Forest Preserve of New York. Though most of the work is related to trail maintenance—by encouraging visitors to use well-marked trails, and limit their wanderings to them, the Sierra Club protects the delicate ecosystems of the park—projects extend to numerous other matters. "Workdays," says one description of a Sierra Club project, "will be divided between cleaning up nearby abandoned mining towns and reconstructing part of the Brown Basin Trail." Says another: "We will re-vegetate campsites." Or "our work will include cleanup and maintenance in and around the most imposing prehistoric ruins of the Southwest"; "we will cut and clear downed trees and underbrush from . . . around Chub Pond north of Old Forge."

Half the days of every trip are devoted to simple enjoyment of the wilderness; half are workdays. Lodging is in rustic cabins, lodges, or tents; cooking is done cooperatively by all participants; companionship is provided by vital, dynamic Americans of all ages. Complete descriptions of each service trip are set forth annually in the January/February edition of *Sierra*, official magazine of the club. For a copy of that listing, send a $2 check to **Sierra Club Outing Department, 730 Polk St., San Francisco, CA 94109.**

PRESERVING THE TRAILS

Slightly different in character is the even more extensive program of volunteer work projects in national and state parks, and national forests, for which the American Hiking Society serves as clearinghouse. Each year it lists several hundred such opportunities, for which food and lodging costs are either nil or nominal; volunteers provide the open-air parks with services that tight budgets will not allow the government agencies themselves to supply. Thus, for two to six weeks people act as unpaid, or nominally paid, "hosts" of campgrounds, build suspension bridges in Yellowstone National Park, weed out non-native plants from Haleakala National Park in Hawaii, spot and record the movements of bald eagles, act as deputy forest rangers or fire lookouts, even help out in the on-site offices of parks and forests. But mainly, in keeping with the core function of the nation's major hiking club, they maintain forest trails—and what "aerobics" that entails! "We clear brush, grub out stumps, trim vegetation, remove downed trees, repair erosion damage, and generally keep trails open . . . using hand tools like shovel, pick, pulaski, and saw. . . . It's strenuous," says an A.H.S. publication.

For information, write for a copy of *Helping Out in the Outdoors: Volunteer Opportunities on Public Lands,* to the **American Hiking Society, 1015 31st St. NW, Washington, DC 20007,** enclosing $3 to cover costs.

REPLACING A RESERVIST

Far less traditional, but fully as vital, is an unusual three-week stint of voluntary effort in the state of Israel, at any time of the year, and free of expense except for air fare (which, on this subsidized program, costs as little as $508 for a student traveling from New York to Israel in off-season, $658 for adults in other months).

But once there, "they" take care of everything else: room and board, even a set of boots and khaki fatigues.

"They" are the Israeli army. As a "Volunteer for Israel"—aged 18 to 70, male or female, Jew or gentile—you're housed at an Israeli military base, working at light, unskilled chores for 5½ days a week (for three weeks) to free up Israeli reservists for actual military training.

At an armored camp near Ashkelon, you grease or paint tanks, tighten the screws on howitzers, make careful inventories of spare parts. At an infantry bivouac in the Negev, you cook for the troops or serve in the mess hall. At a supply depot near Jerusalem, you sort uniforms, pack kit bags, clean rifles, or cut grass.

The working day is from 8 A.M. to 4 P.M. In the evenings, there's a "rec room" and subtitled movies or an Israeli professor (doing reserve duty) happy to deliver a lecture (in English) on the Dead Sea Scrolls or the current Mideast conflict.

You sleep in barracks segregated by sex, but take your meals with both male and female soldiers, enjoying mammoth Israeli breakfasts of yogurt and fresh vegetable salads, eggs, bread, and black coffee.

If, following your stint, you wish to stay on for extra weeks in Israel (this time, at your expense), your air ticket is easily extended for up to 180 days.

Some Americans devote every one of their yearly vacations to the work I've just described—and then can't wait to return. Some older Americans go several times a year.

"It can be tedious," wrote one volunteer-grandmother in her 60s, in a newsletter for alumni of the program. "I packaged coffee beans for distribution to the troops. But I was happy to do it.

"Some grandmothers take their grandchildren to the park—and some grandmothers volunteer for the Israeli army."

At an armored camp in Israel near Ashkelon, you grease or paint tanks, tighten the screws on howitzers, make careful inventories of spare parts.

NEW/FOURTH WORLD MOVEMENT

Annual Report APRIL 1988 - MARCH 1989

(Incidentally, though you assist that army, you do not join it or otherwise endanger your U.S. citizenship.)

Groups depart on three-week programs as often as eight times a month in the busy summer season, four times a month in the winter. Participants apply either to the New York office of Volunteers for Israel or to volunteer representatives. Recently, the organization has begun offering civilian projects as well (such as three weeks of voluntary effort in an Israeli geriatrics center), about which you might inquire when you write or phone.

Contact **Volunteers for Israel, 330 W. 42nd St., Suite 1318, New York, NY 10036-6092 (phone 212/643-4848).**

ALLEVIATING WORLD POVERTY

You perform this next voluntary deed with a highly impressive group. Like the fictitious priest who lived among the lepers, beggars, and cart-pullers of *The City of Joy*—that massive bestseller found on all the newsstands—so permanent members of the Fourth World Movement share the actual lives of the most abject poor in shantytown commu-

nities all over the world. Without making quite the same commitment, nonpermanent "volunteers" spend two weeks each summer in workcamps at the movement's international headquarters in Pierrelaye, France, held late June to mid-July, mid-July to early August, and early to late September. No knowledge of French is needed; total cost for the two-week stay is 420 francs (around $80); work includes carpentry, painting, masonry, cooking, followed by evening discussions and readings, until recently with the movement's much-revered founder, the late Fr. Josef Wresinski. Similar workshops, two summer weeks in length, are currently planned for the Washington, D.C., area; inquire.

Other volunteers devote two months, at any time of the year, to an internship at the movement's Washington, D.C., headquarters, or at the New York City branch office, again working with families living in extreme poverty on projects designed to draw them back into society: street libraries, literacy and computer programs, family vacations. Interns share housing (free) and housing duties with permanent Fourth World members, but are asked to make a small contribution to food costs during the first month only.

Because the movement is painfully strapped for funds, be sure to enclose an already-stamped, self-addressed envelope (and perhaps a contribution, too) when requesting further information and literature: **Fourth World Movement, 7600 Willow Hill Dr., Landover, MD 20785 (phone 301/336-9489)**, or to the New York branch office at **172 First Ave., New York, NY 10009 (phone 212/228-1339)**.

WORKING ON A KIBBUTZ

Finally, a 30-day overseas opportunity for young adults (up to 32 or 40 years of age; see below). That's the minimum stay required to share the life of an Israeli kibbutz, one of the communal societies that contain only 3% of the Israeli population, but produce 50% of its food and none of its crime. A type of collective farm in which property is held in common and children are raised as a group, the kibbutz has long held a strong fascination for Americans, both Jewish and gentile. Responding to a heavy demand, the kibbutz movement cur-rently permits young Americans (18 to 35) of any religion to join their ranks for a one-month (or longer) "workcamp vacation" for a fee of only $65, plus air fare to Israel. Or they accept a slightly older group (18 to 40) on a five-week "Kibbutz/Discovery" program consisting of only three weeks at the kibbutz, one week of archeological digs, and one week on tour in Israel, for a total of $1,890 per person, this time including round-trip air fare to Israel. Workcampers labor in the fields for six hours a day, six days a week, receive all meals daily, and live with a kibbutz family. Other plans requiring longer stays involve language instruction (Ulpan), even university courses. And all are sponsored and operated by the **Kibbutz Aliya Desk, 27 W. 20th St., New York, NY 10011 (phone 212/255-1338)**, which represents an impressive 280 kibbutzim (the plural of kibbutz). Other Kibbutz Aliya Desks (check the phone books) are in Chicago, Los Angeles, San Francisco, Houston, Atlanta, Miami, Denver, Pittsburgh, New Orleans, Cleveland, St. Louis, Boston, Milwaukee, and Philadelphia; write or call them for literature.

The kibbutz movement currently permits young Americans of any religion to join their ranks for a one-month (or longer) "workcamp vacation."

Send Your Child to an International Workcamp!

They Bear No Resemblance to the "Gulag," But Rather to the Best Form of Residential Education, Among Other Young People from Around the World

THIS SUMMER, MANY THOUSANDS OF AMERIcan teenagers will be hurtling through Europe by escorted motorcoach, isolated from the life of that continent by the steel-and-glass enclosure of their buses. They will socialize with one another, speak and hear English throughout, eat in segregated portions of hotel dining rooms, and regard themselves—subconsciously but firmly—as a privileged elite.

A better-informed segment of our youth will be sent by their parents, out of motives of the purest love, to international workcamps. Several hundred such places are found in countries of both Western and Eastern Europe.

There they will perform socially useful projects in the full midst of the European population. They will mix with other international young people, attempt foreign languages, make

> *There, young people will enjoy the satisfaction of worthy efforts, gain an appreciation for the realities of life abroad, and feel their minds stretch and grow.*

lifelong friendships, enjoy the satisfaction of contributing to worthy efforts, gain an appreciation for the realities of life abroad, and feel their minds stretch and grow.

And having paid only their air fare to reach the workcamp, they will receive free room and board once there.

WORKCAMP—REALLY A MISNOMER

"International workcamps"—a horrid term unrelated to the happy atmosphere of the sites—were first formed at the end of World War I. A Swiss pacifist, Pierre Ceresole, conceived of projects in which youth of the former combatants—France and Germany—would work together to clear the wreckage of war. Fittingly, he chose the battlefield of Verdun for the first voluntary "workcamp."

In the several decades since, many hundreds of communities have sponsored similar efforts at other sites in Europe or, in a few instances, in North America. People in each locality propose a socially significant task to be performed by international volunteers, and raise the funds to pay for the modest local lodgings and meals required by the participants. Then, by various means of publicity, for which UNESCO has been the most effective channel in recent times, they invite young people of the world to travel at their own expense to the workcamp site. Once there, on stays averaging three weeks, the volunteers receive free room and board (and sometimes a bit of pocket money) in exchange for a few hours of enthusiastic effort each day.

While no one would denigrate their ensuing accomplishments, it becomes clear that the camaraderie of shared work, and the international understanding it brings about, are as important as the structures they build or the services they render.

What do the young volunteers do? In the midlands of

Volunteers for Peace

England, they take underprivileged children on summer excursions to the sea. On the outskirts of Paris, they fill in for vacationing orderlies at centers for the aged. In the national parks of Germany, they restore hiking trails or clear away debris. And in the slums of Boston, they help to refurbish low-cost housing for the poor.

As many as 1,500 workcamps are operated throughout the year, although the great bulk take place in the summer months.

THE MAJOR SOURCES

Here in the United States, the two major clearinghouses for information on nearly 1,000 international workcamps (they will also book you into them) are: **Service Civil International (SCI/USA), c/o Innisfree Village, Rte. 2, Box 506, Crozet, VA 22932 (phone 804/823-1826)**; and **Volunteers for Peace International Workcamps (VFP), Tiffany Road, Belmont, VT 05730 (phone 802/259-2759)**. SCI requires its overseas volunteers to be at least 18 years of age, and will accept 16-

and 17-year-olds only into its several domestic workcamps scattered around the country. VFP will accept 16- and 17-year-olds at more than 200 workcamps in France, Germany and Spain, in addition to its U.S. workcamps, and enforces an 18-year-old minimum only for the remainder of them.

SCI, with branches ranging from the U.S. to India, is the more strongly ideological of the two; many of its workcamps stress liberal political values or ecological concerns. Recent workcamps have included construction of energy-efficient "hogans" (dwellings) and aid to elderly people on Navajo reservations in the Far West; construction of health-care facilities in Hillsboro, West Virginia; staffing of various European refugee centers for displaced Tamils from Sri Lanka; garage work in Hamburg, Germany, converting trucks into ambulances for the SWAPO movement in Angola.

VFP is less political in its approach. "We believe that any opportunity to come into contact with other cultures is worthwhile," says its co-director, Penny Coldwell. Sample activities include digging water trenches for remote Turkish villages, creating of a community center for newly settled-down gypsies in England, or replanting a park devastated by construction in Greenland.

Interestingly, both programs include numerous camps in Central and Eastern Europe (gardening in Czechoslovakia, forestry in Hungary, repairing the Lidice concentration camp memorial in Poland); and VFP is particularly proud of its 11-year record of sending youthful American participants to several different workcamps in the Soviet Union. For two- and three-week periods in the summer of 1991, international volunteers will join an equal number of Soviet youngsters in cultivating apricot trees at a co-op farm in the Ukraine, working in a nature reserve at the Pushchino Biological Center near Moscow, or attending another, larger (300 participants) "service camp" in Moscow itself. Work fills half a day, discussions and debates the other half, but no proselytizing occurs, claims VFP, and U.S. kids do more than hold their own in the lively afternoon discussions. Unlike other European workcamps, those in the Soviet Union require a payment of $500 to $700 for three weeks by foreign participants.

What does it all amount to? Listen to the returning three-week volunteers. "It was wonderful," said a youngster from Michigan, "to see people working toward a common goal, not as 'Americans' or 'Czechs' or 'Germans' or 'Catholics' or 'Protestants' or 'Jews,' but as people." "I felt so lucky to have befriended people from around the world and across the political spectrum," said another. "There were 60 of us, from 14 nations, and after work we would sit around a campfire. What followed were conversations and arguments, some dancing, and also some people sitting quietly, reflecting. It was during those informal times that I learned the most."

Both the SCI and VFP directories for the coming summer are published in April. SCI's costs $3; VFP's, $10 (but the latter charge also includes subscription to a newsletter and is deducted from any later registration fee). After perusing the several hundred descriptions of workcamps, applicants pay (to SCI) $35 for a U.S. workcamp assignment, $75 for one abroad; and (to VFP) $90 per workcamp in Western Europe, $100 per workcamp in Eastern Europe. Some youngsters attend multiple workcamps in the course of an active summer.

A SIMILAR PROGRAM

A similar but much smaller workcamp program is offered by the official U.S. student travel organization, the **Council on International Educational Exchange (C.I.E.E.), 205 E. 42nd St., New York, NY 10017 (phone 212/661-1414).** Here the literature is free, but a later application costs $125.

While no one would denigrate their accomplishments, the international understanding they achieve is as important as the structures they build or the services they render.

Selfless Vacations, the Jimmy Carter Way

The Rewards of Undertaking an Uncommon Series of "Outer-Directed" Trips

HIS LIFE—COMPARATIVELY SPEAKING—WAS in ruins. He had been defeated for reelection to the presidency. His family business was in debt. Prematurely retired, shaken and adrift, he faced a midlife crisis more intense than most, but similar in essence to that confronting millions of middle-aged Americans.

And so he and his wife traveled. But in a different way. What restored the spirits of Jimmy and Rosalynn Carter, among several major steps, was an uncommon series of selfless, "outer-directed" trips. For them, travel was undertaken to discover new world issues and social needs, and—equally important—to be involved in curing the ills that travel revealed.

The vacation challenge, writes the former president, "lies in figuring out how to combine further education with the pleasures of traveling in distant places, and, on occasion, helping to make the lives of the people you visit a little better." Having done both, the Carters leave little doubt that the activity has launched them on a second, rewarding phase of life.

In a remarkable book published by Random House— *Everything to Gain: Making the Most of the Rest of Your Life*—Jimmy and Rosalynn Carter tell, among other things, of the several life-enhancing travel or travel-related organizations with which they have associated their names, or which they recommend to others. These are: the Friendship Force, Habitat for Humanity, GATE (Global Awareness Through Experience), the Citizen Exchange Council, and the International Executive Service Corps.

THE FRIENDSHIP FORCE

This is already known to many Americans. It is the 13-year-old, nonprofit, Atlanta-based organization founded by the Carters and the Rev. Wayne Smith, which each year sends thousands of adult travelers ("citizen ambassadors") to live

for one or two weeks in foreign homes found in 45 countries, including the Soviet Union. Subsequently, the foreign hosts come here to live in American homes. Since the stay in each case is basically without charge (except for transportation and administration), the cost of a Friendship Force holiday is considerably less than for standard trips to the same destination, and upward of 400,000 people have thus far participated. Upon returning, they continue to exchange correspondence or privately arranged visits with the families they have met. In this way, writes Rosalynn Carter, "friendships are . . . made that can only lead to a more peaceful world."

The Friendship Force

For information on membership in the Friendship Force, and on the 1991–1992 exchanges planned from dozens of U.S. cities, contact **Friendship Force, Suite 575, South Tower, One CNN Center, Atlanta, GA 30303 (phone 404/522-9490).**

HABITAT FOR HUMANITY

This is a less obvious travel resource. Based in Americus, Georgia, near the Carter household in Plains, it was created 15 years ago (before the Carters' involvement in it) to work for the elimination of poverty housing (namely, shacks) from the U.S. and the world. Its founder, a fierce Christian crusader named Millard Fuller, enlisted the assistance of Jimmy Carter in the period immediately following Carter's defeat for reelection.

At Fuller's urging, the Carters traveled by bus to Manhattan, lived in a spartan, church-operated hostel, and worked each day for a week as carpenters in the rehabilitation of a 19-unit slum tenement in New York's poverty-ridden Lower East Side. The worldwide publicity from that volunteer effort made Habitat into a powerful organization that built more than 2,500 houses in 1990 (and a projected 3,000 homes in 1991) in 480 locations in the United States and Canada, and in 26 Third World nations.

What results is not a mere vacation, but the most rewarding interludes of life.

Jimmy and Rosalynn Carter continue to travel periodically to workcamps at these locations.

Though others may recoil from the suggestion that arduous, physical labor on a construction site can be a "vacation" activity, hundreds of Habitat volunteers disagree. To cast their lot with the poor is, for them, many times more refreshing than lazing at a tropical resort. If they have one to three weeks off, they travel to work at scores of Habitat locations in the U.S. and Canada, paying for their own transportation and food, and often receiving accommodations—rather basic—at the site. No prior construction experience is required.

Similar opportunities are now available overseas—in Central and South America, Brazil, India, Zaire, and

Jimmy Carter Work Project, Habitat for Humanity

Malawi—under Habitat's recently instituted "Global Village" program. For one or two weeks, volunteers build housing in those countries under conditions similar to those of the domestic program: they pay for their own transportation there, and for food, although it is sometimes also necessary to pay the cost of simple accommodations as well. Mainly they work alongside the Third World people who will eventually occupy the houses under construction.

For information on how you can devote your vacations to building a "habitat for humanity," or for application forms, contact **Habitat for Humanity, 121 Habitat Street, Americus, GA 31709 (phone 912/924-6935).**

GATE, C.E.C., AND I.E.S.C.

Other Carter-approved travel programs include the **International Executive Service Corps, P.O. Box 10005, Stamford, CT 06904 (phone 203/967-6000),** arranging trips by retired business executives to lend their expertise to would-be entrepreneurs in developing nations; **Citizen Exchange Council,**

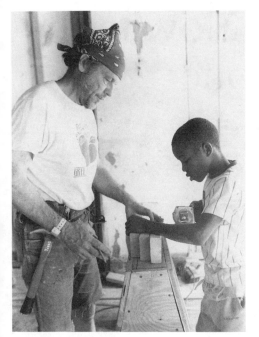

Habitat volunteers at work

12 W. 31st St., New York, NY 10001 (phone 212/643-1985), offering group trips to engage in exchange of views with counterpart organizations in the Soviet Union; and **GATE (Global Awareness Through Experience), c/o Viterbo College, La Crosse, WI 54601 (phone 608/791-0462),** with tours to experience the realities of Third World life, as operated by an order of Catholic nuns, the Sisters of Charity.

For the Carters, as for so many other Americans, simply to lie on a beach, or otherwise turn off the mind, is no longer the sole—or even the wisest—approach to vacationing. Using the mind is a far happier leisure activity. Seeking challenge and new ideas is the way to travel pleasure. A change can help us, in Allan Fromme's words, "become more alive again."

And when the changes achieved through travel are combined with selfless activity—work designed to help others or advance world understanding—then what results is not a mere vacation, but some of the most rewarding interludes of life.

For them, travel was undertaken to discover new world issues and social needs.

A "Mini Peace Corps," Now in the Reach of Everyone

"Working Vacations" to Rural Villages of the Third World

OUR FAMILIES, OUR JOBS, THE NEED TO EARN a living, carry a mortgage, repay a college debt—all these are reasons, imagined or real, that have dissuaded multitudes of Americans from joining the Peace Corps, though they longed to do so. Here was the "ultimate trip," the chance to experience the village life that half of humankind leads, but one unattainable to those of us who can't lightly abandon obligations at home.

Well, now there's a way, and it's a breathtaking, breakthrough travel opportunity achieved after six years of preparatory work by a Minneapolis/St. Paul organization called Global Volunteers. In 1991, they will be offering 54 varied departures of a "working vacation" to rural villages in the Third World—in Mexico, Jamaica, Guatemala, Paraguay, Tanzania, India, and Western Samoa—each lasting a manageable two or three weeks. And each will be available to those with no particular engineering or agricultural skills—like lawyers, let's say, or homemakers from Memphis or Chattanooga.

If all this seems a bit of radical chic, a patronizing, quick trip by dilettantes (as it initially appeared to me), then you'll want to know the following:

Each trip is undertaken at the specific request of the village, for projects they eagerly wish to complete. The long and laborious task of soliciting such invitations has largely occupied the time of the organization over the past six years, and is now complete. No one arrives uninvited, and villagers give a warm welcome to the volunteers who will assist them in programs of education (teaching English, math, or science), health care (building clinics and community centers), and natural resources (securing potable water supplies, reforestation)—all as mapped out by the villagers themselves.

Though each participant stays for only two or three weeks, the projects go on for a much longer time, and are worked on by successive groups averaging 8 to 12 volunteers apiece. As one group leaves, another often arrives, and the work continues unabated.

So great is the gap in formal education between the villagers (many of them illiterate and thus unable to read instructions) and their guests (mostly college graduates) that even the most technically untrained of those volunteers can make a substantial contribution. "I never knew I had these skills," said one middle-aged matron, "but mixing concrete is like baking a cake: you simply follow the recipe."

The initial four or five visits apiece in 1984–1990 to each of the destinations scheduled for 1991 (a total of 39 preparatory trips) were immensely successful. "We built a relationship of trust," says Burnham (Bud) Philbrook, a lawyer and former member of the Minnesota House of Representatives who is president of Global Volunteers. "We showed them that not all Americans were like characters from 'Dallas.'" Currently, the requests for further visits arriving from villages around the world are far greater than the number of volunteers on hand to make the trips.

Among the villages to be visited in 1991 by Minnesota's "Mini Peace Corps" are:

• **Pommern,** in Tanzania, a remote rural community of 3,000 people, to which Global Volunteers was invited by the Tanzanian Lutheran church. There, participants will live for three weeks in an old German mission house built of red clay in 1912, sleeping in separate men's dorms, women's dorms, and a few private rooms for couples, and consuming meals carefully prepared for them by local women. Daytimes, they'll expand a woefully inadequate 16-bed clinic currently serving a dozen surrounding villages, create a secondary school and teach the English-language skills so vital to commercial success in Tanzania, and assist villagers in several water-supply projects.

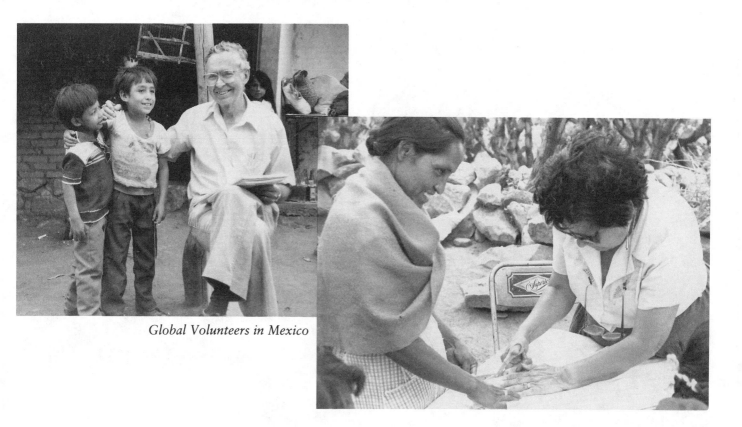

Global Volunteers in Mexico

• **Llanos de Morales,** in Guatemala, at the invitation of a nonprofit, secular Guatemalan foundation. Members will stay for two weeks at a time in the annex to a Catholic church, eating in the backroom of a nearby small *tienda* (store). In a country whose government provides its poverty-stricken villagers with scarcely any training or resources at all, Global Volunteers will run the gamut of development efforts, from renovating an old building into a preschool, teaching English, helping preschoolers to use toothbrushes, coaching volleyball, constructing a community center, and providing assistance in the start-up of small businesses.

• **Leabuu,** in Western Samoa, the independent nation that is far poorer but far lovelier (say several volunteers) than nearby American Samoa. At the invitation of Roman Catho-

lic Cardinal Pio Tafinuu, a native Samoan who wears the traditional "lava lava" skirt, they will stay for three weeks at a time in a church retreat center 20 yards from the Pacific Ocean. Their task: to renovate a large community center that will then serve as the catalyst for a broad range of development projects.

• **Adjuntas,** in Mexico, south of Guanajuato, both the poorest of the villages served by Global Volunteers and also the nearest, and typical of literally thousands of Mexican villages that lack both electricity and running water, requiring villagers to place large buckets on their burros to carry water from locations miles away. And yet, says Philbrook, the village is rich in both culture and a sense of community, and determined to make progress. There are now latrines in

If all this seems a bit of radical chic, relax; each trip is undertaken at the specific request of the village, for projects they eagerly wish to complete.

Volunteers building homes in Jamaica (top) and Guatemala (bottom)

Adjuntas (Global Volunteers built them), and a host of other energizing communal activities, most of them sponsored by the University of Guanajuato, which also coordinated the villagers' invitation to Global Volunteers.

In every village, the organization insists that the ultimate responsibility for development be on the local people, who initiate and supervise every project, using resources on hand and tools they are familiar with. In total agreement with the teachings of the late British economist E. F. Schumacher ("Small Is Beautiful"), Global Volunteers imports no complex devices or machines; if shovels are lacking to dig a well,

they send out no urgent orders for a shovel, but use local implements. While providing assistance, the volunteers learn about community structures, family loyalties, courage in the face of adversity, "receiving far more than we contribute," according to Philbrook.

As one volunteer put it: "I expected to find a sense of futility and hopelessness. I discovered instead a determination of the human spirit to carry on in spite of limited circumstances, an attitude of innovation and make-do, an eagerness to learn new ideas, and hope for their children to have a better life than they've had."

And lest the group be accused of overlooking widespread

Global Volunteers

"I never knew I had these skills," said one middle-
aged matron, *"but mixing concrete is like baking a
cake; you simply follow the recipe."*

poverty and development needs here at home, the organization is planning future projects in American "villages": Native American reservations in several southwestern states, rural towns in the Mississippi Delta or southern Appalachia, Eskimo villages in Alaska. "We couldn't have operated domestically before we had acquired global experience," says one officer. Careful to operate frugally and within their means, the organization claims to be on a firm financial footing, issues impressive literature, and has ambitious plans for the future, of which the "breakout" program in 1990 (as many departures as in the six previous years) provides a glimpse.

Because Global Volunteers is a registered, nonprofit organization, contributions to it are tax deductible; and because the expenses incurred by each volunteer are deemed to be contributions by them, they, too, are deductible. Keep that in mind when considering the modest cost of participating:

$1,150 to $1,210 for two weeks in Mexico, Jamaica, or Guatemala, including round-trip air fare from the United States, and all lodgings and meals; $2,050 for two weeks in Paraguay; $2,250 for three weeks in Western Samoa (including air fare from and to Los Angeles); $2,900 for three weeks in India (including air fare from Boston); $3,200 for three weeks in Tanzania (including air fare from New York). Each of these prices is reduced by federal and state tax savings of as much as 38% for some Americans. And each price includes the services of a trained tour leader, and about $100 per person for project materials (concrete, nails, other construction aids).

To join a "private" Peace Corps sponsoring short-term working vacations, one that has gained my own excited attention to the same extent as the original Peace Corps, contact: **Global Volunteers, 375 Little Canada Rd., St. Paul, MN 55117 (phone 612/482-1074).**

THE NEW WORLD OF TRAVEL 1992

The lifeblood of the Arthur Frommer travel guides is the correspondence received from readers, commenting on the establishments recommended in the texts and recommending new establishments. Each such letter is carefully studied, and when a particular lead seems promising, it is followed up and personally checked.

It is hoped that *The New World of Travel* will receive similar assistance from its readers. A yearly publication, issued near the start of each year, *The New World* will constantly grow. And since much of its content relates to organizations that lack the means to market themselves properly, or come to the attention of a travel journalist, your help is invaluable in alerting me to the organizations—hospitality exchanges, alternative resorts, new travel clubs, and the like—that you have discovered.

If you become aware of a new travel organization, program, or development that deserves to be described in our next edition, *The New World of Travel 1992*, won't you please let me know about it? Send your letters to Arthur Frommer, *The New World of Travel*, c/o Prentice Hall Press, Travel Division, 15 Columbus Circle, New York, NY 10023. All letters will be acknowledged, and all are warmly appreciated, in advance, by the author.

V

LIVING WITH A
PRIVATE FAMILY, BOTH
HERE AND ABROAD

Inexpensive, Short-Term "Homestays," Two Nights to a Week

A Travel Experience That Widens Your Horizons As No Commercial Lodging Could

IN 12 SCATTERED WEEKS OF THE YEAR, HANS and Ilse Sternhagen of Salzburg, Austria, take paying guests into the single spare bedroom of their chalet home.

They do so as much for pleasure as for profit. Though they value the income from that activity, they are far more excited by the chance to converse with exotic visitors, like people from Albuquerque or Santa Fe. They like to linger over a brandy, after a home-cooked dinner of *Beuscherl mit Knödel* (calves' liver with dumplings), and exchange opinions and outlooks with their new overseas friends.

Instead of merely providing a bed, the Sternhagens are sharing their lives.

And that is the essence of a "homestay." It can never be adequately stressed that in the world of travel a homestay is radically different from, and usually infinitely superior to, a guesthouse stay or a bed-and-breakfast stay.

The latter is often supplied by rather jaded individuals who make their living from the rental of multiple rooms in a residence each night of the year. While they may be warm and generous people, their behavior has frequently been affected by too much continual contact with international tourists; they no longer reflect the national attitudes of their nation. In their multibedded guest homes, you receive a room for the night, breakfast the next morning—and little more. You save money, but gain no worthier rewards.

A homestay, by contrast, takes place in the dwelling of a private family with only a room or two to rent, and then only on occasion, simply to supplement their income but not to provide the major portion of it. Here the arrival of a tourist is still an event. After breakfast, the guest stays on to converse, and often to share in daily activities; and returns at the end of the day for dinner. The inclusion of two meals a day, or at least the option for it, is a hallmark of a homestay.

Of the many organizations placing tourists in bed-and-breakfast situations, only a portion offer true "homestays" (single-unit rooms, two meals a day, contact with the family) to people of all ages. The following are typical for:

HOMESTAYS IN CONTINENTAL EUROPE

Though several continent-based organizations provide these arrangements in their own countries (I'll supply an example farther on), a great many travelers prefer using the British firm known as Anglia International, which places homestaying tourists in France, Germany, Italy, Spain, Portugal, Greece, and the Benelux nations; you are thus generally assured that your hosts will be English-speaking. The long-established Anglia, currently headed by Vivienne Bullock, claims to have chosen only such hosts as will pledge "to introduce the guest to family and friends."

"Our kind of tourism," says Mrs. Bullock, "is the dy-

Instead of merely providing a bed, the hosts are sharing their lives. And that is the essence of a "homestay."

namic kind where you get to know the country you are visiting thanks to the people who live there." It differs, she adds, "from the sad kind of tourism where you travel abroad and hardly see anything of the life of the country and never meet any worthwhile resident in that country."

Though Anglia's charges differ from country to country, they average £100 ($190) per person per week for room and "full board"—three meals a day—plus a £25 ($47.50) registration fee to Anglia. Contact **Anglia International, 15 Eastern Ave., Southend-on-Sea, Essex SS2 5QX, England (phone 702/58449).**

An example of the several national agencies arranging English-language European homestays is the Belgian firm known as La Rose des Vents ("The Windrose"), whose per-person-per-night charge of $25 covers a double room and breakfast (dinner is optional) in scores of homes scattered about the tiny country. Descriptions of hosts are especially fulsome: in one location 10 minutes from downtown Brussels, the lady of the house is said to be "a most pleasant woman of style and polish, in her 50s. Her former profession of social worker has developed her natural grace in human contact and in being helpful. . . . Monsieur . . . is a chemical engineer who speaks English." Contact **La Rose des Vents, avenue des Quatre-Vents 9, 1810 Wemmel, Brussels, Belgium (phone 02/460-34-59).**

HOMESTAYS IN BRITAIN

In private homes near lakes, dales, moors, or the sea, in country villages, or in the suburbs of London, Bath, Edinburgh, Oxford, or Cambridge, a many-years-old company called Visit Britain will find you a homestay including two meals a day (breakfast and supper) for as little as £115 ($219) per person per week, plus a one-time registration fee

Homestays in Britain

Wolsey Lodges

to Visit Britain of £35 ($67) per first person traveling, £20 ($38) for the second. That's for a stay in the home of people with "an average standard of living," says proprietress Mary East; you pay another $16 a week to stay with a "high-tariff" family in an "above-average" home. In both instances, according to Ms. East, you "live as the family and often join in their leisure and social activities." For more information, contact **Mary East, Visit Britain, The Old Brickyard, Rye, East Sussex TN31 7EE, England (phone 0797/224-871).**

Two other British firms do much the same thing, but tend to specialize in limited geographical areas:

The 33-year-old Host & Guest Service is a prime source of homestays in London, including some in the most central areas of that sprawling city. On request, they will send you descriptions of 21 host families drawn from a much larger list of Londoners renting a single guest room or two in their town houses or apartments. Surprisingly, these currently go for as little as £10 to £12 ($19 to $22.80) per night per person for room and breakfast in "Category A" homes, £15 to £18 ($28.50 to $34.20) in "Category B," and £20 to £26 ($38 to $49.40) in high-quality "Category C" dwellings—far less than in equivalent hotels or commercial B&B guesthouses, yet for added benefits and more lasting rewards. "To be a paying guest in a private home and live as one of the family," says H&GS proprietress Mrs. Rutter, "is the quickest way to broaden one's horizons." Contact **Host & Guest Service, The Studio, 635 King's Rd., London SW6 2DX, England (phone 71/731-5340).**

A final and much larger (but somewhat costlier) source of budget-priced homestays in Britain is Wolsey Lodges, a loose marketing association of independently owned country houses clustered in the southern half of England, heavily in the Cotswolds and East Anglia, but throughout Scotland and Wales as well. Though some resemble the more commercial variety of bed-and-breakfast, they are all a cut above, and by studying the Wolsey literature carefully, one can find homes owned by Oxford graduates, retired lieutenant-colonels of the Royal Air Force, people actively engaged in demanding professions and business activities. Their charges range from

as little as £18 ($28.50) per person to rarely more than £30 ($57) per person, a cooked breakfast included, and although they engage in none of the elaborate screening and matching of guests with hosts, of the sort promised by the other firms, they offer the opportunity (through careful selection of homes, this time by yourself) to socialize with English people of above-average intelligence and tastes. Contact **Wolsey Lodges, 17 Chapel St., Bildeston, Suffolk IP7 7EP, England (phone 0449/741-297).**

HOMESTAYS IN IRELAND

A 20-year-old school for the teaching of English as a foreign language, whose students stay with private families, the Dublin School of English quickly realized that its homestay arrangements would also be suitable for tourists, and it currently services a great number of them. Homes are pro-

Visiting Ireland

vided throughout the Republic of Ireland, and in Northern Ireland, but travelers using these arrangements in Dublin have the added bonus of enjoying the school's social and touring activities as well. Rates per person per week, for room and "part board" (breakfast and evening meal), in Irish pounds, are IR£135 ($256) in the Dublin area, IR£145 ($275) outside Dublin, IR£145 ($275) in Northern Ireland. Contact the **Dublin School of English Ltd., 10-12 Westmoreland St., Dublin 2, Ireland (phone 773322).**

HOMESTAYS IN INDONESIA

Founded by Mrs. B. Moerdiyono in 1970, when she first welcomed travelers to her own home in Yogyakarta, on the big island of Java, Indraloka Home Stays has become a thriving organization that places tourists with English-speaking private families in every major Javanese location: Djakarta, Yogyakarta, Bandung, Surabaya, Malang, and others. Hosts include university lecturers, teachers, physicians, businesspeople; guest rooms are invariably large and comfortable, with ceiling fans; and Indonesian home-cooking, according to Mrs. Moerdiyono, "far surpasses most restaurant food." Her lodgings, she adds, are particularly popular with "single women traveling alone, and businesspeople tired of the impersonality of a conventional hotel." Rates for 1990 (they may be a bit higher in 1991) were a remarkable $15 per person for room and breakfast, double occupancy; $25 for

Javanese market

single people traveling alone. Other meals—lunch for $4, dinner for $5—are available as options. Contact **Indraloka Home Stays, c/o Mrs. B. Moerdiyono, 14 Cik Di Tiro, Yogyakarta 55223, Indonesia (phone 0274/3614).**

A homestay is radically different from, and usually infinitely superior to, a guesthouse stay or a bed-and-breakfast stay.

Inexpensive, Long-Term Homestays for Three Weeks and More

At Last, the Famed Experiment in International Living Has Extended Its Facilities for Placing Teenagers with Foreign Families, to Permit Adults of All Ages to Enjoy the Same Remarkable Benefits

EVERY AUTUMN FOR THREE OF THE LAST five years, Earlene Richards—a 43-year-old nurse from Milwaukee—has traveled abroad to spend two weeks with a foreign family: a different family, in a different nation, each time. In 1986, Sri Lanka; in 1987, Japan; in 1988, a more familiar stay, in the midlands of England. On each occasion, the cost of her visit was a modest $400, plus air fare. But the experience was priceless.

"When you live abroad as a tourist," she says, "you see the world from your own point of view. When you live with a family, you see things from *their* point of view, and you are never the same again."

Such is the classic "homestay vacation," as operated by the Experiment in International Living. It will come as a surprise to many that the famous Brattleboro, Vermont, organization, long known for its live-with-a-family programs offered to teenagers in summer, or to college students for a semester, is now making the same experience available to adults of all ages and throughout the year, for one to four weeks.

It was inevitable, in my view, that such expansion of its activities would come about. For nearly 60 years, since its founding in 1932 by educator Donald Watt, the Experiment has argued that the family is the finest of all laboratories for learning; that travelers living for a week and more with a foreign family, as unpaid house guests, would receive unique rewards; that sharing the family's daily activities, its values, its circle of friends, would enhance their understanding of the human condition, of cultural differences and human similarities, all in the course of an immensely pleasurable and invigorating vacation experience. Why, then, limit such rewards to youngsters?

Experimenter with Huaorani people

Quietly, and without the publication of a single brochure, the Experiment has now made its international homestays available to people of all ages, as part of any overseas trip; and it is anxious, as recently confirmed to me, to increase the number of adult participants. The sponsor of these "Individual Homestay Programs" is the Experiment's separate "Federation" office in Putney, Vermont, eight miles from the student-and-teenager doings in Brattleboro.

The separate office results from the fact that the Experiment is now an association—a "Federation"—of 27 wholly autonomous Experiment organizations in that many countries on six continents. Each sends travelers of its own nation to enjoy homestays in other member nations, and each has enlisted scores of volunteer host families who—largely without payment of any sort to themselves—accept adult guests for stays of one to four weeks as members of their family, taking all meals and enjoying all family activities. They do so, according to the Federation, to enjoy a cross-cultural experience that also furthers the cause of world peace.

To apply for a foreign homestay, adults should contact **The Experiment in International Living, Federation Office, P.O. Box 595, Putney, VT 05346,** advising the dates and length of stay you desire, and the preferred country. Experiment organizations accepting U.S. adults are in 5 European nations, 5 Latin American republics, and 8 countries in Asia and the South Pacific. Each sets its own policies and conditions. Some permit participation by people of any age, while others stipulate ages 18 to 60; others, 17 to 50, 18 to 40, and so on. Some print their own descriptive literature on adult homestays, which the Federation office will pass on to you.

While the Federation office arranges the homestay, participants make their own travel arrangements. Generally, you will be met by your hosts at the railroad station of their town or city.

Although most host families receive either nothing, or at best a small sum, for your stay with them, each national organization imposes a charge designed to offset the considerable expense of administering the program (and including the small fee to the hosts). Charges vary from country to country, but generally average $250 for a two-week stay by one person, $400 to $500 for a two-week stay by two people,

In Japan with The Experiment in International Living

with small additional sums for extra weeks and slight reductions for a one-week stay. Mexico, Argentina, and the Philippines are among the cheapest nations for an Experiment homestay.

India and Japan are among the most popular destinations. And India's explanatory leaflet is particularly appealing: "We are all the happier to receive you," it says, "because you do not come as the ubiquitous tourist, and instead of being content with 'doing' us, you want to make an effort at understanding us. . . . We also presume you are free of Western misconceptions about our country, [including] those of Oriental splendor (or squalor, as the case may be), snakes, tigers, maharajas, and what not."

In most countries, the homestay is offered in locations remote from tourist-filled capital cities; you cannot choose New Delhi, but rather Hyderabad, or Madras, or Varanasi; not Tokyo, but Nagoya, or Kagoshima, or Niigata. You write a "Dear Family" letter in advance of arrival, bring a

The Experiment has contended for years that the family is the finest laboratory for learning.

Thrashing rice in Bali with homestay families

token gift, and thereafter share the home as a relative would, conversing, relating experiences, enjoying cross-cultural learning.

Bear in mind that the experience is wholly unlike the free two-night or three-night stays available from the Servas organization (11 John St., New York City) as part of a broad, city-hopping tour; here, the stay is a sustained one, and the major—if not the sole—purpose of the overseas trip. The experience is also wholly unlike that of a bed-and-breakfast stay in a foreign guesthouse or pension; the latter is often just that—bed and breakfast—in a structure usually run by a commercial entrepreneur grown jaded by overexposure to a constant daily volume of foreign guests.

"It's unique," said a professor of English whom I interviewed, "a remarkable welcome." He had arranged a Mexican homestay through the Experiment in International Living "to see what life was like within the culture and not as an outside observer. I experienced viewpoints and dealt with people in a way that would have been impossible through traditional tourism."

"The whole community accepted us," said a middle-aged couple who had enjoyed a three-week homestay in Cesme, Turkey, arranged by the Experiment. "They shared everything and answered every question we put to them."

The Experiment also cooperates with the well-known Elderhostel organization to provide Americans over the age of 60 with a one-week homestay program abroad, but this time sandwiched between two weeks of group travel (and classroom instruction) in the same overseas area. For details, contact **Experiment/Elderhostel Homestays** at the Elderhostel headquarters in Boston (see other references to Elderhostel in this book).

But simply to enjoy a remarkably inexpensive individual homestay of one to four weeks, write to the Putney, Vermont, address given elsewhere in this essay. That's the first step of a cerebral travel adventure designed to observe a different system of values and beliefs; to feel part of a family abroad, not simply a tourist; to become directly involved in the community life of another culture; to acquire ease in a foreign language (though English is often spoken); to form an enduring international friendship.

How many of us ever have such an opportunity?

"As a tourist, you see the world through your own eyes; as a homestay guest, you see things through their eyes, and you are never the same again."

Join a "Hospitality Exchange" and Stay for Free Whenever You Travel

It's the Most Logical Idea in All of Travel, and Increasingly Utilized by a Broad Range of People

IN THEORY, AT LEAST, IT'S A SIMPLE IDEA. WE all have spare rooms, spare beds, a cot or a couch. Why not make them available to congenial people when they travel to your home city, in exchange for their doing the same for you upon a visit to their home city—or to the city of another congenial person?

Unlike a "vacation exchange," which involves a meticulously scheduled, simultaneous swapping of homes or apartments, the "hospitality exchange" is a far more casual facility, available at any time. On the eve of a trip, members—in the usual instance—consult a directory of other members, and then phone or write to learn if they can be accommodated. The others—the hosts—do the same when it's their time to travel. Each is received in another's home as a relative would be, either for free or at most for a simple reimbursement of out-of-pocket expenses.

Sensible? Logical? It's more than that. It's like a perfect world, this cooperation among people, like enjoying an extended family all over the world.

But there's a problem: the considerable amount of time spent by the organizer. The practice involves, at least, the periodic publication and distribution of a members' directory, and sometimes even direct assistance from the central organization in making reservations. Because membership fees must be kept modest, and no one earns a living from them, the idealistic founders of many a hospitality exchange have eventually been forced by hard reality to give up the effort.

That's what happened in 1986 to Tom Lynn's Travelers Directory, a 27-year-old nationwide hospitality exchange that was both the "giant" (several hundred members) and pioneer in the field.

But seven other groups continue to carry the torch, and deserve our attention. Each caters to a different type of American:

The Hospitality Exchange, of San Francisco, California,

is the direct successor to the Travelers Directory, a three-year-old project by two of the latter's members—Lee Glickstein and Joy Lily—to perpetuate its membership list, policies, and ideals. Hosts tend to be young, enthusiastic, and low-income, with some stressing that they are able to offer

only floor space (presumably for sleeping bags) to would-be guests (picture a "personals ad" in New York's *Village Voice* and you have an image of the average member). Bookings are made via a thrice-yearly directory sent to all members, but only those willing to appear in it are entitled to receive a copy. Membership is $15 a year, which brings you an immediate March edition of over 300 members (again, only if you're willing to be listed in it). For an application form, contact **The Hospitality Exchange, 116 Coleridge St., San Francisco, CA 94110 (phone 415/826-8248).**

The World for Free, of New York City, is another fledgling exchange entering its third year, but already the possessor of a hundred names and addresses, of which nearly half are found in Europe, including Eastern Europe (Poland especially), half in the U.S., and one apiece in Australia, Peru, Kenya, and Japan. Founded by a former musician, and thus partly oriented to creative people in the arts, it uses a biannual directory to convey offers of hospitality. Sample entry, from a Chicago member: "We are a politically sensitive collective of artists and writers living on the top floor of an old department store, where we have a gallery/performance space, studios, and living areas. We have futons, couches, and hammocks for four people and floor space for a small army. We don't get to travel much, so we appreciate the world coming to our house." Membership is $25 a year. Contact **The World for Free, c/o Seidboard World Enterprises, P.O. Box 137, Prince Street Station, New York, NY 10012.**

Visiting Friends, Inc., of Lake Jackson, Texas, near Galveston, for more standard types, is the Sunbelt specialist among hospitality exchanges, although its 200 members actually reside in over 40 states and four Canadian provinces (in addition to England). Because founders Laura and Tom LaGess believe in protecting the privacy of their members, they publish no directory, but instead themselves respond to requests for housing assistance from members on the eve of a trip. Members supply the cities they plan to visit, and the LaGesses then make reservations for them with guest-accepting hosts in each such city or nearby. Because this entails a good deal of work, a nominal charge is assessed:

$20 for a one- to six-night stay at the first host home (per stay, not per night), $15 for the same stay at each additional host home on the same trip, all in addition to a lifetime membership fee of $25 per couple. From the warm and folksy flavor of the Visiting Friends literature, I would assume that most members are from small towns and of retirement age, in sharp contrast to the counterculture bent of others I've listed. But people of all ages and conditions are accepted for membership, provided only that they "have a clean, comfortable guest room in their own home suitable for one or two adults" (children are not accepted) and "are prepared to have guests at least once a year." Contact **Visiting Friends, Inc., P.O. Box 231, Lake Jackson, TX 77566 (phone 409/297-7367).**

Evergreen Bed and Breakfast Club, of Redondo Beach, California, limits its services to persons over the age of 50— the theory being that mature people prefer accommodating other mature people in their homes. A 700-member subsidiary of the powerful American Bed and Breakfast Association, it charges $40 a year for single membership, $50 for a couple, for which members receive a yearly directory (in which they must also be listed) and the right to enjoy the hospitality of other members for a fee of $10 a night for a single room, $15 a night for a twin. Considering that the charge includes a full American breakfast, these must be the lowest bed-and-breakfast rates in the world. Why the fee at all? Club officials think that the $10 and $15, in addition to offsetting out-of-pocket costs, add a businesslike quality to normal attitudes of hospitality. Enclose a self-addressed, stamped envelope in contacting **Evergreen Bed and Breakfast Club, 1926 S. Pacific Coast Hwy, Suite 217, Redondo Beach, CA 90277 (phone 213/540-9600).**

INNterlodging Co-Op, of Tacoma, Washington, has several hundred members of widely varying ages and backgrounds scattered about the country (though mostly clustered on the two coasts), and can provide accommodations for an initial family fee of $50 to $95 (various membership drives and discounts account for the variance), plus $4 to $5 per person per night paid to your actual hosts for the cost of fresh linen, towels, and other usables. Children with their own sleeping bags pay only 25¢. Founder Bob Ehren-

Unlike the "vacation exchange," which involves a meticulously scheduled, simultaneous swapping of homes or apartments, the "hospitality exchange" is a far more casual facility, available at any time.

Making friends in Spain

heim publishes a directory of membership in September of each year, and requires that members agree to make their own homes available for guests at least three times a year. Contact **INNterlodging Co-Op, P.O. Box 7044, Tacoma, WA 98407 (phone 206/756-0343).**

Globetrotters, of London, is a worldwide organization of largely young, but always intrepid and usually impecunious travelers—the kind that hitchhike across Third World countries, sleeping in village huts and cadging meals; an "anaemic wallet" is actually cited as a prerequisite for membership. Membership fees of $14 per year, $24 for two years, enable you to receive the group's six-times-a-year newsletter, *The Globe,* and the "Globetrotters Directory" listing names, addresses, ages, and travel experience of members, as well as purely optional offers by them of free accommodations. Because a great many members do in fact make such offers of lodging (spare beds or cots in their living rooms or dens), the Directory is a rich source of free travel opportunities, although not primarily designed as such. Contact **Globetrotters Club, c/o BCM Roving, London WC1N 3XX, England.**

And finally, there's Servas, of New York City, similar to a hospitality exchange, but not really so, because members are entitled to receive hospitality without being obligated to provide it; as a Servas member, you can be a "taker," not a "giver," all because thousands of other Servas members around the world are willing to put you up without expecting anything in return; they do so because they enjoy having foreigners in their homes and because they believe the activity furthers the cause of world peace. Applicants pay a fee of $45 and are then screened for membership by a Servas interviewer in their locality; after being accepted for membership, they are then entitled, on the eve of a trip, to receive the names and addresses of hosts in the cities to which they will be traveling. The normal stay with a Servas host is three days and two nights, which may be extended at the discretion of the host. To me, Servas is the most exalted travel organization on earth. Contact **U.S. Servas Committee, 11 John St., Suite 706, New York, NY 10038 (phone 212/267-0252).**

I haven't described Mennonite Your Way because the church-sponsored hospitality exchange of that name, with several hundred members, is a rather restricted organization anxious to confine its services to intensely religious Christians. It shuns publicity, and should be approached, if at all, through your local Mennonite congregation.

But all the rest are anxious to grow, anxious to serve. By simply providing occasional hospitality to their members—an enriching experience—you can then receive hospitality from their members, traveling cheaper and better.

Seven groups carry the torch, alerting the rest of us to offers of hospitality.

Bed-and-Breakfast in a Private U.S. Home

The Use of "RSOs" Has Now Become the Key to Finding a Proper "B&B"

CLINT EASTWOOD'S CARMEL, CALIFORNIA, has banned them altogether. So has trendy Santa Fe. The once-burgeoning bed-and-breakfast industry—a source of livelihood for more than 20,000 American households—is currently beleaguered with threats from zoning officials, angry hoteliers, and frightened neighbors of the B&B proprietors.

To make things worse, numerous Americans are bad-mouthing these unpretentious, overnight lodgings, claiming them to be more expensive, on occasion, than comparable hotels.

What has happened to the B&B movement? In my view, simple growing pains, basic misunderstandings, and nothing more. An activity less than 12 years old (for all practical purposes) is moving into maturity, achieving importance and setting off understandable—if flawed—reactions.

THE B&B BOOM

Although people from time immemorial have been renting spare rooms in their homes to transient visitors, the activity came of age in the United States only with the creation of large-scale "reservations service organizations" (RSOs) in the late 1970s. Such early RSOs as Bed-and-Breakfast Rocky Mountains, Bed-and-Breakfast Nebraska, Bed-and-Breakfast Philadelphia, and scores more (I've listed more than 50 of them in the Appendix to this book) provided the marketing efforts and all-day telephone confirmations in their respective cities, states, or regions that no individual B&B house could afford to supply on its own.

An explosion in the use of B&Bs soon followed. The cost-conscious public, on arrival in a large city, had only to look under "B" in the telephone book to find the area-wide reservations service that could recommend any number of B&Bs and then confirm space at them.

To aid matters more, various telephone companies soon created a "bed-and-breakfast" category in the *Yellow Pages*, enabling travelers to find those few ornery RSO services whose names did not begin with "B": Sweet Dreams and Toast, Urban Ventures, Pinellas County Bed-and-Breakfast, etc.

Suddenly, the public had a surefire means of always uncovering a nearby B&B. But more important, they were

B&B in a Brooklyn, New York, brownstone

able at last to deal only with homes that had been pre-screened for suitability by a larger organization.

The single greatest dread of the traveler—arriving at an improper lodging, to be met by an unshaven and bleary-eyed proprietor—was overcome, and Americans by the tens of thousands began flocking to guest-accepting homes confirmed and vouched-for by a regional "reservations service organization."

THE NEGATIVE REACTION

And then the reaction set in.

First from the hotel industry. Whether America's commercial innkeepers are behind the banning of B&Bs in Carmel and Santa Fe is hard to determine. But there are suspicions of their part in drafting fire regulations that impose unreasonable burdens (in my opinion) on the bed-and-

breakfast industry. A recently enacted New York State fire ordinance (admittedly, the nation's most stringent) requires elaborate sprinklers, expensive extra stairs, special fire doors, of any establishment housing more than four paying visitors on a habitual basis. The application of such rules to an easily evacuated, one-story ranch house or simple two-story home seems a bit much.

Other attempts to put B&Bs out of business have focused on residential zoning laws that forbid the taking of "boarders." But most courts have responded that the boarder ban was meant to refer to guests who were full-time residents of the city, not transient visitors, and that other significant differences also made the rules inapplicable.

> ## *Confusing a B&B inn with a B&B house, disgruntled guests have proceeded to damn the entire movement.*

Such zoning fights—the disputed interpretation of various vague prohibitions against commercial activity—are obviously the result of fears that a steady stream of B&B visitors will cheapen a residential neighborhood, attracting motor vans, backpackers, impecunious wanderers, and the like to an area of quiet homes.

As sensitive as we all might be to such concerns, there seems no evidence at all to support the prediction. B&B houses have no signs outside, nor are they open to walk-in members of the public—as in a hotel—but only to specific individuals who have made reservations in advance. Far from harming a community, experience shows that a thriving bed-and-breakfast industry attracts the best sort of additional tourism: sensitive and reasonably well-financed travelers who prefer the charm of a private home to an impersonal hotel or flashy motel. It brings considerable extra income, even prosperity, to the areas in which those homes are located.

WHY YOU'RE NOT SEEKING A B&B INN

A problem of equal weight has been the adverse reactions of some travelers to the rates charged by B&B "inns," which are frequently higher than in a hotel. Confusing a B&B inn with a B&B house, such disgruntled guests have proceeded to damn the entire movement. It is important that, somehow,

1920 farmhouse, home of Just-n-Trails Bed & Breakfast, Sparta, Wisconsin

both the B&B proprietors and the writers of B&B guide-books adopt a proper, semantic distinction between B&Bs that are inns rather than homes.

A B&B inn is a multiroom structure wholly devoted to transient visitors. It is often a place of exquisite decor, down comforters, punctilious attentions, and cinnamon croissants (or strawberry-flavored quiche) for breakfast. Its prices are, often justifiably, higher than those of hotels.

By contrast, a B&B home is that of a normal, private family that has simply decided to supplement its income by setting aside one or two spare rooms—rarely more—for occasional paying guests. The family does not derive its en-tire income from that activity, but simply an extra $3,000 to $6,000 a year—the average earnings cited by most reports on the B&B industry (supplemented by the family's frequent ability to write off a portion of its home expenses or home purchase price on their taxes).

Places that are B&B houses as opposed to B&B inns continue to charge 40% to 50% less than comparable hotels all over the country. Yet because they are confused with B&B inns, they are suspected of gouging. The industry needs dif-ferent names for different categories.

BECOMING A B&B HOST

What should someone do who is tempted to enter the bed-and-breakfast field? If you, for instance, should have a spare room or two in your attractive and well-located home, should you simply phone up the nearest "reservations service organization" forthwith (they're listed in the *Yellow Pages* under "Bed and Breakfast Accommodations") and ask them to list you? (The RSO fee is usually 20% to 30% of the sums they generate for you.)

Greater deliberation is called for. If you live in a large city, check first to learn whether a local "urban independent night school" (a Learning Annex, Discovery Center, Open

In a B&B home, the family does not derive its entire income from that activity.

University, or some such) is offering a one-night course in "How to Start a Bed-and-Breakfast Business." There you'll learn of additional pitfalls in addition to prospects.

Or else order a copy of one of the several books on the subject, such as *Open Your Own Bed & Breakfast* by Barbara Notarius and Gail Brewer (New York: John Wiley & Sons; $10.95). Its chapters ("Is It for You?" "Financial Considerations," "Advertising," "Working with a Reservations Service," etc.) deal with just about every question you may have.

Ms. Notarius, herself a successful B&B host, has recently formed a consulting service that operates periodic one-day seminars around the country ($150) for would-be hosts of B&Bs, and also provides personal, one-on-one advice to persons contemplating the more serious step of opening a multi-room B&B inn. Contact **Barbara Notarius, INNsider's**

Expertise, Inc., 49 Van Wyck, Croton-on-Hudson, NY 10520 (phone 914/271-6737).

Or for a more intensive look at B&B inns, not homes, order *So . . . You Want to Be an Innkeeper* ($14.95 through the mails from **Professional Association of Innkeepers International, P.O. Box 90710, Santa Barbara, CA 93190 (phone 805/965-0707).** The several authors of this book also issue an innkeeping newsletter and operate three-day workshops ($375) twice a year for people aspiring to enter the field. For information on both, write to the address above.

A wise man once said that Hell consisted of being condemned to stay, each night into eternity, in a different Holiday Inn. Through the judicious use of B&Bs, that need not be your fate.

They provide us with a refreshing and cheaper alternative to the stale and increasingly standard hotel.

B&B homes provide us with a refreshing and cheaper alternative to the stale and increasingly standard hotel.

A New and Better Way to Visit the Soviet Union

The Most Unlikely Organization Has Formed a Successful Network of Private Home Accommodations in Eight Russian and Baltic Cities

THE TYPICAL TOUR OF THE SOVIET UNION IS one that takes you to hotels from which ordinary Soviet citizens are excluded—barred, in effect, by the requirement that all expenditures at those hotels (at bars, shops, and restaurants) be in dollars or other "hard currencies."

The same tour supplies you with three meals a day at those hotels, in the exclusive company of other tourists. You also spend mornings and afternoons with the same fellow nationals, in a sightseeing bus that rushes you from place to place. Evenings, you join still other tourists in visits to theaters or concert halls, always as a group.

The life of Russia you really don't experience. The people of Russia you really don't meet.

There's a better way. A wonderfully simple way. It consists of a 16-day "homestay" in the Soviet Union, spending a week apiece in two different Soviet cities, sleeping in the apartment of an English-speaking Soviet family, taking your meals with them, accompanying them on their daily rounds, meeting their neighbors at vodka-lubricated "coffee klatches," visiting their relatives, even occasionally staying overnight in the tiny *dachas* (country bungalows) that some possess on the outskirts of cities.

And paying several hundreds of dollars less for the entire, superior experience than you would have done for a standard package tour.

Major tour operators to Russia will tell you that no such thing as a homestay tour of the Soviet Union exists. That's because they're tour operators, wedded to the mass-volume hotel arrangements of Intourist, the official Soviet travel agency.

Quietly, but in complete conformity with Soviet law, three residents of Iowa City, Iowa—of all unlikely spots—have formed an organization called Soviet-American Homestays, Inc., that enabled 500 Americans in 1990 to enjoy Soviet private-home vacations, and will do the same for nearly a thousand in the late spring/summer/early fall of 1991. By booking fast, you can be among that fortunate number.

Here is a remarkable travel breakthrough. It came about through the decision of the Soviet government to permit its private citizens to enter into commercial joint ventures with foreigners. The three Iowa organizers of American-Soviet Homestays—Martie Olson, her husband, Byron Olson, and their friend Joe Kinczel—rushed to the USSR upon hearing the news and stole a march on nearly everything else in travel by finding Soviet partners to make and administer homestay

---

It's a remarkable travel breakthrough that came about through the decision of the Soviet government to permit its private citizens to enter into commercial joint ventures with foreigners.

106

American-Soviet Homestays, Inc.

arrangements in eight Soviet cities: Moscow, Leningrad, Kiev, Yalta, Frunze, Tallinn, Riga, and Kaunus.

The last three cities are the ancient capitals of Estonia, Latvia, and Lithuania; a one-week homestay in them is always combined with a prior week in Moscow or Leningrad. Alternatively, passengers can homestay for a week apiece in Moscow and Leningrad, or spend a week in Moscow followed by a week in Kiev or Yalta. Because the stays make no use whatever of hotels in Moscow, passengers are not subject to the three-day maximum stay there imposed by Intourist because of the critical shortage of hotels in that city. In fact, passengers can, if they wish, stay for a full two weeks in Moscow, living all the while with a Muscovite family.

The families are happy to have them for any length of time. Though the literature of American-Soviet Homestays, Inc., is silent on the point, I believe that the stipend paid by the organization to each Soviet host family (rumored to be about $30 per person per day for room and full board) comes as a veritable godsend to those families. That U.S. $30 currently buys almost 200 Soviet rubles, a very considerable sum in that country. The families are also reimbursed by the organization for the costs of public transportation and ruble admission fees incurred in squiring their guests around town.

Whatever their monetary incentive, the Soviet host families appear to be unusually enthusiastic—sometimes even emotionally overwhelmed—over their participation in the program, and anxious to host more visitors. One 42-year-old American reported back that his host couple had gazed at him in complete wonder when he first arrived, and then proceeded to shower him with every conceivable service and attention. "You would have thought they were my parents," he wrote.

To be chosen as hosts, the Soviet family must meet two requirements. First, at least one of them must be fluent in English. And second, they must have a separate room for their guest or guests. Sometimes, in the cramped living conditions of most Soviet citizens, this means that children must vacate their own room in favor of the guests, and move in with their grandparents. On occasion a couple have gladly moved out of their own bedroom and slept in the living room, in order to house a guest in the manner prescribed.

Both the Ohio organization and their Soviet joint venturers (one is a member of the Supreme Soviet, a lawyer) take pains to match up each guest or guests with host families appropriate to their ages and interests: physicians with physicians, teachers with teachers, a couple with a 15-year-old daughter placed with a Soviet family having a teenage daughter. An advance questionnaire is filled out by each traveler for just this purpose. In every other way as well, the trip is a custom-tailored experience, wholly unlike the volume arrangements of Soviet government entities in travel. Having participated in a number of officially sponsored "international peace walks" through the USSR prior to the time when they began American-Soviet Homestays, both Martie and Byron Olson and Joe Kinczel formed a strong aversion to

One host, a lawyer, is a member of the Supreme Soviet.

working with the large bureaucracies that have traditionally monopolized the Soviet travel industry. Whether American-Soviet Homestays can avoid the same impersonal procedures as it grows in size of course remains to be seen.

The stays are offered May 3 through October 7. Each trip is 17 days long and costs $2,390 from New York or $2,690 from Los Angeles, totally inclusive of air fare and all else. Each price, in my experience, is $600 per person less than is usually charged for a hotel-based tour of government guides, canned lectures, prepackaged meals, and sightseeing tours that whiz you from one war cemetery to the next (sometimes as many as nine separate stops at museums and monuments in one single day). Although the standard tour might also take you to more Soviet cities in the course of your two weeks, what's the advantage of that?

For brochures and application forms, contact **American-Soviet Homestays, Inc., Rte. 1, Box 68, Iowa City, IA 52240 (phone 319/626-2125).**

And if in the course of the year, American-Soviet Homestays sells out your desired department date, then consider creating your own homestay tour by dealing directly with one of the several Soviet citizens who are apparently entering into the homestay business. Arriving in the mail the other day (and how he obtained my name and address I have no idea) was a crudely photocopied homestay leaflet from one Mikhail Zykov of 11 Volochaezskaya St., Moscow 109033 (with an alternate mailing address of 19 Poste Restante, 121019 Moscow, USSR), who heads a Soviet organization called World Family. For about $35 a day, they, too, will arrange a Soviet homestay (including all three meals), and will meet visitors upon their arrival at various airports of the Soviet Union.

World Family, according to Mr. Zykov, has numerous branches in the Soviet Union and a large membership. Its purpose: "To contribute to a new type of human coexistence on this planet, not in hostility, competition, and confrontation, but in love, friendship, and creative cooperation."

How the world has changed!

VI

NEW AND CHEAPER LODGINGS, FOR PEOPLE WEARY OF STANDARD HOTELS

Removing the "Youth" from "Youth Hostels"

A Revolution Has Altered the Character of These Inexpensive Lodgings, Making Them Available to Mature Adventurers of Every Age

IT WAS A MIXED-UP SCENE, TO SAY THE LEAST. But strangely affecting. In a corner of the lounge, a middle-aged pianist sat riffling off a Schubert cadenza while a teen-age music-lover turned the pages of her sheet music. At a chessboard nearby, two college students stared at their rooks and knights while a white-haired senior offered occasional advice. And at an overstuffed couch under a notice-filled bulletin board, several eager young people sought travel advice from a couple in their 40s.

If you were now to learn that this jumbling of the generations—young with old, newly retired with newly wed—was occurring not in a school, but in a youth hostel, you'd probably be startled. Unknown as yet to the vast majority of American travelers, every youth hostel organization in the world (other than in the German state of Bavaria) has eliminated the maximum-age limitation on youth-hostel membership or the right to use youth-hostel facilities. A small but growing population of every age and condition—married and single, elderly, middle-aged, baby boomer, yuppie, and preppie—is today flocking to make use of the cheapest lodgings and most dynamic travel facilities on earth.

WHAT IS A YOUTH HOSTEL?

And what are these structures that now accept "young people of all ages"—to use a newly coined slogan of the hostels? They range from ancient castles to modern farmhouses, from Buddhist temples to converted water mills, from rambling Victorian mansions to four-masted sailing ships to glass-walled high-rises in the center of great cities—some 5,000 hostels in all (in 74 different countries), of which 240 are here in the United States. While the beds they offer are often double-decker cots in privacy-lacking dormitories (but segre-

---

They range from ancient castles to modern farmhouses, from Buddhist temples to converted water mills, from rambling Victorian mansions to four-masted sailing ships.

Santa Monica International AYH

Originally a country store

gated by sex, with men in one wing, women in another), their facilities are otherwise comfortable and clean, closely supervised by "hostel parents," social, cheery, priced in pennies— and now multigenerational in clientele, as I was recently able quite personally to confirm.

The scene that began this essay was one I witnessed recently in the public areas of the Washington, D.C., youth hostel short blocks from the White House. I had arrived in Washington on a Friday afternoon, without reservations, never dreaming that every hotel in town would be sold out. They were. Shaken and dismayed, but vaguely aware of the revolution in youth-hostel policies, I rushed from the Capitol Hilton (where I had just been turned down) to the Capitol Hostel, if it could be called that. And moments later I was ensconced in a quite decent (if somewhat dreary) single room at the grand rate of $29 a night, tax included. I could have stayed in the dorms for only $12 a night.

If the locale had been Europe, Mexico, or the Far East instead of Washington, D.C., I could have enjoyed similar facilities for as little as $6, $7, or $8 a night, sometimes with breakfast included. Only in the United States, and only in the nation's capital at that, do youth-hostel prices rise to the princely levels I encountered that night. Almost everywhere else they amount to a near-negligible expense, permitting seniors to enjoy a major extension of their time spent on travels.

Prior to retirement most of those seniors had money but no time. Now they have time but less money. The ability to use $6-per-person hostels instead of $50-per-person hotels suddenly enables mature citizens—even those on Social Security—to enjoy the same three-month stays abroad that many younger Americans experience on their summer vacations. How many retired Americans could undertake trips of that length if they were compelled to pay normal hotel rates on each and every night?

THE "SENIOR" REVOLUTION

What brought about this revolution? Some hostelers point to the laws against age discrimination enacted in numerous enlightened countries. Some mention the growing realization by youth-hostel organizations of their need for income and patronage in those non-summer months of the year when young people are in school and unable to use hostels. Still others suggest that the lowering of age bars, occurring gradually in different countries, came about when hostel-loving "baby boomers" approached their middle years and insisted on the right to continue using hostel accommodations. "Hosteling gets into your blood and you can't get rid of it," say Hal and Glenda Wennberg of central Maryland, who met at a hostel in 1946 and soon were husband and wife. Though the American youth-hostel organization has always, in the-

Star of the Sea AYH-Hostel, Nantucket

Llama trekking is just one of several recreation activities available

ory, been open to people of all ages (unlike its European counterparts), it is only recently that youth hostels have openly advertised the right of seniors to join and participate. In Europe, formal decisions were required, and taken, to accomplish the same goal.

"The reason we use hostels," says an elderly hosteler and former college lecturer from Nebraska, Jane Holden, "is because hosteling is an attitude, not simply a source of cheap accommodations for penniless young people. That attitude never changes. To me, the finest moments of life are in meeting people from different countries and backgrounds, and extending friendship to them. Even if it means trading off a bit of comfort and privacy."

Do mature hostelers find it difficult to mix with members 40 years younger than they? "Not at all," say Edwin and Jeanne Erlanger, hostelers since the mid-1950s. "Once people work together in the kitchen or begin discussing that day's news, the barriers just fade away. Wherever it is—Japan, Austria, Mexico—the generations have far more in common than you'd think." One prominent San Francisco member of Golden Gate Youth Hostels, the sassy, 74-year-old Miriam Blaustein, is also a leading activist in the highly political Grey Panthers. "I am still as youthful mentally as I ever was!" she states. "But I know my limits. I will not

exceed them, nor will I impede what the younger people are doing. My work in youth hostels is part of a broader effort against 'ageism.'"

When seniors first began using youth hostels in heavy numbers, some youth-hostel "parents" (managers) persisted in giving preference in reservations to young members; that's now ended, says an official of American Youth Hostels, Inc., and he has never received a single complaint of age discrimination. Other mature guests were a bit nonplussed by the dormitories assigned to them, although many soon found that hostel managements were at pains to provide them with such private rooms as existed. Still another AYH executive points out that the trend in youth-hostel construction around the world is to rooms housing no more than four or five people, and occasionally to the standard twin-bedded or single-room variety.

An often-heard proposal is formally to eliminate the word "youth" from the organization's title. Though that idea was rejected by the organization's board of directors, individual hostels have taken steps to do just that. In the Washington, D.C., structure, the word "Youth" in a large neon sign has been replaced by the word "International"—Washington International Hostel—and staff members inside patiently explain that the "youth" in the title of their sponsoring organization means "young in spirit" or "young in outlook," and not in chronological terms. As if the dream of Ponce de León were finally at hand, today's mature citizens find "eternal youth" in a youth hostel.

ENTER ELDERHOSTEL

But now a caution. This newly acquired ability by mature and senior citizens to make use of youth hostels should not be confused with a wholly separate program of study tours called Elderhostel. Limited to people over the age of 60 (but open as well to their spouses of any age), "Elderhostel weeks" are conducted by the Elderhostel organization of Boston, Massachusetts, at more than 1,500 universities and other educational institutions in the U.S. and abroad. Domestically, Elderhostel programs last for one week and cost $245 per person, plus the cost of transportation to the site. Internationally, Elderhostel programs are usually of three weeks' duration—a week apiece in each of three foreign centers—and average $2,000 per person, including air fare. In each case participants stay in unused or temporarily vacated university residence halls or youth hostels, receive all three meals each day, and attend at least 4½ hours a day of classroom instruction.

What sort of instruction? The courses range from "Modern Italian History" to theories of Albert Einstein to "The Architecture of Jerusalem"—to any topic at all, in fact, so long as that subject does not deal with problems of aging or other issues uniquely affecting senior citizens. The goal of Elderhostel is to permit senior citizens to remain vital and alive to current concerns, and the formula has proved immensely popular. Reacting to course announcements in Elderhostel's quarterly free catalog (supplemented by intermittent newsletters), nearly 220,000 people over age 60 will pursue such instruction in 1991. That catalog is today stocked in most public libraries, but can also be obtained by contacting **Elderhostel, 75 Federal St., Boston, MA 02112 (phone 617/426-7788)**.

Meanwhile, to simply stay at youth hostels regardless of your age, get a youth-hostel membership card from **American Youth Hostels, National Administrative Offices, P.O. Box 37613, Washington, DC 20013 (phone 202/783-6161)**, or a local youth hostel council in your own city, if one exists. Enclose $15 (plus $1 for postage and handling) if you are 17 and under, or age 55 and older; $25 (plus another dollar) if you are age 18 to 54; $35 for family membership. You'll receive the card, and a manual listing youth-hostel facilities of the United States. For an additional $10.95 (plus $2 for postage and handling), you'll receive a similar but more extensive handbook of youth hostels in Europe and the Mediterranean area, and still another $8.95 (plus another $2 for postage and handling) will bring you the same for Africa, Asia, Australia, and New Zealand. And suddenly a brave new world of remarkably inexpensive lodgings becomes available to you, permitting almost constant travel—month after month—for an outlay that would barely secure two or three nights at the average hotel!

Whether married or single, elderly, middle-aged, or baby-boomer, yuppie or preppie, you may now make use of the cheapest accommodations on earth.

The Rise of the "Private Hostel"

A Hundred Converted Hotels Now Sell Lodgings by the Bed, Not the Room, to Respectable Adults

Like a shadowy presence, without ads or flashy signs, a hundred "private hostels" charging $10 to $17 a night have quietly emerged in America's largest cities. And while their amenities are not of the level of the nation's similarly priced budget motels—Red Roof Inns, Econotels, Motel 6s, and the like—they are not, like the latter, on the outskirts of town, along deadening highways, but in the very center: in the heart of San Francisco or New York, in downtown Los Angeles or near the Chicago Loop, at the harbor of Seattle or a block from the Greyhound Station in Tucson.

They emerged in apparent response to the lodging needs of cost-conscious European and Asian tourists now flooding into the United States. Sensing a profit, or simply wanting to be of aid, an unlikely mix of entrepreneurs and idealists began adopting one of three time-honored approaches toward solving a shortage of transient housing. They bought or leased bankrupt, shabby hotels, and quickly touched them up. They leased a floor or two of a standard modest hotel, and proclaimed the space a "hostel." Or they converted residential or specialized buildings—a winery, a rambling Victorian home—into public-accommodations use. Into the rooms of each such establishment they brought multiple beds (three or four beds per room in most cases, small dormitories of double-decker cots in others), for such is the key to hostel operation, and the secret of their ability to charge less. More beds are packed into a given space than in normal hotels, maintaining income while slashing rates.

When you stay at a "private hostel," just as at an official "youth hostel" you pay by the bed, not by the room. You stay, in the usual case, in a room with strangers of all ages (but of the same sex). Although, if you're traveling as a couple or group, you often occupy the room with people chosen only by yourself, that isn't guaranteed, and the opposite situation is often lauded by the visionary founders of some hostels. "We bring the traveler a new sociocultural experience," I was told by one hostel owner. "Sharing a room with tourists of other nations is a means of breaking down barriers."

I first learned of the new "private hostels" in the *Yellow Pages*. Looking for a hotel, I chanced upon a category called "hostels"; and as goosepimples slowly spread upon my arms, I awoke to the fact that the establishments listed were not the standard "youth hostels," but a new breed of budget lodgings. "Then felt I like some watcher of the skies," in Keats's phrase, "when a new planet swims into his ken."

I have now seen a half dozen private hostels and interviewed (by phone) the managers of others, and here is how they differ from the more familiar youth hostels:

Although both the youth hostels and the new private hostels accept people of all ages—the term "youth" in the title of the former is an increasing misnomer and anachronism—the private hostels tend to attract an older average age range and get fewer actual youths. The private hostels also have smaller rooms and fewer large dormitories, and place no more than three or four beds in their private rooms. That contrasts with the "pack-'em-in," dormitory-oriented philosophy of the youth hostels. "Our guests value the camaraderie of our public rooms and lounges," says one private hostel manager, "but they place a greater emphasis on privacy in their sleeping arrangements." Also, since most private hostels are in former hotels, their rooms are usually equipped with private baths—"private," that is, for the three or four people in that room—with fewer of the larger communal facilities found in youth hostels.

And since the age of the average guest in the private hostels is higher, the latter have fewer of the distinctive, youth-oriented operating policies of the youth hostels: fewer curfews and other forms of strict supervision.

The hundred or so private hostels consist of about 55 fully independent properties and two "chains": the **International Travelers Club** ("Interclub"), headquartered at the **Venice Beach Cotel, 25 Windward Ave., Venice, CA 90291 (phone 213/399-1930)**, and the **American Association of International Hostels (A.A.I.H.)**, headquartered at the **Santa Fe International Hostel, 1412 Cerrillos Rd., Santa Fe, NM 87501 (phone 505/988-1153)**.

"Interclub" properties in Venice, California

A.A.I.H. is a loose marketing organization of 35 independently owned hostels in roughly that many major cities, all using the term "international" in their titles—New Orleans International Hostel, Denver International Hostel, Miami Beach International Hostel—despite the fact that most guests aren't "international" at all, but simply cost-conscious American travelers. The group is headed by a 20-year veteran of American Youth Hostels, who left that organization after acrimonious policy disputes. His new "international hostels" charge a youth hostel–like average of $10 to $12 per person for their occasional dormitories, up to $17.50 per person per night for their more numerous double, triple, or four-bedded rooms, and perpetuate a great many other youth hostel traditions: guests are "requested" (but not required) to perform a few light chores each day (making their own beds, sweeping up), rooms and floors are segregated by sex, and bus station–type lockers are frequently used for luggage and valuables.

Outstanding hostels in the A.A.I.H. chain: Key West, first and foremost (phone 305/296-5719); Orlando, Denver, Santa Fe, and (especially) Huntington Beach, California, the last 40 minutes south of Los Angeles. Guests seem to feel less enthusiastic about the branches in downtown Los Angeles, San Francisco, and Portland (Oregon).

The "Ritz-Carltons" of the private hostels are those of the International Travelers Club. Indeed, some of these $15-

Unlike the budget motels, private hostels are found not on the outskirts, along deadening highways, but in the very center.

Key West Hostel, Florida

a-night (on average) lodgings are so well endowed that they are classified by their sponsors not as "hostels" at all, but as "cotels"—"community hotels"—in which few rooms contain more than three beds. Yet like the others they normally rent by the bed, not the room, and go for $10 to $17.50 per person per night.

The unique creation of two young, international businessmen—Urs Jakob and Klaus Stölting—who had tired of traditional commerce, they are staffed by international volunteers, decorated in wild, eclectic fashion (wall murals, fishing nets, giant plants) to create a "sense of place," occupy period buildings in a number of instances, and adhere to highly liberal policies that encourage constant socializing and parties, that make them—in the words of one guest—"a cross between a YMCA and a Club Med." The "club" currently consists of seven structures in the United States and Canada, and another six in Australia, New Zealand, Switzerland, and Kupang (Timor), Indonesia. Their ideal guest, according to Urs Jakob, is an around-the-world traveler taking six months or so for the trip. A former emphasis on West Coast locations (Los Angeles, San Francisco, Hawaii) has recently been balanced by the decision to open two branches in New York City, of which one occupies the top floor of the large and recently refurbished Carter Hotel on West 43rd Street, off Times Square.

The "cotels," with their notice-packed bulletin boards, paperback libraries, and eager amateur managers—each encouraged to let imagination soar—are all radically different in appearance. The International Travelers Club Cotel in Venice Beach, California, is the old (1901) St. Charles Hotel, a national landmark building that once hosted Charlie Chaplin. Musicians in its café were playing lively folk songs in the course of my own visit. The International Travelers Club Cotel Globe in San Francisco is a mix of hostel rooms (two double-decker beds, $15 per person) and hotel rooms ($17.50 per person double, $30 single), all with private bath and floors with green shag rugs and artfully done oil trims spattered by a volunteer on skateboard. In the less private International Travelers Club Hostel Waikiki, lobby furniture is from a Japanese sushi bar and ceilings are covered by bamboo shoots and beach mats.

At each of the club's hostels or cotels, and in sharp contrast to the "early-to-bed, early-to-rise" atmosphere of the official youth hostels, curfews are unknown and conversations go on late into the night. "People here are adults," says Jakob, "and expected to behave reasonably. We don't treat them as in an institution." Nor is the performance of house chores expected of guests. Perhaps because of that, a great many guests are in their 40s and 50s (though most are 20 to 35), some European, some American, all seeking budget lodgings, but with a social atmosphere.

For a list of leading A.A.I.H. or International Travelers Club hostels or cotels, either contact the organizations named above, or look in the *Yellow Pages* under "Hostels," keeping in mind that these "Poor Man's Hiltons" come and go with dizzying rapidity. The 1989 Manhattan *Yellow Pages* contained such listings, while the 1991 edition—inexplicably—doesn't, despite the thriving current operation of several. Persevere.

More beds are packed into a given space, maintaining income while slashing rates.

In a Housekeeping Van: The Art of "Gypsying"

On No More Than Their Social Security Income, Some Americans Are Able to Keep Constantly Traveling

To ALL THE STANDARD FORMS OF TRAVEL, add a new one: gypsying. It consists of staying constantly on the move—year after year, exploring multiple countries—but living on almost nothing (or, at best, on Social Security income).

And if that seems a pipedream, adolescent and unreal, hold on, reserve judgment. Unending travel, by normal people, is the passionate theme of what may well become a minor travel classic, published in 1988 by John Muir, of Santa Fe, and distributed by W. W. Norton.

The book is *Gypsying After 40*. Its author, Robert W. Harris, is a middle-aged Santa Fe architect who discovered 13 years ago that he had unfinished goals, a passion to view the world, a yearning to return to fundamentals, and a deep concern about the pressured, money-focused nature of his life.

So he became a "gypsy."

Though he and his wife had few resources, their savings sufficed to buy a housekeeping van from a used-car dealer in London. In it, they learned that people can greatly control the level of their material needs (and thus their travel costs), reducing those wants in a drastic degree by simply making psychological adjustments. Living in sturdy but simple clothes, preparing their own meals in the van from foodstuffs purchased en route, using the same unpretentious vehicle for both accommodations and transportation, they learned to live as travelers for a fraction of the sum that others spend as tourists.

And were thus able to travel without cease.

Today they are in their 13th year of continual, "long-term" travel, crisscrossing nation after nation, month after month, on costs that average (independent of the earlier purchase price of the van) a remarkable $1,000 a month—the sum that many retired couples enjoy from Social Security alone. And the resulting character of their life, they believe, makes pitiful the structured, earthbound, higher-spending existence of the rest of us.

Apart from continual spiritual experiences that Harris lyrically describes—"When travel took command of my life, extraordinary events shook the core of my being"—he relearned as a "gypsy" to savor the most ordinary values, patterns, and events of life.

"Poetry and beauty became infinitely more important to us than security.... The arrival of dawn, the goings-on around us—insects moving, animals grazing, farmers harvesting—became spectacles.... Rich curiosity and heightened awareness increased."

No more for them the tourist throngs and standard attractions: "The strong personal character and dignity of people as they live day-to-day became the focus of our

"Thousands of people make long-term travel their main mode of existence and awake each morning as if it were the shining first day of their lives."

inexpensively into living space, cheap to run, and so unpretentious as to offer no target to vandals or thieves. (In some cases, a live-in boat does the job.)

• **"Free camping":** You eschew, to the extent possible, the organized, pay-to-enter campgrounds, and simply park the van at night in legally permitted places: village greens, churchyards, even gravesites, public areas for pasturing sheep, on farms (after permission has been obtained), castle grounds, in city parks, at well-secured freight trucking areas in port cities, alongside marinas or historic ruins (where you tip the guards or invite them for a drink in the van).

"If you free-camp," writes Harris, "you do not need to have a specific destination in mind, nor a campground to reach before dark. You amble along, unhurried.... You savor each moment."

You also meet a better class of people, he implies, "a

travels.... The gypsy life afforded time to cavort with nature, dive into deep wells of reading, warm the fires of friendship, wrestle with meditations."

Most wondrous of all, he discovered, too, that multitudes of others were "gypsying" along the byways of Europe and North Africa, Mexico and the Far West: "Thousands of people make long-term travel their main mode of existence and awake each morning as if it were the shining first day of their lives."

How is it done? How, on a small retirement income, can one travel without let-up? *Gypsying After 40* prescribes a few simple rules:

• **The modest van:** Self-transportation is the key, not a resplendent, gas-guzzling motorhome, but a van converted

woman camping alone at interesting, scenic ruins, busily sketching . . . a large family stopping where they could swim, sun, and fish.''

• **Rural settings:** You stay mainly in small towns or in farm locations, where you live for a quarter of the usual price; you dart daily into the big cities from your rural base, and return there at night.

• **Warm-weather countries:** You of course avoid the colder climes. You traverse the sights of northern Europe only in summer, the Mediterranean countries in spring and fall, North Africa (Morocco, especially) or Mexico in winter.

• **You slow down:** You avoid expense by careful deliberation, and by patience in securing the right air or sea fares.

• And finally: You avoid hotels, restaurants, and high-season tourist locations like the plague.

There is, of course, far more to gypsying than this; it is set forth in 250 closely reasoned pages, available today in most bookstores.

I met Robert Harris and his wife, Megan, at a television talk show on travel. He is a white-haired, white-bearded, ebullient elf of a man, glowing with life and vigor; she, a still-attractive matron-turned-gypsy, is blessed with a glamour undimmed by life in a van.

And what were they confiding to each other in the moments before the broadcast?

Their desire to return to the road.

"Gypsying" consists of staying constantly on the move—year after year, exploring multiple countries—but living on almost nothing (or, at best, on Social Security income).

At Home on the Road: The RV Life

The Range of Motorhome Options Has Greatly Increased Your Ability to Enjoy Meaningful, Low-Cost Vacations in the U.S.A.

IT'S THE OPPOSITE OF CHIC, SOMEWHAT RUS-tic and rough. Yet the fastest-growing means for vacationing in America is the recreational vehicle. And though I be drummed from high society for saying so, the people using them are the finest travelers our country has.

You meet them with increasing frequency. They can be your best friends who have just returned from a three-month trip through the national parks—in a shiny new motor-home—and claim it's the best thing they've ever done. They are your neighbors who have bought a trailer they're going to

use to "winter" in a luxury RV resort of Florida. They are images of yourself as you daydream about getting away from it all, buying a recreational vehicle, and taking off to see the great outdoors, the sights of the Southwest, the scattered grandchildren across the land.

But how do you get started? Buying a recreational vehicle—an RV—is a major investment that can even go over the six-figure mark. Is it worth the outlay? Will you enjoy the lifestyle of the semi-nomad? Will you get restless and claustrophobic, or will you have the travel experience of a lifetime? A bit of analysis is in order:

THE VEHICLES THEMSELVES

"RVs"—a generic term for a conveyance that combines transportation with living quarters—come in two varieties. They can be motorized (like motorhomes or van conversions) or towable units (like travel trailers, truck campers, and folding camp trailers).

The motorhomes, most popular among retired Americans, are built on or as part of a self-propelled vehicle chassis, with kitchen, sleeping, bathroom, and dining facilities all easily accessible to the driver's cab from the inside. They range from 18 to 33 feet in length, can sleep from two to eight people, and cost from $22,000 for "compacts" to $48,000 for larger types, with luxury-status models going way up, to $150,000 and more.

Conversions are cheaper (but smaller). These are vans, originally manufactured by an automaker, that have been modified for recreation purposes through the installation of side windows, carpeting, paneling, custom seats and sofas, and assorted accessories. They can sleep from two to four people, and sell for an average of $19,000.

Travel trailers are hard-sided units designed to be towed by an auto, van, or pickup truck, and can be unhitched from the tow vehicle. They sleep four to eight people, and provide such comforts as kitchen, toilet, sleeping, dining, and living facilities, electric and water systems, and modern appliances. Models range from $5,000 to $36,000, depending on size and features.

Truck campers are camping units that are loaded onto the

bed or chassis of a pickup truck. Many have kitchen and bathroom facilities. They sleep two to six, and go for $2,000 to $10,000.

Folding camping trailers are units with collapsible sides that fold for lightweight towing by a motorized vehicle. Set up, they provide kitchen, dining, and sleeping facilities for four to eight people, and sell for between $1,500 and $8,000.

You can visit friends and relatives anywhere in the country without imposing on them: your RV, parked in their driveway, becomes your own private guest cottage.

THE ADVANTAGES

In an RV, you follow your own totally flexible time schedule, without fixed reservations anywhere, without depending on others (hotels, trains, planes). You don't constantly pack and unpack; in fact, you carry no luggage. You cook when you like, eat out only when you wish, say good-bye to greasy spoons, and usually enjoy home-prepared food.

You can have your pets with you. You can visit friends or relatives anywhere in the country without imposing on them: your RV, parked in their driveway, becomes your own private guest cottage—as well as your summer beach house, your winter chalet.

You make friends easily upon arriving at a camping ground or RV resort. RV-ers are, in general, enthusiasts who love their lifestyle and like sharing it with new people. They are constantly attending rallies, caravans, campouts, meeting with other RV-ers to share common interests.

"It's difficult to be lonely in a campground," one confirmed RV-er told me. "Our luxury RV resort in Florida ($15 a night) was constantly holding social events. Between dinners and galas, folk dances and exercise classes, meeting new people was not only simple—it was unavoidable."

And RV travel is economical. You can purchase fresh local produce on the road and cook your own meals. Your stay at campgrounds is usually nominal ($5 to $20 a night is typical). And there's no one to tip. A recent study showed that an RV vacation cost about half the expense of a car/hotel vacation, one-third the cost of a bus/hotel or train/hotel holiday, and one-fourth the cost of an air/hotel vacation.

In an RV, you follow your own totally flexible time schedule, without fixed reservations anywhere, without depending on others (hotels, planes, trains).

THE DRAWBACKS

But RV travel is not for everyone—it may not be for you. A Philadelphia couple I know who recently spent four months traveling across country in a motorhome issued the following caveats: "Be sure," they said, "you feel extremely comfortable with whomever you will be traveling with; you're going to spend long periods of time in close quarters. Be sure you're an expert driver and enjoy spending long periods on the road. Above all, don't take this kind of trip unless you're extremely flexible, elastic, and able to cope with new situations, which happen all the time. Mechanical breakdowns are not uncommon and you have to be able to handle them without getting upset."

RENTING BEFORE BUYING

Like many first-time RV-ers, my informants began by renting a motorhome, got used to driving a large vehicle and used to spending a great deal of driving time together. Now they're so enthusiastic, they're planning to sell their large suburban home, move into a small apartment, buy an RV, and spend at least six months on the road each year. "The excitement and variety of life cannot be compared with any travel experience we've ever had—and we're experienced foreign travelers," they say. "It's a new kind of life, a brand-new world we never saw before."

THE RENTAL PROCESS

First step is to look in your local telephone directory under the category "Recreation Vehicles—Renting and Leasing." Or you can call one of the three major national companies that have toll-free 800 numbers: **Cruise America (phone toll free 800/327-7778); America En Route (phone toll-free 800/582-8888);** or **Rolling Homes (phone toll-free 800/GET-ANRV).** A fourth major firm, Altman's America, has only a local number (818/960-1884), but you can write

to them: **Altman's America, 6323 Sepulveda Blvd., Van Nuys, CA 91411.** It's also useful to obtain the book called *Who's Who in RV Rentals,* listing the names and rates of more than a hundred other dealers; it's $7.50 from the **Recreation Vehicle Rental Association, 3251 Old Lee Hwy., Suite 500, Fairfax, VA 22030 (phone 703/591-7130).**

Rental costs vary considerably, depending on type of vehicle, when and for how long you want it, season, and other variables. From one such company, I secured a quote of $39 a day plus 39¢ per mile for a particularly elegant 22-foot camper trailer sleeping two adults and two children (and there are cheaper versions, and smaller, 13-foot trailers from other firms). One of the "grander" motorhomes—either a 26-foot Alumalite by Holiday Rambler or a 27-foot Southwester by Fleetwood—will average $600 to $700 a week, plus low-cost mileage (19¢ per mile after an initial number of free miles). But that's for a vehicle that can sleep six people and is fully self-contained, with such added features as a microwave oven, roof air conditioning, its own generator and propane tank (so that a hookup is not necessary), power steering, and almost everything else you can name.

It is usually cheaper to rent from a private individual, but then you must be aware of the risk you take if a breakdown should occur; a private owner can usually do little for you, while with a major company, repairs are either handled on the spot or you are given a new vehicle and put back on the road within 24 hours. Rental dealers may also apply the cost of a rental to a future purchase. They can provide you with broad forms of insurance. Some will arrange tour packages if you're traveling to popular state or national parks or historic landmarks. Others offer orientation sessions and packages that include linens and cookware.

The most important step is advance study and comparison-shopping before you rent. Make sure you understand the terms of the agreement, take your vehicle out for a test spin, and reserve as far in advance as possible. Indeed, the "RV life" is becoming so popular that a reservation several months in advance might not be a bad idea.

The most important step is advance study and comparison shopping before you rent an RV.

Cottages, a New Weapon in the Arsenal of Budget Travel

Costing Far Less Than a Villa or Apartment Rental, They Also House You in Areas Unaffected by Mass Tourism

To GUESTHOUSES AND STUDENT DORMS, HOStels and pensions, to third-class hotels with bathless rooms and private homes with rooms for rent—to all such havens for the budget-minded transatlantic tourist, you can now add a new form of low-cost lodging: the European "cottage." For some of us, these tiny dwellings full of charm can prove the cheapest of all accommodations—and the single best introduction to life in the Old World.

But it's important to know what they are and what they're not.

WHAT IS A COTTAGE?

First, a European cottage is very different in location and appearance from a vacation home. The latter is generally in jam-packed resort areas, near seashores or mountains, in world-famous locations publicized for years. To rent one, you contact an international real-estate broker—like Blanding's, of Washington, D.C., or Villas International, of New York City—and pore over glossy, four-color photos of designer interiors and pastel throw-cushions. You pay a rather hefty price for your two- to four-week rental—about the same as you'd spend here at home—and fly to the remoter airports, like Nice or Rome, to claim your impressive hideaway.

A cottage, by contrast, is almost never in a resort area—else it would have been grabbed up long ago, restyled and

These tiny dwellings full of charm can prove the cheapest of all introductions to life in the Old World.

Heart of England Cottages

refurbished, and thus transformed into a vacation home. Rather, a European cottage will be found in purely rural locations, near prosaic villages or small towns. Most are in walking distance—true—of pubs, shops, or cafés, but often at least a mile or two away.

They also come from another age, and are the sort of structure rarely built today: of stone, small and boxlike, in period designs with tiny windows, sometimes topped by a thatched roof or ancient tiles.

But they are charming and idyllic, full of repose, a refuge from modern pressures. And however basic they may appear, they are today equipped with the simple essentials: private bath or shower, gas or electric stoves, flip-a-switch heating.

Most important, they're cheap. When occupied by four to six people (in a minimum of two bedrooms, but often with three), they rent for as little as $250 a week in winter, $300 in spring, $350 in summer, even at current exchange rates. Because of that, they're rarely (or only reluctantly) handled by traditional brokers or by the trendy travel agencies that deal in Mediterranean villas and Swiss chalets. But more and more Americans have ferreted them out, and at least a half dozen U.S.-based organizations have emerged in recent years to facilitate the process of booking them.

ORGANIZATIONS AND SOURCES OF INFORMATION

Cottages and Castles, of Elkton, Virginia, is the leading source of British cottage rentals, despite having been in business for only four years. It is a venture launched by the publishers of the prestigious bimonthly *British Travel Report*, who are a bit bewildered—from several indications—by the explosive response to their initial cottage offerings. Currently the fledgling organization represents 35 to 40 British brokers with 8,000 cottages to rent. And these—in locations all over England, Scotland, and Wales—can usually be had for a week, and also for two weeks, but rarely for longer than that because of heavy demand. To beat the rental limitations, some avid Anglophiles move from cottage to cottage, spending a week at each.

The average cost? Remarkably low. Some lucky renters pay only $275 a week in low season (November through March), $345 a week in mid-season (April, May, September, and October), $395 a week in high season (June through August)—and those are the total rates for four to six people. Although the charges go higher in upgraded categories, the three cheapest categories (A, B, and C) are hugely popular and highly praised by people who have stayed in them.

Consider, for example, the timbered Churn Cottage near Siddington, Gloucestershire, in the bucolic Cotswolds. Set on a 750-acre farm, but close to the city of Cirencester, its facilities include three bedrooms (for five people), large kitchen and dining room, bathroom, color TV, and garage, in a setting for quiet walks along the River Churn and fishing for local trout, with village shops and pub nearby. Though this one is two categories higher than the A level, it rents for only $375 a week in low season, $425 a week in mid-season, and $475 a week in high season. The last rate works out to barely more than $13 per person per night.

Or try the B-level, thatch-roofed Medieval Cottage in the tiny village of Wrangaton, Devon, 12 miles from the coast at the edge of the Dartmoor National Park, with Torquay and other delightful towns nearby. It offers two bedrooms for four people, a kitchen, lounge, bathroom, color TV, and parking, for approximately $300 a week in low season, $350 per week in mid-season, and $400 a week in high season— $15 per person per day in the last instance.

For a catalog that pictures and describes 500 representative examples of the 8,000 cottages available to you, send $3 to **Cottages and Castles, c/o British Travel Associates, P.O. Box 299, Elkton, VA 22827 (phone 703/289-6514, or toll free 800/327-6097 outside Virginia**), and state your preferences, the dates you need, and the kind of group you are. Within 24 hours Cottages and Castles will propose a specific cottage rental suiting your needs, and everything proceeds from there.

For comparative purposes, you might also send for the programs of two similar organizations: **Heart of England Cottages, P.O. Box 878, Eufaula, AL 36072 (phone 205/687-9800**), enclosing $3.50 for an assortment of cottage brochures, including some for Ireland as well (the $3.50 will be deducted from the cost of any subsequent bookings,

which average $240 a week); and **Eastone Overseas Accommodations, 198 S. Hampton Dr., Jupiter, FL 33458 (phone 407/575-6991,** or their New Jersey branch at 609/722-1010), specifying the location you prefer, and they'll send you photocopies of lengthy listings in the area (no fee is required).

THE GÎTES OF FRANCE

In France, the cottages are 20,000 in number, similarly priced or even lower in cost than the British variety (which is to say, remarkably cheap), and known as *gîtes* (pronounced "zheet"), an antiquated medieval term for "abode" or "lodging." Again they're found mainly in countryside locations, but nowhere near resorts, among populations whose warmth and generosity toward visitors are the very opposite of some Parisian attitudes. From your *gîte,* by bike or rented car, you'll drive to shop in nearby French villages, explore historic sights, enjoy ravishing landscapes, practice your French, and conserve your cash. *Gîtes* rent for as little as $250 a week (for a minimum of four people, remember); a usual high of $450 a week, in a long high season of April through October (though they can run higher in August); and for less than that—say, $200 a week—in March or October. Rentals can be had for a single week, except in July and August, when a two-week stay is required.

Why are the *gîtes* so cheap? Because they're rent-controlled. In the immediate postwar years, when thousands of the French abandoned their ancient residences to move to cities or more modern homes, the French government offered subsidies to preserve and maintain the *gîtes,* on condition that they be offered for vacation rentals at low prices. Today the *gîtes* of France remain a largely governmental institution administered by the 95 *départements* of France, and marketed by the government-sponsored Fédération de Gîtes. With typical French flair, each *gîte* is awarded a symbol of either one, two, or three ears of corn, to rate its comparative quality.

I'm looking at several photographs of *gîtes* as I write these words. One, a charming shuttered cottage with coral-tile roof, as in a van Gogh painting, is 37 miles from the Riviera Coast, in Regusse, the *département* of Var. It's rated three ears of corn, can sleep up to six people, and costs only $329 a week in any month other than July or August (when the charge is $447 a week).

A European cottage is radically different in location and appearance from a vacation home.

Heart of England Cottages

Another, a large and ancient stone-walled structure in St. Germain sur Vienne, in the *département* known as Indre et Loire, eight miles from the renowned Chinon (site of the castle), is also a three-ears-of-corn winner that can house up to five people and yet rents for only $250 a week in April, May, October, and November, $310 a week in June and September, $365 a week in July and August.

The chief U.S.-based source of *gîtes* is **The French Experience, Inc., 370 Lexington Ave., Suite 812, New York, NY 10017 (phone 212/986-1115)**. Write for their catalog, called "France Beyond Clichés," which contains additional information and application forms. And don't confuse the rental of an entire *gîte,* for one to four weeks, with a system for obtaining bed-and-breakfast in private French homes; the latter are called *gîtes de chambres* or *gîtes d'étape,* and I'll have more on those in next year's edition of this book.

In the meantime, picture yourself living like a resident, not a tourist, in France, ensconced in your own private *gîte.* Wandering to a French village market, where luscious vegetables and exquisitely presented cuts of meat are arrayed before you. Standing with your spatula and a *Larousse Gastronomique* in a French kitchen, attempting to outdo Julia Child. Savoring the taste of that fresh mâcon or beaujolais as you pour it from a pitcher into a cool stone mug. Ooh-la-la!

Camping in the Caribbean

On Six Major Islands or Locales, Supervised Sites Await Your Tent—for as Little as $3 a Night

IF YOU'RE LIKE ME, THEN ON YOUR FIRST TRIP to the sultry Caribbean you have at some point asked: "Why am I staying in a hotel? With heat so intense, and nights so balmy, why must I pay a king's ransom for space in a high-rise tower? Why can't I simply sleep on a beach, under canvas, for peanuts?"

Well, glory be, the very same thought has now occurred to a growing legion of open-air entrepreneurs. And today, commercial campsites await your tent in multiple, major Caribbean locations. And I'm referring to organized and supervised sites, attended at night, with showers, toilets, and—often—electricity.

Though some tropical islands forbid camping (Bermuda is one, except for organized Scout groups and the like) and others discourage it (Antigua), while still others permit it but then provide no organized facilities for it (Trinidad/Tobago, Dominican Republic, Grenada), six enlightened locales have made the activity into a major tourist resource:

PUERTO RICO

Puerto Rico is one such place, although it burdens the sport with a touch of bureaucracy, a required permit obtained in the manner explained below. Yet fully seven public beaches (*balnearios*) renowned for their swimming now possess supervised campsites, of which the best endowed (electricity, showers) are at Luquillo and Cerro Gordo. Luquillo, with 58 sites renting for $13 per site per night, $17 with roof, is in eastern Puerto Rico (Rte. 3, km marker 35.4), on a full mile of white sand shaded by majestic coconut palms. Cerro Gordo, with 60 tentsites renting for the same, is in northern Puerto Rico (Rte. 690, near Vega Alta), on a beach almost as grand. More spartan sites lacking electricity (you use lanterns) are: Añasco, in western Puerto Rico (Rte. 3, km 77; $10 per campsite, $30 per cabin); Punta Guillarte, in southeastern Puerto Rico (Rte. 3, km 128, near Arroyo; tentsites for $10, cabins for $30); Seven Seas Beach, near the marina area of Fajardo in eastern Puerto Rico (Rte. 987 connects Fajardo to Seven Seas Beach, where tentsites are $10 a night); and finally, the rapidly developing island of Vieques, off the eastern coast of Puerto Rico (where campsites rent for $10 nightly on Sun Bay—"Bahía del Sol"—off Rte. 997, looking out onto the eerie glow of Phosphorous Bay).

Elsewhere in Vieques, at the feminist retreat called New Dawn, for women only, tents can be pitched on platform sites (limit of three people per site) for $10 a night, $60 weekly, with breakfast and dinner available in the adjoining main house for an extra $15 per person daily. For feminist tenting, write **New Dawn Adventures, 518 Washington St., Gloucester, MA 01930 (phone 508/283-8717), or P.O. Box 1512, Vieques, PR 00765 (phone 809/741-0495).** For all other Puerto Rican camping locations, write for an application form (resulting in a permit) and reservations to **Departamento de Recreación y Deportes, Compañía de Fomento y**

In Puerto Rico, seven public beaches renowned for their swimming now possess supervised campsites—of these, Luquillo and Cerro Gordo have the best facilities.

Public beach in Puerto Rico

Recreativo, Oficina de Reservaciones para Centros Vacca-cionales, Apartado 3207, San Juan, PR 00904 (phone 809/722-1771 or 809/721-2800, ext. 341, and ask to speak with Irma Batista, who speaks English).

BRITISH VIRGIN ISLANDS

The British Virgin Islands are a second renters' heaven. On the islands of Jost van Dyke and Tortola, facilities aren't simply in the form of bare sites for pitching your own tent, but include already erected, two-person tents on elevated wooden platforms, with cot beds, lanterns, linen, and even cooking utensils. Such elaborate canvas lodgings rent to two people for $20 a night ($3 for a third person) at Brewers Bay Campground in Tortola, and for $25 a night ($5 for a third person) at Tula's N&N Campground on Jost van Dyke. Cost-conscious as I may be, I'd still choose the more expensive Tula's on enchanting Jost van Dyke (whose population is all of 130 people), which provides campers with coal or wood for cooking, two restaurants in the area, a grocery store next door, and several rope hammocks along the beach

(a bare campsite at Tula's is $15 for up to three people). The smaller Brewers Bay Campground has freshwater showers (as does Tula's), a beach bar and tiny restaurant, and a beachfront location about three miles from Road Town, with its 1,000 inhabitants, overly urbanized by my standards. For reservations or information, contact: **Tula's N&N Campground, Little Harbour, Jost van Dyke, British Virgin Islands (phone 809/77-40774 or 77-53073); or Brewers Bay Campground, P.O. Box 185, Road Town, Tortola, British Virgin Islands (phone 809/49-43463).** An alternative and perhaps better mailing address for Tula's (your letter will reach them faster) is **P.O. Box 8364, St. Thomas, U.S. Virgin Islands 00801.**

U.S. VIRGIN ISLANDS

The U.S. Virgin Islands offer superlative camping on the stunning, white-sand beaches of the island of St. John, two-thirds of which is a national park. Cinnamon Bay Campground, operated for the U.S. Park Service by the elegant Rockresorts organization, is the standout. Its bare campsites

NEW DAWN ADVENTURES

write **Maho Bay Camps, 17-A E. 73rd St., New York, NY 10021 (phone 212/472-9453, or toll free 800/392-9004 outside New York State).**

BELIZE

Belize (not an island, but a Central American country in the Caribbean) provides camping on its popular *cayes*—thin, water-surrounded, beach-lined strips of land just off its coast. Three of the closely grouped cayes are called the Bluefield Range, and there, at a working, lobster-and-fishing camp known as Ricardo's, sites for erecting your tent are rented for $4 a night; you're then right alongside a group of only slightly more expensive beach huts on stilts in the water, with budget-priced restaurant and constantly staffed office to aid you. Write or phone for information and reservations to: **S & L Travel Services, P.O. Box 700, Belize City, Belize, Central America (phone 011/501/2-77593).** Elsewhere among the cayes, the ultra-budget Caye Caulker has several wooden beachfront "hotels" whose proprietors, I am told by several recent visitors, will permit you to pitch your tent in

(for erecting your own tent) are less than a two-minute walk from the sea; are serviced by a cafeteria, convenience store, lavatories, and shower in separate buildings; and rent for only $10 a day for two people throughout the year, $2 per third or fourth person. Park naturalists attached to the camp lead you on all-day hikes or provide snorkeling instruction. Not within my own definition of low-cost camping, but popular, is a separate section of 54 already erected 10-by-14-foot tents on wooden floors, and with cot beds, stove, ice chest, and utensils; the latter rent to two people for $28 a day from September 1 to December 19, $56 a day from December 20 to March 31, and $40 a day from April 1 to August 31, with third and fourth persons paying $8 extra. For bare sites, book directly with the local manager at **Cinnamon Bay Campground, Cruz Bay, St. John, U.S. Virgin Islands 00830 (phone 809/776-6330).** But for those furnished, luxury tents, contact **Rockresorts Reservations, 850 Third Ave., New York, NY 10017 (phone toll free 800/223-7637).** Down the coast on the same island, the well-known Maho Bay Camps rents furnished, kitchen-equipped, canvas-sided, hillside cottages for $50 (off-season) or $75 (high season) per cottage per night, but those (in my view) can't qualify for low-cost camping status either. Still, if you're interested,

Enjoying Jamaica

Jamaica

back for a uniform $3 per person per night. Here, you simply appear on the spot and ask. And off the southern city of Dangriga (you get there by boat from Dangriga), Tobacco Caye offers already erected, two-person tents for $9 per person, and three meals a day for a total of $15. What's special about Tobacco Caye is that it sits right on the reef, a boon for divers.

For non-caye camping in Belize, at the so-called Hopkins Village of the Garifuna Indians (Afro-Caribbean) in the south of the country, the charge is $2.50 for pitching your tent, or you can rent space in the bunkhouse for $5. (Facilities here are rather primitive, on the beach near a typical Garifuna village, but safe and rewarding). Call Charles Halsall of Personalized Services for reservations, and while you're at it,

Since campsites are also used by the local population, they afford you a rare and rewarding chance to meet the Caribbean people on an equal footing.

ask him about inland camping at Jungle View, in Cayo, near San Ignacio ($8 per campsite for two), or at the Cockscombe Basin Jaguar Preserve and Wildlife Sanctuary (where you pay $6 for accommodations under a roof in the heart of this world-famous reserve).

JAMAICA

Jamaica offers supervised camping, with electricity and running water, in all three of its major tourist areas, but for more than most others charge. Near Montego Bay, Damali Beach Village rents sites for $9 per person (not per site) per night, and will also rent you a tent (if you haven't brought your own) for $4 extra per night. A restaurant, bar, and water sports are all nearby. Contact **Damali Beach Village, Whitesand P.O., Montego Bay, Jamaica (phone 809/953-2387).** At Ocho Rios, Hummingbird Haven charges $7.50 per person per night for a bare site, but has no tents for rent. It does provide showers, toilets and basins, electric lights for campers, and dogs for security. Take the minibus to get there ($2) and not an expensive taxi ($50). And contact **Hummingbird Haven, P.O. Box 95, Ocho Rios, Jamaica (phone 809/974-5188).** Near Negril Beach, on those cliffs with steps descending into the sea, Lighthouse Park offers tent spaces for $8 per person per night; and nearby, for a younger crowd, Negril Roots Bamboo on the beach charges only $4 per person, and also rents tents for $4 more. Contact **Lighthouse Park, West End, Negril, Jamaica (phone 809/957-4346); or Negril Roots Bamboo, Negril P.O., Westmoreland, Jamaica (phone 809/957-4479).** For organized camping in the Blue Mountains of central Jamaica, contact **Jamaica Alternative Tourism, P.O. Box 216, Kingston 7, Jamaica (phone 809/927-2097),** whose president, the dynamic Peter Bentley, is a source for all manner of Jamaica adventure tours.

Since campsites are also used by the local population, they afford you a rare and rewarding chance to meet the Caribbean people on an equal footing, not tourist-to-bellman or tourist-to-chambermaid. And they place you in the open air, among settings of awesome natural beauty.

Honeymooning in Jamaica

The Village Apartment, Your Base for an "Untour"

A Former University Professor Sends Thousands Each Year to Experience the Typical Life of Hamlets Bypassed by Commerce and Tourism

Kaub, Germany, an "untour" village

Housed in a hotel, taking meals in a restaurant, all in the commercial center of a large city, how could one hope to experience the culture and lifestyle of a foreign people?

That was the basic flaw in traditional tourism, as it appeared to a university professor named Harold Taussig, who lived in a suburb of Philadelphia.

So in 1976 he took the usual step of forming a travel company named Idyll Ltd. to provide "untours" for "untourists." These consist of three-week stays in housekeeping apartments located in isolated villages of Austria, Switzerland, Germany, Wales, and Scotland.

Now you probably haven't heard of Idyll, or untours, or untourists, because Professor Taussig doesn't advertise and never has, but relies solely on "word-of-mouth" for his bookings. Nor does he market his untours through travel agents. In that way, he saves a 10% commission and keeps prices low.

But from a total of six clients in 1976, his untours were sold to more than 2,200 customers in 1990, virtually all from personal recommendations. Current bookings indicate an even larger, geometric increase in 1991, despite the current weakness of the U.S. dollar in Europe.

WHAT'S DIFFERENT ABOUT UNTOURS?

How do "untours" differ from the villa rentals of international real-estate brokers? The latter assign you to trendy vacation homes in popular seaside or mountain resorts, intended for and inundated by tourists.

Untours, by contrast, take you to towns that tourists have never heard of, to such unlikely locations as Meiringen,

"Glacier Express" to "untour" destination

Switzerland (pop. 4,000), or to the dozing, dreaming St. Goar, Germany (pop. 2,000).

There you live—usually—in a two-family house, enjoying separate quarters and entrances, but close to foreign, small-town neighbors, downstairs. You shop at the local butcher or grocer, wander to the tiny post office and chat with its one-person staff, share the daily cycles and rhythms of village life.

To an extent currently unknown in the United States, Taussig says, village life remains vibrant and viable in Europe. Governments there subsidize their agriculture and agricultural communities to a far greater degree than here, and villagers need not commute to jobs in larger towns or otherwise forsake their village roots. Accordingly, he claims, the untourist is able to experience the highlights of a rural culture that has hardly changed in hundreds of years.

Among the villages of Europe, he chooses the untouristy

for his untourists, rejecting such well-known, postcard-pretty hamlets as Gstaad or Oberammergau, Zermatt or Velden. "Have you ever wondered," he writes in a 60-page newsletter sent to past and potential untourists, "what these alleged paradises were like before everybody else discovered them?"

They were like Breconshire, he says, the current Welsh location for his untours in Britain; there an Idyll representative, cooking an evening meal of roast lamb for her American guests, sends "her little girl running down the hedgerow to a neighbor's garden to borrow some mint for the sauce.... She has mint in her own garden but it's not exactly the right sort for mint sauce, and she particularly likes the mint picked just minutes before she uses it."

In preparation for their stays at these idyllic Edens, untourists receive a heavy packet of typewritten booklets providing them with hints and rules of conduct, hand-drawn

Untours take you to towns that tourists have never heard.

diagrams ("unmaps") of their airport arrivals and village locations, inked overlays enabling them to decipher European railroad timetables, handy foreign phrases, suggestions for walks and hikes outside each particular village, thumbnail sketches of village personalities, other carefully tested tidbits of information, written as if in a letter to a friend.

Upon arrival, they are met by members of Idyll's staff, who escort them to the village destination, get them settled, and remain accessible throughout the summer in a nearby town for problem-solving and advice.

As if in a co-op, all staff of Idyll Ltd. receive the same salary as Taussig, participate in all decisions on an equal basis with him, and set the profit markup on Idyll's prices at just the level needed to provide each of them with a living wage. Such is Taussig's vision of a "just world," according to him. That policy, and the zero cost of advertising, probably account for Idyll's low prices, which are remarkable indeed in this expensive travel year.

THE DESTINATIONS

Idyll's 1991 untours to Germany (three weeks in length, running from early May through October) include round-trip air fare on Lufthansa between New York and Frankfurt, an unlimited-mileage German railpass for each person, two half-day excursions, and the fully equipped apartment, and cost as little as $1,197 for each of four people traveling together, $1,255 for each of three, $1,374 for each of two.

Idyll's 1991 untours to Switzerland, its most popular program, are also for three weeks, departing on Swissair from New York or Boston at various intervals from early May to late October. They include round-trip air, transfers, excursions, assistance, a "Swiss Holiday Pass" for unlimited

Chalet in Hohfluh, Switzerland, an "untour" apartment

In Switzerland with Untours, Idyll Ltd.

On an "untour," you shop at the local butcher or grocer, wander to the tiny post office and chat with its one-person staff, share the daily cycles and rhythms of village life.

transportation (bus or train) throughout Switzerland, and the apartment for 21 nights, and cost as little as $1,286 for each of four people traveling together, $1,321 for each of three, $1,406 for each of two.

Idyll's 1991 untours to Austria are on Lufthansa to Salzburg (via Frankfurt) from early May to mid-October, and last three weeks; they include transatlantic air, transfers, car or train with unlimited mileage throughout, and the apartment. Rates are $1,364 for each of four people traveling together, $1,452 for each of three, $1,536 for each of two. Add-ons are available from other Lufthansa departure cities in the U.S.

Idyll's 1991 untours to Britain have been revised to focus on Scotland, and are therefore called "Celtic Untours." They will usually consist of three weeks in a Scottish cottage, including air fare and a car once there, and will cost $1,656 for each of four people traveling together, $1,806 for each of three, and $2,178 for each of two. Variations on the above will include two weeks in Scotland and one in Wales, two weeks in Scotland and one in Ireland, or two weeks in Scotland and one in London. (For the week in London, passengers will receive a one-week BritRail Pass in addition to their accommodations.) Figure about $100 more for the variations. Departures are from late April to mid-October.

Two totally new untours for 1991 are the "Glasnost" Untour to Vienna, Budapest, and Prague (a week in each, including transatlantic air fare and transportation between the cities by Danube steamer and rail, costing $1,542 for each of four people traveling together, $1,614 for each of three, and $1,635 for each of two), and the French Untour (three weeks in a private home or apartment half an hour from Avignon, at a cost of $1,550 for each of four people traveling together, $1,703 for each of three, and $1,910 for each of two, including round-trip air from New York, April through October).

For brochures, schedules, ratesheets, and bulky newsletters, contact **Idyll Ltd., P.O. Box 405, Media, PA 19063 (phone 215/565-5242).**

Budget Motels, America's Greatest Travel Achievement

The Advent of Quality Inns into the Under-$30-a-Night Category of Double Rooms Brings Major New Savings to the Vacationing Motorist

WITHIN THE ROOM IS A REMOTE-CONtrolled color television set with built-in VCR; a video vending machine in the lobby supplies first-run movies for the glistening screen. Along the wall stands a mini-bar. On the ledge by a queen-size bed is a pushbutton telephone with speed-dial capabilities for fast phoning—it connects you in a flash, for instance, with a pizza-delivery firm—while an ultramodern GE reverse-cycle air-pump unit heats or cools the room at an instant's touch.

And how much for all these amenities, similar to those in the most deluxe of international hotels?

Just $29 a night, for two people, at the height of the travel season. Per *room*, not per person.

Meet "Sleep Inns," the cheapest of motels, yet equipped, if you can believe it, in the fashion described above. The newest creation of Quality Inns (recently renamed "Choice Hotels")—third-largest hotel chain in the world—Sleep Inns are about to sprout by the dozens, by the scores, and eventually by the hundreds along the highways of America, setting off a titanic battle with the hitherto reigning champion of the low-priced inns, Motel 6.

And we, the public, can only be the winner.

The budget motel is the single greatest achievement of the American travel industry. Modern, and nearly as comfortable as the standard hotel, yet renting for peanuts, it has no major counterpart in any major nation outside the U.S. Abroad, in most large countries, an expenditure of $30 to $40 a night will now barely suffice to rent a pension room for two people in an ancient structure or converted residence, without private bath, and usually without air conditioning, TV, or telephone. Here, the same expenditure at a budget motel places two people in a new facility custom-designed for hotel use, in an air-conditioned room with private bath and TV, with all or most of the other facilities of higher-priced establishments, and often even with swimming pool. What they lack is only large lobbies, conference rooms, elaborate eating places, and items of decor. The difference is often a psychological one, nothing more.

The budget motel was born in Santa Barbara, California, in 1962, with the construction of the first Motel 6, charging, as its name revealed, as little as $6 a night per room. The product was such an "overnight" success that dozens of others soon emulated it. A study by the accounting firm of Laventhol & Horwath identified as many as 50 nationwide chains in the "U.S. economy/limited-service lodging industry," of which 19 chains consisted of more than 50 properties apiece.

WHAT'S BUDGET AND WHAT'S ECONOMY?

But one chain's conception of "economy" doesn't always mesh with another's. Though the initial effort, by Days Inns and others, was to compete with the radically low rates of Motel 6, participants soon began charging a wide range of prices, usually higher ones, and total price confusion reigns today. Some "economy motels" charge in the mid-$20s for a double room, others in the mid-$30s, still others in the mid-$40s, and some, which call themselves economy-style chains, are today building motels to rent in the low $50s per double room.

Nor can one discern the price range of a budget motel from its name. Ha'Penny Inns and Super 8 sound awfully cheap, but aren't at all in the ranks of the truly cheapest.

To make things worse, some budget chains charge a wide variety of rates in a single motel, or charge widely differing rates in differing locations and properties, or increase their rates in peak-season periods, or constantly shift the rates, on

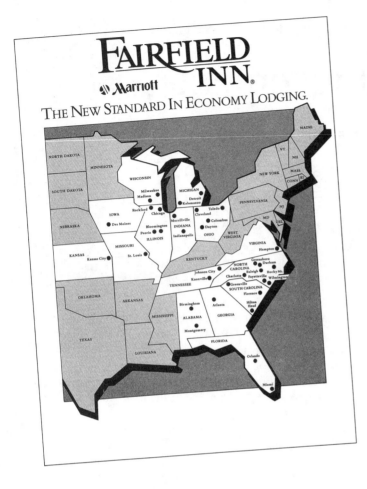

even a daily basis, to match the competition. When the *Consumer Reports Travel Letter* of the prestigious Consumers Union tried to assist its members in gauging the costs of budget motels in its February 1988 issue, it was forced to print such double-room spreads as "$26 to $115" for Rodeway Inns, "$33 to $100" for Ha'Penny Inns, "$23 to $75" for Budget Hosts. Some help!

On a far less scientific basis, I recently wrote for the directories of the 20 largest budget chains (more than 50 properties apiece), and then riffled through the pages to spot the price that most frequently appears for a double room. My survey results in the following groupings:

In the "super-budget" area of motels consistently charging under $30 for a double room, for most of their properties

and most of the time, are three large chains: Motel 6, Scottish Inns, and All Star Inns, with Sleep Inns about to make a breathless appearance. One should note that Scottish Inns and All Star Inns are not entirely consistent in quality or design, as some are formerly independent properties built for "momma-and-papa" operations, and only later acquired or franchised by the larger chains.

Hovering at the very outer edge of the "super-budget" category, just before the next price level, are Budgetels, averaging $32 to $34 for a double room. They're a growing, aggressive chain.

In what we might next call the "standard budget" category of motels consistently charging under $40, but over $34, for a double room are at least Super 8 Motels, Regal 8, Shoney's, and Knights Inns. Add to the lower end of this category National 9 Inns, which sometimes charge even below $34, but also above $34, for a double room. And at the upper end, add such "hybrids" as Susse Chalet, Red Roof, Econo Lodge, and Rodeway, charging from the $30s to the $40s for a double room.

(Interestingly enough, the mammoth Marriott Hotels Corporation was recently poised to enter the "standard budget" field with its new chain of low-priced Fairfield Inns, striking terror into the psyches of the companies listed above. But more recent price announcements for the first of the new Fairfields have led me to conclude that they will be, at best, upper-range "hybrids," charging from the high $30s to the mid-$40s for a double room. Apparently, you have to have budget principles in your very soul to create miracle rates of the Super 8 or Scottish Inns variety.)

The remainder of the big players among the budget chains are those that invariably charge in the $40s for a double room: La Quinta and Friendship Inns are among them. The much-publicized new budget operations of the giant Holiday Inns chain (called Hampton Inns) and Quality Inns (Comfort Inns were their cheap variety, before Sleep Inns) are only barely within economy limits: most double rooms rent for the mid-$40s, and even into the $50s, at Hampton and Comfort.

But once the price structure is understood, where are the budget motels found? Alongside highways, mainly in Sunbelt states, and only recently, and to a lesser extent, in colder climes. That latter phenomenon once caused critics to conclude that flimsy construction, suitable for the South, and lack of expensive heating facilities were the basis of their low

*What they lack are large lobbies and items of decor.
The difference is often a psychological one, nothing more.*

Motel 6

charges. Not so, say the several chain presidents with whom I've spoken; the early Sunbelt locations were chosen to track the most popular vacation movements of Americans throughout the year. Now, with greater experience and momentum, the Northeast, Midwest, and Pacific Northwest are beginning to get their "budget motels."

The chief factor determining where they will be built is the cost of land: a usual, necessary maximum of $7,000 to $10,000 per room, which usually relegates the budget motels to roadside locations on the outer peripheries of cities. Since in-city land costs several times that much (except, say, in Butte, Montana), it isn't likely that we'll be seeing these $25-a-night and $30-a-night rooms in urban centers.

The cost of actually constructing and furnishing a room must then be kept to about $20,000 in order to charge rates

in the upper $20s per room per night. The belief that they can do so, and nevertheless create a superior room, is what has led the executives of Quality Inns to announce the imminent creation of as many as 300 Sleep Inns.

THE NEW "SLEEPS" CHALLENGE MOTEL 6

From their campuslike headquarters outside Washington, D.C., equipped with laboratories and testing machines, sample rooms and architects' tables, Quality Inns has designed an absolutely standard, off-the-shelf, but radically different form of hotel room for Sleep Inns, which franchisees must then construct "as is," under master construction contracts negotiated by Quality Inns. Rooms will be 70% the size of

Sleep Inns are about to sprout by the hundreds along the nation's highways, setting off a titanic struggle with Motel 6.

standard rooms—the key factor in keeping costs low—but so artfully designed, with curving walls for a portion of the bathroom, as to create the appearance of greater space. Acrylic stall showers will substitute for bathtubs.

Only one type of bed has been ordered for Sleep Inns, of the queen-size variety, and only one such bed will be in each room. Travelers seeking twin beds will either need to go elsewhere or rent adjoining rooms. By using such approaches, executives of Quality Inns believe they will be able to equip the rooms with elegant space-age amenities—VCRs and the like—and yet hold rates to the $29 range, competitive with Motel 6 and other super-budget chains.

The first six Sleep Inns opened in 1990 (using prefabrication and other advanced techniques, a 100-unit Sleep Inn can be built in six months). About 90 more will join the chain by the end of 1991, and hundreds thereafter. Contracts are presently being let for the first Sleep Inns, in locations ranging from Pennsylvania to Utah. Inquiries about foreign Sleep Inns have been received from England, Australia, Brazil, and the islands of Tahiti.

And how are they reacting at Motel 6? With 501 dirt-cheap but modern motels presently in operation, all company owned, the pioneering budget hotelier is currently and calmly adding 30 to 40 more Motel 6s each year, and plans to continue doing so on into the foreseeable future. Many new such "6s" are especially planned for the Atlantic seaboard, from which the chain has been conspicuously absent in the past.

"But aren't you concerned about Sleep Inns?" I pressed a succession of Motel 6 executives. "They can say they'll be charging $29 a room," said one, "but they're a franchised operation; how will they keep their franchisees in line?

What's to stop a Sleep Inn from succumbing to temptation and raising the rate when the area is jammed?"

"Do you know what our average room rate will be in 1991?" he continued, with mounting excitement, rising from his chair, and beginning to shout:

"Twenty-six dollars and fifty-four cents!"

Such is the crowning glory of the American travel industry, the one domain in which no one beats us, not even the Japanese.

OBTAINING THE DIRECTORIES

If you're to expand your travel horizons, you'll want to seek out the cheapest of the budget motels for your own next trip. Write for directories to **Motel 6,** 3391 Southern Blvd., Rio Rancho, NM 87124; **Sleep Inns,** c/o Choice Inns, 10750 Columbia Pike, Silver Spring, MD 20901; **Scottish Inns,** c/o Hospitality International, Inc., 1152 Spring St., Atlanta, GA 30309; **All Star Inns,** 2020 De La Vina St. (P.O. Box 3070), Santa Barbara, CA 93130; **Econo Lodge,** 6135 Park Rd., Charlotte, NC 28210; **Budgetel Inns,** 212 W. Wisconsin Ave., Milwaukee, WI 53203; **Super 8 Motels, Inc.,** 1910 Eighth Ave. NE, Aberdeen, SD 57401; **Knights Inns,** 2255 Kimberly Parkway, Columbus, OH 43232; **Regal 8 Inns,** 800 S. 45th St., Mount Vernon, IL 62864; **Susse Chalet Inns,** Chalet Drive, Wilton, NH 03086; **La Quinta Inns,** P.O. Box 790064, San Antonio, TX 78279; **Rodeway Inns,** 3838 E. Van Buren, Phoenix, AZ 85008; **Hampton Inns,** 6799 Great Oaks Rd., Memphis, TN 38138; **Shoney's, Inc.,** 1727 Elm Hill Pike, Nashville, TN 37202; **Red Roof Inns,** 4355 Davidson Rd., Hilliard, OH 43026; or **National 9 Inns,** 9010 Soquel Dr., Aptos, CA 95003.

"Formula 1," Star of Budget Travel to Europe

A Mammoth European Hotel Chain Has Just Created the Cheapest Modern Lodgings on Earth

IF THEY WERE BUILT IN AMERICA, TO THE SAME plans and using the same factory-like methods of construction, they would rent for an astonishing $14 a night per room. As it is, under the costlier conditions of Western Europe (higher land costs, more rigid construction codes), the same rooms in brand-new buildings rent, nevertheless, for only $22 a night—and that's again per *room*, not per person. Employing the most remarkable new techniques in hotel building and room design, a European hotel chain has just created the cheapest modern lodgings on earth.

They're called Formula 1 hotels (or, in the French, Formule 1), and there are already 150 of them, in France, Belgium, the U.K., and Germany, with 900 more planned for construction in a dozen other European countries in the decade ahead. Owned by the Accor group of Paris— operators of Sofitels, Novotels, and Ibis and Urbis hotels, which together constitute the world's largest chain of wholly owned hotels—Formula 1 is surely the single most important development in low-cost tourism in years.

The "formula" is not for everyone. Just 8 feet wide and 12 feet long, Accor's rooms are among the smallest anywhere, yet they are meant to house up to three people (the third sleeps in a bunk bed elevated on a loft-like platform above the double bed). Elsewhere in the room, a triangular sink with hot and cold running water is ingeniously placed in

1000 hotels by the year 2000

Only eight weeks are needed to build a Formula 1 hotel, using prefabricated units that are trucked from a central factory to the site.

Paris

one corner, taking up hardly any room, while a triangular writing desk/makeup counter is in another corner, set flush into the adjoining walls. A television set with built-in alarm clock is suspended high on a wall, angled toward the main bed. Clothing is hung from a rack placed underneath the loft bed, the latter reached by a ladder. And a tiny stool for sitting at the desk/makeup table is pushed underneath that fixture when not in use, enabling guests to walk around the bed. The bed itself takes up almost all space in the room.

Only eight weeks are needed to build a 100-room Formula 1 hotel, using prefabricated units that are trucked from a central factory to the site. And yet the result is a strong, valid building, with interior corridors, a tiny lobby, and an equally small coffee shop with bar and stools, enabling guests to enjoy a self-served continental breakfast. For years, hotel people have talked about "manufacturing" prefabricated hotels in this manner. The French, with their customary verve and flair for futuristic designs, have now done it. Bear in mind that Formula 1s are not at all like the "hotel-coffins" announced several years ago by the Japanese—stacked containers, each large enough to accommodate one supine body—but are composed of stand-up, walk-around rooms, however tiny they may be. Rooms even have a window—one apiece.

While the hotels are open year around, they are staffed only from 6:30 to 10 A.M. and from 5 to 10 P.M., presumably permitting their one-shift personnel to take on other jobs in between. Outside of staffed hours, an automatic, on-site reservations machine makes rooms available to persons seeking them. The latter simply stick their credit cards into a slot, are assigned a room, and are then simultaneously billed for the night on their credit-card account. The doors to their rooms are also opened by the credit card, but only for the amount of time that they are booked. Security is total.

If there is any controversial aspect to the Formula 1 concept—and any main reason why they are so much cheaper than our own Motel 6s, Sleep Inns, Red Roof Inns, and other American budget motels—it is that their rooms are without private bath, although with sinks and hot and cold running water. The showers and toilets are "down the hall"—one such shower-and-toilet room for every four guest bedrooms. The deliberate decision to omit private facilities caused some observers to predict, mistakenly as it turns out, that Formula 1 would not prove popular with the public. In fact, they are nearly always filled. What overcame the earlier, expected reaction, in my view, is the following:

First, a ratio of only four rooms to every shower and toilet is much better than is found in the average European pension or guesthouse. The lines or waits to use such facilities are almost never experienced in a Formula 1 hotel.

Second, an automated chemical method of cleaning such facilities after each use—opening and closing the door, after use, locks the room for a time and starts up machines that

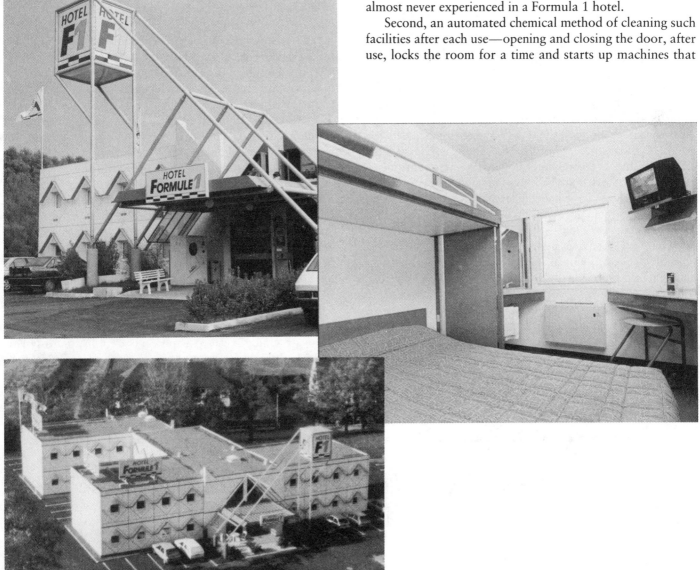

chemically clean the shower, toilet, and floor area—makes each such room far more sanitary than is usually the case, say Formula 1 officials. The room is then reopened through the insertion of the next guest's credit card. Although German law requires that private facilities be attached to each guest room in the Formula 1 hotels planned for Germany, the contrary policy of Formula 1 will remain unchanged for France, the Benelux nations, England, Italy, and Spain, officials insist. In this fashion, they hope to maintain Formula 1 room rates at less than half the prevailing level of other budget facilities, and at half the level that might have been required if Formula 1 hotels had been built with one bathroom to each guest room.

Where are they presently found? Of the 150-some-odd Formula 1s presently open, 140 are in France—at least one apiece in or just outside each of the 100 largest towns of that country.

A dozen or so are on the outskirts of Paris, or otherwise near the French capital. Closest to town are Formula 1s in Aulnay-sous-Bois, Cergy St-Christophe, Cergy Pontoise St-Martin, Conflaus St-Honorine, and Rungis-Orly. A bit farther out are brand-new Formula 1s in Sarcelles, Savigny-Epinay, St-Denis, and Maurepas. Visitors to Paris can save a bundle by staying in a Formula 1 on the outskirts, and then taking the bus or subway each day to the center.

Two Formula 1s are in Belgium, outside Ghent and Namur. One apiece have just opened in Britain and West Germany (which will each possess 150 Formula 1s several years from now). Apart from the Formula 1s planned for Western Europe, units are currently contemplated for Czechoslovakia, Hungary, and Germany, spurred by the surging tourism to Central and Eastern Europe.

Is there a "Formula 1" in the future for North America? It is perhaps significant that the Accor group, parents of Formula 1, in 1990 acquired the Motel 6 chain of the United States. Since the average Motel 6 is like a palace compared with a Formula 1, it would seem to me that space exists for a new category of super-budget hotel undercutting what we have earlier regarded as rock-bottom in prices and amenities. But though I've asked them all, not one Formula 1 official will specify their U.S. plans for either Formula 1 or Motel 6.

Until they do, it at least behooves every budget-minded, Europe-bound traveler to acquire a current list of every Formula 1, their addresses, their phone numbers. To do that, simply contact **Accor, 2 Overhill Rd., Suite 420, Scarsdale, NY 10583 (phone 914/725-5055).**

Is there a "Formula 1" in the future for North America?

Learn to Bargain in the Marketplace of Hotels

By Ridding Yourself of Pompous Dignity, You Can Save Thousands in the Years Ahead

I F THE CLASS—AHEM!—WILL COME TO ORDER, we shall discuss the single most important skill in all the world of travel: how to "bargain down" the price of hotel rooms. That talent can save you thousands in the years ahead.

Start from the premise that nothing in this life is more "perishable" than a hotel room. If such a room should go unrented on a particular night, its value for that night can never again be recouped by the owner of that hotel.

Accordingly, it behooves that owner to rent the room for almost any price rather than leave it unoccupied. Why? Because the cost of placing a guest in the room, as opposed to keeping it empty, is measured in terms of a dollar or two: a change of towels and sheets, a bit of electricity, a cake of soap. A reduced (but still a reasonable) amount of room income is therefore better than no income at all.

Such reasoning has led smart hoteliers the world over to authorize their front-desk clerks to respond favorably to requests for discounts, if that should be what's needed to fill rooms on a slow night. And every nationality of traveler the world over is aware of their willingness to do so, and therefore bargains—except the American.

BARGAINING WITH DIGNITY

Why not Americans? Because to most of us the very act of bargaining is vulgar and degrading.

No one else regards it as such. If you will stand in the lobby of a large Venetian hotel on a November afternoon, when 60% of the rooms in Venice are empty, chances are that you'll soon spot a well-dressed English tourist or an affluent German tourist or a French one approaching the desk and politely stating: "I am looking for a room that costs no more than 50,000 lire" (about $40).

This tourist knows full well that there is no such thing here as a room for 50,000 lire. He is bargaining. He is saying, in effect: "If you will rent me a room for 50,000 lire, I will stay in your hotel. Otherwise, I will stroll down the street and seek another hotel."

In other words, to bargain over hotel rates does not require that you comport yourself like a hysterical fishwife or a tobacco auctioneer. It can be done—as in the above example—with dignity, by indirection.

Often it requires only that you use a "code word" to convey to the desk clerk that you are "shopping." How many times have you heard a traveler inquire as to whether the hotel grants a "corporate rate" or a "commercial rate"— thus bargaining, and usually successfully, for a reduced rate?

What's to prevent you from doing the same? Why can't you name the corporation or firm for which you work and then speculate: "I'm sure we must have a special rate at this hotel." If the hotel is empty and you appear disposed to leave the hotel unless a discount is granted, will anyone challenge the statement? Does anyone really care whether your com-

To bargain over hotel rates does not require that you act like a hysterical fishwife or a tobacco auctioneer.

pany has made such arrangements? Or are they anxious to fill their hotel?

Or else you name your occupation and ask for a reduction based on that. You ask for a "teacher's rate" or for a "student's rate." You request a "civil servant's rate" or a "minister's rate" (that always works). You might as well ask for a "stenographer's rate" or for a "dentist's rate." What matters is that you are subtly (and politely) communicating the message that you will stay at the hotel only if they grant you a discount.

When I was a travel agent, I used to phone from the airport, announce that I was seeking a room, but only if I could have a "travel agent's rate." And in that fashion I was usually able to cut my hotel costs in half.

It just so happened that I was telling the truth—I *was* a travel agent. Yet in 20 years of using the tactic, not once was I ever asked to prove it. For, in reality, the hotels didn't care. If the night was a slow one and they needed the business, they were quite happy to accept any assertion of status as an excuse for cutting the rate and keeping the guest.

Recently I phoned two professors at the prestigious Cornell University School of Hotel Administration to confirm these hotel policies, and although both pleaded to remain nameless, they instantly did.

WHAT NOT TO DO

Why, then, I asked, do some hotel guests encounter rejections of their requests for reductions?

It is primarily because, they replied, most people phone nationwide toll-free "800" numbers to seek reservations and rates. The minions who man the phones at central reservations headquarters of the large hotel chains have no authority to cut rates. Rather, one should place the call directly to the hotel and speak to someone more entrepreneurially inclined. If those local, and directly interested, people are made

Macuto Sheraton, La Guaira, Venezuela

Trump Taj Mahal, Atlantic City

discounts aren't given. A better course, they say, is to phone from the airport or train terminal, and announce from there that you are seeking a room that costs "no more than $—." Such a call is obviously from a "shopper," and the desk clerk will take pains to do what's necessary to make the sale—provided, of course, that the night is a slow one.

Best of all is to write ahead. In scheduling a vacation trip to Barbados or Jamaica in the dead month of June, for

Grafton Beach Resort, Tobago

to know that you will stay at the hotel only if a lower rate is found, they'll often find that rate.

All hotels quote from "the top down," added one professor. "When you tell them the rate is unsatisfactory, they'll quite frequently find a lower one."

The second frequent mistake, say my informants, is to make the request—tired and burdened with luggage—in the lobby of the hotel. Once at the front desk, you are presumed by most hotel personnel to be in no position to walk out if

Never make your reservation through the toll-free 800 numbers; rather, call directly to the hotel and speak to someone more entrepreneurially inclined.

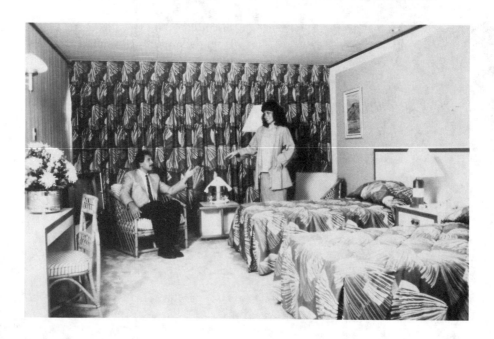

instance, you advise the hotel: "I am planning a stay, but only if I can secure a room for no more than $40 a night." "It so happens we have such a room" will come the instant reply.

"Ask and it shall be given," says the Bible.

The final error, say my academic friends, is to bargain at the wrong time of year. Obviously, bargaining will not work during peak hotel seasons, when hotels are confident they will fill up. But all hotels have slow weeks or months, or slow "down cycles" during a week. Hotels in business centers like New York, Chicago, or Philadelphia are packed to capacity Monday through Thursday, then empty and hurting Friday through Sunday. The traveler who pays full rate—who fails to bargain—on weekend nights is a chump. That traveler is simply subsidizing the weekend stays of package tourists enjoying rooms at half the rate.

Conversely, in resort locations like Atlantic City or Las Vegas, hotels are full on Friday and Saturday nights but often quiet at other times. If you're a Monday arrival at Harrah's or the Golden Nugget, bargain!

In a country that currently deifies the "free market" and worships the likes of Adam Smith and Milton Friedman, isn't it surprising that we as individuals should be reluctant to bargain over the price of a hotel room? Who decrees that hotel rates are fixed in stone? Who denies us the right as free consumers to flex our economic muscle?

Travelers of all nations, unite! You have nothing to lose but your pomposity! You have savings to win!

VII

"COOPERATIVE CAMPING," THE SMARTEST NEW IDEA IN TRAVEL

Sharing the Tasks and the Costs in a 14-Seat Van

It Is a Sensible Travel Method for People Reluctant to Transport Camping Equipment and Vehicle to Areas Overseas or Far Away

"WHEN I USE A WORD, IT MEANS JUST what I choose it to mean—neither more nor less."

Those were the sentiments of Humpty Dumpty in Lewis Carroll's *Through the Looking Glass*. They could have applied to the antics of travel brochure writers in describing the activity of cooperative camping. By refusing to use the term—substituting instead a dozen or so contrived titles that only they understand—the pamphlet authors have so confused matters as to conceal this marvelous travel mode from 80% of the people who could have benefited from it.

Cooperative camping (the name they won't use) is a cheap and sensible travel method for people who haven't the energy, funds, or commitment to buy and then transport their own camping equipment and/or camping vehicle to regions overseas or far away.

The operators of cooperative camping tours print literature in which they describe dozens of potential itineraries throughout the United States, Mexico, and Europe. They schedule departures for each itinerary, take bookings from widely scattered individuals, and ultimately assemble a group of about 14 for each departure.

When the group of 14 reaches the jumping-off point (London, Mexico City, Los Angeles, or New York), they board a 14-person van furnished by the operator and driven by a professional guide—the only paid employee on the trip. The vehicle is already supplied with up to eight state-of-the-art tents, elaborate camping utensils, and (sometimes) sleeping bags—although most companies require that you provide the last. Except for that last item, passengers avoid all the expense and burden of outfitting themselves for camping.

On the first day of the trip, participants vote to establish a "food kitty," fixing the sum they will collectively spend each day for campfire meals. Members of the group, in rotation,

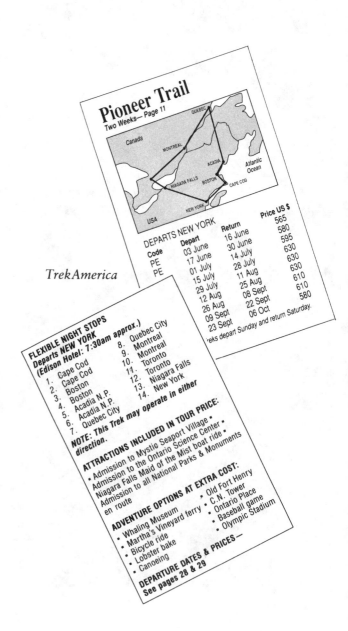

152

Cooperative camping in Monument Valley, Arizona, with TrekAmerica

shop for groceries along the way, and then rotate the cooking and cleaning chores. They each pitch their own tent each night and pack it away in the morning. The driver drives. Since the group carries its own accommodations (the tents) and needn't adhere to hotel reservations, they are able either to follow the preplanned itinerary or make broad deviations from it. They are also able to travel through areas where standard hotels aren't found.

The entire trip is unstructured and fun, close to nature and informal, adventurous, instructive—and cheap. The average cooperative camping tour costs around $35 a day, plus air fare, and plus about $4 per person per day in contributions to the food kitty.

THE MAJOR COMPANIES

So why haven't you heard of it? Blame the following:

TrekAmerica, of Gardena, California, is the largest U.S. operator of cooperative camping tours, but ought to be spanked for semantic inexactness. A "trek" isn't what they

do; in holiday travel, a "trek" is an organized walk along the lower slopes of the Himalayas, Andes, or Swiss Alps, in which porters or pack animals carry your gear. Such adventure travel companies as Himalayan Travel, Mountain Travel, and Journeys operate treks. Cooperative camping tours of the sort organized by TrekAmerica are often to distinctly unadventurous places—Yellowstone, Salt Lake City, Yosemite—but are accomplished through the delightful, semi-adventurous mode of camping.

Despite my quibbles, the company is a superb source of cooperative camping: 32 itineraries through North America, from two to nine weeks in length, with up to two dozen yearly departures per itinerary, at daily costs of $30 to $45, plus air fare, and plus a food kitty of about $30 a week. But passengers are limited to the age group of 18 to 38. For their colorful catalogs, contact **TrekAmerica, P.O. Box 1338, Gardena, CA 90249 (phone 213/323-5775, or toll free 800/221-0596 outside California)**.

Toucan Adventure Tours, of Long Beach, California, offers cooperative camping to offbeat locations in Mexico

Bryce Canyon, Utah, another popular destination

and the United States, and makes them available to people of all ages, encouraging even oldsters to come along. But how does its literature describe the tours? As a "Mexico Toucan Adventure" or as a "Canyon Land Toucan Adventure." Only within the text do you occasionally learn that "many nights we will camp along secluded beaches where we only have to step from our tents to reach the sea. . . . We'll take time to climb a volcano, camp along beautiful mountain lakes, and visit villages where artisans craft fine works."

Toucan studiously avoids "tourist Mexico." Acapulco appears on no itinerary. Rather, from Mexico City you head south into the highlands, to Oaxaca and Tuxtla Gutierrez, or to enchanting San Cristobal de las Casas and Palenque. Or else you travel the length of Baja California, to Santa Inez and Guerrero Negro, to La Paz and Cabo San Lucas. Its tours of the United States are a bit more standard.

Itineraries are usually three weeks in length (but can range from two to eight weeks), cost as little as $615 for two

The vehicle is already supplied with up to eight state-of-the-art tents and elaborate camping gear.

weeks (plus air fare and food kitty), $815 for three weeks, and are scheduled throughout the year. Phone or write: **Toucan Adventure Tours, Inc., 3135 E. 4th St., Long Beach, CA 90814 (phone 213/438-6293).**

Tracks, of London, England (now there's a trendy name describing nothing), raises the formal age limit to 38, but also explains that "travellers who are not in this age range are welcome, so long as they understand that our tours are designed for the 18–38s." Its vehicles (all supplied with camping equipment) traverse every standard European itinerary ("Ten Countries in 23 Days," "Eighteen Countries in 70 Days"), and even branch out to Eastern Europe and Russia, where it warns that "campsites . . . and camping conditions are not equal to those of Central Europe." Unlike the other companies I've surveyed, it frequently assembles larger groups than the standard 14 or so, and reserves the right to use 40-passenger motorcoaches for transportation between camping sites. But the gathering of larger groups results in rates no lower than the others: about $40 a day, plus food kitty. To confuse matters even more, its U.S. representative is a "trekking" organization: **Himalayan Travel, Inc., P.O. Box 481, Greenwich, CT 06836 (phone 203/622-6777, or toll free 800/225-2380 outside Connecticut),** from which four-color brochures are available.

Pioneer Travel Service, of Cambridge, Massachusetts, runs perhaps the most unusual tour of all: cooperative camping and driving through the Soviet Union, on two lengthy itineraries (9 weeks for $3,950, including air fare; 3½ for $3,125, including air fare), ranging from Leningrad to the Black Sea on one route, into Central Asia on another. It imposes no age limit whatever, and attracts half of its participants from noncollege-age adults, the other half from its largely Harvard and MIT base. (Families with children are, however, discouraged.) Surprisingly, the program is now in its 25th consecutive year, receives full cooperation from Intourist, the Soviet travel agency, and yet allows its participants maximum exposure (on campgrounds, in shops, in smaller towns) to Soviet citizens and ordinary institutions of Soviet life. Rave comments from several recent participants lead me to believe that these are among the most rewarding trips around. Contact **Pioneer Travel Service, 203 Allston St., Cambridge, MA 02139 (phone 617/547-1127).**

FROM GEORGIA TO GREAT BRITAIN

A regional tour operator, Wilderness Southeast, of Savannah, Georgia, runs "cooperative camping" tours (they supply the vehicle, tents, and cooking gear; participants pitch the tents and rotate the cooking) to wilderness areas in the Florida Everglades and Okefenokee Swamp, the coastal "barrier" islands of Georgia and South Carolina, the Great Smoky Mountains of North Carolina, and even occasionally to Belize and Costa Rica. Tours are a weekend to a week in

CampAlaska Tours, visiting the state's leading attractions

length; are led by dedicated naturalists; appeal to all age groups, and indeed are sold to people 20 through 70 years of age; and average $70 to $90 a day, all inclusive, plus transportation to the starting point. Though those are high prices for cooperative camping, they are apparently justified by the rather short length of most tours. Already 17 years old, yet little known outside Savannah, the nonprofit organization publishes a compelling, well-organized catalog of trips, and richly deserves attention from all parts of America. Contact **Wilderness Southeast, 711 Sandtown Rd., Savannah, GA 31410 (phone 912/897-5108).**

In Britain, an organization called Travelbug of London operates a remarkably inexpensive 12-day camping/hosteling trip through the length and breadth of England, Scotland, and Wales, for approximately $386 per person

(that's $32 a day), plus air fare to London. Travelbug provides a van and driver, tents, folding camp beds and blankets, all cooking and eating utensils, and operates the tour from April through October. Suitable for people of all ages, it is surely the cheapest approach to Britain presently being offered by anyone. The well-designed itinerary takes in Bath and the Wye Valley, Wales and the Lake District, Edinburgh and York, Warwick, Stratford, and Blenheim, among other locations.

Elsewhere in this 1991 edition of *The New World of Travel,* in the chapter called "26 Varied Travel Organizations," I've described the well-operated and long-established San Francisco company The Green Tortoise, which operates "the foam-rubber bus" (people of all ages ride in it). Although you sleep in the bus, and not in a tent, on those trips,

Participants vote to establish a "food kitty," fixing the sum they will spend each day for campfire meals.

the activity is otherwise akin to "cooperative camping" and should be considered as an alternative to the trips described in this "cooperative camping" chapter.

Of a more standard nature are the trips operated by American Adventures, of Pomfret, Connecticut: camping tours along 21 far-ranging itineraries within the United States, Mexico, and Canada, for up to 13 passengers apiece, most for ages 18 to 38 but some for all ages also, traveling cooperatively. Trips are two to six weeks in length, average $35 a day (plus $5 daily for the food kitty), but require that you make your own way to the starting points, either New York, Los Angeles, Seattle, or Miami. Wonder of wonders, the company places the words "Camping Trips" (in small type) on the front cover of its catalog, and may even go to the title "Tenting Trips" in 1991. Progress! Contact **American Adventures, Inc., 158 Cherry Hill Rd., Pomfret, CT 06259 (phone 203/974-3231).**

A LAST EXAMPLE

Cooperative camping is also the solution to a shortage of tourist housing in Alaska. Already notoriously short of peak-season accommodations, the 50th state is best visited in any event on excursions into its parks and uninhabited wilderness, where few or no lodgings exist. The company that enables you to do so: CampAlaska Tours for tourists of all ages, and for families.

You supply the sleeping bag, they provide all else: 14-passenger vehicle with driver, state-of-the-art tents, other camping gear and cooking equipment (in the classic fashion of "cooperative camping" tours). Tours average $75 a day (plus a food kitty contribution of $6 a day), last 7 to 28 days (but average 12), depart from early June to mid-September, and transport no more than 12 individuals booking each departure (of which more than 100 such departures are available). They leave mainly from Anchorage, and include all overland and ferry transportation, entrance to national parks and campgrounds, services of CampAlaska's guide, and use

In Alaska

of their camping equipment. You visit the continent's most spectacular natural wonders, breathe exhilarating air, go fishing, climbing, trekking, and rafting.

For irresistible literature, contact: **CampAlaska Tours, P.O. Box 872247, Wasilla, AK 99687 (phone 907/376-9438).**

"Overlanding," the Last Great Travel Adventure

In Self-sufficient "Expedition Trucks," Modern-Day Tourists Travel for 7 to 42 Weeks Across Asia, Africa, or South America

WHEN MARCO POLO TRAVELED IN THE 13TH century from Venice to the Chinese court of Kublai Khan, he became the first person to use "overlanding" as a method of tourism. He made scarcely any use of sea routes or even river transport, went for great distances where there were no roads, and slept every night in cloth tents, not inns.

That's "overlanding." And amazingly enough, today thousands of tourists are using much the same methods, as offered by several overland tour companies of Britain, to accomplish journeys almost as long (7 to 42 weeks), just as exotic (trans-Asia, trans-Africa), and nearly as full of insight, learning, and satisfaction.

Overlanding is the closest modern approach to the experience of the great explorers. Although it uses several familiar practices of "cooperative camping" (people become participants in the mechanics of their own trip, sharing the cooking and pitching the tents), it differs in radical respects from the far tamer activities of the cooperative camping tour operators. The latter take you to commercial campsites near large cities or well-visited attractions, and travel from place to place on modern highways, or at least paved ones.

The overlanding companies go on dirt roads, or back-roads, or where there are no roads at all, in underdeveloped areas of untouched fascination, the largely uncharted. Their journeys are through the rawest countryside, not near cities, in circumstances that afford them the closest contact with rural people of Asia, Africa, and South America, their three principal destinations.

Overlanders offer travel adventure and unpredictability (though almost complete safety). On such a trip, you encounter, let's say, a washed-out bridge and must shift routes. You find that sand dunes have shifted and obliterated tracks through the Sahara, and again you improvise. In Zaire, you take out batteries from your own vehicle to start the stilled motor of a ferry that must take you across a raging stream. In Cameroon, you discover that the border to Nigeria has been closed for political reasons, and again you and your group make decisions about where to go next.

RIDING HIGH ABOVE THE GROUND

The key to overlanding is the "expedition truck," usually an open-sided, 20-passenger, British-made Bedford with extremely high ground clearance. This permits the vehicle to drive along a riverbed if the roads have been washed out, to come on and off primitive ferries, to negotiate a boulder-strewn path.

The vehicle has so much storage capacity as to be virtually self-sufficient. It carries 200 gallons of fuel (for a 2,000-mile range), 100 gallons of drinking water, oil enough for 12,000 miles, gas stoves, and a huge supply of food. Do these provisions seem excessive? Well, one particularly important route for overlanders, bringing them to the very heart of the Dark Continent, is from Tamanrasset, Algeria, to Gao, Mali. The distance is 1,000 miles on a soft sand track—up to 10 days of driving—unaided by a single

---

Their journeys are through the rawest countryside, in close contact with rural people.

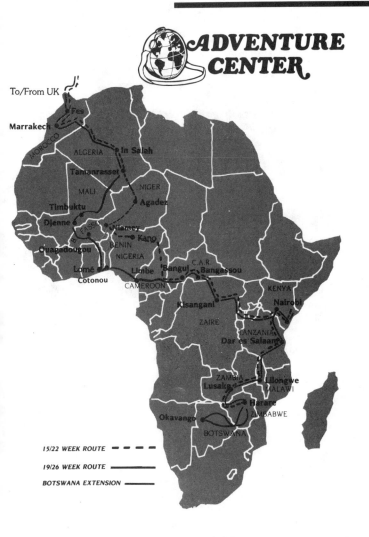

ADVENTURE CENTER

15/22 WEEK ROUTE - - - -
19/26 WEEK ROUTE ————
BOTSWANA EXTENSION ————

Afghanistan routing has eliminated much of the former dramatic encounter with tribespeople and colorful cultures along the way.

Therefore, in recent years, trans-Africa trips have overtaken the trans-Asian jaunts in popularity. People sign up many months ahead for the 15-week trip from London to Dover and Europe, and then through North and Central Africa to Nairobi in East Africa. Or they opt for a longer, 19-week journey that includes West Africa as well.

More recently, a number of one-month to six-month trips through South America—seeking out the unusual and the out-of-the-way—have begun to enjoy heavy bookings. And overland operators have now begun to operate shorter, three-week and four-week varieties as well, such as a three-weeker in Africa, called "Gorillas, Volcanoes, and Pygmies," that starts and ends in Rwanda, but also takes in Zaire and Uganda.

COMPANIES AND COSTS

Astonishingly, most long-term (one month and more) overlanding tours cost only $30 to $40 per person per day, including meals, but plus air fare to the jumping-off point (which is London in most instances). Participants come equipped with only their clothing and a sleeping bag; the overlanding company provides everything else: vehicle, fuel, food, tents, cooking equipment, a driver/leader. One such firm—Guerba Expeditions—provides three paid personnel

filling station, a single store, or a single house, with no wood for a fire and no food nearby. Overlanders value the capacity of their Bedford truck.

The development of such vehicles in the early 1960s gave overlanding its start, on a route much favored by the British and Australian adventurers who make up half the audience for it: from London to central India. For nearly 20 years, until conditions in Iran and Afghanistan became unstable, overlanding companies in Britain sent out many dozens of departures each year on a three-month journey somewhat similar to that of Marco Polo: from Europe to and through Turkey into Persia (Iran) and through what is now Afghanistan to India.

The overlanding companies continue to operate that three-month route to this day (for $2,700), though they skirt through only the barest part of Iran (completely away from Teheran) and substitute the Baluchistan Desert of southern Pakistan for the former route through Afghanistan. Even so, most American participants ask to overfly Iran (and do so), leaving the group in Turkey and then awaiting arrival of the truck in Pakistan. Unfortunately, too, the new Pakistan-for-

A Tuareg watering his camels

An Adventure Center expedition

per truck (a driver/leader, assistant, and a cook), yet charges only $2 to $3 a day more than the others. While all members of a Guerba expedition continue to participate in chores and cooking, they do so to a slightly lesser extent than is usual.

Guerba, from its base in London, takes participants aged 18 through 65 on all their overland itineraries. Another major company, Encounter Overland, of London, limits its passengers to those aged 18 through 40. Though nearly a dozen other companies in Britain offer overlanding tours of differing durations and destinations, and their number is joined by one or two companies in Holland, I am reliably told that Guerba (with 20 expedition trucks) and Encounter Overland (with 40 such vehicles) account for more than 70%

of the market. Of each 20 people who board one of their trucks for this supreme adventure, four or five are generally British, four or five Australian, three from the U.S., three Canadian, two from New Zealand, and two or so are English-speaking northern Europeans.

Both companies are represented in the United States by Adventure Center of northern California, which makes their yearly catalogs available free of charge, and then accepts bookings on their overland programs. And both publications are so colorful, well written, and compelling as to awaken the Marco Polo in each of us. Contact **Adventure Center, 1311 63rd St., Suite 200, Emeryville, CA 94608 (phone toll free 800/227-8747, 800/228-8747 in California).**

The key to overlanding is the "expedition truck," with so much storage capacity as to be virtually self-sufficient.

VIII

NEW MODES OF TRAVEL

Trekking as a Cheap and Fulfilling Mode of Travel

Organized Walks Along the Lower Slopes of the Himalayas, Andes, and Alps

LIKE THE CHARACTER FROM MOLIÈRE WHO suddenly discovers that he's been speaking "prose" all his life, a growing number of Americans have learned that "trekking" is the unfamiliar word for their favorite vacation activity. Though only the barest handful of travel agents understand the term—and some misuse it horribly—international trekking has become a substantial travel activity for at least 20,000 Americans each year, and is currently marketed by upward of five major nationwide organizations.

In oversimplified terms, trekking is walking—the healthiest sport on earth—but walking of a special nature, elevated to a high art and mental adventure.

Unlike the hiking and backpacking pursued by individuals, trekking is an intricate, organized, group activity in which porters or pack animals carry your camping gear, cooking utensils, and food from one overnight campsite to another. Relieved of that weight, you're able to go where roads and paths aren't, through the most exotic of nations, over breathtaking terrain, but without performing feats of endurance or possessing mountaineering skills. Persons in their middle age are a familiar sight on treks, as are families and even seniors into their 70s.

That's not to say that minimal vigor isn't required—it is. Yet hundreds of perfectly ordinary, normally sedentary (even chubby) Americans are today found in such unlikely locations as the historic, 18,000-foot-high base camp in Nepal used by intrepid climbers for the assault on Mount Everest. They get there by trekking—organized walking—without

setting a single metal wedge into stone or tugging a single rope.

And they achieve that forever-memorable trip for total land costs of less than $70 a day (plus air fare to and from Nepal, in this instance); trekking is one of the cheapest of travel modes, considering the distance you've covered and the highly personal nature of your travel arrangements (groups are never more than 15 people in number). No money goes toward hotels or restaurants, because no such places exist in the areas for trekking. Apart from the one-time purchase of tents and gear by the trekking company, labor alone—the chief guide, the cook, the Nepali or Peruvian porters, let's say—are the only major expense of the venture.

TREKKING DESTINATIONS

I used the example of Nepal and Peru advisedly. For reasons not entirely clear to me, almost all international treks are operated to mountain areas of the world: the Himalayas, the Andes, the Swiss Alps in particular. (While you don't go atop them, you walk along their easy lower slopes, usually at elevations of 8,000 to 10,000 feet.) Though it is theoretically possible to trek through lowland valleys supplied with roads, it is apparently felt inappropriate and uninspiring to do so.

The mountain kingdom of Nepal, at the northern border of India, is the chief trekking destination, accounting for nearly 40% of all treks. The associated Indian states of

---

Trekking is walking of a special nature, elevated to a high art and mental adventure.

Kashmir, Sikkim, and Ladakh, and portions of Bhutan, Pakistan, and Tibet, draw another 10% of all trekkers. Together these areas flank the full length of the most remarkable geographical feature on earth—the 1,500-mile-long chain of the Himalayas, the world's tallest mountains.

It was Nepal, almost entirely covered by mountains, that set off the trend to trekking. A country with scarcely any roads at all, isolated from the outside world until the 1950s, its widely scattered mountainside villages harbor 35 different ethnic groups, whose ways of life have been scarcely touched by outside influences.

The people of Nepal have a particular tradition of hospitality to strangers. As you trek the trails from village to village along the south slope of the Himalayas, you are invited to tea in small council chambers, sometimes to stay the night in the homes of villagers or in monasteries.

With unlimited access to the world's greatest mountains, in this peaceful Shangri-La whose half-Hindu, half-Buddhist population coexists without conflict, your own near-spiritual reactions are almost too intimate to describe. You awake at 6:30 A.M., when a cup of steaming tea or coffee is thrust through the flaps of your tent by a member of the cooking staff. Accompanied by experienced Sherpa guides,

you take to the trails, trekking 7 to 10 miles a day at your own pace. The trip starts and ends in the otherworldly capital of Kathmandu, reached by air via New Delhi or Bangkok.

The Peruvian Andes, and that section of it known as the Cordillera Blanca, is next in popularity, accounting for perhaps 30% of all treks. From Lima you fly to Cuzco and there, your gear stowed atop a mountain burro, you embark on a 5-day, 35-mile walk along the ancient Inca Trail to the lost city of Machú Picchú, passing awesome Incan ruins unseen by conventional tourists. Again from Lima, you go by car to Huaraz to embark on an 8-day trek through the heart of Peru's highest mountain area. For an enhanced 11-day (Inca Trail) or 21-day (Inca Trail and Cordillera Blanca) trip of this nature, as packaged by some of the trekking companies, you pay $745 or $1,600, respectively (plus air fare to Peru)—an average of $72 a day for your all-inclusive needs in Peru.

In the Swiss Alps (a 10% share of the trekking industry), hut-to-hut trekking replaces the traditional variety, with vans bringing your food, clothing, and bedding to austere and unattended mountain lodges scattered among the mountain trails, a day's march from each other. The classic trip is of the Mont Blanc massif, on a trail dominated by the tallest of Europe's mountain peaks. Trips cost as little as $895 for

Crossing Annapurna on a Mountain Travel trek

15 days (plus air fare to Switzerland), including lodging, meals, and the services of a support vehicle that moves camp each day.

THE MAJOR TREKKING SPECIALISTS

Himalayan Travel, Inc., of Greenwich, Connecticut, proudly occupies the low end of the trekking industry in price: its consistently low rates for land arrangements ($60 and $70 a day, all inclusive) are matched by similar marvels in air fares, bringing you round trip between New York and Kathmandu for $1,335 to $1,490, plus $16 tax (compared with the $1,600 from East Coast cities and $1,400 to $1,500 from West Coast cities charged by most other companies). How that fare is achieved is shrouded in secrecy and the subject of controversy. Its specialty, naturally, is Nepal (40 different treks there, 200 yearly departures), but all other mountain areas are also offered; and through its representation of a leading British trekking company, Sherpa, an extensive program of low-cost treks in the Swiss Alps, the Pyrénées, the Tyrol and Turkey, is also available. Ask for the Sherpa catalog when requesting other literature from **Himalayan Travel, Inc., P.O. Box 481, Greenwich, CT 06836 (phone 203/622-6777, or toll free 800/225-2380 outside Connecticut).**

Wilderness Travel, of Berkeley, California, is the price competitor to Himalayan Travel, offering similar treks (including those to Nepal and the Alps), but with almost as much emphasis on the mountain areas of Europe and South America, to which more than a quarter of its passengers go. Both the founders of Wilderness Travel have spent considerable time in Peru and the Patagonian region of Argentina and Chile; fittingly, the company's 24-day Patagonia Expedition is a highlight of all trekking programs. Impressive, too, are the expertise and experience of Wilderness's tour leaders, many with Peace Corps backgrounds or graduate degrees in the destinations of the treks. For interesting literature, contact **Wilderness Travel, 801 Allston Way, Berkeley, CA 94710 (phone 415/548-0420, or toll free 800/247-6700 outside California).**

Mountain Travel, of El Cerrito, California, is the largest and oldest of the companies, operating an extraordinary variety of treks on at least five continents. Called "deluxe" by its competitors, its rates—in my reading of them—are only slightly above the industry level: an average of $80 a day in Nepal, from $80 to $130 a day in other mountain regions (plus air fare, of course). Those other areas include India, Peru, Papua New Guinea, Patagonia, Turkey, and Tibet. Like all trekking companies, Mountain Travel provides the tents, foam sleeping pads, and cooking gear; you provide the sleeping bag. For free, four-color literature, contact **Mountain Travel, 6420 Fairmount Ave., El Cerrito, CA 94530 (phone toll free 800/227-2384)**, but for the unabridged, 84-page Mountain Travel catalog, add $2 (which includes postage and handling).

Journeys, of Ann Arbor, Michigan, stresses the cross-cultural aspects of a trek to a far greater extent than the adventure-oriented others. It makes an intense effort to bring about meetings between trekkers and the hill people of each area. Even prior to departure, it involves its trekkers in cultural training for the trip, then delivers daily briefings en route and along the trail by speakers ranging from Buddhist monks and naturalists to ordinary villagers (through interpreters). Specialists to Asia, especially Nepal and Ladakh, since 1978, and highly regarded, even by its competitors, Journeys also offers some departures to Latin America, Japan, and Africa, and charges the "going rate." Contact **Journeys, 4011 Jackson Rd., Ann Arbor, MI 48103 (phone 313/665-4407, or toll free 800/255-8735 outside Michigan)**, for a well-written, well-illustrated catalog.

Above the Clouds Trekking, of Worcester, Massachusetts, is still another small company whose strong suit is Nepal (and the Andes), with Europe (Transylvanian Alps, Ireland) a strong second. "Everest from the East," using the less-traveled route there, is among its innovative, $80-a-day offerings in Nepal; the "Mountains, Monasteries, and Markets" trek is its most popular tour. Like Journeys, the company stresses cross-cultural lessons, and designs its treks to maximize contacts with local residents. For brochures, contact **Above the Clouds Trekking, P.O. Box 398, Worcester, MA 01602 (phone 508/799-4499, or toll free 800/233-4499 outside Massachusetts)**.

Patagonia

Trekking! Is this not the ultimate trip, the answer to the vapid vacation, the plastic "package," the madding throng? "When you have to walk six days to a village," a trekker once told me, "you can be pretty sure it is unspoiled by tourism."

Relieved of your backpacks, you're able to go where roads and paths aren't, but without performing feats of endurance or possessing mountaineering skills.

A Search for Reliable Sources of Bicycle Tours

A Dozen Companies That Take You Biking to All Parts of the World

FRANKLIN ROOSEVELT DID IT IN HIS YOUTH, gliding for weeks along the country roads of Switzerland and Germany in the course of an enchanted summer.

John F. Kennedy, Jr., did it several years ago, on vacation from prep school. And so have many more from other wealthy, or at least moderately well-off, families.

On the lanes and roads of rural France, on the always-level pavements of cycle-loving Holland, over the softly rolling hills of Vermont, in Oregon, and even in Hawaii, increasing numbers of Americans—of ever-increasing age—are flocking to the group bicycle tour.

But why is the activity so expensive—often $110 and $120 a day? Why are bicycle tours more costly, on occasion, than tours by escorted motorcoach? After all, it is you and your two legs that provide the transportation, eliminating a costly vehicle.

Or is that the case?

What most of us fail to consider, in scanning the bicycle brochures, is that a vehicle almost always does accompany the group, to carry luggage. Unless you've opted for the most rugged form of tour, carrying nothing but your cycling costume, a van or truck and a paid driver follow the bicycling tour at a discreet distance.

Because that group is usually limited to 20 or so people, the cost of the vehicle and driver is also divided among fewer people than on a 45-seat motorcoach trip. And because this mode of travel appeals to a more limited audience, all other

costs—marketing of the tour, scouting the itinerary, escorting the group—are also proportionately higher per person.

Thus bicycle tours, except in rare instances (see below), will continue to cost a hefty sum—but one that's justified by advantages aplenty: the best sort of exercise in the open air,

---

Their sometimes hefty price is justified by advantages aplenty: the best sort of exercise in the open air, the closeness to nature and contact with rural people, a relief from urban pressures.

the closeness to nature and contact with rural people, the scenery, and the relief from urban pressures.

But there are pitfalls. They mainly stem from the ease with which underfinanced or inexperienced people can schedule a bicycle tour. Because so many shaky operators flood the mails each year with ill-conceived programs destined to cause trouble, I've sought to ferret out the firms that have made a substantial, long-term commitment to this travel sport. The list is by no means complete; if you know of others, please write to me at the address given in the Preface.

Unless otherwise stated, all tours accept members of any age, provide a supply van, and will rent you a bike (for an extra charge) if you haven't brought your own.

15 BICYCLE TOUR SPECIALISTS

Vermont Bicycle Touring, of Bristol, Vermont: The pioneer in country inn cycling, 20 years old, it operates almost wholly in the unspoiled state of Vermont, with its well-maintained and relatively traffic-free roads. The tours of interest to most are five days long, cost an average of $120 a day, and include two high-quality meals daily and lodging in charming country inns, some of luxury standard. A mouth-watering, four-color, 45-page catalog can be had by contacting **Vermont Bicycle Touring, P.O. Box 711, Bristol, VT 05443 (phone 802/453-4811).** There you'll also learn about an experimental new summer trip to England ($1,599 plus air fare, for 14 days), 10- to 12-day trips to Holland and France for $1,200 plus air fare, and two winter programs to Hawaii and New Zealand. Vermont, however, remains the chief emphasis.

Vermont Country Cyclers, of Waterbury Center, Vermont: The chief competitor to Vermont Bicycle Touring, with similar tour features, prices, and policies, and an excellent catalog. Its five-day tour of the coast of Maine ($120 a day) is a popular addition to its Vermont repertoire, as are several cycling trips to Western Europe, the Caribbean, and other vacation areas of the United States (Colorado, Florida, California). Contact **Vermont Country Cyclers, P.O. Box 145, Waterbury Center, VT 05677 (phone 802/244-8751).**

Country Cycling Tours, of New York City: A well-established (14 years) operator of bicycle tours through the eastern United States and to Europe. Domestic itineraries are particularly novel, and go "island-hopping" in New England (Martha's Vineyard, Nantucket, Newport), to the horse-and-wine country of northern Virginia, along the eastern shores of Maryland; they also include the unique feature of transportation from Manhattan to the place where tours start. To Europe, tours go (for two weeks) to the Cotswolds of England, County Donegal in Ireland, the Loire and elsewhere in France. Lodgings are comfortable country inns in the U.S., two-star or three-star hotels in Europe; two meals a

day are always included; and tours average $140 a day in both the U.S. and Europe, plus air fare. Contact **Country Cycling Tours, 140 W. 83rd St., New York, NY 10024 (phone 212/874-5151).**

Euro-Bike Tours, of DeKalb, Illinois: Well-priced tours of Europe (by the pricey standards of bike touring; about $135 a day, plus air fare), almost all of two weeks' duration. Interesting itineraries (the Dordogne of France, the islands of Scandinavia, Hungary and Austria, the "Romantic Road" of Germany) operate May through early October, on which you receive room, breakfast, and 30% of your dinners, in lodgings ranging from first-class hotels down to intimate inns without private bath. Contact **Euro-Bike Tours, P.O. Box 40, DeKalb, IL 60115 (phone 815/758-8851).**

Tour Prices

	Inn Tour	Camping Tour	# of days/nights	Tour (land cost only)	Bike Rental (optional)	Van Transfer (optional)
CALIFORNIA WEEKENDS						
Alexander Valley						
Alexander Valley	•		2/2	$368	$54	$40
Anza Borrego-Mtn. Bikes			2/2	$179	$54	$40
Anza Borrego-Mtn. Bikes	•		2/2	$374	$54	$40
Bodega Bay			2/2	$179	$54	$40
Bodega Bay	•		2/2	$318	$54	$40
Napa Valley			2/2	$179	$54	$40
Napa Valley	•		2/2	$328	$54	$40
Point Reyes-Mtn. Bikes			2/2	$179	$54	$40
Point Reyes-Mtn. Bikes	•		2/2	$349	$54	$40
Russian River			2/2	$179	$54	$40
Santa Ynez Valley	•		2/2	$317	$54	$60
THE WEST COAST						
Alaska (Price incl. Matanuska River raft trip)			8/8	$1497	$109	N/A
Big Sur Coast			5/5	$998	$99	$55
California Experience (Price incl. skunk train)			5/5	$947	$99	$45
California Experience (Price incl. skunk train)	•		5/5	$597	$99	$45
Gulf Islands (Price incl. sailing)						
Oregon Coast			5/5	$927	$99	$25
Oregon Coast			5/5	$879	$99	$25
Puget Sound (Price incl. all ferry rides)			5/5	$594	$99	$45
Puget Sound (Price incl. all ferry rides)			6/5	$888	$99	$55
Redwood Empire	•		6/5	$599	$99	$55
Wine Country			5/5	$947	$99	$65
Wine Country			5/5	$998	$99	$45
THE SOUTHWEST						
Arizona-Mtn. Bikes	•		5/5	$628	$99	$45
Baja ($100 supplem...)			6/5	$897	$99	...

Backroads Bicycle Touring

Womantrek's "Inner Mongolia" Tour

International Bicycle Tours of Essex, Connecticut: Primarily Holland (though elsewhere in Europe too), for one or two weeks, as organized by a native Amsterdammer, now a longtime resident of the U.S. Tours to Holland include high-quality hotels, with breakfast and three dinners, and cost $850 for one-week tours and $1,200 for two-week tours (not including air fare)—the latter tours work out to about $80 a day, a value. Because the flat terrain of Holland makes cycling easy even for older Americans, some departures are designated for people over the age of 50 only. Contact **International Bicycle Tours, 7 Champlin Square P.O. Box 754, Essex, CT 06426 (phone 203/767-7005)**, and ask, too, about their bike tour to Russia, first time ever (you fly into Warsaw, take a bus to the border, then cycle to Minsk, and from there fly to Moscow, where you stay three days; $2,300 plus air fare, for two weeks).

Butterfield & Robinson, of Toronto: A highly elegant (and expensive) company active as well in the United States. Its major bike program is to Europe (France, Italy, England, especially); uses high-quality villas, castles, country homes, and châteaux; includes two meals a day (with minor excep-

tions) at top restaurants; throws in "wine tastings"; and averages $200 (some tours more, some less) per person per day, not including air fare to Europe. Special student departures cost considerably less. For a 100-page catalog, like a costly picture book, contact **Butterfield & Robinson, 70 Bond St., Suite 300, Toronto, ON, M5B 1X3 Canada (phone 416/864-1354, or toll free 800/268-8415 in Canada, 800/387-1147 outside Canada)**.

Gerhard's Bicycle Odysseys, of Portland, Oregon: From May through September, two-week tours to Germany, Austria, France, and Norway, at $120 a day, plus air fare. All are personally led by German-born Gerhard Meng, now in his 18th year of bicycle-tour operation. Fine country hotels are used; cyclists receive daily breakfast and almost all dinners; several U.S. cycling areas (Maine, Vermont, Virginia, Louisiana, North Carolina) are about to join the roster of itineraries. Contact **Gerhard's Bicycle Odysseys, P.O. Box 757, Portland, OR 97207 (phone 503/223-2402)**.

Backroads Bicycle Touring, of Berkeley, California: All-year-round tours of the western states, Baja California, Hawaii, New Zealand, Tasmania, Bali, and, new in 1991,

France, England, Thailand, and Ireland—all well described in a slick, 62-page free catalog. Groups are of all ages; if seniors find some itineraries too taxing, they can ride in the support van (the aptly named "sag wagon") for part of each day. Tours include three meals daily, plus accommodations in fine inns, and average $120 a day, though some are cheaper. Contact **Backroads Bicycle Touring, 1516 5th St., Berkeley, CA 94710-1713 (phone 415/527-1555, or toll free 800/533-2573 outside California)**. This is a top firm, now in its second decade and growing fast.

Paradise Pedallers, of Charlotte, North Carolina: Two-week and three-week tours of New Zealand, December through March, at the remarkable price of $90 a day (plus round-trip air fare) for inns or motels and two meals a day; and yet a support van accompanies the group, in addition to two experienced guides pedaling alongside. Contact **Paradise Pedallers, P.O. Box 32352, Charlotte, NC 28232 (phone 704/335-8687)**, and ask about their new-for-1991 one-week tours of Bermuda, and North and South Carolina, at the same $90-a-day price.

Arrow to the Sun, of Taylorsville, California: Energetic, exotic tours of Baja California, the central Pacific coast of Mexico, and the Yucatán (in addition to weekend trips through the West), camping out half the nights in tents carried in a support van and supplied by the tour operator, and including three meals a day. Prices average $60 to $70 a day, plus air fare. Write or phone **Arrow to the Sun, P.O. Box 115, Taylorsville, CA 95983 (phone 916/284-6263, or toll free 800/634-0492)**.

China Passage / Asia Passage, of Teaneck, New Jersey: Bicycle tours of China, Thailand, and Indonesia, 16 to 24 nights in duration, all inclusive except for lunch and dinner in Hong Kong. Because of the high air fares, included in tour prices, total charges range from $2,300 to $3,900, but actual land costs average about $115 a day. Contact **China Passage / Asia Passage, 168 State St., Teaneck, NJ 07666 (phone 201/837-1400)**. A high recommendation for this fine company, headed by Frederic Kaplan, author of the definitive guidebook to China, called *The China Book*.

Forum Travel International, of Pleasant Hill, California: In business for 27 years, it claims to be the oldest and largest of America's bicycle operators, but achieves that status in part by representing a number of foreign operators, for which it accepts bookings. Aside from going to all the standard places (it has particularly cheap tours to France), it operates where the others don't: Peru, eastern Germany, Turkey, Czechoslovakia, New Zealand, Hungary, China, Australia. Almost all tours use quality hotels and provide two meals a day and a support van, and average $80 to $120 a day, plus air fare. Contact **Forum Travel International, 91 Gregory Lane, Suite 21, Pleasant Hill, CA 94523 (phone 415/671-2900)**.

Bicycle Africa, of Bellevue, Washington: For a very spe-cial type of traveler, full of adventure and insight, this is a program of three- and four-week bicycle tours to either Kenya, Cameroon, Zimbabwe, or several countries of West Africa, operated throughout the year. Because no traveling van is used, and accommodations are spartan, costs average only $35 to $50 day, including everything except air fare to Africa (around $1,100, round trip, to West Africa; $1,365 to $1,650 to Kenya and Cameroon, respectively). "We journey through cultures, history, landscapes, cuisines, and lifestyles, close enough to touch them," says a spokesperson; "we enjoy

AYH Tour through Austria

Young AYHers

bers strong, this is my own personal favorite of all the programs, a nationwide array of one-week to 10-day tours within the United States, on which no "sag wagon" is provided and leaders are unpaid volunteers. Because of that, costs average only $45 to $55 a day, including all lodgings and meals. You provide your own bike and are responsible for its upkeep. Programs run from late spring to early autumn; sample tours are of the "Northern California Coast" (eight days for $500), "Arcadia (Maine) Hike and Bike" (six days for $300), "Cape Cod and Islands" (six days for $310), "Wisconsin Hills and Valleys" (seven days for $345), "Lake Michigan Shorelines" (Michigan and Wisconsin; seven days for $325), "Colonial Virginia" (seven days for $350)—you get the picture. Tours are always planned to allow maximum independence to participants; you are required to reach the destination each evening, but are otherwise free to wander and detour as you like. Pace is vigorous but not agonizing; changes of clothes are carried in panniers attached to hub caps or in handle-bar bags; groups are limited to 15 people. For detailed listings, contact the **Sierra Club, 730 Polk St., San Francisco, CA 94109 (phone 415/776-2211)**, and send $2 for the yearly, January/February edition of *Sierra,* the club's magazine, which contains a directory listing of all bike tours scheduled for the year.

American Youth Hostels, of Washington, D.C.: The price champion of all the bicycle operators, for people of all ages, its trips average $30 to $40 a day in the U.S., $40 to $55 a day in Europe, including all three meals (cooperatively prepared by the group) daily, but plus air fare to the jumping-off point in the U.S. (air fare to Europe is included in the cost). That's because spartan hostels are used for lodgings, and no van accompanies the group; rather, you balance a knapsack over the rear wheel. Contact **American Youth Hostels, P.O. Box 37613, Washington, DC 20013 (phone 202/783-6161)**.

this fascinating and diverse continent on a personal level not usually attainable by tourists." And, says a recent participant, "the trip, a month long, is worth four years of college anthropology courses; it was the greatest experience of my life." For detailed information and brochures, contact **Bicycle Africa, International Bicycle Fund, 4887 Columbia Dr., South Seattle, WA 98108-1919 (phone 206/767-3927)**.

The Sierra Club, of San Francisco: Operated by the fierce and powerful environmentalist organization, 500,000 mem-

A bicycle-tour operator of particular renown uses high-quality villas, castles, country homes, and châteaux.

Good News for Devotees of the Meandering Cruise by Freighter

After Declining to a Dangerous Level of Capacity, the Passenger-Carrying Freighter Is on the Rise Again

WHAT'S UP WITH PASSENGER-CARRYING freighters? Are they still around? Still a viable vacation possibility for retired Americans with lots of time?

Had those questions been put as recently as four years ago, the answer to them might have been a shaky "No." Capping a 10-year decline, the number of such ships sailing from U.S. ports fell to a paltry 45 or so in 1986. The departure from the field of two major cargo lines, Moore McCormack and Delta; the replacement of several older passenger-freighters with newer, all-freight vessels; a spasmodic reluctance by younger cargo executives to bother with passengers—all threatened to end the activity.

Since freighters are limited to a passenger complement of only 12 persons (otherwise they'd be required by law to carry an expensive doctor), the 1986 decline reduced the U.S. openings to fewer than 400 berths a month.

Gradually, you heard less—saw fewer ads and newsletter mentions—about those long, leisurely sails to Durban and Dar es Salaam, to Mombasa and Yokohama. Die-hards fretted and festered on waiting lists for a year and more; others, more desperate, flew to Hamburg, or Gdynia, Poland, to board the few Europe-originating passenger freighters.

Yet suddenly—in 1987—the picture changed. As with a pendulum, a Hegelian counterreaction, 1987 saw a sharp, upward swing to more than 60 passenger freighters. And 1988 to 1990 still more. A recent, radical mechanization of ship functions has reduced the need for crew, freeing additional cabin space for passengers. A cyclical glut in cargo capacity has forced lines to search for new revenue sources, which can only come from passengers.

Thus the German-owned Columbus Line (phone 212/432-1700) has reentered the field with eight new passenger freighters sailing from both coasts to Australia and New Zealand; the British-owned Pace Line plies the same route with several passenger-adapted ships added in 1989.

Chilean Line double cabin

The Cast Line now carries passengers on a number of vessels from Montréal to Antwerp. Mineral Shipping has assigned additional ships to the classic task of "tramp steaming"—wandering the seas like a driven Ahab, dashing here and there as radio messages direct, changing course in mid-Atlantic to pick up containers from South America, diverting them to the west coast of Africa, and providing 12 lucky passengers with the cruise of their lives.

(By freighter tradition, passengers pay for a fixed number of days; if the trip comes in early, they receive a refund; if it takes longer—as it often does—they receive the extra days free.)

Come 1991, we also see the return of the "cargo liner"— freighters deliberately built to carry 90 and more passengers. The Norwegian-owned Navaran Line will provide us with one such vessel, sailing from the East Coast to South America on a near-regular schedule. Lykes Lines (phone toll free 800/

Freighter World Cruises, Inc.

535-1861) supplies us with another, sailing from East Coast ports to Africa and the Mediterranean.

Waiting lists are thus back to a normal six weeks to four and five months. Last-minute berths are increasingly available. Freighter fans are once again full of expectations and plans.

Why such eagerness? Because the activity is incomparable.

You visit exotic, untouristed ports. Time stretches before you, unlimited, unpressured. You dine with ship's officers, have the run of the ship, attend periodic barbecues on deck and biweekly parties, dart into the galley to fix your own sandwich or pour a beer, as the mood hits. You delight in the intimacy of a lengthy, shared, unstructured experience, gathering at night around the VCR and its extensive library of tapes that all the ships now carry.

You incur half the daily cost of the average passenger liner. While benchmark rates are an average of $90 a day, some budget-style ships charge as little as $70 or $80 a day, some overseas-originating freighters as little as $60 a day.

What is asked of you is flexibility (you rarely know exact sailing dates until a week or so ahead) and time (voyages last for 30 days, 45 days, even 70 and 90 days).

Because of that, passengers are invariably in their 60s and early 70s and retired (unless they're professors on sabbatical or writers seeking seclusion—author Alex Haley sails on three or four freighter cruises each year). Interestingly, most freighter lines have recently raised their maximum age limits from 69 to 79 (and occasionally higher)—a tribute to the increasing vigor of today's senior citizens.

The largest of the passenger/freight companies is the Lykes Line (phone toll free 800/535-1861), with upward of 28 ships in service; Columbus Lines is the next most numerous, with 10 ships. Polish Ocean Lines is among the cheapest ($60 to $85 a day), occasionally sailing from Port Newark.

SOURCES OF FREIGHTER INFORMATION

Freighter World Cruises, Inc., of Pasadena, California, is the base of veteran Mary LeBlanc, an industry pioneer who has personally propelled a number of freighter companies into the passenger business.

She derides the widely held notion that freighter capacity is incapable of meeting the demand. "There is always space around if you don't care where you go," she says. "We can move a person in two weeks. Only when you insist on, say, New Zealand, or hot-weather ports in winter, must you wait three or four months for a ship."

To prove the point, LeBlanc's 26-times-a-year "Freighter Space Advisory," a smartly edited six-page newsletter, devotes itself to photos and descriptions of ships leaving in the next month or two from both U.S. and foreign ports.

The recent show-stopper: a periodic departure from Charleston, sailing to New Orleans, then to Houston, then through the Panama Canal to Sydney, Melbourne, and Brisbane (Australia), from there to three ports in New Zealand, back to the Panama Canal, and finishing in Philadelphia—a full 70 days at sea. Off-season cost (March through September) is $5,190 per person, whether single or double, amounting to $74 a day; in high season (October through May), $8,100 single, $7,300 per person in a double.

Contact **Freighter World Cruises, Inc., 180 S. Lake Ave., Suite 335, Pasadena, CA 91101 (phone 818/449-3106)**, and send $27 for a one-year subscription to the "Freighter Space Advisory"; the same firm then makes the reservations and handles all details.

TravLtips of Flushing, New York, is the other combination freighter–travel agency/newsletter company, except that its publication, a bimonthly, is a slick and elaborate 32-

You visit exotic, untouristed ports. Time stretches before you, unlimited, unpressured. You have the run of the ship, dine with the ship's officers. You delight in the intimacy of a lengthy, shared experience.

Passenger-carrying freighter of the Bank Line

page magazine (*TravLtips*), devoted not only to "freighter-ing" (through first-person accounts by subscribers of their own recent trips), but to exotic or long-term sailings by ordinary passenger ships—the kind that would appeal to the heavily traveled, sophisticated devotees of freighters.

Currently edited and administered by the 37-year-old son of its founder, the late Ed Kirk, the publication/organization is staffed by several experienced reservationists and other cruise experts.

Send $15 for a one-year subscription (and membership),

or $25 for two years to **TravLtips, 163-07 Depot Rd. (P.O. Box 188), Flushing, NY 11358 (phone 718/939-2400, or toll free 800/872-8584 outside New York State).**

Unlike the first two organizations, the 33-year-old Freighter Travel Club, of Roy, Washington, makes no reservations, sells no trips or tickets, and simply confines itself to publication of a monthly eight-page (and rather crudely typewritten) newsletter, whose charming and helpful contents make up for its appearance. Send $18 (for a one-year subscription), or $28 for two years, to **Freighter Travel Club of America, 3524 Harts Lake Rd., Roy, WA 98580,** addressing any specific inquiries to its veteran editor, a walking encyclopedia of freighter lore, Leland J. Pledger.

The larger companies are supplemented by a handful of smaller travel-agency specialists on freighter—usually a single individual—of which **Pearl's Travel Tips, c/o Ilsa Hoffman, 9903 Oaks Lane, Seminole, FL 34642 (phone 813/393-2919),** is perhaps best known for long expertise. Although Pearl passed away in December 1989, her daughter-in-law, Ilsa Hoffman, has succeeded to her large store of information and contacts.

And some of the lines accept direct bookings from the public, without the intervention of an agent. For one such, contact **Lykes Cargo Liner Passenger Service, Lykes Center, 300 Poydras St., New Orleans, LA 70130 (phone 504/523-6611, or toll free 800/535-1861).**

What is asked of you is flexibility (you rarely know exact sailing dates until a week or so ahead) and time (voyages last for 30 days, 45 days, even 70 and 90 days).

The Trend to the Tiny Ship

Increasing Numbers of Vacationers Are Opting for Intimate Vessels Able to Take Them to Secluded Places

ON THE QUAYS LEADING TO A STORE-LINED main street, a scraggly group of hawkers fidgets nervously as they await the imminent onslaught of 1,400 visitors. At curbside stands bearing English-language signs, they will have short minutes to dispose of their cheap straw hats, their gaudy T-shirts.

As the tenders deposit a regiment of humanity from the giant vessel anchored offshore, noise and confusion erupt. A military band blares away. The first arrivals go dashing to a celebrated perfume shop, while others rush to ranks of foul-smelling tour buses or to stand in line for casino admission.

And that is the scene encountered as many as seven times in a single week by Americans sailing through the Caribbean on certain massive cruise ships. Others, repelled by the urban qualities they traveled so many miles to avoid, are opting for a wholly different seagoing experience, on a "tiny" ship—one that accommodates 60 to 150 passengers and goes to quiet ports or secluded beaches.

American-Canadian Caribbean Line

In the British Virgin Islands,
Clipper Cruise Line

In a backlash from current cruise-ship trends (one line is contemplating construction of a 5,000-passenger behemoth), a market is growing for yacht-like vessels with shallow drafts enabling them to go directly onto palm-lined shores or to small marinas in cozy bays.

Their customers often are an affluent but unpretentious lot who relax on board in shorts and sandals, follow no schedules at all, and attend no ship "events"—there aren't any.

Ashore, they dine quietly in the fresh-fish restaurant of a backwater town, or lie reading a paperback novel in a rope hammock, hearing nothing but sea gulls and waves.

Among the "tiny" ships that bring you that form of paradise are:

A market is growing for yachtlike vessels with shallow drafts enabling them to go directly onto palm-lined shores or to small marinas in cozy bays.

WINDJAMMER CRUISES

Like that cabin boy in *Two Years Before the Mast,* you'll stumble in dazed excitement onto the teakwood decks of an actual ocean schooner with sails—as sleek as a greyhound, but with the tiny, cot-equipped cabins you'd expect on so narrow a vessel.

You have the run of the entire ship: bowsprit, rigging, even crow's nest and at the wheel—and are actually encouraged to help the professional crew with steering the ship. Each day you anchor off a quiet beach or tiny port, to which your lunch is brought by kitchen crew wading through the surf. You live throughout in shorts and sandals, in sheer relaxation or happy camaraderie with like-minded, unpretentious, adventure-seeking people from all over the world who have heard of these renowned ships. They range in size from the "giant" S/V *Fantome* (126 passengers) and S/V *Polynesia* (126 passengers) down to the S/V *Flying Cloud* (80 passengers) and M/S *Yankee Clipper* (66 passengers, a former scientific survey ship equipped with two large sails). You sail through the Grenadines, the exotic Leeward Islands of the Caribbean, the British Virgin Islands, and to other highlights of the West Indies. And you pay only $725 to $850 for a six-day cruise in most cabins, plus air fare from the U.S. ($299 from the East Coast, $499 from the West Coast). For details, contact **Windjammer Barefoot Cruises, P.O. Box 120, Miami Beach, FL 33119 (phone toll free 800/327-2601 for reservations or information, 800/327-2600 for brochures).**

AMERICAN-CANADIAN CARIBBEAN LINE

Budget-priced cruises of the Caribbean in winter, the inland waterways of Rhode Island, Montréal, and Québec in summer, on yachtlike ships carrying as few as 60 and 70 passengers apiece. Rates range from a low $95 to $175 per person per day, not including air fare to embarkation cities. On each ship used in the winter season, "bow ramps" allow passengers to walk, not climb, from the ship to the most isolated and inviting beaches. For literature, contact **American-Canadian Caribbean Line, Inc., P.O. Box 368, Warren, RI 02885 (phone 401/247-0955, or toll free 800/556-7450 outside Rhode Island).**

Clipper Cruise Line

177

CLIPPER CRUISE LINE

Elegant luxury yachts carrying only 100 passengers apiece, the *Newport Clipper* and the *Nantucket Clipper* limit themselves to "American" waters, even in the Caribbean. Winter, they ply the Virgin Islands, visiting such peaceful ports as Cruz Bay in St. John and Christiansted in St. Croix. Spring, they explore the "Colonial South"—the ports and historic coastal cities and islands of Florida and Georgia. Summer, they head farther north, to Yorktown, Annapolis, Chesapeake City, Newport, and Nantucket. For all their exquisite attentions and amenities, prices are not extreme: $200 to $250 per person per day for most cabins, but plus a specially reduced air fare to embarkation points. For literature, contact **Clipper Cruise Line, Windsor Building, 7711 Bonhomme Ave., St. Louis, MO 63105 (phone 314/727-2929, or toll free 800/325-0010 outside Missouri).**

OCEAN CRUISE LINES

On the borderline of bigness, this company's 250-passenger *Ocean Islander* has all the facilities of a much larger ship, but the intimacy of a private yacht. In the summer of 1991 (early May to late September), it will cruise between Venice and Nice, and between Venice and Istanbul, yet at the surprisingly low rates of as little as $170, an average high of $300, per person per day (plus air fare from the U.S. to Italy). For literature, contact **Ocean Cruise Lines, 1510 S.E. 17th St., Fort Lauderdale, FL 33316 (phone 305/764-5566, or toll free 800/338-1700).**

Tobago

You have the run of the entire ship: bowsprit, rigging, even crow's nest and at the wheel.

WINDSTAR SAIL CRUISES

The newest (1987), longest (440 feet), tallest (masts 20 stories tall), and maybe largest of the world's sailing ships is the *Wind Star,* berthed at the island of Barbados, from which it makes weekly one-week cruises to such magical spots as Mustique, Bequia, Tobago Cay, Palm Island, St. Lucia, and other unlikely ports of call (for the standard ships). It places its passengers in cabins 185 square feet in size, and plies them with every luxury (like impulsively buying 300 pounds of lobster at a native market for consumption at a beach barbecue that day). The total passenger complement is 148, on ships whose sails are directed by computer; the mood is casual elegance, the charge about $300 per person per day— which is not as high as you'd expect for an experience as exclusive as this. A sister ship, the *Wind Song,* sails year round from Tahiti, while still a third vessel of identical size and design, the *Wind Spirit,* sails along the French and Italian Rivieras in summer, the islands of St. Thomas, St. Barts, St. Maarten, and Virgin Gorda in winter, all for approximately the same rates (which do not, however, include air fare to and from embarkation points). For details, contact **Windstar Sail Cruises, Ltd., 300 Elliot Ave. West, Seattle, WA 98119 (phone 206/281-3535 or toll free 800/258-7245 for information, 800/626-9900 for brochures).**

I have not mentioned the *Sea Goddess* ships of the Cunard Lines because their rates are truly high, and out of reach for the great majority of our readers; nor have I included several vessels whose 500-passenger size disqualifies them from inclusion in this discussion. Here we're interested in proving that "Small Is Beautiful." Viva the smaller ship!

Windstar Sail Cruises

Sailing the Tall Ships

Low-Cost Schooner Cruises for Non-Standard Sailors

WHAT DO YOU DO IF YOU'RE LURED BY the sea but you can't stand the increasing sameness, the crushing uniformity, of the world's large cruise ships?

It's a growing problem. As cruising becomes big business, conducted by billion-dollar corporations, ships are becoming alike in their atmosphere, amenities, and programs. All feel compelled to offer mindless, Las Vegas–style revues at night, Bingo in the afternoon, mass aerobics and jogging tracks, crowded shore excursions, and big movie theaters. Though each will claim to have distinct characteristics—"Italian-style cruising," computer classes, lectures by ecologists—in my opinion there's not a dime's worth of difference between most of them.

Unless you're talking of the "Tall Ships." In full-masted schooners, carrying 30 to 90 passengers, under canvas sails billowing in the wind, a small but select number of American vacationers are enjoying the classic thrills of the sea as it used to be, in the days before "The Love Boat" converted a rather elitist intellectual activity into a robotlike, mass-volume routine. Those lucky few are also paying half the cost of a standard cruise, about $100 to $120 a day.

But the schooners aren't for everyone. Cabins are tiny, beds are often bunks, meals family style and without choice, planned activities few, and nightlife nil. Instead of pursuing an active schedule, passengers simply stretch out on deck to peruse a paperback, go snorkeling when the mood hits, stroll deep in thought along the undeveloped beaches that shelter the ship by day. Does that sound bad? It's exactly the reason why many Americans wouldn't dream of cruising except in a "Tall Ship."

The wind-driven vessels (they all have supplementary motors) making regular weekly cruises throughout the year, and accepting bookings from the public at large, are—as best I can determine—17 in number: 5 operated by Windjammer Barefoot Cruises, Inc., and 12 offered by a total of five other firms. Windjammer created this travel mode back in 1947, and is said by some to have grown a bit jaded, though others still sing its praises. The remaining firms have all emerged in the past decade to do battle with Windjammer, and perhaps try harder.

Except for Blackbeard's Cruises and Bounty Voyages (see below), all the lines operate their one-week trips on a rather truncated basis: their ships usually stay in the port of embarkation for an initial night, and then spend five remaining nights at sea—not really a full week. Some ships do, other ships don't, provide private facilities; read the brochures carefully. But all supply a wonderful closeness to the sea and nature, a devil-may-care informality, a loosening of habits and inhibitions—and isn't that what a vacation is for?

Windjammer Barefoot Cruises, Inc., P.O. Box 120, Miami Beach, FL 33119 (phone toll free 800/327-2601, 800/432-3364 in Florida), has—as earlier noted—a multiple fleet (five schooners) and the largest ships (carrying 66 to 126 passengers apiece, double the capacity of the other lines), but those attributes of size aren't regarded as advantages by everyone; some prefer the greater intimacy, camara-

---

Here is what cruising was like before "The Love Boat" converted a rather elitist intellectual activity into a standard holiday of rote-like scheduled events.

derie, and informality of the other lines. One of its fleet, the *Mandalay*, undertakes successive 13-day cruises of the Caribbean (West Indies and Grenadines) for prices ranging from $1,350 to $1,550 per person for most cabins, while the others house you for one night in port and then for five at sea (British Virgin Islands, West Indies, and Grenadines) for $710 to $850 per person; they charge only $1,350 to $1,550 per person, however, for those staying on board for 12 consecutive nights. Since the ships vary their itineraries each week, never repeating an island in succession, numerous passengers opt for the two-week pattern, and spend their two intermediate nights exploring the port of embarkation on foot, returning each night to the ship for meals and bed. Islands from which Windjammer sails throughout the year include Antigua, Tortola, St. Maarten, Trinidad, and Grenada. Islands visited: dozens. And inexpensive air fares are made available by the line to each departure point.

Blackbeard's Cruises, P.O. Box 661091, Miami Springs, FL 33266 (phone 305/888-1226, or toll free 800/327-9600 outside Florida), operates three 65-foot sloops, housing 22 passengers and six crew members apiece, that make seven-day/six-night cruises from Miami to the Bahamas, primarily for diving. Boats leave Miami on Saturday afternoons throughout the year, return the following Friday morning, charge $599 per person for the entire week, take you for three to four dives a day off the boat, then spend the nights in calm anchorages on the placid "lee" side of Bimini, Freeport, or the Berry Islands. Can you go if you're not a diver? Absolutely, says the small firm (in business for 12 years), provided you're not expecting a "shuffleboard [activity-filled] cruise." Rather, the nondiver will pass the time "snorkeling off the beach, shell-hunting on deserted islands . . . staying up late for conversation under the stars . . . or simply sleeping in."

Yankee Schooner Cruises, P.O. Box 696, Camden, ME 04843 (phone 207/236-4449, or toll free 800/255-4449 outside Maine), sails the chilly waters of Maine in summer and early fall (late June through mid-September), then repeats its pattern of continuous one-week cruises in the U.S. and British Virgin Islands from early December to late April. This is a one-ship firm, but what a ship: the 137-foot schooner *Roseway*, built in 1925 of sturdy oak, with varnished mahogany walls throughout and other elegant fittings for its complement of 36 passengers. You board on Sunday afternoon, then sail with the tide on Monday, returning to port (Camden in Maine, St. Thomas in the U.S. Virgin Islands) by midday Saturday. Cost is a uniform $535 for Down East Maine cruises, but varies with cabin category in the Virgin Islands—$725 per person in a Pullman berth, $745 in a quad, $795 in a double cabin. This time, scuba-diving is not at all stressed (although available), but snorkeling is, along with swimming, beach lolling, windsurfing, shelling, and reading.

Dirigo Cruises, 39 Waterside Lane, Clinton, CT 06413

Sir Francis Drake, *Tall Ship Adventures*

(phone 203/669-7068), operates the 95-foot, traditionally rigged (as in the 1860s) schooner *Harvey Gamage* on consecutive one-week cruises, winters in the West Indies (most from St. Thomas, but on four occasions in January and February from St. Maarten), summers along the east coast of the United States. From mid-November through April, passengers board on Sunday afternoon, disembark at noon the following Saturday, and pay $595 for adult passage ($495 if they're senior citizens), $495 if they're 13 to 18, $445 if they're 12 and under. Summer dates and rates aren't yet fixed for 1991. Passengers are encouraged to assist the crew, but spend most of their time swimming, snorkeling, or navigating the two small sailboats carried aboard.

Cabins are tiny, beds are often bunks, meals family style and without choice, planned activities few, and nightlife nil.

Tall Ship Adventures, Inc., 1010 S. Joliet St., Suite 200, Aurora, CO 80012 **(phone toll free 800/662-0090)**, operates the most elegant of the authentic sailing ships—the 36-passenger *Sir Francis Drake*—with private "heads" and showers for every cabin, full-size double beds in some, and elaborate meals. Its one-week rates are thus a bit elevated, but still well below those of standard cruise ships: $895 per person in a cabin with upper and lower beds, $995 with side-by-side beds, $1,095 with double bed and upper bed, $100 for children under 12 sharing a cabin with their parents. For this, you cruise in winter (summer rates are $100 less per person) through both the U.S. and British Virgin Islands, visiting St. Thomas, St. John, Jost van Dyke, Peter Island, Dead Man's Chest, Cooper's Island, Tortola, and Virgin Gorda. And at night you enjoy what most schooners deliberately omit from their facilities: a lounge with stereo, video, and TV.

Finally, **Bounty Voyages, c/o Worldwide Adventure, 920 Young St., Suite 747, Toronto, ON, M4Y 3C7, Canada (phone toll free 800/387-1483)**, is an Australian fleet of six tall ships, of which five are fairly small vessels carrying 14 to 30 passengers, plus 6 to 8 in crew, with most people aboard occupying rather modest compact bunks and cabins; the sixth is a luxurious three-masted barquentine housing 50 guests in cabins with private facilities. Ships sail in New Zealand waters from December through March, then from April through November head to the islands of the South Pacific (Tahiti, Fiji, Samoa, Cook Islands, Tonga) and Australia's Great Barrier Reef. Most voyages are of 14 days' duration and cost a uniform $1,825 ($130 per day) per person, plus air fare, but are also available for both lesser and longer periods of time.

Merely to scan the illustrated pages of each company's brochure is to thrill to an eternal urge. "Oh, I must go down to the seas again," wrote poet laureate John Masefield, "To the lonely sea and the sky/ And all I ask is a Tall Ship/ And a star to steer her by."

Country Walking Tours Are Another Major New Discovery

Walking Inn to Inn, While a Van Carries Gear Ahead

ARE YOU A "CLOSET" WALKER? WHILE others jog on their vacations, or go bicycling or white-water rafting, do you simply sneak off to walk, in utter bliss, for miles and miles?

If so, you're one of a growing number of Americans who go away to walk—even to places thousands of miles from home. They believe, along with the American Heart Association, that brisk walking is the most healthful holiday sport, as aerobic as running (and far easier on the joints), and the best possible way to approach the life and people of an unfamiliar destination. The popularity of walking has resulted in the emergence of a surprising number of walking-tour operators covering every part of the globe.

With some operators, you walk inn to inn while a van carries your gear ahead or brings you lunch. With others, you remain three or four days at a time in one base—a country hotel or a cluster of B&Bs—and walk from there. While England is clearly the most popular destination for walking vacations, few of the world's flatlands are spared attention by walking-tour operators. I've surveyed 11 major ones:

Elegant Ambles, P.O. Box 91254, San Diego, CA 92109 (phone 619/222-2224), is the Tiffany's among them, supplying custom-tailored walks, not set departures, to any size group, even a party of two. "We're like architects building the product you want," says founder Larry Forman, a professor of computer sciences at San Diego City College, who recently arranged for one couple on tour to meet James Herriot of *All Creatures Great and Small* fame. Tours run two to three weeks, go anywhere (but mainly to England, Scotland, Switzerland, and New England) and cost $95 to $295 per person per day (plus air fare), depending on style of travel. Groups are booked months ahead, but individuals can call to ask whether they can be attached to one.

Hummingbird Nature Tours, 22374 Lougheed Hwy., #31, BC, V2X 2T5, Canada (phone 604/467-9219), is a surprising Canadian source for well-operated U.S. walking tours in New Mexico (in May and September, for eight days, at a cost of $830 from Albuquerque); in Mount St. Helens, Oregon (in July, for one week, price pending); along the Oregon coast (in August, for one week, at a cost of $755); and around San Diego County (in December, for one week, at a cost of $675 from San Diego). Tours are led by naturalists or archeologists, all emphasize health food–oriented meals, none involve the hard walking of dramatic elevation changes or difficult terrain, and all drive you from one walking area to another (you do not hike "from inn to inn").

Billy Platypus Australia, R.R. 1, Box 10A, Clifton, KS 66044 (phone toll free 800/633-8032), operates tours "which leave you fitter, not fatter" (their words), between Melbourne and Sydney from December through February and in April and October. Their 11-day "Walkabout" re-

Oeschinen Lake in the Bernese Oberland, Switzerland

quires no hiking experience or extraordinary vigor, but is designed for active people anxious to meet Australians and enjoy the odd appearance of the Australian bush. Walkers occasionally go horseback riding on a remote sheep ranch, swim off the unspoiled beaches of Cape Conran, or wander from barbecue to barbecue on the outskirts of Canberra. The cost is $1,390 to $1,475 per person, plus air fare to Melbourne.

Vermont Walking Tours, P.O. Box 31, Craftsbury Common, VT 05827 (phone 802/586-7767), runs weekly five-day walking tours on fixed dates from May through June and September through October, along backroads and wilderness paths in the sparsely settled northeastern section of Vermont. You start at 9:30 A.M., walk 5 to 10 miles, eat lunch delivered by van, and are then driven back to your starting point: a charming, lakefront cottage where you room and take your meals. Experienced guides accompany you at every step. The cost is $375 and $425 per tour. Add air fare to Burlington, or bus or train fare to nearby Montpelier.

Four Seasons Walking Vacations, P.O. Box 145W, Waterbury Center, VT 05677 (phone toll free 800/244-8751), is still another Vermont specialist combining overnight stays-with-meals at charming inns, with guided walks from inn to inn, over weekends or for three to five days during midweek, from late May through late October. Walks average five to seven miles a day, by brooks, along streams, and through fields of wildflowers, at costs averaging $289 for a full weekend (all inclusive) and $659 for a five-night walk during midweek (all inclusive). A charming, bearded young Vermonter named Bob Maynard, a veteran of 10 years of leading bicycling vacations for Vermont Country Cyclers, has turned to walking with the formation of Four Seasons Walking Vacations.

Knapsack Tours, 5961 Zinn Dr., Oakland, CA 94611 (phone 415/339-0160), despite its name, says that backpacks are never needed on its four tours each year, to Switzerland (in June, for three weeks, costing $2,195, not including air fare), to Yosemite (in July, for two weeks, costing $1,000), to the Canadian Rockies (in September, for 11 days, costing $850), and to New England (in early October, for seven days, costing $970 and walking inn to inn). Vans carry luggage. Daily hikes are four to six hours long each day.

Walking tours are as aerobic as running (and far easier on the joints), and the best possible way to approach the life and people of an unfamiliar destination.

Walking through Iceland

Walking to Machú Picchú

Obviously, these tours are cheaper than some others I've cited, primarily because Knapsack searches out modest lodgings appropriate (in my view) to the unpretentious nature of the activity.

New Age Health Spa, Neversink, NY 12765 (phone toll free 800/NU-AGE-4-U), better known for its Catskill Mountains diet farm, operates walking tours to the world's most exotic locales in winter and spring. Each tour is accompanied by Werner Mendel or Stephanie Paradise, noted advocates of New Age health therapies, which means that health food is obtained for participants every day—even in deepest Borneo. Recently scheduled (with air fare extra for all) were trips to the Costa Rica rain forest (in January, for nine days, at a cost of $995), to New Zealand (in February, for 12 days, costing $1,355), to the Thailand hill tribes (in April, for 11 days, costing $999), to Mexico's Copper Canyon (in May, for seven days, costing $655), and to Machú Picchú (in June, for eight days, costing $585).

Samvinn Travel, 12 Austurstraeti (P.O. Box 910), Reykjavik 121, Iceland (phone 354/1-69-1010), operates both 11-day walking tours (usually $1,095) and 5-day walking tours (for $525) of largely uninhabited areas of Iceland, with accommodations in schools and huts scattered among eerie lava fields and craters. On most tours, a bus takes participants from base to base for daily hikes. Dates are late June through August; add air fare to Iceland. Write for a compelling catalog.

Ryder/Walker Alpine Adventures, 87 Morse Hill Rd., Millerton, NY 12546 (phone 914/373-7005), is perhaps the nation's leading source of one- and two-week walks through the Swiss Alps (Zermatt, Saas-Fee, Wengen, Kandersteg, and Pontresina) and other high mountain regions of Europe (Scottish highlands, Bavaria-Appenzell), from late May through September; these are walks, not climbs. In Switzerland, walkers stay at a base hotel for a week at a time, embarking on daily hikes; elsewhere they move more frequently from place to place. Figure about $185 a day, plus air fare, for most tours.

Back Trails Tours, 2316 Galewood, Anchorage, AK 99508 (phone 907/276-5528), founded seven years ago by two school principals, operates a seven-day walking tour of Alaska's Kenai Peninsula in July and August from Anchorage. The price is $1,250 per person, all inclusive except for air fare, for the ultimate in walks: passing moose and migrating ducks, seeing salmon on spawning runs, encountering 35 varieties of wildflowers, the awesome scenery of this northern wilderness—never viewed as well as through this mode of travel.

Tours of Britain, 5757 Wilshire Blvd., Suite 214, Los Angeles, CA 90036 (phone 213/937-0494), markets a series of rather expensive one- to two-week walks May through September, traversing 5 to 12 miles a day through five regions of Britain: the Cotswolds, the Devon coast, Dorset, Scotland, and Exmoor. Tours are operated by a group of expert local guides called Greenscape Ltd.

"We walk through picturesque villages and farmyards, over tranquil paths and pastures with newborn lambs. We stop at pubs and tea shops along the way, look up history in the village church, speak with people in their gardens," says a representative. A charge of $200 a day covers all costs in Britain; air fare is extra.

As for other walking tours of Britain, a group known as the Rambler's Association, at 4 Wandsworth Rd., London, publishes a magazine called *The Rambler,* which describes walk opportunities and lists organized tours throughout the country.

But some avid walkers are upset about the commercialization of strolling through Britain, believing the activity should always be do-it-yourself in style, *sans* tour operators. Such is the belief of Richard Hayward, of Seattle, Washington, who teaches classes in the area about the joys of unorganized walking tours.

The whole point of walking, in Hayward's view, is to meet people of the host country. It is especially easy, he says, to meet Britons, "for whom walking is a national pastime. They care about the countryside, and if they meet you in that setting, their old-world reserve melts away and you are one of them. Organized walking tours can be a waste of time and energy because you don't meet the people as readily."

Hayward has compiled a list of books that supply itineraries for independent walking tours of England and Wales. For a copy, send $3 and a stamped, self-addressed envelope to **Richard Hayward, British Footpaths, 914 Mason St., Bellingham, WA 98225.**

While others sit solidly in a bus, gaining pounds by the mile, the smart traveler walks, and gains health, in addition to contact with people, nature, life.

While others sit stolidly in a bus, the smart traveler walks.

IX

ENLARGING YOUR MIND THROUGH STUDY VACATIONS

A Yank at Oxford—or Cambridge (Summer Style)

Short Summer Study Courses at the Great British Universities Offer an Unusual Supplement to the Standard English Holiday

THEY ARE KNOWN AS "QUADS" BECAUSE THEY spread between the enclosing wings of a quadrangular building, and they are magical beyond compare—otherworldly and still, their silence challenged only by the chirpings of a thrush, yet the very air within seems to pulse with the joy of human achievement, 800 years of learning. They are the "quads" of the colleges at Oxford and Cambridge, some so old that one built in the 1300s is still known as New College.

Who among us hasn't dreamed of studying there? How many of the most eminent Americans still harbor a secret disappointment over having failed to win a Rhodes Scholarship or some other form of admission to the ancient universities of Britain?

Well, life in this instance affords a second chance (for a week to a month, at least). From late June through early September, most of the major British universities—Oxford and Cambridge among them—offer study courses of one, two, three, four, and six weeks' duration, to overseas visitors of any age, with adults quite definitely preferred. While a summer week or more in the quiet, near-deserted quads isn't quite the opportunity you may have craved in younger days, it provides a memorable communion with these awesome institutions, and a learning experience that has edified and enchanted many discerning visitors before you.

By the end of spring, the undergrads of Oxford and Cambridge, in their abbreviated black cloaks flung over tweedy suits and dresses (you won't be wearing one), have all departed for the beaches and hills; but instruction in summer is by the unvarnished "real thing": eminent dons (teaching masters) who pursue a clipped and no-nonsense approach to learning that contrasts quite refreshingly with some American pedagogy. The mind responds—stretching to accommodate difficult concepts and queries, directly and sometimes brutally put. At night you join your instructors in the always-active pubs of the university towns, enjoying conversation as heady as a glass of good brandy. Though individual tutorials aren't provided to summer students, opportunities abound to continue classroom discussion in less formal settings.

In all other respects the experience is reasonably akin to that of British university life. You live in the temporarily vacated quarters of an Oxford or Cambridge student. You dine at the long, wooden refectory tables of an Oxford or

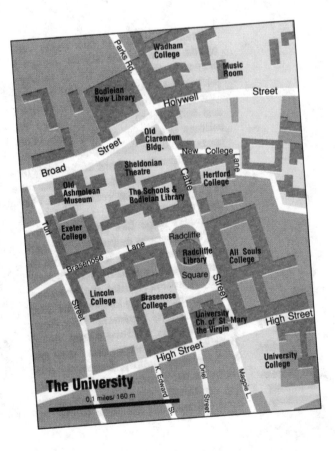

Oxford, from Magdalen College Tower

While a summer week or more in the quiet, near-deserted quads isn't quite the opportunity you craved in younger days, it provides a memorable communion with these awesome institutions.

The Bridge of Sighs at Hertford

Summer scholars

Cambridge dining hall—though "High Table," the elevated realm from which faculty members take their wine-accompanied meals, is normally vacant at these times. You roam the stacks of the historic Bodleian Library of Oxford, browse among ancient tomes in the hush of Cambridge's Pepysian Library, lie on the sunlight-flecked grass as you cope with the heavy reading load that most courses entail.

CURRICULA

What courses do you pursue? While Shakespeare and other giants of English literature dominate the lists—and attract the greater number of international students—most remaining studies deal with contemporary aspects of British life and institutions: "Political Thought in England," "The English Educational System," "The United Kingdom Economy," "History of English Painting," among a wide selection of others.

The top summer programs are those offered by departments of the two great universities that concern themselves with extension or continuing education. Cambridge's "official" program, the International Summer School, offers the broadest choice of courses and, unlike Oxford, makes no great point of imposing deadlines for application. It operates a first "term" of four weeks in July, a second "term" of two weeks in early August, permits you to take either or both, and charges upward of £725 ($1,305) for the first term and £425 ($765) for the second. Charges include all tuition, a single room in a university residence, the services of a "scout" to clean your room (but not otherwise to wait upon you), and two meals a day (breakfast and dinner) in a soaring Gothic hall of ancient stone. For catalog and application forms, contact **The Director, Board of Extra-Mural Studies, Madingley Hall, Madingley, Cambridge CB3 8AQ, England (phone 0954/210636)**, and specify your preference among the International Summer School, Literature Summer School, and Art History Summer School, attended in total by more than 1,500 people each year.

Oxford's "official" summer course is a six-week session from July to mid-August, for which three-week enrollments are also permitted (and heavily chosen by most people attending). Here, all students pursue the single theme of "Britain: Literature, History, and Society from 1870 to the Present Day," vividly presented in an integrated series of

King's Chapel, Cambridge

Instruction in summer is by the unvarnished "real thing": eminent dons (teaching masters) who pursue a clipped and no-nonsense approach to learning.

more than 50 lectures by noted Oxford academics (including such major "names" as Professors Richard Ellman, A. H. Halsey, Terry Eagleton, and Christopher Ricks). Tuition for the entire six-week term is £1,290 ($2,322) and about half that for three-week sessions, which includes your room (in Exeter College, founded in 1314) and all three meals daily—as well as the occasional invitation to dine at "High Table" with tutors and lecturers. For further information, contact the **Summer School Secretary, Department for External Studies, Rewley House, 1 Wellington Square, Oxford 0X1 2JA, England (phone 0865/270360).** For applications, contact **U.S. Student Programs Division, Institute of International Education, 809 United Nations Plaza, New York, NY 10017 (phone 212/883-8200).**

If the "official" programs are full, or you have only two weeks available for study, you can opt for a number of "unofficial" courses organized by various Oxford and Cambridge dons on a purely private, entrepreneurial basis; the latter simply rent the use of classrooms and lodgings, and announce their own programs, some for durations of as little as two weeks. Typical are the courses offered at Oxford in "Modern British History and Politics" by the so-called Institute for British and Irish Studies; these are given in July and early August, for either two, three, four, or five weeks, intensively from 9 A.M. to 6 P.M., for a cost to you of about $800 a week, including tuition, lodging, all three meals daily, and weekly theater tickets and excursions. Contact the Institute c/o its U.S. representative, **Dr. E. C. Johnson, IBIS, Camford House, Almont, CO 81210 (phone 303/248-0477, or toll free 800/327-4247 outside Colorado),** or call the institute directly in England (phone 0865/270980). Dr. Johnson and the institute (both highly regarded by me) also offer summer programs for adults in history, literature, and international law at Trinity College, Dublin, and University College, London.

No one suggests that courses such as these should be the sole activity of a British vacation; they can be combined, instead, with the most standard sightseeing and recreation. But what an opportunity awaits! The smart traveler seizes the chance, if the chance exists, to experience these hallowed institutions of learning in the manner they deserve: not as casual tourists, but as students, in the endless quest for light.

Meet the Danish "Folk High School," and Never Be the Same Again

A Winter Week or Two at a Residential College for Adults

WE BEGAN THE DAY SINGING. FROM OUR places at a table of polished light pine, drenched in the sunlight reflected from a silver fjord, we sang a secular hymn to life and brotherhood, to goodness and sharing. "Would you care to attend my seminar this morning?" asked a young Danish beauty as she passed me a breakfast bowl of peaches and yogurt. "I shall be inviting people from other disciplines to help me over a rough spot in my paper on producer cooperatives."

I was at a Danish folk high school (*folkehøjskole*), more properly translated as a "people's college," one of 102 such residential centers of adult education in Denmark, of which two are conducted in English. They represent a massive contribution by Denmark to educational policies emulated all over the world, and they can be visited this coming fall and winter, for stays of as little as one and two weeks, by "intelligent travelers" from the United States and Canada.

WITHOUT TESTS OR ADMISSIONS

A "folk high school"—the basic characteristics are easy to describe, but infinitely more complex in their application. There are no entrance requirements or admission exams, hence "folk" (meaning open to all). Students are adults, of postschool age (hence "high school," the term used sensibly, without the unfortunate meanings we Americans ascribe to the words). The schools are residential, and thus radically different from those attended on adult-education programs in other lands. Folk high school theorists believe that adults, throughout their lives, should periodically wrench themselves from familiar routines and accustomed settings to go live in a rural residential college with their fellow citizens of all income classes, in a spirit of equality. In Denmark a full 20% of the current population has passed through a folk high school at least once.

They are a massive contribution by Denmark to educational policies emulated all over the world, and can be visited for periods of as little as one or two weeks by travelers of all ages.

Elsinore, Denmark

Within the schools there are no tests, no final examinations, no certificates or degrees awarded. Learning is for the sheer love of learning. Students and teachers are equals. They are collaborators in the quest for learning. Though teachers initiate some discussions, they quickly cede to their students, and allow inquiries to develop as they naturally do. "It is not the teachers who ask their students questions," explains one folk high school principal, "but the students who interrogate their teachers."

The focus is always on discussions, oral presentations, lively seminars in which students confront their preconceptions and prejudices, their inner and often unexamined be-

liefs. A goal is to achieve democratic communication between people of widely divergent backgrounds. Another goal is to tap creative talents lying hidden or subordinated to the harsh realities of earning a living. A Danish farmer with gnarled hands checks into a folk high school near Aalborg for one month; there he applies himself to easel and canvas, determined to give vent to a hitherto-submerged artistic urge. An operating-room nurse positions herself at a desk near a window looking out onto vistas such as Ibsen might have seen and patiently begins writing a play. While pursuing a thousand different educative tasks, students rediscover their better selves, delight in their nationhood, experience maturation. They study not a single practical subject, but return instead to the liberal arts: poetry, philosophy, history, music. "What did you get out of it?" was the challenge posed to an American businessman completing a two-week stint at one of the two English-language folk high schools. "I got absolutely nothing out of it," he replied, "but I left with my spiritual batteries recharged."

Some observers credit the high Scandinavian regard for law and various forms of community cooperation—including the vaunted Scandinavian cooperative movement itself—to the 140-year-old tradition of the folk high school.

ONE IS MORE TRADITIONAL

Of the two English-language folk high schools in Denmark, one is very much in that tradition, while the other has passed light-years beyond even the radical formlessness of most schools. The "traditional" establishment is the International People's College (Den Internationale Højskole) at Elsinore, an hour by train from Copenhagen, in a Scandinavian-modern complex of low, glass-sided buildings on expansive grounds. Recognized (and subsidized) by the Danish government, it earns that support by officially offering 26 one-hour classes a week and by publishing a printed, purported curriculum of subjects ("alternative societies," "comparative religion," "life in the Third World"), but there all resemblance to the usual college ends. New subjects spring spontaneously to life, wholly unplanned subject matter grips the imagination of a particular term, while students rush to complete projects and papers that they themselves have conceived. Drawing its student body half from English-speaking Danes, half from other widely scattered nations, and employing as "faculty" (read: fellow students) a Greek sociologist, a Ugandan lawyer in exile from successive regimes, an Australian poet, an Indian playwright—some without actual academic credentials—the school shimmers with international vitality, excites even the casual visitor. Tuition, reduced by government grants, runs to all of $210 per week, including all three meals each day and lodging in single rooms.

While most students attend the International People's College for periods of four months and more in the fall/winter season, reserving short courses for the summer, the school will occasionally accept three-week and four-week students in winter, if space exists, and particularly if they start near the January 27 opening of a winter term. Address your applications to the white-bearded, cigar-smoking, prominent Danish educator Eric Hojsbro-Holm, who heads the school. He's a notorious "softie" about making a place available for American adults anxious to attend, if only for a fortnight or so. Contact **Den Internationale Højskole, Montebello Alle 1, Elsinore 3000, Denmark (phone 02/213-361).**

The competing English-language folk high school has no problem at all in accepting short-term students. The New

Den Internationale Højskole

Experimental College (NEC) will eagerly clasp you to its side at any time of the winter, for as little as one, two, or three weeks, and regardless of whether it has on-premises sleeping space still available for you; if it doesn't, it will board you at nearby, comfortable farmhouses or at modern hotels less than six miles away.

THE OTHER FAR MORE RADICAL

So radical in approach as to lack recognition and subsidy from even the permissive Danish government, NEC is still a highly regarded institution lauded by such celebrated educators as Harold Taylor and Paul Goodman. Yoko Ono and the late John Lennon are among its "graduates." Located at the crest of a gentle hill overlooking a Danish fjord at the northern tip of the Jutland peninsula, it enjoys an enthralling setting supplemented by the comforts of a sprawling Danish farmhouse capable of housing about 38 students. Because of its lack of subsidy, it charges $210 a week for those able to pay, for tuition, room, board, evening sauna, and assignment to a sleep-inducing, overstuffed leather chair in an extensive, quiet library sprinkled with U.N. publications, among its other resources.

At NEC there are no regular or recurring classes at all, not even an initial published curriculum. There are, in fact, no paid faculty members, no "teachers" at all. Every individual pursues his or her study interests, without interference or outside influence, the only element of discipline being the requirement to report, at a Saturday-morning meeting, on what they have done the preceding week. If students should feel an earlier need for reporting their results to others, or obtaining comments from them, they "announce" a class or seminar, which they then present, and which others are free to attend or not, as they see fit. They select their own educational goals, define their own education, conduct a raging inner battle, award their own "certificate of completion" to themselves. In effect, they commence a lifelong process of continually discovering what it is they wish to learn and how to go about doing so. They learn best, according to NEC, when that discovery is their own.

Throughout this process of self-realization, akin almost to a self-analysis, NEC remains almost coldly neutral. When outsiders "ask the question 'but what do you do there—what do people learn?'" writes founder Aage Rosendal-Nielsen, age 69, "we take our stand and . . . simply refuse to answer the question."

There is still social interaction. You, as a scholar/student, attend the seminars so continually announced by others. You participate in the *ting*—a Scandinavian-style town-hall frequently invoked to pose a general question to the assemblage; anyone can call a ting. At a Friday-evening "celebration meal," you dress for a special candlelight meal at which volunteers deliver speeches on their work or thoughts. You converse on walks into the heather-covered hills. And occasionally at night you relax within a sometimes-coed sauna so hot as if almost symbolically to burn away the inhibitions, unthinking patterns, communications barriers, or narrow provincial attitudes with which you entered NEC.

To attend the NEC at any time of the year, but especially in winter, and for as little as a week or two, write to **New Experimental College, Skyum Bjerge, Thy, 7752 Snedsted, Denmark (phone 07/936-234).** The school is reached from the airport of either Thisted or Aalborg, 50 or so minutes by S.A.S. jet from Copenhagen, or 6½ hours by train from Copenhagen's central station. You will never be the same again—and isn't that the hallmark of intelligent travel?

NOTE: In a late development occurring just as this 1991 edition of *The New World of Travel* was going to press, NEC appears likely to be moving to other, and possibly multiple, locations in Denmark. The Thisted site has been sold but may continue to be used for educational purposes. Letters to the above address will be forwarded to NEC's management, who have assured me they will respond with up-to-date information.

Folk high school theorists believe that adults, throughout their lives, should periodically wrench themselves from familiar routines to go live in a rural residential college.

Low-Cost Language Schools Abroad

The Careful Use of Travel to Acquire Fluency in a Foreign Tongue

"OF COURSE YOU DON'T GET OUR BUSIness! Of course we don't send you our orders! You don't speak our language!"

Such words of reproach from a normally courteous European surprised even the speaker, stirred some long-smouldering resentment, led to further indictment.

"It isn't that we're asking you to engage in technical discussions with us. But at a simple dinner party you can't carry on the most routine conversation with the lady on your left. You Americans take the cake!"

Why, among all the achievers of the world, do the overwhelming number of Americans fail to possess a second language? Or a third?

Sheer indolence is a first explanation. Torpor. Thoughtless indifference, largely stemming from unpleasant, subconscious memories of uninspiring language courses at ol' State U. Mistaken smugness ("they all speak English"). And failure to make the proper use of travel opportunities. Since languages can be acquired with surprising ease in situations where you are "immersed" in them, the mere decision to travel *solo*, unaccompanied by English-speaking spouse or companion, can yield the most remarkable results. When that vacation trip is further pursued at a European language school, in an off-season period when the tourists have fled and all you hear is one foreign language, at breakfast and in classes, on television and at the movies, in restaurants and bars, one language unendingly—the results are astonishing indeed. You speak!

This fall and winter a great many bright Americans will enhance their cultural perspectives, careers, and lives by pursuing short language courses overseas, partially funded by European governments. They will achieve fluency, or near-fluency, in one of four major European tongues—French, Spanish, German, or Italian—at schools whose glorious traditions, European settings, and remarkably low costs provide the greatest of travel pleasures in addition to instruction.

Most of the schools share common features, of which the most important is the timing of one-month classes to begin near the first of each month; schedule your applications and arrivals accordingly. Most will provide you with lodgings in the homes of private families, where you'll again be immersed in the local language. State-operated schools are usually considerably cheaper than private ones, without a loss of quality or intensity. Schools in secondary cities will send you to cheaper accommodations than those in famous ones: thus the families with whom you'll stay in Perugia will charge a third of what you'll pay in Florence.

You choose from the following:

The mere decision to travel solo, unaccompanied by English-speaking spouse or companion, can yield the most remarkable results.

FOR FRENCH

Ancestor to all the great European language schools, founded in 1883 to advance French culture and the French language to all the world, is the powerful Alliance Française. Directly funded (in part) by the French Foreign Ministry, it operates low-cost French-language schools in more than 100 nations, but its soul remains in a great gray building on Paris's Left Bank, at boulevard Raspail 101, steps away from the trendy cafés, art galleries, and way-out boutiques of the busier boulevard St. Germain.

In the large stone courtyard of the giant school, teeming with Egyptian caftans, African turbans, Canadian blue jeans, the atmosphere may be international but only one language is spoken: French. And French is spoken at every moment and exclusively throughout the day, in the very first class you attend, in the on-premises cafeteria where you take your meals, at theatrical performances and lectures in the school's auditorium. You are in class at least 3½ hours a day, then in earphone-equipped language laboratories for supplemental practice, then at near-mandatory social events—yet you pay only 520 francs ($100) a week, quite obviously subsidized, for all tuition, and house yourself in any of dozens of inexpensive Left Bank hotels clustered in this section of the Latin Quarter; there, too, you hear and speak French exclusively.

Alliance Française classes must be taken for a minimum of four weeks, starting at the beginning of each month, and application should be made at least a month in advance. For further information and forms, write: **Alliance Française de Paris, boulevard Raspail 101, 75270 Paris CEDEX 06, France.**

FOR ITALIAN

Choosing from a score of major, Italy-based Italian-language schools, the clear consensus of the experts (I've spoken with three) favors the state-operated University for Foreigners of Perugia (Università Italiana per Stranieri) and the Cultural Center for Foreigners of Florence (Centro Culturale per Stranieri). Both are in that broad region of Italy (Tuscany and Umbria) where the purest form of Italian is said to be spoken.

At Perugia, an Intensive Preparatory Course (5½ hours of classroom instruction a day, of which 2 hours are devoted to conversation and language laboratories) is priced at only 400,000 lire ($300) for a month—$75 a week. A normal beginner's course (4 hours a day), for either one, two, or three months, costs only 150,000 lire ($140) per month. Compare those rates with what you'd pay to a private language school at home!

Nonintensive courses start every two weeks, and may be taken for as little as a month. Students attend classes in a vast, baroque-style palazzo, stay with Italian families in private homes ($110 a month), and take their meals ($1.25 apiece) in one of two University of Perugia canteens. Weekends, they journey for culture and conversation to nearby Assisi, Orvieto, Spoleto.

At the more leisurely Florence school, where classroom time occupies only 2½ hours a day, but is supplemented with homework and language labs, courses run for 10 weeks, start at regular quarterly intervals, and cost 350,000 lire ($262) for the entire term, independent of room-and-board costs. If you're fixed on Florence but can't stay 10 weeks, or can't get into the official school, try the one-month, four-hour-a-day sessions of the prestigious but private (and costlier) Dante Alighieri Society ($275 a month, not including room and board).

Write for information and/or application forms to: **Università Italiana per Stranieri, Palazzo Gallenga, piazza For-**

Munich

tebraccio 4, 06100 Perugia, Italy; Centro Culturale per Stranieri, Università degli Studi, via Vittorio Emanuele 64, 50134 Florence, Italy; or Società Dante Alighieri, via Gino Capponi 4, 50121 Florence, Italy.

And for a list of additional language schools in other Italian cities, contact the **Italian Cultural Institute, 686 Park Ave., New York, NY 10021 (phone 212/879-4242)**, or one of their branch offices: in Chicago at **500 N. Michigan Ave., Suite 530, Chicago, IL 60611 (phone 312/822-9545)**; or in Los Angeles at **12400 Wilshire Blvd., Suite 310, Los Angeles, CA 90025 (phone 213/207-4737)**. Alternatively, contact **Louise Harber, Foreign Language Programs, P. O. Box 5409, Grand Central Station, New York, NY 10163 (phone 212/662-1090)**, who represents several such schools in Italy, and can also arrange for you to study Italian in the actual home of an Italian language teacher, living there as well.

FOR GERMAN

The influential world role of German commerce and culture (1 out of every 10 books on earth is published in German) lends continuing importance to German-language study. Germany's own government provides heavily subsidized instruction via its Goethe Institutes, of which more than 100 are found in 60 countries, and 13 are maintained in Germany itself. The latter are marvelously diverse, in both large cities (Munich, Berlin), university towns (Göttingen, Mannheim), and idyllic countryside locations (Prien and Murnau in rural Bavaria).

If you've the time for an eight-week course, you can make your own selection of a Goethe Institute (and city) from the 13 available. Busier people able to devote only four weeks to it are confined to three locations: Rothenburg-ob-der-

Berlin

Tauber (that perfectly preserved medieval village on the "Romantic Road" near Nuremberg, from June through January), Prien (an hour from Munich, December through March only), and Boppard (in the Valley of the Lorelei, along the Rhine, from February through May).

In each you are given 24 hours a week of classroom instruction, supplemented by at least 10 hours a week of private study, and additional sessions of conversation with German residents dragooned in for the purpose. Each institute makes all the arrangements for your room and board with a private family, and charges a total for the entire month—tuition, materials, room, and board—of 2,060 marks (approximately $1,200).

For further information and application forms, contact **Goethe House, 666 Third Ave., New York, NY 10028 (phone 212/972-3960)**. The U.S.-based branch will then forward your completed form to the Goethe Institute you've selected.

FOR SPANISH

Salamanca is the place. Emphatically. Without a second thought. It is the heart of Old Castile, where Spanish is noble and pure, untainted by the Gallego accents of the northwest, the Catalán of the east, the assorted dialects of the south.

Its monumental University of Salamanca (dating from 1226) is one of the world's oldest. Together with similar medieval academies in Padua and Bologna, it developed an early tradition for attracting international students, and that reputation—even stronger today—has a wholesome impact on language studies there. Because students are from dozens of countries scattered from Japan to Yemen, the only common language among them is Spanish. You either speak it or suffer muteness.

Though Salamanca is only 2½ hours from Madrid, it is no Madrid in cost: $14 a day is more than enough for room and all three meals at scores of guest-accepting private homes. And tuition at the private language schools is as low as the University of Salamanca's, enabling you to study one-

The brightest of travelers achieve fluency, or near-fluency, in one of the four major European languages at schools whose glorious traditions, settings, and remarkably low costs provide the greatest of travel pleasures in addition to instruction.

On the Left Bank, near the Alliance Française

on-one with your teacher, or in small groups of seven or eight, for as little as you'd pay elsewhere in a class of 20. I like, for that reason, an intensely personal school called Salminter (Escuela Salmantina de Estudios Internacionales), which charges only $300 per month for four hours of instruction, five days a week.

Dominant among the other all-year-round private schools is the Colegio de España, whose intensive four-week course starting at the beginning of every month (four hours daily, in classes limited to 15 students) costs a remarkable 32,000 pesetas ($320) a month, to which you add about $90 a week for room and board. Weekends, its students travel by short bus rides to Ávila, Segovia, and Valladolid, though the older adults among them (like me on previous trips) scarcely budge from a sidewalk café seat on the historic plaza Mayor—barred to traffic, and like a baroque drawing room, except out-of-doors. Churches and museums with the next-equivalent of Goyas, Velázquezes, and El Grecos are short steps away.

When people ask why I don't prefer the more accessible Spanish-language schools of Mexico to those of Spain, I answer diplomatically that Mexico is Mexico, but Spain is . . . well, Spain.

For applications or further information on the Salminter school, write or phone **Salminter, calle Toro 34-36, 2nd floor, 37002 Salamanca, Spain (phone 023/211-808).** For the larger Colegio, contact **Colegio de España, calle Compañía 65, 37008 Salamanca, Spain (phone 023/214-788).** For enrollment in Spanish-language courses at the equally reputable Colegio Miguel de Unamuno in Salamanca, contact the **Language Studies Enrollment Center, P.O. Box 5095, Anaheim, CA 92814 (phone 714/527-2918).**

If, on the other hand, you would prefer to pursue your language studies in Madrid, you would do well to contact the five-year-old **Domine Escuela de Español, calle José Abascal 44, 1 dcha., 28003 Madrid, Spain (phone 01/442-83-33 or 01/442-83-55),** highly recommended to me by several recent visitors there, but costlier than the Salamanca schools.

The Love Boat and the Learn Boat

Expedition Cruising Brings Education to the High Seas

YOU STEP ABOARD TO THE STRAINS OF Vivaldi and search in vain for a single casino. At night you amuse yourself not in a seagoing cabaret, but in that long-forgotten art of serious conversation with fellow passengers, over a brandy in a relaxing lounge. If a film is shown, it's of exotic tribespeople in an actual setting or of hump-backed whales off the Patagonian fjords.

And when you retire to cabin or bunk, you're first handed a half-hour's reading for the day ahead.

You've heard of the "Love Boat." Now meet the "Learn Boat." Though it may seem like a contradiction in terms, the combination of cruising and education is creating a potent new vacation lure for thousands of intellectually curious Americans.

Every week nearly a dozen small ships—and their number seems to be growing—depart from Mediterranean, Central and South American, and South Pacific ports on so-called expedition cruises staffed by naturalists, anthropologists, and cultural historians.

The major programs are four in number:

SWAN HELLENIC CRUISES

Cheapest of the lot—a remarkable value—are two-week cruises of the eastern Mediterranean aboard the 300-passenger M.T.S. *Orpheus,* operated continuously from mid-March to early December each year by the distinguished Swan Hellenic organization of the venerable P & O Lines of Britain.

Here you look in depth at the origins of the Greco-Christian-Judaic civilization, accompanied at all times by a minimum of five—often as many as six—British university lecturers, museum people, clergy, and authors. The dean of Merton College, Oxford, frequently lectures on board and ashore. So do several professors of ancient history at Cambridge, the archeology editor of *The Illustrated London News,* a former dean of Salisbury Cathedral, a director of the Imperial War Museum.

"I so treasured our afternoon at Ephesus," wrote one passenger, "because as we sat in the theater, the guest lecturer read to us from Acts 19 and instantly brought alive the story of the silversmiths who demonstrated against St. Paul in defense of their livelihood—the making of idols to the goddess Diana."

Aboard the Sea Cloud, *Salen-Linblad Cruising*

Society Expeditions

They depart from Mediterranean, South American, and South Pacific ports, staffed by naturalists, anthropologists, and cultural historians.

Travelers photographing King penguins, Society Expeditions Cruises

For such a profound combination of cultural discovery and water-borne pleasures, 16 days in length, you pay a total of $4,300 (in the bulk of cabins), which includes round-trip air fare between several U.S. East Coast cities and London ($200 more from the West Coast), and round-trip air between London and either Athens, Thessaloniki, Venice, or Dubrovnik, from which the ship departs. You're put up for two nights at a first-class hotel in London (one night before the cruise, one night after), and then cruise for a full 14 nights to the "isles of Greece," the coasts of Turkey, Yugoslavia, Bulgaria. The trip is so very all-inclusive—such a splendid example of the refreshing British insistence on moderate travel costs—that even the daily shore excursions (with their eminent lecturers) are thrown in at no extra charge.

Swan Hellenic Cruises are represented in the U.S. by **Esplanade Tours, 581 Boylston St., Boston, MA 02116 (phone 617/266-7465, or toll free 800/426-5492 outside Massachusetts).** Contact them for a fascinating catalog.

SOCIETY EXPEDITIONS

Now you're on voyages of daring (but deluxe) exploration and discovery, into the most mysterious and remote regions of the earth: the islands of Borneo, Indonesia, and the South Pacific, the Antarctic, the Amazon, and Papua New Guinea.

On a Society Expedition, the bent is distinctly naturalistic or anthropological, far less historical or archeological than the themes of Swan Hellenic. You visit untouristed shores,

Each Society Expeditions voyage is accompanied by a team of naturalists, marine biologists, and (sometimes) anthropologists.

not ports, making landfall on motorized rubber landing boats called "Zodiacs."

Thus conveyed, you go to otherwise inaccessible villages or riverbanks, where at night the beat of a shaman's drum raises appeals to ancestral spirits. You walk among upright penguins gathered by the hundreds on a shore of the Falklands. You meet and interact with Amazonian natives. To avoid "polluting" their natural or cultural life, your visits are scheduled for widely scattered dates.

The trips are realized aboard three luxuriously fitted ships: the 160-passenger *Society Adventurer*, 140-passenger *World Discoverer*, and 96-passenger *Society Explorer*, all large vessels, but with the shallow drafts, specially ice-hardened hulls, and bow-thrusters required for expedition cruising.

Each voyage is accompanied by a team of naturalists, marine biologists, and (sometimes) anthropologists. You sail with the likes of Dr. Johan Reinhard, noted anthropologist; Peter Harrison, who has won international acclaim with his books on sea birds; or Frank Todd, former senior research fellow at Hubbs Sea World Research Institute.

All three ships go circumnavigating the globe, on different itineraries, throughout the year. Passengers, essentially, book segments of the voyage—usually from two to several weeks—and are flown to and from ports at both ends of the segment. Costs average $350 a day for the bulk of cabins and trips.

For a set of mouthwatering, award-winning, large, glossy brochures, contact **Society Expeditions, 3131 Elliott Ave., Suite 700, Seattle, WA 98121 (phone 206/285-9400, or toll free 800/426-7794 outside Washington)**.

WORLD EXPLORER CRUISES

This next one's a pipsqueak of a company, as such fleets go, with only one ship, the S.S. *Universe*. But it provides a serious learning experience, in addition to considerable value: two-week cruises of Alaskan waters each summer (May to the end

Jungle river exploration in "Zodiacs"

Society Expeditions Cruises

of August, 1991) for the same price that many others charge for a one-week cruise (about $1,900 for most cabins on most sailings). How is it done? By eliminating glitzy, Las Vegas–style revues; by serving three normal meals daily, and a couple of snacks, in place of the six Lucullan orgies of eating featured on other lines; by catering to serious, unpretentious people more interested in the daily lectures by eminent natu-

ralists the S.S. *Universe* carries aboard than in expensive cocktail lounges and seagoing casinos. In short: your type of ship. Contact **World Explorer Cruises, 555 Montgomery St., San Francisco, CA 94111 (phone 415/391-9262, or toll free 800/854-3835).**

SALEN-LINDBLAD CRUISING, INC.

This final firm operates the smallest of expedition ships, some carrying as few as 36 passengers, in addition to such "larger" vessels as the 250-passenger *Adriana* (cruising the coast of West Africa). An example of the smaller variety, and its major pride, is the new *Caledonian Star,* sailing the Red Sea and the Indian Ocean on trips of 12 to 19 days apiece, for prices averaging $4,000 to $5,000 per person, not including air fare. On the larger (164 passengers) and even newer (October 1990) *Frontier Spirit*, whose captain (Heinz Aye) has been called "the Captain Cook of the 20th century," passengers will sail the waters, and visit the shores, of Antarctica in winter, the South Pacific and Great Barrier Reef in spring, and the Northwest Passage in summer, at rates of $300 to $400 per person per day. The average trips are two or three weeks in length.

Other year-round programs of Salen-Lindblad: To West Africa and New Guinea; to Indonesian waters, embarking from Djakarta on a 36-passenger luxury catamaran yacht (world-renowned divers and naturalists accompany you); to Baja California for diving; and to the Galápagos Islands (a specialty). Seasonal programs: along the Volga River of the Soviet Union, and to the North Cape of Norway. For brochures, contact **Salen-Lindblad Cruising, Inc., 133 E. 55th St., New York, NY 10022 (phone 212/751-2300, or toll free 800/223-5688).**

So what will it be, the "Love Boat" or the "Learn Boat," the libido or learning? Some say that expedition cruising allows the best of both.

The Arts-and-Crafts Vacation: A Sign of Our Times

Back to Basics, on a Vacation Devoted to Acquiring a Manual Skill

THEY RESEMBLE RESORTS, WITH THEIR OUT-door pools and tennis courts, their wooden lodge buildings and country barns, their guests in skimpy sports clothes.

But there all likeness ends. Within the barns are lathes and looms, potters' wheels and blacksmith's forge, all heavily in use throughout the day by guests in throes of creation. At a growing number of residential countryside crafts centers, more and more Americans are devoting their vacations to the mastery of a folk manufacture—the ability, say, to make a ladderback chair or an earthenware vase, a hand-bound book or a rough wool cloak.

For them, the activity is a rewarding expression of art, a satisfying connection with the past, a deeply pleasurable return to human basics (in a time of high technology), and therefore the best possible use of leisure time.

Six awesomely scenic locations are especially active in the world of arts-and-crafts vacations:

Penland School, of Penland, North Carolina, an hour's drive from Asheville, is the big one, a sprawling complex of 50 buildings on 450 acres of Blue Ridge Mountain land. A pioneer in creating new American forms of craft art, it urges its guests to let their imaginations soar, tolerates outlandish experiments, even uses a bevy of Macintosh computers to enhance students' "vision" (by devising new geometrical forms). "We blur the overlapping lines between fine and applied arts," says the school's director. The new approach is

Arrowmont School of Arts and Crafts

Within the barns are lathes and looms, potters' wheels and blacksmith's forge, all heavily in use by guests in throes of creation.

then applied to all the standard materials—wood, clay, fibers, glass, iron, metals, and paper—and results each week in countless varieties of stunning products emerging from classes taught by eminent figures. Sessions run from mid-March to mid-November; are 2, 2½, and 4 weeks in duration; are open to students of all levels of skill; and average $200 a week, plus room-and-board fees of $170 (dorms) to $360 (double with private bath) per person per week. For more information or reservations, contact **Penland School, Penland, NC 28765 (phone 704/765-2359).**

Anderson Ranch Arts Center, at Snowmass Village, Colorado, is a somewhat costlier alternative of equal fame; it's found in the Rockies, 10 miles west of Aspen, 200 miles from Denver, at an elevation of 8,200 feet. Many of the nation's most renowned craftspeople—prize winners, manufacturers of crafts, academics in the field—come here each summer (late May to mid-September) to teach one- and two-week classes in woodworking and furniture design, ceramics, and bookmaking (just those three crafts, and no others), in addi-

tion to courses in photography and painting. Some have such outstanding reputations that they attract other professionals, who make up a third of some classes otherwise composed of sheer novices—the advantages for these beginners are obvious. Interdisciplinary studies combining people from different fields are especially interesting at this high-quality gathering of leaders in crafts instruction, all in a setting of old ranch buildings refurbished to provide considerable comfort in both lodgings and labs. Tuition, including lab fees, is usually $280 for one week, $425 to $475 for two weeks, to which you add room-and-board costs of $235 to $325 a week, depending on room category. For further information, contact **Anderson Ranch Arts Center, P.O. Box 5598, Snowmass Village, CO 81615 (phone 303/923-3181).**

Arrowmont School of Arts and Crafts, in Gatlinburg, Tennessee, a mile down a scenic road from a main entrance to Great Smoky Mountains National Park, is another nationally known visual arts complex, particularly noted for its instruction in odd new techniques: patination of metal, an-

Library bulletin board, Arrowmont School

odizing of aluminum, granulation of sterling silver, combining "media" on cloth; it is also, according to one faculty member, "the wood-turning capital of America" (and teaches the standard crafts as well). One- and two-week sessions are offered in March, June, July, and August, to persons of varying skills, including those of no previous crafts experience at all. Some students, energized by creative excitement, work up to 15 hours a day in well-equipped workshops or in the 4,000-tome library of arts and crafts. On average, figure on costs of $320 to $405 a week for everything. For further information, contact **Arrowmont School of Arts and Crafts, P.O. Box 567, Gatlinburg, TN 37738 (phone 615/436-5860).**

Augusta Heritage Arts Workshops, at Davis & Elkins College in Elkins, West Virginia, at the edge of the Monongahela National Forest, differs sharply from the others in its emphasis on traditional crafts—not innovative ones—designed to preserve and transmit a proud Appalachian heritage of designs. Accordingly, classes are in such homespun subjects as stonemasonry, quiltmaking, knifemaking, blacksmithing, basketry, folk carving and whittling, bobbin lacemaking, spinning, and log construction. Nevertheless, director Doug Hill contends that some classes here—"contemporary quilt design," "create your own weaving"—are moving old-style crafts into the future. There are five separate summer weeks, early July to mid-August (you can sign up for one or more weeks); tuition averages a low $225 a week; and room and board adds only $150 a week more and is provided in college residence halls and dining rooms. Contact **Augusta Heritage Arts Workshops, c/o Davis & Elkins College, 100 Sycamore St., Elkins, WV 26241 (phone 304/636-1900, ext. 209).**

John C. Campbell Folk School, in Brasstown, North Carolina, a 365-acre campus nestled between the Smokies and the Blue Ridge Mountains, is still another of those primarily regional schools that seek to instruct in traditional, southern Appalachian crafts, and not in the unrestrained modern approach to the decorative arts. Most courses are confined to such old-world pursuits as spinning, knitting, and quilting, woodcarving and pottery, blacksmithing, enameling, chairbottoming and the like, all heavily functional—the abstract is generally eschewed. Still, the spirit here is dynamic and joyous, and courses (one and two weeks in length) are offered

Papermaking at Arrowmont

from February to mid-December, at times when other schools are closed. Most students pay around $340 a week for everything (room, board, tuition, lab fees), but that charge can rise by another $100 for certain wood-turning and metal-finishing courses. For more information, contact the **John C. Campbell Folk School, Brasstown, NC 28902 (phone 704/837-2775, or toll free 800/562-2440).**

Haystack Mountain School of Crafts, in Deer Isle, Maine, is the only northeastern location among the major crafts centers, overlooking the Atlantic Ocean from a spectacular wooded slope. A much-discussed architectural achievement, it consists of two dozen shingled structures—some lodgings, some workshops—with high-pitched roofs, all connected by wooden walkways elevated from the ground. Here, from

"We blur the overlapping lines between fine and applied arts," says a director of the summertime center.

Appalachian crafts, Augusta Heritage Arts Workshop

mid-June through mid-September only, roughly 80 students at a time, of all ages and degrees of skill, including beginners, come together in successive one-, two-, and three-week sessions to study crafts of clay, fibers, glass, metals, and wood, in studios that never close—they remain open for inspiration around the clock. High standards, intense activity; charges total (for room, board, shop fees, and tuition) $515 for one week, $940 for two weeks, $1,355 for three weeks, in accommodations ranging from open bunkhouses to twin-bedded rooms with private bath. For more information, contact **Haystack Mountain School of Crafts, Deer Isle, ME 04627 (phone 207/348-2306).**

For summertime crafts courses in Britain and Mexico, contact the **National Registration Center for Study Abroad, P.O. Box 1393, Milwaukee, WI 53201 (phone 414/278-0631)**, requesting their free catalogs entitled "Britain Art and Craft Programs" and "Craft Workshops in Mexico." And for tours of the studios of noted craftspeople all over the world, contact **Craft World Tours, Inc., 6776 Warboys Rd., Byron, NY 14422 (phone 716/548-2667).**

X

VACATIONING FOR HEALTH, AT A MEDICALLY SUPERVISED RESORT

It's Smart to Vacation at a Reducing Center

Our Own Durham, North Carolina—"Fat City"— Has Become Dieting Capital of the World

WE FELT A BIT SHEEPISH AS WE ENTERED the steakhouse, carrying our tiny scales and concealed measuring cups.

But we needn't have worried. Here in Durham, North Carolina, dieting capital of the world, people are used to the sight of overweight visitors on a "dining out experience." Every week of the year, hundreds of reducers from across the country are in attendance at four different nutrition/exercise schools in this key southern hub, with its equable climate and accessible location.

Some come because they are seriously obese and with associated illnesses; others, simply to devote their vacation time to the loss of 10 or 15 pounds of excess weight. And why not? What better use of leisure than to improve one's health?

AT THE MECCA OF FAT

I arrived in winter, flying from the February storms and sub-zero chills of the Northeast into the brisk but springlike weather of the Raleigh/Durham Airport, which is fast becoming a major destination for more and more airlines (American, USAir, others).

By the time I left six days later, I had lost seven pounds. But more important, I had gained lessons of nutrition that dozens of earlier diet books and articles had always failed to drive home. Durham's success, in my view, results from the unique quality of a residential dieting experience, in which one is wrenched from normal routines, isolated from family pressures, and forced to reflect without distraction upon a lifetime of thoughtless and destructive eating habits.

While most short-term "fat farms" and fad diets have an overwhelming record of recidivism—people quickly regain the weight they've lost—some of Durham's establishments claim a 70% record of "wins": patients, upon returning home, either maintain their weight loss or continue to drop additional pounds.

That's probably because most of the Durham centers preach the use of a balanced assortment of popular foods, close in taste and appearance to the average American diet, but prepared without harmful fats and saturated oils, and served in moderate—but filling—portions. Though most Durham programs restrict their patients to a daily intake of only 800 calories over the two- to four-week duration of their stays (a quantity of food that, to my surprise, proved entirely adequate and caused no great discomfort), their aim is to prepare the student for resumption of a far more normal, but properly chosen, 1,200- to 1,500-calorie diet upon returning home.

The lesson is taught in a hard, daily round of classroom lectures, seminars, laboratory workshops, and one-on-one consultations.

My own "rehabilitation" occurred at what may well be the largest of the Durham schools, Duke University's Diet

What better use of leisure time than to improve one's health?

At Duke University Diet and Fitness Center

and Fitness Center ("DFC"), where my fellow students, among others, ranged from a seriously overweight minister of the Gospel, to a portly legal aid lawyer, to an only slightly pudgy drama teacher from a midwestern high school. Despite the wide diversity of weights and backgrounds, there emerged a touching camaraderie among us, sensitive and supportive. Though we joked about food, we knew the depth of commitment on each one's part to break harmful eating habits.

At night we drove with one another to various Durham movies so that we could fill the hours between dinner and bed, but unaided there by a single kernel of popcorn, let alone the buttered kind. One afternoon and evening we ourselves planned and prepared a festive, calorie-conscious banquet. Accompanied by a nutritionist, we shopped at a supermarket, bought only the healthiest of ingredients, cooked the meal in one of Duke's well-equipped kitchens, and then consumed it—blackened redfish, baked potato, a Caesar salad without a single yolk, an exquisite Key lime parfait of skim milk, egg whites, and sugarless pudding—at candlelit tables.

Daytimes, we flocked to the gym for low-impact aerobics, later in the day to a heated pool for water aerobics. We walked and cycled, played hilarious games of volleyball, memorized calorie-counts in our moments of rest. One memorable night we had our restaurant experience and learned

213

how to cope with the realities outside our diet center. But mostly we went to class after class, consultation after consultation, with nutritionists, behavioral psychologists, and fitness experts.

FOUR CENTERS

All this costs considerably less than a trendy spa (the cheaper ones are usually $1,400 a week) or a Pritikin Longevity Center (the two most prominent charge $8,000 single, $6,000 per person double, for a month). At Duke's DFC, the fee even for single patients is $2,900 for two weeks, only $3,600 for four weeks, and covers everything except lodging: meals, exercise, complex medical and psychological evaluations, swimming and gym work, classroom lectures, seminars, and workshops. Most participants then stay in a $45-a-night, one-bedroom apartment in Duke Towers (a comfortable, modern, but low-rise hotel) across the road, or in a number of cheaper (as little as $450 a month) nearby motels (and one large B&B house) recommended by the DFC. For brochures and application forms, contact **Duke University Diet and Fitness Center, 804 W. Trinity Ave., Durham, NC 27701 (phone 919/684-6331).**

Space doesn't permit a lengthy discussion of Durham's several other diet centers. Structure House follows much the same approach as at the DFC, but with a far greater emphasis on behavioral and psychological counseling, and is nearly the same size. It maintains its own lodgings on its own impressive grounds and rarely permits its patients to live "off campus." Guests may stay from one to eight weeks, and total charges, including meals and lodging, run $1,200 for one week, $2,300 for two weeks, $4,200 for four weeks, to cite but a few examples. Contact **Structure House, 3017 Pickett Rd., Durham, NC 27705 (phone 919/688-7379, or toll free 800/553-0052).**

DUPAC (Duke University's Preventive Approach to Car-

Preparing a low-calorie meal at Duke's Diet and Fitness Center

Structure House facilities

*Durham's success results from the unique quality of
a residential dieting experience, in which one is wrenched
from normal routines, isolated from family pressures, and forced
to reflect without distraction upon a lifetime
of destructive eating habits.*

diology) emphasizes cardiovascular fitness, gained through diet and exercise, with weight loss simply an added dividend. It is visited, in roughly equal portions, either for preventive purposes or following an actual heart attack. And it requires a four-week stay. Four-week charges for meals, exercises, medical tests, and supervision amount to approximately $3,000; but participants provide their own lodging, which most do by staying either at the Duke Motor Lodge, the Durham Sheraton, the Brownstone Inn, the Campus Oaks Apartments, or other such lodgings. Contact **DUPAC, Finch-Yeager Bldg., Box 3022, Duke University Medical Center, Durham, NC 27710 (phone 919/681-6974).**

Rice House (the Kempner Clinic), in a modest white frame residence, prescribes a far more radical regimen than the other three (initially, simply rice and fruit), provides little behavioral counseling or fitness exercises, and is primarily for seriously ill or seriously obese persons who need to lose weight fast and massively. Although administrators of several other diet centers disagree with its approach, they always speak of it with great respect; but a stay there, in my opinion, is to be prescribed only by your physician.

Rice House is administered from the more elaborate offices of the **Kempner Clinic, Box 3099, Duke University Medical Center, Durham, NC 27710 (phone 919/286-**2243), where patients undergo an exhaustive, initial checkup ($600 to $1,200). After that, they pay about $1,100 per month for continual medical evaluations, lab tests, and those three—spartan—daily meals at the modest Rice House. The program is apparently based on the belief that modifications to the normal American diet—the goal of the other centers—are not sufficient, but rather a wholly new and healthier diet (low salt, low protein) must be substituted; and people need also to be taught to eat far less.

As for me, I'll stick with the more moderate adjustments to the typical American diet prescribed by DFC; they seem capable of being sustained after you have returned home from Durham—and isn't that the point?

Bear in mind that some dieters simply check into a low-cost motel in Durham for a week or two, without entering a center, and take their meals at the several Durham restaurants that now cater to them and cook in fat-free, low-calorie style. Other such lodgings have instituted a program of on-site low-calorie meals, and added the services of a doctor who calls at the hotel. For only $245 per person per week (sometimes less), you'll be given room and board (carefully prepared diet food) at the **Heart of Durham Hotel, 309 W. Chapel Hill St., Durham, NC 27701 (phone 919/688-8221).**

On the Trail of Eternal Youth, at a European Spa

Can 200 Million Europeans Be Wrong? Or Is There Validity to the Treatments at European Health Resorts?

As I LOWERED MY LIMBS INTO THAT UN-heated tub of carbonated water, piped in from peat bogs of the Belgian Ardennes, I felt slightly chilly, faintly embarrassed, and more than a bit dubious about the whole thing.

Yet in 20 minutes my arms and legs were as heavy as lead, my head dropped to my chest, and I could barely stagger to a nearby cot before falling asleep. Hours later I awoke vigorous and refreshed.

I was at a "baths establishment" in the Belgian city of Spa, taking a cure of the sort pursued each year by hundreds of thousands of Europeans.

American doctors think "water cures" are unscientific garbage. European doctors think American doctors, on this point, are boobs.

For centuries, physicians overseas have been sending their patients to spas chosen as carefully as specific medicines for particular ailments—this spa for arthritis, that spa for asthma, still another for neuritis or gallstones or worse. And today so many thousands of Americans are following their lead that a small but thriving segment of the travel industry—close to a dozen U.S. tour operators—has emerged to package the transatlantic health vacation as its sole activity.

The Swiss Spas

Despite the progress achieved in today's medical science, the bathing cure, a many-thousand-year-old therapy, has lost none of its significance. In Swiss health resorts one finds the quiet and relaxation one needs, far from everyday psychological stress, noise and struggle for existence. The cure in its various applications affords the physiological stimuli that are necessary to stir up the curative power within the body.

American doctors think "water cures" are unscientific garbage. European doctors think American doctors, on this point, are boobs.

BEAUTY VS. HEALTH

Why the trend to foreign spas? Let me suggest a reason or two.

Compared with a European spa, the average American spa is like an elementary school next to Harvard, like a pickup softball team next to the New York Mets. Such dazzling resorts as The Golden Door, La Costa, The Palms, and Rancho La Puerta are almost wholly concerned with diet, exercise, and massage. Their aim is cosmetic; their methods are hardly the stuff of medical journals.

European spas pursue therapy, the prevention of illness. They operate under strict medical supervision and are recognized by national health plans, which reimburse their costs (if a doctor has prescribed the treatment) to residents of all European Community countries. They screen patients and turn away those for whom their particular treatments are inappropriate. In short, they practice a form of "alternative medicine," stressing natural, health-giving substances in the earth, waters, and minerals around us, or biological substances taken from our fellow animals.

Though none of this has impressed the American medical profession, neither did acupuncture years ago, or the Lamaze method for natural childbirth, or numerous other overseas-originating practices until they were forced upon our M.D.s by popular insistence. That thousands of distinguished European doctors opt for spa therapy is unsettling at the very least, and indicates the wisdom of keeping an open mind.

Certainly no such doubts are harbored by the tour operator specialists in the health-and-fitness field. "Have you ever noticed," says Gerie Tully of Santé International, "that many Europeans are far less prone to winter colds and other common ailments than we are here? They visit a spa once a year, for two weeks or so, and renew themselves for the next 12 months." "While the statistics are difficult to verify," says Willy Maurer of Distinguished Spa Resorts, "there is simply no denying the effectiveness of spa therapy. Too many centuries have proven it, too many case studies, too many strong reactions. And remember: this is the chosen course of highly intelligent people, in mature, sophisticated nations."

Though overseas spas are frequently identified with mineral waters and hot mud—"thermal cures," "bal-

Jericho Spa Tours

neotherapy," "taking the waters"—their concerns extend to three other significant treatments: live-cell injections (heavily done in Switzerland), Procaine-based cures (Romania), and anti-psoriasis regimens (Israel, in resorts along the Dead Sea). For each there's a tour operator (or several), and each has a "package" for every purse.

LIVE-CELL THERAPY

Not the dream of Faust, or eternal youth, but at least a slowing of the aging process is the aim of this radical treatment created by the legendary Paul Niehans in the early 1930s, at his Clinic La Prairie near Montreux. Niehans, who remained active until the age of 89, administered the therapy to thousands of rather affluent persons (including Pope Pius XII, Winston Churchill, and Joan Crawford), and his clinic has since given it to a total of 50,000 seekers from around the world. Fetal cells from an unborn lamb are injected into the muscles; because the embryo has not yet developed the properties that would normally cause it to be rejected by other human tissues, it remains in the body, causing other cells to stay active and dynamic (so goes the theory).

As you'd expect, the treatment is fiendishly expensive in the main Swiss clinics: as much as $6,500 plus air fare at the ultra-deluxe Biotonus Bon Port Clinic (classic Niehans injections) overlooking Lake Geneva; $7,500 to $8,500 for six nights at Clinic Lemana ("cell-vital" injections) near Montreux; but only $4,300 for a week at the still highly reputed Baxamed Institute for Revitalization (classic Niehans) in Basel—including full board at all such centers.

Cheaper versions are had outside of Switzerland. In London, the much-publicized "youth doctor," Peter Stephans, injects a serum of cells and placenta, at fees, including examination and post-injection care, of about $1,950 (but without room and board, for which patients make independent arrangements). In Montecatini, Italy, Dr. Antonio Caporale charges $3,000 (including room and board) for injections of a carefully prepared "biological cocktail" (and also provides a nine-week supply of suppositories containing such cells for continuing treatment). And in Paris, the president of the International Association of Physicians for Age Retardation,

the English-speaking Dr. André Rouveix, charges approximately $1,350 (without room and board) for his own approaches to cell therapy (which include placenta "implants") at his heavily visited Clinique Nicolo.

For one-week packages using the services of the above three physicians, or for a stay at the Transvital Center in Switzerland, contact **Santé International, 55 Park Ave., Suite 1 NW, New York, NY 10016 (phone 212/779-8333)**; its president, Gerie Tully, a former patient of Dr. Stephans and recipient of such therapy, is a stunning blonde looking 15 years younger than her true age. For one-week packages to La Prairie, Biotonus, Lemana, or the Baxamed Institute in Switzerland, contact **Distinguished Spa Resorts** (formerly Health and Fitness Vacations), **2911 Grand Ave., Coconut Grove, FL 33133 (phone 305/445-3876, or toll free 800/FITNESS outside Florida)**.

PROCAINE-BASED THERAPIES

One of the rare chemicals used at European spas, Procaine is a derivative of Novocaine, widely reputed to dilate the blood vessels and thereby bring greater oxygen to tissues and cells from increased blood circulation. Mixed with other substances into a serum known as Gerovital H3 and Aslavital (both denied admission into the U.S. by the F.D.A.), it is administered to many thousands of elderly Europeans each year as a treatment for diseases and declines of the aged. But though the substance is found in every spa (and in unauthorized forms, highly controversial and of disputed effectiveness, in European pharmacies), the cognoscenti get their Procaine in Bucharest at the clinics and resorts founded by the late Prof. Dr. Ana Aslan, who created Gerovital and Aslavital in the mid-1950s, and remained active until her mid-80s.

The key Procaine clinics are at the modern Flora Hotel in the parks district of Bucharest, and the more traditional Otopeni Sanatorium on the outskirts of the city, about eight miles away; both provide the classic Gerovital H3 and Aslavital treatments. The key tour operator is **Litoral Travel, Inc., 124 E. 40th St., New York, NY 10016 (phone 212/986-4210)**, charging a winter-season (Novem-

---

For centuries, physicians overseas have been sending their patients to spas chosen as carefully as specific medicines for particular ailments—this spa for arthritis, that spa for asthma, still another for neuritis or gallstones or worse.

ber through March) price, at either establishment, of $1,615 for two weeks, $2,020 for three weeks, including round-trip air from New York on Pan Am or Tarom Romanian Airlines. Since full board, laboratory tests, and daily treatments are also included, the value is considerable. For comparisons, you might also request the Romanian brochures of **Health & Pleasure Tours, 165 W. 46th St., New York, NY 10036 (phone 212/586-1775, or toll free 800/443-0365 outside New York).**

ANTI-PSORIASIS TREATMENTS

Called "climatotherapy"—climate therapy—it consists of only sea and sun. But it's pursued in the briny sea and ultraviolet sun found only at the lowest point on earth, along the shores of the Dead Sea in Israel, 1,300 feet below sea level. There, in waters with the world's highest concentration of salts, whose constant evaporation produces a mist that prevents sunburning rays from reaching the earth, victims of skin-blemishing psoriasis lie safely under the burning sun and bathe for half an hour daily in the jelly-like sea.

What results is like a biblical miracle: remission of psoriasis for substantial periods in a remarkable percentage of cases. The subject of weighty medical studies for more than 20 years, the benefits of these Israeli spas are today confirmed by exact clinical data of which other therapies can only dream; many physicians are no longer skeptical—and one weeps for psoriasis sufferers who are unaware of the healing Dead Sea.

Along the Dead Sea, the specialist spas for psoriasis are the Moriah Gardens (not to be confused with the Moriah Dead Sea Spa), Galei Zohar, the Hotel Lot, and Ein Bokek. The major U.S. tour operator for them is **Jericho Spa Tours Company, 555 Fifth Ave., New York, NY 10017 (phone 212/286-9291, or toll free 800/538-8383 outside New York State).** And the rates are unusually moderate by spa standards: in a seven-month, split off-season (June through August and November through February) prices average $1,100 to $1,400 for two weeks (the suggested bare minimum), $1,900 to $2,600 for four weeks (the recommended stay), including two meals a day and all treatment, but with air fare extra. Summer is the best time for treatment.

WATER CURES

And finally you have the classic treatments—"carbogaseous baths," "fango mud," "vapor inhalations," underwater massage, saunas, "Kneipp foot baths," "thalassotherapy," "algae baths," and repeated draughts of mineral water—as practiced with exquisite deliberation (different treatments, different spas, for different ailments) at quite literally hundreds of spas in Italy, Austria, Yugoslavia, France, Belgium, Germany, and Switzerland. While your average celebrated U.S. spa charges $1,800 a week and up (to as much as $3,000 a week at The Golden Door) for its "beauty care" and "weight loss," a European spa can be had for as little as $600 a week in the Yugoslavian locations, for an average of $1,200 a week (depending on spa) in Italy (where Abano, Montecatini, and Ischia are the key names), and for $1,250 and up per winter week in Switzerland. The properties and programs are all lavishly described in glossy catalogs mailed free by Santé International and Distinguished Spa Resorts from the addresses set forth for them above.

THE ULTIMATE QUESTION

Is there anything to it? I tend to think there is; but whether or not, it is surely the worst smugness, a form of jingoism, to dismiss the claims of European spas out-of-hand and without investigation, as so many do.

Shakespeare warned that "there are more things in heaven and earth, Horatio, than are dreamt of in your philosophy." Perhaps there is more to medicine than the chemical-based prescriptions of U.S. doctors.

Spa on the Dead Sea, Jericho Spa Tours

Vacationing at a Holistic Health Resort

A New Variety of Spa, Not for Weight Reduction, Not for Stress Reduction, But for "Wellness"

"MACHINES RECEIVE PREVENTIVE MAIN-tenance; why not people? Why should we wait until illness strikes us down before we attend to our health?"

With those words, a wise old doctor once explained to me why he had turned at the end of his career to the practice of "holistic" medicine. An eminently sensible approach to life, with which almost no one can disagree, holistic methods of strengthening the body to fend off future illness have attracted the attention of millions of Americans, and created a thriving vacation industry of "holistic health farms" and "holistic health resorts."

None of these institutions, to my knowledge, disavows traditional approaches to medicine. "Holistic physicians" will readily prescribe an antibiotic for infection, or even perform surgery if it is needed.

But the same physicians believe in supplementing the standard therapies with alternative ones: better nutrition, exercise, stress reduction, and relaxation. People, they claim, should actively pursue "wellness" before they become sick, a process—essentially—of self-education and modifying life-styles. The decision to vacation at a "wellness spa"—holistic centers where guests receive "preventive health workups" and seek to adapt to a healthier mode—is an obvious first step.

HEARTWOOD INSTITUTE

On 200 acres in the mountains of northern California, five hours by car north of San Francisco, this is the classic "holistic retreat," and astonishingly cheap: it charges $420 a week in single rooms, $350 per person in doubles, $280 on a campsite, including three vegetarian meals a day and use of sauna, hot tub, and pool. Accommodations are mainly bunk-houses with small, simple rooms, not far from a "community

Heartwood Institute

222

X-country skiing on Crescent Lake

The yurt covered in snow, Northern Pines

center" and restaurant in a picturesque log lodge with outside dining deck. When guests arrive to pursue a one-week or two-week "wellness retreat," trained counselors aid them to choose from a variety of therapies in massage and bodywork, nutrition and exercise, at nominal extra costs. The institute's credo? That illness results from imbalances in the body's normal state; that balance can be restored, as it often is in Asian medicine, by alternative therapies such as acupuncture or Ayurveda, lifestyle changes, modified nutrition, herbal preparations, homeopathy, still other treatments. Throughout the year, more intensive workshops are then scheduled at Heartwood in the full range of therapies under study by holistic practitioners: massage and yoga, "bodywork" and hypnotherapy, "energy balancing" and hydrotherapy—all,

It seems a sensible approach to life, with which almost no one can disagree.

of course, for tuition charges (though fairly reasonable ones) not imposed upon people participating in a simple retreat. For information, contact **Heartwood Institute, 220 Harmony Lane, Garberville, CA 95440 (phone 707/923-2021 or 707/923-3182).**

Rates at other "holistic resorts" vary widely from those of Heartwood, and from each other.

NORTHERN PINES HEALTH RESORT

For instance, in the lake district of southern Maine near Portland, about 2½ hours by car from Boston, Northern Pines Health Resort charges $506 to $675 per person for a full week, for which it places you in lakefront log cabins or rustic country cottages on 80 acres of pine forests and rolling hills. Although some guests here simply lie in a hammock and read for that week, most pursue an active daily schedule of exercises, hikes, canoeing, sailing, swimming, and classes in

aerobics, yoga, nutrition, stress management, weight control, shoulder massage, and "morning stretch." Meals, served in a large, lakeside lodge, are vegetarian, but supplemented twice a week with fish and eggs; and rates throughout the year, including all three such meals, classes, hot tub, sauna, and use of boating equipment, are $506 per person per week in a lakeside cabin, $563 in a better hillside or "yurt" lodging, $675 in a cedar or pine cottage. Add 25% for stays in July and August; subtract around 25% in winter. For information, contact **Northern Pines Health Resort, Rte. 85 (R.R. 1, Box 279), Raymond, ME 04071 (phone 207/655-7624).**

MURRIETA HOT SPRINGS RESORT

Ninety minutes south of Los Angeles, on 47 acres of rolling hills dotted with palm trees, this is a rather upscale version of the more typical health farm, with Spanish-style buildings, tiled walks, and elaborately manicured grounds. Yet rates

Tai Chi Class

"Country Roads Hike," Bluegrass Spa

At poolside, Bluegrass Spa

are rather reasonable by health-spa standards: $795 per person per week in a double room ($945 single), including all three vegetarian meals daily, spa mineral baths with "energizing bodywrap," exercise program, mud bath, and full use of all hot-springs pools and saunas. Accommodations are in cozy cottages or terraced lodgings. Throughout the day, courses in stress management, exercise, diet, bodywork, "awareness," and health information are presented to guests free of charge. For information, contact **Murrieta Hot Springs Resort, 28779 Via Las Flores, Murrieta, CA 92362** **(phone 714/677-9661, or toll free 800/322-4542 outside California).**

HARBIN HOT SPRINGS

On 1,100 wooded acres in a valley of northern California, 2½ hours by car from San Francisco, Harbin Hot Springs is a simpler (rooms without private bath), and far less expensive West Coast alternative to Murrieta; guests enjoy the very same species of natural, warm mineral-water pools (one of

Holistic physicians believe that people should actively pursue "wellness" before they become sick, a process—essentially—of self-education and modifying lifestyles.

Bluegrass Spa

112° Fahrenheit, open all night and all year), but stay in dormitories, unpretentious private lodgings, or even on campsites. In addition to soaking (without speaking, a requirement) in the celebrated hot springs, hiking, sunbathing, and enjoying—according to one staff member—a "meditative atmosphere," guests sign up for one of numerous courses in exotic massage—Swedish, shiatsu, acupressure, watsu (water shiatsu)—at rates as low as $15 per bout of instruction. Room rates per person are $70 a week on campsites, $115 a week in dorms, $175 a week in rooms ($100 for the second person), to which you add $12 a day for two vegetarian meals. For information, contact **Harbin Hot Springs, P.O. Box 82, Middletown, CA 95461 (phone 707/987-2477 or 707/987-0379).**

BLUEGRASS SPA

In the rolling horse country of central Kentucky a few miles north of Lexington, Bluegrass Spa is an antebellum mansion with large white columns, set on expansive lawns amid clusters of guesthouses and spacious exercise facilities. Rooms are quite comfortable, almost elegant. Your day begins with yoga; goes on to include fitness and nutrition lectures, tai-chi exercises, walks and jogging, swimming and saunas, country-road biking and spa aerobics; and ends with optional massage and Jacuzzi bathing. Meals are mainly vegetarian, but often with chicken or fish, and always low in fat, salt, and sugar. High-season rates are $1,677 per person for a seven-night week, in double-occupancy rooms (but only $1,474 per person in shared triples or quads, $1,892 in singles), including meals, classes, and use of all fitness facilities, as well as complimentary transportation to and from Lexington Airport. For information, contact **Bluegrass Spa, 901 Galloway Rd., Stamping Ground, KY 40379 (phone 502/535-6261).**

For reasons of space, I have obviously compressed the theories of "holistic health" into almost absurdly simple form. For a more complete exposition, request a program guide of the Heartwood Institute described above, enclosing $2 to cover costs.

Vacations at Pritikin Centers Are High Priced But Healthy

Bland Meals and Mild Exercise at Miami Beach and Santa Monica

THE GOOD NEWS IS THAT THE APPROACH seems to work, restoring your health, increasing your longevity.

The bad news is that it's rather expensive: an average of $3,900 for two weeks, $6,500 for a month, even when two people are taking the "cure" together.

Yet Americans continue to throng the Pritikin diet centers, devoting their two- to four-week vacations to a disciplined regimen of bland meals and mild exercise. And a major expansion of the Pritikin facilities—as planned by the 38-year-old son of the company's founder, the late Nathan Pritikin—will soon bring Pritikin-style vacations or treatments into the geographical reach of more and more people.

Residential Pritikin centers are currently in operation in Santa Monica, California, and Miami Beach, Florida. Each advances the message first proclaimed by Pritikin in 1974: that most of the major degenerative diseases of our time—heart disease, diabetes, atherosclerosis—are largely caused by excessively high blood-fat levels, and that their prevention and cure could be brought about by reducing those levels through diet and exercise.

Sounds commonplace now, doesn't it? But it was revolutionary then. Heart-disease patients were being routinely treated by drugs and surgery, told to avoid exercise, and then sent back to eating the standard American diet of meat, eggs, and dairy products.

Instead, Pritikin advocated a diet that consisted of only 10% fat and only 15% protein, but a full 75% complex carbohydrates, the last mainly from fruits, vegetables, and whole grains. He counseled an avoidance of all extra fats and oils (other than those naturally in grains and lean meats), all simple sugars (honey and molasses as well as sugar), all salt, coffee, and tea, and all foods rich in cholesterol (eggs, shellfish, animal organs and skin).

And each Pritikin patient or vacationer, regardless of age, was to engage in daily exercise, mainly walking.

On such a program, he maintained, the middle age of life could be stretched to cover the years between 40 and 80, rather than those from 40 to 60. Old age would begin at 80, not at 55 or 60.

Pritikin staff will cite all sorts of statistics—I won't repeat them here—to bolster their claims that the treatment has had remarkable results for the 50,000-odd people who have thus far passed through the three residential centers. What is unarguable is that strong word-of-mouth comment has kept both facilities busy and well occupied, despite the founder's death from leukemia in 1985.

PROGRAMS, COSTS, AND MEALS

Each center offers programs for 13 and 26 days. The shorter course is for those overweight or interested in preventing future illness or reducing stress, or who have hypertension or mild diabetes (currently treated by oral medication). The

Each of the centers advances the claim that most degenerative diseases are caused by excessively high blood-fat levels.

Exercise three times a day

The meals are reportedly much better than in the early years of Pritikin; they are largely vegetarian but with some fish or chicken served several times a week.

second program, while available to anyone, is primarily designed for those suffering from the more serious health problems of heart disease, insulin-demanding diabetes, obesity, gout, and claudication.

No matter which program you select, you're busy from early morning till early evening, taking pre-breakfast walks along the beach or on country lanes, exercising three times a day, attending cooking classes, lectures, or supermarket expeditions.

Personalized medical supervision is a major feature of the program. Depending on their health needs, guests are assigned to a specialist in either cardiology or internal medicine (Pritikin physicians are all Pritikin enthusiasts and live the programs themselves).

As for the meals, they are—reportedly—much better than in the early years of Pritikin. Although no extra fat is added to foods, and no salt, sugar, or caffeine is permitted,

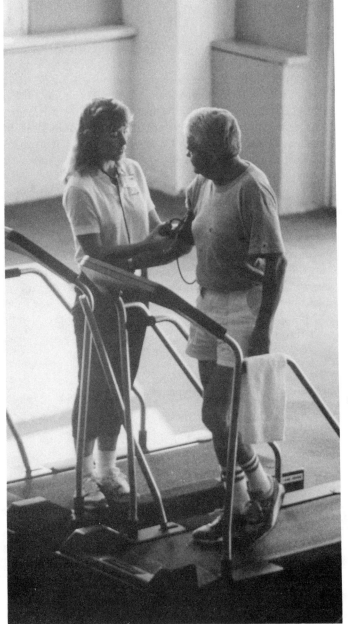

Checking blood pressure, Pritikin

chefs still manage to turn out tasty fare. Meals are largely vegetarian, but with some fish or chicken served several times a week. You eat five times a day, so you never get hungry. Snacks might consist of vegetables and soup, Pritikin "chips" and salsa, fresh fruits. Dishes include "enchilada pie," potato pancakes, Moroccan orange-and-carrot salad, sweet-and-sour cabbage, ratatouille, paella, vegetable pot pie, and yogurt-marinated chicken. Desserts might be carrot cake or strawberries Romanoff.

For all this, you pay a substantial price if you are traveling alone, but considerably less on a per-person basis if you are with a spouse or companion. For a 13-day session, in-

Each Pritikin patient or vacationer is busy from morning till early evening, taking pre-breakfast walks, exercising three times a day, attending cooking classes and lectures.

cluding medical costs, the fees average $5,500 or so for one person, but only $7,900, at most, for two. For a 26-day session, fees are as much as $8,900 for one person, but only $13,000 for two. Major-medical plans may cover that portion of the cost that is attributed to medical attention. And some guests have been known to treat the entire expense as tax deductible, provided they have been directed to take the program by their doctor (consult your tax adviser about IRS regulations).

Is it necessary for the Pritikin experience to be so very expensive? Physicians with whom I've spoken think it well worth the price and not out of line with costs in the more exclusive spas (not to mention alternative costs of surgery, hospitalization, time lost from work).

The other, lower-cost alternative is a planned new chain of health-and-fitness clubs for people over 40, embodying the Pritikin principles. Three are currently in operation in Los Angeles and Houston, with several more due to open soon. These, in essence, are "outpatient" facilities, with Pritikin-style restaurants on the premises and a 30-hour program of instruction presented three nights a week for four weeks, all at the moderate charge of $300 to $400.

VACATIONING AT THE RESIDENTIAL FACILITIES

Meanwhile the better course—if you can afford it—is to spend a two-week or four-week vacation at an actual Pritikin residential facility. The **Pritikin Longevity Center, 1910 Ocean Front Walk, Santa Monica, CA 90405 (phone toll free 800/421-9911, 800/421-0981 in California)**, is the largest (150 guests) and the mother center (some would call it the "mother church"). It enjoys a superb beachfront location facing 10 miles of boardwalk, on which, conceivably, you might walk from Malibu to Palos Verdes.

The somewhat similar **Pritikin Longevity Center, 5875 Collins Ave., Miami Beach, FL 33140 (phone 305/866-2237, or toll free 800/327-4914 outside Florida)**, is housed in a small resort hotel on an ocean beach that is swimmable year round. A recent expansion of facilities permits the center to accommodate up to 132 guests at a time. There's a large beachfront pool, and an oceanfront gym.

At both centers, visitors are welcome to take a free tour. At Miami Beach, says the general director, you may even be invited to take a meal with guests.

THE NEW WORLD OF TRAVEL 1992

The lifeblood of the Arthur Frommer travel guides is the correspondence received from readers, commenting on the establishments recommended in the texts and recommending new establishments. Each such letter is carefully studied, and when a particular lead seems promising, it is followed up and personally checked.

It is hoped that *The New World of Travel* will receive similar assistance from its readers. A yearly publication, issued near the start of each year, *The New World* will constantly grow. And since much of its content relates to organizations that lack the means to market themselves properly, or come to the attention of a travel journalist, your help is invaluable in alerting me to the organizations—hospitality exchanges, alternative resorts, new travel clubs, and the like—that you have discovered.

If you become aware of a new travel organization, program, or development that deserves to be described in our next edition, *The New World of Travel 1992*, won't you please let me know about it? Send your letters to Arthur Frommer, *The New World of Travel*, c/o Prentice Hall Press, Travel Division, 15 Columbus Circle, New York, NY 10023. All letters will be acknowledged, and all are warmly appreciated, in advance, by the author.

Vacationing with the Seventh-Day Adventists

A Less Costly Form of Pritikin-like Treatments for Mature Americans

YOU ARE 55 AND YOU FEEL YOURSELF—faintly but perceptibly—slowing down. You are overweight and high in cholesterol. You are anxious and stressed. You have heard of the Pritikin Centers, where health can supposedly be restored, but you can't afford the tab (as much as $7,000 for a month).

So what do you do?

You call the Seventh-Day Adventists (and I am perfectly serious). For prices averaging $3,000 a month they offer residential health retreats all across the U.S.A., where diet, exercise, and atmosphere are akin to those maintained in the costly health resorts, but at less than half the price.

Stress reduction

The Adventists have long been known for their interest in health and nutrition, and for the consequent longevity of their lives. Studies in California have revealed a much lower incidence of heart attacks and strokes among them, as compared with other population groups in the state. Early in the century an Adventist named Kellogg began producing strange but effective breakfast foods called "wheat flakes" and "corn flakes," while his brother in the same town founded the famous Battle Creek (Michigan) Sanitorium. Today Adventists operate large and prestigious hospitals—notably, Loma Linda in California and Castle Medical Center in Hawaii—from which smaller, no-frills, nonprofit, inexpensive health retreats have been spun off.

DIET AND EXERCISE, NOT RELIGION

At each such center the policy is determinedly vegetarian. Adventists are normally advised (but not required) to consume a purely "Vegan" diet of fruits, vegetables, legumes, and for those able to handle them, modest amounts of such high-fat foods as nuts, avocados, and olives. Scarcely any "free fats"—i.e., those not found in whole foods—are used.

Which means no butter or marmalade on rolls, no oils in salad dressings, and foods sautéed in water rather than oil (the Adventists and the Pritikin people are in agreement on the virtual elimination of "free fats"). Complex carbohydrates are the basis of their diet (again in agreement with Pritikin; Pritikin, however, does allow small amounts of poultry, fish, and dairy products).

For all its spartan features, Adventist food can be surprisingly tasty. At my own recent lunch in the Adventist-run Living Springs of Putnam Valley, New York, I took repeated helpings from a buffet of salad, steamed vegetables, and cashew chow mein.

Careful attention to diet is combined, at the centers, with exercise in the open air, sunbathing, a mammoth intake of water (six to eight glasses a day), hydrotherapy treatments (saunas, alternate hot and cold showers), and temperance: the total avoidance of coffee, alcohol, tobacco, and irritating spices.

Those strictures are translated into programs that begin early in the morning with brisk outdoor walking, followed by a hearty breakfast, daily lectures by physicians, hydrotherapy, classes on remedies utilizing water, vegetarian cooking classes, more walking, a large meal at lunch, educational seminars, more walking or exercising, a light evening meal, then perhaps a slide show on some aspect of health.

"Hands-on" at Hartland

What does not take place is religious proselytizing. "People of all persuasions and no persuasion come here," says Leatha Mellow of the center known as the Weimar Institute, in California. "We've had Catholic priests, Jews, Christians, and atheists. We do maintain a spiritual emphasis, but it is nondenominational and nonsectarian."

In health matters, by contrast, the centers are fierce advocates. Like Pritikin, they believe a proper diet can avoid the major degenerative diseases of our time—heart disease, diabetes, atherosclerosis—and pursue their cures intensively in two- to four-week programs at the various locations.

THE EIGHT MAJOR CENTERS

Living Springs Lifestyle Center, 136 Bryant Pond Rd., Putnam Valley, NY 10579 (phone 914/526-2800, or toll free 800/729-9355): In the foothills of the Berkshire Mountains, about an hour's drive from New York City, it is a large but homey building overlooking an 18-acre pond with swans. Guests occupy attractive private and semiprivate rooms, all with private bath, for which they pay weekly year-round rates (Memorial Day through Labor Day) of $599 in a semiprivate room, $788 in a private room, $1,072 for two people

What does not take place is religious proselytizing.

staying together, including all three meals daily and all treatments.

Hartland Institute of Health and Education, P.O. Box 1, Rapidan, VA 22733 (phone 703/672-3100, or toll free 800/763-9355): On over 700 acres of gently rolling hills, an hour from the Blue Ridge Mountains and two hours from Washington, D.C. When its current expansion program is completed by the spring of 1991 it will house up to 30 guests in two lodges. Programs are 25 days long, and cost $3,750 for one "patient," $2,750 for a companion patient, $1,250 for a companion not undergoing treatment. Says head nurse Linda Ball: "We believe services like these should be made available to everyone, and not just those with a lot of money. Some people call and say, 'I'll pay any price.' Others still say, 'I can't afford it.'"

Wildwood Lifestyle Center and Hospital, Wildwood, GA 30757 (phone 404/820-1493, or toll free 800/634-9355): A modern facility on 500 acres of trails and hills, at an elevation of 700 feet, between Mount Raccoon and Mount Lookout. Rooms are attractive, and each has its own sunny patio. On a 24-day program, rates are $3,495 in a semiprivate room, $4,095 for a private room with bath, $3,927 for a private room with shared bath. On the 17-day program, rates in a semiprivate room are only $2,895; a private room with bath is $3,320, $3,201 without bath.

Uchee Pines Health Conditioning Center, Rte. 1, Box 440, Seale, AL 36875 (phone 205/855-4764): In a climate that is generally warm the year round (though rainy in winter), this is a country house set in 250 wooded acres, with lovely gardens and trails. An 18-day program is offered, at charges of $2,595 for the first "patient," $2,395 for a patient/companion. Occasionally guests will be accepted for shorter programs, and fees will then be prorated.

Poland Spring Health Institute, RFD 1, Box 4300, Summit Spring Road, Poland Spring, ME 04274 (phone 207/998-2894): Smallest of the retreats (10 guests only), but with a broad variety of activities, including cross-country skiing in winter. It is an old New England farmhouse with attached barn housing the guests and various hydrotherapy facilities. Down the road is a clinic with medical offices. Rates are $745 a week for semiprivate rooms, $950 a week for private rooms; but most rooms share a bath. The average stay is two weeks. And, oh yes, this is the same Poland Spring of the world-famous mineral waters; the institute has its own well, and guests therefore drink the same water as in the bottled product.

Weimar Institute, P.O. Box 486, Weimar, CA 95736 (phone 916/637-4111, or toll free 800/525-9191): It enjoys the most idyllic of Adventist retreat locations—on some 450 acres in the foothills of the Sierras, about 50 miles northeast of Sacramento, off Interstate 80—but is atypically expensive: $4,275 for the first "patient" on a 19-day program, $3,575 for that patient's companion. Guests do a great deal of walk-

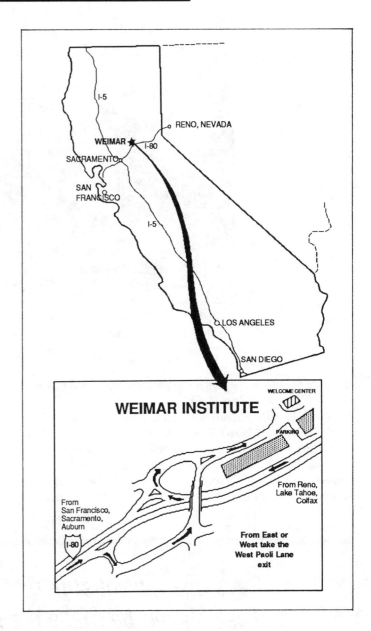

ing through hundreds of acres of hiking trails, and occupy rooms that are all supplied with private bath.

Black Hills Health and Education Center, P.O. Box 19, Hermosa, SD 57744 (phone 605/255-4101 or 605/255-4687): In the Black Hills of South Dakota, in a scenic valley surrounded by rimrock cliffs, this is a "change-your-lifestyle" retreat whose diet is free from refined products and cholesterol, low in fat and salt. Daily exercise is stressed, including visits to a large, natural indoor pool fed by hot springs; physical examinations and numerous blood-chemistry tests are administered by a medical doctor. The emphasis is on a 25-day program costing $2,200 for a single room (including meals and all else), $1,600 per person dou-

Total Health Foundation

ble, only $1,400 per person if you park your own motorhome on one of the center's camping sites.

Total Health Foundation, P.O. Box 5, Yakima, WA 98907 (phone 509/965-2555): An 18-room country mansion in fruit orchards of the Yakima Valley, 10 miles from Yakima; it's operated by a number of physicians who first subject patients to a complete medical evaluation and then supervise a program of meals made up solely of natural foods, and considerable physical therapy. For a 10-day program the charge is $1,995 in a private room, $3,490 for a 19-day program, $4,095 for a 25-day program. A companion participating in the program pays 20% less. Some (but not all) insurance programs cover a part of the treatment at T.H.F.

Write for literature, then call. Staff members at all eight centers are, in my experience, gentle, caring people.

Says one Adventist nurse: "We believe services like these should be made available to everyone, and not just those with a lot of money."

Vacationing, for a Change, at a Whole-Grain Resort

At Macrobiotic Centers Clustered on Both Coasts, the Cuisine Is as Soothing as the Setting

JUST AS YOU OCCASIONALLY NEED A VACAtion (which is presumably why you are reading this book), so does your stomach occasionally need a vacation. Both can achieve that restful interlude at a macrobiotic center, of which our nation has a dozen. Without necessarily subscribing to the tenets of macrobiotics—a diet of cooked whole grains and vegetables—you can turn for a time to a gentler form of life, lacking in stress, free of fats, and full of companionship among the most amiable people.

Many thousands of Americans make an exclusive use of the macrobiotic cuisine, which they often first encounter and learn to prepare at residential centers clustered on the two coasts.

Contrary to a popular misconception, macrobiotics has no necessary connection to Zen, Zen Buddhism, or even Buddhism, although a great many of the last persuasion adhere to the theory. It is a purely secular approach to nutrition based on the teachings of the late George Ohsawa, born in Japan, who believed in essence that people should live in harmony with what he perceived as natural cycles and elements of the physical universe. Thus they should eat only those foods that had grown for centuries in the places where those people lived. They should, in the United States, emphasize grains, the staff of life, supplemented by vegetables, beans, vegetarian soups—on occasion a bit of fish.

Translating those ingredients into tasty meals takes skill.

Accordingly, all macrobiotic centers include cooking courses in their schedules, taught to all guests. Yet even in the hands of a gourmet cook, the subtly flavored macrobiotic dishes are bland compared with the steak and potatoes of the average American diet, and thus offer a radical change of pace—a soothing one—to the average American.

You pursue that relaxing course in centers operated by disciples of Ohsawa, of whom Japanese-born Michio Kushi on the East Coast and Herman Aihara on the West Coast are certainly the most prominent. Out of a dozen possible choices, you may want to request schedules and literature from:

THE THREE MAIN CENTERS

Vega Study Center, of Oroville, California: Ninety minutes north of Sacramento, in an old and sleepy town of Victorian homes and later shops and stores of the 1920s, is this large, residential, teaching base of Herman and Cornellia Aihara. Their courses (including "hands-on" cooking classes) run for one to two weeks throughout the year, and cost $545 for one week, $1,095 for two weeks, with full board. Guests live in shared rooms with pine beds and wonderfully firm futon mattresses; wake at 7 A.M. for meditation, Eastern-style exercises, and tea; attend lectures delivered by the charming Aihara himself; and eat classic macrobiotic meals often pre-

Just as you occasionally need a vacation, so does your stomach occasionally need a vacation.

235

Herman and Cornellia Aihara, Vega Study Center

building is an old mansion with spiraling wooden staircases and stone fireplaces for cool evenings. It is an appropriate setting for the calm and gentle lectures of Michio Kushi and his wife, Aveline. Seven-day residential seminars on emotional harmony and healthy food preparation cost approximately $800 for a shared room and all meals. A unique opportunity to study with the "master" (although sometimes he's not in attendance; check first). Write or phone the **Kushi Foundation, Berkshire Center Program, P.O. Box 7, Becket, MA 01223 (phone 413/623-5742)**.

Lady Diane's, on the island of Jamaica: A lavishly decorated macrobiotic hotel near the airport of Montego Bay, with superb views of the bay. There's no classroom instruction, but an imaginative macrobiotic cuisine enhanced with Jamaican touches for holiday purposes: breakfast might consist of hot grits, turnips, miso soup, and whole-wheat biscuits. Rates for room and full board at the charming seafront resort, for a full seven-night week, are $679 per person (double occupancy), and include shiatsu massage. Contact **Lady Diane's, 5 Kent Ave., Montego Bay, Jamaica (phone 809/952-4415)**.

pared by Cornellia. Contact **Vega Study Center, 1511 Robinson St., Oroville, CA 95965 (phone 916/533-7702)**, for an interesting catalog.

The Kushi Foundation, in the Berkshires of western Massachusetts: Placid and still, on 600 mountain acres, its main

THE SUMMER CAMPS

And then there are the macrobiotic summer camps, for a cheap, refreshing, and restorative holiday in the open air. Try the 200-guest International Macrobiotic Institute Summer

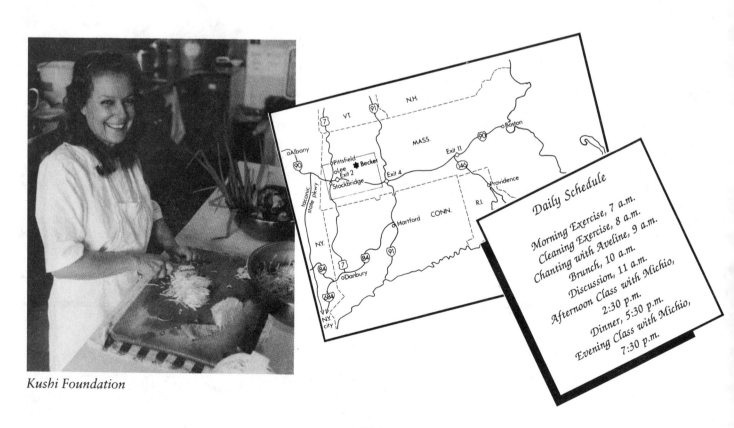

Kushi Foundation

Daily Schedule

Morning Exercise, 7 a.m.
Cleaning Exercise, 8 a.m.
Chanting with Aveline, 9 a.m.
Brunch, 10 a.m.
Discussion, 11 a.m.
Afternoon Class with Michio, 2:30 p.m.
Dinner, 5:30 p.m.
Evening Class with Michio, 7:30 p.m.

Camp, always in July, in a comfortable hotel in the Swiss Alps, near Kiental (approximately $500 per person for the week)—contact its U.S. agent: **Macrobiotic Center of Baltimore, P.O. Box 445, Timonium, MD 21093 (phone 301/628-0880)**; the Macrobiotic Summer Conference, in August at Simon's Rock of Bard College in the Berkshires of Massachusetts near Great Barrington ($600 to $900 per person for the week, depending on the accommodations)—contact the **Kushi Foundation, Macrobiotic Summer Conference, P.O. Box 7, Becket, MA 01223 (phone 413/623-5742)**; the Mid-Atlantic Summer Camp, usually held for a week in mid-June, in the Pocono Mountains of Pennsylvania ($495 for all meals and dorm accommodations in rustic cabins)—contact **Macrobiotic Center of Baltimore, P.O. Box 445, Timonium, MD 21093 (phone 301/628-0880)**.

I have, in my description of macrobiotics at the beginning of this chapter, compressed a complex subject into a simplistic and inadequate paragraph. I have failed, in particular, to explore the emphasis of the theory on the need to properly balance the expansive (*yin*) and contractive (*yang*) varieties of food, and their counterparts in other areas, or the claims that a macrobiotic way of life can prevent or cure serious illness.

All this you'll hear—and more—in one of the most restful interludes of your life, as you grant time off to your overworked and suffering stomach.

Macrobiotics is the theory that people should live in harmony with the natural cycles and elements of the physical universe.

America's Cheapest High-Quality Spas

Vacations for Health and Reducing, at Less Than $1,100 a Week

WHY PAY $3,000 A WEEK WHEN ALL YOU receive at lunch are a carrot-raisin salad and a tiny baked apple? When the "program" consists of your own physical exertions in jogging, bending, stretching, and leaping? When "optional entertainment" consists of a five-mile hike along mountain trails that are free of charge to all?

Too many Americans have been discouraged from booking a spa vacation by the frightening rates of the famous resorts—the only ones of which you hear. At the elegant Golden Door and Canyon Ranch, at Maine Chance and Doral's Saturnia, prices do indeed often start at $2,800 to $3,000 for a week and quickly climb from there. Even at the several well-known "budget" versions of the glitzy names (Rancho La Puerta, Heartwood), weekly rates average $1,400 to $1,700, to which a hefty air fare need be added.

Unadvertised, and largely unknown outside their immediate areas, are at least 30 locally marketed spas in every region of the nation that, in my opinion, will provide you with the very same reductions of weight and stress, the very same toning of muscles and spirit, for under $1,100 a week, and often for considerably less than that.

They deserve to be better known. For as modest as they may look, these spas provide the very same well-planned meals totaling 900 to 1,200 calories per day, the same hyperactive regimen of group aerobics and individual workouts, the same walks in the open country air, the same instruction in proper nutrition and behavior modification.

The best establishments I've found are listed below. Unless otherwise noted, the rates cited are for a full seven-day stay in establishments with active programs of exercise and instruction, and serving nothing other than low-calorie meals.

Jimmy LeSage's New Life Spa, in Stratton Mountain, Vermont, 3½ hours by car from Boston, 4½ hours from New York City, charges $990 per person double in spring, $1,090 in summer, and $100 more for a single room. It has somewhat the reputation of a marine boot camp, with its seemingly endless regimen that begins at 7:30 A.M., and includes such frolics as a five- to seven-mile morning hike, aerobics and "aquarobics," lower-body workouts, upper-body workouts, and afternoon mountain walks (straight up and down), all coming blessedly to an end at 5 P.M. with a final half hour of easy-motion yoga. Calorie intake is limited to 800 to 1,000 per day; it is claimed that guests lose seven to eight pounds a week for men and four to five pounds for women. This resort has been highly regarded for 14 years,

---

They provide the very same well-planned meals totaling 900 to 1,200 calories per day, the same hyperactive regimen, the same workouts, walks, and instruction.

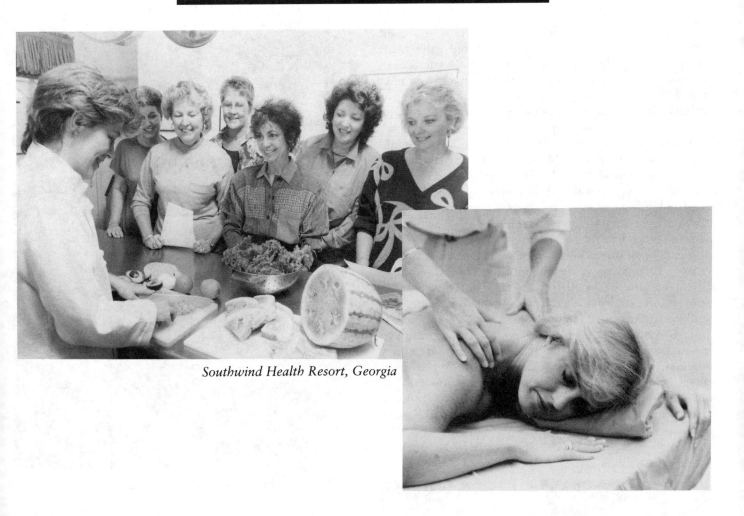

Southwind Health Resort, Georgia

and is the place to which Mel Zuckerman, founder of Canyon Ranch, comes to spend his own summer vacation. The setting is breathtaking, in the mountains of a popular winter ski area that is used for spa purposes only from March through September. For additional information, contact **Jimmy LeSage's New Life Spa, c/o Liftline Lodge, P.O. Box 144, Stratton Mountain, VT 05155 (phone 802/297-2534.)**

The National Institute of Fitness, near Ivins, Utah, in the southwest corner of the state, 120 miles north of Las Vegas, charges $474 per person in quads, $539 in triple rooms, $639 in double rooms, $899 in singles. "For the price we charge," says the institute's owner, "we are the number one fitness resort of the world." Amazingly enough, I have heard similar raves from several people who paid recent visits. Guests stay in futuristic two-story geodesic-type domes, on a desert floor flanked by canyon walls of red sandstone; they work out on the most modern sports equipment, swim in a large heated indoor pool, engage in numerous exercise classes daily, eat meals designed to cut fat and cholesterol, and often experience dramatic reductions in blood pressure and clothing

sizes. For further details, contact the **National Institute of Fitness, 202 N. Snow Canyon Rd. (P.O. Box 938), Ivins, UT 84738 (phone 801/673-4905).**

The Wooden Door, at Lake Geneva, Wisconsin, 90 minutes by car or bus from Chicago's O'Hare Airport, charges $525 per person for five nights in bunk-like facilities in cabins, $625 in standard beds and rooms. The name—a dig at you-know-who—tells it all. This is an impassioned, nononsense program of weight-and-inch reduction, operated (unfortunately) for women only at a 43-acre rented church camp along the famous lake. Exercise is continuous, meals are rigidly limited to 1,000 calories daily, and cabin-lodges are rustic but spacious and comfortable, with indoor showers and plumbing. Sessions take place during a dozen scattered weeks of the year, and usually run from Sunday through Friday. For exact details, contact **The Wooden Door, P.O. Box 830, Barrington, IL 60011 (phone 708/382-2888 or 708/983-5055).**

Southwind Health Resort, near Cartersville, Georgia, charges $995 per person for shared accommodations (the resort will match you up with a roommate if you come alone). Another establishment for women only, this is the tiniest of the inexpensive spas, housing only 16 guests in its sprawling three-story southern country home. It promises complete "rejuvenation," and therefore supplements the standard low-calorie meals and high-energy workouts with classes in "stress reduction," "self-esteem management," wardrobe, and skin care, among others. Contact the **Southwind Health Resort, 932 Old Altoona Rd., Cartersville, GA 30120 (phone 404/975-0342, or toll free 800/832-2622).**

The New Age Health Spa, of Neversink, New York (in the Catskill Mountains), 2½ hours by car from New York City, charges summer rates of $669 to $849 per person double (depending on room size), and $1,069 to $1,339 single; fall and winter rates decline by as much as $100 per person. Though innovative and open-minded, it is no more "New Age" than many other classic spas I've visited, and it is scarcely different from other, far more expensive resorts. The facilities are extensive (indoor pool, well-equipped exercise rooms, saunas, etc.), meals are high quality but meant to ensure weight loss, rooms are rustic and plain but entirely pleasant, management is passionate (not to say fanatical) about current-day theories of good nutrition (low fat, low sodium, low calorie) and exercise, and the setting—on a hillside overlooking a vast expanse of other rolling green hills—is as awesome as you'd wish. For further details, con-

Lake Austin Resort, Texas

The Palms at Palm Springs, California

tact the **New Age Health Spa, Neversink, NY 12765 (phone 914/985-7601, or toll free 800/NU-AGE-4-U).**

The Shangri-La Health Resort, in Bonita Springs, Florida, roughly halfway between Fort Meyers and Naples on the state's west coast, has rates of $525 per person double in winter, $560 single. This retreat is quite unlike the others previously mentioned in its emphasis on "natural health" methods that stress the consumption of raw foods (vegetables, fruits, nuts), sometimes eaten "monotrophically" (one food at a time per meal). Aside from four cooked dinners a week (like a rice casserole, a buckwheat kasha, a lentil chop suey), all other meals are raw, from the freshest of organically grown legumes and such. A fanatically loyal repeat clientele of raw-food vegetarians account for most of the occupancy in this 14-acre expanse of multiple buildings, jogging paths, game courts, heated pool, and more. For literature, contact the **Shangri-La Health Resort, P.O. Box 2328, Bonita Springs, FL 33959 (phone 813/992-3811).**

The Palms at Palm Springs, in Palm Springs, California, a two-hour drive from Los Angeles, has rates of $938 per person double (plus 12% service charge), $175 more for a single room, during the high winter season; less for a room with shared bath. As glamorous as you might wish, located in an area of elegant resorts, the Palms offers you a choice of 16 optional fitness classes a day in addition to meals limited to a spartan but well-balanced 750 calories per day, which virtually guarantees a daily weight loss of nearly a pound. Though it only barely fits within our budget standards, the Palms' desert mountainscape and good-quality lodgings make it a value. For details, contact **The Palms at Palm Springs, 572 N. Indian Ave., Palm Springs, CA 92262 (phone 619/325-1111).**

The Lake Austin Resort, about 30 miles from Austin, Texas, charges $643 to $703 per person double in summer/fall, $790 to $850 in winter/spring, and $200 to $250 more for a single room. At this complex of rustic-style buildings in the rolling hill country of Texas, men consume 1,200 calories daily, women get 900 calories, derived from low-fat foods made tasty by dousing them with the salsa stacked on every table, or by nibbling ever-present jalapeño peppers with your unsugared bran cereal—true southwestern touches. A jam-packed exercise schedule is accompanied by classes in behavior modification (including a visit to a supermarket for unlearning bad habits in selecting food). An enthusiastic staff of fitness experts works alongside guests in 45-minute sessions of aerobics and toning in pools and gyms. In late November and all of December until Christmas you'll often find reduced prices at this leading health center. For complete details, contact the **Lake Austin Resort, 1705 Quinlan Rd., Austin, TX 78732 (phone 512/266-2444, or toll free 800/847-5637).**

The Carmel Country Spa, in Carmel Valley, California, inland from Carmel and Monterey, charges $770 per person double, $1,050 single. In addition to prescribing a spartan 700- to 800-calorie-a-day regimen, this establishment pursues such a no-nonsense approach to exercise that it makes each such session near mandatory: "You will return to the pool at 2 P.M. for Aquathinics," "You will begin Hatha Yoga at 3:30 P.M.," "You will break for a cup of hot potassium broth at 10:30 A.M.," etc., states the rather threatening schedule. Spirits are lifted by the spa's breathtaking Shangri-La—like setting and year-round temperatures in the mid-70s, all in a mountain-flanked valley of northern California, a 40-minute hike from the beach-lined Pacific coast. Rooms are well furnished and located in small hillside cottages reached by picturesque paths. Additional luxuries include an Olympic-size pool and hot tubs. For further information, contact the **Carmel Country Spa, 10 Country Club Way, Carmel Valley, CA 93924 (phone 408/659-3486).**

Deerfield Manor, in East Stroudsburg, Pennsylvania, two hours from New York City, has rates of $620 to $675 per person double, $120 more for single rooms, and a $100-per-

Deerfield Manor, Pennsylvania

Woods Fitness Institute, West Virginia

week supplement to all rates for July and August stays. This is a large and sprawling country home on 12 acres of Pocono forest that offers comfortable air-conditioned rooms with private bath, several lounges, a heated outdoor pool and separate gym, carefully prepared meals limited to 750 to 900 calories daily, a small but caring staff of physical therapists, and a full-scale program of aerobics and body workouts, extensive hiking, swimming exercises, and yoga and relaxation techniques. Book and music libraries supplement a video collection for quiet evenings leading to an early bedtime. Mainly for women, but occasionally booked by men and couples, Deerfield Manor is open from late April to mid-November only. For details, write or call **Deerfield Manor, R.D. 1, Rte. 402, East Stroudsburg, PA 18301 (phone 717/223-0160, or toll free 800/852-4494).**

The Lakeside Health Resort, in Lake Elsinore, California, roughly halfway between Los Angeles and San Diego but slightly inland, is currently closed for renovation but will reopen in late spring of 1991, with probable rates of $776 per person double, $1,007 in a single room. This one-story-high motel structure has impressive facilities (outdoor and indoor pools, exercise gym, weights room, aerobics workout room, sauna, and whirlpool), tasty but low-calorie meals, and a comprehensive daily program—from 7 A.M. to 7 P.M., as active as any—of supervised exercises and instruction in healthy living. For complete details, contact the **Lakeside Health Resort, 32281 Riverside Dr., Lake Elsinore, CA 92330 (phone 714/674-1501).**

The Woods Fitness Institute, in Hedgesville, West Virginia, a two-hour interstate drive from Washington/Baltimore, features rates of $692 to $802 (the first for "fitness cottages," the second for rooms in the main lodge) per person per week, double occupancy, and $851 to $961 in single rooms. The institute is actually a program, not a sepa-

For all who have stood dumbfounded and aghast at the sky-high rates of the nationally known "fat farms," here is good news.

rate establishment, that is operated year round in the larger context of the 2,000-acre Woods Resort and vacation-home community. Most fitness participants are grouped close together in their housing arrangements, and take low-calorie family-style meals at specially designated tables in the main restaurant of the resort. I'm concerned about this proximity to nonspa guests, and additionally point out that the exercise program here consumes only five hours a day (fewer than at the others I've named). Still, the institute's moderate price structure, serious approach, and scenic setting, alongside a vast 23,000-acre nature preserve, entitle it to be considered. For more information, contact the **Woods Fitness Institute, P.O. Box 5, Hedgesville, WV 25427 (phone 304/754-7977, or toll free 800/248-2222).**

The Oaks at Ojai is 50 miles east of Santa Barbara, California. A usual average of $800 to $900 per week per person in double rooms, a stiff $1,115 in singles, slightly more for double-occupancy cottages away from the main lodge, all plus a 12% service charge, make this a high-end budget selection. Impressive in both its fervor and facilities, the rustic (beamed ceilings, stone fireplaces) but elegant Oaks is a fitting country-inn addition to the art colony town of Ojai, offering a remarkable program of nearly 20 daily exercise classes and lectures. Meals are frequently gourmet in quality, but made without salt, white sugar, or white flour and containing a total of only 900 or 1,100 calories daily. Equipment and exercise areas are of top quality, as is the large staff that attends to a varied clientele of both sexes and all ages. For more information, contact **The Oaks at Ojai, 122 E. Ojai Ave., Ojai, CA 93023 (phone 805/646-5573).**

Next time you go on vacation, consider trying a cheap or moderately priced spa. Isn't the active pursuit of health a better use of leisure time than simply loafing for a week or two?

Golf as exercise, The Woods

The Cheap New Spas of Mexico and the Caribbean

Six Resorts for Less Than $650 a Week

D O YOUR PULSES TWITCH WHEN YOU READ the rates of U.S. health resorts? Does vision blur, and pounding set in, at the sight of a $2,000-per-week, per-person, price tag for aerobics-and-avocado?

As in so many other instances in travel, a trip beyond our borders can sometimes achieve the very same vacation experience for far less money. Though low-cost spas do exist at home (and are increasingly available), I've been struck by the growing popularity of six dirt-cheap health resorts and spa-type hotels in Mexico and the Caribbean. And while the

Taxco, Mexico: Nearby is the Ixtapan Resort Hotel

Instituto de Vida Natural, Rio Grande, Puerto Rico

added air fare may consume part of the savings, isn't the foreign setting a plus?

Consider the following:

Rio Caliente, Mexico: In the valley of a remote pine forest about an hour by taxi from the airport of Guadalajara, Rio Caliente is Mexico's holistic-health-inclined, yoga-oriented, New Age–style spa and mineral hot springs. Guests—who represent a broad range of ages, backgrounds, and inter-ests—"take the waters" in one of four heavily salted (of lithium and selenium) and mineral-rich pools or in a natural steam room; alternate between meditation, yoga, tai-chi, aquatic and non-impact aerobics, hiking, or horseback rid-ing; and consume a slimming, vegetarian diet low in sodium and fat. Various forms of massage, and the services of an M.D./acupuncturist, are available on the grounds. Bear in mind that the social program and setting are not for swingers

As in so many other instances in travel, a trip beyond our borders can achieve substantial savings.

or other standard resort types; that children are not admitted; and that a pervasive, stressless, hush prevails over the 30 acres of stunning terrain, in a constantly moderate climate. For all this, you pay only $46 or so dollars a day for room and all three meals, and a remarkable $15 for each one-hour massage, $8 for detoxifying mudwraps. Request bookings or brochures from **Barbara Dane Associates, 480 California Terrace, Pasadena, CA 91105 (phone 818/796-5577).**

Ixtapan, Mexico: The closest Mexican equivalent to our own luxury spas, the large (250 suites) and well-equipped Ixtapan Resort Hotel and Spa emphasizes its thermal pools and Roman baths, but also takes pains to limit its spa guests to 800 calories a day of well-prepared diet meals. On the all-inclusive, Sunday-to-Sunday spa program costing only $650 per person double occupancy, and $830 single, guests take a daily morning walk followed by aquatic exercise, steam bath and daily massage, facial, and gymnastics. Then, three times a week, and also included in the price, they receive mudwraps and loofa baths, hair treatment, manicures, and pedicures, staying all the while in attractive junior suites that would cost far more in the U.S. Don't confuse this location with Ixtapa on the Pacific coast; this is near Ixtapan de la Sal, south of

Instituto de Vida Natural

Mexico City, and also near the silver-producing city of Taxco. For brochures or bookings, contact **E & M Associates, 211 E. 43rd St., New York, NY 10017 (phone 212/599-8280, or toll free 800/223-9832).**

Villa Vegetariana, Cuernavaca, Mexico: Fresh vegetarian meals heavy in fruit—pineapple, mango, watermelon, papaya, mamey, chico, and guava—are the theme and chief treatment of this "naturism" resort (not to be confused with a nudist "naturist" resort), but those are supplemented by daily aerobics and other exercise classes, mudpacks, tennis, pool, sauna—and cooked vegetables, topping off the fruit. Guests are told they can lose between 5 and 10 pounds a week, in addition to achieving considerable rejuvenation. All this costs only $300 a week (and as little as $225 if you share a room), all inclusive, for pleasant accommodations with private bath in a well-tended setting of arcaded walkways around a large patio and pool. And location is the famous and sometimes rather elegant suburban community of Cuernavaca—the so-called City of Eternal Spring—50 miles south of Mexico City. The exact address is **Villa Vegetariana Health Resort, Pino 114, Sta. Maria Ahuacatitlan, Cuernavaca, Morelos 62100, Mexico (phone 73/13-10-44),** but write for brochures to the resort at **P.O. Box 1228, Cuernavaca, Morelos 62000, Mexico.**

Instituto de Vida Natural, Rio Grande, Puerto Rico: A small, holistic health farm in the foothills of the El Yunque rain forest, the Instituto is open year round for both day visitors and overnight guests, but is most interesting for its series of five-day workshops scattered throughout the year (usually over Memorial Day in May, mid-September, Thanksgiving, mid-January, and mid-March). These cost an all-inclusive total of $495 per person, and deal with varying topics of mind/health relationships, as presented by psychoanalyst Dr. Jane Goldberg of New York and Boston. Participants engage in aquatic exercises and mountain trekking, eat the freshest of vegetarian meals, and have plenty of free time—after their classroom sessions—for ocean swimming. For a simple and unstructured stay outside the workshop periods, the rate can decline to $50 per person per night, double occupancy, including meals, or to $75 a night for single rooms (but the Instituto can sometimes arrange shares). More complete information on both options is had by writing or phoning **Dr. Jane G. Goldberg, Ph.D., 222 Park Ave. South, #6D, New York, NY 10003 (phone 212/260-5823).**

Baños de Coamo, Puerto Rico: This one is only for taking a classic "water cure." Built around a forcefully gushing, thermal hot springs, the modest country inn with 48 air-conditioned but rather plain rooms is nevertheless an officially designated *parador* of the Puerto Rican government. Its rates are marvelously low—$48 for one person, $59 for two, not including meals—but virtually all you do for health is

El Yunque rain forest

bathe in the therapeutic hot waters that Ponce de León also experienced in his quest for the Fountain of Youth nearly 500 years ago (Franklin D. Roosevelt was a more recent visitor). Two swimming pools (one with the thermal waters), a tennis court, and a restaurant complete the amenities; but only a half hour away by car is Ponce, second-largest city of Puerto Rico, with its famed Ponce Museum of Art, newly restored Perla Theatre, and other attractions. Contact **Baños de Coamo, Road 546, Coamo, PR 00640 (phone 809/825-2186).**

Lady Diane's, Montego Bay, Jamaica: The Caribbean's only "macrobiotic resort," Lady Diane's serves the severe grain-and-vegetables diet advocated by the late George Ohsawa. Usually, a yoga instructor is also in residence, or comes to conduct a daily exercise program, and there is much jogging by guests, some tennis at a next-door court, and swimming off a pocket-handkerchief-sized beach or in the pool. Since the 15-room hotel sits at the end of a cul-de-sac facing the sea, it is unusually quiet and without traffic. Remarkably for the Caribbean, you pay only $81 a day per person for room and all three macrobiotic meals, double occupancy, including service charge and tax. Contact **Lady Diane's, 5 Kent Ave., Montego Bay, Jamaica (phone 809/952-4415).**

At one location, you bathe in the same hot-water spring that Ponce de León tested for his "Fountain of Youth."

XI

NEW DESTINATIONS FOR BETTER AND CHEAPER TRIPS

Thailand, a Travel "Must" in Every Season

. . . And the Important Activities Include a Trip to the Hill Tribes

WHEN THEY HEARD I WAS PLANNING A summer trip to Thailand, my friends were aghast. "It's the monsoon season!" they cried. "You'll float away! No one goes there in summer."

No one except hundreds of thousands of Europeans, Japanese, Australians, Singaporeans, and other Asians, all having a perfectly wonderful time. Such is the nonsense about climate—"England is unbearable in January," "Rio is freezing in July"—that discourages so many Americans from traveling to destinations during their most desirable, off-season months.

While June through August is indeed the time of tropical downpour ("monsoon") in Southeast Asia, most of the rains are concentrated cloudbursts of, at most, an hour's duration, occurring late in the day or even at night. By timing your touring, and taking shelter for a short while when necessary, you enjoy a normal stay in what is perhaps the most dynamic touristic situation on earth.

Thailand (the former Siam of *King and I* fame) is booming. With nearly five million visitors in 1989, and more than that in 1990, it has joined the ranks of the mega-destinations.

Part of the reason is price. Except at the grand hotels, tourists can eat for $1 simply by patronizing the tiny local restaurants that number in the thousands in Bangkok alone.

"$5-a-day" living is alive and well in Thailand!

Then, by carefully selecting a guesthouse in any Thai town, rooms are secured for as little as $4 a night—and that's for two people. "$5-a-day" living is alive and well in Thailand!

The economy is also booming, at a rate of increase that topped 10% in 1989, and figures to do almost as well in 1990. With its relatively stable political conditions (won at the cost of a government dominated by the military) and huge, cheap labor force, the nation is attracting new factories and investments diverted in part from Hong Kong and, more recently, China. Cranes and construction are everywhere, as manufacturers rush to erect assembly lines for their labor-intensive activities.

The result is a near-constant condition of traffic gridlock in Bangkok, the most monumental crush of autos, buses, trucks, and motorcycles of any city. Unless you time your movements with surgical precision to avoid the heaviest flow, you find yourself spending an hour or two in a taxi or *tuk-tuk* (tiny three-wheeled vehicles rented for a pittance) to reach even nearby points. There is no subway.

So tourists take to the river—the muddy and broad Chao Phraya—which courses in a loop through the center of Bangkok, servicing its key attractions. From any number of hotels, you wander on foot to crude riverside landings where public express boats (fares: 15¢ to 35¢) or specially hired under $1 "needle boats" take you on a fast and wind-blown ride past exotic markets and slum dwellings to the magnificent Buddhist temples and complexes of such temples on or near the river's edge. Bangkok's Grand Palace is the most magnificent of these, a glittering fairyland of multiroofed, fire-spewing structures and conical monuments covered with glass and mosaics in the most brilliant tones of yellow and red. The nearby Wat (temple) Phra Kaeo, housing the sacred Emerald Buddha, and the adjacent (to the Grand Palace) Wat Po, with its 140-foot-long Reclining Buddha, are nearly as impressive, as is the more ancient Wat Arun (Temple of the Dawn) on the other side of the river.

All these stellar sights of Bangkok, as well as its several floating markets and crocodile farm, are easily and cheaply viewed by boat and on foot, without the need to enter a single taxi, tuk-tuk, or bus.

Other Bangkok residents beat the traffic jams by casually hopping aboard the rear seat of one of the thousands of motorcycles that also fill the thoroughfares and easily weave into and out of the traffic. Spotting a well-dressed woman who you could swear was the wife or girlfriend of the man driving the motorcycle, you are then amazed to see her alight at a street corner, hand a small coin to the driver (for the ride), and coolly stroll away.

While traffic problems can be wearying, all is redeemed by the sunny dispositions, the warm and generous natures, of the Thai people, a joy to meet. Buddhists to an overwhelming

Karen tribeswomen, near Chiang Mai

extent (90% to 95% of the population), their religion is one of the world's most tolerant and open-minded, not to say permissive. As always in travel, it is vital to steep yourself in the culture (including the religion) of the nation before arriving there; and for Thailand, such books as the recently published *Living Buddhism* by Andrew Powell (New York: Harmony Books, 1989) are invaluable.

Even without attempting a book-length study, every traveler can at least peruse the brief discussions of Buddhism in such widely available sources as the *Encyclopaedia Britannica*. Reading there of the young Indian prince (Siddartha Gautama) who left his family's palace in the mid-500s B.C. to pursue first enlightenment, and then nirvana, the tourist's eye is trained to see (and understand) the tens of thousands of images of the Buddha in Thailand—here a Buddha meditating, there a Buddha reclining on his side before death. The unique Theravada form of Buddhism that prevails in Thailand sees Buddha as a supremely wise philosopher, not as a divine being. The Thais appear to downplay all other aspects of the supernatural to a greater extent than do most other

Thailand is a Third World nation invaluable for the insights it provides into pressing issues of our time.

Ayutthaya

people, despite the frequent presence of tiny "spirit houses" that serve almost as a joyful tribute to nature in the front yards of houses and buildings all over Thailand.

To reach the essence of Thai culture, the single indispensable day-trip from Bangkok is to the Buddhist ruins of Ayutthaya, the ancient capital of Thailand that was demolished by Burmese invaders in the 18th century. Going one way by riverboat, the other way by bus (1½ hours), you view a broad variety of country and small-town sights, which reach their apotheosis in the magnificently preserved and/or restored temples, palaces, fortresses, and gates of the once-great city.

From Bangkok, most European tourists head next to the nearby beaches of Pattaya City or the more remote seaside pleasures of the island of Phuket, to the south. Americans, in general, do not follow their lead (or find it sensible to have flown several thousands of miles just to lie on a beach). Those who do, prefer the more tasteful resort settings of Phuket to the increasingly crowded, often-shabby aspects of Pattaya; the latter area also houses a considerable spillover

from the amazingly prolific nighttime bar scene (with famous "bar girls") of Bangkok.

Rather, most U.S. visitors immediately fly on from Bangkok to the city of Chiang Mai in the north, primarily for the direct factory-outlet shopping—better than Bangkok's—in the area around that town of 200,000 residents (no longer the sleepy place portrayed in the guidebooks). On a one-day "industrial tour" of Chiang Mai's outskirts, made either by tour bus or in a cheap tuk-tuk that you have rented yourself, you go to a succession of paper-umbrella factories (featuring hand-painted parasols), leather-goods factories, teakwood-furniture factories, silver works, jewelry firms, ceramics factories, jade carvers, lacquer manufacturers, and—most important of all—to the mills weaving renowned Thai silks (of intense, radiant hues) and then working them into suits, dresses, blouses, sarongs and bathrobes, scarves, and neckties. Buying directly from the manufacturer, one seems to do better than at the famed Night Market of Chiang Mai or in the shopping centers of Bangkok, and certainly better than in the pricey Jim Thompson's, the best-known silk outlet of

Bangkok, which is thronged at all hours with affluent tourists.

From Chiang Mai, a three-hour ride by bus or car takes you farther north to the town of Chiang Rai in the area of the "Golden Triangle," where Thailand abuts Burma and Laos. In Chiang Rai, a visit to a travel agency will result the very next day in a one-night or two-night trek to the isolated hill tribes living on mountain peaks overlooking the border. It's a singular, mind-boggling experience, and one that's described directly below.

Thailand is a Third World nation valuable for the insights it provides into pressing issues of our time (population growth, famine and poverty, drug cultivation, exploitation of cheap labor and women, authoritarian governments). But it is also a developing nation, in which a growing middle class coexists with a much larger population of very low income or impoverished and where legislators debate whether to enact Thailand's first "social security" system (which they were doing at the time of my visit).

For its Asian culture and economic development, for low costs and charming people, Thailand is currently a "hot" destination that should be on anyone's travel list. And there's still another aspect of Thailand that almost alone is worth the trip:

A VISIT TO THE HILL TRIBES

In the mountains of northern Thailand, above the teakwood forests and rice fields of the Mae Kok Delta, a broad range of Western tourists—from youthful backpackers to middle-aged professionals—are currently enjoying what may be the world's last real opportunity to share the life of an isolated and primitive people, scarcely removed from the world of a thousand years ago. If you are to join them, you must do so quickly, because the very contact between the modern visitors and their innocent hosts is gradually erasing the differences between them.

Though pockets of primitive people survive throughout the world—in Papua New Guinea, for one, or in the Amazon or deepest Mongolia—none can be seen with the ease or lack of substantial expense that attends a trek to the hill tribes of Southeast Asia. And none, to my knowledge, permits visitors to sleep overnight in their villages as the hill tribes do—and as I did.

In contrast to the lengthy preparations for a trek through the Himalayas or Andes, an impulse decision—made in your comfortable Bangkok hotel room—transforms you into a Thailand trekker within 24 hours. You need no special equipment other than jeans, sturdy walking shoes, and a T-shirt, and you can book onto a hill-tribe trek lasting only one, two, or three days, although the very limited one-day variety is scarcely advisable.

The trek begins with a one-hour flight from Bangkok to Chiang Mai in the north of Thailand. The nation's second-largest city, but with only 200,000 residents, Chiang Mai is a once-sleepy, temple-bestrewn cultural center now transformed by tourism into a teeming bazaar of shops and small factories (on the outskirts) of arts and crafts.

It is in Chiang Mai, from any of a score of travel agencies, that arrangements can be made for a hill tribe trek. I made mine with Fairyland Tours, which assigned a former hill-tribe member—Asoepa (pronounced "Ah-soo") Saenya—as the trekking guide; he was an inspired choice. Depending on the number of people in your party, the journey is priced at $40 to $100 per person for a two-day/one-night version, all included. Never buy the trek from the costly tour desk in your hotel.

Even cheaper arrangements can be had from the travel agencies in the actual jumping-off point for the trek, which is the smaller town of Chiang Rai, three hours by car or public bus (85 baht, $3.40) from Chiang Mai. The winding, hilly ride from Chiang Mai to Chiang Rai takes you to the northernmost part of Thailand near the borders of Burma and Laos, adjoining the infamous "Golden Triangle" area, where much of the world's opium is said to be grown (its production is banned in Thailand). As you bounce along for most of the morning, the view outside is of endless rice fields flooded a foot thick. Barefoot peasants in conical bamboo hats—an affecting scene, unchanged for centuries—stand jackknifed over the water as they press each shoot of rice into the muddy earth.

Once in Chiang Rai, at a crude, wooden landing on the Mae Kok River, you transfer to a narrow motorized "needle boat" for a further ride of 1½ hours into the jungle area

A Karen village

leading to the hill tribes. Your possessions have been reduced to a single khaki rucksack carrying a change of underwear and socks and a canteen of distilled water, but now you have been joined by porters carrying bags of vegetables and chicken and additional water for your meals in the mountains.

By now you have left civilization altogether. There are no nearby roads, not even the rural village scenes that dot the route between Chiang Mai and Chiang Rai. You begin to perceive ponderous shapes lumbering through the thick reeds at the river's edge: elephants. And then, at a muddy riverbank, you disembark onto a path leading to a cluster of thatched huts. Here members of a partially abandoned hill tribe, the Karens, live suspended, as it were, halfway between the near-isolation of the peak dwellers and the more modern life of Chiang Rai.

A young Karen *mahout* (elephant driver) helps you into a basket-like platform atop a wrinkled elephant, and forthwith you embark on another 2½-hour leg of your trip to the hill tribes: a swaying, bucking, somewhat precarious journey as the giant beast steps carefully along muddy jungle paths leading upward, always upward. This time you are passing terraced rice paddies that actual hill-tribe people have carved from the mountain slopes and then cultivated with water borne there in bamboo pipes. Each morning from their mountain homes the tribespeople descend several thousands of feet to eke out a marginal existence from the poor mountain lands on which their rice and vegetables are grown.

Mercifully, the elephant ride ends, only to be followed by a 2½-hour climb on foot up mountain paths that zigzag through even thicker jungle vegetation. We are now above the clouds. Though the climb is arduous and sweaty, it requires no mountaineering skills and can be accomplished with periodic rest stops by mid-lifers like myself.

And then, in open sunlight, the jungle growth ends and you step into a scene of prehistory.

In front of you is a mountaintop village of 30 or so huts made solely of thatch and reeds and bamboo mats affixed with wooden pegs to crude posts, all beige and gray. It is a sight of the sort that Gauguin saw, or that Margaret Mead studied. Without a single device or machine, without running water or even lanterns, without vehicles or signs, without literacy or news—humankind in a state of nature.

Ranged in a central clearing, without advance notice of your arrival, are women of the hill tribes in their normal dress, but so colorful as to dazzle the senses. Around their heads are elaborate beaded caps with high protruding mane-plates of beaten silver behind their knotted hair. From ear to ear hang multihued, multistrand necklaces that loop beneath their chins. Some of the glitter comes from ancient Tibetan coins sewn to the caps. The nomadic hill tribes are a people of vaguely Tibetan origin who have progressively moved south to Burma and Thailand in numbers of several hundred thousand, but scattered among temporary villages averaging no more than 100 or 150 people apiece. They are animists, believing in earth spirits, and recognize no modern nation.

As dusk falls and workers return from the fields, we tourists wander the village in complete freedom, gazing at the pre-evening activities, while the hill people gaze back at us in friendly, innocent curiosity. Half-clad children scamper about among the cows, chickens, dogs, and pigs that mix in playful confusion with the human beings of whose life they are a part. As in the Middle Ages, the animals eat and sleep in or near the same structures that house their masters.

It is evening. The women—but not the men—light clay pipes of tobacco. The men squat upon their haunches and heatedly discuss village policies. To an extent unknown in the modern world, conversation is their chief distraction.

Later, in the hut of the chief on a mat of woven rush, we eat the dinner that our trek guide has prepared. On another section of the mat, and in an adjoining room, the chief and his family and friends eat their more heavily spiced meal of rice and vegetables. We glance at our hosts, who grin back sheepishly at us.

There is no verbal contact between us; their language isn't even Thai. But a different form of communication passes between us. We are observing their society, their living quarters, their evening meal.

The chief's wife hands us lighted tapers to illuminate the hut in which we are to sleep. As we bed down for the night on hard raised pallets of bamboo, other people of the village stroll inside to gaze innocently at us, our clothes, our equipment. Later, we awake feeling a bit astonished that we have spent not simply a daytime interlude but overnight with a primitive people—and we sense how increasingly natural it is for us to be among them.

Though pockets of primitive people survive throughout the world, none can be visited as easily as the hill tribes of Southeast Asia.

Each one of us, as the visit lengthens, grows more absorbed in thought. We are assessing the difference between civilization and a life in nature; we are weighing both the pains and rewards of a bygone life, when matters were simpler.

We spend a final hour or so simply strolling among the villagers, watching as they pound their corn, attend to their children, feed their animals. As we take our leave, we buy several trinkets from the colorfully clad women. They, in dignified response, give each of us a free necklace of beads, from which a small gourd hangs.

Afterward: a three-hour walk down another part of the mountain, through jungle-like vegetation, passing radiant waterfalls; a ride by van on rutted paths to the main road outside Chiang Rai; a bus for three hours to Chiang Mai and a modern hotel where musicians play Cole Porter melodies from the stage of a slick coffeeshop.

And that—as it now seems hard to believe—was a travel experience I had at a day's remove from the bustling city life of Bangkok in the company of other worldly tourists from developed nations. Who knows how long the same will remain available, and with its present rewards?

The Undiscovered Caribbean

33 Barely Visited Islands Afford a Unique Vacation to the Discriminating Traveler

FOR AMERICANS OF TASTE AND INTELLIgence, much of the Caribbean has been ruined. On island after island, the building of multiple high-rise hotels, squeezed side by side onto a single beach area (I'm thinking, for instance, of Aruba), has wrought terrible damage to the fragile atmosphere of these once-innocent spots.

On some islands, casino activity now dominates all other attractions. Slick shopping malls, like the ones we have at home, are replacing the smaller commerce of before. Hawkers roam the beach, pestering you to buy. The motors of waterski boats shatter the calm.

But just when everything seemed gloomiest, along comes an important guidebook to provide us with relief. It's called *Undiscovered Islands of the Caribbean*—the author is California travel agent Burl Willes—and it was recently published by John Muir of Santa Fe and distributed to bookstores by W. W. Norton of New York ($14.95).

In it you'll learn of those peaceful locales where people can still string a hammock to a pair of palms and recline therein with a paperback novel for the entire day, always without another soul in sight and with no sound other than the lapping of waves. Where they can walk barefoot down the near-deserted streets of a town and then through swinging doors into a wooden bar, where they are greeted with smiles by the denizens within. Where tiny restaurants prepare the fish that they have caught that morning and serve it with slices of lemon on a wooden plank.

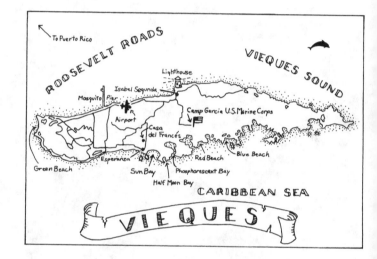

"Undiscovered islands"? Willes isn't referring, of course, to the totally unknown—uninhabited—islands; those aren't of use to anyone. Rather, his definition is of islands without high-rise or substantial (100-room) hotels, that are endowed instead with a scattered handful of tiny lodgings, guesthouses, or private homes accepting guests. In his book he describes 33 such places, out of a potential total of 100 islands meeting his criteria for gentle, natural vacations. The

---

Here are peaceful looales without another soul in sight, and no sound other than the lapping of the waves, where people string their hammock to a pair of palms and read Proust or Joseph Campbell.

256

remainder will presumably be treated in a subsequent, expanded edition of the current guidebook.

Where are these magical isles? Five, he says, are cayes of the stable Central American nation of Belize, none with a grand hotel, but all with the modest two-story variety. Five are charming islets of the Grenadines (Carriacou, Petit Martinique, Union Island, Mayreau, and Canouan), three are off the large French island of Guadeloupe (Marie-Galante, Terre de Haut, Terre de Bas), four are off the coasts of Venezuela (Isla de Coche, Isla de Cubagua) and Puerto Rico (Vieques, Culebra), and seven are dots of land in the Turks and Caicos (Pine Cay, North Caicos, Middle Caicos, South Caicos, Salt Cay Island, Grand Turk Island, and Providenciales).

Three are in the Leeward Islands (Saba, Barbuda, Monserrat), three are in the Bahamas (Green Turtle Cay, Long Island, the Exumas), and two are off Mexico's Yucatán peninsula (Isla Mujeres, Isla Holbox). Only in his naming of bustling, burgeoning Isla Mujeres do I take issue with Willes. And his inclusion of Puerto Rico's Vieques—where numerous developers have big plans—is perhaps arguable as well.

To Willes's credit, he does not include or describe those

virtually private islands, like Mustique, where wealthy individuals have built homes that they then rent on occasion to the public. Rather, his recommendations are of breathtaking bargains, which often charge as little as $20 to $50 for a double room, and only rarely go higher than that. That's because the little-known lodgings on the "undiscovered" islands are small 10-room hotels or guesthouses converted, in most cases, from former residences and operated in simple style.

Take, for example, Posada Vista Mar on Vieques, where, according to Willes, "an unbelievably thoughtful Vieques woman named Olga rents out a half dozen small, clean but spartan rooms behind her screened-in restaurant. The sound of crickets and the island's famous tree frogs creates a vibrant chorus at night, and the bleating of Olga's goats combines with the crowing of roosters in the early morn. When it was time for us to catch a ferry to Fajardo, Olga woke us up before dawn, served us 'coffee on the house,' and said goodbye with a kiss. Rates are $25 per night, including tax."

Here tiny restaurants prepare the fish that they have caught that morning and serve it with slices of lemon on a wooden plank.

Are these, however, desperation prices for unsuitable lodgings, offered by a desperately poor people? I put these questions to Burl Willes in a recent telephone interview:

"I don't consider them poor," he responded; "they are happy people, with a pride in their island community that is often lost in larger cities or countries. Perhaps they are poor by our standards, but on small islands the people share, they don't starve, and they're delighted to pick up this small extra income for rooms that are simple but clean and dignified."

"On these islands," he continued, "you travel as a visitor, not a tourist. The people are easier to meet, and are grateful for your visit."

"How difficult is it to reach the tiny islands?" I asked. "A fifteen-minute plane ride, perhaps a one-hour ferry ride, at most, from the larger island to which they're adjacent. That's all that is required, yet so few of us take that extra step."

Now more of us will, thanks to *Undiscovered Islands of the Caribbean*. And be assured that most of Burl Willes's recommendations are of higher-quality lodgings than Olga's, though no less gracious, no less refined.

THE NEW WORLD OF TRAVEL 1992

The lifeblood of the Arthur Frommer travel guides is the correspondence received from readers, commenting on the establishments recommended in the texts and recommending new establishments. Each such letter is carefully studied, and when a particular lead seems promising, it is followed up and personally checked.

It is hoped that *The New World of Travel* will receive similar assistance from its readers. A yearly publication, issued near the start of each year, *The New World* will constantly grow. And since much of its content relates to organizations that lack the means to market themselves properly, or come to the attention of a travel journalist, your help is invaluable in alerting me to the organizations—hospitality exchanges, alternative resorts, new travel clubs, and the like—that you have discovered.

If you become aware of a new travel organization, program, or development that deserves to be described in our next edition, *The New World of Travel 1992*, won't you please let me know about it? Send your letters to Arthur Frommer, *The New World of Travel*, c/o Prentice Hall Press, Travel Division, 15 Columbus Circle, New York, NY 10023. All letters will be acknowledged, and all are warmly appreciated, in advance, by the author.

A Mixed Bag of Pleasures on the Island of Bali

Though No Longer Without Problems, It Is Culturally Enriching and Dirt-Cheap

THE TERM "TROPICAL PARADISE" WAS ONCE synonymous with the Indonesian island of Bali.

It no longer is. Bali's capital city of Denpasar is overcrowded and a bit honky-tonk, and its much-depicted beaches are today lined with hotels, discos, beach vendors, and masseurs who often plead and shout at you to use their embarrassingly cheap services.

But if Bali is no longer floral headdresses and grass skirts, it is nonetheless an exciting and culturally enriching destination, and one of the cheapest on earth. What's important is that you know where, and where not, to go.

Of the three main beach areas, one—the elegant Nusa Dua—is scarcely Balinese at all, unless you count the artificial Bali-style façades pasted onto its five-star resorts. This is where pampered tourists go, to a wide shopping boulevard with immaculate boutiques and an attractive beach that could be anywhere in the world.

The beach area of Sanur is only slightly better, though a deluxe Bali Hyatt and equally deluxe Sanur Beach Hotel are jarring notes on a scene that begins to partake of what you expected to find in Bali. At least here you can enjoy the famed low prices of Bali: $30 to $35 for a double with bath and two breakfasts at such comfortable lodgings as the Queen Bali Hotel, a block from the beach; $30 to $45 per double in modern bungalows surrounded by graceful gardens and Balinese stone temple motifs at the Bali Sanur Bungalows; only $2 for a steak dinner at the Mango Restaurant, and only $3.50 per person for a stunning Indonesian *rijstaffel* of varied dishes—grilled chicken on bamboo sticks, with peanut sauce, shrimp curry, and a dozen other courses on tiny plates. Even the high-quality Bali Beach Hotel here charges only $20 for its multicourse Beach Buffet dinner and dance performance under the stars, all to the strains of gamelon music and softly clashing cymbals. The downscale Kuta Beach area is Bali's most popular, with its smooth white sand that stretches

for miles and is dotted with palms. But this is the haunt of Australian young people—including a few rowdy surfers, not exactly intellectual types. Still, their presence here, and the weak purchasing power of the Australian dollar, support a broad industry of budget-priced facilities.

Even "upscale" hotels in the Kuta Beach area—like the new Sahid Bali Seaside Cottages—charge an average of only

$60 a night for a double room. In the town of Kuta itself, amid busy streets of stores, clubs, and restaurants, less expensive cottages/rooms/pensions—basic but clean—cost $20 for an air-conditioned double with private bath and hot water; $15 per double with fan only, bath and hot water; $12 with fan and bath but no hot water; and an amazing $6 for two people without private bath. And breakfast is included!

Kuta's room bargains are matched by those of its restaurants and shopping. In my own favorite restaurant, patronized by that small sliver of book-reading tourists (it's called Made's Warung, and you eat on a tiled balcony under a bamboo roof), fruit salad with black rice is the equivalent of 65¢, and nasi campur (white rice mixed with up to seven kinds of meat, with coconut sauce and peanuts) is well under $1. This you wash down with draughts of a potent rice drink known as an "Arak Attack," at 45¢ a cup.

And in the shops of Kuta, prices are far lower than in many other Balinese locales: under $15 for snakeskin shoes and sandals custom-made in the color of your choice, under $25 for leather suitcases, $10 for stylish batik sundresses, about $12 for elaborate sterling-silver bracelets.

In Kuta, you begin to glimpse the all-pervasive role of the Hindu religion in Bali, so different from the prevailing Islamic culture in the rest of Indonesia. Brightly colored offerings of flowers, food, and incense, placed on coconut palms as an offering to dead relatives and the gods, are so thickly placed that you must literally maneuver your way around them when walking down the street, even Kuta's main shopping strip. You would not see these in such profusion in Nusa Dua or Sanur.

Some tourists choose Kuta as their base, for its low costs and ample nightlife, but then flee from the beaches (not the best aspects of Bali) for daily excursions into the more important inland and mountain areas, all less touched by tourism, more thoroughly Balinese. Transportation is so cheap in Bali that some even skip the more basic forms of getting about—so-called *bimos* (public pickup trucks) costing under $1 to any point in Bali, motorcycles for $5 a day, rental cars for

Rice terraces

With new friends at Tjetjak Inn, Ubud

Balinese dancers

$15—and hire a van-with-driver for the day and early evening, for only $40. By comparison-shopping to find a driver capable of providing the cultural/historic context of what you are viewing, you are able to properly visit the chief attractions of Bali.

These are, first, its major hillside and lakeside temples in constant, daily use by the Balinese (conduct yourself with proper respect inside); then, the healing rituals, crematory funerals, and remarkable fire-dance ceremonies held daily in several key villages. Then, too, several villages each specialize in a single craft—stonecarving in Batbulan, silver working in Celuk, woodcarving in Mas—and a skilled driver-guide can direct you to them. Finally, lively "night markets" (kerosene-lit stalls and carts), not at all oriented toward tourists, flourish in Denpasar and at least a dozen other towns.

My own driver-guide, in one day, took us (among other places) to little-known hot springs scattered about the island, then to drink coconut wine cross-legged on a mat with elders of his village, then to four different night markets barely touched by the outside world.

Rather than base myself in Kuta, however, I'd opt for the best of all worlds by skipping the beaches altogether and heading directly to the mountain town of Ubud, which approximates and sometimes surpasses what travelers dream of finding in Bali. Here, nestled in brilliant-green mountains and rice terraces, a community world-renowned for its paintings carries on a daily round of art and ritual, more visibly than in any other part of Bali, while accommodating tourists at the same time. The tourists are also different here; quiet and respectful, sometimes wearing the traditional sarong, they go

Balinese dance show

strolling a short distance outside town and soon pass farms and then participants in religious processions. Village women lead the march, their heads stacked high with brightly colored, pink-and-green temple offerings. At night, the same tourists sit on platform balconies built into the hills and listen to gamelons and the sound of the Campuan River.

The lodgings of Ubud are outstanding. My idea of paradise is a cluster of bungalows with patios and thatched roofs called the Tjetjak Inn, all built alongside a hill above the river, and all with sweeping views. You awake here to the sounds of the river and its traffic, and glimpse workers gathering thatch across the river. You sunbathe on nearby boulders and swim in the river, and the price of all this is $12 per cabin, including a hearty breakfast for two, eaten on the porch. Less scenic (but still adequate) rooms in private homes rent for under $5 per double, with bath and breakfast, but without hot water or flush toilets. And in the center of Ubud, wonderfully picturesque and historic, is a former palace com-

What's important is that you know where, and where not, to go.

plex, Puri Saren Agung, charging $32 per double room, including breakfast.

Shops in Ubud sell carved and painted wooden art (masks and mobiles of painted fish or birds) for $8.50 to $11, carved and painted frames with floral motifs for $4.50 to $20, silver jewelry for $1 to $25, and of course a massive array of paintings—the town's specialty—for widely varying prices, but cheap.

Although you can take a thrice-daily $1.50 shuttle bus from Ubud to the beach area of Kuta, a great many visitors in Ubud travel on to the far less crowded beach at Candidasa, in eastern Bali, another approximation of a "tropical paradise."

Here, residents and especially fishermen outnumber the tourists, and you see a steady stream of Balinese walking back and forth to the beach with various varieties of work on their heads. Temples decorated with streamers and food offerings adorn the scene; the mood is quiet but somehow celebrational. Rates for simple but clean rooms in Candidasa range from $7 (no hot water) to $22 (air-conditioned, hot water), and there are far more basic quarters for under $5 per double. For another $5 you rent a motorbike, and for still another $15 a guide who comes with his or her own motorbike. And thus equipped, you chug from Candidasa to the former Balinese capital of Singaraja (stopping to buy bananas for the

Balinese mountains and hillside temples

onslaught of friendly monkeys that await you on the ride), to the enchanting Lake Batur, the northern beach of Lovina, and numerous traditional villages where bones of the dead are prominently on display.

As you can see, the Hindu culture of Bali, and its superb natural sights, are all accessible, and accessible cheaply, to the tourist who avoids the heavily touristed beach areas to the south. It all depends on knowing where to go

Garuda Indonesian Airlines flies to Bali from Los Angeles for as little as $1,155 round-trip. So does Continental Airways (via Guam), Qantas (via Australia), and Malaysian Airlines (via Kuala Lumpur). Other airlines fly to Jakarta, from where you connect to Bali.

Monkey Forest Road

THE NEW WORLD OF TRAVEL 1992

The lifeblood of the Arthur Frommer travel guides is the correspondence received from readers, commenting on the establishments recommended in the texts and recommending new establishments. Each such letter is carefully studied, and when a particular lead seems promising, it is followed up and personally checked.

It is hoped that *The New World of Travel* will receive similar assistance from its readers. A yearly publication, issued near the start of each year, *The New World* will constantly grow. And since much of its content relates to organizations that lack the means to market themselves properly, or come to the attention of a travel journalist, your help is invaluable in alerting me to the organizations—hospitality exchanges, alternative resorts, new travel clubs, and the like—that you have discovered.

If you become aware of a new travel organization, program, or development that deserves to be described in our next edition, *The New World of Travel 1992*, won't you please let me know about it? Send your letters to Arthur Frommer, *The New World of Travel*, c/o Prentice Hall Press, Travel Division, 15 Columbus Circle, New York, NY 10023. All letters will be acknowledged, and all are warmly appreciated, in advance, by the author.

Five Small Towns Prove That Historic Preservation Brings Touristic Wealth

Though Hardly Household Names, They Enjoy a Steady Flow of Visitors

Madison, Indiana; Guthrie, Oklahoma; Rugby, Tennessee; Stevensville, Maryland; and Las Vegas, New Mexico (not Nevada, but New Mexico)—these aren't exactly household words. Each is a tiny village, or at best a small town of fewer than 14,000 souls. And none is near a great natural wonder or other touristic sight. Yet each enjoys a thriving tourist trade that fills its hotels, restaurants, and shops on weekends in winter, and throughout the week at other times. And why?

Because each has preserved its past. Each has had the presence of mind to banish development to the outskirts of town, to prohibit the high-rise and the shopping mall near the center, to preserve and maintain historic structures as precious jewels. Therein lies a lesson for scores of other American communities with similar potential.

The tourism enjoyed by these small towns is based on an aspect of human nature: the satisfaction people derive from communing with the past. People travel in part for that reason. They gain solace, strength, or inspiration from a contact with structures of earlier times, feel part of humankind, less alienated and apart; they seek roots. Though historic preservation is not undertaken for touristic reasons—but rather to preserve the continuum of culture, the basis of civilization—it throws off important dividends to the industry of tourism.

And therefore when people feel uncertain about whether to prevent the real-estate developers from placing parking garages or gas stations in their historic downtown districts, they might want to ponder the achievements of five small towns that have followed the course of preservation—unyielding hostility to the forces of commercial greed.

F.C. Bonfils Building (1890), Guthrie, Oklahoma

State Capital Printing Company Building (1902), Guthrie

De Steiguer Building (1890)

MADISON, INDIANA

In a valley of the Ohio River, and alongside that river, Madison's downtown stretches for dozens of blocks without a single high-rise, a scene of gentle beauty. Here is found every major example of 19th-century architectural style: Gothic, Georgian, Regency, classic revival, Federal, Americanized Italian villa, and—of course—Victorian, all fiercely protected against demolition and replacement.

Has commerce suffered from these limits placed upon the developers? Exactly the opposite has occurred, say numerous spokespeople; Madison is a vital, bustling, modern city whose normal commerce is simply enhanced by tourism to its downtown area, whose entire expanse has now been placed on the National Register of Historic Places. For accommodations, try the Broadway Historic Hotel (operating since 1859), the Victoria Inn, Cliff House, or one of the numerous historic bed-and-breakfast homes. To reach Madison, simply drive for less than two hours from either Louisville, Kentucky, or Cincinnati, Ohio.

STEVENSVILLE, MARYLAND

On Kent Island, in Chesapeake Bay, within commuting distance of Baltimore, Washington, D.C., and Annapolis, Stevensville is the smallest of the recent success stories, but thriving and growing not only in a commercial sense, but in its opportunities for residential living in town houses and apartments. And yet the developer of this once-typical turn-of-the-century Eastern Shore town has been scrupulous in maintaining the Victorian character of the town's period structures, unaltered by a single new façade, a single neon sign. Those buildings were saved when the simultaneous construction (in the 1950s) of the Chesapeake Bay Bridge and busy Maryland Rte. 50 drew traffic away from the rail and port facilities located near the enchanting Victorian town. While other areas of Kent Island erupted into shopping malls and the like, Stevensville slumbered until taken in hand by a businessman with a sense of taste. Even his new office building there is only two stories high and in traditional style. If you do decide to visit, you'll want to stay at the nearby Kent Manor Inn, built in 1820, which has 25 super-comfortable rooms. From the eastern end of the Chesapeake Bay Bridge, turn down Maryland Rte. 18 to reach Stevensville.

Foucart Office Building (1891), Guthrie

GUTHRIE, OKLAHOMA

Nearly 100 years ago the great Oklahoma land rush brought thousands in a single week to create the town of Guthrie in Victorian style and splendor. The first capital of Oklahoma, by 1910 Guthrie had over 50 miles of sidewalk lined by handsome buildings of every sort, but then declined with startling suddenness when the capital moved 28 miles south to Oklahoma City. As other Oklahoma cities "boomed"—replacing their historic centers with ugly high-rise offices—Guthrie remained unaltered, and today enjoys the largest commercial historic district in the National Register of Historic Places: 100 Victorian business buildings, 2,300 certifiably Victorian homes, an amazing treasure unmarred by modern towers. Looking for the "Old West"? You'll find it in Guthrie. And a lively array of rodeos and ranch shows, resident theaters and museums, keep things lively beyond the lure of architecture.

Each has had the presence of mind to banish development to the outskirts of town.

Las Vegas, New Mexico

La Castaneda Hotel, built by Fred Harvey in 1898

LAS VEGAS, NEW MEXICO

Long overshadowed by its namesake in Nevada, Las Vegas was once the supply city for a vital fort guarding the Santa Fe Trail, then a key stop on the Atchison, Topeka and the Santa Fe railroad. By 1882 it was nearly the size of Albuquerque and Denver, but then ceased growing as additional rail lines bypassed its own. Today, with 900 buildings on the National Register, its decades-long economic torpor is viewed as a blessing, and tourism is increasingly pushed as a major activity. Though heavily visited, it is not nearly as "touristy" as Santa Fe, and its several historic districts—with their many stone residences and stone commercial buildings—provide a fascinating glimpse into American history. For lodgings, try for a room at the imposing La Castaneda Hotel, built by Fred Harvey in 1898.

Though historic preservation is undertaken to preserve the continuum of culture, the basis for civilization, it throws off important dividends.

Las Vegas

View from Plaza, Las Vegas, New Mexico

RUGBY, TENNESSEE

An "intentional community" founded in the 1880s by English author Thomas Hughes (*Tom Brown's Schooldays*), who envisioned it as a rural cooperative, yet with high-peaked Victorian buildings and ornamental gardens. Though the gentlemen farmers he attracted there never really succeeded in an economic sense (some dressed for tea at 4 P.M.), the village survived and today zealously maintains and preserves its 17 original structures (which include a church, schoolhouse, public library, and bookshop, all built in the 1880s). Thousands of visitors stop by each month, at this location in the Cumberland Plateau of eastern Tennessee, some staying at B&Bs maintained in historic homes. Rugby can be visited from March 1 to December 15.

Costa Rica, for a Different Sort of Tropical Vacation

On the T-Shirts of the Teenagers Here, the Words "Costa Rica Air Force" Are Emblazoned Near the Neck; Filling the Space Below Is a Huge Dove

THEY ABOLISHED THE ARMY HERE MORE than 40 years ago, and have lived in perfect peace and tranquillity ever since. They enjoy the highest per-capita income in Central America, a fully functioning democracy, the presence of North American retirees totaling 35,000 people, and a president who won the Nobel Peace Prize for his plan to end the fighting in nearby Nicaragua and El Salvador.

But the beaches are 80 miles from the capital city, and the seaside hotels are small lodgings that haven't yet attracted masses of foreign visitors. While that's a disturbing fact for traditional tourists, it's a positive plus for special ones. Costa Rica is the destination par excellence for people seeking the pleasures of the tropics without the pressures of crowds and casinos. It affords you a chance to experience Central America without danger, to explore and discuss the politics of the region with open-minded, uncoerced residents, to combine rest for the body with stimulation for the mind, pleasure with learning.

But what exactly do you, as a tourist, do there? Because the capital city of San José is in a central valley, 80 miles from the sea on either side, your initial activities are different from those you scheduled for more standard tropical destinations located on a coast, near beaches. Here, before attending to countryside pleasures, you first experience the distinctly urban life of a great Central American center, conversing with its highly opinionated, politically alert people, visiting attrac-tions of cultural interest, taking Spanish lessons, attending highly charged lectures (in English) on social and regional concerns.

THE LIFE OF SAN JOSÉ

The opening step is a remarkably cheap and effective, three-day "crash course" in the Spanish language at the Instituto Universal de Idiomas in the heart of downtown San José, Costa Rica's capital. For six hours a day on each of three days (Tuesday, Wednesday, and Thursday) each week, their university-level instructors will provide you with a basic underpinning in that useful subject for a total charge of only $85, and a $15 registration fee. Reserve your place by contacting the **Instituto Universal de Idiomas, P.O. Box 219-2120, San José, Costa Rica (phone 23-96-62).**

More serious travelers will opt for a one-month course in Spanish (three hours a day for five days a week, for four weeks) at the same instituto, costing an equally remarkable total of only $225, including materials and registration. To ensure your immersion in the subject, the instituto will then arrange your room and board with one of 20 Costa Rican families in the area, for $85 a week, including all meals and laundry service. Classroom instruction is with a usual total of three or four other students, a maximum of six. Private lessons, either supplementing the group instruction or substitut-

The country is peaceful and stable, its cities calm and well ordered.

Forester Institute, Los Yoses

ing for it, are $9 an hour, which contrasts radically with what you'd pay for Spanish instruction here at home.

A shorter, but perhaps more elaborate, introduction to the language and culture of Central America, in a country club–like setting within the elegant residential neighborhood of Los Yoses (20 minutes by bus from downtown San José), is provided by the Forester Institute; its classrooms enjoy an awesome view of the surrounding mountains, and the chirping of birds.

At Forester, you choose from either two-week, three-week, or four-week classes (maximum of eight students per class) in either "Language" or "Language and Culture." The former involves four hours a day of instruction; the latter supplements classroom instruction with daily excursions, cultural activities, and conferences (on both political and cultural themes). On both programs, students are placed with carefully selected but non-English-speaking Costa Rican families where they receive a private room, breakfasts, dinners, and laundry service.

Charge for Forester's language program, including the homestay, is $560 for two weeks, $700 for three weeks, $840 for four weeks. The more extensive language-and-culture

program (including the homestay) runs $680 for two weeks, $880 for three weeks, $1,080 for four weeks. Contact Forester's U.S. representative: **Charlene Biddulph, 249 S. U.S. Hwy. 101, Suite 226, Solana Beach, CA 92075 (phone 619/943-0204).**

Two final examples of Costa Rica's programs for total immersion in the Spanish language start, first, with David Kaufman's Centro Linguistico CONVERSA, in a large and rambling farmhouse atop a hill about three miles from the center of San José. There, you'll be brought each morning by Jeep from your lodgings with a Spanish-speaking private family in the nearby town of Santa Ana, and given 5½ hours daily of classroom instruction in addition to other practice sessions exclusively in Spanish. After four weeks, you speak! Total cost of the four-week course, taught every month but December, and including all lodging, meals, tuition, everything: $1,452 for one person, $2,703 per couple. Contact **Centro Linguistico CONVERSA, Apartado no. 17, 1007 Centro Colón, San José, Costa Rica (phone 21-76-49).** The Centro's U.S. representative is Dr. Brian Adams, phone 800/292-9872, who will be happy to provide you with additional information. That toll-free number is his wife's travel agency; leave your name and number, and Dr. Adams will phone back.

Or try the month-long "total immersion" regimen of the ICAI organization (described more fully below) for $1,200. That includes room and board with a private family, tuition, classroom materials, excursions, cultural and sightseeing activities, and instruction in classes limited to six students. For information, contact the organization's U.S. office: **ICAI School of Languages, P.O. Box 5095, Anaheim, CA 92814 (phone 714/527-2918 or 213/383-4064).**

Students of Forester Institute

REALITIES OF CENTRAL AMERICA

With or without a knowledge of Spanish, you can attend courses presented in English on the present-day realities of Central American societies at the Central American Institute for International Affairs ("ICAI") in San José, founded in part by the Organization of American States. ICAI offers numerous short-term (three weeks to one month) programs co-sponsored by about a dozen U.S. universities, to which outsiders are admitted, but only if they have some college training or other background in the social sciences. Lecturers are leading scholars or political figures of Central America; classes are supplemented by field trips, such as to a Nicaraguan refugee camp in Costa Rica's Limón Province; and students are housed (room and two meals a day) with Costa Rican families. Though prices vary, figure about $900 for a three-week course of instruction, including room and two meals a day. For information, contact **Roberto de la Ossa, Director, ICAI, Apartado Postal 3316, San José, Costa Rica (phone 33-85-71 or 55-08-59 in San José).**

More casual learning, and again usually in English: at the Monday evening lectures of the Quaker-run **Friends Peace Center** in San José, or at their periodic, frequent workshops, many of which are conducted in English (phone first— 33-61-68—to determine if they are). And you can browse through numerous hard-to-find newspapers and magazines dealing with Central American issues at the center's extensive library. Its address, in the strange directional terms of San José, but comprehensible to any taxi driver, is: "c 15 a 6, no. 13-36." Taxis to most points in San José are rarely more than $1 in cost.

If you would simply like the experience of living with a Costa Rican family on your visit to San José, contact **Señora Soledad Zamora (phone 24-79-37)**, who serves as a one-woman booking agency for nearly 80 such families in and around the city (and mainly in the suburb of San Pedro, 15 minutes out). For a $15 fee, Señora Soledad will place you with a family that charges $7 to $12 a day, full board. Since she does not speak English, ask to speak with her daughter, Silvia, or with one of the American students usually living at Señora Soledad's home, if you yourself do not speak Spanish. Staying with a host family, you soon will.

COSTS AND CULTURAL OPPORTUNITIES

For the standard tourist to Costa Rica desiring standard accommodations, the choices are broad and at wonderfully low rates. They range from such standouts as the deluxe Corobici Hotel (as little as $66 for a double room) to the tourist/first-class Gran Hotel Costa Rica ($52 per double) and Ambassador Hotel ($40 for a double), to the charming Pension Don Carlos ($30 per double) to the more basic Costa Rica Inn ($14.50 per double) to the Toruma Youth Hostel ($2.45 per person per night). Restaurants offer meals with music at such outstanding values as El Balcon de Europa (Costa Rican dishes from $2 to $4.85) and Miró's Bistro (a giant platter of rice with shrimp for $3.30). Nightlife is cen-

tered at El Pueblo, a sparkling-white village of Spanish colonial architecture whose varied components—discos, bars, restaurants with guitar players and accordions—could not be exhausted in a week of going out each night. At the complex's La Cocina de Leña restaurant, where musicians wander in to play, a mammoth plate called "gallo pinto" (mixed rice and beans, meat, eggs, and sour cream) sells for the Costa Rican equivalent of $2.70.

Suitably housed and fed in the year-round, spring-like climate of San José, you then attend symphonic or dance performances (tickets for under $5) at the famed National Theater; visit the art exhibits and presentations at the Costa Rica–North American Cultural Center; wander among the modern art, primarily by Central American artists, at the Galería J. Garcia Monge or in the galleries of the Central Bank on the Cultural Plaza; view pre-Columbian art at the National Museum of Costa Rica.

But mainly you meet the politically alert, fiercely independent people of Costa Rica, and hear their varied reactions to conditions in Central America and policies of other nations toward Central America. And then, if you wish, you can head to the beaches, surrounded by jungle-like national parks.

INTO THE COUNTRY

When you then strike out into the hinterland, your vacation is again utterly different from what you've experienced in more standard resorts, in high-rise hotels. It is not only different, it is more human, more removed from urban atmospheres, better.

Because the Costa Ricans are fiercely determined to protect their beach areas from the excesses of a Miami or Acapulco, they have limited seaside hotels to the height of a palm tree, and placed many of them back from the sea, on hillsides or enveloped by trees. About the closest equivalent to a standard resort area is that sector (actually a province) of Costa Rica's Pacific coast called Guanacaste, where the several small one- and two-story hotels on four particular beaches—Tamarindo, Ocotal, Condovac, and Flamingo— are the chief draws, but charge no more than $37 to $50 for a single room, $47 to $70 for a double, even in high season. Those rates contrast sharply with the levels of other tropical countries available to North Americans.

Amazingly, you can fly from San José to Guanacaste for

In rural Costa Rica

Here are the pleasures of the tropics without the pressures of crowds and casinos

only $11 each way, or go by bus for infinitely less, or drive there from San José in four hours on the Pan American Highway.

Rather than stay at the resorts of Guanacaste, however, I'd pursue the more exotic pleasures of the nation's national parks and nature reserves, teeming with wildlife and wonders. They are the true, standout attractions of Costa Rica.

MANUEL ANTONIO NATIONAL PARK

Reached by air from San José for only $7.50 each way, this 1,700-acre preserve on the Pacific Ocean is a series of crescent-shaped, white-sand beaches surrounded by lush tropical jungle and verdant volcanic cliffs; mention its name to a "Tico" (a Costa Rican) and you'll provoke exclamatory superlatives, sighs, and dreamy smiles. It is one of the few places on earth where you can luxuriate on a beach and experience jungle (including white-faced monkeys) at the same time. You walk to the beaches along well-marked jungle paths, enjoy breathtaking views of azure seas and sharp cliffs from atop lookout areas on Cathedral Point (a bit more difficult to reach), view wildlife in a hundred forms, then frolic in the warm surf with Tico families, who later tap and sway to salsa music—and prepare enormous lunches for their beachside stays.

Although campers can remain overnight in the park, at designated sites (receiving fresh water, bathroom facilities, and picnic tables, for 50¢), the hotels are outside its grounds, but immediately alongside or less than two miles away. The top lodgings are the Spanish-colonial duplex villas of La Mariposa, built into the otherwise-untouched, lush countryside, with one of the world's most spectacular ocean views and Costa Rica's highest rates: $75 per person per night, including breakfast and dinner served in an elegant pavilion amid jungle flowers and palms. You dine to the strains of classical music, enjoying such treats as stuffed quail baked in red wine or heart-of-palm brioche. For reservations (which

La Mariposa Hotel, near Manuel Antonio National Park

In the Tilaran Mountains

you will need here), phone toll free 800/223-6510 in the U.S., or directly to La Mariposa in Costa Rica at 77-03-55.

Lesser priced, but perfectly adequate and just as exotic: the small Hotel Divisamar, directly across the road from La Mariposa ($34 double, without meals), and the nearby Hotel Karahe ($34 double), the latter with a moderately priced restaurant. Rock-bottom in cost, but proper: the Costa Linda Youth Hostel, accepting people of all ages, for $4 per bed per night.

MONTEVERDE CLOUD FOREST RESERVE

By express bus from San José ($3.40), or by rental car, a great many visitors schedule time for still another major attraction: the mystical, cloud-enshrouded, 25,000-acre reserve of Monteverde in the Tilaran Mountains, 6,000 feet above the sea. Protected and maintained by a world-renowned, Quaker-founded science institute, it harbors hundreds of varieties of mammals and birds (including the mythical Quetzal and the elusive golden toad; you'll almost certainly spot the

former), lush jungle with 80 miles of wood- or rock-carpeted trails, waterfalls, orchids, and a dense shroud of white cloud—you feel somewhere between land and sky. For $49 per person, including all three meals, you can stay in the lodge/farm known as the Hotel Montana (call 61-18-46 in San José for reservations) or for $25, including meals, in the Belmar Hotel or Pension Quetzal, or for $18, including all three meals, in the Flora Mar, or for $3 a night, without meals, in the dormlike "field station" of the Tropical Science Center ("T.S.C.", headquartered at Apartado 8-3870, San José 1000, Costa Rica, phone 22-62-41; phone them in advance for a bunk). And at the club known as the Golden Toad in the nearby town of Santa Elena, Latin and rock music is played most nights.

THE JUNGLE TRAIN

Still other visitors take the six- to eight-hour trip on the slow "Jungle Train" from San José to Limón, where they proceed by bus for another hour to the 1,500 acres of coral reef that make up Cahuita National Park of Costa Rica. After that

Sights from the Jungle Train

day-long ride through tropical vegetation and coffee plantations along mountains and in green valleys, so close to village life as to enable eye contact with Ticos going about their daily business, they repair for rest to the pleasant Hotel Cahuita ($15 per very basic double room), with garden, pool, and patio restaurant. In the park, snorkeling equipment is rented for $5.40 to explore the exquisite coral reef.

Some of these sights, and still others, can be managed on shorter day-trips from San José (where a dozen travel agencies will make the arrangements), but staying overnight or for several nights at small lodgings affords you a different and better contact with the primeval life of tropical jungles, mountains, and sea—the kind of experience that used to be the accustomed lot of travelers before high-rise hotels standardized the world.

For assistance in visiting these and other attractions of Costa Rica, I like the services of OTEC, a well-staffed, nonprofit organization of student travel that specializes in trips and discounts for the young, but actually handles the needs of all ages and of nonstudents. They're found on the second floor of the Victoria Building in San José ("a 3, c 3/5"; phone 22-08-66), where they answer questions and offer to make you one of their traveling groups, which brings you a radical saving from the price levels of other commercial tour operators. Contact them ahead of time if you're planning a special interest or group tour of Costa Rica, by writing: **OTEC, P.O. Box 323, San José 1002, Costa Rica.**

For additional information on this inexpensive and inspiring nation, contact the Miami office of the **Costa Rica Tourist Board (phone 305/358-2150, or toll free 800/327-7033 outside Florida).** The national carrier, LACSA, and Eastern Airlines, service San José directly from several U.S. cities, and numerous other airlines go there via their own national gateways.

An Introduction to Belize

Shunned by Many Because of Its Location in Central America, It Is Peaceful, Stable, Filled with Activities—and Cheap

WEATHER-BEATEN WOODEN HOMES AND streets made of white sand. "Hotels" with 10 rooms and "restaurants" with five tables. Barefoot informality and yarn-spinning residents with all the time in the world. Electricity that doesn't always work, schedules that aren't always met.

If you're yearning for the Caribbean as it once was, you'll find it in the Caribbean's newest nation, Belize, only nine years removed from its former status as British Honduras. Two hours by air from Miami, and yet touristically underdeveloped, it awaits you on the edge of Central America—some would say "on the edge of the world"—just below the Yucatán peninsula of Mexico, between Guatemala and Honduras.

Beach-lined "cayes" of Belize

It is remarkably peaceful, stable, democratic. Though its tiny population (175,000 people in an area the size of Massachusetts) is split among a dozen ethnic groups—Mayan Indians, Chinese, "Anglos," Créoles, Hindus, mestizos, Hispanics, even a recent community of horse-and-buggy Mennonites—they live in perfect harmony, enjoy a British-style parliamentary government, intermarry, and serve as a lesson for all of us. What's more, their official language is English!

As for its touristic attractions, Belize possesses the second-longest (after Australia) barrier reef on earth, a teeming coral formation of sea life, shapes, and colors that draws scuba-divers and sailors from around the world. Along the reef are then dozens of "cayes" (pronounced "keys")—narrow, beach-lined islands of remarkable beauty, dotted with small hotels (often 10 rooms apiece) of modest, friendly pretensions.

On the mainland, only one major city is found, of no great visitor interest. This is Belize City, with only 60,000 people, but site of an international airport well serviced by a number of carriers (I'll list them later). From here, you take smaller planes to the cayes.

Inland of Belize City is of greater appeal: 65% of the country's land area is uninhabited jungle—supporting jaguars, no less—and scattered about are relics, temples, even cities, of the once-mammoth Mayan civilization that flourished from the 3rd to the 10th century in what is now Belize.

You have two vacation choices, therefore, on a trip to Belize, and many tourists combine them both. You can sun, swim, sail, or scuba-dive on and off the cayes. Or you can explore the inner mainland, pursuing bents of archeology, wildlife and other natural history, Mayan ruins and culture, all forms of jungle adventure travel.

THE MAINLAND

The region on the mainland best suited to accommodate tourists is the Cayo District (two hours by car from Belize City), which has several exotic but comfortable lodges, and is accessible to the formidable Mayan ceremonial site of Xunantunich and the impressive natural wonders of Mountain Pine Ridge. Alternatively, you go south down the coast to Dangriga, viewing the world's only jaguar preserve and the life of Garifuna Indians, who allow visitors (if they're so inclined) to participate in their rituals. Because life hereabouts is rustic, with treacherous roads and nonexistent (usually) signposts, you accomplish all this not by self-drive car, but on organized small-group tours operated weekly and well by several Belizean tour operators. In my opinion, it's best to pursue the mainland portion of your trip first (say, for four days) and follow up with R&R on those sunny, pleasant cayes for two or three concluding days of your trip.

Upon the mainland, so rich is the Mayan heritage of Belize, so diverse its wildlife and flora, that the resulting travel choices are fairly dizzying.

If you can somehow manage the time, sign on for Charles Halsall's 12-day/11-night "In Search of the Ancient Maya" (as little as $1,485 per person, and virtually all-inclusive; contact **S & L Travel Services, P.O. Box 700, Belize City, Belize, Central America (phone 2-77593)**, which takes you to a dozen ancient ceremonial centers, Mayan trading sites, excavated village ruins dating as far back as 2,500 B.C. Your stops include Altun Ha (the country's most extensively excavated Mayan pyramids, mounds, ball courts, burial chambers, reservoirs) and Xunantunich (tallest man-made structure in Belize, with elaborate stucco friezes); and then your tour darts over the Guatemalan border to view the grandeur of famous Tikal (a Mayan royal city flourishing from 600 B.C. to A.D. 950, when it was mysteriously aban-

doned). On the way, while still in Belize, you visit the current "digs" at Caracol, which university archeologists believe will ultimately unearth a pre–Classic Age Mayan city three times as large as Tikal and every bit as grand.

Or if you're inclined to less vigorous touring, but in the same prime location (the well-located Cayo District), you can contact the English couple who own the palm-thatched safari lodge called **Chaa Creek Cottages, P.O. Box 53, Cayo, Belize (phone 92-2037)**, from which every standard tour is offered. Charges here are $62.50 per person per night, double occupancy, including all three meals. Or you can stay at the newer, basic but charming, **Windy Hill Cottages (phone**

Temple of Xunantunich

You have two vacation choices on a trip to Belize—you can sun, swim, sail, or scuba-dive on and off the cayes, or you can explore the inner mainland in pursuit of Mayan ruins and culture, wildlife, and other natural history.

92-2017), where double rooms rent for a total of $60 a night, breakfast for two included. Finally, if you're not up to a jungle camp at all, you can simply base yourself (for $45 double) in the hillside **San Ignacio Hotel, P.O. Box 33, San Ignacio, Cayo District, Belize (phone 92-2034)**, booking one-day tours, or hiking on your own, from there.

Whatever your hotel choice, you must be sure to include a visit to the mile-long Panti Trail, in the same area and of considerable historic and perhaps scientific interest. It's lined with the remarkably diverse plants, bushes, and trees supplying herbal substances used as medicines by the ancient Mayans, all according to formulas handed down from generation to generation and today known to a 92-year-old Mayan/Belizean priest/doctor (read: medicine man) named Eligio Panti. For six years now, scientists headed by Dr. Rosita Arvigo have been "debriefing" Don Eligio of his secrets, attracting attention from learned groups ranging from the New York Botanical Garden to the National Cancer Society. They also conduct guided tours of the trail (daily except Monday, $12), commenting on the strongly apparent-medicinal properties of the growths (a tree bark that cures dysentery, a leaf that stops bleeding).

And don't laugh: fully 25% of the world's commercial medicines are derived from plant-based chemicals found in tropical regions (according to Dr. Arvigo).

The Panti Trail begins at Dr. Arvigo's home, "IX Chel" (named for the Mayan goddess of medicine), just beyond San Ignacio off the Western Hwy. The great Mayan ceremonial site of Xunantunich is not far away. To contact Dr. Arvigo for a guided group tour of the Panti Trail ($30 per group), write: **Dr. Rosita Arvigo, General Delivery, San Ignacio Post Office, Cayo District, Belize, or leave a message at 92-2188.**

THE CAYES

After an active and sometimes tiring exploration into the interior, a great many visitors turn to those restful strips of water-surrounded land along the barrier reef.

Ambergris Caye is the most highly developed of these narrow lines in the sea, and that mark of distinction will come as a surprise when you first arrive by small plane at the sleepy frontier town of San Pedro, "capital" of Ambergris Caye. It consists of exactly three white-sand-covered "avenues," the unpretentiously named Front, Middle, and Back Streets. On Front (also known as Beach) Street, within the five intersecting blocks of the city center, are small hotels and cabañas (40 of them), interspersed with the basketball court, police station, town hall, school, and local discothèque (Big Daddy's).

On Front Street, the Holiday Hotel ($74 per double room), features the colorful tales and excellent cuisine of the charismatic Celi McCorkle, whom many call the "mother of tourism" in Belize. Farther along, the Coral Beach is a favorite of divers and operated by the "father of diving," Allan Forman, who offers low rates ($50 for the average double room) and generous, family-style meals. You can stay at the Sun Breeze Beach Resort ($90 for a double room, and home of the island's windsurfing school), at Ramon's Reef (in charming, waterside cabañas priced at $110 a day, double), or on the edge of town in the costlier ($95, double) Paradise Hotel much favored by Francis Ford Coppola.

It is also possible, either by simply applying door-to-door, or by using the advance services of Charles Halsall of S & L Travel Services in Belize City (address and phone number above) to obtain $40-a-night rooms at such family-run lodg-

Dr. Rosita Arvigo on the Panti Trail

Exploring on horseback

ings as the San Pedrano and its several affiliates run by four brothers and sisters.

From all these havens, the barrier reef is less than a mile out into the sea, supplying not simply the site for snorkeling and dives, but a wonderfully protected area for invigorating sailing and windsurfing; "there's always a breeze in Belize," goes a local saying.

For on-the-spot information and assistance in San Pedro, contact Pany Arceo (phone 26-2136); he's a dynamic fisherman-turned-guide who offers insight, instruction, and excursions in bonefishing, snorkeling, diving, and bird-watching at considerably lower cost, and with far greater knowledge, than others I've met. Or seek out his sister, Shelley Prevett, who operates the moderately priced and popular restaurant, The Hut ($10 for turtle curry). She provides hard-to-get information (babysitters, air charters, local black-coral-jewelry makers), and will also prepare your own fish catch at half the normal menu price.

The lower-priced, budget alternative to Ambergris

Caye—if you can imagine such a thing—is **Caye Caulker**, a few miles farther south in the sea. With only two streets along the beach, it's like a stage setting for a W. Somerset Maugham play, and hotel rooms are widely available for $15 to $30 a night, while several inexpensive "restaurants" are in people's homes. At the popular Tropical Paradise hotel, $30 will get you your own cabaña by the sea. Caye Caulker, though, can be reached only by boat from Belize City (on several services operated daily except Sunday), while Ambergris Caye is more easily serviced by air.

Other cayes (often with only a single hotel apiece) are more difficult of access, and thereby more exclusive: Caye Chapel (the 32-room Pyramid Resort), St. George's Caye (St. George's Lodge), South Water Caye (Blue Marlin Lodge), Glover's Reef (Manta Reef Resort), and Caye Bokel (the fishing-oriented Turneffe Island Lodge, $160 a day per per-

Cayo

son for room and all three meals, unlimited use of fishing boats, gas for the boats, and guides, all for the purpose of seeking six-pound bonefish, the chief activity), among them. An exception to the pricey tone of the less accessible cayes is Bluefield Range Cayes (a group of three), where beach huts on working lobster and fishing camps rent for under $25 a night. Ricardo's Beach Huts, also offering tent sites for $2.50 per person per night, is one such place.

SOME ADDED POINTS

As we go to press with this 1991 edition of *The New World of Travel*, a new resort area of Belize—in the tiny fishing village of Placencia, on a charming peninsula in the south of the country—is coming up fast in popularity, for its fishing, diving, and general ambience. It may currently be the country's fastest-growing area for tourists, and already offers several small hotels and lodges with accommodations for $20 a night, plus several rooms in private homes for as little as $4 a night. I'll report further on Placencia in the 1992 edition, but I urge you to inquire about facilities from the information sources listed below.

The chief recreational activity of Belize? Diving. The chief drawback? Car-rental rates—as much as $80 a day. The high season in Belize? November through April, when travelers planning to use standard rooms should not arrive without reservations.

RESOURCES FOR TOURING

Always bear in mind that the relative newness of tourism in Belize adds to its appeal, but also has its drawbacks. Tourists are often surprised to find no air conditioning in many hotels (unnecessary, say the Belizeans, because of their cooling trade winds). And visitors should also be prepared for occasional electricity shortages and lack of hot water, particularly inland. Bring a spirit of adventure—and an open mind.

Your best contact for preparing a trip to Belize is **Tropical Travel Representatives, of Houston, Texas (phone 713/688-1985, or toll free 800/451-8017 outside Texas).** A combined travel agency and tour operator, its founders,

Placencia

Caye Caulker is like a stage setting for a W. Somerset Maugham play, and hotel rooms are widely available for $15 to $30 a night.

Tommy and Jerisue Thomson, are so enchanted with the country that they exchanged wedding vows on its white sands six years ago. They also publish a quarterly newsletter, *Belize Travel News*, which is widely distributed by the Embassy of Belize and the Caribbean Tourist Association and available to their clients. Other Belize-specializing U.S. travel agents include the high-volume **Ocean Connections (phone 713/486-6993, or toll free 800/331-2458 outside Houston)**, and **Triton Tours (phone 504/522-3382, or toll free 800/426-0226 outside Louisiana)**.

Another excellent Belize information resource and travel coordinator is **Charles Halsall of S & L Travel Services** in Belize City (see above for address and telephone number). He has a wealth of information and welcomes inquiries that state budget limitations and personal interests. For ultra-cost-conscious travelers whom the U.S. agents cannot accommodate, Charles's services will be well worth the time of a letter or the cost of an overseas telephone call.

Good background reading for Belize is the book *Jaguar* by Alan Rabinowitz (published by Arbor House).

Four airlines service Belize from the States, usually for a round-trip "add-on" fare from Miami of $254, a bit more from New Orleans and Houston. **Tan Sahsa Airlines (phone 305/526-4300, or toll free 800/327-1225, 800/432-9818 in Florida)** operates daily service at that rate from Miami, four times a week from New Orleans, thrice weekly from Houston; it also provides advantageous "through" fares from other cities, such as from New York for $498 round trip.

Continental Airlines (phone toll free 800/231-0856) and **TACA International Airlines (phone 305/526-6795, or toll free 800/535-8780 outside Florida)** offer similar services. Continental charges a dramatically low $290 round-trip from Houston. TACA goes there from Los Angeles ($556), San Francisco ($660), New Orleans ($325), and Houston ($325).

This winter in the Caribbean, you have a choice.

You can crowd into a high-rise hotel and fight for a place at a noisy pool.

Or you can go to Belize.

Guess which I'd choose.

Hot Turkey

Tourism There Is Booming as the World Awakens to Its Attractions and Low Rates

NO DESTINATION ON EARTH HAS CREATED more tourist excitement this year than Turkey. As if Aladdin had suddenly rubbed his lamp to give the Islamic world its first big travel hit, Turkey is today awash with visitors throughout the year, bestrewn with new hotels in construction, covered with touring motorcoaches.

Why did it happen so late? What delayed the advent of Turkey into massive tourist popularity? Though many will cite the remarkable cheapness of a Turkish vacation—decent hotels for $20 a night; colorful meals of lamb shish kebab, eggplant, and juicy tomatoes for $3; in-city transportation via group taxi (*dolmus*) for 30¢—Turkey has always been that cheap, even cheaper a decade ago.

The explanation seems to stem from political changes that bode well for the long-term health of tourism in Turkey. Stable, democratic, civilian government seems to have been achieved after a period of intermittent military rule. No longer do fanatical religious parties control the Ministry of Tourism, from which they frequently sought to block incoming tourism and the liberalizing influences it brought. Most important, Turkey is currently attempting to enter the Common Market (the European Community) and is supporting the application with widespread advertising and exhibitions that stress its openness to commerce and visitors.

Turkey is a pleasant way-station to the Muslim world, a partially Westernized country that nevertheless grounds its culture and religion on the Koran, a safe and familiar base for commencing your study of Middle Eastern institutions.

Though there are mosques everywhere, and veiled women, there's none of the tension felt in similar countries, and people are friendly to foreigners. Signs are in Roman letters, not Arabic script; hotels serve cocktails and wine; the female tourist is tolerated at restaurants and cafés, even alone; and women of the West are able to move about without harassment or scorn, at least in the larger cities and at beachfront resorts.

For tourists, as I've already noted, the country is remarkably cheap, the cheapest of any European nation. With Spain increasingly costly, and Greece getting there, the budget-conscious traveler is especially attracted today to Turkey.

EXPLORING ISTANBUL

You start, of course, in Istanbul, the former Constantinople. Once the capital of Christianity, then of the great Ottoman Empire, its downtown is a startling forest of needle-like spires sticking into the sky from the minarets of more mosques than you are ever again likely to see in one location.

The key attractions are rather conveniently grouped on a peninsula of sea-surrounded land known generally as Sultanahmet. Here is the rich Topkapi Palace, where a series of often decadent, occasionally impressive, sultans, pashas, and caliphs once disported themselves in sensual style, both at water pipes (still seen at cafés in Istanbul) and with harem dancers; the exhibits inside are disappointing, but the harem exquisite. More impressive, just outside the palace walls, are

No longer do fanatical religious parties control the Ministry of Tourism.

St. Sophia, Istanbul

the Museum of Oriental Art (with Hittite ruins), the Archeological Museum, and the Museum of Tiles.

From there you easily stroll to the massive Blue Mosque, removing your shoes to enter inside; and then, across the way, to Aghia Sophia, once the largest domed church in all of Christendom, now a mosque but still bearing Byzantine mosaics of biblical scenes.

From the grand mosques, a street called Divan Yolu leads to the Grand Bazaar (Kapali Carsi), perhaps the largest covered bazaar in the world. As you near the vast emporium, numerous "kebab" restaurants tempt you with savory scents and displays of grilled lamb or chicken kebab or sausage kebab, accompanied by that supreme achievement of Turkish farmers: succulent fresh tomatoes, the highlight of a meal that rarely exceeds $3 in cost. As you then pass into the four-block-wide labyrinth of shops that make up the bazaar, you catch your breath at the bargains that smart shopping can secure: excellent leather wallets for under $6, pantaloon-like "harem pants" for the same, full-length leather coats that can be negotiated down to $200, pages from medieval illuminated Islamic manuscripts—a superb gift—for $10.

The bulk of visitors, after touring Istanbul, head to inexpensive beach resorts on the Antalyan portion of Turkey's Mediterranean coast, but I'd suggest the coast just outside the port city of Izmir ($40 by air from Istanbul); there you can combine sea-bathing with a one-hour trip by *dolmus* or taxi to the unforgettable Roman ruins at Ephesus, where Paul preached. After all, you didn't fly 4,500 miles from the U.S. just to lie on a beach.

CAPPADOCIA

An even better course is to follow up Istanbul with eerie Cappadocia, the highlight of all Turkish visits, in my view, and a great wonder of the world. It is the province of volcanic rock in central Turkey to which tens of thousands of Christians fled in the 7th century from Muslim persecution. And there they proceeded to build and inhabit underground cities—whole cities—carved from the volcanic stone.

Although a military airport at Kayseri, in Cappadocia, receives civilian flights from Istanbul twice a week ($40 for the trip), the timing of that facility permits its use only in one direction—one way, in other words. The other leg is best accomplished by flying from Istanbul to Ankara ($45) and boarding a bus from there for a five-hour ride to Nevsehir, largest city in the region. Motorcoaches leave Nevsehir every two hours and charge only $3.50 for the five-hour journey.

Does all this seem overly fatiguing? Not once have you

Uçhisar, Cappadocia

seen Cappadocia. The trip begins in ordinary style, but gradually, in the triangle of land formed by the towns of Nevsehir, Avanos, and Urgup, you encounter a weird alternation of terrain in shapes you have never before seen: cream-colored hills of solid rock undulating like folds of satin, alongside high, conical mounds formed from the eroded volcanic ash of eruptions occurring a millennium ago. Suddenly, within these strange, cone-shaped forms, you take in hundreds upon hundreds of large, oblong, man-made holes cut into the face of each monolith.

It was through these openings that fleeing Christians built whole cities in the rock: churches adorned with fresco paint-

Women of the West are able to move about without harassment or scorn, at least in the larger cities and at beachfront resorts.

ings, refectories, dormitories, workrooms—all ingeniously carved, and then hidden from view by giant boulders over each entrance. Gazing at them, wrote a young American tourist, Tracie Holder, in a recent letter to me, "I had feelings of wonderment—wonder that these early inhabitants could have thought to hew entire cities from solid rock. To me, Cappadocia attests not simply to the determination of a particular people at a particular time, but to the timeless human spirit which creates civilizations in the face of adversity."

Most visitors to Cappadocia stay in the pleasant town of Urgup, in one of a cluster of small hotels ranging from the comfortable, swimming-pool-equipped Kaya Otel ($58 per double room, including breakfast for two), Boybas Motel ($53 double), and Turban Motel ($43 double, yet also with swimming pool), to the simple but adequate Pinar Otel ($12 per double room) and other more basic lodgings renting for as little as $10 and $8 per double room. Others prefer to stay closer to the Open Air Museum at the village of Goreme (really, a wide spot in the road), at the three-story, red-stucco Pala Otel, paying $17 for a double room and two breakfasts.

For meals, I like the Restaurant Allah Allah in the Cappadocian city of Avanos, on the Red River, where my party of four once paid a total of $20 for appetizers, melon, dolmades (stuffed grape leaves), shish kebab of lamb and chicken, Russian salad, wine, and strong Turkish coffee (sweet, in thimble-like cups).

Turkey is an important country of 55 million people, almost the size of France or Germany. And as you may have guessed, it's also a sybaritic experience at the lowest of costs. Get there before it's too late.

Galata Bridge, Istanbul

A Visit to Sedona, America's Newest "Hot Spot"

In High Desert Country, Surrounded by Soaring Red Rocks

FOR YEARS IT FLOURISHED "UNDERGROUND," a travel secret as closely guarded as the name of a favorite Paris bistro or a cheap Hong Kong tailor.

Suddenly, Sedona, Arizona, has surfaced. Not only once, but perhaps half a dozen times in late 1990, travel colleagues have pulled me aside to whisper that a hot new destination—Sedona—was coming on strong. And I, as a long-time ad-

mirer of that little, two-traffic-light, 4,300-foot-high mountain village, have enthusiastically agreed.

You've seen Sedona before, sometimes as a setting for western movies (*Harry and Tonto*, *Apache*, *Midnight Run*) and car commercials, but more often on your trips to the Grand Canyon. Halfway between Phoenix and that big, big ditch, Sedona is used in summer as a rest stop, lunch break, or

Oak Creek Canyon

Chapel of the Holy Cross, Oak Creek Canyon

short overnight respite by hundreds of thousands of Canyon-bound motorists or motorcoach touring groups, who give it the briefest treatment. Now, the smartest among those tourists are stopping by in other seasons, and for a much longer time.

One reason is climate. Higher (and therefore cooler) than Phoenix, lower (and therefore warmer) than nearby Flagstaff, Sedona has four mild seasons a year, and a vegetation that runs to several shades of green. True, it is winter here now, but that means morning temperatures in the high 30s, sunny afternoons in the mid-50s and often higher—and cool nights. Snowbirds from the cold midwestern states seem invigorated by the mild—but not the balmy—temperatures of Sedona's winter.

Another lure is scenery of the most remarkable sort.

Nestled among gigantic red rocks that point a thousand feet and more into the dazzlingly blue Arizona sky, Sedona is simply one of the great natural beauty spots of the planet.

If all it had were scenery and climate, however, Sedona would not be the lively, sophisticated town that is currently attracting such attention. Some of those latter characteristics are lent by an influx of modern nonconformists, drawn here by the same red rocks that Native Americans of past centuries regarded as sacred sites for ceremony and ritual. Proponents of the "New Age" movement consider Sedona to be one of the world's major "power spots" because of its so-called energy "vortexes," a name applied to electromagnetic-energy fields that can be felt at many spots in Sedona. Thousands of metaphysical seekers—some serious, some silly—have converged on the area in recent years, giving rise to lively book-

Its growth derives from an increasing realization that Sedona enjoys the best of two Arizona worlds.

stores (Eye of the Vortex and Golden Word); an actual, downtown Center for the New Age; numerous crystal shops; and highly sophisticated restaurants.

Where the New Age alights, other forms of commerce follow. Drawn in part by the reputed energy of the rocks, but more by the light and the landscape, some 200 artists and perhaps another 200 craftsmen currently work here and show their creations in numerous galleries and shops. The Sedona Art Center is their chief headquarters, as well as a site for a wide variety of performing arts activities, including classes, concerts, and theatrical productions.

Elsewhere in Sedona, galleries and shops are clustered in the re-creation of a Mexican arts-and-crafts village called Tlaquepaque, so charming with its tiled patios, adobe walls, cast-iron gates, fountains, and flowers. Other artists of the Southwest display in a complex called Hohzo, or at Elaine Horwitch's gallery on Schnebly Hill Road, or along the town's "main street" in "uptown Sedona." In Hohzo, you should not fail to visit Garland's Navajo Rugs, which contains the world's largest selection of them. Garland buys directly from Navajo weavers who visit the store daily—I saw one of them on my own most recent visit—and this enables the famous emporium to offer very fair prices. Upstairs is Kopavi, which works with Hopi Indians in the sale of traditional Indian jewelry, drums, baskets, and textiles.

Shopping completed, you'll of course want to visit the red rocks, mighty canyons, gorges, and creeks of Sedona's backcountry. Apart from endless hiking trails (well described in locally published books available everywhere), there are several popular Jeep or four-wheel-drive tours. Each such tour company has exclusive rights to various trails (in order to protect the environment), so you can safely take multiple tours and experience something new each time.

Pink Jeep (**phone 602/282-5000, or toll free 800/283-3328**) is Sedona's largest tour company, and the only one authorized to take passengers into the Broken Arrow Trail in the Coconino National Forest. Theirs is a rugged, roller coaster of a ride, and sometimes the Jeep seems to hug the cliff downward at an almost impossible angle. But all is forgiven when you step out and find yourself standing high atop Submarine Rock, surveying the vast panorama of rocky cliffs surrounding you.

Marty Wolf's Earth Wisdom Tours (**phone 602/282-4714**) features experiential journeys that put one in touch with the teaching of the Native Americans—their myth, lore, and various methods of natural living and healing. So credible are these tours, led by highly sensitive guides, that one of them, the "Earth Medicine Workshop," is now accepted by several schools as a continuing-education credit for nurses. (Tours are for either half a day, a full day, or even for three to five days.) Highly recommended as well are the tours run by **Time Expeditions** (**phone toll free 800/937-2137**), which has exclusive rights to visit an untouched 12th-century cliff dwelling deep in the Sedona "outback."

Of course, all the companies run Vortex Tours. And if **Pete Sanders**, an MIT-trained specialist in brain science and author of the bestselling *You Are Psychic* (Macmillan) is at his home base during the time of your visit (**phone 602/282-9425** to learn), take one of his. Sanders purports to teach his clients how to discover the so-called vortex energies, and to use them as "turbo boosts" for developing spiritual and psychic skills.

If you have time for more, you'll want to visit highlights of the Verde Valley near Sedona: Montezuma's Castle National Monument, Montezuma's Well, Tuzigoot National Monument (Indian cliff and hill dwellings), and the impressive Yavapai Apache Museum near the entrance to Montezuma's Castle. Fort Verde, also nearby, was built in 1871, and served as the base for U.S. military operations to subdue the Apache, a rather infamous phase of our history. A visit to Jerome is also worthwhile; the old copper mining town, with its switchback streets, now hosts a thriving artists' colony, and has shops, galleries, and restaurants. And finally, you can use Sedona as your base for visiting the Grand Canyon, 100 miles north via Flagstaff.

A word of caution: Even the most avid booster of Sedona, the most frantic real-estate broker, is concerned that people will make a too-hasty decision to move to Sedona; they need, according to my informants, a preliminary stay of two weeks or more, a longer-than-usual holiday here. "Be careful," says Gene Munson, a highly respected senior citizen in his late 70s (at least), who retired here in 1966 after a career as a management consultant: "Beauty overwhelms people. They make decisions too quickly, then live to regret them."

Sedona, says Munson, is a city of "self-starters"; it is not for people "who want everything laid out and planned for them," as (presumably) in such other Arizona retirement centers as Sun City. Like many others, Munson warns that retirement to even a Shangri-La–like Sedona may not be the panacea people think it is; away from the noise and confu-

Its other major feature is an influx of New Agers, some serious, some silly.

Pink Jeep takes passengers into the Broken Arrow Trail

sion of the big city, inner concerns and anxieties may become more apparent.

The other problem is cost. Though it may not seem expensive to people from California or the Northeast, real estate in Sedona will appear costly indeed to retirees from other parts of the country: a median of $168,000 for a one- or two-bedroom house, $205,000 for three bedrooms, $225,000 for four bedrooms, according to a report given to me by Foothill Realty of Sedona. The median cost of a residential lot is $69,000; of a mobile home lot, $25,250.

But other communities immediately surrounding Sedona are considerably less expensive, and you'll want to rent a car on your visit to check them out. Helen Brown, a realtor with Foothills South, points, as one example, to the Wild Turkey development in the village of Oakcreek (near uptown Sedona), where town houses start at $55,000—and that would be for a two-bedroom structure near the golf course. And patio homes (with garage) are available in Oakcreek from $75,000, with view of nearby Bell Rock, one of the major "vortex" or energy points of the area.

For those who want larger lots with their homes, Brown suggests they settle in Cornville, about 10 miles from Sedona. For $80,000 to $100,000, they can get a small home with an acre of land. Cornville is more rural, has good soil for growing, and a more desert-like environment; but it has no red rocks or pine trees of the famed Sedona variety.

Another affordable area in the surrounding Verde Valley countryside is Cottonwood, where lots are one-third the price of those in Sedona, and where smaller houses might begin at $50,000; condos, at $40,000. Prices for all goods and services are generally lower in Cottonwood, where many Sedonans do their basic marketing and shopping. Keep in mind, to balance the picture, that Cottonwood is a service area rather than a resort town, and for loyal Sedonans, it's just too far from the rocks and the magic.

Apart from the real estate, you'll want to check the activities in the course of your exploratory stay in Sedona. The retirees with whom I've spoken seem to find it an extremely congenial place, and many keep busy "from morning 'til night." The Sedona Health Spa at the lovely Los Abrigados Resort is one of their favorite places. So is the Sedona Arts Center, where many take classes; it offers art shows, exhibitions, and many events in the performing arts. Concerts by the Flagstaff and Phoenix Symphonies are big draws, as are two chamber-music groups and two theater companies, which often utilize the talents of retired Hollywood actors. Local clubs and organizations have something for every interest, from gardening and genealogy to quilting, tap dancing, astronomy, and preserving the environment.

As for the metaphysically oriented crowd, they enjoy an even more crowded, virtually nonstop, calendar of events. A publication called *Creative Happenings*, available at the bookstores and at the Sedona Center for the New Age, lists workshops, lectures, and classes taking place daily, in such subjects as shamanism, healing, Kundalini yoga, numerology, UFOs, and world-healing meditation.

Where do you stay on your visit to Sedona? In the "luxury" range, **L'Auberge de Sedona (phone 602/282-1661, or toll free 800/272-6777)** offers the ultimate in French Provincial charm, rooms with views of the canyon, and rates of $90 to $135 a night for two people. **Los Abrigados Resort (phone 602/282-1777, or toll free 800/521-3131)** is like a south-

L'Auberge de Sedona

Sedona

western hacienda, with Spanish-style plazas, whispering fountains, and winding walkways, and suites from $125 to $185. **John Gardiner's Enchantment,** located in the midst of a "vortex" in scenic Boynton Canyon, is a top-of-the-line tennis ranch in which casitas start at $180, breakfast included.

In the middle range, **Sky Ranch Lodge** (phone 602/282-6400), atop Airport Hill, another "vortex" area, offers stunning views of the town, a swimming pool, and 98 units averaging $70 a day. **Bell Rock Inn** (phone 602/282-4161), in the village of Oak Creek, offers 47 pleasant units, a heated pool, and rates of $40 to $94. And it's hard to beat the prices at **Black Forest House** (phone 602/282-2835), where German hosts Hans and Rosie offer simple motel rooms, with TV, refrigerator, and microwave, from $50 double. Their weekly rate of $250 is perhaps the lowest in town.

Among the bed-and-breakfasts, **Sipapu Lodge** (phone 602/282-2833), in West Sedona, offers large rooms with private baths, a welcome for pets and children, and a hearty southwestern breakfast in a spacious, ranch-style home decorated with Native American artifacts. Rates are $50 to $80 a night, double.

For all sorts of helpful information on Sedona, contact the **Sedona Chamber of Commerce, P.O. Box 478, Sedona, AZ 86336 (phone toll free 800/288-7336).**

An Ode to Eastern Long Island

Cherished by New Yorkers as Among the Finest Vacation Areas on Earth, It Is—Inexplicably— Unknown to the Rest of the Country

Whenever I am asked to name the area of my favorite beach vacations, I always disappoint people by responding: eastern Long Island. As a travel lunatic who has been to hundreds of seashores all over the world, I am sup- posed to come up with places queer or exotic, like Pattaya Beach in Thailand or Rostock on the Baltic Sea.

Yet eastern Long Island it is. By a long shot. Beyond dispute. Stubbornly. Till the day I die.

Farm stand along Montauk Highway 27, East Hampton

And it dismays me to realize that while other New Yorkers will understand my choice, almost no one else will. Outside the Empire State, Americans are abysmally unaware of one of the most glorious holiday regions on earth.

The narrow strip of land called Long Island is a largely rural, 130-mile-long extension of a portion of New York City. Along its southern shore on the Atlantic Ocean, about an hour by train from the city, there begins one of the world's longest continuous beaches, extending to the east for more than 60 miles.

It's a remarkable beach, of soft white sand, 50 and more yards deep, flanked by high protecting dunes, and lashed by strong waves topped with foam, invigorating to ride or confront.

So vast is the long, long beach of eastern Long Island that even the multitudes of summer visitors are lost upon it. I once

An hour by train from New York City, there begins one of the world's longest continuous beaches, a marvel of fine white sand.

Montauk Point Lighthouse

took a French friend to a stretch of sand outside the town of Quogue, and his mouth dropped open. It was the first time in his life that he had encountered a beach that was not literally covered with bodies, each allotted his or her own two-foot-wide pallet, as at Nice, Cannes, or St-Tropez. Here, 30 yards or so separated most sunbathers.

At intervals along the shore, a few miles inland from the beach, are picture-book villages revered by most New Yorkers but unknown to others, and strangely absent from novels or films: Westhampton, Speonk and Quogue, Water Mill, Bridgehampton and Amagansett, Montauk and Sag Harbor (the last facing away from the Atlantic), plus a dozen noteworthy others. F. Scott Fitzgerald placed his *Great Gatsby* on Long Island, but not along the sea, and I suspect that the hundreds of prominent writers and artists who currently inhabit the shores of eastern Long Island are anxious to guard their havens from greater renown.

Summer homes in these parts are fiendishly expensive to rent, but hotels and other lodgings are normally priced, no worse than in other vacation areas, and the budget-minded visitor can find low-cost B&Bs and moderately priced motels. From those they can then descend upon the beaches—all open to the public—or rent fishing boats for adventurous excursions onto the sea. At Montauk especially, but at other ports as well, a series of marinas harbor charter boats of every style and size.

What gives eastern Long Island its special flavor is a unique blend of worldly sophistication and country appearance. This, after all, is where New Yorkers vacation. Famous-name shops of Fifth Avenue alternate with homespun general stores. A small filling station will display a large stack of the *New York Times* for Sunday readers; *Vanity Fair* is on the shelves of 7-Elevens. On the main street of Sag Harbor, a movie theater shows only the most avant-garde of foreign films, while at the entrance to Easthampton, the John Drew Theater previews the most experimental of plays.

The Ozarks it's not.

And yet on the roads leading to the several towns are countless country-style vegetable-and-fruit stands of nearby farms. As one of the great produce-growing areas of America, both the eastern and central parts of Long Island yield tons of sweet corn, juicy tomatoes, sugary strawberries and peaches, excellent potatoes and onions, plus every other legume. And vacationers often make a daily visit to the stands to ensure that their table will bear only the freshest of foods. Some even go so far as to pick the fruits and vegetables themselves, in the fields directly behind the stands.

You eat here magnificently, of Long Island cherrystone clams and steamers, of scallops and swordfish, of Long Island duckling and home-grown asparagus. At one enormous restaurant called Gosman's Dock, cantilevered over a part of the port of Montauk, and partly outdoors, hundreds of diners feast on superb fresh lobster prepared in every way, and then they puzzle aloud—as I often have—as to why Gosman's lobsters are so very much better than any they've had elsewhere. My French friend, observing the summer gaiety of the wooden dining deck of Gosman's, remarked quite rapturously that it reminded him of a scene by Cézanne. He was similarly impressed by the meals—and especially the wines—of the dining room of the American Hotel in Sag Harbor, surely one of the nation's finest.

Wine, locally produced, is the latest attraction of eastern Long Island, although most of it is from vineyards and wineries of the so-called North Fork of Long Island's eastern end, away from the trendy towns of the South Fork on the Atlantic. Near Jamesport, Mattituck, and Cutchogue on that North Fork, such increasingly distinguished vintners as Pindar, Palmer, and Hargrave run free public tours and tastings of their cellars, and distribute a great deal of their product to the restaurants nearby.

Apart from wining, dining, bathing, sailing, fishing, hiking, playing, and movie/theater-going, what else do you do in eastern Long Island? You visit dozens of historic landmarks, some dating from colonial and revolutionary times, and take in the important and engrossing whaling museums found in several towns. You book yourself on a day-long whale-watching cruise from Montauk (phone 516/728-4522), or go to yard sales found everywhere, or to summer festivals found weekly, or to famous shops in every town. You participate in every form of recreation and relaxation, browse through frequently encountered bookstores, attend the numerous summer lectures. And when your needs are occasionally urban, you board the Long Island Rail Road for an easy 2- or 2½-hour ride into midtown Manhattan.

For a visiting Frenchman, it was the first time in his life he had walked on a beach not covered with bodies.

Don't get me wrong. I love an occasional stay in Acapulco or Aruba, a few days of bathing at Rimini, an autumnal sojourn on the Costa del Sol of Spain. But where can you have all the pleasures of a renowned beach, and at the same time enjoy phones that work, water that's drinkable, and morning delivery of a meaty English-language newspaper?

Eastern Long Island, that's where.

For directories of accommodations and restaurants, attractions, events, and activities, contact the **Long Island Tourism & Convention Commission, The Nassau Veterans Memorial Colosseum, Uniondale, NY 11553 (phone 516/794-4222, or toll free 800/441-4601).**

THE NEW WORLD OF TRAVEL 1992

The lifeblood of the Arthur Frommer travel guides is the correspondence received from readers, commenting on the establishments recommended in the texts and recommending new establishments. Each such letter is carefully studied, and when a particular lead seems promising, it is followed up and personally checked.

It is hoped that *The New World of Travel* will receive similar assistance from its readers. A yearly publication, issued near the start of each year, *The New World* will constantly grow. And since much of its content relates to organizations that lack the means to market themselves properly, or come to the attention of a travel journalist, your help is invaluable in alerting me to the organizations—hospitality exchanges, alternative resorts, new travel clubs, and the like—that you have discovered.

If you become aware of a new travel organization, program, or development that deserves to be described in our next edition, *The New World of Travel 1992*, won't you please let me know about it? Send your letters to Arthur Frommer, *The New World of Travel*, c/o Prentice Hall Press, Travel Division, 15 Columbus Circle, New York, NY 10023. All letters will be acknowledged, and all are warmly appreciated, in advance, by the author.

XII

NEW WAYS TO
VISIT OLD
DESTINATIONS

The Other London

By Scorning to Fall into a Tourist Mentality, Visitors Can Greatly Enrich Their Stays in Britain's Capital

I'T'S PLEASANT, OF COURSE, TO VIEW THE Changing of the Guard, the Beefeaters at the Tower, the face of Big Ben. But is it worth a trip to London—worth the expense, worth the effort—to do just that and nothing more?

I don't think so. Without exposure to the current life of London—the lectures, seminars, and socials, the conferences and classes, where residents mix and mingle—a trip confined to the tourist sights of Britain's capital seems a feeble diversion, a bowl of soup without salt.

How do you, the tourist, meet the people and taste the life of this great English-speaking city?

A first step is the purchase of one of three weekly magazine calendars: *What's On* (60p, $1.08), *Time Out* (£1, $1.80), and *City Limits* (90p, $1.62), sold at all London newsstands. Comprehensive to an extent that's never remotely achieved in their U.S. counterparts, each reviews not only the scheduled concerts, plays, and films of the city, but also dozens of other communal gatherings: meetings of clubs and associations open to all, evening lectures and speeches all across the city, galas and parties, serious dialogues and workshops with political, social, or interpersonal themes. If nothing else, the British are joiners, sensitive to causes, and their confabs listed in the three London weeklies are open to people of all backgrounds, and almost always for free.

The tourist who treads off the beaten path—to the weekly debates of the Shavian Society, the numerous public lectures of the Social Democrats, the Thursday poetry readings of the Keats Foundation—becomes a traveler, not a tourist, and enjoys the opportunity to experience other outlooks, a distinctive national culture, an encounter with foreign residents.

PUBLIC AFFAIRS AT THE UNIVERSITY OF LONDON

But as broad as their coverage is, the London weeklies are relatively mainstream in their approach. Moving to more exotic realms, or to more specialized concerns, requires a trip to the bulletin boards of the central campus of the University of London. Take the Tube (the Underground, or subway) to the Russell Square stop and ask for instructions to nearby Gower Street (site of the university's North Cloister Building, Darwin Theatre, and Birkbeck College) and Malet Street (housing Senate House). At the North Cloister Building, a monitor flashes news of unusually erudite but utterly free lectures of the day, all open to the public at large. At the Darwin Theatre, free lunchtime lectures on Tuesday and Thursday from 1 to 2 P.M. run the gamut of disciplines from physics to fine arts (phone 387-7050, ext. 2043, for advance information). And at Birkbeck College, large posters announce one-time colloquiums and lectures by titled speakers or eminent dons (teaching masters) on "Proust's Recherché,"

Without exposure to the life enjoyed by residents, a trip confined to the tourist sights of London is a feeble diversion.

"The Greenhouse Effect," "Problems of the Inner City," both in midafternoon and early evening, open to all, student and nonstudent alike, and free when last I looked.

At Senate House, in addition to finding the ubiquitous bulletin boards with their posters of daily free events, you can pick up a map and catalog of all the schools' faculties and departments, enabling you to pinpoint even the most ultra-specialized lectures. At the School of Oriental and African Studies, you may discover: "Today—Tea and Biscuits at 4:45 P.M., then lecture ('Indigenous Agricultural Revolutions') at 5 P.M., free." At the Center of Near and Middle Eastern Studies: Tuesday at 5:30 P.M., "Tribe and State in Libya," free; Thursday at 6 P.M., "Ancient Arab Politics," free. Attending are London's brainiest folk, all amenable to continued conversation after the lecture.

Unfortunately, there is no one central source for all the university's free daily lectures; you simply have to wander from building to building to track down the offerings.

ADULT EDUCATION INSTITUTES

For discussions of a less exalted nature, among ordinary residents of London of all ages, the places to visit are the 20-some-odd adult education institutes (nighttime instruction, mainly) found in all sections of the city. Though the curricula here are of semester-long duration, each school is festooned with posters of both daily and weekly events: tea dances, let's say, on Monday afternoon; Saturday classes on paper-making and other crafts; one-time lectures (open to all) in Chinese culture—those were some recent selections I found at the Camden Institute on Longford Street, NW1 (phone 388-7106). Other centrally located adult education institutes are: the Central Institute, Stukeley Street, Drury Lane, WC2 (phone 242-9872); the Westminster Institute, Hallfield School, Inverness Terrace, W2 (phone 286-1900); the Mary Ward Institute, Great Ormond Street (phone 831-7711); and the Islington Arts Centre, Shepperton Road, N1 (phone 226-6001), offering seasonal workshops in music, art, and dance, at which outsiders can "drop in" (audit) for a single session at a cost of £2.25 ($4.05).

THE "GREEN" LIFE OF LONDON

And how about spending a weekend in one of the green areas of London, assisting residents to restore and protect the natural environment? Every Saturday and/or Sunday of the year, the British Trust for Conservation Volunteers (c/o The London Ecology Centre, 80 York Way, N1; phone 278-4293) operates a wide range of "day projects" for British people from every walk of life: hedgelaying in North London, tree planting in the East End, creating wildlife areas on formerly developed sites. Minibuses leave at 9:30 A.M. from various pickup points and drive participants to the

project areas, where tools and instruction are provided. And are tourists invited to join the hardy, affable British volunteers? Yes! says a BTCV official in a recent letter to me. "No need to be a London resident. Anyone can turn up for these tasks; they are free, and all that's needed is a packed lunch. We supply soft drinks, biscuits, and (grotty) coffee."

Weekend-long "residential" projects (you stay Friday and Saturday nights in the countryside outside London, in Kent, Sussex, Surrey, or Essex) are also run by BTCV throughout the year, attracting volunteers of every age and condition, usually dynamic, outgoing Britons. Participants bring old clothes and a sleeping bag, stay in dwellings ranging from youth hostels to village halls, and receive food, transportation, and accommodation for the grand total of £3 ($5.40) per day. "Everything is very informal," adds the BTCV spokesperson, "and it isn't necessary to have experience in the field of conservation."

Here, on your overseas trip, is a meaningful travel experience. Isn't it better than shuttling about in a glass-enclosed tour bus with other Americans and paying an overpriced $150 per night in a crowded hotel?

ST. JAMES'S

And then you have the multiple activities of London's strangest theological center. Though it's a 300-year-old church, with a pastor as devout as any, St. James's of London bears no resemblance to your ordinary house of worship.

It swings. It trembles. With yoga classes, New Age lec-

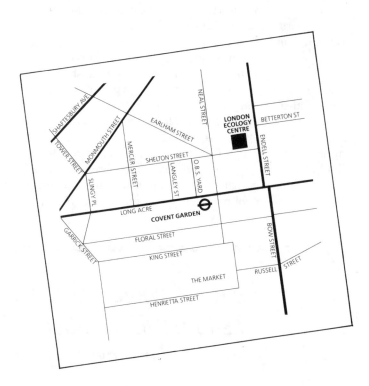

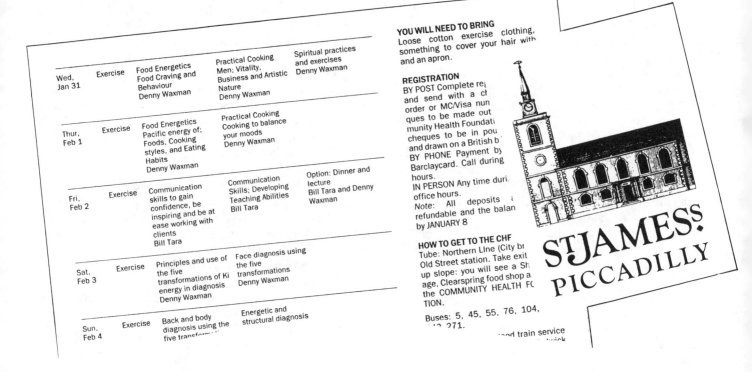

Wed, Jan 31	Exercise	Food Energetics Food Craving and Behaviour Denny Waxman	Practical Cooking Men: Vitality, Business and Artistic Nature Denny Waxman	Spiritual practices and exercises Denny Waxman
Thur, Feb 1	Exercise	Food Energetics Pacific energy of: Foods, Cooking styles, and Eating Habits Denny Waxman	Practical Cooking Cooking to balance your moods Denny Waxman	
Fri, Feb 2	Exercise	Communication skills to gain confidence, be inspiring and be at ease working with clients Bill Tara	Communication Skills; Developing Teaching Abilities Bill Tara	Option: Dinner and lecture Bill Tara and Denny Waxman
Sat, Feb 3	Exercise	Principles and use of the five transformations of Ki energy in diagnosis Denny Waxman	Face diagnosis using the five transformations Denny Waxman	
Sun, Feb 4	Exercise	Back and body diagnosis using the five transf...	Energetic and structural diagnosis	

YOU WILL NEED TO BRING
Loose cotton exercise clothing, something to cover your hair with and an apron.

REGISTRATION
BY POST Complete re[
and send with a ch
order or MC/Visa num
ques to be made out
munity Health Foundati
cheques to be in pou
and drawn on a British b
BY PHONE Payment by
Barclaycard. Call during
hours.
IN PERSON Any time duri
office hours.
Note: All deposits a
refundable and the balan
by JANUARY 8

HOW TO GET TO THE CHF
Tube: Northern Line (City br
Old Street station. Take exit
up slope: you will see a Sh
age, Clearspring food shop a
the COMMUNITY HEALTH FC
TION.
Buses: 5, 45, 55, 76, 104,
...3, 271.
...od train service

St JAMESS PICCADILLY

tures, seminars on personal relationships, flamenco guitar concerts. And it invites casual visitors, including tourists simply passing through, to join its constant daily doings, in a location only three short blocks from Piccadilly Circus.

No better way exists to escape the often artificial confines of the tourist and move instead into a real-life setting of dynamic Londoners. Every day of the week, St. James's offers either lectures, one-night classes, crafts markets, meetings of the William Blake Society (the famed English poet and visionary painter was baptized here), workshops (in ecumenical theological literature ranging from the Bhagavad Gita to the Hebrew Talmud), lunchtime recitals, evening concerts (of atonal strains), one-day instruction ("Awakening the Heart through Painting," "Introduction to Meditation"), and other communal events too numerous to list. Far from confining its schedule to church members, it openly solicits visitors of all religious persuasions from around the world to join the British at this "international centre for healing, fellowship and reconciliation . . . a place for prayer, worship and celebration . . . a forum for the arts."

Failing, and slated to become a museum (the building is by Sir Christopher Wren), St. James's was revived in 1980 by its then-new rector, the Rev. Donald Reeves, whose Christian teachings encompass political concerns of international security ("The Roots of Violence," a recent lecture) and daring theological speculations ("ideas which provide creative and spiritual alternatives to currently accepted Western thought"). You have only to enter this Anglican/Episcopalian center and its charming interior coffeeshop (Wren's), and scan a daunting array of notices and posters, to be swept up into an active stratum of London life that virtually guarantees you will get to interact with the people. St. James's is at 197 Piccadilly (phone 734-4511), near both the Piccadilly Circus and Green Park subway stops.

Here, 24 hours a day, seven days a week, sensitive visitors join members of London's Anti-Apartheid Alliance in picketing the South African Embassy.

SPECIAL INTERESTS

And next, depending on your interests, you can seek out further encounters—an enlightening immersion into the actual life of British citizens—in at least eight other areas of London life.

Quaker London

Just as ecumenical, the worldwide Religious Society of Friends (Quakers) was founded in Britain in the 17th century and today maintains a remarkable 49 meetinghouses in London, of which the most central are the large and gracious **Friends House** on Euston Road (phone 359-1525), across from the Euston Station Tube stop, and the smaller **Westminster Friends Meeting House** at 52 St. Martin's Lane (phone 743-2994), near the Charing Cross or Leicester Square Tube stop; both are filled with posters and notices of meetings and lectures open to all. Gentle and tolerant, the London Friends seem even more involved in outreach to newcomers/visitors and in social/political issues (peace studies, nonviolence, the Third World) than elsewhere. Their meetings provide an excellent opportunity to get to know these impressive Londoners.

Feminist London

The venue now is London's largest bookstore devoted solely to women's causes, the important **Sisterwrite** at 190 Upper St. (phone 226-9782), near the Highbury/Islington Tube station. Its corridor space, in effect, is one vast bulletin board of events, classes, and group discussions. Visiting feminists will find several of their British counterparts almost always in attendance, in addition to learning about such gatherings as a full-day conference on "Women's Well-Being," another on the problems of "Fat Women," and still another on the shared thoughts of "Older Women"—with foreign participants eagerly invited (all these were recently offered).

Poetic London

In the land of Byron, Shelley, and Keats, poetry is celebrated by the unique **National Poetry Centre**, at 21 Earls Court Square (phone 373-7861). Several times a month (write or phone for the schedule), except in July and August, Britain's leading contemporary poets convene at the centre to read their poetry before an avid audience that after the reading heatedly discusses the work among themselves, and often repairs to nearby coffeeshops or pubs with newly made friends, including those from abroad. Admission costs £2.50 ($4.50).

Walkers' London

The increasingly popular walking tours of London (you meet at a designated subway exit and then are led through a historic district by an informed guide) are patronized as much by Londoners as by tourists, and are thus an excellent way to meet the British. Although there is no comprehensive list of walking-tour companies, five seem to be mentioned with particular frequency: **Citisights**, 145 Goldsmiths Row (phone 739-2372), operating on weekends throughout the year and on scattered weekday dates, for £3.50 ($6.30)—their "Victorian London" tour is an especial bestseller; **London Walks**, 10 Greenbrook Ave., Hadley Woods, Herts (phone 441-8906), which also charges £3.50 ($6.30) for such theme walks as "Jack the Ripper's London" or "In the Footsteps of Sherlock Holmes"; **Streets of London**, 32 Grovelands Rd. (phone 882-3414), which has daily walks for £3.50 ($6.30) devoted to such themes as "The London of Henry VIII," "Literary London," or "Aristocratic London"; **John Muffty's Historical Tours**, 3 Florence Rd., South Croydon (phone 668-4019), offering daily strolls costing £3.50 ($6.30) that cover such topics as "Pirates, Smugglers, and Pressgangs," "The Real London Eastenders," or "A City in the Blitz," among others; and **Londoner Pub Walks**, c/o

Mysteries

Peter Westbrook, 3 Springfield Ave. (phone 883-2656), who has led a group every Friday evening for the past 21 years for a £3.50 ($6.30) charge.

Political London

Since April 1986, 24 hours a day, seven days a week, members of the **City of London Anti-Apartheid Group** have been inviting outsiders to join them in picketing the South African Embassy to protest that country's racial policies. They con-

duct a well-attended rally on the perpetual picket line every Friday at 6 P.M., and then invite all pickets to attend a group meeting nearby at 8 P.M.; phone 837-6050 for details. Alternatively, visitors wishing to participate in the frequent periodic meetings and vigils of the **Campaign for Nuclear Disarmament,** 22 Underwood St. (phone 250-4010), are best advised to pick up a copy of the monthly magazine *Sanity* at newsstands or direct from the organization; it lists each such event, both current and several weeks in advance. Elsewhere

If nothing else, the British are joiners, and their meetings listed in the three London weeklies are open to all and almost always free of charge.

in London, the **Conservative Party Bookshop,** 32 Smith Square, near Westminster (phone 222-2004); the **Labour Party Bookshop,** 150 Walworth Rd., near the Elephant & Castle Tube stop (phone 703-0833); and the **Social Democratic Party Bookshop,** 4 Cowley St., near the Westminster Tube stop (phone 622-3811)—all frequently display notices of periodic political seminars open to all and scheduled on a near-weekly basis.

New Age London

The city's major bulletin board for lectures, one-day classes, and workshops in psychic phenomena, from Tarot to acupuncture, from rebirthing to regression, is at the sprawling multiroom shop called **Mysteries,** at 9 Monmouth St. (phone 240-3688). Equipped with its news of weekend festivities, LRT (loving relationships) lectures, and the like, you'll quickly connect with other devotees of these notions. Elsewhere in London, holistic health and Eastern approaches to well-being are the theme of the large **East-West Centre,** minutes from the Old Street Tube stop (use Exit 6). In the lobby of its Community Health Foundation, and on every stairwell, are leaflets and postings of activities, including numerous events (like a Friday dinner-and-lecture series) particularly appropriate for short-term tourists in London.

Ecological London

The **London Ecology Centre,** 80 York Way (phone 379-4324), is an impressive hub of activity and second headquarters for more than 70 ecological organizations that hold near-daily get-togethers open to all in the meeting space above the main floor containing a café, giftshop, and bookstore. A visit will give you an overview of Britain's activity in environmental protection. You'll be able to converse with London's ecologists, who seem calm and confident despite their obvious concern over the continual political battles they must wage. To find out more about the meetings of the new "Green Party," call the main office at 673-0045.

Library London

And finally, keep in mind that, just as in U.S. cities, the libraries of London are posting places for community activ-

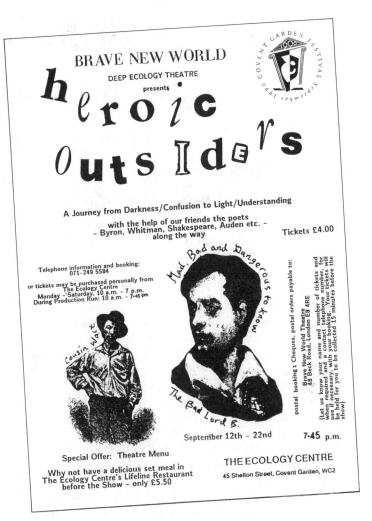

ities and neighborhood lectures, classes, and workshops. Walking into the Westminster Public Library recently, I learned of and then attended that night a free lecture by the headmaster of an Oxford college on "Dynamics of Darwinian Evolution." I will remember that evening, and the ensuing conversations with dynamic Londoners, long after the Changing of the Guard fades from memory.

St. James's of London bears no resemblance to your ordinary house of worship.

In London the Real Action Is "On the Fringe"

Britain's "Off-Off-Broadway" Theaters—Often Difficult to Find—Provide Dramatic Excitement, Unsettling Ideas, and Low Ticket Prices

MY FRIEND BILL, FROM ATLANTA, GEORgia, is a thoughtful man who reads good books and subscribes to brainy periodicals. But when he travels to London, he turns off his mind.

"I hear you can now get tickets to *Starlight Express*," he said, referring to the roller-skate operetta. "And Mary knows a broker who has seats for *Cats*."

Are mindless musicals the only theater reward of a trip to London—or to New York, for that matter? For millions of Americans, the opportunity to enlarge their horizons at night, to escape the ordinary and encounter new ideas, is almost always squandered on their trips to a theater capital by just such a limited choice. And the reason, in part, is a woeful failure on the part of major newspapers in those cities to alert the visitor to the full range of theater opportunities.

In London, the shows patronized by tourists are nearly always those of the West End, in and around Leicester and Trafalgar Squares. In Manhattan, the same are confined to the side streets of Times Square, the so-called Broadway theaters.

Most of these standard productions, in the opinion of a growing number, have been paltry and unworthy ventures, distinctly inferior to the current level of films, either plotless collections of song (*Black and Blue*), superficial farce (*Run for Your Wife*), or tired perennials (*The Mousetrap*). Of the plays on Broadway at any given moment, nowadays only one or two are of real importance (currently, and just barely, *The Grapes of Wrath*), while in London's West End the number rises to perhaps two or three (currently, *Orpheus Descending* with Vanessa Redgrave, *Richard III* with Derek Jacobi).

For pith, for substance, for excitement on the stage, the informed theater-goer turns to the several score "Fringe theaters" of London. Yet to the tourist reading the London dailies, these are like quasars of a black hole, invisible and unseen. Although an occasional London newspaper will briefly list half a dozen of the major Fringe productions, none of the dailies pays them more than the scantiest attention.

What causes a London theater to be regarded as "on the Fringe"?

Unlike the Off-Broadway theaters (fewer than 499 seats) or Off-Off-Broadway theaters (fewer than 100 seats) of New York City, the Fringe theaters of London are distinguished from those of the West End by their location—which is usually outside the central Piccadilly Circus–Leicester Square–Trafalgar Square area. Yet from many hotels, they are no farther by subway than are the better-known playhouses, a matter of half an hour at most. They also charge far less for their seats: an average of £5 to £9 ($9 to $16.20) at most, including an occasional compulsory membership fee, as contrasted with a current average of £15 ($27) for most orchestra seats in the West End.

For pith and substance, the informed theater-goer turns to the several score "Fringe" productions of London.

Last week, in the 60 or so theaters of the Fringe (some large, some small), theater-goers could see plays by Sartre and Sophocles, by Ibsen, Chekhov, and Strindberg, by Arthur Miller and Bertolt Brecht. They could watch a theatrical exposé of women's prisons in Britain, performed by ex-inmates; attend a revival of *The Royal Hunt of the Sun* by Peter Shaffer (who wrote *Amadeus*); see socially provocative works by modern playwrights like *The Lover* by Harold Pinter, or politically provocative works like *A Common Woman* by the Italian anarchist Dario Fo. They could thrill to Shakespeare's *Timon of Athens* performed by an all-female cast, or encounter dozens of other dramatic thunderbolts engaging the mind.

To obtain a complete current listing of all Fringe productions, the tourist needs to purchase one of three weekly magazines of London events: either *Time Out* (£1, $1.80), *What's On* (60p, $1.08), or *City Limits* (90p, $1.62), sold at most newsstands and exhaustive in their coverage of Fringe theater schedules, locations, phone numbers, and prices; they also provide a very brief description of each play.

Then, to obtain reservations for the Fringe, one simply phones the theater in question or, better yet, goes to a single, central Fringe theater box office in the lobby of the mainstream Duke of York Theatre on St. Martin's Lane, WC2 (phone 379-6002).

What's especially delightful about the Fringe theaters is that most are like community centers, offering not simply a performance, but often a restaurant on premises (for pre- or post-performance dining), scheduled workshops, lectures and seminars during the day, art or photo exhibits, an occasional bookshop, even babysitting "night care" rooms for the infants of theater-going parents. In other words, they are full-scale British institutions which also make it possible for tourists to mingle with a dynamic set of English people and occasionally to meet them—something harder to do in the commercial, tourist-jammed settings of the West End theaters.

Among the more prominent of the Fringe theaters, of near-consistent excellence, are these:

Riverside Studios, Crisp Road, Hammersmith, W6 (phone 748-3554), houses, in addition to its stage, a continuing art exhibition, a restaurant-café, and an excellent theater bookshop, plus ongoing courses, lectures, and workshops.

Institute for Contemporary Arts, The Mall, SW1 (phone 930-6393). Artistic and experimental, it presents mainly "performance pieces," mostly multimedia or dance in place of regular narrative theater. Its lecture series, known as "Guardian Conversations," features new and established writers, critics, poets. Its three exhibition galleries have a major reputation in the British art world.

Drill Hall Arts Center, 16 Chenie St., WC1 (phone 637-8270), is a block from the University of London, and is well known for its vegetarian restaurant, The Greenhouse,

and its evening babysitting services. Three on-site rehearsal studios are used for classes ranging from aerobic exercises to a study of feminist writers.

Almeida Theatre, Almeida Street, Islington, N1 (phone 359-4404), frequently features international theater as performed by visiting troupes from abroad.

Lyric Studio, King Street, in Hammersmith, W6 (phone 741-2311), attracts well-known performers, and frequently previews shows before their move to the West End. For example, *House of Bernarda Alba* by García Lorca, starring Glenda Jackson, tried out here (at low ticket prices) before it moved to a more prestigious stage.

King's Head Theatre Club, 115 Upper St., N1 (phone

226-1916), is housed in the space above a popular pub, and offers meals before the show.

Age Exchange Theatre, 11 Blackheath Village, SE3 (phone 318-9105), devises plays of life in past times based on the "oral histories" it obtains from elderly Londoners.

Soho Poly Theatre, 16 Riding House St., W1 (phone 636-9050), presents works of new British playwrights.

AND IN NEW YORK...

In New York, information on alternative theater is a bit more readily accessible than in London—but only slightly so: a fairly comprehensive listing of the 40 or more Off-Broadway plays and musicals currently running ($25 for the average ticket, as compared with the $40, $45, and more charged for Broadway shows) appears daily in the *New York Times,* but not always in the other papers.

As for the 50 or so Off-Off-Broadway productions in small 100-seat houses ($8 to $15 per ticket), these appear in full only in the Sunday edition of the *New York Times,* and rarely in the other papers. Rather than look for those fleeting mentions, avid theater buffs pursue Off-Off-Broadway by purchasing the weekly *Village Voice* or *West Side Spirit,* and obtain a less comprehensive review of Off-Off-Broadway in *The New Yorker* and *New York* magazines.

As a New Yorker myself, and a frequent theater-goer, I rarely attend the Broadway shows; I find them too often obvious and contrived, designed for the tired suburbanite, the harried tourist, a form of "aspirin for the middle class," in the words of a wag. For me, the unique impact of theater—a special artistic and cultural experience, unlike that of a film—is found Off- or Off-Off-Broadway or on the Fringe, and I urgently suggest that you try the same on your own next trip to London or New York.

But to the tourist reading the London dailies, "Fringe theaters" are like quasars of a black hole, invisible and unseen.

A Visit to the New Paris

Five Recent Additions to the "City of Light" Have Made It the World's Unchallenged Leader

However magical it has always been, it has been made better. In 10 years, the great city of Paris has acquired five monumental new attractions. And suddenly, what was once a mere equal among the several top capitals of the world is today, in my opinion, the indisputable leader, without peer or contender. It stands alone.

If your own last visit to the "City of Light" was more than three years ago, then you haven't felt the combined impact of the five new wonders—the d'Orsay, the Picasso, the Beaubourg, La Villette, and the enhanced Louvre—as a single experience. That treat, a form of cultural gluttony, is at last fully available, and best pursued from mid-November through mid-April, when the city's trade shows abate a bit and hotel occupancies drop. Then you can tour the museums in comparative calm; pay as little as $60 a night for a double room in a charming small hotel; devour bistro meals that engage your senses, indeed lift you to the skies, for all of $25.

The **Picasso Museum** (opened in September 1985) should perhaps be your first choice. In the resplendent Salé mansion built in the 17th century in the historic Right Bank district of the Marais, the French government has mounted a permanent display of nearly 200 paintings from Picasso's own collection, his obvious favorites, together with ceramics and sculptures acquired in payment of the massive estate taxes levied upon the artist's death. And though you may think you have earlier experienced the titanic genius of this 20th-century master, you will be stunned—left weak but uplifted—by the works on view. Some are seen here for the very first time; all are grouped into the major periods or styles through which the artist passed, and all are brilliantly described in posted commentaries translated into English.

The **Beaubourg** (1978), or **Centre Georges Pompidou**, oldest of the four, is Paris's block-long collection of 20th-century art, reached on foot and with ease from the Picasso Museum. In a giant building as modern and joyful as its contents—with incongruous façade of water pipes, ducts, struts, and metal spars—visitors enter a tube of glass and ride up the outer wall to a top-floor permanent collection of surrealists, expressionists, post-impressionists, cubists, pop artists, and more, from Matisse and Mondrian to Andy Warhol and Salvador Dalí. Outside are street buskers encouraged to entertain, while along one side—and often missed by tourists—is a water-filled playground for a team of impishly comic industrial robots, all dipping, dousing, and spraying water from garden-hoselike appendages. What other city would have had the audacity to place such a fanciful construction into a traditional area?

La Villette, as it's commonly called (because of its location next to the Porte de Villette Métro station), is the brand-new science and industrial museum of Paris, resembling a world's fair of several structures. Although only a portion of the ambitious project is completed, what you will see today is a display of ultramodern technology ranging from rockets, robots, and lasers to humanlike computers. In the style of so many museums, visitors are encouraged to step through and/or handle the items on display, but what distinguishes this exhibition is its vast size, surely larger (when completed) and more varied than any other on earth. It should be seen.

It provides a kind of cultural gluttony, best experienced from November through mid-April.

Picasso Museum

Centre Georges Pompidou

The **d'Orsay Museum** (early 1987) is the other recent addition to the list of not-to-be-missed Parisian attractions, and the subject of reams of recent travel literature. In its showing of 19th-century masterworks of art, especially those of the French impressionists—Monet, Cézanne, Degas, Toulouse-Lautrec, Renoir—it provides a logical prelude to the more recent art of the National Museum of Art and the Picasso. And though I personally find it to be a confusing place with its 80 different galleries, its impact is staggering as one explores the vast floors of a magnificent railroad station converted at great expense into an elegant museum of size and grandeur. It fills the niche between the largely ancient art of the Louvre, and the modern and contemporary art found elsewhere in Paris.

And then there's the enhanced and expanded **Louvre**, entered through the glass pyramid designed by I. M. Pei.

A brilliant pyramid. With its futuristic spaceship-like form and transparent modern walls, juxtaposed against the ancient ornate face of the grand palace, it reminds you that several hundreds of years have passed since construction of the latter. It makes "time visible." It does not detract from the Louvre and its courtyard, as an opaque building would have done, but highlights it, proclaims its age. With the vast public space underneath it, greatly increasing the exhibition

La Villette Park, near the Museum of Science and Industry

A pyramid that makes "time visible."

areas of the Louvre, Paris has taken a further quantum leap in its visitor facilities.

As always, the glue that binds together your activities in Paris is food. If you carefully avoid the restaurants that cater to tourists, and patronize only those supported by residents, you will eat magnificently at moderate cost. Recently I strolled along the Seine at night until I was out of range of the bright lights, and there, *Voilà!*, was a restaurant filled to every seat with Parisians. They did not let me down. I began with a salad of mixed greens topped with razor-thin shavings (to keep the price down) of pâté de foie gras, the whole sprinkled with a subtle dressing. I had sole with oysters under a light pie crust with deep-green stringbeans (*haricots verts*) alongside. I had three desserts—brie, crème brûlée, a strawberry tart—with black coffee. And earlier, a half bottle of white Mâcon-Village. The tab? Just $25 for a meal that caused me to sing and leap my way home.

Friends who had dined that same evening at a better-known "name" restaurant—filled with Japanese, and other affluent foreigners—ate dismally at three times the cost. In Paris, if the restaurant is a household word, you're 10 years too late.

Food and fine art, culture and cuisine, sights of the most awesome beauty—all this adds up to Paris, and Paris today, in my stubborn view, is the top attraction on earth.

THE NEW WORLD OF TRAVEL 1992

The lifeblood of the Arthur Frommer travel guides is the correspondence received from readers, commenting on the establishments recommended in the texts and recommending new establishments. Each such letter is carefully studied, and when a particular lead seems promising, it is followed up and personally checked.

It is hoped that *The New World of Travel* will receive similar assistance from its readers. A yearly publication, issued near the start of each year, *The New World* will constantly grow. And since much of its content relates to organizations that lack the means to market themselves properly, or come to the attention of a travel journalist, your help is invaluable in alerting me to the organizations—hospitality exchanges, alternative resorts, new travel clubs, and the like—that you have discovered.

If you become aware of a new travel organization, program, or development that deserves to be described in our next edition, *The New World of Travel 1992*, won't you please let me know about it? Send your letters to Arthur Frommer, *The New World of Travel*, c/o Prentice Hall Press, Travel Division, 15 Columbus Circle, New York, NY 10023. All letters will be acknowledged, and all are warmly appreciated, in advance, by the author.

Guided Walks Through the Cities of Europe

Unlike the Standard Bus Tours, Which Pander to the Lowest Tastes and Understanding, They Provide Penetrating Insights into the Essence of Each City

YOU MEET THEM AT A CAREFULLY PRESCRIBED address ("the northwest corner of Kongens Nytorv"), or under a famous statue, or along a bridge. They await you in clean but scruffy clothes—a worn tweed jacket, a frayed and mended shirt—for none earns more than a marginal living.

But in their eyes, their manner, their speech, glows pride in their profession. And in the next two hours, they are exuberant, they literally bounce, as they share an overweening love for the city they inhabit by escorting you on a walking tour of a tiny portion of it, a historic quarter, a cluster of ancient homes.

All over Europe, unauthorized, unlicensed entrepreneurs have set themselves up as one-person tour companies to provide the visitor with a view of "Europe on foot."

They gain their clientele through leaflets scattered in budget hotels, or via index cards tacked to subway bulletin boards, or—if they're lucky—through a guidebook mention.

And would you believe it? Tourists in large numbers are responding, as the realization spreads that intimate walk-throughs provide the finest possible experience of Europe.

IN COPENHAGEN

The pioneer in the art is a 60-ish former motorcoach guide named Helge Jacobsen, a Dane. A little more than 20 years ago he sent me a letter, which I printed in a book then called *Europe on $5 a Day*. "I am tired," he wrote, "of having to speak two, three, or even four languages on the same bus, and of rushing by everything of interest in a hurry. The best way to see any city is on foot." And thereafter followed a list of multiple walking tours offered weekly from April through mid-June and daily from mid-June through mid-September.

Mr. Jacobsen has been leading such tours ever since. Recently, I appeared for his Saturday-afternoon walk through the bohemian Christianshavn district of Copenhagen, and was regaled for 2½ hours (along with 10 other tourists, some touring with him for the third consecutive day) by a witty, intelligent, deeply felt commentary on a single but important urban quarter constructed in the 17th century. The tour—like the performance of an accomplished actor, against a backdrop of period courtyards, cul de sacs, and small churches into which we strolled—was the stellar high-

In a number of capitals, unlicensed, unauthorized entrepreneurs have turned themselves into one-person tour companies to conduct the visitor on walks through historic areas.

Christianshavn district, Copenhagen

light of my short Copenhagen visit, and cost all of 20 kroner ($3.35). For additional information on seven different daily walking tours, contact **The Guide-Ring, 91 Kongelundsvej, Copenhagen (phone 51-25-90)**.

IN STOCKHOLM

The Swedish equivalent of Mr. Jacobsen's enterprise is a tiny firm called **Old Town Walks**, for which tourists are asked to gather daily in summer at 6:30 P.M. in front of the Obelisque on Slottsbacken; no advance reservations are necessary. Price of the two-hour tour: 20 Swedish kronor ($3.56); theme is the daily life of Stockholm through the ages.

IN LONDON

The many historic districts of London, with their intimate courtyards and curving lanes too narrow for traffic, are custom-made for walking tours, and no fewer than a dozen tiny companies vie for the patronage of intellectually curious tourists. Every day of the week, March through October, at 11 A.M. and 2 P.M., and some evenings as well, they offer "Legal London," "Literary London," "Aristocratic London" (Mayfair and St. James's), "Historic Pubs," and other crowd-pleasers of two hours' duration, for a uniform £3.50 ($6.30) per tour. You meet each time at a designated subway exit. For other details, see the "Walkers' London" section of the chapter on "The Other London."

The most distinctive of the companies, but perhaps too drily intellectual for some tastes, is Citisights. Founded by professional archeologists in 1981, it reflects their tastes with such predictable themes as "Celtic London," "Roman London," "Medieval London," and "Victorian London," to name but a few. For further information, contact **Citisights, 145 Goldsmiths Row, E2 (phone 739-2372).**

City Walks, Streets of London, and London Walks are all fierce competitors of Citisights, and a bit more popular in their approach. All lay a heavy emphasis on such sure-fire themes as "On the Trail of Jack the Ripper," "In Search of Sherlock Holmes," "Ghosts, Ghouls, and Haunted Taverns" (an evening walking tour), and "The World of Charles Dickens," and all charge a standard £3.50 ($6.30) per two-hour tour. But each company stresses its own periodic "exclusives" (which are soon imitated by the other firms).

Currently, City Walks is particularly proud of its two-hour "Beatles' London" (on Wednesday at 11 A.M.), which takes you past the place where John and Yoko first met, to the recording studios where renowned albums were made, and to the present-day site of Paul McCartney's office. For complete details, contact **City Walks, 9 Kensington High St., W8 (phone 937-4281).**

Streets of London features as its current "exclusives" "The London of Henry VIII," "Islington—A London Village," and "In and Out of Fleet Street—Home of Sweeney Todd." For more information, contact **Streets of London, 32 Grovelands Rd., N13 (phone 882-3414).**

At London Walks, the emphasis is on "The Historic City" and "The Famous Square Mile." For current details, contact **London Walks, 10 Greenbrook Ave., Hadley Wood, Herts EN4 (phone 441-8906).**

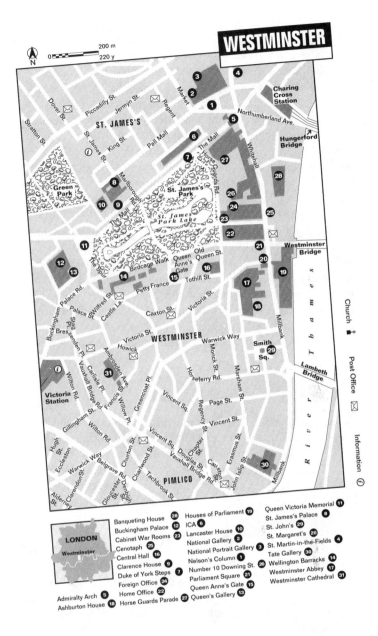

"I am tired," he wrote, "of having to speak two or three languages on the same bus, and of rushing by everything of interest in a hurry. The best way to see any city is on foot."

Typical of the smaller one-person walking-tour operators is John Muffty's Historical Tours, with guaranteed near-daily departures in every month but December. I particularly like his "Inside Some Hidden Interiors of Old London," which takes you to a 16th-century dining hall still in use, a 12th-century church, and to the 18th-century Old Curiosity Shop, among others. Contact Mr. Muffty at **Historical Tours, 3 Florence Rd., South Croydon, CR2 (phone 668-4019).** Or consider Peter Westbrook's Londoner Pub Walks, leaving from the Temple Underground station at 7:30 P.M. every Friday of the year. For complete details, contact **Peter Westbrook, 3 Springfield Ave., N10 (phone 883-2656).**

A variant on the standard walking tours of London are the one-hour backstage tours of famous London theaters offered by Barbara Kinghorn's Stage by Stage Ltd. for £5 ($9); these are given Tuesday through Saturday at 11 A.M. A different theater is visited each day, and brought alive for you by one of a dedicated staff of actors and actresses. Bookings are made at the **Edwards & Edwards desk in the British Travel Centres at 12 Regent St. or 156 Shaftesbury Ave. (phone 379-5822)** or directly from Stage by Stage (phone 328-7558).

IN BRUSSELS

The one-man **Babbelbus** organization (his name is Philippe Baeyens) runs three-hour English-language walking tours of the central city daily except Monday from April through September at 10 A.M., for 220 Belgian francs ($6.87), including a drink at the end, at a typical workingfolks' tavern in the Marolles district. Phone 673-1835 for all the details.

IN ROME

And finally, an order of Dutch nuns conducts walking tours of sights in the Eternal City—an entire morning devoted to one building, or to one of the Catacombs, or to a section of the Vatican Museum—for tourists seriously interested in history and culture. Tours leave on Tuesday, Thursday, and Saturday at 9:30 A.M., except in August, from the Foyer Unitas in the lovely Pamphili Palace at via di S. Maria del Anima 30, and a small contribution to their work (the equivalent of a dollar or two) is asked at the end. Always phone 686-5951 for reservations.

City Hall of Brussels

Puerto Rico, Turnabout in the Caribbean

Because It Has Preserved Its Own Culture and Civilization, Our Own American Commonwealth Is Again King of the Tropics

THE RESURGENCE OF TOURISM TO PUERTO Rico is one of the big travel stories of the year. Suddenly, from San Juan to Mayagüez, from Ponce to Dorado Beach, developers are rushing to complete new hotels and marinas on a coastline that now receives more visitors each year than any other island in the Caribbean.

Gone are the days of shuttered resorts, or of other lodgings visibly deteriorating before your eyes. As of this writing, all except El Conquistador have reopened (and it soon will), some in better shape than ever before. The old Normandie, near the Caribe Hilton, has reemerged as an elegant pink-walled Radisson. The sprawling Cerromar Beach, under new Hyatt management, sports a $4-million winding river of a swimming pool that's one of the great wonders of the resort world. In Old San Juan, period buildings of the 17th century have been restored and are as impressive as they once were.

No one better deserves such a turnaround than the Puerto Ricans. To come from a week among them, as I recently have, is to be refreshed and enlightened by a generous, warm-spirited people. As their economy has improved—and it continues to do so, with discernible dips in unemployment and poverty, the building of a major middle class, a near-halt in emigration elsewhere—so has their mood. Pride breeds security, and the old chip-on-the-shoulder days of *West Side Story* are like ancient history, replaced by almost unvarying courtesy, a dignified hospitality, and a sense of caring for the visitor.

Add to this a series of concrete improvements in tourist conditions. Apart from massive recent investments of private and government funds in hotels and attractions, four other factors, in my opinion, contribute to the upswing of tourism to Puerto Rico:

1. Cost. Although hotel prices here are marginally higher than on many other islands, everything else is dramatically

La Fortaleza

Beach on Vieques

El Cristo Chapel, Old San Juan

Here tourism doesn't dominate the scene, as on so many smaller islands.

La Casa Blanca, San Juan

cheaper. Food is reasonably priced, and meals in Puerto Rico are delicious, featuring many more fresh ingredients than are normally found in the Caribbean. The visitor delights in a broad range of just-caught seafood, accompanied by plantains and corn sticks (*sorullitos*), excellent local beer (try the India brand), and that most celestial of Puerto Rican specialties—a distinctively prepared, subtly flavored side dish of rice and beans.

2. Culture preserved. On this island of three million people, tourism is a relatively small activity, however large in numbers (it accounts for only 6% of the gross national product), and doesn't dominate the scene, as on so many smaller islands. Except in Old San Juan, the tourist is often invisible, and the Puerto Ricans are absorbed in their own concerns, their own history and language, their own boisterous politics. To me, this provides the best kind of setting for tourism, enabling those visitors to enjoy a foreign society and not a copy of their own.

3. Variety. A full 100 miles long and nearly 35 miles wide, Puerto Rico is a large island of cities and villages, mountains and rural valleys, rolling hills with cattle grazing,

parks and beaches, theaters and schools. Evening cultural activities are abundant, and every sort of enterprise—from tuna canning to the production of pharmaceuticals, from Spanish-language Shakespeare (Raul Julia frequently returns to perform it) to scuba-diving schools and thoroughbred racetracks—flourishes both day and night.

4. Ease of access. The decision by American Airlines to make San Juan its major "hub" to the Caribbean has brought dozens of daily flights to Puerto Rico from cities all over the U.S. Thousands of people headed for other islands are now brought first to San Juan, and an increasing number of them are staying over for a few days en route. No other tropical island enjoys such convenient nonstop access to and from so many major U.S. cities.

Most visitors stay, of course, in the high-rise seafront resort hotels of San Juan; but other areas and categories seem far more desirable:

• **Off-beat Vieques and Culebra.** Off the east coast of Puerto Rico, reached by small plane or ferryboat, the cozy, country-like, laid-back, and barely developed isles of

Vieques and Culebra, with small hotels and guesthouses only, are becoming increasingly popular among unpretentious, intelligent "beachcomber" types. Here's the Caribbean as it was 30 years ago.

• **The low-cost beach hotels of the west coast.** A very special type of American, anxious to holiday among Puerto Rican vacationers, will head to the sprightly holiday areas at Boqueron Beach and Boqueron Bay, and to the *paradores* (country inns) on both the western and northwestern coasts. At Boqueron, high-season rooms can be had for as little as $40 a night, and though they're in modest structures they are clean and comfortable, and are located smack in the heart of a bustling Spanish-style vacation industry, alongside an array of low-cost seafood restaurants, one better than the next. At the *balneario* (supervised public beach) of Boqueron, cottages housing up to six people can be rented for $40 a night

On the West Coast

They are absorbed in their own concerns, their own history and language, their own boisterous politics.

Horned Dorset Primavera Hotel, near Rincón

El Yunque rain forest

total, even in the winter months (which are a low-season period for the Puerto Ricans themselves). Though Boqueron is nearly three hours by car from San Juan Airport, it's a prime choice for cost-conscious Americans willing to adapt to local conditions and amenities. They'll enjoy the dividend of closeness to the Puerto Rican people as the latter pursue their own vacations.

• **The exquisite seaside haciendas.** Finally, tourists of the most highly refined tastes will opt for the elegant period seaside estates of Puerto Rico that have been converted into intimate high-quality hotels. The latest, completed just two years ago, and destined to become a jet-setter's favorite, is the 26-suite Horned Dorset Primavera Hotel near Rincón, on the west coast, just 15 minutes by car north of Mayagüez. In its third winter of operation, rates will be $190 to $210 per large double room (expect a 30% reduction of rates in summer) for elaborate Spanish-style accommodations with canopied beds and luxury fixtures. My own room, with heavy mahogany antiques and an opulent bathroom, hung over the crashing waves of the Caribbean. I took cocktails in a well-stocked paneled library, supped gourmet dinners served by white-gloved waiters (five courses cost an astonishing $35), relaxed on a golden beach and on the powder-blue chaises longues at the quiet swimming pool area, almost as if I were the house guest of a titled Spanish family. Two former college professors—Kingsley Wratten and Harold Davies of Horned Dorset restaurant fame in upstate Leonardsville, New York—are the proprietors of the Horned Dorset Primavera, which serves as a model for what can be done with stately but ancient homes. For reservations, contact **Horned Dorset Primavera Hotel, Apartado 1132, Rincón, PR 00743 (phone 809/823-4030).**

What's ahead for Puerto Rico? The chief construction of future world-class hotels is taking place on the eastern and northeastern coasts of the island: an elegant Ritz Carlton near Humacao, two 400-room Princess Hotels near Rio Grande, a luxury Trafalgar House hotel near Ceiba, and the Western Hemisphere's largest marina (600 slips) almost next door.

Meanwhile, bustling hotel lobbies are a tribute to the spirit of the Puerto Rican people, who fought to erase an unfortunate image, and once again stand revealed as the gracious hosts they are.

THE NEW WORLD OF TRAVEL 1992

The lifeblood of the Arthur Frommer travel guides is the correspondence received from readers, commenting on the establishments recommended in the texts and recommending new establishments. Each such letter is carefully studied, and when a particular lead seems promising, it is followed up and personally checked.

It is hoped that *The New World of Travel* will receive similar assistance from its readers. A yearly publication, issued near the start of each year, *The New World* will constantly grow. And since much of its content relates to organizations that lack the means to market themselves properly, or come to the attention of a travel journalist, your help is invaluable in alerting me to the organizations—hospitality exchanges, alternative resorts, new travel clubs, and the like—that you have discovered.

If you become aware of a new travel organization, program, or development that deserves to be described in our next edition, *The New World of Travel 1992*, won't you please let me know about it? Send your letters to Arthur Frommer, *The New World of Travel*, c/o Prentice Hall Press, Travel Division, 15 Columbus Circle, New York, NY 10023. All letters will be acknowledged, and all are warmly appreciated, in advance, by the author.

A Trip to the Other Hawaii

If Our Vacation Budget Confines Us to the Tourist-Jammed Island of Oahu, How Can We Nevertheless Escape the Tawdry?

WALL-TO-WALL HOTELS. AWESTRUCK, FIRST-time visitors in matching muumuus or gaudy shirts. Fast-food restaurants with lines stretching far outside. Hokey Hawaiian performers leading organized songfests and drawn-out chants of "ah-loh-hah."

And if you present a tour voucher upon arrival at Honolulu airport, you get kissed on the cheek. No voucher, no kiss.

HAWAII'S TOURIST GHETTO

Let's face it: some sections of modern-day Hawaii, especially overbuilt Waikiki, leave much to be desired. Some visitors to the 50th state are less than enchanted with the development of mass-volume tourism there, and seek an option—a pathway to the "other Hawaii," the "real Hawaii."

So do many longtime residents of Hawaii's heavily populated Oahu, who feel resentful of tourism, even enslaved by it. That, in part, is why Waikiki remains "ghettoized," in the words of a University of Hawaii anthropologist. And as he further notes, that's just fine for many locals. It gives them the rest of the island to enjoy for themselves, a space in which they needn't be endlessly reminded of Hawaii's dependence on tourism.

The thoughtful visitor follows the same path, to areas of Oahu outside of Waikiki, and to the people who work in or inhabit those areas. But it isn't easy—it requires sensitivity and work.

The key word is "respect." That's the quality voiced to me by a dozen residents as lacking in tourists to Hawaii, and the essence of what would otherwise give them access to the "real Hawaii." People here have an overweening appreciation for courtesy—perhaps a by-product of the Japanese culture of the islands' largest ethnic grouping. They like questions to be prefaced with "Excuse me, could you please tell me? . . ." And if the resulting conversations should lead to an invitation to someone's home, where shoes are left outside the door, leave yours outside also. "Don't ask if you should take your shoes off. Just do it," said a long-suffering Hawaiian of my acquaintance.

PEOPLE PLACES

Certainly the finest place to meet or mingle with the locals is the Ala Moana Shopping Center, largest outdoor shopping mall in the world, with close to 200 shops. Its Makai Market features dozens of food stalls offering international cuisine at low prices (less than $5 for large portions), and there you join locals in that ultimate conversational "bond" between tourists and residents: food.

After walking around the mall, go across the street to the pleasant Ala Moana Park, which has grass, picnic tables, and a lovely beach favored by locals. You can bring lunch from the Makai Market, or stop off at the Ala Moana Farmer's Market behind the nearby Ward Warehouse shopping complex; the latter features specialty foods of Hawaii: for example, a Hawaiian plate, from Haili's Hawaii, of lau-lau (dumplings made of ti leaves and stuffed with meat or fish), poki (raw fish), lomi salmon (smoked with tomatoes and onions), poi (sticky, pudding-like starch made from taro root), and haupia (coconut pudding), for a total of $3.60. And you won't see a single other tourist.

TRAVELING ELSEWHERE

For getting about and meeting friendly folk at the same time, the essential device is Honolulu's wonderfully efficient and inexpensive public transporation system, TheBUS (60¢ to any point in Oahu; call 531-1611 for the routes, and request a copy of the free brochure "Hawaii Visitors Guide to TheBUS." According to many locals, use of TheBUS distinguishes locals from tourists. If you are friendly, you will soon

Maui

The Big Island

find yourself in conversations about the food and weather, which often lead to weightier things. Cultivate the habit of listening to the residents; one local's explanation to me of what makes tourists so offensive is that they are "abrupt" and cut people off.

THE NONPROFITS

In preference to the commercial attractions and events assaulting you from every poster and glossy ad-filled brochure, patronize the attractions that aren't operated for money. Go to the **Campus Center of the University of Hawaii at Manoa** and look at any of the numerous bulletin boards publicizing time and location of such cultural events as a Western Samoan music concert. Pick up a copy of the weekly *University Bulletin* (at Brachman Annex no. 6), which lists several activities each day, including art exhibitions, theatrical productions, films, and lectures (a recent example: a breakfast meeting to discuss "The Pacific Attitude Toward Work"). Visit the University Bookstore for its "Hawaiiana section" of works on whatever aspect of Hawaii most interests you: from poetry and healing practices to mythology, ethnic difficulties, marine biology, whatever.

You can plan your activities, read your books, or perhaps participate in lively discussions at the **Coffeeline**, 1820 University Ave., open Tuesday through Saturday for both breakfast and lunch. A comfortable, open-air but roofed meeting place for the university community, the Coffeeline serves healthy, old-fashioned cooking at low prices (seafood gumbo, biscuits, lime pie, and coffee for $3; meals are prepared by food science/nutrition teacher Brigitte Campbell and the students she trains). You can also go to the sometimes boisterous university hangout, **Manoa Garden in Hemenway Hall,** open weekdays only: from 10:30 A.M. to 8 P.M. when school is in session, from 11 A.M. to 6 P.M. during vacations.

And then there's the **East-West Center,** established by Congress in 1960 to "bring together people from the United States, Asia, and the Pacific in studying and seeking solutions to problems of social, economic, and cultural change." By dropping in at Burns Hall on the East-West Center campus (adjacent to the university), you can pick up a copy of the event-listing *Centerweek.* From it, I was recently able to attend a free storytelling event by Hawaiian, Samoan, and Maori performers, "Na Mo'olelo O Ka Pakipiki—Legends of the Pacific" (followed by an engrossing, lively discussion). You can also scan the more detailed bulletin called "Today at the East-West Center" posted in Burns Hall, or phone 944-7283 for schedule information. Be sure to ask how early you should arrive to obtain a seat.

Along the Hamakua Coast, the Big Island

Manoa Falls, Oahu

MORE OPTIONS

The thoughtful visitor can also obtain information on Hawaiian ethnic festivities by reading the local newspapers (*Star-Bulletin* and *Honolulu Advertiser*), or by calling the **Hawaiian Visitors Information Office** (phone 923-1811). There you'll learn about such celebrations as the Japanese Bon Dance, which takes place at temples for the purpose of sending ancestral spirits to the "other world." Or you'll be given word of cultural activities in which you also can partici-

pate, such as Japanese tea ceremonies. If you'd prefer to arrange for this particular item on your own, contact the **Urasenke Foundation of Hawaii** (phone 923-3059), which offers tea ceremonies to the public on Wednesday and Friday from 10 A.M. to noon.

An excellent way to have a taste of Oahu's Asian communities is to **walk around Chinatown.** Wander down the main street, Mauna Kea, and look in the glass windows to see people making leis. Sample local foods—yellow bean cake and lotus root candy. Ask to be directed to a Chinese herbalist, Dr. S. Yee (on Mauna Kea Street), who charges $25 for acupuncture treatment and herbal prescriptions, and by whom several of my Hawaiian friends swear. Stroll through the **open-air market** on King Street (most active on Saturday mornings), which displays produce, poultry, and exotic fish. Eat dim sum (assorted dumplings) for lunch, or at the famous Wo Fats, at the corner of Hotel and Mauna Kea Streets, for which dinner reservations are required. Take in the **Kuan Yin Temple** on Vineyard Street, whose impressive statues, altars, offerings, joss sticks, and incense reflect a mix of Confucian, Taoist, and Buddhist influences.

And if you must take a tour, at least opt for a walking tour of Chinatown. Both the "Chinese Chamber" (phone 533-3181) and the Hawaiian Heritage Center (phone 521-2749) offer full-scale explorations on foot of Chinatown and the Old Oahu Market District, dropping in at a Chinese noodle factory, cake shop, acupuncture clinic, herb shop, open-air fish market, and Asian food processor—a total of three hours and only $4. Both depart at 9:30 A.M., on Tuesday in the case of the Chamber, on Wednesday and Friday in the case of the center.

AROUND THE ISLAND

Now let's escape the city altogether and taste the pleasures of the "other Oahu." Following which, I'll talk about specific institutions that introduce you in general to the "other Hawaii."

THE ROAD LESS TRAVELED

Kamehameha Hwy. is your "yellow brick" path to the dream of Hawaii; it almost circumscribes the island, along the ocean on one side, with farmland and sloping volcanic hills on the other (where you'll see families hanging octopus to

A thoughtful visitor runs from the tourist ghetto of Waikiki.

dry in the sun). In a rental car (as little as $23 for the day), you'll find numerous points from which to enjoy beaches unspoiled by tourists or development, cane fields, quaint towns, fruit stands, and lunch wagons. One visitor at a roadside pay phone was recently overheard calling home to complain about learning of this "paradise" so late in her stay.

For surfing and such, you use **Sandy Beach** on the far side of Hanauma Bay, or **Sunset Beach** on the north shore (but beware the dangerous waves). For simply enjoying the ocean and clear air, **Waimanalo Beach Park** and **Kailua Beach Park** are favorites of the residents whose town sits on their shores. **Haleiwa,** also on the north coast, is the quaint village site of still another charming beach.

Closer to Honolulu is the suburb of **Kailua,** with its soft, white sand beach of Lanikai flanked by aquamarine waters; from here you can take a 3½-hour excursion by inflatable boat (and for $45) to five uninhabited islands and a legendary sea cave—the kind of approach to unspoiled, breathtaking nature that many visitors mistakenly assume can be had only on the more expensive outer islands of Hawaii. Contact **Windward Expeditions (phone 808/263-3899)** for reservations. In Kailua, too, is the moderately priced **L'Auberge Swiss, 117 Hekili St. (phone 263-4663** after 2 P.M. for dinner reservations), which many regard as among the islands' best.

In the course of your self-drive journey prior to reaching the Kamehameha Hwy. you can stop to visit **Manoa Falls,** an easy, one-mile hike through lush tropical rain forest entered by scarcely any tourists; if they did, they'd enjoy a major reward: a freshwater pool created by the gentle but high-up cascade. Drive to **Paradise Park** at 3737 Manoa Rd. (a popular tourist attraction for bird enthusiasts), but head behind the parking lot to the well-marked but scarcely used road leading to the falls.

And for other "roads less traveled," inquire of the **Sierra Club of Hawaii (phone 946-8494)** about their $1 hikes through still other unspoiled terrain of Oahu. These are generally scheduled for every Sunday (but occasionally on Saturday) and are often available on the other islands too.

THE INSTITUTIONS THAT ASSIST YOU

Kawaiahao Church at 957 Punchbowl St. in Honolulu, which many call the Westminster Abbey of Hawaii, dates back to 1842 and figured prominently in the early Christian period as the church of the Ali'i (chiefs and chieftesses). Viewing the 21 graceful and lifelike portraits of the Ali'i here gives one a sense of the former Hawaiian kingdom and its rulers. Services, though open to everyone, are still conducted partly in the Hawaiian language, and there's no more awesome experience than the Sunday 10:30 A.M. program, suffused with the true aloha spirit, and frequently attended by

parishioners dressed in the pageantry of Hawaii's past—not, mind you, to entertain the tourist, but in celebration of their heritage.

The **Bishop Museum,** at 1525 Bernice St., displays relics of the art, transportation, war practices, and worship of ancient Hawaii. It's important, too, and charges an entrance fee of $5 for adults, $2.50 for children 6 to 17.

The Mission Houses Museum, also in downtown Honolulu at 553 S. King St., where it displays home and workplace furnishings of 19th-century Protestant missionaries, is less interesting for its contents, in my view, than for its frequent (call for the schedule) guided walking tours of the historic downtown center of Honolulu. Tours depart from the museum on several days of the week, cost $7 for adults and $2 for children, require reservations (phone 531-0481), and are another introduction to the "other Hawaii."

The other Oahu

Kawaiahao Church, Honolulu

The Honolulu Academy of Arts, 900 S. Beretania St., is home to one of the world's finest collections of Asian arts, and is unusually pleasant to visit in its airy setting of court-yards with sculpture gardens. Open free of charge six days a week (closed Monday), it also offers classes, lectures, and films on the culture and art of Asia, the Pacific, and Hawaii, and serves lunch in its café for $5.95.

Temari Center for Asian and Pacific Arts, 1329-A Tenth Ave., provides semester-long courses to residents in Asian crafts, but also serves the tourist by scheduling single-evening lectures and demonstrations in such subjects as lei-making ($15 for three hours) or Japanese paper-making ($60 for a Friday-night lecture followed by Saturday and Sunday work-shops). Phone 808/735-1860 for detailed information.

DISCOVERING AUTHENTIC CULTURE

Tune your Walkman or your transistor radio to AM 1420—KCCN—the island's only Hawaiian-music radio station. Watch the newspapers for appearances by the Brothers Cazimero (best known of all the contemporary Hawaiian music groups), the Makaha Sons of Niihau, the Sons of Hawaii, or the Kahuano Lake Trio.

Waimea Falls Park, at 59-864 Kamehameha Hwy. in Haleiwa, on the north shore (phone 638-8511), offers exact performances of the original hula—considerably different from the contrived variety performed at Waikiki's Royal Hawaiian Shopping Center—daily at 11:30 A.M. and 1, 2:30, and 4 P.M. Additionally, a covey of shrines, burial caves, ancient game sites, waterfalls, and arboretums make the park well worth visiting, even for its steep admission charge of $10 for adults.

"Luaus" are another means for entering into the life of Hawaii, but only if they are of the kind designed for local residents. Watch the newspapers or bulletin boards for announcements of one of the periodic community-sponsored luaus that rarely cost more than $10.

NONSTANDARD RESORTS

Finally, with their otherworldly airs, their remoteness from industrial concerns, their mid-ocean location, it was inevitable that the islands of Hawaii would become capitals of the "New Age."

And that's exactly what is happening. Though Honolulu and its crowded Waikiki Beach have remained determinedly mainstream—with fast-food restaurants and souvenir stands at every turning—the remainder of the lush Pacific state is sprouting everywhere with "holistic spas," "Buddhist retreats," "channeling centers," and "meditation lodges." Even the recently built $300-a-night Hyatt Regency Waikoloa on the Big Island of Hawaii has announced that its central health facility will be devoted to "A New Age Restorative Approach" ("A.N.A.R.A.") consisting not simply of spa-like treatments, but of therapies with "depth and meaning ... promoting a state of inner peace," according to a Hyatt official.

Should you, who may have no sympathy at all for New Age concepts, nevertheless consider the use of such facilities for your next Hawaiian vacation? Yes, in my view, for the following reasons:

• The New Age resorts of Hawaii are all far from the overly developed areas, in remote settings of untouched, awesomely lovely nature. They assure you a noncommercial vacation.

• Their cuisine avoids the gluttony and overindulgence of the tourist restaurants; you'll feast on bran muffins for breakfast, on tofu and sprouts for lunch.

• They tend to be cheaper than the standard resorts in all but a few instances. And finally,

• They put your own, standard views to the test, provoking thought, perhaps awakening your mind to new values, at least reducing stress and anxiety.

All this is found on three particular islands:

Maui

Here's the most visible evidence of the burgeoning new philosophy in the form of countless herbal and health-food stores, holistic medical centers, offices of "transformational counseling," and alternative bookstores, along the length of Central Avenue in the town of Wailuku, a short drive from the airport. The impressive commerce attracts large numbers of sympathizers from the mainland, who congregate particularly among the New Age books and crystals on sale at **Miracles Unlimited, 81 Central Ave., Wailuku,** where they gaze at a notice-filled bulletin board and peruse Suzi Osborn's monthly "Island Calendar of Events" listing massage classes, fire dance celebrations, acupuncture demonstrations, nutritional lectures, and other such esoterica across the island. Phone 244-7400 for Suzi.

Maui's key New Age resort, though tiny in size, is Old Maui Zendo, a former Buddhist monastery taken over four years ago by a 29-year veteran of detective work in Los Angeles, Rick Smith, who himself had experienced a life-change in the awesome natural setting of the tropics. He thereupon resolved to create a center for other establishment people—standard, conservative types who had not yet been exposed to the liberating ideas of the newer generation. "My ideal guests," he recently told me, "are Mr. and Mrs. Middle America, usually 40 to 60, who've been stuck in certain phases, but are ready to open up to a beautiful place."

A single big house with an enormous porch, Old Maui

The quality voiced as lacking in tourists to Hawaii is "respect."

At Plantation Spa, Oahu

Larger, and altogether different in mood, is the several-structure retreat complex known as Hale Akua, which consciously caters to persons already well versed in New Age approaches; neophytes, or nonbelievers, would not, in my view, be comfortable in this million-dollar estate whose ideal guest, according to manager Donny Regalmuto, is "arty, together, clear-minded, and happy." On the awesome tropical estate with seaside views are hot tubs, a large swimming pool, waterfalls, fountains, and considerable classroom space for periodic workshops on topics dealing with frontiers of the mind. Expect to pay about $55 to $65 a night for most double rooms, and to prepare your own meals in the kitchen facilities of each building. Write for a schedule of retreats to: **Hale Akua, P.O. Box 1425, Paia, Maui, HI 96753.**

Hawaii

Less evident to the eye, the New Age facilities of the Big Island are still vital and popular. The leading New Age location is a laid-back retreat called Kalani Honua, consisting of 32 rooms grouped into four wooden lodges, rustic but elegant, on 20 acres of scenic lawns and forests about a mile from a black sand beach (and 30 miles down the coast from Hilo). Though outside groups schedule one-week workshops there during much of the year, individuals are always welcomed to occupy the small but charming rooms, and to imbibe meals prepared with a careful attention to good nutrition—for example, homemade granola, sprouted-grain bread with fresh berry topping, and fresh fruit, for breakfast. Hiking is particularly popular, to hidden lagoons, lava tubes, natural steambaths, and volcanic lakes. Room and board: a remarkable $50 per person per day, on average, exclusive of optional workshop costs. Contact **Kalani Honua, Intercultural Conference and Retreat Center, R.R. 2, Box 4500, Pahoa, HI 96778 (phone toll free 800/367-8047, ext. 669).**

On the same island, Wood Valley Retreat is a Tibetan Buddhist center (actual Buddhist temple and adjoining two-story residence) nestled in the woods near Pahala. Contemplation and calm prevail here, as contrasted with the sharing and sociability of other centers. Prices for retreats vary greatly, but often range about $40 a day for room and full board. Contact **Wood Valley Retreat, P.O. Box 250, Pahala, HI 96777 (phone 808/928-8539),** or send $5 to receive its mailings.

Oahu

The pickings here are slimmer, but accessible even to visitors staying at the standard hotels. By scanning the large bulletin board at the **Sirius Bookstore, 2320 Young St., Honolulu,** open until 7 P.M. on weekdays, until 6 P.M. on Saturday, you'll learn of a wide range of New Age seminars and meditations in the area away from Waikiki, and especially about the

Zendo lodges fewer than 20 guests at a time, but looks out onto vast grounds filled with surprises: natural pools, waterfalls, hot tubs. Instruction is informal and eclectic, often unplanned, and by tai chi masters or lecturers on mythology, who make periodic, unscheduled appearances. Total charge for a full week, including airport pickup, room, three meals daily, and all surprises, is exactly $1,000 for single occupancy, only $750 per person double, plus air fare—of course—to get you there. Contact **Rick Smith, Old Maui Zendo, 915 Kaupakalua Rd., Haiku, Maui, HI 96708 (phone 808/572-8795).** And contact Rick as well for information on the cheaper ($100 for a weekend) New Age activities (retreats, workshops, conferences) at the adjoining Akahi Farm, through which you must pass to reach Old Maui Zendo. Akahi Farm sleeps 50, in rooms far less elaborate than at Zendo's, but still comfortable.

popular yoga classes taught for 19 consecutive years (and for $6 per hour) by the much-respected Rick Bernstein at the Kilauea Recreational Center, two miles from Waikiki, at 9 A.M. on Tuesday and Thursday, and at other times (Tuesday and Thursday at 5:30 P.M., Saturday at 9 A.M.) in the airy structure behind the Japanese temple in Oahu's Nu'uanu Valley. Phone 924-6615 to speak with Rick.

A better base than a standard hotel would be Oahu's small Plantation Spa, occupying elegantly manicured grounds on the north shore, near Ka'a'awa. It qualifies for the New Age with its emphasis on preventive health, warding off illness with yoga, aerobics, and a lacto-vegetarian cuisine, but its hefty rates are very much of the "Old Age": $1,250 per person for a six-night, Sunday-to-Saturday stay, all inclusive. Contact: **The Plantation Spa, 51-550 Kamehameha Hwy., Ka'a'awa, Oahu, HI 96730 (phone 808/237-8685).**

Even if you stay on Oahu, you can visit the more exotic New Age facilities on Maui and the Big Island by flying there for a day visit; Aloha Airlines charges only $50 for any point-to-point trip within the islands.

Use of "TheBUS" distinguishes locals from tourists.

Tropical Trekking—A New Hawaiian Holiday

Through a Tangle of Jungle and Undergrowth, Waterfalls and Rain Forests, Mountains and Coral Reefs

IT SEEMS AN OXYMORON, A CONTRADICTION in terms, a just plain absurdity. To the first-time visitor engulfed by the crowds at Waikiki, the skyscrapers of Honolulu, the traffic gridlock of Kalakua Avenue, the notion that Hawaii can be visited for its wilderness aspects seems farfetched indeed.

Yet most of Hawaii remains a wilderness, a natural tangle of jungle and undergrowth, waterfalls and rain forests, mountains and coral reefs. Based on those riches—the perfect ingredients for adventure touring—a dozen, quite remarkable residents have begun operating tours that differ radically from the standard urban variety. And though their client base is still small, it is growing fast, and posing a strong challenge to the mass-market firms.

Here are a few of the "dissidents" in Hawaiian travel:

HIKE MAUI

The 47-year-old Ken Schmitt, owner of Hike Maui, brings greater-than-usual academic training (in anthropology, archeology, and geology) and vivid wilderness experience to Hawaii's second-most-popular island. When a hurricane destroyed the boat he had been using in the charter business, he went to live in the jungle/forest for an extended camping trip that lasted three years. No one knows the backcountry of Maui better.

Schmitt leads hikes nearly every day of the year. They include a redwood forest trek, one to the waterfalls at Hana, others to coastal or mountain areas; but the hallmark trip—8 to 11 hours long—is into the other-worldly domain of Haleakala Crater, a panorama of changing colors, endemic plants and flowers, birds, and other wildlife, that Schmitt calls "a natural temple."

The accompanying commentary is both learned and inspiring. "What I aim to do," says Schmitt, "is to teach people how to be comfortable in nature, especially by using the knowledge of ancient peoples.

"This is particularly important to us today," he says. "What would we do if our homes were destroyed? I'm talking not simply of survival, but of how to enjoy living in the wilderness." Some fledgling hikers, excited by Schmitt's prescriptions on their one-day hike, decide to do a week-long trip with him to learn more.

Most hikes start at $60 per person, and range to $80 or $90 for Haleakala (less for children). Schmitt will work with a minimum of two people, a maximum of six. When you

> "Our trips," says an operator of Hawaiian adventure tours, "not only remove people from the framework of a standard vacation, but from the enclosures of a nine-to-five office job as well."

Swimming and snorkeling off the Big Island

phone his office and specify the date of your desired trek, he'll either advise you of the destination for that date or—if nothing is scheduled—permit you to pick the hike. Contact **Hike Maui, P.O. Box 330969, Kahului, Maui, HI 96733 (phone 808/879-5270).**

PACIFIC QUEST

Perhaps the leading adventure-tour company of Hawaii, so popular that reservations at least three and four months in advance are often required, Pacific Quest is the creation of Zane Bilgrave (a former "experiential educator" working out-of-doors with children under the auspices of the Hawaii Department of Education) and his wife, "M.J.," a former ranger at Volcanoes National Park. They now have a staff of several others who accompany scores of departures each year, each limited to between 10 and 16 people. Participants can be of any age and degree of experience, provided only that they regard themselves as active, adventurous sorts with a strong interest in the natural and cultural history of Hawaii.

Each day of the tours—there are 14-day, 8-day, and 1- to 5-day tours available—focuses on a unique aspect of Hawaii, almost always associated with its ecological environment. One day participants will be walking up a mountain and swimming under a waterfall; another day they may be horseback-riding, swimming, and snorkeling. "And that," says Bilgrave, "leads to a heightened awareness of each day. It may even give people a different perspective on their lives when they return home. They try to get more out of each day. They begin to spend more time outdoors. Our trips not only remove them from the framework of a standard vacation, but from the enclosures of a nine-to-five office job as well."

Three basic tours are offered. The most popular, "Quest Hawaii" is a 14-day trip to the islands of Kauai, Molokai, Maui, and the "Big Island" of Hawaii. Cost is $1,650 per person, which includes all lodging, ground transportation, inter-island flights, activities, instruction, and most meals. Nights spent camping alternate with stays in rustic inns. There is no backpacking.

"Crater Comforts" is an eight-day, three-island trip to

333

Descending a mountain slope to Halape, Wilderness Hawaii

son includes seven days of sailing, all food, captain and crew, snorkeling, and fishing equipment.

Contact **Pacific Quest, P.O. Box 205, Haleiwa, HI 96712 (phone 808/638-8338, or toll free 800/367-8047, ext. 523).**

WILDERNESS HAWAII

Reflecting the approach of the international "Outward Bound" movement, this company helps travelers to go beyond their usual limits of endurance or daring. Its founder, a 37-year-old outdoorswoman named Shena Sandler, has been leading her own challenging wilderness courses since her work with the Hawaii Outward Bound School in 1977–1980.

Although Sandler devotes much of the summer to a program for teenagers, she offers four-day courses for co-ed adults or women-only in other seasons. These consist of backpacking expeditions to the southern coast of the Big Island, costing only $300 per person, and open to people of not backpacking-type skills and without equipment (Sandler provides the necessary gear and food).

First day, participants engage in a demanding hike down a mountain slope to Halape, a remote salt-and-pepper beach that few tourists ever get to see. There, one can sleep either on the beach or in a grove of coconut trees. For two full days there's swimming, snorkeling in a protected lagoon, underwater photography, and a visit to a lava tube a mile away to view the petroglyphs of an ancient archeological site. On the fourth day the group hikes back up the mountain.

Says Shena Sandler: "People enjoy the company, the sense of safety we provide, and the feeling of being taken care of. Plus they have a sense of accomplishment and adventure with a trip like this; some people have significant experiences, especially if they are not familiar with the wilderness."

Contact **Wilderness Hawaii, P.O. Box 61692, Honolulu, HI 96839 (phone 808/737-4697).**

EYE OF THE WHALE

These, next, are largely marine trips, with no camping or backpacking, but rather accommodations aboard sailing yachts (on the sea-borne portions of each journey) or in scenic inns and comfortable bed-and-breakfasts on shore.

Kauau, Lanai, and Maui. Days are spent hiking the Na Pali coast, "zodiacking" (sailing by motorized, rubber boat) to Lanai, and hiking the summit trails of Haleakala. This one costs $995 to $1,080 per person, depending on group size.

And finally, "Hawaiian Sailing Adventures" is a seven-day sail to Lanai, Maui, Molakai, and Oahu, on a fully equipped 35-foot Coronado sloop. Cost of $1,092 per per-

Most of Hawaii remains a wilderness, a tangle of jungle and undergrowth, waterfalls and rain forests, mountains and coral reefs.

Always, the focus is on the natural history of Hawaii, and all activities are "hands on," from helping to sail the ship to recording vocalizations of whales and dolphins. Your guides: a dynamic young couple, Mark and Beth Goodoni, she an experienced naturalist and educator, he a licensed U.S. Coast Guard captain and naturalist.

One seven-day trip led by them, "Earth, Fire, & Sea," begins on the west coast of the Big Island of Hawaii, and includes a stay in remote Waipio Valley (for flora identification and photography), a hike across the crater floor of Kilauea (world's most active volcano), and three days aboard ship devoted to whale-watching, exploring a coral reef, and sailing instruction. Total cost, virtually all inclusive: $995 per person.

A second trip of five days' duration is called "Whale Tales" and operates in winter, when hundreds of humpback whales come to breed off the west coast of the "Big Island." This time for $975 per person, including meals and lodging, instruction and sailing, participants assist in collecting data on the giant mammals, photo-identifying individual humpback whales, and recording their mating songs for a research institute.

A third trip of 10 days' duration, the company's only land-based variety, is called "Hawaiian Odyssey" and takes you hiking through each of Kauai, Molakai, and the Big Island of Hawaii, with meals and overnights in B & B inns; $1,275 per person.

Contact **Eye of the Whale, P.O. Box 1269, Kapaau, HI 96755 (phone 808/889-0227, or toll free 800/657-7730).**

PACIFIC OUTDOOR ADVENTURES

Finally, in a safe and stable, inflatable kayak (with one or two paddlers), this company takes intrepid tourists on a five-day expedition to the spectacular coast of Molakai, which claims to have the world's tallest seacliffs. Safety is always paramount: paddlers go downwind and avoid any areas of rough water, storm, or high surf. You also snorkel, swim, and hike, attend a campfire dinner, and sleep under canvas and the stars. At $850 per person, it is the firm's most popular trip and, according to a spokesperson, "almost anybody can do it." One-day trips for $45, on the windward side of Oahu, are also available.

Contact **Pacific Outdoor Adventures, P.O. Box 61609, Honolulu, HI 96822 (phone 808/988-3913, or toll free 800/52-KAYAK).**

"Earth, Fire & Sea" trip, Eye of the Whale

The Other New York

A World of Cultural Riches, Known to the Resident But Too Often Denied to the Tourist

I SOMETIMES WEEP TO THINK OF THE LIMITED enjoyment and experience that most tourists derive from visiting New York.

To those of us who live here, the city—with its unparalleled cultural opportunities—is an endless source of new ideas, dynamic and stimulating. To the tourist confined to the standard attractions designed for the tourist, it is too often hackneyed and contrived, mindless and superficial.

So what to do? On your own next trip to New York, try alternating the usual sights with the following eight nonstandard activities:

1. Go to a Speech: With its massive, concentrated population of politically sensitive people from scores of ethnic and national backgrounds, New York plays host each night to dozens of free or inexpensive lectures, seminars, protest demonstrations, and gatherings on every subject. Pick up a copy of the *Village Voice* (from any newsstand), turn to "Listings," and under the subhead called "Cheap Thrills" (meaning events that are either free or less than $2.50 in cost) you'll find announcements of verbal fireworks occurring nightly throughout Manhattan, on the part of speakers ranging from opposition leaders of Angola to spokespersons for Ralph Nader. Provocative as they are, the meetings gain additional interest from the intense, intellectual New Yorkers who at-

tend, and both—the meeting and the audience—are fully accessible to the visiting tourist.

2. Enter the New Age: New York's Open Center is the nation's largest facility for inquiries—mostly in the form of nightly, one-time lectures, daylong weekend workshops, and group discussions—into the spiritual speculations and psychological experiments of those who champion "holistic health" or "New Age" thinking. Whether it be theories of meditation, reincarnation, or healing, or simple personal growth from advanced psychological approaches, you'll find it here nearly every day of the week, sometimes for free, never for more than a nominal charge. And you'll meet a special type of open-minded, modest, questing New Yorker of every age. For schedules, write or phone **New York Open Center, Inc., 83 Spring St., New York, NY 10012 (phone 212/219-3739)**. And for numerous other such daytime or evening meetings sponsored by dozens of other New Age groups in New York, pick up the newspaper called *Free Spirit* at most health food or New Age bookstores, such as the one at 78 Fifth Ave., between 13th and 14th Streets.

3. Folkdance in the Big City: Every Sunday evening in Earl Hall on the campus of Columbia University (and for only $4), every Friday evening at the Ethnic Folk Art Center at 131 Varick St. (for about the same), avid folkdancers from

---

People and ideas—the key to a rewarding vacation—lend a new dimension to the experience of New York.

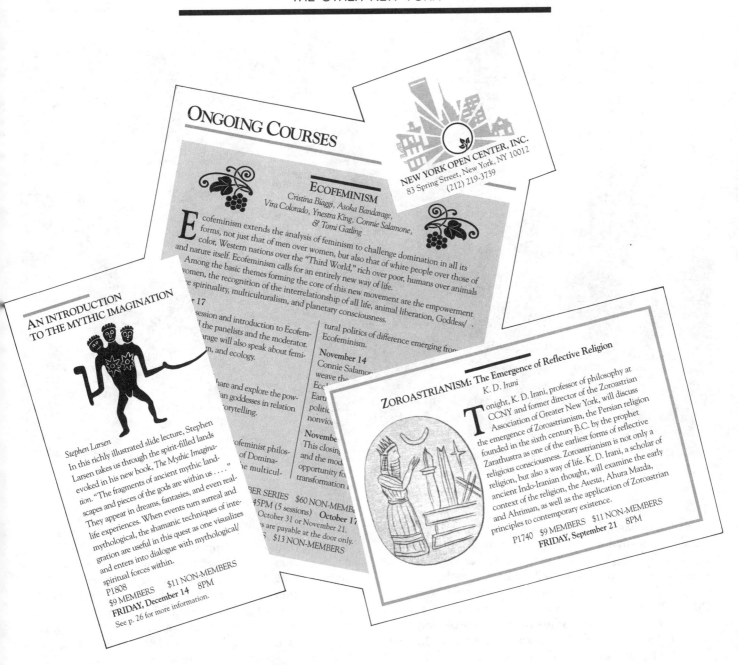

ONGOING COURSES

NEW YORK OPEN CENTER, INC.
83 Spring Street, New York, NY 10012
(212) 219-3739

ECOFEMINISM

*Cristina Biaggi, Asoka Bandarage,
Vira Colorado, Ynestra King, Connie Salamone,
& Tomi Gatling*

Ecofeminism extends the analysis of feminism to challenge domination in all its forms, not just that of men over women, but also that of white people over those of color, Western nations over the "Third World," rich over poor, humans over animals and nature itself. Ecofeminism calls for an entirely new way of life.

Among the basic themes forming the core of this new movement are the empowerment women, the recognition of the interrelationship of all life, animal liberation, Goddess/ re spirituality, multiculturalism, and planetary consciousness.

...r 17

... session and introduction to Ecofem- ...l the panelists and the moderator. ...arage will also speak about femi- ...m, and ecology.

...hare and explore the pow- ...an goddesses in relation ...orytelling.

tural politics of difference emerging fro... Ecofeminism.

November 14
Connie Salamo... weave the... Eco... Eart... politi... nonvio...

Novembe...
This closin... and the mod... opportunity fo... transformation...

...ofeminist philos- ...of Domina- ...he multicul-

...BER SERIES $60 NON-MEMB... ...45PM (5 sessions)   **October 1...** ...October 31 or November 21. ...s are payable at the door only.
$13 NON-MEMBERS

AN INTRODUCTION TO THE MYTHIC IMAGINATION

Stephen Larsen
In this richly illustrated slide lecture, Stephen Larsen takes us through the spirit-filled lands evoked in his new book, *The Mythic Imagina- tion.* "The fragments of ancient mythic land- scapes and pieces of the gods are within us . . . ," They appear in dreams, fantasies, and even real- life experiences. When events turn surreal and mythological, the shamanic techniques of inte- gration are useful in this quest as one visualizes and enters into dialogue with mythological/ spiritual forces within.
P1808 $11 NON-MEMBERS
$9 MEMBERS
FRIDAY, December 14   8PM
See p. 26 for more information.

ZOROASTRIANISM: The Emergence of Reflective Religion
K. D. Irani

Tonight, K. D. Irani, professor of philosophy at CCNY and former director of the Zoroastrian Association of Greater New York, will discuss the emergence of Zoroastrianism, the Persian religion founded in the sixth century B.C. by the prophet Zarathustra as one of the earliest forms of reflective religious consciousness. Zoroastrianism is not only a religion, but also a way of life. K. D. Irani, a scholar of ancient Indo-Iranian thought, will examine the early context of the religion, the *Avesta*, Ahura Mazda, and Ahriman, as well as the application of Zoroastrian principles to contemporary existence.
P1740 $9 MEMBERS $11 NON-MEMBERS
FRIDAY, September 21   8PM

all five boroughs of the city engage in nonstop, joyous folk dancing of every variety. Newcomers and novices are ac- cepted without question, and no better way exists to meet New Yorkers of every background, every age. Simply stand outside the line or circle until you've learned the step, and then break in. For still other folkdance evenings at other city locations, phone the Folk Phone at 212/666-9605.

4. Attend Daytime Museum Lectures: Every one of the city's major museums—the Metropolitan Museum of Art, the Museum of Modern Art, the Guggenheim Museum, the Museum of Natural History—offers daytime lectures for free or for a nominal charge, attracting New Yorkers of a highly developed artistic or scientific sense. The "Gallery Talks" of the Metropolitan Museum of Art ("Masters of the Early 20th Century" and "Buddhist Gilt Bronzes of China" were two recent themes) are especially popular, and take place daily except Monday, sometimes several times a day. Phone 212/879-5500 for specific talks or printed schedules.

5. Head Off-Off-Broadway: As the expensive Broadway theaters ($30 to $40 the average seat) turn increasingly to an escapist tourist or suburban audience, with flashy but vapid musicals and predictable plays, the serious, resident theater- goer heads Off-Broadway (about 30 shows nightly, in smaller theaters) or even Off-Off-Broadway (as many as 80

New York Open Center

shows nightly, scattered about the city). The latter are found in tiny loft or basement stages seating fewer than 100 people, and there—behind the ugly façade of run-down buildings—beauty emerges, excitement prevails. To see experimental, avant-garde productions, revivals of classic works, new and serious efforts by young playwrights, consider taking in an Off-Off-Broadway show—and you may never again return to the larger houses. Full listings of Off-Off-Broadway plays are found in the Sunday theater/arts section of the *New York Times*, or in the weekly *Village Voice*, with partial listings in *New York* magazine.

6. Attend an Acting Class: The atmosphere of New York is considerably affected by the presence here of thousands and thousands of aspiring actors and actresses, and it's fascinating, in my view, to see them at work in the city's many acting schools, whose tuition they manage by waiting on table in hundreds of restaurants. The famous **Herbert Berghof Studio** (one such school) will permit outsiders to visit a class (your choice of acting technique, scene study, or voice) for a fee of $1.50 per two-hour session; and it's the only one, in my experience, to do so. Phone 212/675-2370 for specifics. As a related activity, take a tour behind the

The city is host each night to scores of inexpensive lectures, readings, seminars, gatherings on every subject . . . all fully accessible to the visiting tourist.

Abby Aldrich Rockefeller Sculpture
Garden, Museum of Modern Art

"Herbs in New York City"
workshop, Learning Alliance

scenes of a major theater. **Backstage on Broadway** runs one a day, at 10:30 A.M., which includes a one-hour lecture by a theater professional (actor, director, or stage manager) costing $7. Phone 212/575-8065 for details.

7. **Take a Walking Tour:** In sharp contrast to the once-over-lightly approach of the escorted motorcoach tours, walking tours explore a particular area or activity in depth, and each is led by an individual literally in love with the city—the monetary rewards are slight. You'll tour with a small, intimate group, visiting neighborhoods and institutions that are highlights of the actual, workaday city. Each week, *New York* magazine lists at least 20 ad hoc walking tours in its "Cue Listening" section, but two year-round operators of multiple walking tours are **Adventure on a Shoestring** (phone 212/265-2663) and **Sidewalks of New York** (phone 212/517-0201), both charging about $10 a tour.

8. **Enroll for a One-Night Course:** A scattered 10 U.S. cities have one apiece of those trendy, new night schools that teach an entire course in one evening session of three hours; New York has four. On most nights of the week, tourists can join advice-hungry New Yorkers for instruction costing $20 to $25 in subjects ranging from career planning to computer usage to personal relationships to preparing sushi and sashimi. Some take the course as much to meet other class members as for the advice, but whatever your aim, you'll gain an insight into the urban life of still another slice of the population. Of the four schools, two—the **Learning Alliance**, at 494 Broadway, New York, NY 10012 (phone 212/226-7171), and the **92nd Street Y**, at 1395 Lexington Ave., New York, NY 10128 (phone 212/996-1100)—deal primarily with subjects of serious political and social concern. The other two—**Discovery Center**, at 245 W. 72nd St. New York, NY 10023 (phone toll free 800/777-0338), and the **Learning Annex**, at 2330 Broadway, New York, NY 10024 (phone 212/580-2828)—are considerably lighter in their themes. Write or phone for catalogs covering the period of your own visit.

Though none of these eight activities will ever replace or pose a threat to the standard commercial approaches to New York—the round-Manhattan sightseeing cruises, the skyscraper observation towers, the big Broadway musicals—don't they add a new dimension to your New York stay? Don't they begin to afford you a glimpse into how some New Yorkers make use of the enormous cultural resources of their city? If people and ideas are the key to rewarding, fulfilling travel, shouldn't some of the eight be added to your own itinerary?

The Future of Mexican Vacations

Pitfalls, Prospects—and Where to Go

THE ATTITUDE OF MOST AMERICAN TRAV-
elers toward Mexico has always been one of love and hate. We dislike the occasional stomach upsets (*turista*), the pestering vendors, the crowded airports and flights. Yet so great is our affection for the colorful culture and setting of Mexico that it overcomes all doubts. In 1990, nearly 7,000,000 international visitors—most of them Americans—came to vacation in Mexico and made it the eighth-largest tourist destination on earth.

In May of 1990, I attended the mammoth, annual travel trade show of the Mexican government in Acapulco, known as the Tianguis (from the Mayan for "marketplace"). And there it became perfectly clear that, for good or ill, Mexico would loom even larger in the vacation plans of us North Americans throughout the 1990s. Never before in travel history has a government made a more determined effort to build tourism into its leading industry.

The plans are staggeringly ambitious: a literal doubling of Mexico's incoming tourists—to an annual figure of 10 million international visitors—by the end of the presidential term of Carlos Salinas de Gortari in early 1994. To that end, billions of pesos will be invested in 50,000 new hotel rooms; $33 million will be spent on overseas advertising in 1991 alone; restrictions will be lifted on incoming charter flights and anyone will be permitted to land; U.S. motorcoach operators will be permitted to drive their massive busloads of seniors right across the border and then—without changing vehicles—into the heart of the country. For the American travel industry, it's a whole new ballgame.

But can the quality of Mexican tourism survive the increase? In those coastal locations where gringos already overflow the sidewalks and turn once-quaint fishing villages into cheap bazaars, is it possible to import still more camera-toting couples without destroying the charm of Mexico?

There's no easy answer. Already, the single most heavily visited Mexican destination—the island of Cancún, off the Yucatán peninsula—is readily conceded by Mexican officials to be no longer Mexican in character but rather "Caribbean." Defending the rather high hotel rates of Cancún in relation to those in the rest of Mexico, they argue that Cancún's competition is other islands of the Caribbean and not the rest of Mexico. Therefore, they say, Cancún's price level is relatively low.

(Elsewhere in the Caribbean, one island after another is presently attributing its recent calamitous winter season to the lower-cost competition from new hotels in Cancún. One such deluxe property, the recently opened Hotel Club las Velas, the "Sails," offers a totally all-inclusive rate—room, meals, water sports, and all the daiquiris you can drink—for $130 per person per day, fully 30% less than at equivalent, but older, hotels in Jamaica.)

It is apparently the plan to create several more Cancúns, not only in new locations, but by adding to the resort capacity in older ones. Thus, a project called "Acapulco Diamante," at the extreme end of and beyond the great seaside bay that made Acapulco famous, will soon add 10,000 rooms to the legendary strip of Mexico's first "Riviera." Already, a new Hard Rock Café, which does battle each night

In those coastal locations where gringos already overflow the sidewalks and turn once-quaint fishing villages into cheap bazaars, is it possible to import still more camera-toting couples without destroying the charm of Mexico?

341

with a giant, new discothèque called Extravaganza, further lessens the feeling that you are in Mexico when you are in Acapulco.

An even larger resort development along the Bays of Huatulco, on the Pacific coast 200 miles south of Acapulco, is currently under construction, with four hotels (including a Sheraton and a Club Med) already open. Because the new development is nowhere near a traditional Mexican city, it, too, will be an isolated resort area, like Cancún, with nothing Mexican about it. Only the smaller resort community now abuilding at Los Cabos, at the southern tip of Baja California, seems both ecologically and culturally sensitive. Even the small cultural gains represented by the aesthetic Los Cabos are overcome by the immense, further development of sprawling Puerto Vallarta farther to the south, which continues to grow in a helter-skelter, unplanned, and—to my mind—unattractive, shabby, urban fashion.

The winter before last, at Christmastime, I escaped the crowds of Puerto Vallarta (where I had been staying) by flying to Mexico City, of all places. And there, in a setting blessedly free of tourists, I wandered with delight to great museums, galleries, theaters, and shops, through ranks of mariachis and alongside murals of Orozco and Rivera, to pyramids and pre-Columbian excavations.

Imagine: To avoid the excesses of tourism, I had to flee to the nation's capital!

What other Mexican locations can a sensitive traveler choose for a satisfying vacation? More than ever before—and as simple-minded as the advice may seem—you must go to where the free-spending, disco-craving, shopping-mad tourists aren't

• Go, for instance, to the **State of Chiapas** at the extreme southern tip of Mexico bordering Guatemala. Visit its en-

Mexico City

342

Diego Rivera mural, Mexico City

hotels claim they can renew your energies, and even cure or reduce arteriosclerosis, neurasthenia, and outbreaks of the skin.

• Go to **Zacatecas**, in the state of Zacatecas, a city of 500,000 residents whose vast central area is almost entirely colonial, with scarcely a single modern construction. Ten minutes from town is the renowned Convent of Guadalupe, with its marvels of handcrafted and painted art.

• Go to that circlet of well-preserved 17th-century Spanish colonial cities that surround the capital, about a three-hour drive away: **Patzcuaro, Querétero, Guanajuato.** Here you have culture treasures, charming hotels with interior courtyards, classic Mexican cuisine—and only a handful of North American tourists.

• Go, if you insist on a Pacific-coast beach resort, to the uncrowded southern half of the **State of Jalisco**, halfway between Acapulco and Mazatlán, and to such quiet resorts as the Hotel Coasta Careyes. From its solitary position on a private bay, it resembles the kind of place to which Mexico-bound jet-setters headed in the 1960s, and yet it charges a high-season average of only $90 for doubles, from $120 to $180 for suites (but much more for casitas). You get there by flying to Manzanillo, an hour's drive away.

• And finally, go to **Mexico City**, heart and soul of the nation. Go to its archeological museum, among the greatest in the world. Go to the daily (late afternoon) flag-lowering ceremonies by a battalion of troops in the plaza of the Na-

chanting colonial city of San Cristobal de las Casas, and then book a burro trip into the mountains, where anthropologists have paved the way for safe and satisfying visits among Indian communities. Then go to the large town (60,000 people) of Tuxtla Gutierrez, capital of Chiapas, for a view of contemporary Mexican life.

• Go to **Oaxaca**, growing in tourist popularity but not yet inundated by it. Visit nearby Monte Alban, stroll through flower markets and crafts fairs, dwell again upon many vestiges and remains of the Spanish conquistadors.

• Go to the **State of Michoacan** and, in a rental car, follow the "hot springs route" from the state's eastern border to the northwest end of Lake Chapala. Top thermal resorts along the way, with pleasant rooms, meals, and heated mineral baths: San José Purua, in the village of Jungapeo; Agua Blanca, five miles from San José Purua; Atzimba, near the town of Zinapecuaro; Santa Rosa near Tuxpan. Staff at these

> *And yet the Mexicans hope to double their current, massive levels of tourism—50,000 new hotel rooms will be built.*

tional Palace. See the nearby Diego Rivera murals. Attend the Ballet Folklorico, or go to Garibaldi Square for the nightly impromptu concerts by mariachi bands looking for bookings. And stroll, in perfect serenity, past the enticing shop windows for the Zona Rosa. Unjustly maligned by exaggerating travel writers, in the same way that New York often

Lake Chapala, Guadalajara

is, Mexico City is as safe today as any large U.S. city for tourists taking reasonable precautions.

A vast country that's nearly a quarter the size of the United States, Mexico has scores of compelling attractions and locations that haven't yet caught the attention of mass-volume tour operators. By traveling on your own to the places they've overlooked, you still have a few remaining years to enjoy the Mexico that once was, the delightfully foreign country just south of the border. But rush—because more and more of it is growing less and less foreign each passing month.

XIII

COST-CUTTING CLUBS AND ORGANIZATIONS, COST-CUTTING DEVICES FOR TRAVEL

26 Varied Travel Organizations That Bring You Better, Cheaper Travel

Clubs and Exchanges, Schools and Retreats, Passes and Programs, Fitting into No Established Categories—An Assortment of Travel Firms That Can Change Your Travel Life

IF ADAM SMITH RETURNED TO LIFE (AND I'M referring to the 18th-century economist, not the current-day journalist), he'd be rather pleased with the travel industry: it's largely a free-market dream. Except for the transportation element of it—increasingly dominated by a few large carriers—the activity consists of thousands upon thousands of relatively small and little-known entrepreneurs scrambling to improve upon their competitors' products.

Among those mini-units are a thousand particular firms whose approach to travel, in my view, is meaningful, innovative, and exciting, and it is that charmed number of organizations—1,200 or so, to be exact (see the index at the back of this book)—that account for the bulk of our discussion.

A remaining 26 firms fail to fit, however, into any of our preceding categories. Hence the following chapter dealing with a few last miscellaneous and sometimes rather odd organizations that can nevertheless have a major beneficial impact on your next trip:

1. THE ULTIMATE TRAVEL CLUB

Its only membership requirement is that you have "an anemic wallet," and a zest—despite that condition—to rove the farthest reaches of the world. Its members of all ages make the readers of my $40-a-day books seem like plutocrats. They walk across all of Nepal; take local buses, regional jitneys, occasional mule trains, to cross the wastes of sub-Saharan Africa; sleep in the huts of Indonesian villages, cadge meals at the communal fires of New Guinean fisher-men, trade bars of soap for trinkets crafted in the yak tents of Ladakh.

And then they return home to tell about it, at monthly public meetings in St. Martin's Lane, London; in southern California or New York; or in the pages of their six-times-a-year newsletter, *The Globe*.

Surely the most distinguished travel group on earth—despite their "anemic wallets"—is the 42-year-old **Globetrotters Club, c/o BCM Roving, London WC1N 3XX, England** (an oddly truncated, but perfectly adequate, mail-drop address). Since officers are all volunteers lacking a full-time office and frequently changing, they use that simple pickup point to receive membership applications and communications. The fee is $14 per year, $24 for two years, for receiving *The Globe* every other month, as well as *The Globetrotters Directory*, listing names, addresses, ages, and travel experience of members (be sure to provide that information while applying), as well as purely optional offers by them of free accommodations or advice to other members. Because a great many members do, in fact, make such offers of lodging (in spare beds or cots of their living rooms or dens), the *Directory* is a rich source of free travel opportunities, though not primarily designed as such.

London Globetrotters (and visitors from abroad) meet at 3:30 P.M. the second Saturday of each month in the Friends Meeting House, 52 St. Martin's Lane (entrance at 8 Hop Gardens), London WC1; monthly sites and dates for the same in New York, Toronto, and southern California are listed in *The Globe*—as are those accounts of members' adventures in touring the Third World.

2. NETWORKING THE "A.T.s"

"Appropriate Technology" or "Alternative Technology" ("A.T.") is a massive worldwide movement of people who believe in a simpler, gentler, human-scale life, non-industrial, cooperative, participatory—the dramatic opposite of the factory-polluted, harshly competitive, and hierarchical world of autos and metallic wastes in which most of us live. Its advocates are found in every nation, on organic farms and in vegetarian restaurants, at "New Era" bookshops and solar-energy centers, in consumer co-ops and small utopian communities. And because they believe in pressing their views on others, they are the easiest people on earth to get to know. Regardless of your own beliefs, you add a new dimension and intellectual growth to your travels when you meet and interact with these mild-mannered but highly motivated, free-thinking people.

But how do you meet them? Though it wasn't intended for that purpose, the quarterly newspaper/newsletter called TRANET, for *Transnational Network for Appropriate Technologies,* is a highly useful "guidebook" to alternative technology people in every nation. Its primary goal is to apprise alternative technology advocates of developments in their specialties in other lands. But recent editions have contained extensive directories of addresses for the specific purpose of encouraging well-focused, carefully planned, international travel by persons exploring A.T. Thus, issue 48 listed 200 sources of "alternative travel," while issue 42 listed organizations engaged in "cross-cultural, people-to-people linkages" across national boundaries; by contacting them, one arranges to meet "people who are changing the world by changing their own lives . . . adopting alternative technologies." Issue 43 was called "Alternatives Down Under" and provided the addresses of scores of contacts in Australia and New Zealand for experiencing those approaches. Issue 51 has a similar directory to alternative movements and peoples in the otherwise highly conformist nation of Japan, and issue 53—published in 1989—did the same for Southeast Asia.

Such contacts are the supreme essence of meaningful travel, says TRANET. Journeys should produce not simply a "tolerance" of foreign people, but "a love of our differences. . . . We need to invite them to our homes, to visit them in theirs. We need to participate in their alternative celebrations, to eat their foods, to honor their ceremonies, to explore their wild places, to understand their human-rights issues, to see how they confront their governments."

Though a year's subscription to TRANET is a hefty $30, back issues will be sent to you for $5 apiece. You'll want to start with the remarkable directory to Australia and New Zealand (no. 43), then perhaps go to the earlier one on "People-to-People Networking" worldwide (no. 42). Contact **TRANET, P.O. Box 567, Rangeley, ME 04970 (phone 207/864-2252).**

3. THE OTHER ELDERHOSTEL

You've just been placed on your third waiting list for a popular Elderhostel course; your first two choices are hopelessly sold out. Soaring in popularity, the 15-year-old system of foreign and domestic study tours for seniors over 60 is expected to draw more than 200,000 participants in 1991, causing a moderate, but still irritating, number of "closeouts."

So try Interhostel. It's administered by the same University of New Hampshire officials who created Elderhostel, but then "spun it off" when the baby grew too big for the campus. The university continues to operate Interhostel, which this time sends people over the age of 50 to pursue intensive two-week tours and bouts of classroom instruction at foreign universities around the world. While topics are a bit more general and geographical than Elderhostel's, they're taught by leading academic figures. Price: $1,295 to $1,595 for two weeks, including everything (housing in university residences, all meals, all tuition) except air fare, usually from Boston or New York.

For information, contact **Interhostel, University of New Hampshire, Division of Continuing Education, 6 Garrison Ave., Durham, NH 03824 (phone 603/862-1147 Monday through Friday from 1:30 to 4 P.M. EST).**

4. THE "READER'S DIGEST" OF TRAVEL

Once a week throughout the year, Miriam Tobolowsky of West Los Angeles—a part-time English teacher—travels to a

Its only membership requirement is that you have "an anemic wallet," and a zest—despite that condition—to rove the farthest reaches of the world.

public library to scan the Sunday travel sections of two dozen major newspapers. Pausing for breath, she then proceeds to read every major U.S. magazine, searching for their occasional words on travel. That done, she composes highly abridged "précis" of the latest travel news and publishes them in her bimonthly newsletter, *Partners-in-Travel*.

No matter how extensive your own reading of the travel press, you will always encounter surprising new tidbits of travel lore in her chatty but incisive condensations. Though her focus is on the mature traveler, and her newsletter was initially intended as a match-up service for retirees seeking travel companions (and still performs that function), *Partners-in-Travel* is fast emerging as a valuable compendium of travel discoveries that would otherwise appear in only isolated form, lost to the great majority of us.

Where else would you learn about a club for single people owning recreational vehicles ("Loners on Wheels")? Or about swim-up blackjack tables in Las Vegas, a golf school for senior citizens, a pet hotel in Arizona? One issue even preserves the advice of a certain Arthur Frommer (on how to override the airline computers when they show an absence of discount fares) for those deprived communities, dark holes of ignorance, where this book isn't sold.

A subscription to *Partners-in-Travel* (still devoted in part to "Travel Personals") is $40 for a year. Contact **Partners-in-Travel, P.O. Box 491145, Los Angeles, CA 90049 (phone 213/476-4869).**

5. CHEAPEST CARIBBEAN CRUISES

It's not a sailing offered by the lower-quality ships, or even a cruise heavily discounted in price by the cruise "bucket shops." Rather, it's a cruise on which four people squeeze into a single cabin. Though travel agents told them they were crazy to try, a small but distinguished tour company called Singleworld (formerly known as Bachelor Party Tours) recently offered to guarantee quad accommodations for individuals traveling alone. By stuffing four unrelated people (of the same sex, of course) into a quad "room," Singleworld reduces the price of some one-week Caribbean cruises to less than $800 a person, including round-trip air transportation to the embarkation point.

Do people then chafe at their cramped condition? Are they at each others' throats after only a few hours? Not so, says Singleworld—they're rarely *in* the cabin assigned to them!

For a free catalog of Singleworld's offerings, contact **Singleworld, P.O. Box 1999, Rye, NY 10580 (phone 914/967-3334, or toll free 800/223-6490).**

6. CATTLE-HERDING HOLIDAYS

Consider, now, the latest initiative of the tireless Patricia Dickerman of New York City.

In 1948, alone in a battered coupe, she bumped along the rural dirt roads of America, persuading skeptical farmers to accept her guests and thus create a new holiday industry and a new source of income for themselves: farm vacations. She later did the same at working ranches. Her classic book of 1949, *Farm, Ranch, & Country Vacations* ($12 postpaid from Pat Dickerman, 36 E. 57th St., New York, NY 10022), updated approximately every three years, is the oldest continually published travel guide in America.

Now, fulfilling everyone's secret desire to lead the life of a cowboy, she arranges for actual participation by us city types in real-life cattle drives in Wyoming, Arizona, Colorado, New Mexico, and Montana, moving herds to pastures with better grass. Costs average $85 to $110 per person per day, including everything: chuckwagon meals, tents or sleeping bags under the stars, your own horse to ride. If nothing else, says Pat, "you'll have a new respect for a hamburger and the hard work that goes into producing it."

For a free newsletter on cattle drives, send a self-addressed, stamped no. 10 envelope to **Adventure Guides, Inc., 36 E. 57th St., New York, NY 10022 (phone 212/355-6334).**

7. MEXICO STUDY GROUPS

Gayle Savelsberg, of Phoenix, Arizona, is a retired teacher who felt that school-based Spanish-language courses were lacking in one key element: immersion in the home life of a Spanish-speaking family.

So she darted from Cuernavaca to the Yucatán, from San Miguel de Allende to Guadalajara, laboriously persuading Mexican families to put up students (aged 15 to 85) in their homes, on a three-meals-a-day basis. That exposure to everyday Spanish, coupled with four hours a day of instruction in distinguished Mexican schools, catapulted her courses over those of the competition—while keeping prices at rock-bottom levels.

The study tours last for 30 days, are each accompanied by Gayle (who stays near you, but at a discreet distance, and without intruding into your Spanish-speaking life); and they are operated at renowned "institutos" or "academias" in San Miguel and Cuernavaca in summer, in Mérida and Cuernavaca in winter. Rates are a remarkable $1,195 for 30 days (thus, $39 a day), including everything (housing, meals, instruction) but round-trip air fare to Mexico.

Contact **Mexico Study Groups, P.O. Box 56982, Phoenix, AZ 85079 (phone 602/242-9231).**

8. A REPUTABLE STUDENT EXCHANGE

The very finest form of travel, bar none, is a several-month stay in a foreign home, enjoyed in the teenage years of one's life. I weep for those students who miss out on these life-

Mérida, for language study

enhancing, maturing experiences simply because their schools haven't publicized the offerings (which happens more than you'd expect).

The solution: Acquire the information yourself and then deal directly with the sponsoring organization.

A 115-page publication from the Council on Standards for International Educational Travel describes the student programs offered by 54 reputable U.S. organizations and provides the facts for selecting the group from which to request further information. Listed are not simply the "giants"—Experiment in International Living, Youth for Understanding, American Field Service—but also the smaller, specialized ones as well, like the Educational Foundation for Foreign Study ($3,880 to $4,520 all inclusive, for 10 months in Europe with volunteer host families, while attending European public schools; note its full scholarship for students creatively talented in the arts); or the Iberoamerican Cultural Exchange Program ($500 for a six-week stay with a Mexican family, $1,700 for a full school year, excluding air fare). Scholarship aid is heavily stressed.

Request the *Advisory List of International Educational Travel and Exchange Programs 1991–1992* from **CSIET, 3 Loudoun St. Lessburg, VA 22075 (phone 703/771-2040)**, and enclose $6.50 for the cost of the booklet, postage, and handling.

9. WORLD'S FINEST CRUISE VALUE

Forget the source and focus on the price. You pay as little as $125 a day (plus air fare), perhaps an average of $140 a day (more familiar cruise ships average $200 to $225). You cruise with largely English-speaking passengers on unusual routes through the Baltic Sea, or to the North Cape (of Norway) or the South Pacific, or you sail around the world in 100 days for as little as $10,000.

Only thing is: you do it on a Soviet ship. Proud possessors of the world's largest passenger-carrying fleet, the Russians have launched a determined effort to enter the international cruising market. And thousands of British vacationers, Germans, and more recently Americans have responded favorably, booking themselves onto the world's cheapest ocean-going cruises.

From Tilbury, England, on the River Thames, the 17,000-ton *Kareliya* and *Azerbaidzhan* sail in summer on 14-day itineraries along the fjords of Norway's North Cape, and on alternate departures through the Baltic to Helsinki, Stockholm, Copenhagen, Gdynia (Poland), and Leningrad—the last visited on group excursions requiring no visas. In spring and fall the same large ships depart from Genoa or Venice to wander the eastern Mediterranean, and then go to the Greek Islands and Turkey, occasionally darting through the Black Sea to Yalta or Odessa (again no visa needed). In December, and again from Tilbury, the *Azerbaidzhan* sets off to sail around the world (at even lower daily rates than its normal $125 minimum).

From Bremen, Genoa, or Venice, the M/V *Odessa* makes similar 14-day cruises, but is best known for its yearly round-the-world sailings, on which 50% of all passengers are now Americans. From Australia, the M/V *Belorussiya* cruises through the South Pacific.

Meals on board are "continental," with Russian touches: borscht among the soups, chicken à la Kiev and beef Stroganoff among the entrées. Entertainment is so-called international cabaret adapted to Russian talents: balalaika groups perform, and sailors dance the *kasatski*. But movies, thankfully, are U.S. or British, all cabin and deck staff are reasonably multilingual, and politics is never discussed. "You are in America when you use the ships catering to the U.S. market," says a Soviet shipping official, "but on our ships, you are in Europe more than America."

For brochures and sailing schedules, contact the U.S. general agent for the Soviet shipping lines: **International Cruise Center, Inc., 250 Old Country Rd., Mineola, NY 11501 (phone 516/747-8880, or toll free 800/221-3254).**

10. KING OF THE DISCOUNT BOOKS

Though more than two million are sold each year, scarcely a copy appears in bookstores, and use of the so-called Entertainment Books is thus confined to those relatively few savvy Americans who purchase them from nonprofit clubs, service groups, and other civic organizations. Yet each book entitles the bearer to near-50% discounts at restaurants, sporting events, movies, live theaters, and other recreational facilities, even at scattered hotels in that person's home city—or in the 73 other major U.S. cities for which Entertainment Books are published.

Bulky as dictionaries, the books consist of perforated discount coupons offering "two-for-one" dining or admissions, or straight 50% reductions, at scores of establishments. Some 111 books are published each year, one for each of the 104 largest American and Canadian cities and regions, plus 7 international destinations.

Of course, the discount doesn't always work out to 50%. When two of you order a $15 and $11 entrée, respectively, at a listed restaurant, it is the cheaper entrée (the $11 one) that comes free; and drinks and dessert aren't included in the "two-for-one" offer. As for the hotel discounts, a major portion of them are valid for lightly booked weekend stays only. Yet though the dining discount works out to 30% on average, and some of the weekend hotel discounts are of dubious value, the savings overall are substantial indeed. Two million families wouldn't budge from their homes without their Entertainment Books.

Individual-city books cost $25 to $45 apiece, depending on the city, and often pay for themselves in one or two days of travel or use. Almost all are sold in bulk to nonprofit organizations that then quietly resell them to members in fund-raising programs. But since Entertainment Publications, Inc. (a 30-year-old publicly owned company), has offices in most of the largest cities, they can usually be contacted directly by the public (and books purchased) by simply looking up the words "Entertainment Publications" or "Entertainment Passbooks" in your local phone directory. Or you can go directly to the headquarters of **Entertainment Publications, Inc., 2125 Butterfield Rd., Troy, MI 48084 (phone 313/637-8400).** If you do contact them directly, consider buying the condensed one-volume nationwide Entertainment Book called *Travel America at Half Price* ($26.95).

11. THE SECOND NIGHT FREE

With nearly two million members currently enrolled, the Encore Travel Club of Lanham, Maryland, has become the largest discount organization in travel history. Reason: It has signed 2,300 hotels to provide "the second night free" to Encore members (usually without weekend limitations). Thus, stay for two nights and you pay for only one; stay for seven nights and you get two free nights; and so on. If you are constantly traveling and staying in hotels, you can scarcely afford not to join (membership is $48 a year).

But will success spoil (or even ruin) Encore? As an ever-greater percentage of the American public joins, won't these 2,300 hotels find that they are giving discounts to almost everyone, thus eliminating the potential for purely incremental business that led them to give "the second night free"? That's a problem that puzzles me. Still, until the day when hotels dig in their heels and say no to Encore's entreaties, it remains an attractive organization for frequent travelers. And it supplies its members with a growing list of other services: the lowest air fare available on domestic flights, a six-times-a-year magazine listing discounts on tour programs and packages, still more.

For further information, or to join, contact **Encore Travel Club, 4501 Forbes Blvd., Lanham, MD 20706 (phone toll free 800/638-8976).**

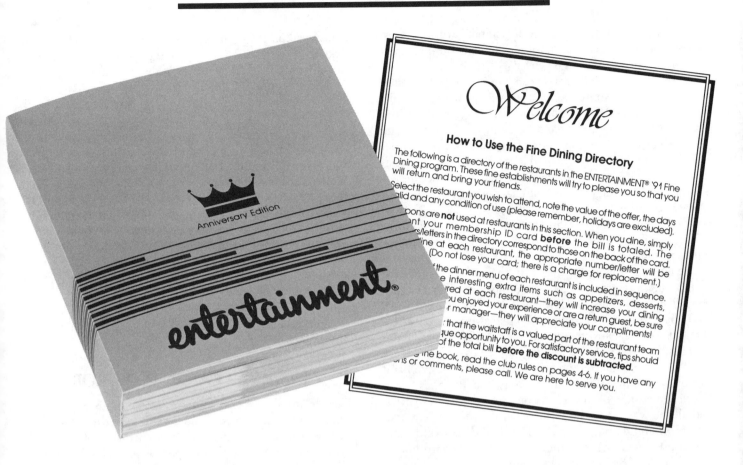

12. FINDING THE "POOR MAN'S SPA"

A glossy four-color publication called *Spa-Finders* ($4.95 through the mails) is currently enabling a narrow segment of the public (those who know about it) to enjoy wholesome spa vacations here in the United States at a fraction of the cost that others incur. It achieves that feat simply by revealing the existence of a broad range of spas heretofore known only to spa-lovers residing in the immediate vicinity.

A cottage industry by normal commercial standards, the average U.S. spa is a small, family-owned resort hotel, chronically strapped for cash and barely able to advertise outside its own small region.

There is no trade association of spas, no publication devoted to the activity.

The industry has for years been dominated by the glitzy names—La Costa, The Golden Door, Maine Chance—charging a king's ransom for a week of their health-bestowing attentions. Most Americans have consequently assumed these slimming spa vacations to be outside their financial reach.

Unless they had a copy of *Spa Finders,* that is. A remarkable product of nationwide research, presented with glamorous flair but punctilious attention to detail (prices to the penny, seasons, facilities), it claims to contain listings and descriptions of all major U.S. spas, bar none, alerting us to underutilized facilities that have long catered to a purely local clientele. Included are places with all the features and facilities of the big-name resorts—Jacuzzis and rubdown tables, saunas, aerobics, and scientifically measured meals—but at rates as low as $400 a week for room, all meals, and all traditional spa treatments and programs. Some of the establishments in it are making their first appearance before a nationwide audience.

(*Spa Finders* also lists and describes the higher-priced varieties, of course, but proudly claims to be the first such publication to gather particulars on every one in every price range, in a widely dispersed activity.)

For a copy of the 132-page magazine-size catalog, send $4.95 to **Spa-Finders, 784 Broadway, New York, NY 10003 (phone 212/475-1000, or toll free 800/ALL-SPAS)**.

13. BRITAIN WITH ELSIE

"Elsie from England" is a Cockney from south London named Elsie Dillard, who immigrated to the state of Washington in 1957, tried her hand at real estate and insurance, but preferred offering advice to friends about travel to the

British Isles. "You don't want a dull hotel," was her most frequent litany. "I've got this darling bed-and-breakfast house for only 32 shillings 6 pence."

Soon she was a retail travel agent, and then a wholesaler, the single leading source to other travel agents of low-cost bed-and-breakfast accommodations in scores of locations throughout England, Scotland, Ireland, and Wales. Her product currently ranges in price from $30 per person per night (breakfast included) for the standard English guesthouse, to $40 for an upgraded version that can sometimes be a comfortable country estate. (She charges $10 additional for every reservation made.) And although her clientele originally was mainly travel agents from the western states, she is perfectly willing (indeed, eager) to deal directly with the public from every state.

If you've a craving for the "real England," call Elsie for even a single reservation in a single location. Or else put yourself entirely in her hands for a full three-week tour. She'll start you in a B&B in London, then place you in a self-drive car, and provide you with other prepaid B&Bs for all remaining nights, as you follow a classic, planned-by-Elsie itinerary into Wiltshire (Somerset) and the West Country (Devon and Cornwall), up to Bath and through "the Potteries" into North Wales, thence to Chester, on up to the Lake District, and all the way up to the Hebrides and northern Scotland, then south to Edinburgh, and into York, the Cotswolds, and Heathrow or Gatwick Airport for the homeward-bound flight. With pre-reserved, classically British, marvelously cheap guesthouse rooms all the way! Write or phone "**Elsie from England**," P.O. Box 5107, Redondo, WA 98054 (**phone 206/941-6413**).

14. VACATIONS FROM A BARTER FIRM

"Barter" is the exchange of product for product, and nowhere is the activity more intensely pursued than in the travel industry. Airlines trade seats for radio commercials, cruise ships trade cabins for stationery and supplies, hotels trade rooms for ads on the sides of buses. Since each of the "traders" has unused capacity or excess merchandise, they are exchanging items that might have gone unsold in any event—thus the trade costs them nothing (so goes the theory).

But who ends up sitting in the airplane seats, or sleeping in the hotel rooms and cruise-ship berths, that have been "bartered"? Since there's an obvious limit to the number of trips that radio station personnel and staffs of advertising agencies can themselves use (or else they'd be on perpetual vacation!), the excess "travel credits" are sold by dozens of so-called barter companies to large corporations or special groups, at prices heavily discounted from normal levels. Among those firms, a small but growing number (a handful,

really) are currently selling their credits—sharply reduced air tickets, cruises, car rentals, tour packages, hotel stays—directly to individual members of the public, among others.

In the Southeast, the behemoth of the barterers is **Lino and Associates, 6534 Central Ave., St. Petersburg, FL 33707 (phone 813/384-6700)**, and it is willing to deal with the public (I asked). Call, write, or visit, and you'll pick up a broad variety of trips and tickets at substantial discounts. In the East and West, the leading firms are, respectively, **Travel World Leisure Club, Inc., 225 W. 34th St., Suite 2203, New York, NY 10122 (phone 212/239-4855, or toll free 800/444-TWLC)**, and **Communications Development Corp., 1454 Euclid St., Santa Monica, CA 90404 (phone 213/458-0596)**. Both sell deeply discounted tour packages, cruises, and air tickets, and have no objection to selling them in "ones and twos," to even a single person or couple contemplating a trip. For precisely what were these tours, cruises, and tickets originally exchanged? For a TV spot late at night, or a billboard in the country, or even a paint job in the airline's office!

15. "RV" TRAVEL TO EUROPE

Ever heard of "caravanning"? People with recreational vehicles—motor homes, camper vans—meet up at a departure point and travel as a group to attractive destinations. There they use their bed-equipped devices for overnight accommodations, but every day board a single sightseeing motorcoach for touring, exactly as they would on a standard, escorted tour.

Popular for many years within the United States, "caravanning" is now being offered to Americans for touring overseas. How? By flying recreational vehicle enthusiasts to a foreign site, and there providing them with rented, foreign recreational vehicles, again as part of a group.

Creative World Rallies and Travels, 606 N. Carrollton Ave, New Orleans, LA 70119, (phone 504/486-7259, or toll free 800/REC-VEES outside Louisiana), is by far the leader in the activity. Although is has been organizing domestic group trips for 14 years, its overseas caravans—on which travelers drive a motor home temporarily assigned to them—are of far more recent vintage. First introduced a few years back in the form of a single departure using rented British camper vans to tour the U.K., the program has grown in 1991 to include three scheduled caravans to Australia and New Zealand, one ambitious trip to Eastern Europe (fly to Munich and pick up a German motorhome there for touring through Germany, Poland, and Czechoslovakia), one through Scandinavia, one of "Alpine Europe" (Austria, Switzerland, and Bavaria), one again to the British Isles—always in spring, summer, and fall.

Durations of stay are lengthy—they average 32 days—and yet the cost is less than $3,900, including round-trip air from Atlanta (or, if requested, from other U.S. cities), a large number of restaurant meals en route, extensive sightseeing, use of the motor home, all campsite fees, and group leaders. "For what other people spend for two weeks staying in hotels," says Creative World's founder and president, 41-year-old Bill LaGrange, "we can provide five and six weeks abroad in a motor home." And is this not an exceptional travel method, staying close to the land and peoples of the countries you visit?

16. VISITS TO A "HOMESTEAD"

Next, a short trip to bask in the glow of the late Scott Nearing, who remained handsome, vigorous, and creative until his recent death at the age of 100. He, as you may recall, was the 1920s radical ousted from teaching positions because of his far-advanced views. Whereupon he and his wife, Helen, determined to end their dependency on society by moving first to Vermont and then to an abandoned farm in Maine, where they developed the practice of homesteading to a fine art: producing goods and services for their own consumption, self-sufficiently, without the intervention of a market or the use of cash.

A stream of books from their fertile pens—*Living the Good Life, Continuing the Good Life,* and *Simple Food for the Good Life,* among others—brought thousands of visitors each year to their Forest Farm and stone house built with their own hands, where Helen and Scott demonstrated the virtues of a fresh-food diet, gardening, composting, pond and dam building, and lectured on other, broader social themes. Despite Scott's death, 86-year-old Helen is still willing to receive visitors, provided they make advance contact with the nearby **Social Science Institute, Harborside, ME 04642 (phone 207/326-8211)**, to which royalties from the Nearings' books are assigned, and which also sells their books through the mails (request a catalog). According to Helen Nearing, it is possible to visit Forest Farm during the summer and fall. She devotes the other seasons to travel and writing. Accommodations and meals are available in the town of Blue Hill, approximately 20 miles away.

Care to change your life? The farm and books of Scott and Helen Nearing have done that for multitudes before you.

17. FOAM-RUBBER BUS TRAVEL

From the innards of a large motorcoach, all the seats have been removed and then replaced by a foam-rubber platform. Why? So that 35 adventurous souls can stretch out to sleep, their heads on knapsacks or rolled-up coats, while the bus hurtles through the night. Daytime, the same passengers recline in varying positions, while some strum guitars or play the classics on a reedy flute. In vehicles so oddly outfitted, enabling an obvious lowering of travel costs (and an obvious camaraderie), the most casual (but perhaps the most insight-

ful) of American tourists are today exploring geographic wonders of the U.S.A., Mexico, and Canada.

Some use the foam-rubber method to cross the country. Once every two weeks or so from May through September, from each coast (New York and Boston in the East, Los Angeles and San Francisco in the West), buses of the celebrated Green Tortoise line embark for an 11-day transcontinental adventure traversing 5,000 miles each way, yet costing only $279 per person. The buses drive mainly at night. In the day, passengers go river-rafting on the Colorado, explore major national parks (Bryce, Zion, Yellowstone, Badlands, Tetons, depending on itinerary), and go wandering about all over the continental states.

Other Green Tortoise trips go to Baja California and mainland Mexico in the winter, to Yosemite throughout the year, up and down the West Coast. Though singles predominate, Green Tortoise urges—and receives—patronage from families and senior citizens. On one four-week tour to Alaska, the average age aboard was 45.

On all trips, passengers contribute about $6 each per day to a food "kitty" used to purchase vittles for a twice-daily cooperative cookout. Breakfast is coffee, eggs, and rolls purchased at various truckers' stops, or else "gourmet vegetarian" if participants are bestirred to purchase and prepare the necessary ingredients.

One of the few survivors of a number of alternative bus companies established in the late 1960s—they included the Briar Rabbit and the American Gypsy—Green Tortoise is no Greyhound, but still a flourishing company that publishes an irresistible periodic tabloid, *Tortoise Trails,* about its most recent tour successes. For detailed information, contact **Green Tortoise, P.O. Box 24459, San Francisco, CA 94124 (phone 415/821-0803, or toll free 800/227-4766 outside California)**.

18. BRITISH MOTOR HOMES

Ever vacationed in a recreational vehicle? Then why not do so in Britain? The campsites and trailer parks there are as numerous as here, and large fleets of what the English call "motor caravans" are available for rental from numerous firms at rates of $364 to $483 a week for the June-July-August use of a "camper/van" sleeping four adults, while larger and more luxurious motor homes in summer go for $427 to $533 a week (sleeping four) and for $490 to $623 a week (sleeping six); rates are considerably less in all other months, and cover everything except gasoline, food, and nominal charges for campsites. In a vehicle fully equipped with beds and sleeping bags, toilets, and all cooking and eating utensils, you'll wander the British Isles without fear of high hotel rates or fully booked hotels, and share the company of camping English people, all at marvelously low rates. Among the largest of the British firms (300 motor homes for rent) is **Apex Leisure Hire, London Road, Staines, Middlesex, U.K. TW18 FJJ (phone 07/8446-3233)**, represented in the United States by **Professional Representatives, Inc. (phone 818/507-1151 in Los Angeles, or toll free 800/421-8905, 800/223-7422 in California).**

19. THE WORLD'S CHEAPEST SKIING

It costs only $488 to $598 for seven nights, including round-trip air fare from London, round-trip airport-to-hotel transfers, top-quality hotel accommodations, two meals daily, round-trip transportation daily to the ski slopes, and all lift tickets. Where? Bulgaria! In a major effort to attract international business, the official Bulgarian tour company and airline have enlisted various airlines to fly skiers from London to Frankfurt, where they then connect with Balkan Airlines to Sofia and its modern high-rise Rodina Hotel. From there,

they ski daily on Mount Vitosha, a half hour from the Bulgarian capital. For $20 to $30 more—a usual total of $949 in February and March, less at other times—skiers can opt to be lodged in the largest ski resort of the Balkans, the five-slope Borovets, about 45 miles south of Sofia. Since two meals daily and all lift tickets are again included in the price, a Bulgarian ski vacation is about the cheapest currently available in the world. And a conversation-stopper too. Contact **Balkan Holidays U.S.A., Ltd., 161 E. 86th St., New York, NY 10028 (phone 212/722-1110).**

20. A NEW MATCH-UP SERVICE

Like several other firms, the new Odyssey Network of Wellesley, Massachusetts, helps single people find other singles with whom to travel—but with a twist. Odyssey limits its services to women seeking other women with whom

Winter ski resort, Pamporovo, Bulgaria

Borovets, leading ski resort of the Balkans

to travel, and that decision has catapulted the company to an early success (apparently, the overwhelming number of people seeking travel companions are women wishing to travel with other women). Odyssey charges only $20 a year and already has several hundred members, for whom it arranges not only independent trips but also share arrangements on group trips and cruises. Participants complete a questionnaire and are then matched up with other members by Odyssey's staff. Obviously, Odyssey also benefits from commissions earned on the trips it sells. Contact **Odyssey Network, c/o Charles River Travel, 118 Cedar St., Wellesley, MA 02181 (phone 617/237-2400).**

21. A FOLKDANCING TOUR OPERATOR

Karl Finger is a composer/guitarist who conducts two-week international folkdance tours on which his American participants do the dancing, not just the looking. In Yugoslavia, for

instance, they bus from one folkdance festival to another, periodically flinging themselves from the vehicle to dance with Yugoslavian country folk, learning the steps as they go along. It's a remarkably popular program, booked by folkdance lovers from 18 to 80, and now entering its 15th year. Upcoming tours: Christmas to Mexico; summer to Alaska and Bulgaria (for the famous Koprivshtitsa Festival), autumn to Turkey. Destinations change each year, and in the case of European trips cost around $2,100 to $2,300, including air fare. Contact **Karl Finger, 36 Plaza St., Brooklyn, NY 11238 (phone 718/783-0500).**

22. AUSTRALIAN HOMESTAYS, FARM-STAYS, PUB-STAYS

Unlike their reserved British forebears, the Australians—from all accounts—are often excited to have foreign visitors in their homes; it enlivens their daily routine, breaks their isolation (especially in Outback farms). Result: Several hun-

A Bulgarian ski vacation is about the cheapest currently available in the world.

dred families have signed on to lodge you and to share their lives for rates of only $23 per person per night, double occupancy, in "pub accommodations" (small inns attached to or over friendly pubs), $35 in private homes (this time with breakfast included), $87 on farms (including all three meals daily and transfers from the nearest transport terminal). Less than three years old, the program is already attracting hundreds of bookings from gregarious cost-conscious Americans who "mix-and-match" homestays, farm-stays, and pub-stays in locations all over Australia, and use various unlimited-mileage pass programs for air travel within the country. It's available from a major firm: **Guthrey's Pacific, 2182 Dupont St., Suite 213, Irvine, CA 92715 (phone 714/752-8322)**.

23. A BROKER OF GREEK VILLAS

Renting a villa on a Greek island costs as little as $700 on the smaller islands, $900 on the larger ones, per person, double occupancy, for two full weeks in high season, including round-trip air transportation between London's Gatwick Airport and Greece; you fly nonstop to Kos, Rhodes, Crete, or Mykonos, and either stay on one of those major islands in the Aegean, or take a short onward ferry ride (again included in the price) to one of the smaller islands of Patmos, Leros, Kalymnos, Symi, Paxos, or Kythira. An organization called **Twelve Islands and Beyond, 5431 MacArthur Blvd. NW, Washington, DC 20016 (phone 202/537-3550)**, makes all the arrangements except your flight from the U.S. to London. Surely these are among the cheapest villa rentals in Europe, and yet they are found in the highly desirable, indeed enchanting world of Homer's *Iliad* and *Odyssey,* in traditional stone houses near an attractive inland village, often with orange and lemon trees growing in the garden or with olive orchards nearby.

24. CHAUTAUQUA

From late June to the end of August, the village of Chautauqua, New York, 100 miles from Buffalo, is filled to the eaves—and I use the word advisedly—with 10,000 visitors

Ballet at Chautauqua Institution

at a time, all in search of intellectual stimulation, spiritual balm, and cultural enrichment. If you're to be among them, or at least housed in acceptable accommodations, you've got to make your reservations early in winter.

Chautauqua, once described as an "intellectual Club Med," is a Victorian village frozen in time, virtually unchanged from its appearance in the 1890s. Then, and through the 1930s, it was a cultural capital of America, a

Odyssey limits its services to women seeking other women with whom to travel, and charges only $20 a year.

Chautauqua

national forum whose "institute" sponsored book clubs and traveling speakers (the "Chautauqua circuit") to bring new ideas and the latest developments to communities across the nation. Its own lecture platform welcomed the key celebrities of the time—Ulysses S. Grant and Theodore Roosevelt, Leo Tolstoy and Amelia Earhart; its meeting halls housed important world conferences.

Today, in summer, the multiple theaters, concert stages, lecture halls, conference and classrooms, and giant 6,000-seat amphitheater of Chautauqua provide a dizzying daily array of morning, afternoon, and evening speeches and seminars, concerts, recitals, and performances of every sort—English-language opera, theater, orchestras, political and inspirational talks, educational courses, arts and crafts workshops, and Great Books seminars—supplemented by all the standard summer recreations. Speakers in 1990 ranged from David Eisenhower, historian and grandson of the late president, to Frank Carlucci, former secretary of defense, to Harrison Salisbury, noted former foreign correspondent, to Roger Rosenblatt, TV "essayist."

"Gate tickets" to all daily events and courses at Chautauqua cost a reasonable $13 to $16 for the day, $22 for both day and evening sessions for adults (but only $125 per week), free for children 12 and under. To this you add widely varying accommodations and meal costs (all quite reasonable) in Chautauqua's dozens of hotels, apartments, inns, and bed-and-breakfast homes, which expand each summer to accommodate thousands each night. But to get the best rooms at the best prices—sometimes to get any room at all—you should reserve before spring, or by mid-spring at the latest.

For literature or for a free accommodations directory, write or phone **Chautauqua, P.O. Box 1095, Chautauqua, NY 14722 (phone 716/357-6200 or 716/357-6204)**. For bookings, or immediate information, call the **Accommodations Referral Service (phone 716/357-6204, or toll free 800/333-0884)**.

25. "HUCK FINN UNIVERSITY"

Build a better mousetrap in travel and America rushes to your door. With rates reaching $300 a day and more for those big, glitzy riverboats that go up and down the Mississippi, two young women from Rock Island, Illinois, built a 40-foot, 12-passenger houseboat to do nearly the same thing for far less

"Sometimes we'd have that whole river to ourselves for the longest time. Yonder was the banks and the islands, across the water . . . and maybe you could hear a fiddle or song coming over . . . It's lovely to live on a raft."

Huckleberry Finn

(you don't sleep aboard, but rather at historic country inns on shore, when the boat docks for the night). Calling their venture "Huckleberry Finn University" after the immortal Mark Twain lad who floated a raft on the mighty river with the runaway slave, Jim, they operated two pilot cruises in 1988, a "raftful" of sold-out, five-day cruises in 1989–1990, and will be expanding to two-day, three-day, four-day, and five-day floats in 1991. The season is May 25 to October 1, at various stretches of the river between St. Paul and St. Louis; the cost averages $150 a day, including cruise, lodgings, and two meals daily; and each departure focuses on a different theme from the rich history, architecture, and folklore of the river. If this operation doesn't soon grow to a whole fleet of ships, I'll eat my hat. For brilliant literature contact **Huckleberry Finn University, c/o Detours, 1705 Second Ave., Suite 422, Rock Island, IL 61201 (phone 309/788-8687).**

26. SERVAS

Finally, and for every trip, you'll want to know of Servas, to me the most exalted travel organization on earth, which arranges for you to stay for free in the homes of thousands of Servas members around the world—not simply in terms of occupying a bed, but even to the extent of sharing family tables for meals, and without being obligated to provide reciprocal hospitality at some later date in your own home. And why do they do this? Because Servas members believe that such people-to-people contacts serve the cause of world peace. An outgrowth of the peace movement, Servas has built its remarkable roster of thousands of hospitality-givers over more than 40 years, and yet maintains a relatively low profile in the United States.

Applicants are screened for membership (through interviews designed to weed out frivolous seekers of cheap "crash pads"), membership fees of $45 a year are charged, and free stays in any one city are theoretically limited to three nights—although the last provision is meant, in my experience, simply to give hosts a graceful out if unusually obnoxious types should appear on their doorsteps ("I'd love to house you for longer, but the rules won't permit me . . . "). A great many Servas travelers, known to me, invariably stay for a week and longer in the homes of their hosts. If you're endowed with the proper attributes—you enjoy meeting people, conversing with them and ascertaining their views, sharing the daily rhythms of their lives—then you'll want to join Servas. Contact **U.S. Servas Committee, 11 John St., Suite 706, New York, NY 10038 (phone 212/267-0252).**

Reductions in Price for the Traveling Theater-Goer

Discount Ticket Stands Have Proliferated Throughout the Country— and Around the World

TRAVELERS TO NEW YORK CITY USUALLY PAY $30 to $45 and more for the average theater seat. Residents of New York City frequently pay $15 to $22 for the very same seat.

Travelers to London, Paris, and a dozen other major theater cities almost always pay the same full price. Knowledgeable residents there often pay half.

Surely the largest single gap in travel information relates to the half-price facility for theater-going that's made available in every major theater city of the world. Though guidebooks often refer to the famous half-price "TKTS" (tickets) booth in New York's Times Square, they almost always overlook the very same facility in a dozen other towns, thus depriving their readers of an important opportunity to save.

All the booths below sell same-day tickets (when available) for half the normal price, plus a small service charge (usually 75¢ to $2). Some also sell full-price tickets for future dates, but that's not the main reason for patronizing them.

London: The half-price booth on Leicester Square, clearly marked and easily found, sells tickets to all 40 or so West End theaters, and for some concerts too, and is open daily except Sunday from noon to 2 P.M. for matinees and 2:30 to 6:30 P.M. for evening shows.

Paris: Just behind the Madeleine Church on the Right Bank (place de la Madeleine, 15; Métro stop is Madeleine), the Kiosque Théâtre sells hitherto-unsold seats at half price on the day of performance, and is open Monday through Saturday from noon to 8 P.M. and on Sunday from noon to 4 P.M. Tickets are often available for concert recitals and variety cabaret, in addition to the standard plays and musicals.

Sydney, Australia: You pick up last-minute half-price tickets for theaters, and for musical and dance events as well, at Martin Place, City Center, on Castlereagh Street; open weekdays from noon to 5:30 P.M. and on Saturday from noon to 5 P.M.

Toronto: "Five Star Tickets," at two locations—the main lobby of the Royal Ontario Museum, and on Yonge Street near Dundas Street, outside the Eaton Centre—sells half-price tickets to the great majority of the city's plays and musicals, including those of small nonprofit companies. It's open Monday through Saturday from noon to 6 P.M. and on Sunday from 11 A.M. to 2 P.M.

New York: There are three "TKTS" booths attracting heavy patronage: on a traffic island in Times Square (at 47th Street, open daily from 10 A.M. for matinee seats, from 3 P.M. for evening performances), in the World Trade Center (building 2), and at the corner of Court and Montague Streets near Borough Hall in Brooklyn (the latter two are open Tuesday through Friday from 11 A.M. to 5:30 P.M. and on Saturday from 11 A.M. to 3:30 P.M.). New York also operates a Music and Dance booth selling day-of-performance half-price tickets to concerts, recitals, and ballet, on 42nd Street be-

The smart traveler buys tickets as residents do—on the day of performance, for half price.

tween Fifth and Sixth Avenues, just alongside Bryant Park; open Tuesday through Saturday from noon to 2 P.M. and 3 to 7 P.M. and on Sunday (selling Monday seats as well) from noon to 6 P.M.

San Francisco: Its "STBS" (pronounced "Stubs") booth on Union Square (at 251 Stockton, between Post and Geary Streets) is an "interdisciplinary" outlet selling half-price tickets for theater, music, and dance, open Tuesday through Saturday only (it sells Sunday and Monday tickets on Saturday) from noon to 7:30 P.M. On the weekend when I researched this chapter, it had half-price tickets available to 17 shows—pity the uninformed tourist who paid full price!

Minneapolis/St. Paul: In this highly active center of the performing arts, half-price tickets are broadly available, Tuesday through Saturday from noon to 6 P.M., at the "Tickets to Go" outlets in the IDS Center of downtown Minneapolis, and in the Town Square of St. Paul; Sunday tickets can be purchased on Saturday. These are almost always for theater performances only, but occasionally as well for the St. Paul chamber orchestra and mime troupe.

THEATER DIRECTORY

BROADWAY

TOMORROW AT 8
"EXCITING, THRILLING AND VERY, VERY FUNNY." —Liz Smith
RON PERLMAN BRADLEY WHITFORD
A FEW GOOD MEN
Mon.-Sat.8;Mats.Wed.& Sat.at 2
Telecharge (212)239-6200(24hrs/7days)
Groups (212)239-6262.Also at Ticketron
•Music Box Theatre,239 West 45th St.

TOMORROW AT 8PM
Telecharge:(212)239-6200(24hrs/7days)
ANDREW LLOYD WEBBER'S
NEW MUSICAL
ASPECTS OF LOVE
Mon.-Sat. 8PM, Wed. & Sat. 2PM
Groups:(212)239-6262.Also at Ticketron
•Broadhurst Theatre, 235 W.44th St.

MATINEE TODAY AT 3
MATINEES WED., SAT. & SUN.
B'WAY's 1989 TONY AWARD
WINNING MUSICAL!
BEST PERFORMANCE BY A LEADING
ACTRESS IN A MUSICAL
BEST COSTUME DESIGN
BEST CHOREOGRAPHY
BLACK AND BLUE
Tues.-Sat. at 8; Mats Wed & Sat 2;Sun. 3
Ticketron Phone Charge: (212) 246-0102
Group Sales: (212) 398-8383
•MINSKOFF THEATRE 200 W. 45 St.

BOX OFFICE OPENS TOM'W AT 10AM!
THE MAN, THE MUSIC...THE LEGEND
BUDDY
The BUDDY HOLLY Story
Performances Begin October 23,1990
Eves. Tue.-Sat. at 8, Mats. Sat. at 2.
Sun. at 3: $47.50, 42.50, 32.50, 15.
Sun. at 7: $42.50, 37.50, 27.50, 15.
Telecharge (212) 239-6200(24hrs/7days)
Group Sales (212) 239-6262 or 398-8383
•SHUBERT THEA.225 W.44, NYC 10036

Today at 3.Mon & Tues at 8
THE ANDREW LLOYD WEBBER/
T.S.ELIOT INTERNATIONAL AWARD
WINNING MUSICAL
CATS
Mon-Wed,Fri at 8,Sat 2 & 8,Sun 3:Wed.2
Telecharge (212)239-6200(24hrs/7days)
Groups (212)239-6262.Also at Ticketron
•Winter Garden Thea.50 St.& B'way

TODAY AT 3PM
WINNER! 6 TONY AWARDS
including BEST MUSICAL
WINNER! BEST MUSICAL
1990 N.Y. Drama Critics Award
1990 Outer Critics Circle Award
1990 Drama Desk Award
JAMES NAUGHTON GREGG EDELMAN
CITY OF ANGELS
with RENE AUBERJONOIS
Book by LARRY Music by CY Lyrics by DAVID ZIPPEL

CALL TICKETRON TODAY!
(212) 246-0102 (24hrs/7days)
12 WEEK LIMITED ENGAGEMENT
BEGINS NOVEMBER 3, 1990
TOPOL
FIDDLER ON THE ROOF
GROUP SALES: (212) 398-8383
Tues-Sat at 8, Sat at 2, Sun at 3: $55.00, 50.,45.,35. Wed at 2: $45.00,40.,35.,25.
Enclose a stamped, self-addressed envelope and alternate dates along with check or money order made payable to:
•Gershwin Thea.222 W.51 NY,NY 10019

Mon & Tues at 8
1990 Winner of 5 Tony Awards
Best Direction of a Musical
and Best Choreography Tommy Tune
1990 Drama League Musical Theatre
Award Dir/Chor Tommy Tune
1990 Astaire Award
Best Choreography
1990 American Dance Award
"THE BEST! THE MUSICAL WINNER OF THE SEASON." —Time Magazine
GRAND HOTEL
The Musical
Mon-Sat at 8, Mats Wed & Sat 2
$16 Student tkts at B.O. subj. to avail.
Ticketron 212-246-0102 24Hr/7 Days
Groups Call(212)398-8383
•MARTIN BECK THEA.302 W.45th St.

TODAY AT 3PM SHARP!
LINDA LAVIN
GYPSY
THE 1990 TONY AWARD WINNER!
Tues.-Sat. 8, Mats. Wed. & Sat. 2, Sun. 3
CALL TICKETRON:(212)246-0102
(24 Hours a Day/7 Days a Week)
GROUP SALES (212)398-8383
•ST.JAMES THEA.246 W.44 St.

TODAY AT 3PM &
TUESDAY AT 8PM SHARP!
Latecomers Will Only Be Seated At A Suitable Break In The Performance.
LES MISERABLES
CALL TELECHARGE TODAY: 239-6200
24 Hrs a Day/7 Days a Week
MAIL ORDERS NOW: Tues.-Sat. 8PM, Mats: Sat. 2PM, Sun. 3PM & Special perfs: Mon. Oct. 8 at 8PM & Mon Dec. 31 at 8PM: Orch. & Front Mezz.: $60; Rear Mezz.: $42.50, $25. Wed. Mats. 2PM: Orch. & Front Mezz.: $50; Rear Mezz.: $37.50, $22.50. Checks payable to Les Miserables, PO BOX 998, NY, NY 10108. For Theatre Parties Contact Your Theatre Party Agent.
GROUP SALES: 398-8383 or 239-6262
•Broadway Thea.Broadway at 53rd St.

TODAY AT 3PM
1990 TONY AWARD WINNERS
MAGGIE SMITH
MARGARET TYZACK
LETTICE & LOVAGE
A New Comedy by
PETER SHAFFER
Tues.-Sat. 8; Mats.: Sat. 2, Sun. 3
Telecharge (212)239-6200(24hrs/7days)
Groups (212)239-6262.Also at Ticketron
•BARRYMORE THEA.,243 W.47th St.

Box Office opens Tom'w at 10AM
CALL Telecharge Today: (212) 239-6200
4 WEEKS ONLY!
OCTOBER 2nd thru 27th

BOX OFFICE OPENS TOM'W AT 10AM
CALL TELECHARGE TODAY:
(212) 239-6200, 24Hrs/7 Days
PERFORMANCES BEGIN OCT. 2
ONCE ON THIS ISLAND
a new musical
Booth Theatre, 222 W. 45th St.

Call Ticketron Today: (212) 246-0102
6 WEEKS ONLY! DEC. 11 -JAN. 20
CATHY RIGBY
is
PETER PAN
Tue at 7:30 -ALL SEATS $35.
Wed -Sat 7:30, Sat 2, Sun 3: $50, 45, 37.50. Wed at 2, Fri Dec 28 at 2,
Tue Jan 1 at 3: $45, 40, 32.50.
Groups: (212) 398-8383
Lunt-Fontanne 205 W 46 St NYC 10036

TODAY AT 3
"ENCHANTING, CHARMING MYSTERIOUS!"-Oliver, New Yorker
"A WINNER."—Wm. Henry III, Time
Timothy Hutton Barnard Hughes Mary-Louise Parker
in
PRELUDE TO A KISS
Tue-Sat 8; Mats Wed & Sat 2, Sun 3
Ticketron: 246-0102/Groups: 398-8383
•HELEN HAYES THEA. 240 W. 44 St.

Previews Begin Nov.2 Opens Nov. 11
Call TICKETRON Today:(212) 246-0102
"A CELEBRATION OF LOVE." —London Times
NIGEL HAWTHORNE JANE ALEXANDER
in
SHADOWLANDS
A Love Story
Tue-Sat 8; Mats Sat 2, Sun 3: $42.50, 37.50, 32.50. Wed 2: $37.50, 32.50, 27.50. Group Sales: 398-8383.
Make checks payable to:
Brooks Atkinson 256 W 47 St NY 10036

Box Office opens Tom'w at 10AM
Previews Begin Nov. 1; Opens Nov. 15
JAMES CLAVELL'S
SHOGUN
The Musical
Call Ticketron Today: (212) 246-0102
GROUPS: (212) 398-8383
Tue-Sat 8;Mats Sat 2,Sun 3: $55,45,35.
Wed Mats at 2: $47.50, 37.50, 27.50.
MARQUIS THEA.1535 Bway NYC 10036

Performances Begin Sept 25!
STAND-UP TRAGEDY
by BILL CAIN
Directed by RON LINK
Tele-Charge (212)239-6200
Box Office (212)764-7070
Group Sales (212)889-4300
Tue-Sat 8; Mats Wed & Sat 2, Sun 3
Special Perf. 10-1 at 8
Criterion Center: 1530 B'way at 45th

TODAY AT 3
1990 PULITZER PRIZE WINNER!
CHARLES S. DUTTON
THE PIANO LESSON
by AUGUST WILSON
directed by LLOYD RICHARDS
Tues.-Sat.8;Mats.Wed;Sat at 2, Sun.at 3
Ticketron 212-246-0102(24hrs/7days)
Group Sales (212) 398-8383
WALTER KERR THEATRE
219 W. 48th St. (212) 582-4022

Limited Engagement/Perfs begin Oct. 23
THOSE WERE THE DAYS
A New English-Yiddish Musical Revue
Mail Orders and Group Sales Now
Call For Tickets: (212) 683-7816
Tue, Wed, Thu at 8; Sun at 2 & 6: $35.
Sat at 8: $40. Mats Wed & Thu at 2: $25.
EDISON THEA. 240 W 47 St. NYC 10036

OFF-BROADWAY

Special Priority Calls Today: 239-2570
BEGINS NOVEMBER 6th
"REALITY IS FOR PEOPLE WHO CAN'T HANDLE FANTASY."
AND BABY MAKES SEVEN
A New Comedy by Paula Vogel
Directed by Gordon Edelstein
WESTSIDE THEA. W. 43rd St & 9th Ave

Extended Indefinitely! Today at 3 & 7:30
"GREAT THEATRE!" —The Nation
"TRIUMPHANT!" —New Yorker
BY AND FOR HAVEL
AUDIENCE by VACLAV HAVEL
CATASTROPHE by SAMUEL BECKETT
ALL TIX: $20. —HIT-TIX: 564-8038
Tues-Fri 8, Sat 2 & 8, Sun 3 & 7:30
Houseman Theatre Center 450 W. 42 St.

Tonight at 7
THE RIDICULOUS THEATRICAL CO.
Presents
Charles Ludlam's
CAMILLE
A tearjerker
Tue-Fri at 8, Sat & Sun at 7
B.O. 691-2271 or HIT-TIX 564-8038
Charles Ludlam Thea. 1 Sheridan Sq

TODAY AT 3 & 7
CLOSES 10/2 for VENEZUELAN TOUR
RE-OPENS 1/9/91
"A TRAILBLAZER!" —N.Y. Times
PAMELA ROSS
IS
CARRENO
A MUSICAL PLAY
WED-SAT 8, WED & SAT 2, Sun 3 & 7
TICKETCENTRAL: (212) 279-4200
GROUPS (212) 866-4368
INTAR THEATER 420 W. 42nd Street

Begins Fri. Evg. at 8
"A MUSICAL OF JUBILANCE AND COURAGE." -Rich, NY Times
FALSETTOLAND
music and lyrics by WILLIAM FINN
directed by JAMES LAPINE
the Playwrights Horizons production

TODAY 3 & 7
"LEAVES THE AUDIENCE SHOUTING FOR MO'!" —Time Magazine
FURTHER MO'
The NEW New Orleans Musical!
TICKETMASTER: 307-7171/
GROUPS: 889-4300
Tue.-Fri. 8, Sat. 6 & 9, Sun. 3 & 7
The Village Gate, 160 Bleecker St.

PERFS BEGIN OCT. 23
Call now for tickets 496-6486
or Hit Tix 212 564-8038
LIFE ON THE THIRD RAIL
A romantic comedy
Tues-Sat 8, Mats Wed & Sat at 2, Sun. 3
Thea. at Saint Peters Church
Citicorp Cntr. Lex. & 54th St.

TODAY AT 2
JASON ALEXANDER
PEGGY CASS
CHARLES KEATING
BILL McCUTCHEON
in
LIGHT UP THE SKY
A Comedy by Moss Hart
Directed by Larry Carpenter
Tue-Sat at 8; Mats Wed, Sat & Sun at 2
ROUNDABOUT THEATRE COMPANY
100 East 17th Street 420-1883/1360

"FUNNY AND MOVING." -NY Post
"WARM AND WISE!" -Newsday
MEN OF MANHATTAN
Scenes of New York City Gay Life
A New Comedy by JOHN GLINES
Wed-Fri at 8; Sat at 6 & 9; Sun at 7
Tickets $20; Phone Res: (212) 869-3530
COURTYARD PLAYHOUSE
39 Grove St

The Stillwaters Theatre Company
MIDSUMMER
a new comedy-drama by Paul Parente
Directed by Rick Lombardo
Tues.-Sat. at 8; Sat. at 2: Sun. at 3
Special Perf. Mon. Sept. 10 at 8 and
Tues. Sept. 11 at 6:45pm
Call TicketCentral 212-279-4200
The Nat Horne Theatre 440 West 42 St

Previews Wed. Sept. 19, 11pm
Premieres Oct. 3, 11pm
All Seats $22.50 Free Midnight Snack
MURDER AT MIDNIGHT
All new audience participation murder mystery—You can die laughing!
Tues. 8pm, Wed.-Fri. 11pm, Sun. 10pm
Ticketron 246-0102 Box Off: 838-8528
Theatre East, 211 E. 60th St, NYC

TODAY at 3
5th SMASH YEAR!
WINNER 4 1986
OUTER CRITICS CIRCLE AWARDS
BEST OFF-B'WAY MUSICAL
"DELIGHTFUL!" —N.Y.Times
NUNSENSE
The Worldwide Musical Comedy Hit!
239-4321; HIT-TIX: (212) 564-8038
Tue-Sat at 8; Mats Wed & Sat 2; Sun 3
Douglas Fairbanks Thea.,432 W. 42 St

TODAY at 3 & 7
"FUNNY, SERIOUS, SUSPENSEFUL, INVOLVING, DISTURBING AND ABOVE ALL EXPERTLY CRAFTED."
—John Simon, New York Mag.
OTHER PEOPLE'S MONEY

"A TRANSCENDENT THEATRICAL EXPERIENCE" —Frank Rich, NY Times
TODAY AT 3
LINCOLN CENTER THEATER
presents
SIX DEGREES OF SEPARATION
by John Guare
Directed by Jerry Zaks
Tue-Sat 8; Mats Wed & Sat 2, Sun 3
MITZI E. NEWHOUSE THEATER
Tele-Charge (212)239-6200
Groups (212) 362-4411
Performance Length 1:30

TODAY AT 3 & 7
"RUN, FORGET ABOUT WALKING TO THE LAMB'S!" —NY Post
"WITTY & REFRESHING!" —NY Times
SMOKE ON THE MOUNTAIN
a new comedy musical
Wed 2 & 8, Thu & Fri 8, Sat 2&8, Sun 3&7
Tickets and Info CALL: 997-1780
LAMB'S THEATRE 130 West 44th St.

Joseph Papp
presents
THE PUBLIC THEATER
FINAL PERFS. TODAY AT 3 & 8
Manbites Dog Theater Co. Production of
INDECENT MATERIALS
based on the words of Senator
Jesse Helms and Larry Kramer

Quiktix: ½ Price distributed day of perf. only 1PM Mats. 6PM Eves. Subject to availability

Charge Tix:598-7150/Groups:398-8383
The Public Theater,425 Lafayette St.

TODAY AT 3
Holiday Perfs. Sun. 9/23 & 9/30 7:30PM
"A STIRRING PRODUCTION!"
—Howard Kissel, Daily News
THE ROTHSCHILDS
A Tale of Romance, Risk and Reward
Book by Sherman Yellen Music by Jerry Bock Lyrics by Sheldon Harnick
Based on "The Rothschilds"
by Frederic Morton
Starring Mike Burstyn
Directed by Lonny Price
Tues-Sat 8, Mats. Wed & Sat 2:30, Sun 3
For Tickets Call (212)254-6330
Group Sales (212)889-4300
Circle in the Square Thea. (Downtown)
159 Bleecker St.

"MIX & MATCH MAGIC."
D. Richards, Washington Post
"A GENDER-BENDING, PANSEXUAL ROMP" —D.C. Paper
Cornerstone Theater Company's
THE VIDEO STORE OWNER'S SIGNIFICANT OTHER
Sept 12-29 ONLY; Tue-Fri 8; Sat 3 & 8
Tix $12-18; Tue-Pay What You Can; TDF
Charge Tix: (212)-366-6134
St. Clement's Church, 423 W. 46th

TODAY AT 2, WED. 7
"A HIT!" —People Magazine
TONY N' TINA'S WEDDING
TUES.-SAT. 7, SAT. & SUN. 2
Ceremony: St. John's, 81 Christopher St
Reception: Vinnie's, 147 Waverly Pl.
TICKETCENTRAL: (212) 279-4200

Washington, D.C.: "TICKETplace" is the spot, at F Street Plaza between 12th and 13th Streets NW, open from noon to 2 P.M. on Monday and 11 A.M. to 6 P.M. Tuesday through Saturday; you purchase Sunday tickets on Saturday. You can also phone 202/842-5387 to learn what half-price tickets are available that evening—a service most other cities don't offer.

Boston: "BOSTIX," in Faneuil Hall Market Place, at the corner of Congress and State Streets, is occasionally stocked with same-day half-price tickets for sports events, in addition to the more usual reduced-price seats for theater, music, and dance. Open Tuesday through Sunday from 11 A.M. to 5 P.M.

Chicago: "HOT TIX" discounts to nearly 50 theaters, from locations at 24 South St. in the heart of the Loop, the Park Square Atrium in Oak Park, and 1616 Sherman Ave. in Evanston. Figure hours of 10 A.M. to 3 P.M. generally, but until 6 P.M. at the Loop location, Tuesday through Saturday; Sunday tickets can be purchased on Saturday.

Denver: The "Ticket Bus"—a bright-red British double-decker—is parked at 16th and Curtis Streets, downtown, from noon to 6 P.M. on weekdays and 11 A.M. to 3 P.M. on Saturday (when you can also buy half-price Sunday tickets).

San Diego: Try "Auto Tix" in the lobby of the Spreckels Theatre at 121 Broadway, at the corner of First Avenue; open Tuesday through Saturday from 10 A.M. to 6 P.M. On Saturday you can purchase not only Saturday tickets but those for Sunday and Monday as well.

Pittsburgh: "TIX," at U.S.X. Plaza, at the corner of Grant and Sixth Avenues, open Monday through Saturday from 11 A.M. to 6 P.M., is a final half-price outlet for tickets to theater, music, and dance. Buy Sunday tickets on Saturday.

You might want to keep this chapter in mind for a future trip, because—to my knowledge—news of such reductions is rarely conveyed to tourists, and certainly isn't available from another single source. But at the very least, it may cause you to make inquiries about half-price tickets whenever you travel to a theater town. Like airplane seats and cruise-ship cabins, theater seats are perishable commodities—and wherever that's the case, discounters are at hand.

Like airplane seats and cruise-ship cabins, theater tickets are perishable commodities—and wherever that's the case, discounters are at hand.

XIV
TRAVELING IN THE MATURE YEARS

Our Greatest Retirement Bargain —Extended-Stay Vacations

A Month in Spain for $895, Including Air Fare—and Similar Stays in Yugoslavia and Australia

IF I COULD BESTOW AN ACADEMY AWARD FOR travel, it would be to the operators of extended-stay vacations to Spain, Yugoslavia, and Australia in the winter months. Next to the values offered by these one-month (and longer) sojourns, all other tour programs seem tawdry rip-offs, high-priced scams.

I am standing, in my fantasy, on the great curving stage of the Dorothy Chandler Pavilion in Los Angeles. I rip open the envelope and shout to the world: "The winners are" (pause): "Sun Holidays of Stamford, Yugotours of New York, and Aero Tours International—for their 'Extended Stays'!"

And as they drag me to a psycho ward (overlooking the blue Pacific), I struggle to explain the concept:

Almost by definition, an extended-stay vacation takes place overseas in the off-season setting of a popular summer resort.

The hotels are desperate. Built to accommodate the great warm-weather crowds, they now stand empty and losing in the chillier months. Along comes a U.S. tour operator with the following pitch: "If you will rent us your rooms for $6 a night, we'll fill them off-season with retirees staying for at least 30 days. You'll still lose money, but you'll lose less. And your staff will be happy to stay active and receiving tips."

To the airlines, a similar appeal: "Our one-month clients don't need the popular dates. Give us seats for $300, and we'll fill your flights on Tuesday nights."

To the public: "Why go in the winter to a mildewed motel and the plastic meals of fast-food chains? We'll fly you for less to glamorous foreign resorts. Sure, it's no longer hot in those places. But it's sunny and mild, and filled with exotica."

Thousands of mature U.S. travelers (and their numbers are growing) now say "Yes" to these attractive offers. They receive one of the great travel bargains, which seem particularly well packaged by the following:

SUN HOLIDAYS, TO SPAIN'S MEDITERRANEAN COAST ($895)

The undoubted price champion of the extended-stay companies, Sun charges a flat $895 in January, $905 in February and March, for a full winter month on the Costa del Sol of Spain, including air fare. It flies you there and back from New

Scene on the Costa del Sol

Village of Andalucia

York, Boston, Chicago, or Miami ($156 more from Chicago or Miami) on Iberia Airlines, meets you at the airport of Málaga, and transfers you by bus to the modern, high-rise Timor Sol Apartments on the beach of bustling Torremolinos (Europe's most heavily visited resort city in summer) with its dozens of hotels and varied tourist facilities. And there you stay for four weeks in a studio apartment with fully equipped kitchen, either making your own meals or taking them at restaurants nearby, enjoying maid service, an entertainment program, and the mild winter climate of Spain's southernmost shores (where it's too chilly at that time for ocean swimming, but otherwise entirely pleasant—and emptied of its often-oppressive summer crowds). For $124 more per person, you get a one-bedroom apartment for the month; for $85 per person per week, you get additional weeks. And thus, for as little as $1,235 per person, including air fare, you can stay for a full eight weeks on the Mediterranean coast of Spain!

Almost by definition, an extended-stay vacation takes place overseas in the off-season setting of a popular summer resort.

Sun Holidays has been operating these tours in close concert with Iberia Airlines for 10 years. Though a dozen other companies attempt the same thing—including such well-known senior-citizen specialists as Grand Circle Travel and AARP Travel Service, no one else comes remotely close in price or value. An Oscar is clearly deserved. For a colorful free catalog describing several such lengthy stays in various resort areas of Spain, and a similar miracle of pricing for one-month winter vacations in Venezuela, near Sorrento, Italy, and on the Algarve coast of Portugal, contact **Sun Holidays, 26 6th St., Stamford, CT 06905 (phone 203/323-1166, or toll free 800/243-2057 outside Connecticut).**

YUGOTOURS, TO THE DALMATIAN COAST ($1,295)

Some nine years ago, the leading tour company of Yugoslavia—a remarkably elegant organization despite its somewhat brutish name—discovered ahead of everyone else that a large number of Americans could greatly enjoy a long-stay winter vacation in the then largely empty modern hotels of the medieval resort cities of the Dalmatian (Adriatic) coast of Yugoslavia.

Some 50,000 U.S. travelers, mostly 60 and older, have since leaped at the chance. Somehow they sensed that the colorful atmosphere, setting, cuisine, and deliciously old-fashioned pace of these ancient ports would provide a unique vacation. They had heard, of course, that the Dalmatian coast was among the most scenically awesome spots on earth. And they were soon to learn that it is also remarkably cheap.

Today, from a busy office in New York's Empire State Building, Yugotours publishes an eagerly awaited, and quite handsome, 36-page catalog of "extended stays" in the fall, winter, and early spring to Dubrovnik, Opatija, and Lovran, among other places. Their rates are like from a Slavic fairy-tale. They include not only air fare and accommodations, but two meals a day—and other remarkable features (like a trip by passenger steamer between one resort town and another, on tours that feature more than one resort).

Yugotours, to the Dalmatian Coast

Postojna, Yugoslavia

The best of the tours (but not the cheapest) are those assigning you to Dubrovnik for six weeks. For a grand total of $1,295, $1,355, or $1,415 per person (depending on dates), you fly on JAT Yugoslav Airlines from New York or Chicago ($80 to $100 more from Chicago) to Zagreb, proceed from there by steamer to the walled city of Dubrovnik, stay in modern seaside hotels with heated swimming pools, eat two meals a day, and receive all sorts of charming extra features: cocktail parties and candlelight dinners, a Dalmatian band at several meals, orientation tours, films about Dubrovnik and Opatija, and much else. This short summary can't begin to do justice to the program as a whole.

From all resorts you have cheap, and almost daily, optional excursions to a variety of enchanting, unspoiled villages and seaside locations—especially to those in historic Montenegro: Sveti Stefan and Fudva, the Bay of Kotor. So hand me that golden statuette for Yugotours! And for a free catalog, contact **Yugotours, 350 Fifth Ave., Suite 2212, New York, NY 10118 (phone 212/563-2400, or toll free for information 800/228-1063 outside New York, for reservations 800/223-5298 outside New York).**

AEROTOURS, TO AUSTRALIA'S "GOLD COAST" ($2,075)

Here is the sole exception to the "off-season" timing of most extended stays: our American winter is Australia's summer, and the ocean is filled at that time with swimmers, who later bask in the 80° sun. The low value of the Australian dollar, which sells for only U.S. 80¢ (you greatly increase the value of your money there), explains why the 10-year-old AeroTours International can sell such a reasonably priced, month-long holiday to a peak-season resort so far away.

For a per-person (double occupancy) total of $2,075

from April through August, $2,285 from September through November, and $2,495 from December through March, AeroTours will fly you round trip from the U.S. West Coast

The Great Barrier Reef, Australia

direct to Brisbane and then bus you 40 minutes south to the 26-mile-long beach known as the Gold Coast; it is lined with luxury hotels, condominiums, and even a casino or two. Near a town called Surfers Paradise (its actual name), you'll stay for a full month in a 15-story beachfront apartment-hotel (the South Pacific Plaza) in a balconied studio with wall-to-wall carpeting, fully equipped kitchen, and dining nook. Downstairs are restaurants, shops, squash and tennis courts. Fifteen minutes away are rain forest–covered mountains with horseback and walking trails, and some of the finest wildlife sanctuaries of Australia.

When you consider that the peak-season air fare from the West Coast to Australia alone is $1,545, you glimpse the value this package represents. And if you can yourself improve on the air fare to Australia—using a local bucket shop, for instance—AeroTours will sell you just the accommodations, at a considerable saving. Once in Australia, you enjoy marvelously low prices for everything else, including the memorable trip to the Barrier Reef.

Persons of any age can book these tours (and so can retirees of any age on the programs of Sun Holidays and Yugotours).

For brochures and further details, contact **AeroTours International, 36 E. 3rd St., New York, NY 10003 (phone 212/979-5000, or toll free 800/223-4555 outside New York City)**. And for giving me this chance to tell you about AeroTours, I want to thank the Academy, my travel agent, the Mobil Road Atlas, my typewriter repair shop . . .

Why endure a shabby Miami motel and fast-food chains when Spain awaits?

The Battle for the Older American Traveler

Four Major Travel Firms Are Following a Unique Approach in Their Sale of Vacations to Seniors

IN THE WORLD OF TRAVEL, WHAT DO OLDER Americans really want?

That inquiry is the topic of the year among airlines and tour operators. As if, without warning, a new planet had swung into their sight, they've discovered that a startling percentage of all travel expenditures are made by people 55 and older. Not yuppies, not preppies, not even baby boomers, but rather senior citizens are today the "name of the game" in travel.

Young folks, it appears, go to the movies; older ones go on vacation.

"Our senior citizens," says one tour operator, "are feeling better about themselves, and that's why they're traveling more. They're healthier, living longer, more affluent. They have a new conviction that life is to be enjoyed for quite a while more, and this fairly recent attitude makes them the fastest-growing segment of the travel market."

Given that fact, it is surprising, as an initial note, to find so few companies serving the needs of the older American traveler. Apart from local motorcoach operators and purely ad hoc programs by regional firms, only four really major U.S. companies deal exclusively with the marketing and operation of far-ranging tours for seniors, and three of these are headquartered in one city: Boston. They are: Saga Holidays, Grand Circle Travel, Inc., Elderhostel, and AARP (American Association of Retired Persons) Travel Service.

Having journeyed to Boston to view the first three, and phoned the fourth in California, I've been alternately impressed, startled, dismayed, and educated by several uniform ways in which they do business. Traveling seniors may want to consider the following observations on the major "tour operators for older Americans":

THEY MAINLY SELL "DIRECT"

Not one of the "big four" deals with travel agents or sets aside a single percentage point of income for the latter. Each one heatedly insists that the processing of seniors' tours is a specialty requiring direct contact between them (the tour operators) and their clients (the actual senior travelers), usually via toll-free "800" numbers. Because the four firms adhere fiercely to their position, their brochures and catalogs are unavailable in travel agents' racks and can be obtained only by mail. Nor do they advertise in the general media. If you are not already on their mailing lists, you must specifically request their brochures by writing to the addresses listed above. Once you do, you'll soon receive a heavy packet of attractive four-color literature and application forms.

Not yuppies, not preppies, not even baby boomers, but rather senior citizens are today the "name of the game" in travel.

THEY CATER TO "OLDER" AMERICANS

Although people can theoretically use the services of the senior-citizen tour operators when they reach the tender ages of 50, 55, or 60 (50 for AARP, 55 for Grand Circle, 60 for Saga and Elderhostel), in practice they don't. The average age of Grand Circle's clients is 67, that of the others only slightly less. The apparent reason is that Americans no longer feel removed from younger age categories until they reach their early or mid-60s. Advances in health care and longevity, better diets, and attention to exercise keep most of us youthful and vigorous into our late 50s, and reluctant to cease socializing—or vacationing—with younger people. (I recall growing apoplectic with rage when, on my 50th birthday, the mail brought an invitation to join AARP.) Who any longer even retires at the age of 65?

THEIR CLIENTS INSIST ON THE EXCLUSION OF YOUNGER PASSENGERS

But when those mid-60s are in fact reached, the newly elder turn with a vengeance to services of the specialists. After an initial reluctance to confine their travel companions to a single age group, today's 65-year-olds discover that they are of a different "mind set" from their younger co-citizens. Brought up during the Depression, sent to fight or work in World War II, denied the easy travel opportunities enjoyed by our blasé younger set, they better appreciate the joys of international travel, react with gratitude and awe to wonders of the world, enjoy the companionship of people who feel the same way.

THEY POSSESS A HISTORICAL PERSPECTIVE DENIED TO THE YOUNGER GENERATION

Clearly, they share a wealth of experience and a common outlook; come from an education in the broad liberal arts as contrasted with the crudely materialistic, vocational outlook of so many of today's youth. And when they travel with younger people, they are often upset by the young folks' failure to share the same values or to be familiar with the events that so shaped their own lives. What mature American can enjoy a trip through Europe or the South Pacific with people who are only dimly aware of Franklin Roosevelt or Winston Churchill, of Douglas MacArthur or Field Marshal Rommel, of the Invasion or the Holocaust? Accordingly, they respond with eagerness to tour programs limited to persons of their own age.

THEIR CLIENTS RECEIVE DISTINCTLY DIFFERENT, CUSTOM-TAILORED TRAVEL ARRANGEMENTS

In addition to confining their groups to an older age range, the major tour companies earn their allegiance by providing arrangements that are significantly different from those designed for a general clientele. "We avoid the modern hotels, with their small public spaces, their in-room videos and bars," explains a specialist. "We look for traditional buildings with large lobbies for congregating and sitting—our clients prefer camaraderie to in-room movies! We also insist on a location within distance of everything important."

"We pace our tours to avoid overly long hours on a bus," explains another. "But we keep our passengers active, always on the move. Older travelers have had enough of sitting around at home; they want constant experiences and encounters."

Though the tours are of a longer duration than the normal variety, they are rarely for more than three weeks at a time. "People in retirement like to take two and three trips in a year," says the president of one firm. "They tour a particular destination for two or three weeks, then want to try something else."

In planning tours for the older American, the great majority of departures are scheduled for off-season periods—not in July or August to Europe, for instance, but in the "shoulder" and "off-peak" months when retired people are the best possible prospects for travel. "We get better rates for them that way," says a tour official. "And they're better appreciated at that time by the suppliers. They get more and better attention."

Tour companies earn their allegiance by providing arrangements that differ significantly from those designed for a general clientele.

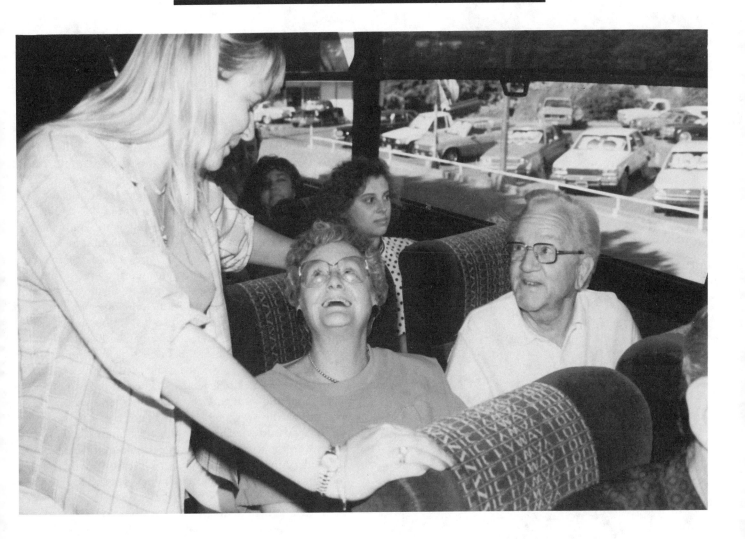

BUT THEIR PRICES ARE HIGHER THAN THE NORM

So much for the good news. The bad news is that the tours planned for senior citizens only are generally higher priced than similar trips sold to all ages. This is not to say that the former do not use better hotels, provide closer and more personal attention, supply more tour ingredients. They may or may not. But except for Elderhostel—whose prices are truly remarkable—not one of the senior-citizen specialists has opted to service the needs of intensely cost-conscious Americans; their tour products are generally $100 to $300 higher than the motorcoach programs or "stay-put" holidays available from several of the low-cost tour operators serving a general public, sometimes for suspiciously similar features. This, to me, is a serious mistake on their part, limiting their programs to an upper-middle-class clientele and bypassing the budget-limited majority of the older gen-

eration. When a tour company—perhaps a wholly new one—begins offering modestly priced tours for exclusive use by older citizens, it will, in my view, be flooded with bookings (as Elderhostel is).

THE PROGRAMS THEMSELVES

What do the specialists offer, and how do they differ one from the other? Here's a quick rundown:

Saga Holidays, 120 Boylston St., Boston, MA 02116 (phone 617/451-6808, or toll free 800/343-0273 outside Massachusetts), is perhaps the largest of the lot, resulting from the activity of its British parent company, which each year sends over 250,000 senior citizens on vacation. To tap into that major movement (and the bargaining power it represents), the U.S. organization routes most of its transatlantic tours through London, there to combine its older American travelers into one group with older British and Australian

Mediterranean Highlights

Great Capitals of Europe

Saga Holidays Club and receive a quarterly magazine supplemented by newsletters. The latter's most appealing feature is a page of travel "personals"—older people seeking other older people to join them on a trip.

Saga's major stock-in-trade is escorted motorcoach tours: heavily (and throughout the year) within the United States, heavily in Europe, but also in Mexico, in Australia and the Far East, and in South America. Although it also offers cruises and extended stays, it is the escorted motorcoach, competitively priced, that most of its clients demand.

Grand Circle Travel, Inc., 347 Congress St., Boston, MA 02210 (phone 617/350-7500, or toll free 800/248-3737), is the oldest of the U.S. firms dealing only with senior citizens, but recently rejuvenated through its acquisition by an enterprising travel magnate, Alan E. Lewis, who has injected considerable new resources and vigor (quarterly magazine, *Pen Pal,* and travel-partner service) into it. In business for 33 years, it enjoys a large and loyal following, who respond especially to offers of extended-stay vacations in off-season months, and to low-cost foreign areas with mild climates. The greater number of Grand Circle's passengers are those spending, say, 2 to 20 weeks on the Mediterranean coast of Spain, in a seaside kitchenette apartment supplied with utensils, china, and cutlery. Others go for several weeks to Dubrovnik on the awesome Dalmatian coast of Yugoslavia, or to Portugal and Madeira, the Canary Islands, the Balearics. Wherever, the tour company argues (and quite successfully) that older Americans can enjoy a "full season" at these exotic locations for not much more than they'd spend to Florida or other domestic havens. While neither Spain nor Yugoslavia offers swimming weather in winter, their low prices enable seniors (even those living mainly on Social Security) to vacation in dignity, enjoying good-quality meals and modern apartments in place of the fast-food outlets and shabby motels to which they're often relegated here at home. Grand Circle's extended stays are supplemented by nearly a dozen other programs—Alaskan cruises, Canadian holidays, tours to Europe and the Orient—booked by thousands, but not yet as popular as those "stay-put" vacations for several weeks in a balmy, foreign clime.

AARP Travel Service, 100 N. Sepulveda Blvd., Suite 1010, El Segundo, CA 90245 (phone toll free 800/227-7737), is the "new kid on the block," less than 10 years old, but obviously destined for big things. As the official travel arm of the 30-million-member American Association of Retired Persons, it draws upon a massive potential following and contacts them quickly and efficiently via the organization's impressive bimonthly magazine, *Modern Maturity,* sent to all members. They, in turn, can request upward of 30 separate travel catalogs dealing with cruises, escorted motorcoach holidays, "long stays," and jaunts of every description.

But though the audience is on such a mass scale, the programs themselves are operated for AARP by a "carriage

passengers. Such blending of English-speaking nationalities adds "zip" to any tour, they claim, and I agree. On board the buses, frolicsome passengers quip that Saga means "Send-a-Granny-Away" or "Sex-and-Games-for-the-Aged" (the latter very much tongue-in-cheek).

Headed by an ebullient walrus-mustached former educator named Jerry Foster, a onetime official of Elderhostel, the Saga staff also provide technical travel arrangements for Elderhostel's programs (see below) to Britain, Ireland, Spain, Portugal, and Turkey—a potent endorsement. Saga's passengers (who must be 60 or older) are later invited to join the

Alaskan cruises

trade" tour operator, Olson-Travelworld, known for its quality accommodations, careful attention to travel details, and substantial price structure. Olson, in its early stewardship of the AARP program, has surprised the travel trade by placing a heavy emphasis on cut-rate cruises; it offers (with considerable success) a lengthy series of sailings on celebrated ships already heavily patronized by seniors, but discounted for the AARP membership by as much as $150 to $1,000 per person. While the strong response to these oceangoing values has tended to overshadow the remainder of the program, AARP's buses, planes, and tours are operating to every major destination.

Elderhostel, 75 Federal St., Boston, MA 02110-1941 (phone 617/426-7788), is, in a nutshell, the much-discussed, increasingly popular, nonprofit group that works with 1,400 U.S. and foreign educational institutions to provide seniors 60 and over with residential study courses at unbeatable costs: $245 per week for room, board, and tuition (but not including air fare) in the U.S. and Canada; an average of $2,000 for three weeks abroad, this time including air fare. Accommodations and meals are in student residence halls or underused youth hostels.

Those are the "nutshell" facts, which can't do justice to the gripping appeal of Elderhostel's course descriptions. Who can withstand "The Mystery and Miracle of Medieval Cathedrals" (taught at a school overlooking the Pacific)? Or "Everything You Always Wanted to Know About Music But Were Too Afraid to Ask" (at a university in Alabama)? Or "Gods, Kings, and Temples" (at a classroom in Cairo)? They make you yearn to be 60!

With more than 250,000 traveling students anticipated for 1991, Elderhostel is the once-and-future travel giant,

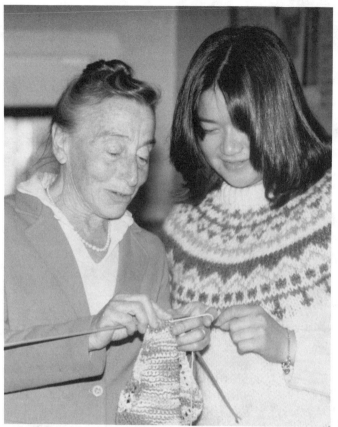

Elderhosteler

fervently acclaimed by its elderly devotees. "Thank you, Elderhostel!" wrote one senior in a recent publication. "We've built beaver dams in Colorado, explored temples in Nepal, ridden outrigger canoes in Fiji, sat on the lawn sipping coffee at Cambridge University, eaten with our fingers at private homes in Bombay, where they venerate older people!"

THE PRICES THEY CHARGE

Those are the four specialists. Why aren't they (with the exception of Elderhostel) cheaper? With such huge resources and immense followings, the senior-citizen tour operators are capable of achieving major price breakthroughs for their elderly clientele. The disquieting thing is that they don't.

In the area of extended stays, a well-known nonspecialist, **Sun Holidays, 26 6th St., Stamford, CT 06905 (phone 203/323-1166, or toll free 800/243-2057 outside Connecticut)**, takes people of all ages to modern apartment-hotels on Spain's Costa del Sol, in winter, for a charge per month (the first month) of $895 per person, including round-trip air fare from New York on Iberia Airlines. Two of the major senior-citizen specialists (I am of course excluding Elderhostel)

charge $100 to $400 more on most of their winter departures for virtually the same one-month stay (although the costlier tour includes a night, with meals, in London at both the start and end of the trip, and a slightly larger apartment). The senior-citizen companies also include insurance worth about $30.

In the field of escorted motorcoach tours, the well-known **Trafalgar Tours,** selling to young and old alike, charges $1,688 for a 15-day tour of Britain, air fare included, and $1,888 for a classic 16-day tour of Europe, air fare included. One of the major senior-citizen specialists (I am again excluding Elderhostel) charges $1,899 for a 16-day tour of Britain, air fare included, and charges $2,159 for a quite similar 17-day tour of Europe, air fare included. Another so-called specialist charges over $2,000 for nearly everything. While hotels on the highest priced of these tours are marginally better than Trafalgar's, they do not support (in my opinion) a differential of that magnitude; and most other features of the tours are similar.

Should companies be surcharging the senior citizen by

Saga Holidays to the Orient (Thailand here)

Hong Kong, an AARP destination

$100 to $400 per person for the right to travel only with other senior citizens? Shouldn't older Americans, of all people, enjoy the lowest of travel costs? Especially when they are dealing directly with the tour operator, saving that company a travel agent's commission?

In private conversations, travel industry people will speculate as to whether the senior-citizen companies are relieved of normal competitive pricing pressures by the semi-captive nature of their clientele—who have no independent travel counselor to steer them to a cheaper course. Whether or not this is so—whether, as the companies claim, their tours are worthier because of their attention to needs of the elderly—those prices quite obviously need some analysis, and perhaps revision.

Traveling Alone in the Mature Years—Plight or Opportunity?

The Problem Is Not Confined to Women; the Question Should Be Rephrased to Ask: "Can a Single Woman, or Single Man, Travel Enjoyably Alone? And Can This Be Done at a Mature Age?"

OUT-OF-BREATH AND WEARY, I END MY eager speech—that overlong lecture on travel that I deliver, somewhere, each month—and throw open discussion to the floor. Within four minutes, never more, it comes, that inevitable, inescapable, and utterly harrowing question: "Can a single woman travel safely, and enjoyably, alone?"

Amazing how persistent the inquiry, how it reveals a major, near-universal concern among a large portion of all potential travelers.

The questioner is usually a widow in her late middle age, her forehead furrowed with worry. She explains that she and her husband had enjoyed memorable trips abroad, that travel for her is a cherished activity, but that now she is anxious, even frightened, about undertaking further journeys on her own.

As she talks, a nervous movement occurs in the auditorium among men of a similar age. Though they—the men—never initiate the question, they now lean forward in rapt attention, concentrating on every word. And suddenly it is obvious: the problem is not confined to women; the question should be rephrased to ask: "Can a single woman, or a single man, travel enjoyably alone? And can this be done at a mature age?"

THE GLIB RESPONSE

Though my answer, generally, is "Yes," I wish I could state it with greater conviction than I do. But the issue is complex, surrounded by ifs, perhaps, and maybes.

In this respect I differ from a great many more impulsive travel lecturers who teach one-evening courses at urban night schools, under the title "Traveling Solo: The Joys of Going It Alone." These people claim that we should always travel unaccompanied, even if we don't have to. Why? Because such is the road to romance and adventure, to chance encounters with foreign citizens, invitations to foreign homes. And the practice, as they tell it, is deliciously selfish: you do only what you desire, without compromise. You do not alter your itinerary or schedule to suit the tastes of another human being. For the first time in your life, you are *free*.

The message of these trendy singles (almost all in their mid-20s) is of course based on the assumption that a compatible travel companion doesn't exist; that, almost as if by some law of nature, two people traveling together must necessarily have widely divergent views, inclinations, and tastes. Having themselves never experienced true friendship, love, or compatibility, they proclaim the resounding advantage of traveling alone.

I can't go quite that far. For surely, only the most naïve pollyanna can believe that the pleasure of traveling with a cherished companion—the joy of sharing reactions to renowned sights and experiences—can now be duplicated or replaced in the absence of that person. At best they can be experienced differently, with adequate enjoyment, but not usually with the profound satisfactions of discovering them in the company of a like-minded friend.

THE ALTERNATIVES TO SOLITUDE

Therefore, before I discuss the ways to enjoy a solitary holiday trip, to "make a go" of traveling alone, it's important to note that you don't have to. By simply mailing $5 for a three-year membership in the Saga Holidays Club operated by

376

Study tours are one possibility

Saga Holidays Ltd., 120 Boylston St., Boston, MA 02116 (phone 617/451-6808, or toll free 800/343-0273 outside Massachusetts), or $5 for a similar membership in the Grand Circle Travel Club, operated by **Grand Circle Travel, Inc., 347 Congress St., Boston, MA 12210 (phone 617/350-7500, or toll free 800/248-3737)**—both of them companies dealing exclusively in travel for mature persons—you can obtain the names of potential companions for your next trip. Both clubs distribute quarterly magazines with "Pen Pal" or "Penfriend" features listing dozens of applications by mature singles for travel partners. These, in effect, are "travel personals," but proper to a fault, and fascinating to read as they detail the varied goals of the mature, experienced travelers submitting them.

For more extensive listings (over 200 "travel personals" per bimonthly publication), send $40 for a one-year subscription to **Partners-in-Travel, P.O. Box 491145, Los Angeles, CA 90049 (phone 213/476-4869)**. Its newsletter, issued every 60 days, is by the irrepressible Miriam Tobolowsky, who attracts a zestful following and ads peppered with jaunty exhortations: "Let's go—life is for living!" One recent listing assures that the applicant is "caring and considerate, but won't hover. Want ardent traveler who travels light, dependable driver, honest and open communication, brisk walker." Though Partners-in-Travel does not limit its services to mature persons, a full 70% of its subscribers appear to be over 50, most in their early 60s.

And for a near-guarantee that you will find a suitable

Before discussing the ways to travel alone, it's important to note that you don't have to.

travel "match-up," but at rates varying from $3 to $11 per month (with a six-month minimum), contact **Travel Companion Exchange, P.O. Box 833, Amityville, NY 11701 (phone 516/454-0880)**, founded by the well-known travel figure Jens Jurgen. His is the most elaborate of all travel match-up services, supplying you with literally thousands of available listings, all carefully grouped by computer into helpful categories ("special interests," "special travel plans," and the like) to enable a wise choice.

TRAVELING ONLY WITH SINGLES

As a substitute for seeking a travel companion, one can travel with groups consisting only of singles. Although the prestigious **Singleworld Cruises & Tours, Inc., P.O. Box 1999, Rye, NY 10580 (phone 914/967-3334)**, does not limit participation to mature persons only, its programs are heavily booked by the mature, and its tours are only for single people. Join them and your problems of "singlehood" vanish.

Loners on Wheels, Inc., 808 Lester St., (P.O. Box 1355), Poplar Bluff, MO 63901 (phone 314/785-2420), is still another travel organization confined to singles. An RV club, it forms caravans of singles only, and takes them to rallies and campouts all over the country and occasionally to Mexico too. Annual dues: $24, plus an initiation fee of $5 (the first year only).

ACTIVITIES WHERE IT DOESN'T MATTER

Your other option is to travel abroad with groups pursuing an intense social, political, scientific, or educational purpose. In that context, the fact that some are singles, some couples, becomes of minor significance: people are engaged in a communal activity, living helter-skelter in group lodgings, so intent on their work that they mix and mingle easily.

The study tours operated by the famous **Elderhostel, 75 Federal St., Boston, MA 02110-1941 (phone 617/426-7788)**, are that kind of program. Elderhostel sends people over the age of 60 to attend one- to three-week classroom courses of instruction in the U.S. and around the world, using university residence halls—sometimes even dormitories, segregated by sex—for lodgings. It makes no guarantee

of single or double rooms, charges one standard fee without single supplement, and thereby attracts a heavy number of singles to its continually fascinating curriculum (singles make up a full 30% of Elderhostel's volume, and two-thirds of those singles are women). But because Elderhostel passengers are focused so intently on ideas outside of themselves, the fact that they are alone or accompanied dwindles in importance, fades from consciousness; and people glory in the camaraderie and joint activities of the entire group.

The trips sponsored by **Earthwatch, P.O. Box 403N, Watertown, MA 02272 (phone 617/926-8200)**, are also that sort of program. It sends its volunteers on scientific research projects (tagging fish, measuring acid rain, interviewing rural residents), making use of a catch-as-catch-can array of housing accommodations (local schools and community centers, tents, and private homes) in which people are lodged as conditions permit. Its charges ("contributions") are uniform per person, with no single supplement, and the composition of its "teams" is heavily slanted to singles. "We were an unlikely group," wrote one recent Earthwatch participant, "... a history teacher from Ohio, a Long Island college student, a retired real estate investor from Arizona...." A full 20% of all Earthwatch volunteers, I am told, are 56 to 65 years old; nearly 10% are over 65.

Similar in character, largely erasing the distinction between couples and singles, and attracting a heavy percentage of singles, are the "adventure tours" (camping safaris, treks in Nepal and the Andes, outdoor nature expeditions) sponsored by an increasing number of tour operators. Though they require a certain minimum vigor (but less than you might think), they cater to people of all ages, attract a heavy turnout of mature singles, and house them in tents or improvised accommodations. Scan the catalogs of **Overseas Adventure Travel, 349 Broadway, Cambridge, MA 02139 (phone 617/876-0533, or toll free 800/221-0814)**—which carried an 82-year-old woman on a recent camping safari to Tanzania—or **Sobek Expeditions, Inc., P.O. Box 1089, Angels Camp, CA 95222 (phone 209/736-4524, or toll free 800/777-7939)**, for additional examples of purposive trips in which all participants became undifferentiated members of a cohesive group, without regard to marital status. The same applies to volunteer "workcamp" tours engaging in socially conscious projects around the world: contact **VFP International Workcamps, Tiffany Road, Belmont, VT 05730**

As a substitute for seeking a travel companion, one can travel with groups consisting only of singles.

(phone 802/259-2759), and specify the trips open to all ages; or to politically oriented trips, some heavily feminist in nature, organized by such as **Global Exchange, 2940 16th St., Suite 307, San Francisco, CA 94103 (phone 415/255-7296).**

While all such trips appeal to only a segment of the mature audience, they provide the perfect antidote to the "single travel blues."

It is primarily—let me suggest—on the standard, traditional trips, with their single supplements and couples-only atmosphere, that the problems of traveling alone are most sharply felt.

ENJOYING THE STANDARD TRIPS

So how, then, do you travel alone for normal sightseeing or recreational purposes? How, as a mature single person, do you best vacation in new lands, or travel to visit important cultural exhibits or simply to refresh the mind and body?

The problem centers on that edifice known as a hotel—that ultimately boring and impersonal institution, with its inescapable "single surcharges." (One wise observer recently speculated that Hell consists of being condemned to stay, unto eternity, in a different modern hotel each night.)

The obvious solution is to avoid the use of standard hotels and replace them with a people-friendly form of lodgings. Staying with families while abroad serves the triple purpose of avoiding loneliness, gaining new friendships and insights, and lowering costs: you not only escape from that burdensome single supplement, but start from a radically lower base of costs. Indeed, some mature singles even lower their lodgings expense to zero by joining the public-spirited, worldwide membership of **Servas, 11 John St., Suite 706, New York, NY 10038 (phone 212/267-0252),** which believes that free and frequent people-to-people contacts, through home visits, serve the cause of world peace. On the eve of a trip, they obtain from Servas the names and ad-

Seniors at a workcamp

Scenes from a camping safari

dresses of families in every major city who have expressed their willingness to receive other Servas members into their homes (for short stays) free of charge, because they believe in the profound moral aspect of such hospitality. (Yearly fee for Servas membership: $45.)

Other mature singles opt for a more commercial form of homestay, but inexpensive and without the single supplement, by utilizing the services of homestay organizations in every major country. For a comprehensive list of several dozen national homestay organizations (and of other interesting travel activities), send $5.95 (plus $1 for postage and handling) to **Pilot Books, 103 Cooper St., Babylon, NY 11702,** for a copy of the 72-page *Vacations with a Difference*. This little book lists homestays in Canada, France, Australia, Tahiti, and Scandinavia; homestays with Unitarians, humanists, Mennonites, and Quakers; homestays with farmers and wine growers; homestays for as little as $85 a week, including all meals. What you yourself may have

done as a teenager—a month and more abroad with a foreign family—is now available in your mature years, and for reasons obvious and profound, no other travel experience quite compares to it.

The most relaxed and adventurous of mature singles stay in youth hostels both here and abroad, now that the international youth-hostel organization has removed all maximum-age restrictions on the right to use their facilities. Particularly in the fall and winter months, when young people are in school, the predominant clientele of many youth hostels is today middle-aged and elderly! But even when one shares these multibedded rooms or dorms with young people, one pays an inexpensive charge, without a supplement. And one stays in a lively setting of international conversations and encounters. For information, contact **American Youth Hostels, Inc., P.O. Box 37613, Washington, DC 20013 (phone 202/783-6161).**

One rather affluent and mature U.S. lawyer of my acquaintance, who has traveled extensively by herself in the South Pacific, actually favors hostels, though she could afford much better. "They offer a wonderful way to meet people, including local people traveling in their own country," she points out. "The kitchen is a great social center, with perhaps 12 people each attempting to cook dinner for one—a hilarious scene. By the time the various dinners are ready, you're all old friends."

REVISING YOUR ATTITUDES

If, despite this advice, you're determined to keep going on the standard trips and to use standard hotels, you may need a new mental outlook for coping with the problems of solitary travel—a confident and positive outlook. Though at the outset I was careful to stress my own view that traveling in twos is usually superior to traveling alone, there are nonetheless some attractive aspects to the latter experience.

You might regard that first experience as a zesty challenge, a chance to shape yourself for the better. Whatever your usual personality, you must of necessity attempt to be more outgoing and convivial.

Introduce yourself to the people around you. Ask other tourists for advice on restaurants and sights. Suggest the sharing of a meal at some celebrated establishment. Just as the same human necessities breed invention, so traveling by oneself often leads to increased openness, receptivity to new people and ideas, greater self-assurance and pride.

Among some single travelers—certainly not all, but some—the experience soon takes on a mood of surprised exhilaration. They find they're more sensitive to the people and culture of the destination. The absence of a familiar companion removes them from the familiar cocoon of their own language and culture, and teaches them a new language, a new culture. (And, incidentally, traveling alone is the fastest—some say the best—way to learn another language).

These new solitary travelers become less self-conscious. After that first nerve-wracking dinner alone in a large hotel restaurant—when every eye seems focused, accusingly, on them—they suddenly realize that in reality no one is terribly concerned with or interested in the fact that they are dining alone. It is a liberating bit of knowledge. On all subsequent evenings they bring a book or magazine to the dinner table, and revel in the luxury of thus relaxing at a high-quality meal.

Though it may not be all that it once was, traveling while alone is soon recognized to be immeasurably more satisfying

On tour in Jaipur, India

than the alternative: moping at home alone. And with every succeeding trip, the experience gains in pleasure, ease, and depth; it keeps us alive. As that canny voyager (Miriam Tobolowsky) who operates Partners-in-Travel puts it: "Travel isn't something you do in old age; it is something you do *instead of* old age."

Travel is thus far too important to be dispensed with when a companion is unavailable; it is part of a civilized life, our birthright. The most vital of our fellow humans travel, whether alone or not—and so should you!

Some Travel Options—Good, Bad, and Indifferent—for the Mature American

As the Travel Industry Scrambles to Win Over the Senior Citizen, a Mixed Bag of Programs Emerges

MAYBE IT'S MY WIDENING GIRTH, MY whitening hair, my increasing nostalgia for "slow music." But the travels of senior citizens interest me more and more, and provoke these comments on recent developments.

That 10% Lure: Call me a grouch, but I'm not impressed with the discounts for mature travelers offered by most hotel chains and airlines. In the majority of cases these consist of 10% reductions off room rate or air fare. Since that's the exact amount that hotels and airlines pay out to travel agents, and since most senior-citizen travel programs require (in effect) that passengers avoid the use of travel agents in making reservations, the hotels and airlines are frequently saving 10% on their senior-citizen programs—and then simply passing on that 10% saving to the senior citizen.

In other words, they're not spending a red cent to obtain their senior business. Which seems a bit chintzy.

BEST HOTEL BETS

Does anyone do better by America's elderly? A few do. And they deserve acclaim as a means of nudging the others to do more. Here's a sampling:

Sheraton Hotels: Though they caution that the discount can be withheld during periods of peak business, and is not applicable to minimum-rate rooms, virtually all Sheratons give a 25% discount to persons 60 and older. Phone toll free 800/325-3535.

Ramada Inns: Many (about three-quarters) give the same 25% off to persons 60 and up. Phone toll free 800/2-RAMADA.

Marriott Hotels: At more than 128 Marriotts in the U.S., Europe, and the Caribbean, a discount of up to 50% off

Rehearsal for retirement: a meaningful research trip

published rates is given to persons 62 years of age and older, and 25% off on lunches and dinners (the latter whether you're a guest or not). Reductions are subject to availability and occasional seasonal closeouts, and require advance reservations at the reduced rate. Phone toll free 800/228-9290.

La Quinta Inns: Offer 15% off to people age 55 and older. Phone toll free 800/531-5900.

Holiday Inns: Give 20% off room rates, 10% off meals, to those over 50 joining their Mature Outlook club for $9.95 a year. Phone toll free 800/336-6330 for membership and to learn the identities of participating inns.

Days Inns: From 15% to 50% (usually 15%) off at 850 participating inns, hotels, suite-hotels, and "Day Stops," to

members (50 years and older) of their September Days Club; send $12 to September Days Club, P.O. Box 4001, Harlan, IA 51593 (phone toll free 800/344-3636).

Howard Johnson's: Take 15% to 30% off for seniors 60 years and older at more than 85% of the nation's H.J. hotels. Phone toll free 800/634-3464.

AIRLINE OFFERINGS

As for the airlines, some of them also confine their senior-citizen air-fare discounts to 10% and simply pass on the 10% they've saved by subtly influencing senior citizens to book direct. In fairness, they also provide self-promoting newslet-

Call me a grouch, but I'm not impressed with the discounts for mature travelers offered by most hotel chains and airlines.

The Algarve coast of Portugal, Lifestyle Explorations

ters for senior travelers, and diverse other discounts and features (for hotels, car rentals, and the like). Some, in handsome style, give 15% off to travelers 65 and older, while other airlines sell coupon booklets or yearly $1,600 or $1,900 passes for extensive travel.

Such programs have been overtaken by events. The introduction of radically reduced "MaxSaver" fares, and the continuation of "SuperSaver" fares—as little as $99 to fairly distant points—lessens the worth of these programs considerably. Unless one travels with absurd frequency, it is often cheaper simply to pay individual advance-purchase rates than to commit to the use of a yearly pass.

Clearly, unless the airlines now devise new programs keyed to the levels of, and kept below, their own "Saver" fares, they must—in my view—brace for outcries of protest from the seniors who purchased their fixed-price coupons or year-long passes.

REHEARSALS FOR RETIREMENT

Happier news—of a bright, new use of holiday travel to scout potential sites for retirement. Though the idea is obvious, it's easier said than done.

When middle-aged people go off to test the retirement attractions of Florida or Arizona, of Costa Rica or Cuernavaca, they often return as uncertain as when they left. Simply to look at a retirement area is not to ensure that you obtain reliable, relevant information about its suitability for retirement. For the latter, you need to meet with real estate people and lawyers, with municipal officials and other retirees.

So reasoned Jane Parker, a retired schoolteacher of Modesto, California. And thereupon she formed a tour company called Lifestyle Explorations that performs all the advance preparations for a meaningful research trip. Arriving at the destination, her groups engage in scheduled interviews, appointments, seminars, and briefings on the pros and cons of that area's retirement possibilities. The information is supplied by on-the-spot specialists, who undergo a withering cross-examination by tour participants; the latter stay at the area's best hotels and enjoy gala dinners while doing so.

Lifestyle Explorations' most popular trip is to Costa Rica. Three are scheduled each year, in February, July, and November, and at least two of these consist of two groups at one time. Price for the 12-day journey is $1,520 per person from Miami, with a single supplement of $360.

Twice a year, Lifestyle Explorations takes groups to the Algarve coast of Portugal and Spain's Costa del Luz (on the Mediterranean). The 15-day trip is $2,645 per person, with a $300 single supplement, and can be booked by up to 35 people per departure.

In the offing: tours to Uruguay and Argentina, costing $2,390 out of Miami, $2,560 out of Los Angeles, per person, double occupancy.

For additional information, or to book, contact **Lifestyle Explorations, World Trade Center, Suite 400, Boston, MA 02210 (phone 508/371-4814).**

In contrast to Lifestyle Explorations, which takes you to cheap foreign countries for the purpose of scouting their

Argentina is a popular destination for retirement

Another bright firm takes you to Sunbelt cities of the U.S. for the purpose of visiting multiple "adult communities."

desirability as eventual retirement sites, another travel firm called National Retirement Concepts takes you to Sunbelt cities of the U.S. for the purpose of visiting multiple "adult communities." You go for a week to Arizona, let's say, spend four nights in Phoenix, three nights in Tucson, and visit five retirement communities in the former, three in the latter, meeting community representatives and residents. The price of $675 covers motorcoach transportation within the state, accommodations, and most meals, to which you add air fare from your own home city. Other destinations include: Arkansas (where condos and homes cost as little as $40,000), North and South Carolina, Florida, and southern California. Founder of N.R.C. is a 16-year veteran of the group-travel business, Janet Lampert, and I predict a bright future for her "look before you leap" approach to retirement planning. Contact **National Retirement Concepts, c/o Lampert Tours, 1454 N. Wieland Court, Chicago, IL 60610 (phone 312/951-2866, or toll free 800/888-2312 outside Illinois).**

A "CLUB MED" FOR SENIORS

At $23 to $30 per person per day (based on double occupancy), including two large meals daily, private facilities, and morning-till-night activities—all limited to people over the age of 60, from November until May 31—that, in a nutshell, is the pricing policy of "Florida's Club Meds" for senior citizens: four large hotels in highly desirable cities on the west coast of the Sunshine State.

These are not, of course, real "Club Meds"—that's only my term for them. The owning company is Senior Vacation Hotels of Florida, in business for 27 years—longer than any Club Med in the Western Hemisphere.

But the offerings—and atmosphere (adapted for an older generation)—are almost those of a Club Med: you receive not only your room but also two grand repasts daily, parties, live entertainment and free movies, bus excursions, theme nights, beach trips, and more—for one fixed, and remarkably low, price.

What's the catch? Well, first, there's the required minimum age, and I should point out that most guests appear to be over the age of 65 (but they're an unusually lively lot of over-65ers). More important, you must normally stay for a minimum of one month, usually starting at the beginning of the month. Provided you do, you pay only $700 per person per month (based on double occupancy) in November, December, April, and May, $895 per month in January, $975 per month in February and March. Single supplement runs about $175 per month in all seasons.

The hotels in question are the large Sunset Bay and Courtyard in St. Petersburg, the Regency Tower in Lakeland, and the Riverpark in Bradenton. For a lively four-color brochure on these veritable "Club Meds for Senior Citizens," and for application forms, contact **Senior Vacation Hotels of Florida, 7401 Central Ave., St. Petersburg, FL 33710 (phone 813/345-8123, or toll free 800/247-2203, 800/872-3616 in Florida, 800/843-3713 in Canada).**

The "Auditing Senior," a New Travel Opportunity

Better Than Any Other Study Vacation, But Virtually Unknown and Largely Unutilized

OF ALL THE TRAVEL PRIVILEGES ENJOYED BY senior citizens, one in particular is virtually unknown and largely unutilized, and yet it is the most valuable of them all. I'm talking about the right to "audit" courses free of charge (or for a nominal sum), at dozens of state and city universities, in the course of a vacation spent in the dorms of those institutions. Though the housing element of the activity is available, for practical purposes, only in summer, the free-course privileges are offered throughout the year to seniors 60, 62, or 65 years of age and older (depending on the university), who then make their own housing arrangements for the nonsummer months in motels or B&B's nearby.

The right to "audit" a class should not be confused with the Elderhostel programs sometimes operated at the same institutions; the latter are special, one-week study programs offered exclusively to senior citizens, who attend them as a group. Nor should the participation in university classes on an "auditing" basis be mistakenly compared to the special summer programs for adults or adult alumni ("campus vacations") that some dozen or so universities offer.

The auditing privileges are better. They involve the right to attend *any* class offered by a university—any out of the hundreds and hundreds offered—with the single exception of "labs" and language courses, for which auditing would be inappropriate. Though permission of the instructor and dean is usually required, such permission is rarely denied.

It is true that most senior auditors are asked not to engage in class discussion, as that would reduce the discussion time available to matriculating students—the ones who take tests and examinations, receive grades and course credits. Auditors are listeners, visitors; they pursue learning solely for the sake of learning, take no examinations, and receive no grades or credits—the best of all possible worlds, in my view. But they obviously derive the same rewards of learning, the same technical stimulation, provided they are sufficiently self-disciplined to perform all advance-reading assignments for the class.

How did the virtually expense-free right of senior citizens to audit university courses get started? Not one of the 50 universities I've contacted has been able to supply me with a coherent history of the practice, or point to a single earlier-published article on the subject. In some instances, state legislatures apparently directed their universities to permit the practice and either waive or reduce the fee to seniors. In others, it appears to be a university administrator who initiated the idea, and other schools copied it.

Some universities restrict the right to residents of their own state; others throw open the privilege to residents of any

Auditors are listeners, visitors; they pursue learning solely for the sake of learning, take no examinations, and receive no grades or credits—the best of all possible worlds.

state. Here is a state-by-state analysis of fifty such programs, starting with the universities that accept "auditing seniors" from all over America:

• **Ohio State University:** By command of the legislature, anyone 60 or older from any state can audit classes free of charge ("Program 60"), and there is no restriction on participation in class discussion. Currently, up to 200 seniors do so at any one time, by traveling to Columbus, Ohio, for 5-week courses in summer, 10-week courses ("quarters") all other times; obviously, they can stay for less than 5 or 10 weeks by dropping out before that time. For information, write to the Office of Continuing Education, 152 Mount Hall, 1050 Carmack Rd., Ohio State University, Columbus, OH 43210.

• **University of Illinois:** Persons 65 and older, from anywhere, can audit as many courses as they like, other than labs or physical education classes, for a token fee of $15 per course (which run, in summer, for either four or eight weeks). But auditors have no university privileges (housing, meal plans), and must fend for themselves in that regard. For more information, write to the Office of Administration and Records, Room 10, Henry Administration Building, 506 S. Wright St., Urbana, IL 61801.

• **University of Connecticut:** Seniors 62 and older can audit as many classes as they choose a for one-time fee of $15. No requirements of state residence, and housing is available in summer on a space-available basis for $56 a week in dorms, $67 a week for a 15-meal plan. Phone 203/241-4724 for an application form to attend classes at the campuses in either West Hartford or Storrs, Connecticut.

• **University of Oklahoma:** Seniors 65 and older may audit courses free of charge, but have no access to university housing or meal plans. Write to the Office of Admission and Records, University of Oklahoma, 1000 Asp Ave., Norman, OK 73109.

• **University of North Carolina:** Nonmatriculated students of any age, and from any state, can audit courses for $10 per course, if they have the instructor's permission. Summer courses are presented in two 5½-week sessions; but no assistance is given for housing or meals. Write for details to the University of North Carolina at Chapel Hill, CB#3340, 200 Pettigrew Hall, Chapel Hill, NC 27599-3340.

• **University of Maine:** Residents of the state over 65 years of age can audit courses for free, while nonresidents of the same age pay a reasonable $69 per "credit" for classes of either three, five, six, or eight weeks' duration. Rooms in

SESSION 7 - JULY 2 - JULY 20
Three Week Session

Course Reference Number	Course Code	Section Number	Title	Credit Hrs.	Days	Time	Room
S7010	ANT491	001	Intercultural Understanding	3	M-F	9:15-12:00	355 S
S7020	ART498	001	Directed Study in Studio Art: Photography	3	M-F	8:00-11:00 11:30-2:00 9:15-12:00	CR 119 BW
S7030	BUA202	002	Principles of Accounting II ($15.00 Course Fee)	3	M-F	9:15-12:00	155 S
S7040	ECO420	002	Intermediate Microeconomics	3	M-F	9:15-12:00	220 LH
S7050	EDB204	002	The Teaching Process	3	M-F	9:15-12:00	206 NV
S7060	ENG123	002	Introduction to Fiction	3	M-F	9:15-12:00	204 NV
S7070	ENG472	001	Teaching of English in the Secondary School	3	M-F	9:15-12:00	202 LH
S7080	FRE101	001	Elementary French I	3	M-F	9:15-12:00	219 LH
S7090	GER101	001	Elementary German I	3	M-F	9:15-12:00	204 LH
S7100	LIB500	010	Graduate Seminar in Liberal Studies: German and American Romantics				
S7110	MCB440	001	Introductory Immunology	3	M-F	9:15-12:00	150 HR
S7120	RUS101	001	Elementary Russian I	3	M-F	9:15-12:00	218 LH
S7130	PAA100	001	Foundations of Public Administration	3	M-F	9:15-12:00	19 SN
			Psychology of Adolescence	3	M-F	9:15-12:00	219 LH
				3	M-F	9:15-12:00	108 BD
				3	M-F	9:15-12:00	220 LH

University of Maine summer programs

University of Maine at Orono

university housing are also made available: $80 a week in singles, $69 per person per week in doubles, 21 meals a week for $75. For more information, write to the University of Maine, 122 Chadbourn Hall, Orono, ME 04469.

• **University of Wisconsin:** Persons 62 and older, from any state, may audit courses free of charge, both in summer and all other seasons. To encourage them to do so, various "private" (i.e., commercially operated) residence halls, like The Towers (502 N. Frances St., Madison, WI 53703), offer them attractive rates for rooms and meals in summer. Write to Summer Sessions and Inter-College Programs, University of Wisconsin, 905 University Ave., Madison, WI 53715.

• **UCLA:** Permits visitors from anywhere to audit any number of courses (subject only to the instructors' permission) for a one-time total fee of $175; exempted from that privilege are language courses and science labs. On-campus housing is available for six weeks in summer for a total

charge of $750, including 21 full meals a week. Phone 213/825-8355 to be placed on a mailing list for next summer's catalog.

• **Boston University:** Under the university's "Evergreen" program, senior citizens (60 and older) from anywhere can audit courses for $10 per course, throughout the year. Currently, the university receives from 200 to 300 senior auditors per semester, and does make some university housing available to them in summer. Write to the Evergreen Program, Boston University, 808 Commonwealth Ave., Boston, MA 02215.

• **University of San Diego:** Auditors of any age are admitted from any state, and pay half the normal tuition; since the average course costs $960, that works out to $480, for courses lasting 12 weeks in fall and spring, 3 and 6 weeks in summer. University housing is sometimes available for $100 to $160 per person per week, double or single. For details, write to the Office of Admissions, San Diego State University, San Diego, CA 92182.

• **University of Kansas**: Persons 62 and over can audit as many courses as they wish, for free; but auditors aren't entitled to housing or meal plans. Write to Office of Student Relations, 122 Strong Hall, Lawrence, KS 66045.

• **University of Texas**: Persons 65 and older, from any state, may audit courses—as many as they like—free of charge; but receive no concession in price on taking courses for credit. They pay a small "library fee" for use of the library, but receive no housing or meal plans. Write to Office of the Registrar, Registrar's Mailroom, Austin, TX 78712, enclosing $1 for handling and mailing of the brochure and course schedule.

• **University of Wyoming**: Persons 65 and older can take classes (even for credit) entirely free. And on-campus single rooms are available to them in summer at $429 for eight weeks. Write to Division of Admissions, University of Wyoming, Box 3435, Laramie, WY 82071.

• **University of New Mexico**: Seniors 65 and older can take classes (auditing or for credit) entirely for free. While they have library privileges, they have no on-campus housing or meal plans. Write to The Admissions Office, University of New Mexico, Albuquerque, NM 87131.

• **University of Arkansas**: Persons 60 and over can either audit or takes courses for credit, free, and are eligible for university housing and meals if they take a full-course load. A single room with all three meals daily is $1487.50 per semester; a single room without meals is $15.85 a day in summer. Phone 501/575-5555, requesting an adviser assigned by the Returning Students Association. No requirement of state residence.

• **University of North Dakota**: Anyone of any age, from any state, can audit courses for a fee of $9 per credit (the average course carries two to four credits). Although housing and meals plans aren't available to auditors, meals can be purchased by anyone at university dining halls. Write to Enrollment Services, Box 8135, University Station, Grand Forks, ND 58202.

• **Eastern Kentucky University**: Senior citizens from any state, 60 and over, may audit any course for free, and enjoy university housing ($834 per semester for a single room) and meal plans ($860 per semester for 20 meals a week), along with library privileges. Write to Admissions Office, 203 Jones Building, Richmond, KY 40475.

• **University of Alaska**: Persons 60 and older can take or audit any course, free of charge. They have library privileges, and—if they are enrolled for as many as 12 credit hours—housing privileges (whose costs vary in different residence halls) and meal plans (three meals daily for an entire semester, $775). "Our student body is very impressed by persons in their mature age who wish to continue their education," says admissions officer Pamela Guzzy. Write to Admissions Office, 102 Signers Hall, University of Alaska, Fairbanks, AK 99775.

• **University of Nevada**: Fall and spring semesters only, persons from any state, 62 and older, can audit courses free of charge; during summer sessions, oddly enough, they pay 50% (about $44 per credit) of the normal tuition charge. University housing ($2280 per year, no meals) is available to seniors pursuing a minimum of ten credits. Write to Office of Admissions Records, University of Nevada, Reno, NV 89557.

• **University of Massachusetts**: By state law, seniors 60 and over, from any state, can take up to six credits per semester (or summer session) free of charge, and are entitled to rooms in dorms for $1113 per semester, plus $50 registration fee. And they can sign on for 19 meals per week for the highly reasonable charge of only $834 per semester. Write to Admissions Office, University of Massachusetts, Amherst, MA 01003.

• **University of Tennessee**: Since the passage of a law in 1977, auditing of courses is free to seniors 60 and over. They receive library privileges, too, but no housing or meal plans. Write to Evening School Offices (which handle the program for the entire university), 451 Communications Building, University of Tennessee, Knoxville, TN 37996-0341.

• **University of Nebraska**: Out-of-state residents, 62 and over, pay half the normal $138-per-credit out-of-state charge to audit classes; residents of that age pay half the normal $51-per-credit residents' charge. But no assistance is given with housing or meal plans. Write to Student Records Office, 107 Administration Building, University of Nebraska, Lincoln, NS 68588-0416.

• **University of Mississippi**: "Mature citizens" from any state, 65 and older, can enroll for up to four credit hours per semester absolutely free, and can apply for university residence halls and meal plans, subject to availability. One such applicant, in his late 70s, who feared his hearing wasn't good enough to take classes, was advised to tape the lectures as a method of filling in what he failed to catch. The approach

Though permission of the instructor is usually required, it is rarely denied.

Auditing seniors at leisure

worked fine. Write to Office of Academic Matters, University of Mississippi, University, MS 38677.

• **Idaho State University:** Anyone from any state, 60 and older, may audit by paying a flat fee of $20, plus $5 per credit—the average course being for three credits (i.e., three hours a week for one semester). Seniors are also eligible for university housing and meals: $2400 to $2600 for a single room throughout the year, all meals included. Write to Enrollment Management Services, Box 8054, Idaho State University, Pocatello, ID 83209.

• **University of Vermont:** Holders of the "Green Mountain Pass" (available from any town clerk in Vermont), who are 63 or older, receive free tuition for as many classes as they choose, and are also eligible for on-campus housing ($1493 per semester) and meals ($808 per semester). "Younger students love the benefit of having elderly people in the class," says the school's registrar. Write to Continuing Education, 322 South Prospect, University of Vermont, Burlington, VT 05405.

• **University of Utah:** Persons 62 and older, but this time

residents of the state only, can audit as many classes as they wish for a flat $10 fee per quarter (business management classes, art classes and labs excepted). They also use the library and computer center for free, the gymnasium and all other recreational facilities for an activities fee of $2.50 per quarter, and can buy books of meal tickets for $5 a meal. But housing assistance isn't provided. Write to the Center for Adult Transitions, University of Utah, 1195 Annex, Salt Lake City, UT 84112.

• **University of Washington:** Under the state's "Access Program," state residents only, 60 and over, can audit for free, in effect, by simply paying a one-time, $5 registration fee. No housing or meal plans, however. According to university officials, history and English are the most popular courses for seniors, and professors welcome their presence in history courses particularly, as many of them lived through the events studied. Write to Student Service, University of Washington Extension, 5001 25th Avenue N.E., Seattle, WA 98195.

• **University of Rhode Island:** State residents only, 60 and older, are entitled to a waiver of all tuition charges other than a $10 registration and $10 activities fee, but receive no housing or meal plans. Write to the College of Continuing Education, University of Rhode Island, 199 Promenade Street, Providence, RI 02908.

• **University of Georgia**: Except at the law and medical schools, state residents 62 years of age and older can take up to three five-hour classes per semester for free. They can also secure university housing for only $500 per quarter. Write to Office of Admissions, 114 Academic Building, University of Georgia, Athens, GA 30602.

• **State University of New York**: At every one of the many campuses of this system, state residents 55 and older can audit classes (other than language or lab courses) free of charge, but only during the standard school year, and not in summer. Library privileges are also granted, but not housing or meal plans. Write to the branch you desire to attend—as, for instance: Office of General Studies, University Library Basement #66, State U. at Albany, 1400 Washington Avenue, Albany, NY 12222.

• **University of South Carolina**: State residents age 60 and up can attend classes free of charge, and rent a double room in university residences for the entire year, for $2700 per person, including three meals a day. Write to Adult Student Services, 900 Assembly Street, University of South Carolina, Columbia, SC 29208.

• **University of Montana**: State residents 62 and older pay $15 for registration, and $25 per credit for most courses. Single rooms cost them only $96 per quarter, all three meals daily $538 per quarter. Write to Financial Aid Office, University of Montana, Missoula, MT 59812.

• **University of New Hampshire**: Residents of the state, 65 and older, can take up to two courses at a time for free, by paying a single $15 registration fee. Library privileges, yes; housing or meal plans, no. Write to Department of Continuing Education, 6 Garrison Avenue, University of New Hampshire, Durham, NH 03824.

• **University of Hawaii**: In the normal school year only, residents 60 and older can take courses free of charge. They receive library privileges as well, but aren't eligible for housing or meal plans. In summer, strangely enough, they receive only a $40 discount off the total normal charge for tuition. Write to Special Programs, Bachman Annex 10, 1630 Bachman Place, Honolulu, HA 96822.

• **University of Delaware**: State residents, 60 and older, can take as many classes as they choose, for free. Non-residents, joining the "Academy of Lifelong Learning" for an $80-a-year charge, can audit one course, attend a separate lecture series, and participate in various social activities. Housing ($329 for five weeks) and meal plans ($395 for five weeks, with three meals daily) are available only during a summer session of five and seven weeks' duration.

• **University of Minnesota**: State residents only, 62 or older, can audit classes for free at all state campuses throughout the year; they join each class on a space-available basis after the first day of instruction. University housing? It's sometimes available, mainly in summer. Write to Student Relations, University of Minnesota, 150 Williamson Hall, 231 Pillsbury Dr. SE, Minneapolis, MN 55455.

• **University of Virginia**: State residents only, 60 and up, can audit up to three courses for free during summer sessions. Single rooms are also made available to them, for $54 a week. For more information write to the Summer Session, 209 Garret Hall, University of Virginia, Charlottesville, VA 22901.

• **University of Maryland**: Under the "Golden I.D." program, seniors 60 and up, but state residents only, can audit up to three courses at a time for free, at any time. While auditors aren't eligible for housing or meal plans, they do have library privileges. Write to Undergraduate Admissions, University of Maryland, Mitchell Building, College Park, MD 20742.

• **University of Colorado** (at Boulder): At the Boulder campus only, state residents aged 55 and older can audit for free, but aren't eligible for campus housing or meal plans. The registrar with whom I spoke recalls overhearing an effort of an 18-year-old freshman to persuade a 70-year-old auditor not to drop a class they were attending together. Phone 303/492-8484.

Several state universities offer no such privileges or programs to senior citizens. They are: University of Iowa, State University of Pennsylvania, University of West Virginia, University of Alabama, University of Missouri, University of Arizona, and Indiana University (although the last institution, according to Dr. Blake of the admissions office, hopes to offer such a program in the future). About three other universities—University of Michigan, University of Louisiana, and South Dakota State University—information has proved almost impossible to obtain. Let's hope all the holdouts adopt the course of the vast majority.

As for the private universities, I phoned a dozen, and found that none attempted to encourage auditing by senior citizens, with the faint exception of Columbia University in New York City, which drops the charge per course to $150 for persons 62 or older belonging to the University's "Lifelong Learners Program." Again, let's hope for improved, future enlightenment on the part of those richer schools.

Sometimes it seems, from the evidence all about us, that seniors are relegated for their leisure activities to cheap bus tours taking them to Atlantic City or Las Vegas, where they stand dumbly all day in front of slot machines. Fortunately, the opportunities are broader and better, if only information comes their way. Life-enhancing study privileges await them at enlightened U.S. universities, if they will but travel there for an adventure of the mind.

XV

NEW SOURCES OF TRAVEL INFORMATION

The Emergence of "Alternative" Travel Magazines

Meet *Transitions Abroad, International Travel News,* and *Great Expeditions*

THE CURRENT CONDITION OF THE STANDARD consumer travel magazine in America is a national disgrace, a public outrage.

Their theme is "Lifestyles of the Rich and Famous." They are not written for real people planning real vacations, but for some mythical jet-setter possessing endless resources and time.

When I read their featured articles—"Where Princess Di Shops," "Where Madonna Stays"—I say aloud: "Who cares?" We—by which I mean the average travel magazine readers—are not going to stop at these shrines to conspicuous consumption, but at the kind of affordable establishment that would never conceivably grace the pages of *Condé Nast Traveler* or *Travel & Leisure*

While some of the travel magazines give an occasional fleeting glance to subjects of "practical travel," their attention on these occasions is brief and almost furtive, as if it were unnatural to consider information of actual utility. Obviously, their editors would prefer to experience the 71 rooms of Caroline Hunt's $450-a-night Hana Maui Hotel in Hawaii, or that secluded Florentine villa where Gucci, Pucci, and Agnelli dine for $200 a meal.

So where does the traveling consumer go for useful, comprehensive magazine treatment of travel? To the "alternative" travel magazines of North America, all virtually unknown and rarely found on newsstands, of which there are three to recommend:

TRANSITIONS ABROAD

Transitions Abroad is the bimonthly, 62-page, black-and-white magazine of Prof. Clayton A. Hubbs of Hampshire College in Amherst, Massachusetts (where, in addition to teaching comparative literature, he spends much time advising students on overseas study opportunities). *Transitions*, as it is popularly known, deals with learning vacations. It was originally intended, in 1977, for students or teachers planning long stays abroad, and much of the magazine still deals with formal study opportunities, classroom style, or with trips of three months and more.

But gradually Hubbs has been expanding his coverage and shortening the duration of time to which the rest of the magazine has relevance. A major segment of readers are now in their early 40s—definitely not students—and much of the publication teaches them do-it-yourself methods for trips of under a month that are totally self-planned, fiercely independent, and designed to experience the current-day realities, politics, and cultures of foreign countries. Thus a recent issue carried such articles as "Bangkok Survival Kit: What You Need to Live in Thailand's Metropolitan Capital," "Tourism and Ecology," "Cutting Costs on Travel to Asia," and "Independent Travel in Indonesia," among others.

Other bimonthly issues deal each year with Europe and the USSR (March), the Mediterranean basin (May/June), the

---

The standard travel magazines? Their theme is "Lifestyles of the Rich and Famous."

Americas and Africa (November/December). A directory issue in July contains broad listings of travel programs, facilities, and resources.

A single cavil: Provocative as they are, the articles in *Transitions* are sometimes lacking in the specifics needed by would-be travelers. A recent report on inexpensive living in Bali contained not a single specific address to contact or patronize.

But those are major flaws in a constantly improving magazine, whose subscription costs $18 for one year, $34 for two

---

While some of the standard publications pay a fleeting glance at subjects of "practical travel," their attention on those occasions is almost furtive, as if it were unnatural.

years, and $50 for three years. Contact **Transitions Abroad, 18 Hulst Rd. (P.O. Box 344), Amherst, MA 01004-9970 (phone 413/256-0373)**.

INTERNATIONAL TRAVEL NEWS

International Travel News, published out of Sacramento, California, since 1976, is this time a monthly with a format even plainer than that of *Transitions*: black-and-white cover and 80 or so newsprint pages.

But there all resemblance ends. While *Transitions* readers are mainly in their 40s or younger, 80% of *I.T.N.*'s audience is over the age of 52. And while *Transitions* readers would never dream of going on an organized tour, most of *I.T.N.*'s travelers are inveterate users of "packages," which they then describe on the pages of *International Travel News* in copious detail.

In fact, most of *International Travel News* is reader-written, and consists of no-holds-barred, first-person accounts of the tours and offerings of Messrs. Gateway/Globus, American Express, Caravan, and the like. The emphasis is always on value for money spent. While *I.T.N.*'s reader-journalists are perhaps a bit more idealistic and adventurous than the average traveler, what they are really interested in is getting a fair shake, and woe to the tour company that consistently disappoints them.

The other half of *International Travel News* consists of regular monthly features reviewing many scores of new developments and travel products—some of them tedious and mundane, others genuinely helpful—in dozen different areas headed: "Airlines" (interesting new fares), "Exchange Rates," "Lodgings" (special deals at hotels), "Tours," "Mildly Adventurous Travel" (for people over 50), "All Aboard" (train travel), "Focus on Archeology," "Cruises," "Secret Corners" (new destinations). Most of the compilations are prepared by voluntary, part-time correspondents, who reportedly receive about 50¢ per column inch for their labors, and obviously don't depend on it for a living. They pepper their columns with outspoken views and brutal travel facts: outbreaks of hepatitis in certain heavily visited destinations, massive currency fluctuations hindering travel to others, stern warnings to avoid travel to particular nations. Advertiser-driven they're not.

Though *International Travel News* has less of an emphasis on people-to-people contacts than I would like, and seems unconcerned with the new forms of "life enhancement" travel that have captivated so many, it is an excellent monthly source for the mainstream traveler, especially those interested in "packages" and organized tours. A free sample copy is available on request, and one-year subscriptions are priced at $15, two-year ones at $29. Newsstands don't see this magazine. Contact **International Travel News, 2120 28th St., Sacramento, CA 95818 (phone 916/457-3643)**.

GREAT EXPEDITIONS

Great Expeditions is a quarterly, English-language Canadian magazine that is primarily devoted to exploring unusual travel destinations off-the-beaten-track; a recent issue advocates skiing at a winter resort in northeastern China, traveling to the Orinoco Delta of Venezuela or the tropical rain forest of Costa Rica's Osa Peninsula, camping in Zimbabwe. While the locales are adventurous choices, the modes of visiting them aren't, and rarely include the acrobatic feats—mountaineering, white-water rafting—of traditional "adventure travel."

"Our type of adventure involves getting on a rickety, old, Third World bus," says *Great Expeditions* publisher Craig Henderson, "one filled with chickens and goats, and not knowing where you're going to end up."

Great Expeditions was first published in 1978 by a travel-loving Canadian geologist who had experienced difficulties in finding trip companions to join him in horseback-riding through the "outback" of the Mexican desert or canoeing in the Arctic. An early inducement to subscribe, still offered today, were unlimited free classified ads that readers may place for adventuresome travel companions or other travel-related purposes.

Under its new publisher, Craig Henderson, *Great Expeditions* has supplemented its continuing emphasis on out-of-the-way destinations with three supplementary themes: cultural encounters, socially responsible tourism, and budget-priced travel. That broadened coverage, and a handsome, four-color cover (the rest is black-and-white), have greatly increased circulation, especially from U.S. travelers, who now make up fully half of all the magazine's subscribers. It may go to six-times-a-year frequency in the coming months.

The 44-page *Great Expeditions* is found on a few scattered newsstands in New York and the Pacific Northwest, but is best obtained by taking out a five-issue subscription for $18, or a 10-issue plan for $32. Contact **Great Expeditions, P.O. Box 8000-411, Sumas, WA 98295-8000 (phone, 604/852-6170 in British Columbia)**.

Meanwhile, why haven't the mainstream travel magazines begun to emulate the increasingly popular approaches of the "alternative" ones? Travel is changing. A recent Lou Harris survey finds that 40% of all international travelers now claim that they travel for "life enhancement" reasons: to improve their minds, gain new perspectives, and meet new people. With scarcely a reference to these strongly emerging trends, the glossy slicks keep prancing as they always have, ecstatic over the latest three-star restaurant, breathless about a five-star hotel, concerned with little else.

As if the reason we travel is to eat in restaurants and stay in hotels.

Five Directories That Can Change Your Travel Life

Their Information Is Often Odd and Unusual, Little Known, Riveting— and Valuable

INFORMATION CAN OFTEN BE THE KEY TO AN outstanding vacation or a properly priced one. Stumbling on a travel article, overhearing a travel remark, or—better yet—discovering a directory of unusual travel opportunities can frequently lead to a memorable or less expensive trip.

Here are five little-known directories dealing with travel problems or opportunities that I would describe as follows:

SCENIC BYWAYS

The secondary roads of America—the rural two-laners passing through small towns and villages, along picturesque farms and past mills and shops—have been dealt a mighty blow in recent years by the great Interstates, which have caused them to lose the bulk of their traffic. And yet, diminished as they are, some of them struggle valiantly to attract tourism with their local cafés and yard sales, their small museums and roadside vegetable stands, their classic American scenery. Many a motorist bored by the sameness of the Interstates ("Burger King, 10 miles") has been sent into raptures by the occasional discovery of a stretch of rural road lined with tasteful, country-like commerce and sights.

But how do you find those desirable stretches? Although one or two guidebooks have compiled the outstanding itineraries through national forests and other specialized locations (try *National Forest Scenic Byways* by Beverly Magley, published by Falcon Press of Billings, Montana, 1990), the more general lists are found in free brochure-directories issued by state tourist offices. Thanks to the efforts of 32 national tourism organizations that make up the **Scenic Byways Coalition, 1331 Pennsylvania Ave. NW, Suite 726, Washington, DC 20004 (phone 202/662-7420)**, some 23 states now have "scenic byways" programs and issue free literature identified by the precise term "scenic byways." They are: Alaska, California, Colorado, Iowa, Maryland, Michigan, Minnesota, Nevada, New Hampshire, New Mexico, New York, North Carolina, Ohio, Oregon, Pennsylvania, South Carolina, Tennessee, Utah, Vermont, Virginia, West Virginia, Wisconsin, and Wyoming.

Another group of states, mainly in the West, have "backcountry byways" programs and literature dealing with even more primitive roads—sometimes unpaved—in the undeveloped public lands of the federal Bureau of Land Management (not to be confused with the national parks).

For directories of the scenic byways, contact the state tourist offices (in the capital cities) of the states listed above. For directories of the backcountry byways, contact the nearest office of the Bureau of Land Management. Thus equipped, you'll escape the monotony of the great Interstates, and enjoy that "sense of place" that can only be provided by the so-called secondary roads.

One such publication deals with secondary roads— the kind that don't appear in million-copy atlases.

THE TRAVELING INTERN

In the offices of U.S. senators and representatives, in museums across the country, in scientific laboratories, political think-tanks, theaters, newspapers, radio and TV stations, and in business trade associations, many thousands of college-age people work as "interns" for short periods of the year, either for free or at best for a small, subsistence stipend. "Internship" is perhaps the most dynamic travel experience available to anyone, uprooting them from accustomed settings in favor of the nation's most glamorous locales. And because the internships are largely without pay, they are not difficult—or overly difficult—to get.

Remarkably, the same opportunities are now increasingly available to adults of all ages, even to those retired, and for periods of as little as three weeks, which makes the "internship" into a broad new form of vacation activity. If you consult the 350-page *National Directory of Internships*, sold for $24 by the **National Society for Internships and Experiential Education, 3509 Haworth Dr., Raleigh, NC 27609 (phone 919/787-3263)**, you will find that a small percentage of the internships listed, but a goodly number, are now available not only to "undergraduate and graduate students" but also to "persons with career work experience, mid-career and retired persons." And they are available for periods considerably shorter than the semester once required.

Interns at Saint Peter's College

Thus Congresswoman Pat Schroeder takes oldsters as interns, as do Congressman John Spratt, Congressman William Gray, Congressman Bryan Dorgan, the Democratic National Committee, and politicos of every other ilk. People of all ages can currently "intern" for a short period with *Common Cause* magazine, the National Audubon Society, the National Trust for Historic Preservation, the Joffrey Ballet of New York City, the Denver Art Museum, and numerous other institutions of distinction and acclaim. Though some may disagree, I can't conceive of a more rewarding vacation experience than to travel to a major city and there associate with the highly motivated people who staff our nation's most important offices of science, government, public affairs, theater, communications, the environment, and international relations. Simply secure a copy of the directory listed above.

TOURS OF EASTERN EUROPE

The use of a computer to compare the costs of multiple tour packages to the same destination continues to reveal the most puzzling variances. A computer-using firm called Tourscan discovered wide differences in price among hundreds of programs to the very same hotels in the Caribbean, Hawaii, and Mexico. A firm called **D. H. Doelker, Inc.,** headed by travel agent Deborah Doelker, found similar anomalies among African safaris.

The very same Mrs. Doelker—whose office is at **301 E. 63rd St., New York, NY 10021 (phone 212/888-7596, or toll free 800/882-5537)**—has now made a computer analysis of 165 tour programs to Eastern Europe and the Soviet Union, with the same surprising results: prices per night (including air fare) that range all the way from $93.33 at the low end (Cosmos Tours, 20 nights to Russia, Eastern Europe, and Scandinavia) to $1,331 at the peak (Abercrombie & Kent, 5 nights aboard the *Anna Karenina*, a luxurious Soviet train), with the great majority falling in the $200-per-night range, from $202 at the low end to $299 at the peak. On a 20-night tour, that $90-per-night difference can amount to $1,800 per person.

Quite obviously, some of the differences are explained by the short duration of some tours, which amortizes the round-trip fare among fewer days, and makes their per-night price appear higher. Some tours use better hotels or include more features than others, which again explains some of the differences in rate.

But experienced people in this field will tell you that most trips to Eastern Europe, and especially to the Soviet Union, are remarkably similar in hotel levels and features. The difference in price, therefore, is often because of differing markup policies by the tour operators. To learn how your own tour may differ from others on the market, write for a free copy of Mrs. Doelker's four-page, computer-printed directory.

Prague, Czechoslovakia

UNBIASED HOTEL DESCRIPTIONS

A large percentage of the nation's travel agencies subscribe to a thick, looseleaf directory designed for travel professionals and known as the "Star Service"; its listings will startle you. In small type, packed to each page, it hurls forth lengthy, well-written critiques of the world's leading hotels—some 10,000 of them—and of all the world's cruise ships, in terms so brutally frank as to make the average travel guidebook seem bland by comparison.

Of one well-known Parisian hotel, Star Service reports that "once enviable standards of comfort and decor have been compromised by sloppy maintenance and poor taste (such as imitation leopard skin upholstery), and [the] physical structure experiences occasional hot water shortages and plumbing problems. To top it off, an extremely limited staff is aloof." Of a famous Times Square hotel in New York: "Discriminating individuals should not expect much and would do well to look elsewhere." Of a widely marketed

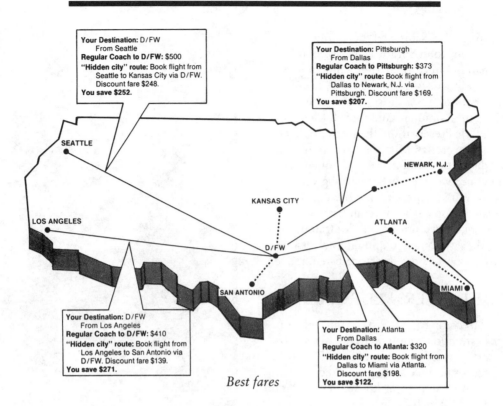

Your Destination: D/FW
From Seattle
Regular Coach to D/FW: $500
"Hidden city" route: Book flight from Seattle to Kansas City via D/FW. Discount fare $248.
You save $252.

Your Destination: Pittsburgh
From Dallas
Regular Coach to Pittsburgh: $373
"Hidden city" route: Book flight from Dallas to Newark, N.J. via Pittsburgh. Discount fare $169.
You save $207.

Your Destination: D/FW
From Los Angeles
Regular Coach to D/FW: $410
"Hidden city" route: Book flight from Los Angeles to San Antonio via D/FW. Discount fare $139.
You save $271.

Your Destination: Atlanta
From Dallas
Regular Coach to Atlanta: $320
"Hidden city" route: Book flight from Dallas to Miami via Atlanta. Discount fare $198.
You save $122.

Best fares

cruise ship: "Despite recent improvements, [the] ship shows her age, and the musty smell of seawater is prominent, especially in the inside cabins."

Appraisals in the looseleaf directory, the size of a New York telephone book, are periodically updated by substitute pages.

On the eve of any holiday trip or cruise, you owe it to yourself to consult the latest Star Service write-up of the hotels or ships you are about to use. You can do that by subscribing (phone 215/630-1804), but that's expensive ($210 a year). A better course is to visit your local travel agency and politely ask to peruse their copy; 6,000 U.S. travel agents have it on their shelves.

BEST FARES

So fluid and chaotic are domestic air fares that some Americans despair of finding the lowest rates for their trips through the U.S.A. Help has arrived in the form of a monthly directory called *Best Fares* that lists the lowest rates from 33 major U.S. cities to dozens of other domestic locations.

To those of us who previously felt, for instance, that the Pan Am and Trump "shuttle" fare of $119 for the one-way flight between New York and Boston, or between New York and Washington, D.C., was the cheapest possible price for the trip, *Best Fares* lists several other airlines that periodically make the trip for as little as $67, and several cheaper fares (as little as $79) that are occasionally available even on the Pan Am and Trump shuttles. The same variety of pricing is revealed for scores of other prominent city-pairs.

Now the very same information is available on the airline computer systems used by travel agents, who can just as easily determine the cheapest fare. But the possession of *Best Fares* can enable traveling consumers to make better use of their travel agents—for example, by reminding those consumers to contact their travel agents a specified number of days in advance in order to secure an advantageous fare. Or to request a ticket from their travel agents for certain days of the week, when cheap fares are available.

Subscriptions, though, are costly: $78 a year. If you're interested, write to **Best Fares, 1506 W. Pioneer Pkwy., Suite 121, Arlington, TX 76013 (phone 817/261-6114).**

Another seeks out faulty plumbing and other defects of well-known hotels.

APPENDIX

24 Outstanding
Discount Travel Agencies

THOUGH SOME CALL THEM "bucket shops," they are simply discounters of air fares performing a function no less proper or respectable than the activities of discount pharmacies, discount record stores, discount clothing shops.

Primarily, they sell airfares to international destinations at discounts of as much as 30% and 40%. Because these tickets come from prestigious airlines, which make them available through selected retail outlets, the bucket shops have to possess some "standing"—a relationship with an international airline—to remain in business. And I, for one, have not yet heard of a single instance among them of blatant skullduggery, financial insolvency, or irresponsibility (stranding of passengers).

In the main text of this book, I've discussed the buckets at length, and provided the names of half a dozen. Here, now, is a more comprehensive listing of 24, out of the 100 or so that presently operate in U.S. cities.

EAST COAST

Access International, Inc.
250 West 57th Street
New York, NY 10107
(phone 212/333-7280)
Claims to be the nation's largest bucket shop, but has recently scaled down its operations to a more limited level, purportedly to provide better service. Offers seats from 20 U.S. cities to 32 European cities, at rates as low as $340 round-trip between New York and London, $440 to Paris, $520 to Rome. "We advertise a genuine price," says owner Christopher Lascoutx, "and include

all surcharges in our prices. We assume the public is intelligent. We issue tickets the day after we receive payment, and Federal Express the tickets at our own expense."

Apex World Travel, Inc.
46–46 Vernon Boulevard
Long Island City, NY 11101
(phone 718/784-1111, or toll free 800/ 666-0025 weekdays only)
Wide range of sharply discounted air fares to Asia: Jakarta, Bangkok, Singapore, Taipei, Tokyo, and Hong Kong. Also, the South Pacific (Guam, Australia) and Europe.

Euram Tours
1522 K Street NW
Washington, DC 20005
(phone 202/789-2255, or toll free 800/ 848-6789)
Discount fares to Europe (both East and West) and South America, year round. "We can waive the advance-purchase requirement on excursion fares and still bring you a price lower than the excursion rate." For people concerned about the nonrefundable nature of most discount fares, they provide cancellation insurance at a nominal rate. Sample fares: $199 to London, one way from New York only; $550 round-trip from Washington, D.C., to Belgrade.

Getaway Travel, Inc.
1105 Ponce de Leon Boulevard
Coral Gables, FL 33134
(phone 305/446-7855, or toll free 800/ 683-4447)
Discounts on fares primarily to Europe, but often to South America and the Orient as well. "We accommodate people planning late."

GO Voyages, Inc.
404 Park Avenue South
New York, NY 10016
(phone 212/481-7500, or toll free 800/ 366-1456)
Another large French company, it is the deadly adversary of Nouvelles Frontières (below), and claims to cut the one-way New York–Paris fare to as little as $235. On several other routings, it offers competitive rates to additional European cities from New York and Los Angeles, occasionally from Baltimore, Chicago, and Miami as well.

Japan Budget Travel
9 East 38th Street, Room 203
New York, NY 10016
(phone 212/686-8855)
Though nearly every employee is Japanese, with less-than-fluent abilities in English, it nevertheless pays to endure the language difficulties—their values are that good. Is primarily engaged in selling air fares to Japan at heavily discounted levels, but also has packages for sale, to both Japan and Europe. Sells Northwest and Japan Air Lines tickets to Japan at the last minute; maintains office hours Monday through Friday only, from 9:30 A.M. to 5:30 P.M.

Maharajah Travels
393 Fifth Avenue
New York, NY 10016
(phone 212/213-2020, or toll free 800/ 223-6862 outside New York State)
Another prominent New York discounter (40,000 passengers in 1990), with a toll-free "800" number for out-of-state clients. Primarily to Europe, but also to Central and South America, Africa, India, Singapore, Tokyo, and "Around the World" (via 150

itineraries on the last quest, costing as little as $1,400). It will also handle hotel reservations.

Nouvelles Frontières
12 East 33rd Street
New York, NY 10016
(phone 212/779-0600, or toll free 800/ 366-6387)
The New York branch of Europe's largest discounter, the French-owned firm cuts prices to all of Europe and Africa, but is particularly effective for bargain-basement rates to Paris. Example: Peak summer-season price of $439, Wednesday departures only, round-trip from New York. All telephone reservationists are bilingual in French.

Pan Express Travel, Inc.
25 West 39th Street, Suite 705
New York, NY 10018
(phone 212/719-9292)
Has remarkable discounted air fares to Africa, islands of the Caribbean, and South America, in addition to the standard European destinations. In fact, claims to be the only East Coast discounter able to get severely discounted rates to Africa. Example: $1,059 round-trip between New York and Nairobi. Also offers "around-the-world specials" for as little as $1,399, without penalties for en route changes of itineraries or dates.

Sun International Travel
6000 Dawson Boulevard
Norcross, GA 30093
(phone 404/446-3111, or toll free 800/ 521-4161)
Sells Japan Air Lines tickets at "wholesale rates"; in phoning, ask for "wholesale division." Best current bargain: round-trip flight between Atlanta and Tokyo for $935.

Transpacific Delight, Inc.
97 Bowery
New York, NY 10002
(phone 212/925-8080)
A long-established specialist to Tokyo, Hong Kong, and Bangkok. It will send you there for an amazing $799 (and less) round trip from the East Coast, provided you agree to go on an indirect route involving stops. "Those who know Asia, know us" is the slogan of this firm that claims to be the oldest East Coast discounter to the Far East.

The Vacation Outlet
(in Filene's basement)
Washington Street
Boston, MA 02108
(phone 617/267-8100)
Sells tours and packages—rarely air fares alone—at sharply discounted prices, primarily to resort destinations. Open Monday through Friday from 9 A.M. to 6 P.M., on Saturday from 10 A.M. to 3 P.M., and claims to be the nation's only "retail travel store." Operates in a bustling, invigorating atmosphere as a result of its location in one of the busiest retail department store basements. Many packages sold are of the last-minute variety, but departures are available several weeks ahead.

MIDWEST

Japan Budget Travel (Illinois)
104 South Michigan Avenue, Suite 700
Chicago, IL 60603
(phone 312/236-9797, or toll free 800/ 843-0273)
Sells air tickets only, at substantial discounts, from the Midwest to the Far East. And has been doing so, reliably, for eight years. Offices also in Houston (phone toll free 800/445-5265) and Atlanta (phone toll free 800/782-7718).

McSon Travel, Inc.
36 South State Street
Chicago, IL 60603
(phone 312/346-6272 or toll free 800/ 622-1421)
Discounted air fares (reduced by 15% to 35%) to Europe, the South Pacific, and the Far East, from a firm in business for 10 years now.

Ryan's Regent Travel
7218 West Touhy Avenue
Chicago, IL 60648
(phone 312/774-8770)
Discounted air fares to Ireland, their main interest. Largest Irish specialist in the Midwest.

SOUTHWEST

Euro-Asia, Inc.
4203 East Indian School Road, Suite 210

Phoenix, AZ 85018
(phone 602/955-2742)
Proud to be called a "discount travel agency." Its international tickets are both transatlantic and transpacific, at considerable reductions; and it also discounts tours and hotels in Asia.

WEST COAST

Airkit
6043 Hollywood Boulevard
Los Angeles, CA 90028
(phone 213/482-8778)
Los Angeles branch of the recently opened New York discounter of the same name (see above, under "East Coast"). Europe only.

All Unique Travel
1030 Georgia Street
Vallejo, CA 94590
(phone 707/648-0237)
Needs three weeks' advance notice to procure you a good discount on tickets to Mexico, Hawaii, Europe, and the Middle East. Has especially good rates to Madrid. Its motto: "Why spend it here when you can spend it there?"

Community Travel Service
5299 College Avenue
Oakland, CA 94618
(phone 415/653-0990)
Particularly good discounts on air fares to the Orient, but discounts to anywhere. Best bargain for 1991: West Coast–Bangkok for $746 round-trip.

Cost Less Travel, Inc.
674 Broadway, Suite 201
San Francisco, CA 94133
(phone 415/397-6868)
Discounts of 25% to 30% on most international air fares, specializing in the Orient. Mr. Wong is the man in charge, a careful, punctilious gentleman.

Express Discount Travel
5945 Mission Gorge Road
San Diego, CA 92120
(phone 619/283-6324)
The heavyweight of the West Coast shops. Air-fare discounts of up to 50%; discounts of 20% to 30% on tour programs. Handles South America, Europe, and Asia, but from West Coast cities only.

Express Fun Travel, Inc.
1169 Market Street, Room 809
San Francisco, CA 94102
(phone 415/864-8005)
Sells discount tickets to the Orient, often at reductions of 30%.

Sunline Express Holidays
607 Market Street
San Francisco, CA 94105

(phone 415/541-7800, or toll free 800/877-2111 seven days a week)
"We're the lowest on the West Coast," they claim—to Europe, Mexico, South America, Hawaii, and Australia. "Our discounts range up to 40%; our prices are sometimes cheaper than the children's fare!" Best bargain for 1991: San Francisco to London for $450 round-trip.

Travel Team
4518 University Way NE
Seattle, WA 98105
(phone 206/632-0520)
The price leader in Seattle, primarily on tickets to Europe. Experienced agents. In business for 12 years, they've now opened a second office, at 25 Central Way, Kirkland, WA 98033 (phone 206/822-0521).

13 Reliable "Distress Merchants" of Travel (Offering Last-Minute Discounts)

FROM TIME IMMEMORIAL, TRAVel suppliers have sold off their last-minute remaining space at distress prices. As departure dates have neared, panic has set in. Employees of cruise ships and charter operators, of tour companies and hotel chains, have leaped to the phone to call relatives and friends, offering them the chance to purchase unsold cabins or seats at drastically reduced levels. At that late stage in the travel process, any sum received for a remaining cabin or seat is better than none. It is "found money."

Some tour operators even maintained lists of people who could travel on short notice. The bulletin board in a large urban hospital would periodically blossom with notices of last-minute travel bargains for nurses and doctors. Certain preferred unions would be alerted to phone their retired members with offers of seats at such low prices as to be irresistible.

Against such a well-known practice, it is not at all surprising that commercial entrepreneurs would finally attempt to organize what had earlier been random and unplanned. What is surprising is that it took them so long. Only within the past five years have "distress merchants" or "distress travel clubs" fully caught the public's attention with bargain offers for travel departures scheduled for the very next week, or even short days ahead.

With some exceptions, the clubs charge a yearly membership fee, which enables their members to use a toll-free line to listen to recorded messages of that week's bargains.

Or they receive a periodic newsletter of bargains. Provided they have flexible work schedules and can literally leave "on a moment's notice," the members can cut their travel costs by as much as 60%.

There is nothing mysterious or arcane about it. Most travel products are totally "perishable" in nature, and must be sold for a particular date or departure, or else their value for that departure is lost forever for the producer of the product. Hence it behooves them to work with the "distress merchants" in disposing of their unsold product.

Here are 12 reliable sources of "distress travel products." My own recommendation as to which you should join: the club nearest your own city. I have the impression (and may be wrong) that each excels at departures from its own immediate vicinity.

Moment's Notice, Inc.
40 East 49th Street
New York, NY 10017
(phone 212/486-0500 or 0503)
Perhaps the oldest of the lot, Moment's Notice is a recent subsidiary of the longer-established Matterhorn Club, which for 22 years has been offering sale-priced cabins, airline seats, and tour places to its members. Its departures are mainly from the East Coast, split almost evenly between New York and Florida. Members receive access to a "hotline phone number" to hear recorded messages of what's available in the days ahead, as well as a quarterly written

update, all for a yearly membership fee of $45 (valid for the member and any number of that member's travel companions). Gil Zalman is the club's experienced founder.

The Short Notice Program
4501 Forbes Boulevard
Lanham, MD 20706
(phone toll free 800/638-0930)
An activity of the Encore Travel Club, but entirely separate from that group, and requiring an independent membership fee: $36 per year, for single travelers and traveling families alike. Upon joining, you're told a number to call for tapes updated weekly of travel products offered at discounts of as much as 50%—but last minute in nature. The "hotlines" are to New York, Maryland, Chicago, and Los Angeles area codes; for reservations, you're permitted to use a toll-free "800" number. Credit cards are used to book, and tickets and tour documents are either mailed or waiting for you at the airport counter or dock. A generous offer is the right to cancel with full refund within a full year of joining if services should seem unsatisfactory.

Spur-of-the-Moment Cruises, Inc.
10780 Jefferson Boulevard
Culver City, CA 90230
(phone 213/839-2418, or toll free 800/343-1991 outside California)
The chief West Coast "distress merchant," it deals only with cruises, but charges no

membership fee for the right to use its services. Rather, you simply dial its "hotline" number—which is 213/838-9329—and hear a six-minute tape recording of all the distinguished ships sailing from ports all over the world that have sharply discounted cabins for sale in the two to three weeks ahead; your savings can be as much as 50%. "We're America's clearinghouse for last-minute unsold cruises," says owner Duke Butler. A recent example of its values was a departure from a Brazilian port of a ship that first stopped at Bahia and Rio, then crossed the South Atlantic to Dakar and Casablanca, and eventually went to both Barcelona and Genoa. Normal price, including air fare from Miami to Brazil, and from Genoa back to the U.S.: $2,800 (for the entire 18-day sailing). Spur-of-the-Moment's price (including air fare): a remarkable $1,689, less than $100 a day. Other similar "coups": seven days in the Caribbean, including air fare from the West Coast, $729 (reduced from $1,400); a seven-day cruise of Alaskan waters, $699 (reduced from $1,250).

Stand-Buys, Ltd.

49 Music Square
Nashville, TN 37203
(phone toll free 800/255-1488)

In business for 10 years, and therefore one of the founders of this segment of the travel industry, Stand-Buys charges $45 per household per year for access to its hotline number, announcing discounts for the purchase of unfilled space on charter flights, cruises, and tours. You also receive a quarterly newsletter, and an "International Travel Card" granting you 50% off at nearly 3,000 hotels. In some of its literature the organization promises a complete refund of the membership fee if you find its services unsatisfactory within 30 days of joining.

Last Minute Travel Club, Inc.

132 Brookline Avenue
Boston, MA 02215
(phone 617/267-9800, or toll free 800/ LAST-MIN)

Though some of its products depart from New York, the overwhelming number leave from Boston, and its members are heavily New England based. Membership, sometimes without charge, covers you, your family, or a travel companion, and results in your receiving a monthly newsletter and access to a 24-hour hotline (phone 617/267-2225). David Fialkow and Joel Benard are the founders, the latter the son of a prominent tour operator. Samples of their recent values: seven nights in Jamaica, air and hotel, $249; seven nights in Cancún, air and beachfront hotel, $179; round-trip air to Orlando, $99.

Worldwide Discount Travel Club, Inc.

1674 Meridian Avenue, Suite 300
Miami Beach, FL 33139
(phone 305/534-2082)

Every third week (that's 17 times a year), it mails you a closely typed letter, front and back, listing imminent departures of tours and/or cruises leaving from Atlanta, Boston, Chicago, Los Angeles, Miami, and New York, on which seats or cabins have been radically discounted in price. You then phone a toll-free number to book the trip you desire. Membership is $40 a year for a single traveler, $50 for a family. The club has been in business for several years.

Entertainment Hot Line Travel Club

2125 Butterfield Road
Troy, MI 48084
(phone 313/637-9780)

A subsidiary of the large, publicly owned company that publishes the famous "Entertainment" discount coupons (74 volumes dealing with the 74 largest cities of the U.S.). It purports to operate nationwide (recent departures from New York, Los Angeles, Detroit, Chicago, Philadelphia) and to bring members savings of up to 65% on last-minute travel merchandise. Membership fee is $35 per year, which includes spouse, dependent children, or a traveling companion, and the fee will be refunded in full within 30 days of joining if you are not satisfied with the club's initial services.

Discount Travel International, Inc.

Ives Building, Suite 205
Narberth, PA 19072
(phone 215/668-7184, or toll free 800/ 334-9294)

Claiming to be the nation's largest "distress merchant," it charges $45 a year for membership (applying to anyone living in the same household), for which members receive a toll-free, short-notice hotline phone number. By dialing, one receives word of imminent departures from one's own area, on which discounts of 35% to 70% are given. Additional benefits of membership: free membership in the Privilege Hotel Discount Program, entitling you to 50% discounts at nearly 1,200 hotels; a small discount coupon book (for hotels, cars, movies); a second hotline service for condos around the world; a 5% cash bonus on any domestic air fare purchased through the club; a 7% discount on any standard non-distress charters, tour packages, or even cruises.

Vacations to Go, Inc.

2411 Fountain View, Suite 201
Houston, TX 77057
(phone 713/974-2121, or for general information, toll free 800/338-4962)

Headquartered in Houston, it maintains telephone numbers (but not offices) in 110 cities for imparting "regionalized" information of imminent departures; usually these are departures from another major city, for which "add-on" fares for connecting flights are added to the price. Yearly membership is $19.95 (for the entire household), which brings you the special number to call from your city. You hear a hotline announcement changed two to three times a week. You also receive, for your yearly membership, a free quarterly magazine on travel, which lists future bargains and vacation values (including cruise discounts).

Vacation Hotline

1501 West Fullerton Avenue
Chicago, IL 60614
(phone 312/880-0030, or toll free 800/ 423-4095)

Specializes in charter flights and vacation packages based on the use of charter transportation. Is heavily oriented to Midwest departures, and to such prominent Midwest charter-tour operators as Apple Vacations, Funway/Funjet, MTI, Hudson Holidays, and Club Med. As president Michael Dorman explains the system: "If you have the flexibility to wait until a week or two prior to departure to make reservations, we will book you with these charter operators at reduced rates. There is some risk in doing this, as not all destinations on all dates are reduced, but those people who are willing to do so can pick up remarkable savings.

Whenever the charter companies do not sell all their seats and hotel rooms, they put them on sale for as much as 30% to 50% off the regular rates.... We advise clients to call us seven to ten days prior to planned departure dates." From the Midwest, last-minute sales are also possible.

Cruises of Distinction
460 Bloomfield Avenue

Montclair, NJ 07042
(phone 201/744-1331, or toll free 800/ 634-3445)
By paying $39 for an "Instant Notice Service," one is informed by phone or first-class mail of outstanding last-minute cruise opportunities discounted up to 50%. If you then book the cruise, your $39 payment is credited toward the price of your cruise tickets.

Voyager Cruise Club
4919 Canal Street
New Orleans, LA 70119
(phone 504/482-1572, or toll free 800/ 274-1572)
Membership is free; simply phone and have your name added to the list. Thereafter you receive a monthly postcard listing cruise departures for the next 60 days on which cabins are discounted by as much as 50%.

36 Student Travel Agencies at Home and Abroad

THE CLOSEST THING WE HAVE to an "official" student travel agency in the United States is the Council on International Educational Exchange (C.I.E.E.). An activity funded by several hundred U.S. colleges and universities, the council is our nation's representative to the International Student Travel Conference. It issues the vitally important International Student Identity Card (ISIC), which entitles students to stay and eat at student hotels and restaurants around the world, and to receive important discounts—or even free admissions—at theaters, museums, and other like facilities. It offers working vacations for American students in Britain, Ireland, France, Germany, New Zealand, and Costa Rica; operates cheap transatlantic charter flights; and provides cheap intra-European air or rail transportation. And finally, it provides longer-term study opportunities for Americans: semester-long and full-year stints at famous universities around the world.

Usually, you secure these services simply by visiting the "student exchange" office or "travel office" on your own campus, which frequently turns out to be a representative of C.I.E.E. But a better course is to visit—if you can manage to do so—a full-scale Council Travel Office, of which there are 31:

COUNCIL TRAVEL OFFICES

CALIFORNIA

Berkeley

2511 Channing Way
Berkeley, CA 94704
(phone 415/848-8604)

La Jolla

UCSD Student Center B-023
La Jolla, CA 92093
(phone 619/452-0630)

Long Beach

5500 Atherton Street, Suite 212
Long Beach, CA 90815
(phone 213/598-3338)

Los Angeles

1093 Broxton Avenue, Suite 220
Los Angeles, CA 90024
(phone 213/208-3551)

Sherman Oaks

4515 Ventura Boulevard, Suite 250
Sherman Oaks, CA 91403
(phone 818/905-5777)

San Diego

4429 Cass Street
San Diego, CA 92109
(phone 619/270-6401)

San Francisco

312 Sutter Street
San Francisco, CA 94108
(phone 415/421-3473)

919 Irving Street, Suite 102
San Francisco, CA 94122
(phone 415/566-6222)

CONNECTICUT

New Haven

Yale Co-op East
77 Broadway
New Haven, CT 06520
(phone 203/562-5335)

GEORGIA

Atlanta

12 Park Place South
Atlanta, GA 30303
(phone 404/577-1678)

ILLINOIS

Chicago

29 East Delaware Place
Chicago, IL 60611
(phone 312/951-0585)

MASSACHUSETTS

Amherst

79 South Pleasant Street
Amherst, MA 01002
(phone 413/256-1261)

Boston

729 Boylston Street, Suite 201
Boston, MA 02116
(phone 617/266-1926)

Cambridge

1384 Massachusetts Avenue
Cambridge, MA 02138
(phone 617/497-1497)

MINNESOTA

Minneapolis

1501 University Avenue SE, Room 300
Minneapolis, MN 55414
(phone 612/379-2323)

NEW YORK

New York City

205 East 42nd Street
New York, NY 10017
(phone 212/661-1450)

New York Student Center
356 West 34th Street
New York, NY 10001
(phone 212/695-0291)

35 West 8th Street
New York, NY 10011
(phone 212/254-2525)

OREGON

Portland

715 S.W. Morrison, Suite 600
Portland, OR 97205
(phone 503/228-1900)

RHODE ISLAND

Providence

171 Angell Street
Providence, RI 02906
(phone 401/331-5810)

TEXAS

Austin

1904 Guadalupe Street
Austin, TX 78705
(phone 512/472-4931)

Dallas

Executive Tower Office Center
3300 West Mockingbird Lane
Dallas, TX 75235
(phone 214/350-6166)

WASHINGTON

Seattle

1314 N.E. 43rd Street, Suite 210
Seattle, WA 98105
(phone 206/632-2448)

OVERSEAS

GERMANY

Bonn

Thomas Mann Strasse 33
5300 Bonn 2
(phone 0228-659-746)

FRANCE

Paris

31 rue St-Augustin
75002 Paris
(phone 42-66-40-94)

51 rue Dauphine
75006 Paris
(phone 43-26-79-65)

16 rue de Vaugirard
75006 Paris
(phone 46-34-02-90)

Nice

10 rue de Belgique
06000 Nice
(phone 93-87-34-96)

Bordeaux

9 place Charles-Gruet
33000 Bordeaux
(phone 56-44-68-73)

Lyon

9 rue des Remparts d'Ainay
69001 Lyon
(phone 16-78-42-99-94)

JAPAN

Tokyo

Sanno Grand Building
14–2 Nagata-Cho, 2-Chome
Chiyoda-ku
Tokyo 100
(phone 03-581-5517)

STUDENT TRAVEL NETWORK

Still another source of student travel services is the Student Travel Network, operated in the U.S. by the Australian-owned STA Travel Group—probably the world's largest student travel organization. Although it issues student cards and organizes student tours and exchange programs, its particular specialty is the sale of low-cost, cut-rate international air tickets on scheduled flights. Like a giant student-oriented "bucket shop," it negotiates with the world's most prestigious carriers to permit students to occupy their seats at stunning rates: as little as $520 round-trip between Los Angeles and London, $549 round-trip to Tokyo. And it provides these prices to people up to the age of 35.

STA offices in the U.S. (others are in Europe, Asia, and the South Pacific) include:

CALIFORNIA

Los Angeles

7204 Melrose Avenue
Los Angeles, CA 90046
(phone 213/934-8722, or toll free 800/777-0112)

San Francisco

166 Geary Street, Suite 702
San Francisco, CA 94108
(phone 415/391-8407)

San Diego

6447 El Cajon Boulevard
San Diego, CA 92115
(phone 619/286-1322)

MASSACHUSETTS

Boston

273 Newbury Street
Boston, MA 02116
(phone 617/266-6014)

NEW YORK

New York City

c/o Whole World Travel
17 East 45th Street, Suite 800
New York, NY 10017
(phone 212/986-9470, or toll free 800/777-0112)

20 of the Nation's Leading Discount Cruise Agencies

THESE ARE COMPANIES THAT cut the cost of a cruise to almost anywhere—and not simply on imminent departures; their reductions apply to sailings many months ahead. Enjoying a special relationship with major cruise-ship lines, they have been known to sell berths and cabins for as much as 40% off published rates. Although other cruise-ship specialists may, quietly, offer the same savings—and therefore I don't mean to imply that "the 20" are your only source of discounted tickets—the firms listed below are open and unabashed about their willingness to cut the cruise-ship rates: some of them send massive mailings to potential cruise-ship passengers, while others even advertise in public periodicals that they offer cruise-ship savings.

White Travel Service, Inc.
127 Park Road
West Hartford, CT 06119
(phone 203/233-2648, or toll free 800/ 547-4790)
A source of remarkable savings and discounts on cruises throughout the year, it is headed by the ebullient Edie White and her son, Rick, who have themselves personally sailed on most of the major ships in service today. Free quarterly newsletter, available at request.

Cruises of Distinction, Inc.
460 Bloomfield Avenue
Montclair, NJ 07042
(phone 201/744-1331, or toll free 800/ 634-3445)
Headed by a former cruise-ship executive,

Michael Grossman (former marketing vice-president of Norwegian American Cruises), who left the industry to concentrate on discounting fares in retail sales to the public. Publishes a remarkable, quarterly catalog of discounts far into the future, and also operates an "instant notice" service for last-minute bookings (see the list of "distress merchants" elsewhere in this Appendix).

Cruises International, Inc.
1050 South Roselle Road
Schaumburg, IL 60193
(phone 708/893-8820, or toll free 800/ ALL-SHIPS)
The Chicago-area powerhouse of the cruise-ship market, selling its space at considerable reductions, in many cases, off published fares. Prepares free, custom-created "cruise profiles" for clients. In business for 12 years.

Edna Leah Frosch/Lifeco
1300 Post Oak, Suite 1600
Houston, TX 77056
(phone 713/626-4000)
Headed by prominent longtime travel agent Edna Leah Frosch, it offers major discounts on numerous sailings each month, and advertises their availability via a jaunty, periodic newsletter sent to a large mailing list. How does she secure such remarkable discounts? "Because I have the clout of being 76 years old and on the board of the Cunard and Princess Lines," says Edna Leah.

Esther Grossberg Travel, Inc.
6300 West Loop South, Suite 360
Bellaire, TX 77401

(phone 713/666-1761)
Another major Sunbelt retailer, it appears to have the same broad inventory of heavily discounted departures on nearly all the major lines. Many years in business.

Blitz World Cruise Center, Inc.
8918 Manchester
St. Louis, MO 63144
(phone 314/961-2700)
Big in the Midwest; throws in free travel insurance, in addition to discounts ranging from 10% to 50%. Motto is: "Service plus savings."

Cruise Reservations, Inc.
8975 N.E. Sixth Avenue
Miami, FL 33138
(phone 305/759-8922, or toll free 800/ 892-9929)
Because of its location in the "cruise capital of the world," it claims to enjoy particularly close relationships with numerous lines, resulting in discounts of "hundreds of dollars" on air/sea programs, as much as 40% off list.

Cruisemasters, Inc.
3415 Sepulveda Boulevard, Suite 645
Los Angeles, CA 90034
(phone toll free 800/242-9444, 800/ 242-9000 in California)
Cites discounts of up to 50% on up to 1,000 cruise departures yearly; will provide informative brochures that describe ships personally sampled by staff members. Rick Kaplan is the president of this long-established company.

The Travel Company
3351 El Camino Real, Suite 250
Atherton, CA 94027-3844
(phone 415/367-6000, or toll free 800/ 367-6090)
In business for more than 22 years, and quite substantial (claims, in fact, to be the largest cruise-only agency in the world), it publishes a "1991 Discount Cruise Catalog," available free for the asking. Promises discounts "up to 50% and more" on numerous sailings.

The Cruise Market Place, Inc.
939 Laurel Street
San Carlos, CA 94070
(phone toll free 800/826-4333, 800/ 826-4343 in California)
Will mail information, or advise over the phone, on discount opportunities as high as 50% on a broad range of sailings. A long-established firm, it publishes a twice-yearly catalog of discount possibilities.

Cruise Pro, Inc.
2900 Townsgate Road, Suite 103
Westlake Village, CA 91361
(phone toll free 800/222-SHIP, 800/258-SHIP in California)
Represents 18 cruise-ship companies, and has built a considerable reputation from its policy of major discounts on their sailings. Nine years old and therefore a pioneer in the "cruise-only" business. Ask for Mr. Seeley, an officer of the National Association of Cruise-Only Agencies, who has himself sailed on more than 60 cruises.

Cruises, Inc.
2711 James Street
Syracuse, NY 13206
(phone 315/463-9695, or toll free from outside New York State 800/854-0500)
"Certified and bonded," it publishes a free 16-page newsletter detailing its special offers and discounts on cruises throughout the world. Escorts many of the groups it sends on board; claims to be one of the top 10 heaviest producers of cruise sales in the nation.

Landry & Kling, Inc.
1 Gables Water Way
1390 South Dixie Highway, #1207
Coral Gables, FL 33146
(phone toll free 800/431-4007)
Josephine Kling and Joyce Landry are the two former cruise-ship officials making up this cruise-only travel agency, a rather elegant firm serving an affluent clientele. Because of their heavy volume of cruise sales, they claim to obtain group space and group rates on numerous sailings, and pass on the savings to their clients. Literature is sent to their clients on a near-quarterly basis.

Bee Kalt Travel, Inc.
2805 North Woodward Avenue
Royal Oak, MI 48072
(phone 313/288-9600, or toll free 800/ 284-KALT)
A reputable, old-line travel agency (at least 30 years old) that is nevertheless one of the largest cruise discounters in the metropolitan Detroit area. Its discounts are substantial ones.

Segale Travel Service
2321 West March Lane
Stockton, CA 95207
(phone 209/952-6606, or toll free 800/ 341-2928, 800/531-3734 in California)
The local American Express affiliate in its area, it enjoys major sales of cruises, and often offers its cruise products at substantial discounts off published levels.

Golden Bear Travel, Inc.
16 Digital Drive, Suite 100
Novato, CA 94949
(phone 415/382-8900, or toll free 800/ 551-1000, 800/451-8572 in California)
A standard travel agency, but one that maintains a busy "discounted cruises department"; the latter not only sells reduced-price cruises to the public, but also wholesales them to other travel agencies.

Vacations at Sea
4919 Canal Street
New Orleans, LA 70119
(phone 504/482-1572, or toll free 800/ 274-1572)
Claims to sell more cruises (at heavy discounts) than any other agency in Louisiana. Accepts credit cards without reducing the discount, operates a club for last-minute sailing opportunities, and maintains a cruise-video library (you pay postage).

Cruise Specialists, Inc.
221 First Avenue West, Suite 110
Seattle, WA 98119
(phone 206/441-7447, or toll free 800/ 544-AHOY)
Operated by Janet Olczak, who worked as a registered nurse on ships for 10 years; she's been on 200 cruises, and now specializes in six cruise lines from which she gets very special prices—up to 50% off—for her clients. What's more, every one of her staff is a former cruise employee.

Cruise Consultants Company
100 North East Loop 410, Suite 500
San Antonio, TX 78216
(phone 512/349-7700, or toll free 800/ 533-9001)
Savings of up to 40%, primarily on the more exotic cruises—to the South Pacific, the Orient, and Europe. Many escorted programs; many cruises for mature and elderly travelers. Cruise Consultants is headed by Jay Silberman, a former president of the National Association of Cruise-Only Agents.

The Cruise Line, Inc.
260 N.E. 17th Terrace, Suite 201
Miami, FL 33132
(phone toll free 800/327-3021, 800/ 777-0707 in Florida)
A final big one, in business since 1983, it operates in the heart of a major port for cruise embarkations and thus stays in the closest contact with numerous cruise-line officials. Major discounts on most sailings, plus Miami hotel discounts for pre- or post-cruise stays. For special bookings, problems, inquiries, ask to speak with vice-president Don Lansky, or even President Larry Fishkin.

Five Major
"Vacation Exchange" Clubs

"**V**ACATION EXCHANGES" are organizations that enable you to swap your home or apartment for the home or apartment of a foreign resident (or one in another part of the country) during the periods of your respective vacations.

The swap is a simultaneous one, for a period of time that the two of you have selected. Having made the arrangements through an exchange of correspondence (usually), you settle upon the date and advise the other of where the door key (and sometimes the car keys) can be found. On that date, you pass in midair, so to speak. You fly to Edinburgh, let's say, or to the south of France, and the other flies to your home in Albuquerque. Each of you receives the lodging element of your vacation absolutely free. And each enjoys a unique vacation abroad, as a resident of a new state or foreign country and not as a mere tourist.

I've listed below five major agencies that can help you make home exchanges, either for short- or long-term stays. In each case, you're the person who handles the details: you study the directories issued by each organization, find a suitable prospect, then send letters and pictures and work out a mutually satisfactory agreement. I've also listed one agency that will do the work for you, charging a fee for the service. Specific details follow under each listing:

Vacation Exchange Club
P.O. Box 820
Haleiwa, Honolulu, HI 96712
(phone 808/638-8747)

Granddaddy of all the U.S. exchange services, begun in 1960 and operating continuously ever since (something of a record in a business that is notoriously short-lived). Two directories are published yearly, the first on February 15, the second on April 15; they include some 6,000 listings in the United States and 40 countries that span the globe. A fee of $30 entitles you to receive both directories and be listed in one of them.

Intervac U.S.
P.O. Box 190070
San Francisco, CA 94119
(phone 415/435-3497)

Chief competitor to the Vacation Exchange Club, and (apparently) gaining fast, it's been around for nearly 25 years and is currently owned and managed by Paula Jaffe and Lori Horne. They publish three catalogs—in February, March, and May—listing 7,500 homes or apartments in 35 countries, four-fifths of them outside the United States, mainly in Europe. For a single payment of $35, you receive all three catalogs and are listed.

Worldwide Exchange
1344 Pacific Avenue, Suite 103
Santa Cruz, CA 95060
(phone 408/425-0531)

Their directory lists not only 1,000 homes in the U.S. and Europe available for exchange, but also several hundred bed-and-breakfast accommodations available for rental. Current (1991) printouts are available for $9.95, whereas the charge for listing a home is $19.95, $6 more if you wish to include a

photograph. As with all the firms thus far described, you do all the matchmaking yourself, utilizing the leads set forth in the directory.

Loan-a-Home
2 Park Lane, Apt. 5-E
Mount Vernon, NY 10552

This is for long-term stays, suitable primarily for retired Americans or academicians (the latter comprising the bulk of Loan-a-Home's clients). Ms. Muriel Gould of Loan-a-Home publishes the only directories that specialize in such extended stays, either as exchanges or as rentals at both ends if an exchange is not feasible (her members, as noted, are mainly academics on sabbatical, or business people transferred elsewhere for a year or two). A good portion of her listings are of second homes purchased for investment purposes, and therefore presumably available even on an open-ended basis. She also has a section on vacation housing, since many of the long-term rentals are available for short periods as well.

Loan-a-Home's directory is unique in that there is no charge for a listing; but if you want your own copy of the directory and its supplements (directories are published in June and December, supplements in March and September), you pay $35 for one directory and supplement, $45 for two directories and two supplements. Ms. Gould earns her income from sales of the directory, and charges no commission on the arrangements made; the latter are your concern, in any event.

Better Homes and Travel
185 Park Row, Box 878
New York, NY 10038
(phone 212/349-5340)
These are the people to contact if you crave a home exchange but don't wish to make the arrangements yourself. The organization will send you questionnaires, ask for inte-

rior and exterior photos of your home, then try to match you up with someone whose lifestyle and surroundings are compatible with yours. There's a one-time registration fee of $50, then a closing fee of $150 to $525, depending on duration of the exchange and whether it is for foreign or domestic locations. Considering that this

service saves you the phone calls, letters, wires, and sheer amount of time that may be involved in arranging an exchange, it's not a bad investment. Exchanges are usually for summer or holiday periods, but the group can also handle sabbaticals.

54 of America's Foremost Bed-and-Breakfast Reservations Organizations

ORIGINALLY, WHEN THE MOVE-ment started, each bed-and-breakfast house advertised itself—in local media—or simply hung out a "B&B" shingle on the white picket fence. That proved increasingly unsatisfactory to the out-of-state travelers seeking B&B accommodations. Most found themselves unable to use these fine, cheap, and unpretentious lodgings because they were unable to ascertain names and addresses, and were also apprehensive about staying in a home about which they knew nothing.

Enter the bed-and-breakfast reservations organization. Regional in scope, each representing about 100 homes, these firms perform the function of prescreening—inspecting each lodging to ensure its suitability for transient visitors. They also have the wherewithal to advertise (a bit), and to maintain extensive phone lines and reservations personnel.

Of the 200 or so bed-and-breakfast reservations organizations in the U.S., the following seem to be outstanding, based either on a perusal of their literature or on actual phone conversations with nearly three-quarters of their owners.

In booking a B&B, be sure to make a sharp distinction between "bed-and-breakfast homes" and "bed-and-breakfast inns." The first is simply a private home or apartment occupied by a family that supplements its normal income by occasionally renting out a spare room or two to overnight visitors. The second—the "inn"—is a little hotel whose proprietors rent out multiple rooms each night and earn their living

from doing so; they also specialize in touches like quiche for breakfast, or cinnamon toast, fresh flowers daily in a bedroom vase—you get the picture. The bed-and-breakfast inns can often be more costly than a hotel, whereas a B&B house is supposed to charge 50% less than prevailing hotel rates in its area.

It's unfortunate that this semantic overlap occurred in the bed-and-breakfast field; a different name should really be found for the bed-and-breakfast inns. When I refer to a B&B, I mean a low-priced room in a private home—the term's initial meaning.

ALASKA

Alaska Bed and Breakfast
P.O. Box 21890
Juneau, AK 99802
(phone 907/586-2959, or toll free 800/627-0382)
Owner Mavis Hanna represents 42 Alaskan homes, including interesting "cove" houses with panoramic views. The structures tend to be large, and often the bedrooms have their own wood stoves; locations are convenient to fishing, boating, and sightseeing. And rooms range in price from $40 to $65 nightly, which is cheap for Alaska.

ARIZONA

Bed and Breakfast in Arizona
P.O. Box 8628
Scottsdale, AZ 85252

(phone 602/995-2831, or toll free 800/266-7829)
Has 100 houses throughout the state, charging an average of $60 a night in high season. Owners Tom Thomas and Trisha Wills stress the advantages of the locations, the comforts, hospitality, and cleanliness of the houses they offer.

CALIFORNIA

Bed and Breakfast International (San Francisco)
1181-B Solano Avenue
Albany, CA 94706
(phone 415/525-4569)
Jean Brown claims that her agency is the oldest bed-and-breakfast reservations service, offering over 300 homes in the Bay Area and throughout all other parts of California. Double rooms range from $40 to $80 a night. Homes are found in Los Angeles, Santa Barbara, the Wine Country, even in Sausalito (houseboats), and are well described in a brochure available free for the asking (but enclose a self-addressed, stamped, no. 10 envelope).

America's Co-Host Bed and Breakfast
P.O. Box 9302
Whittier, CA 90608
(phone 213/699-8427)
Coleen Davis heads this dynamic organization, and prepares fascinating write-ups of the houses and proprietors she represents. Example: "California bachelor who loves to cook will prepare mouthwatering break-

fasts. His interest in fishing and hunting as well as his expertise with horses will allow you to feel you've had some time away from the daily grind. $50 per night, double." Houses are found in all parts of the state, and most rooms range from $45 to $70.

B&B of Southern California

1943 Sunnycrest Drive, #304
Fullerton, CA 92635
(phone 714/738-8361)
The area covered ranges from Los Asos to San Diego. Rates are $45 to $90 single, $55 to $95 double, plus a $5 service charge, with most doubles renting in the $55-to-$65 range. Phone on weekdays only.

COLORADO

Bed and Breakfast Rocky Mountains

P.O. Box 804
Colorado Springs, CO 80901
(phone 719/630-3433)
Coordinator Betty Ann Field handles over 100 homes and inns in Colorado, Utah, and New Mexico. Accommodations range from budget to luxury mansions, with a heavy concentration in the ski areas (Ms. Field is herself an expert skier and can give much good advice in that area). Unhosted B&Bs are also available. Rates range from $35 to $95 per room, but most fall in the $50-to-$90 range. Hours are 9 A.M. to 5 P.M., weekdays only.

CONNECTICUT

Nutmeg Bed & Breakfast

P.O. Box 1117
West Hartford, CT 06127
(phone 203/236-6698 weekdays from 9 A.M. to 5 P.M.)
Nutmeg is now eight years old and represents about 160 host homes ranging from simple rooms in apartments to luxurious suites in mansions. Though owner Michelle Souza is heavily involved in corporate relocation of employees (for whom she obtains temporary accommodation), she stresses her continued loyalty to the classic tourist. Her rooms are classified as "C-Conventional" (modest homes in nice neighborhoods, non-adjoining or adjoining baths, with room charges of $45 to $55 a night); "Q-Quality" (lovely homes in excellent neighborhoods, adjoining or non-adjoining baths—usually private—with room rates of $65 to $80 a night); and "D-Deluxe" (luxurious estate homes, private baths and other private entry, some with kitchenettes, all renting for $85 to $95 per room per night). Surcharge for one-night stays in high season: $10.

DELAWARE

Bed and Breakfast of Delaware

3650 Silverside Road (P.O. Box 177)
Wilmington, DE 19810
(phone 302/479-9500)
Millie Alford handles period homes in the "quaint old town" of New Castle, as well as comfortable modern homes outside Wilmington and in the Chadds Ford area of Pennsylvania. Ten of her properties are on the National Historic Registry, several are near museums, and others are near or on the beach. Rooms average $45 a night for singles, $65 for couples or families.

DISTRICT OF COLUMBIA

Bed and Breakfast Ltd. of D.C.

P.O. Box 12011
Washington, DC 20005
(phone 202/328-3510)
An assortment of about 70 homes in every major area of the city; some of the houses are rambling Victorian mansions featured on local house tours. Rates range, in this high-priced city, from $35 to $75 a night for singles, $10 to $20 more for each additional person.

FLORIDA

B&B Suncoast Accommodations

8690 Gulf Boulevard
St. Pete Beach Island, FL 33706
(phone 813/360-1753)
Though owner Danie Bernard specializes in Florida's west-coast beach towns on the Gulf of Mexico, she also has registered host homes in and near Orlando, Delray Beach, Sarasota, Palm Harbor, Jacksonville Beach, Naples, Neptune Beach, Tampa, St. Petersburg, Winter Park, Clearwater, and Tarpon Springs. Standard B&B runs $40 to $55

double; better amenities, $50 to $60; "exceptional homes," $60 to $80.

B&B of the Florida Keys, Inc.

P.O. Box 1373
Marathon, FL 33050
(phone 305/743-4118)
Features 15 homes throughout the Keys. All are on the water, air-conditioned, and include a complete breakfast. Most rooms range from $40 to $60 a night.

GEORGIA

Georgia Bed and Breakfast

2472 Lauderdale Drive NE
Atlanta, GA 30345
(phone 404/493-1930)
Lists 60 homes all over the Atlanta area, most on routes of public transportation. Homes are mostly modern, yet double-occupancy rooms start at $35. "Gracious hospitality—we pride ourselves on that—at a modest rate," says Erna Bryant, owner-operator of Georgia Bed and Breakfast.

Division of Tourism

Georgia Department of Industry, Trade, and Tourism
P.O. Box 1776
Atlanta, Ga 30301
(phone 404/656-3590)
By writing to this address you can obtain the "Georgia Bed and Breakfast" brochure, a free pamphlet listing 100 excellent bed-and-breakfast homes in all parts of the state.

HAWAII

Bed and Breakfast Hawaii

P.O. Box 449
Kapaa, HI 96746
(phone 808/822-7771, or toll free 800/733-1632)
This firm pioneered in developing a broad network of bed-and-breakfast accommodations in Hawaii, at considerably lower nightly costs than are offered by hotels. Double rooms start at $45 and go up to a top of $60 in most (not all) cases. A new guidebook/directory of 150 host homes, called "Bed and Breakfast Goes Hawaiian," costs $10.95 from the firm, through the mails.

ILLINOIS

Bed and Breakfast of Chicago, Inc.
P.O. Box 14088
Chicago, IL 60614-0088
(phone 312/951-0085)
Mary Shaw handles 60 properties, half of which are unhosted apartments with continental breakfast left in the refrigerator. Apartments overlook key neighborhood attractions, often with views of the Chicago skyline and Lake Michigan. Double-occupancy rooms range from $50 to $75; self-contained apartments, from $65 to $100, for the most part.

INDIANA

Amish Acres
1600 Market Street West
Nappanee, IN 46550
(phone 219/773-4188)
Richard Pletcher represents about 30 homes in the Nappanee area. Most are family homes in the Amish community, and houses tend to be large and comfortable; some are working farms. Rooms average $45 a night for two.

IOWA

Bed and Breakfast in Iowa
P.O. Box 430
Preston, IA 52069
(phone 319/689-4222)
Maintains an inventory of more than 40 private homes, most in rural locations. Some overlook the Mississippi River; others are old mansions filled with antiques. Travelers, it is claimed, are treated like members of the family. As owner Wilma Bloom likes to say, "You're not buying a room, you're buying a memory." Most double rooms range from $45 to $55 nightly; singles, from $30 to $45.

KENTUCKY

Ohio Valley Bed and Breakfast
6876 Taylor Mill Road
Independence, KY 41051
(phone 606/356-7865)
Nancy Cully represents approximately 75 rooms in Victorian mansions, rural retreats, town houses, and urban condos. Homes are located in southern Ohio, northern Kentucky, and southeastern Indiana. Rooms range from $35 to $95 a night, but average $40 to $50 for a double; all are carefully inspected before being listed by the organization, and many are air-conditioned.

LOUISIANA

Southern Comfort B&B Reservations
2856 Hundred Oaks Avenue
Baton Rouge, LA 70808
(phone 504/346-1928 or 928-9815, or toll free 800/749-1928)
Operated by Susan Morris and Helen Heath. Their rates range from $37.50 for a single, $40 for a double, to $150; but 90% of all doubles are $75 and up because, claims Southern Comfort, they are in historic homes. Why not request the unhistoric? While reservations services are free to you upon simply phoning the firm, they'll also send you a descriptive directory of all their homes for $3.50.

MAINE

Bed & Breakfast Downeast, Ltd.
Box 547, Macomber Mill Road
Eastbrook, ME 04634
(phone 207/565-3517)
Represents 100 homes in rural or town locations statewide, including 14 working farms. Homes are situated by the ocean, on islands, mountains, and "everywhere," boasts owner Sally Godfrey. A free brochure and a $3 directory are provided on request. Doubles range from $45 to $80 a night, but average $50 to $60, and they have quite a few for $45 to $55.

MARYLAND

Traveller in Maryland, Inc.
P.O. Box 2277
Annapolis, MD 21404
(phone 301/269-6232)
Disposes of more than 150 accommodations all over the state, many on or close to the water. "We shine in Annapolis, Baltimore, and the Eastern Shore," says manager Greg Page. Rates are $55 to $75 and up per room per night (but there are plenty at $55); each guest is the only guest taken at a time; and all hosts are extensively interviewed before being listed. Reservations should be made by phone and are always confirmed promptly by a friendly staff. Hours are Monday through Thursday from 9 A.M. to 5 P.M., on Friday from 9 A.M. to noon.

MASSACHUSETTS

Bed and Breakfast Cambridge &
Greater Boston
P.O. Box 665
Cambridge, MA 02140
(phone 617/576-1492)
Fifty homes in locations claimed to be the best in the area: Back Bay and Beacon Hill, downtown Boston and Harvard Square, M.I.T., Tufts, and Boston College, Brookline, Lexington, and surrounding towns. Rates are rather high, perhaps because of that: $45 to $65 for singles, $60 to $95 for doubles, with bathless doubles averaging $65. But owner Pamela Carruthers argues that her rates have not increased, while others' have. Phone Monday through Friday from 9 A.M. to 6 P.M. or on Saturday from 10 A.M. to 3 P.M.

Bed and Breakfast Associates Bay
Colony, Ltd.
P.O. Box 57166
Babson Park Branch
Boston, MA 02157
(phone 617/449-5302)
Has 125 homes, both downtown and suburban, Victorian and Federalist, modern as well. Owners Arline Kardasis and Marilyn Mitchell emphasize the firm's "concerned matching" of client to host and location. Double rooms range from $75 to $95; singles, from $55 to $75.

New England Bed and Breakfast
1045 Centre Street
Newton Centre, MA 02159
(phone 617/244-2112 or 498-9819)
Fifty generally less-expensive homes, charging $45 to $65 double, $35 to $50 single, with no extra fees or taxes—a promise (but there's a $10 surcharge for a one-night stay). All are within 15 and 20 minutes of

downtown Boston via public transportation, and always within walking distance of a subway or bus stop. Handles properties throughout the rest of the state too.

Berkshire B&B Homes
P.O. Box 211
Williamsburg, MA 01096
(phone 413/268-7244)
Represents 90 homes in western Massachusetts and eastern New York. It specializes, in particular, in aiding parents with college-age students to tour schools in the area (Amherst, U. Mass., Smith, Wellesley, and others). Singles run $35 to $75; doubles, $45 to $85, with at least half in the lower range. Phone weekdays from 9 A.M. to 6 P.M. or Saturday from 10 A.M. to 1 P.M.

House Guests Cape Cod & the Islands
P.O. Box 1881
Orleans, MA 02653
(phone 508/896-7053, or toll free 800/ 666-HOST)
Places guests at over 100 homes—some historic, some beachfront—on Cape Cod, Nantucket, and Martha's Vineyard, at costs averaging $75 (with private bath and breakfast for two) in high season, plus a one-time $15 booking fee. Its 68-page lodgings directory is particularly well done.

MISSISSIPPI

Southern Comfort Bed and Breakfast
2856 Hundred Oaks Avenue
Baton Rouge, LA 70808
(phone 504/346-1928 or 928-9815)
This organization headquartered in Louisiana is your best source of bed-and-breakfast reservations, at pre-inspected homes, in neighboring Mississippi.

MISSOURI

River Country Bed and Breakfast, Inc.
1900 Wyoming Street
St. Louis, MO 63118
(phone 314/771-1993)
Michael Warner, a woman (her first name *is* Michael), is the owner and founder of this 10-year-old firm that represents over 200 rooms in 100 locations scattered through

Missouri and adjacent parts of Illinois. Most doubles here rent for $50 to $70, most singles from $30 to $60.

MONTANA

B&B Western Adventure
P.O. Box 20972
Billings, MT 59104
(phone 406/259-7993)
Has 60 homes in Montana, Wyoming, and eastern Idaho, including ranch homes and mountain retreats near trout streams and lakes. Average double-room price: $65. "We cater to the western fantasy," says owner Paula Deigert. Phone weekdays from 9 A.M. to 5 P.M. in summer, but only from noon to 5 P.M. the rest of the year.

NEVADA

Nevada Commission on Tourism
Capital Complex
Carson City, NV 89710
(phone 702/687-4322, or toll free 800/ 237-0774)
Will send a free pamphlet listing each and every bed-and-breakfast accommodation in the state. Simply phone, or write to the above address.

NEW HAMPSHIRE

New Hampshire Bed and Breakfast
RFD #4, Box 88
Meredith, NH 03253
(phone 603/279-8348)
Owner Ernie Tadder says he "can offer just about any type of accommodation to guests." He has 60 urban and country homes located statewide; some are on the ocean, lakes, or in the mountains. A few have swimming pools, or offer cross-country skiing out the backdoor. Rates range from $40 to $80 a night, including a full breakfast, and only personally inspected homes are taken on for representation.

NEW JERSEY

Bed and Breakfast Adventures
103 Godwin Avenue, Suite 132
Midland Park, NJ 07432

(phone 201/444-7409, 609/344-6166, or toll free 800/992-2632)
Features over 600 rooms in homes ranging from modest bungalows to large country estates. Manager Aster Mould claims to have interesting accommodations scattered all over the state, including converted grist mills, stately country homes, and an artist's studio. Doubles range in most instances from $40 to $55 a night.

NEW MEXICO

Bed and Breakfast Rocky Mountains
P.O. Box 804
Colorado Springs, CO 80901
(phone 303/630-3433)
They represent around 20 properties that are concentrated in four cities—Albuquerque, Taos, Santa Fe, and Las Vegas. Rooms cost $39 to $120 double.

NEW YORK STATE

Bed and Breakfast USA
Old Sheffield Road
South Egremont, MA 01258
(phone 914/271-6228)
For accommodations outside New York City, in every major area of the state, this organization is unbeatable. Its 40-page directory listing hundreds of homes is a superb introduction to the world of B&B. Most rooms rent for $40 and $50 (again, outside of New York City), plus a $15 booking charge to Bed and Breakfast USA. Some Manhattan homes are also found in the directory. (Don't be confused by the Massachusetts address, just across the state line from New York; their specialty is still the State of New York.)

Rainbow Hospitality
466 Amherst Street
Buffalo, NY 14207
(phone 716/874-8797)
B&Bs in the northwestern corner of New York State, including Niagara Falls, Chautauqua, Rochester, Lewiston, and Buffalo. Georgia Brannir, an especially gracious proprietress, places clients in over 60 homes charging no more than $50 to $60 single, $55 to $65 double. The phone is answered from 9:30 A.M. to 5 P.M. on weekdays and 9 A.M. to noon on Saturday.

NEW YORK CITY

Urban Ventures, Inc.
P.O. Box 426
New York, NY 10024
(phone 212/594-5650)
Represents a remarkable total of more than 1,000 accommodations in Manhattan, Brooklyn, Queens, and "waterfront New Jersey" (Hoboken, Jersey City, etc.), although most are in Manhattan. Their "hosted" accommodations include a continental or larger breakfast, and range in cost from $45 to $60 a night for a single room, $55 to $80 for a double, while "unhosted" lodgings start at $70. "All homes are thoroughly screened and very clean," claims the owner of Urban Ventures, who has operated the service for nearly 12 years.

Abode B&B
P.O. Box 20022
New York, NY 10028
(phone 212/472-2000)
Offers B&Bs in town houses, high-rises, walk-ups, and brownstones—most in Manhattan, a few in Brooklyn Heights—requiring a minimum of a two-night stay. Groups can be lodged in a fashion that keeps all members close to one another. The charge for hosted apartments: a rather high average of $70 to $80 per double room, but for "charming apartments decorated very attractively," according to the proprietor of Abode B&B. Unhosted apartments (they come with a refrigerator stocked with staples) start at an average of $80 a night, single or double.

City Lights Bed and Breakfast
P.O. Box 20355
Cherokee Station
New York, NY 10028
(phone 212/737-7049)
Represents 200 homes, most in Manhattan, but also in Brooklyn and Queens, and charges $60 to $90 a night for a double room in hosted lodgings, $40 to $70 for singles. Dee Staff-Nielsen is the proprietor; she assures that "all accommodations are personally inspected to make certain they come up to our standards. We insist that the personality of the host be reflected in the home. Our hosts are all professional people, from the theater to politics to medicine. And

we obtain evaluations from every single guest. If there is a complaint, we make sure it is remedied or we no longer represent that lodging."

New World Bed & Breakfast, Ltd.
150 Fifth Avenue, Suite 711
New York, NY 10011
(phone 212/675-5600, or toll free 800/443-3800)
One of the largest of the New York City firms, representing 100 to 150 fully inspected Manhattan homes and apartments. The aim is to offer rates 50% less than exorbitantly high New York City hotel charges. Thus B&B prices range from $50 to $80 single occupancy, $50 to $90 double occupancy. If those seem high, wait until you inquire about rates at a hotel! Kathleen Kruger is president of New World.

NORTH DAKOTA

The Old West Bed-and-Breakfast
P.O. Box 211
Regent, ND 58650
(phone 701/563-4542)
A limited selection of large, rural homes, including one with a swimming pool, another with a Jacuzzi. Owner Marlys Prince boasts that his hosts are hospitable and themselves well traveled, and tend to serve large ranch breakfasts. Homes are located near the scenic Badlands, good hiking, horseback riding, and fishing. Rooms average only $30 a night.

OREGON

Bed and Breakfast Oregon
2321 N.E. 28th Avenue
Portland, OR 97212
(phone 503/287-4704)
Owner Milan Larson places visitors in more than 250 moderately priced homes—$40 to $60 single, $55 to $65 double—throughout the state.

NW Bed and Breakfast Travel Unlimited
610 S.W. Broadway
Portland, OR 97205
(phone 503/243-7616)
Represents 325 bed-and-breakfast properties in 100 communities of Oregon, includ-

ing Portland and Eugene, and in California, Washington, Hawaii, and British Columbia. Most charge $40 to $55 for a double.

PENNSYLVANIA

Bed and Breakfast of Philadelphia
P.O. Box 252
Gradyville, PA 19039
(phone 215/358-4747, or toll free 800/733-4747)
Offers 100 homes in the metro area and surrounding suburbs, including a dozen renovated 18th-century homes. Some are within walking distance of Independence Hall in the city; most are in the suburbs or countryside. Highly refined in their tastes, the two women who manage B&B of Philadelphia are both careful to place their clients in a congenial and compatible setting, and will also handle requests for Valley Forge, New Hope (in Bucks County), and the Brandywine Horse Country. In most instances, double rooms range from $40 to $80 a night (and average $70); singles, from $30 to $60.

B&B of Southeast Pennsylvania
146 West Philadelphia Avenue
Boyerstown, PA 19512
(phone 215/367-4688)
Here's your source for lodgings in the Pennsylvania Dutch Country, all up and down Lancaster County and the Lehigh Valley. Singles run $30 to $70 and doubles go for $55 to $95, with most rooms falling halfway along each range.

RHODE ISLAND

Bed and Breakfast of Rhode Island
38 Bellevue Avenue (P.O. Box 3291)
Newport, RI 02840
(phone 401/849-1298)
Lists over 120 homes throughout Rhode Island and nearby Massachusetts. Many are historic structures from the 1700s, and a few are on the waterfront. "Of course, you're never far from the water in Rhode Island," remarks president Joy Meiser. Her hosts are mostly professionals, including oceanographers, psychologists, and antiques dealers. Rooms average $65 to $75 for a double. Belongs to Bed and Breakfast Reservation Services of New England, an

association of bed-and-breakfast reservations organizations in all six New England states, enabling any member to book a continuous itinerary through Connecticut, Rhode Island, Massachusetts, New Hampshire, Vermont, and Maine.

Anna's Victorian Connection
5 Fowler Avenue
Newport, RI 02840
(phone 401/849-2489)
Offers a giant range of homes in all price categories and throughout the state, hosted by everyone from psychologists to sculptors, in structures running the design gammut: Victorian (lots of those), Greek Revival, colonial, beachfront, modern. In season, singles ranges from $35 to $55, and doubles are slightly more; out of season, everything is negotiable. Susan White, a guidance counselor, is co-owner; her partner is a nurse, and the two have run this B&B service for eight years.

SOUTH CAROLINA

Historic Charleston Bed and Breakfast
43 Legare Street
Charleston, SC 29401
(phone 803/722-6606)
Has 70 rooms in scattered houses, all historic, all in the heart of Charleston, one dating back to 1713, some in carriage houses adjacent to a main mansion (and thus affording considerable privacy). Charlotte Fairey heads the service, and stresses that reservations well in advance are needed for the busy period of March through June, and especially for weeks of the Spoleto Festival U.S.A. in Charleston (during May). While double rooms range all the way from $65 to $125, most are found halfway along that spread.

TENNESSEE

Bed and Breakfast Hospitality of Tennessee, Inc.
P.O. Box 110227
Nashville, TN 37222
(phone 615/331-5244)

Fredda Odom takes reservations for nearly 100 homes well scattered around the state. Houses are located in every sort of region, urban and rural. Some are on the National Historic Register; and although the latter rent for as much as $110 a night, the normal bed-and-breakfast homes (not inns) start as low as $50 a night for two persons.

TEXAS

Bed & Breakfast Texas Style, Inc.
4224 West Red Bird Lane
Dallas, TX 75237
(phone 214/298-5433 or 298-8586)
Offers bed-and-breakfast homes in 51 Texas cities, from Austin to Wimberley, from Dallas to Waxahachie, in every important location. Ruth and Don Wilson are the owner/directors, and place the biblical adage, "In this place will I give peace . . ." at the bottom of their letterhead stationery. Their rates extend from $40 to $85 for a double, but fully a third range from only $40 to $50. A top operation.

UTAH

Bed and Breakfast Rocky Mountains
P.O. Box 804
Colorado Springs, CO 80901
(phone 303/630-3433)
Represents 20 properties in the state, including three in Salt Lake City. Two in that city charge as little as $35 and $40 for a double.

VERMONT

Vermont B&B Reservation Service, Inc.
P.O. Box 1
East Fairfield, VT 05448
(phone 802/827-3827)
Represents 60 homes throughout the state, all providing—in the words of their motto—"the gracious alternative." Singles are $40 to $75, and doubles run $55 to $100 for most, plus a one-time reservation

fee of $15. For $25, you can make unlimited reservations in the course of a year.

VIRGINIA

Bensonhouse of Richmond, Inc.
2036 Monument Avenue
Richmond, VA 23220
(phone 804/353-6900)
Offers 40 homes in Richmond, Williamsburg, Petersburg, Bowling Green, Fredericksburg, Orange, and the Northern Neck of Virginia; many are in historic districts. Owner Lyn M. Benson takes special care to select enthusiastic hosts who will take special pains to entertain their guests. The agency's emphasis is on older homes, and rates average $55 to $85, but with occasional "inns" going as high as $100.

WASHINGTON

Pacific Bed and Breakfast
701 N.W. 60th Street
Seattle, WA 98107
(phone 206/784-0539)
Features a wide variety of private rooms averaging $45 to $85 a night. "People are usually amazed at what I offer," says founder Irmgard Castleberry, who handles waterfront cabins, private apartments, and full-scale houses located throughout the state, and in Victoria and Vancouver, B.C. Her directory is available for $5.

NW Bed and Breakfast Travel Unlimited
610 S.W. Broadway, Suite 606
Portland, OR 97205
(phone 503/243-7616)
Represents 300 to 400 properties up and down Oregon, and several in neighboring British Columbia, Canada, as well as Washington, California, and Hawaii. Numerous houses charge only $40 to $55 for a double room, to which you'll need to add a one-time usage charge of $10 to the organization. For a one-year membership, including receipt of their comprehensive directory, families pay $25; only $9.50 (including postage and handling) for the directory alone.

The 10 Top Travel Values of 1991

GREECE

At 150 drachmas to the dollar, Greece's currency is the only one in Western Europe to have weakened, not strengthened, against the dollar since 1985. Consequently, double rooms at deluxe hotels (except for the most celebrated varieties) rent for $80, and at "A"-class hotels for only $40. In Athens, a first-class meal with wine, for two, is under $40; on the islands, the same meal for two is only $20. Here is Europe as it used to be.

CRUISES TO ANYWHERE

With several mammoth new ships scheduled to enter service in the spring of 1991, a prevailing overcapacity will become a serious glut, and discounts are expected to grow in size and frequency. Throughout the year, smart consumers purchasing their berths or cabins from cruise specialists should be able to pick up Caribbean holidays on a broad variety of lines for as little as $1,299 per person for an entire week, including round-trip airfare from many U.S. cities. That figure represents a reduction of as much as $400 off standard rates.

IN-CITY HOSTELS

Responding to a pervasive demand, American Youth Hostels has embarked on the creation of hostels in the downtown areas of America's largest cities. With the recent opening of its midtown facilities in New York and Los Angeles (Santa Monica), AYH becomes a major, domestic resource for cost-conscious travelers of any age.

EUROPEAN BUDGET MOTELS

The race is on to build hundreds of modern, low-cost, highway-based lodgings—similar to our own Motel 6s and Red Roof Inns—in several European countries. With the completion of 150 "Formula 1s" in France (see the discussion in Part VI of this book), and the decision by other European chains (including Concorde of France) to compete in the rock-bottom category, smart tourists will henceforth plan their trips to make use of these new facilities, which rent for as little as $22 per room per night, for as many as three people.

WARSAW, BUDAPEST, PRAGUE

Valuing their currencies at their true, debased levels for the first time in years, the countries of which the above are capitals have become remarkably cheap for Western tourists, except only at hotels of international chains (Hilton, Marriott, Inter-Continental, and the like). Staying at budget facilities (including private homes), and taking meals where the locals do, budget-oriented tourists now travel for costs reminiscent of the 1960s.

BALI

Making a careful choice of beach areas and budget hotels, life here is remarkably cheap, and seems probable to remain so through 1991, setting off a flood tide of tourism to this vacation center of Indonesia.

ZIMBABWE

Possessing fine lodges and resorts in heavily stocked game parks, this emerging African nation is priced at half the levels of nearby Kenya and Tanzania for safaris and camping expeditions. Yet it is just as pleasant, perhaps more stable, and eager for international tourists. Victoria Falls, viewed in its natural setting and without the commercialism surrounding, say, of a Niagara Falls, is a mighty extra bonus.

CAIRO

Its tourism having plunged because of recent developments in the Middle East, hotel and other rates are lower than ever, and can be reduced even more through bargaining. The same distance from Iraq as Chicago is from Boston, it is a safe destination, in addition to being unusually cheap for unpretentious, carefully selecting tourists.

OAXACA, MEXICO

Rapidly growing in tourist appeal, this capital of southern Mexico is nevertheless replete with facilities that have not yet been overwhelmed by tourism from the north, and continue to be priced at Mexican—not American—levels. For lodging and meals, you will pay a third the charges of an Acapulco or Cancún; and, most important, you will experience a rich, impressive culture.

KISSIMMEE, FLORIDA

The poor cousin of Orlando, Florida, it is placed just as close (and in some instances closer) to the key Walt Disney World attractions, and yet it charges bargain rates throughout the year. That's because the setting is highway-garish, with no sense of status; but the family on a tight budget will find it a godsend. Here, in all but a few, peak-season weeks, you'll find some motels charging $30 or so for a room housing two adults and two children, and restaurants galore with family-style rates.

Photo Credits

Adventure Center, pp. 151, 160, 363
Alaska Division of Tourism, pp. 155, 156, 157
American-Canadian Caribbean Line, Inc., p. 175
American-Soviet Homestays, Inc., p. 107
American Youth Hostels, Inc., pp. 111 (bottom), 112 (top); photo by Robert Berwyn, p. 109; by Torsten Blackwood, p. 112 (bottom), 161, 170; by Ken Genser, p. 111 (top); by David Kalter, p. 169
Ananda Ashram, p. 22
Arrowmont School, photos by Cynthia Huff, pp. 207, 208, 209
Augusta Heritage Center, pp. 58, 210
Australian Tourist Commission, pp. 361, 368
Balkan Holidays U.S.A., Ltd., pp. 354, 355
Bed & Breakfast on the Park, pp. 101, 102, 103
Belgian National Tourist Office, photo by C.G.T. Dessart, p. 316
Belize Tourist Board, pp. 277, 278 (bottom), 281, 282
Biological Journeys, photos by Ron LeValley, p. 65
Bluegrass Spa, pp. 224, 225, 226
Breitenbush Community, photo by Peter Moore, p. 19 (bottom)
British Tourist Authority, pp. 44, 189, 191, 307
Buddhist America: Centers, Practices, Retreats, photos reprinted by permission of John Muir Publications, Santa Fe, New Mexico, p. 68
Cedok Czechoslovak Travel Bureau, photo by Dalibor Kusák, p. 399
Chautauqua Institute, pp. 356, 357
Clipper Cruise Line, pp. 176, 177
Cooper, Douglas, p. 326
Costa Rica Tourist Board, pp. 272, 273, 275, 276
Cruise America, pp. 121, 122, 123
Cunard, p. 373
Danish Tourist Board, p. 194; photo by Ellen Thoby, p. 314
Deerfield Manor, p. 241
Den Internationale Højskole, p. 195
Duke University Diet & Fitness Center, p. 213
Experiment in International Living, p. 198; photo by Rucina Ballinger, p. 97; by Bob George, p. 98; by Nanci Leitch, p. 100, 374; by Richard T. Parsons, p. 89, 95; by Ruth Wilmot, p. 96
Eye of the Whale, p. 335
Findhorn Foundation, pp. 12, 13, 14
Forester Institute, p. 271
Foundation for Feedback Learning, p. 18
Freighter World Cruises, pp. 171, 173
French Government Tourist Office, pp. 144, 201, 310, 311
Friendship Force, p. 81
Friendship Tours, courtesy of Jo Taylor, p. 29 (bottom)

Geografix, Inc., p. 315
German National Tourist Office, pp. 199, 200
Global Volunteers, pp. 71, 85, 86, 87; photo by Michael Helft, p. 87 (bottom)
Grafton Beach Resort, Black Rock, Tobago, p. 149 (right)
Guthrie, Oklahoma Chamber of Commerce, pp. 265, 266, 267
Gypsying After 40, reprinted by permission of John Muir Publications, Sante Fe, New Mexico, p. 119
Habitat for Humanity, p. 83; photo by Paul Obregon, p. 82
Hartland Institute of Health and Education, p. 232
Hawaii Visitors Bureau, pp. 325, 328
Heart of England Cottages, Inc., Eufaula, Alabama, pp. 91, 125, 126, 128
Heartwood Institute, p. 222
Henry S. Jacobs Camp, p. 70
High Wind Farm, photo by Doug Green, p. 10
Himalayan Institute, p. 24
Hollyhock, pp. 6, 379
Iceland Tourist Board, p. 185 (top)
Idyll, Ltd., pp. 134, 135, 136, 137
Instituto de Vida Natural, pp. 245, 246
International Tour Management Institute, p. 371
International Travelers Club, p. 115
Jericho Spa Tours Company, pp. 218, 220, 221
Just-n-Trails Bed & Breakfast, p. 104
Key West International Hostel, p. 116
The Kringsten Agency, p. 249
Kushi Foundation, p. 236 (bottom)
La Sabranenque, p. 73
Lady of the Lake, photo by Chris Anderson, p. 57
Lake Austin Resort, photo by Tomás Pantin, p. 240 (right)
Las Vegas, New Mexico Chamber of Commerce, p. 268; photo by Mel Schieltz, p. 269
L'Auberge de Sedona, pp. 292, 293
Learning Alliance, photo by Angie Chen, p. 339 (top)
Lifestyle Explorations, pp. 383, 384, 385
Long Island Tourism & Convention Commission, pp. 294, 296
Lowman, Cherry, p. 33
Macuto Sheraton, La Guaira, Venezuela, pp. 148, 150
McGivern, Morgan, p. 295
Mexican Ministry of Tourism, pp. 244, 342, 343, 344, 349
Motel 6, p. 141
Mountain Travel, pp. 164, 165
Museum of Modern Art, © 1990 Scott Fances, p. 339 (bottom)
National Audubon Society, photos by W. Perry Conway, pp. 43, 44, 45
National Society for Internships and Experiential Education, p. 398
New Routes, Inc., photo by Ruth Rohde, p. 38 (bottom)

New York Open Center, p. 338
Northern Pines, p. 223
Oglebay Dance Camp, p. 60
Omega Institute, photos by Mark Sternfield, pp. 3, 4, 5
Overseas Adventure Travel, pp. 159, 380
The Palms, photo by Heather Molnor, p. 240 (left)
Plantation Spa, p. 330
Pritikin Longevity Centers, pp. 211, 214, 228, 229
Puerto Rico Tourism Company, pp. 130, 247, 317, 318, 319, 320, 321
Robert Reid Associates, p. 274
Salen-Linblad Cruising, Inc., photo by Tom Ritchie, p. 202
Sedona Chamber of Commerce, pp. 288, 289
Shenoa Retreat Center, photos by Kathleen Thormod Carr, pp. 1, 7, 8
Sivananda Ashram Vrindavan Yoga Farm, p. 23
Sivananda Yoga Vedanta Centre, p. 21
Skidmore College Special Programs, p. 54
Smith College Adult Sports & Fitness Camp, p. 53
Smithsonian Associates Travel Program, pp. 64, 381
Society Expeditions Cruises, p. 203; photos by Wolfgang Kaehler, pp. 187, 205; by T.C. Swartz, p. 261; by Werner Zehnder, pp. 204, 206
Southwind Health Resort, p. 239
Structure House, p. 215
Sun Holidays, Inc., pp. 364, 365
Swan Hellenic Limited, p. 63
Swiss National Tourist Office, p. 184
Tall Ship Adventures, Inc., p. 181
Theatre Development Fund, p. 345
Total Health Foundation, p. 234
Tourism Authority of Thailand, p. 252
TrekAmerica, pp. 153, 154
Trump Taj Mahal, Atlantic City, p. 149 (left)
Turkish Culture & Information Office, pp. 285, 286, 287
Undiscovered Islands of the Caribbean, reprinted by permission of John Muir Publications, Santa Fe, New Mexico, pp. 256, 257
University of Maine, photos by Jack Walas, pp. 377, 389
Vaida, Andi, pp. 26, 27, 28, 29 (top), 30, 32, 34, 94, 178, 185 (bottom), 259, 260 (top), 262, 263, 264, 278 (top), 279, 280, 303, 304, 324, 327, 393
Vega Study Center, p. 236 (top)
Volunteers for Peace, p. 79
Wilderness Hawaii, pp. 299, 333, 334
Windstar Sail Cruises, Ltd., p. 179
Wolsey Lodges, p. 92
Woods Fitness Institute, pp. 231, 242, 243
Womanship, p. 38 (top)
Womantrek, pp. 25, 35, 36, 37, 168
World Fellowship Center, photo by Gina Bilander, p. 49
Yugoslav National Tourist Office, pp. 366, 367

We have endeavored to obtain the necessary permission to reprint the photographs and drawings in this volume and to provide the proper copyright acknowledgments. We welcome information on any error or oversight, which we will correct in subsequent printings.

Index

About the Author

Arthur Frommer is a graduate of the Yale University Law School, where he was an editor of the Yale Law Journal, and he is a member of the New York Bar. After service with U.S. Army Intelligence at the time of the Korean War, he practiced law in New York City with the firm of the late Adlai Stevenson until the growing demands of travel writing and tour operating required his full attention. He is the author of *Europe on $5 a Day* (now in its 34th yearly edition as *Europe on $40 a Day,* the largest-selling travel guide in the United States), guidebooks to Belgium, New York, and Amsterdam, and two books dealing with legal and political subjects. In New York, he is an active trustee of the Community Service Society, the nation's largest and oldest antipoverty organization. He writes a weekly nationally syndicated newspaper column on travel and hosts "Arthur Frommer's Almanac of Travel" on the national cable television network, The Travel Channel. He is also the founder of Arthur Frommer Holidays, Inc., one of the nation's leading international tour operators, and lectures widely on travel subjects.

Notes

NOW, SAVE MONEY ON ALL YOUR TRAVELS!
Join Frommer's™ Dollarwise® Travel Club

Saving money while traveling is never a simple matter, which is why the **Dollarwise Travel Club** was formed 31 years ago. Developed in response to requests from Frommer's Travel Guide readers, the Club provides cost-cutting travel strategies, up-to-date travel information, and a sense of community for value-conscious travelers from all over the world.

In keeping with the money-saving concept, the annual membership fee is low—$20 for U.S. residents or $25 for residents of Canada, Mexico, and other countries—and is immediately exceeded by the value of your benefits, which include:

1. Any TWO books listed on the following pages.
2. Plus any ONE Frommer's City Guide.
3. A subscription to our quarterly newspaper, *The Dollarwise Traveler*.
4. A membership card that entitles you to purchase through the Club all Frommer's publications for 33% to 40% off their retail price.

The eight-page *Dollarwise Traveler* tells you about the latest developments in good-value travel worldwide and includes the following columns: **Hospitality Exchange** (for those offering and seeking hospitality in cities all over the world); **Share-a-Trip** (for those looking for travel companions to share costs); and **Readers Ask . . . Readers Reply** (for those with travel questions that other members can answer).

Aside from the Frommer's Guides and the Gault Millau Guides, you can also choose from our Special Editions. These include such titles as *California with Kids* (a compendium of the best of California's accommodations, restaurants, and sightseeing attractions appropriate for those traveling with toddlers through teens); *Candy Apple: New York with Kids* (a spirited guide to the Big Apple by a savvy New York grandmother that's perfect for both visitors and residents); *Caribbean Hideaways* (the 100 most romantic places to stay in the islands, all rated on ambience, food, sports opportunities, and price); *Honeymoon Destinations* (a guide to planning and choosing just the right destination from hundreds of possibilities in the U.S., Mexico, and the Caribbean); *Marilyn Wood's Wonderful Weekends* (a selection of the best mini-vacations within a 200-mile radius of New York City, including descriptions of country inns and other accommodations, restaurants, picnic spots, sights, and activities); and *Paris Rendez-Vous* (a delightful guide to the best places to meet in Paris whether for power breakfasts or dancing till dawn).

To join this Club, simply send the appropriate membership fee with your name and address to: Frommer's Dollarwise Travel Club, 15 Columbus Circle, New York, NY 10023. Remember to specify which single city guide and which two other guides you wish to receive in your initial package of member's benefits. Or tear out the next page, check off your choices, and send the page to us with your membership fee.

FROMMER BOOKS
PRENTICE HALL PRESS
15 COLUMBUS CIRCLE
NEW YORK, NY 10023
212/373-8125

Date _____

Friends: Please send me the books checked below.

FROMMER'S™ GUIDES

(Guides to sightseeing and tourist accommodations and facilities from budget to deluxe, with emphasis on the medium-priced.)

☐ Alaska $14.95	☐ Egypt $14.95	☐ Northwest $15.95
☐ Australia $14.95	☐ England & Scotland $14.95	☐ Portugal, Madeira & the Azores . . $14.95
☐ Austria & Hungary $14.95	☐ Florida $14.95	☐ Scandinavia (avail. May '91) . . $15.95
☐ Belgium, Holland & Luxembourg $14.95	☐ France $14.95	☐ South Pacific $14.95
☐ Bermuda & The Bahamas $14.95	☐ Germany $14.95	☐ Southeast Asia $14.95
☐ Brazil $14.95	☐ Italy $14.95	☐ Southern Atlantic States $14.95
☐ Canada $14.95	☐ Japan & Hong Kong $14.95	☐ Southwest $14.95
☐ Caribbean $14.95	☐ Mid-Atlantic States $14.95	☐ Switzerland & Liechtenstein . . $14.95
☐ Cruises (incl. Alaska, Carib, Mex, Hawaii,	☐ New England $14.95	☐ USA $16.95
Panama, Canada & US) $14.95	☐ New Mexico (avail. June '91) . . $12.95	
☐ California & Las Vegas $14.95	☐ New York State $14.95	

FROMMER'S $-A-DAY® GUIDES

(In-depth guides to sightseeing and low-cost tourist accommodations and facilities.)

☐ Europe on $40 a Day $15.95	☐ Hawaii on $60 a Day $14.95	☐ Scotland & Wales on $40 a Day $13.95
☐ Australia on $40 a Day $13.95	☐ India on $25 a Day $12.95	☐ South America on $40 a Day . . . $15.95
☐ Costa Rica; Guatemala & Belize	☐ Ireland on $40 a Day $14.95	☐ Spain on $50 a Day $15.95
on $35 a day (avail. Mar. '91) . . $15.95	☐ Israel on $40 a Day $13.95	☐ Turkey on $30 a Day $13.95
☐ Eastern Europe on $25 a Day . . $15.95	☐ Mexico on $35 a Day $14.95	☐ Washington, D.C. & Historic Va. on $40 a Day. . . $13.95
☐ England on $50 a Day $13.95	☐ New York on $60 a Day $13.95	
☐ Greece on $35 a Day $13.95	☐ New Zealand on $45 a Day . . . $13.95	

FROMMER'S TOURING GUIDES

(Color illustrated guides that include walking tours, cultural and historic sites, and other vital travel information.)

☐ Amsterdam $10.95	☐ Hong Kong $10.95	☐ Scotland $9.95
☐ Australia $10.95	☐ London $10.95	☐ Thailand $10.95
☐ Brazil $10.95	☐ New York $10.95	☐ Turkey $10.95
☐ Egypt $8.95	☐ Paris $8.95	☐ Venice $8.95
☐ Florence $8.95	☐ Rome $10.95	

FROMMER'S CITY GUIDES

(Pocket-size guides to sightseeing and tourist accommodations and facilities in all price ranges.)

☐ Amsterdam/Holland $8.95	☐ Las Vegas $8.95	☐ Rome $8.95
☐ Athens $8.95	☐ Lisbon/Madrid/Costa del Sol . . $8.95	☐ Salt Lake City $8.95
☐ Atlanta $8.95	☐ London $8.95	☐ San Diego $8.95
☐ Atlantic City/Cape May $8.95	☐ Los Angeles $8.95	☐ San Francisco $8.95
☐ Barcelona $7.95	☐ Mexico City/Acapulco $8.95	☐ Santa Fe/Taos/Albuquerque . . . $8.95
☐ Belgium $7.95	☐ Miami $8.95	☐ Seattle/Portland $7.95
☐ Berlin (avail. Mar '91) $8.95	☐ Minneapolis/St. Paul $8.95	☐ St. Louis/Kansas City (avail. May '91) . . $8.95
☐ Boston $8.95	☐ Montréal/Québec City $8.95	☐ Sydney $8.95
☐ Cancún/Cozumel/Yucatan $8.95	☐ New Orleans $8.95	☐ Tampa/St. Petersburg $8.95
☐ Chicago $8.95	☐ New York $8.95	☐ Tokyo $7.95
☐ Denver/Boulder/Colorado Springs . . $7.95	☐ Orlando $8.95	☐ Toronto $8.95
☐ Dublin/Ireland $8.95	☐ Paris $8.95	☐ Vancouver/Victoria $7.95
☐ Hawaii $8.95	☐ Philadelphia $8.95	☐ Washington, D.C. $8.95
☐ Hong Kong $7.95	☐ Rio $8.95	

SPECIAL EDITIONS

☐ Beat the High Cost of Travel . . . $6.95	☐ Marilyn Wood's Wonderful Weekends (CT, DE,	☐ Swap and Go (Home Exchanging) . . $10.95
☐ Bed & Breakfast—N. America . . $14.95	MA, NH, NJ, NY, PA, RI, VT) $11.95	☐ The Candy Apple (NY with Kids) . . $12.95
☐ California with Kids $15.95	☐ The New World of Travel (Annual sourcebook	☐ Travel Diary and Record Book $5.95
☐ Caribbean Hideaways $14.95	by Arthur Frommer for savvy travelers) $16.95	☐ Where to Stay USA (From $3 to $30
☐ Honeymoon Destinations (US, Mex & Carib) $14.95	☐ Motorist's Phrase Book (Fr/Ger/Sp) $4.95	a night) $13.95
☐ Manhattan's Outdoor Sculpture $15.95	☐ Paris Rendez-Vous $10.95	

GAULT MILLAU

(The only guides that distinguish the truly superlative from the merely overrated.)

☐ The Best of Chicago $15.95	☐ The Best of London $16.95	☐ The Best of Paris $16.95
☐ The Best of France $16.95	☐ The Best of Los Angeles $16.95	☐ The Best of San Francisco $16.95
☐ The Best of Hawaii $16.95	☐ The Best of New England $15.95	☐ The Best of Washington, D.C. . . $16.95
☐ The Best of Hong Kong $16.95	☐ The Best of New Orleans $16.95	
☐ The Best of Italy $16.95	☐ The Best of New York $16.95	

ORDER NOW!

In U.S. include $2 shipping UPS for 1st book; $1 ea. add'l book. Outside U.S. $3 and $1, respectively.
Allow four to six weeks for delivery in U.S., longer outside U.S.
Enclosed is my check or money order for $_____

NAME _____

ADDRESS _____

CITY _____ STATE _____ ZIP _____

1290